D1422690

Inside

Microsoft®

SQL
Server™ 7.0

Ron Soukup
Kalen Delaney

Microsoft Press

PUBLISHED BY
Microsoft Press
A Division of Microsoft Corporation
One Microsoft Way
Redmond, Washington 98052-6399

Library of Congress Cataloging-in-Publication Data
Soukup, Ron.
    Inside Microsoft SQL Server 7.0 / Ron Soukup, Kalen Delaney.
        p.   cm.
    ISBN 0-7356-0517-3
    1. Client/server computing.   2. SQL Server.   I. Delaney, Kalen.
  II. Title.
  QA76.9.C55S68   1999
  005.75'85--dc21   99-13769
                                                             CIP

Printed and bound in the United States of America.

1 2 3 4 5 6 7 8 9   WCWC   4 3 2 1 0 9

Distributed in Canada by ITP Nelson, a division of Thomson Canada Limited.

A CIP catalogue record for this book is available from the British Library.

Microsoft Press books are available through booksellers and distributors worldwide. For further information about international editions, contact your local Microsoft Corporation office or contact Microsoft Press International directly at fax (425) 936-7329. Visit our Web site at mspress.microsoft.com.

Acquisitions Editor: Ben Ryan
Project Editor: Michelle Goodman
Technical Editors: Dail Magee Jr., Jean Ross

To Kay, Kelly, and Jamie,
for your love and support during
the years of ship crunch.
And to the SQL Server Development Team.
Working with you has been the greatest
privilege of my career.
—Ron Soukup

For Dan,
forever.
—Kalen Delaney

CONTENTS SUMMARY

CONTENTS

PART II: ARCHITECTURAL OVERVIEW

CHAPTER THREE

SQL Server Architecture 75

CHAPTER FIVE

Databases and Database Files **179**

CHAPTER SIX

Tables **213**

CHAPTER SEVEN

Querying Data   299

CHAPTER EIGHT

Modifying Data   391

PART IV: PERFORMANCE AND TUNING

FOREWORD

This is the definitive companion to Microsoft SQL Server 7.0. Ron Soukup and Kalen Delaney offer the joint perspective of the developer and the user in an extremely readable presentation. Ron led the SQL Server development team for a decade. Kalen has been working with the application designers and developers for almost that long. This is their guide to why SQL Server is the way it is and how it should be used. This book perfectly complements the reference material in SQL Server Books Online.

The book begins with the inside story of how the PC database giant Ashton-Tate partnered with Microsoft and then-startup Sybase to bring SQL to the OS/2 marketplace. The book goes on to trace the incredible history of the product and the partners. Ron and Kalen's firsthand account makes this a must-read. I cannot think of a more amazing story in our industry.

This book then takes the reader on a whirlwind tour of SQL Server, describing the key features and pointing out some highlights. It looks "under the hood" and describes how SQL Server works inside. Novice users might find this information too detailed, but it lays the groundwork for much that follows.

The book goes on to explain how to design for SQL Server—giving sage advice on application design, database design, physical data layout, and performance tuning. Ron and Kalen base their advice on having watched customers use (and misuse) the product for many years. SQL Server and the Microsoft Windows NT environment are unique in many ways. Although the book covers the standard design issues, it focuses primarily on the features that are unique to SQL Server. Incidental to this, Ron and Kalen show many of the pitfalls and common errors that designers and programmers make. They also impart their wisdom on what makes for both good and bad database design. Anyone planning to perform an implementation using SQL Server would do well to read this book first.

This book covers virtually all the extensions that SQL Server has made to the standard SQL language. Ron and Kalen take pride in describing these features. They often explain why these features were introduced, how they compare to the competition, and how they work. This book is not an SQL tutorial, but it does an excellent job of covering the intermediate and advanced features of SQL and SQL Server. The descriptions are accompanied by detailed examples that are included on the companion CD.

The book also explains how to install, administer, and tune SQL Server. The chapters covering these topics contain essential information that I had never seen explained anywhere else. It is very easy to get started with SQL Server—perhaps too easy. Some customers just install it and start using it without thinking much. Ron and Kalen walk the designer through capacity planning; hardware acquisition; Windows NT, network, and RAID configuration; SQL Server installation and licensing; security policies; operations procedures; performance measurement; and performance tuning. The book provides a valuable checklist for anyone planning to set up or operate a SQL Server system.

You'll find several chapters devoted to understanding performance, concurrency, and recovery issues. Throughout the book, you'll notice an emphasis on designing for client-server and Internet environments. In these environments, the server must process business-rules (stored procedures) or set-oriented requests, rather than record-at-a-time requests. The book explains both traditional Transact-SQL stored procedures, as well as user-defined external procedures and OLE Automation procedures.

Ron and Kalen give a clear picture of how SQL Server transactions work. The book first presents tutorial material on the ACID properties, isolation levels, and locking. It then explains how SQL Server performs locking, logging, checkpointing, and recovery. It also explains how SQL Server uses the Windows NT Cluster feature for high availability. This presentation is exceptionally clear. Understanding these issues is crucial to designing high-traffic and high-availability SQL Servers.

SQL Server database replication is also described in depth—especially the features that are new in version 7.0.

Ron and Kalen have constructed the essential companion to SQL Server. This firsthand account of how SQL Server works, why it works that way, and how to use it will be an invaluable reference for administrators and designers alike. We are all glad Ron and Kalen took the time to write this book. I certainly learned a lot from it, and I know you will too.

Jim Gray
Senior Researcher
Microsoft San Francisco Research Lab

PREFACE

I'll confess right here. I'm a SQL Server junkie. I want to know everything I can about how SQL Server works, exactly what the internal data structures look like, and what every bit in every status field means in the system tables. A full list of all the undocumented trace flags and DBCC commands would be my idea of the perfect birthday present.

I also feel like I was born to be a teacher. No matter how late I've been working or how hard it is to get myself out of bed in the morning, when I stand in front of a classroom, I'm in my element. I love sharing what I know about SQL Server, and I get even more excited when I have students who want to know about things that I've never even thought about.

When I was asked to write the update for Ron Soukup's masterpiece, my first thought was that no one besides Ron could do the topic justice. But then I decided to look at the challenge of the book as the ultimate training assignment, with thousands of students in the classroom. If I was going to write any book on SQL Server 7, this would be the one. The topics it covers are all the ones that I love learning about and sharing. The topics it doesn't talk about are the ones that I haven't spent too much time with and don't really consider myself an expert on.

In Ron's preface to the first edition, he likens his love for SQL Server to his love for a child. I'll go one step further. Writing this book was like carrying and delivering a child. Not too stressful at first (I never did have much morning sickness) and lots of eager anticipation. But during the last few months, I felt like it would go on forever. It would never end! But now it has, and you have this book in your hands and are reading it.

Ron's preface mentions that this book is *not* an introductory treatise on SQL Server, and I want to emphasize the same point. This book delves deep into the internal workings of SQL Server and expects that you, the reader, have some experience with the SQL language and SQL Server already, as well as a fair amount of general technical sophistication.

This book, as the name implies, deals with the way SQL Server works on the *inside*. SQL Server 7 includes a wealth of new peripheral tools, but you'll have to get the details about them in other books. This book doesn't talk about client programming interfaces, heterogeneous queries, or replication. There are also some internal operations that aren't discussed, such as security and database backup and restore. I had to draw the line somewhere, or the book would have been twice as long and I would still be writing it and avoiding calls from my editors asking when the next chapter would be arriving. I hope you find value here, even if I haven't covered every single topic that you would like to know about. You can let me know what you'd like to learn more about, and maybe there'll be a second volume to this book one day. Or maybe I can refer you to other books or whitepapers. You can contact me through my Web site, at http://www.InsideSQLServer.com.

My editors insisted that this second edition wasn't supposed to be a new features guide or an upgrade book. However, I knew that lots of people who have used SQL Server for years would be reading this, and I felt it necessary to compare areas of behavior where drastic changes occurred. New users can just ignore any references to what SQL Server used to do and appreciate all the wonderful things it does now.

To help you appreciate some of the wonderful features even more, the companion CD includes a whitepaper section, which serves as a complete reference to the Transact-SQL language, including all the system stored procedures. Although this is a Microsoft Word document, it is actually intended for use on line, as many of the elements of a syntactic construct contain links to the further description of that element. When using the document on line, you can simply click on the colored element and be repositioned at the document with more details describing that element. I am grateful to Frank Pellow for sharing this document. He has included his e-mail address within the document and invites comments and suggestions from readers.

Now comes the part I have looked forward to the most (besides holding a published book in my hands). I get to thank all the wonderful people whose enthusiasm and generosity have made writing this book not only possible but almost a pleasure.

Thanks to Ron Soukup, for writing the first edition, and giving me his "seal of approval" for undertaking the second edition. Thanks to my editor at *SQL Server Professional Journal,* Karen Watterson, for opening so many doors for me, including passing my name on to the wonderful people at Microsoft Press.

The SQL Server development team at Microsoft has been awesome. David Campbell can never, ever be thanked enough, as far as I'm concerned. His enthusiasm for the book seemed to exceed my own at times, and his technical knowledge and clear explanations were priceless, as well as seemingly limitless. Goetz Graefe, Sameet Agarwal, Mike Habben, Wei Xiao, Nigel Ellis, Eric Christensen, Ross Bunker, Alazel Acheson, Lubor Kollar, and Shaun Cooper opened their doors to me and responded to (sometimes seemingly endless) e-mails. Cesar Galindo-Legaria, Peter Byrne, Greg Smith, Michael Zwilling, Jeff Alger, and Alan Brewer also offered valuable technical insights and information. Other members of the development team provided answers to e-mails, and I hope they all know how much I appreciated every piece of information I received. I am also indebted to Joe Marler and Bob Ward, who aren't really on the development team per se, but the technical information they were willing to share was just as valuable and their pride in SQL Server and dedication to the user community was evident in every e-mail I received from them.

A special thanks to several Microsoft program managers: Richard Waymire, for being a friend as well as a technical resource; David Marshall, for helping pull so many pieces together for the general architecture section in Chapter 3; Bob Vogt, who never seemed to tire of sharing all he could about his special projects, the Index Tuning Wizard, and SQL Server Profiler; and Hal Berenson, who was a tremendous help on the update of the history section in Chapter 1.

I received tremendous support from Ryan Trout and Tom Kreyche of the SQL Server marketing team, who provided advance copies of whitepapers, sample exercises for exploring new features, as well as T-shirts and toys bearing the SQL Server logo. Thank you so much for everything, especially your big smiles every time I stopped by.

Ryan Labrie made it possible for me to start down the long road of learning about SQL Server 7 shortly after the Beta 1 release by inviting me to help develop training materials for SQL Server 7. Rick Byham traveled down that long road with me as we worked together to produce the course, and we were able to spend every day for months doing nothing but learning about and playing with this powerful new version. I am grateful for that opportunity.

I found that other SQL Server trainers were the best help in digging into certain new behaviors and trying to figure out experientially what was really happing. Thanks to Glenn Christensen for posing so many puzzling questions and Kimberly Tripp-Simonnet for wonderful ideas about how to explain things. Don Vilen deserves special thanks for trying to talk me out of writing this book; he said it would be much too much work. You were right, Don, but I did it anyway.

My editors at Microsoft Press deserve thanks also. Ben Ryan, my acquisitions editor, got the ball rolling. Michelle Goodman, the project editor, made sure the chapters kept coming, and my terrific technical editor, Dail Magee Jr., made sure they turned out well. But of course, Dail couldn't do it alone so I'd like to thank the rest of the editorial team, including many of you whom I never met. I know you worked endless hours to help make this book a reality.

Some people might think that working as an independent consultant and trainer would get lonely, as I don't have coworkers to chat with every day in the office. But I've got something even better. As a SQL Server MVP, I work with a dozen other SQL Server professionals to provide online support on the public newsgroups in the SQL Server forums. We share a private newsgroup with two Microsoft Support Engineers who serve as our interface with Microsoft, and through this newsgroup and yearly conferences and summits, I have gotten to know this group personally. Endless gratitude is due Neil Pike for his amazing generosity, both professional and personal. Neil, you are truly an inspiration. Roy Harvey and Brian Moran offered much needed moral support whenever I asked for it, and more importantly, when I didn't. To you three, and to the rest of the MVP crew: Tibor Karaszi, Ron Talmadge, Gianluca Hotz, Tony Rogerson, Bob Pfeiff, Steve Robertson, Trevor Dwyer, Russell Fields, and our Microsoft support buddies, Shawn Aebi and Paul Wehland, I'd like to let you know that being a part of your team has been the greatest honor and privilege of my professional life. I could not imagine working with a more dedicated, generous, and talented group of people.

There's another group of people without whose support and encouragement this book would have never seen the light of day. My husband Dan never faltered once in his absolute confidence in me and his endless encouragement. My multitalented daughter Melissa, who will be graduating from Tulane University this spring, has always been an awesome role model for me. She's someone who can make up her mind to do something or learn something and then just do it. My three sons Brendan, Rickey, and Connor, who are growing up to be generous, loving, and compassionate young men, have been the source of countless hugs and kisses and undreamed of patience and acceptance. I am truly blessed. It's done, guys, and now we're off to Disneyworld!

Kalen Delaney, 1999

PREFACE TO THE FIRST EDITION

For me, Microsoft SQL Server has been a labor of love. I lived and breathed this product for years, and I look at it not unlike how I look at my children—with immense love and pride. I've helped nurture the product from its infancy, through some very tough years, to its current success. I've lost many nights' sleep, upset that some customer was disappointed with it. Fortunately, I've also had many more thrills and moments of rejoicing—like when a customer speaks glowingly of SQL Server or when we win another award. Yes, the analogy to a child is the closest thing I can think of to describe my feelings about SQL Server. Like people who have always thought that one day they'd write the Great American Novel, I felt a need to finally put down in words some hopefully unique knowledge and *opinions* I have regarding SQL Server.

This book is *not* an introductory treatise on SQL Server, although it does include one introductory chapter (Chapter 2). In Chapter 1, I discuss the history of the product (which I lived), from SQL Server's inception and partnership with Sybase to its current success. But beyond these early chapters, the book is very detailed and written for those who want to dig deeply into SQL Server. This book is a suitable read for those who have worked with SQL Server for years already. It will also be of interest to experienced database professionals new to SQL Server who are developing or considering new development projects.

In this book, I focus on the "back-end" capabilities of the database engine. Topics include choosing appropriate hardware for SQL Server, effective use of the SQL language, writing correct queries, common mistakes, consistency and concurrency tradeoffs, data storage and structures, locking, and scrollable cursors. Performance considerations are covered throughout the book. The final chapters (Chapters 14 and 15) discuss specific performance issues, but because they assume that you've gained much knowledge from reading earlier chapters in the book, I strongly discourage you from jumping directly to those chapters.

When I planned the book, I felt it was necessary to describe how SQL Server works before going into the product's functional capabilities. But that presents a "chicken-or-the-egg" problem: what should I introduce first? I decided to include architectural information near the beginning of the book—Chapter 3 provides an in-depth discussion of how SQL Server works. If you are already familiar with the functional aspects of SQL Server, I think you'll benefit most from this chapter. If you are new to SQL Server, I encourage you to go back and read Chapter 3 again in a couple months after you've gained more familiarity with the product. I think you'll get a lot more out of it. Initially, simply try to absorb just the basics.

I've included little discussion of client programming issues, such as which development tools to use or details about ODBC programming. If you need information about these topics, see the Suggested Reading section near the end of the book. And I'm sorry to say that there is little discussion of the replication capabilities of SQL Server. (This is also a little embarrassing because I recently took charge of managing the Replication Unit within the SQL Server development team.) But, like software, this thing had to eventually ship, and replication ended up on the "cut" list. I promise that we're doing so many exciting new things in replication for the next version that I knew I would have to almost completely rewrite any replication section before long anyway. (And a very good whitepaper about SQL Server replication capabilities is included on the companion CD.)

This book has a healthy smattering of my personal opinions about many issues in software and database development. Software development is still at least as much an art as a science, and there are different schools of thought and different approaches. Healthy, even if heated, debate is one of the things that make software development so much fun. I elected to be pretty candid and direct with my opinions in many places, rather than keep the book bland and neutral. Some people will no doubt disagree strongly with some of my opinions. That's fine. I respect your right to disagree. But I do hope you can read and accept the book for its overall merits, even if you disagree with a few topics. And, of course, the opinions I present here are mine alone and not necessarily those of Microsoft.

Now I have many people to thank. Without the product, there would be no book. So my thanks must first be to my fellow SQL Server "old-timers," who bootstrapped the product. Working with you was an amazing, unforgettable experience. We worked 80 hours a week far more often than not, but we loved it. No one deserves more credit for SQL Server's success than Rick Vicik. I'm sure Rick is a genius, but he has the rare trait among those with genius IQs of being perfectly pragmatic. He's a doer, and no one works harder or more passionately. He led the development team by sheer example. And what a team. Without the other old-timers like Mike Habben, Lale Divringi, Peter Hussey, Chris Cassella, Chris Moffatt, Kaushik Chodhury, Dave Fyffe, Don Reichart, Craig Henry, Jack Love, Karl Johnson, Ted Hart, Gavin Jancke, Dan Tyack, Trish Millines, Mike Ervin, Mike Byther, Glen Barker, Bryan Minugh, and Heidy Krauer, there simply would be no Microsoft SQL Server today. And the early documentation team of Lesley Link and Helen Meyers, and the original marketing team of Dwayne Walker, Gary Voth, and Dan Basica, made SQL Server a product, not just software. It took this unique and special blend of people to make this product and to make it viable. There are, of course, many others of great talent who have joined the SQL Server team during the last few years. But if not for the extraordinary efforts of the original, very small team, there would be no SQL Server now. Be proud and always remember what we did together.

We needed and were backed up by a great customer support team, anchored by Andrea Stoppani, Gary Schroeder, Rande Blackman, Joe Marler, Vaqar Pirzada, Damien Lindauer, and James McDaniel (several of whom are now on the SQL Server development team). You often went above and beyond the call of duty. Thank you.

Turning toward the book, I want to extend special thanks to Lesley Link. Lesley did the huge job of editing this book entirely in her "spare time" (which meant many late nights and early Sunday mornings). She really committed to editing this book because of the pride and ownership she, too, feels in the product. But while I wrote the bulk of the book more or less on a sabbatical leave, Lesley edited while she continued in her more than full-time job as the manager of the SQL Server documentation team. There is no better editor in the business. And thanks to her production team, especially Steven Fulgham, Christine Woodward, Pat Hunter, and Rasa Raisys, for helping prepare the book.

Thank you to those who provided invaluable technical reviews of various sections, especially to Jim Gray, Rick Vicik, Mike Habben, Peter Hussey, Don Vilen, Dave Campbell, and Lale Divringi. The mistakes that no doubt remain are mine alone.

Special thanks go to Gary Schroeder, who authored the Microsoft internal documentation for the on-disk data structures that I made use of when describing disk and table formats. And thanks to Betty O'Neil, who revamped and reorganized much of the internal design documentation that I used as a resource when writing.

Finally, thanks to the staff at Microsoft Press: David, Lisa, John, and those of you I never met but knew were there, who guided me through the publication process.

This is the first book I've written. I've shipped a lot more software than books. I've learned there are a lot of similarities. Like the last 10 percent takes 90 percent of the time. And that when it's done, you always have this nagging feeling that you'd like to do some part over and could do it much better the second time around. After all the demands and grief I gave them over the years, I know that the documentation team that formerly reported to me has taken great delight in watching me write and seeing me struggle to complete this work. And just as software is never perfect, neither is this book. I've always found that fact painful in shipping software—I always want it to be perfect. And I find it painful now. I wish this book were perfect, and I know it's not.

But, as I always remind my development team, "Shipping is a feature." So, after a long labor, I have shipped.

Ron Soukup, 1997

PART I

OVERVIEW

4141 417b000c 015858

0xc2b000

xc2b000 pg=0 obj id=
=0 indid=0 freeoff=3
revpg=0 objid=4
d=0 freeoff=30
040 x17b000c 0158585

43040 06030

THE EVOLUTION OF MICROSOFT SQL SERVER: 1989 TO 1999

In 1985, Microsoft and IBM announced "a long-term joint development agreement for development of operating systems and other systems software products." This announcement was the beginning of OS/2, a successor to the Microsoft MS-DOS operating system. OS/2 would be a more complete and robust operating system. It would exploit the powerful new personal computers based on the Intel 80286 processor. It would allow multitasking applications, each with its own address space and each running in the safe ring 3 of the Intel four-ring protection scheme of the 80286. Machines sold in 1986 would be vastly more powerful than the original IBM PC (an Intel 8088–based machine) of just a couple years earlier, and OS/2 would signal a new age in harnessing this power. That was the plan.

OS/2 was formally announced in April 1987, with shipment promised by the end of the year. (OS/2 version 1.0 was released to manufacturing on December 16, 1987.) But shortly after the joint declaration, IBM announced a special higher-end version of OS/2 called OS/2 Extended Edition. This more powerful version would include the base OS/2 operating system plus an SQL database called OS/2 Database Manager. OS/2 Database Manager would be useful for small applications and would be partially compatible (although not initially interoperable) with DB/2, IBM's flagship MVS mainframe database, and with the lesser-used SQL/DS, which ran on slightly smaller mainframe computers using the VM or VSE operating systems. OS/2 Database Manager would also include Systems Network Architecture (SNA) communications services, called OS/2 Communications Manager. As part of its sweeping System Application Architecture (SAA), IBM promised to make the products work well together in the future. (Database Manager later evolved into today's DB2/2.)

But if IBM could offer a more complete OS/2 solution, who would buy Microsoft OS/2? Clearly, Microsoft needed to come up with an answer to this question.

In 1986, Microsoft was a mere $197-million-per-year business, with 1153 employees. (Ten years later, Microsoft had revenues of nearly $6 billion, with almost 18,000 employees.) Microsoft's products were entirely desktop focused, and the main bread-and-butter product was MS-DOS. Client/server computing was not yet in the vernacular of Microsoft or the computer industry. Data management on PCs was in its infancy. Most people who kept data on their PCs used the wildly popular Lotus 1-2-3 spreadsheet application to keep lists (although many were discovering the limitations of doing so). Ashton-Tate's dBASE products (dBASE II and the recently released dBASE III) had also become popular. Although a few other products existed, such as MicroRim's Rbase and a relatively new product from Ansa Software called Paradox, Ashton-Tate was clearly king of the PC data products. In 1986, Microsoft had no database management products. (Beginning in 1992, Microsoft would go on to tremendous success in the desktop database market with Microsoft Access and Microsoft FoxPro.)

IBM's Database Manager wasn't in the same category as products such as dBASE, Paradox, and Rbase. Database Manager was built to be a full-fledged, blood-and-guts database (with atomic transactions and a full SQL query processor), more similar to traditional minicomputer-oriented or mainframe-oriented systems such as IBM's DB/2, or Oracle, or Informix. Microsoft needed a database management system (DBMS) product of the same caliber, and it needed one soon.

Microsoft turned to Sybase, Inc., an upstart in the DBMS market. Sybase hadn't yet shipped the first commercial version of its DataServer product (which it would do in May 1987 for Sun workstations running UNIX). Although certainly not a mainstream product, the prerelease version of DataServer had earned a good reputation for delivering innovative new capabilities, such as stored procedures and triggers, and because it had been designed for a new paradigm in computing: *client/server.*

As is true in all good business exchanges, the deal between the two companies was a win-win situation. Microsoft would get exclusive rights to the DataServer product for OS/2 and all other Microsoft-developed operating systems. Besides getting royalties from Microsoft, Sybase would get credibility from Microsoft's endorsement of its technology. Even more importantly, Sybase would gain a beachhead among the anticipated huge number of personal computers that would be running the new OS/2 operating system.

Because the transaction-processing throughput of these OS/2 systems wasn't expected to be high, Sybase could use the systems to seed the market for future sales on the more powerful UNIX system. Microsoft would market the product in higher volumes than Sybase could; it simply wasn't economically feasible for Sybase's direct sales force to deliver what would essentially be the first shrink-wrapped release of a full-fledged, blood-and-guts database to PC customers. Higher volumes would help Sybase win more business on its UNIX and VMS platforms. On March 27, 1987, Microsoft president Jon Shirley and Sybase cofounder and president Mark Hoffman signed the deal.

In the PC database world, Ashton-Tate's dBASE still had the reputation and the lion's share of the market, even if dBASE and Sybase DataServer offered capabilities that were extremely different. To gain acceptance, this new, higher-capability database management system from Microsoft (licensed from Sybase) would need to appeal to the large dBASE community. The most direct way to do that, of course, was to get Ashton-Tate to endorse the product—so Microsoft worked out a deal with Ashton-Tate to do just that.

In 1988, a new product was announced with the somewhat clumsy name *Ashton-Tate/Microsoft SQL Server*. Although not appearing in the product's title, Sybase was prominent in the product's accompanying information. This new product would be a port of Sybase DataServer to OS/2, marketed by both Ashton-Tate and Microsoft. Ashton-Tate had pledged that its much anticipated dBASE IV would also be available in a Server Edition that would use the dBASE IV development tools and language as a client to develop applications (for example, order-entry forms) that would store the data in the new SQL Server product. This new client/server capability promised to give dBASE new levels of power to support more than the handful of concurrent users that could be supported by its existing file-sharing architecture.

Ashton-Tate, Microsoft, and Sybase worked together to debut SQL Server on OS/2. (This was the first use of the name *SQL Server*. Sybase later renamed its DataServer product for UNIX and VMS *Sybase SQL Server*. Today Sybase's database server is known as *Sybase Adaptive Server*.)

The first beta version of Ashton-Tate/Microsoft SQL Server shipped in the fall of 1988. Microsoft made this prerelease version available at nominal cost to developers who wanted to get a head start on learning, developing for, or evaluating this new product. It shipped in a bundle known as the NDK (network development kit) that included all the software components needed (provided that you were developing in C) to get a head start building networked client/server applications. It included prerelease versions of SQL Server, Microsoft LAN Manager, and OS/2 1.0.

Ron's Story

In 1988, Ron Soukup was working for Covia, the United Airlines subsidiary that provided the Apollo Reservation System and related systems for airport and travel agency use. He had spent the previous five years working with the new breed of relational database products that had appeared on the minicomputer and mainframe computer scene. He had worked with IBM's DB/2 running on MVS; IBM's SQL/DS running on VM; and Oracle, Informix, and Unify running on UNIX. Ron viewed PC databases of the day essentially as toys that were good for storing recipes and addresses but not for much else. He used a PC for word processing, but that was about it. At work, they were beginning to use more and more LAN-based and PC-based systems, and Ron had begun doing some OS/2 programming. When he heard of the NDK, with this new SQL Server product that had been mentioned in the trade press, he ordered it immediately.

The NDK was very much a beta-level product. It didn't have a lot of fit and finish, and it crashed a couple of times a day. But from practically the first day, Ron knew that this product was something special. He was amazed that he was using a true DBMS *on a PC(!),* with such advanced features as transaction logging and automatic recovery. Even the performance seemed remarkably good. Having used mostly minicomputer and mainframe computer systems, he was most struck by the difference in PC response time. With the bigger systems, even a simple command resulted in an inevitable delay of at least a couple of seconds between pressing the Enter key and receiving a reply. PCs seemed almost instantaneous. Ron knew PCs were fast for local tasks such as word processing, but this was different. In this case, at one PC he entered an SQL command that was sent over the network to a server machine running this new SQL Server product. The response time was a subsecond. He had never seen such responsiveness.

Ron's initial kick-the-tires trial was encouraging, and he received approval to test the product more thoroughly. He wanted to get a feel for the types of applications and workloads for which this interesting new product might be used. For this, Ron wanted more substantial hardware than the desktop machine he originally tested on (a 10-MHz 286 computer with 6 MB of memory and a 50-MB hard drive). Although SQL Server ran reasonably well on his desktop machine, he wanted to try it on one of the powerful new machines that used the Intel 80386 processor. Ron was able to procure a monster machine for the day—a 20-MHz 386 system with 10 MB of memory and two 100-MB disk drives—and was the envy of his division!

In 1987, Ron and a colleague at Covia had developed some multiuser database benchmark tests in C to help them choose a UNIX minicomputer system for a new application. So Ron dusted off these tests and converted the embedded C to the call-level interface provided in SQL Server (DB-Library) and ported these benchmarks to the PC. Ron hoped that SQL Server would handle several simultaneous users, although he didn't even consider that it could come close to handling the 15 to 20 simulated users they had tried in the earlier minicomputer tests. After many false starts and the typical problems that occur while running an early beta of a version 1.0 product, he persevered and got the test suite, 2000 lines of custom C code, running on a PC against the beta version of SQL Server.

The results were amazing. This beta version of SQL Server, running on a PC that cost less than $10,000, performed as well and in many cases better than the minicomputer systems that they had tested a few months earlier. Those systems cost probably 10 times as much as the PC that Ron was using, and they needed to be managed by a professional UNIX system administrator. Ron knew the industry was in for a big change.

In May 1989, Ashton-Tate/Microsoft SQL Server version 1.0 shipped. Press reviews were good, but sales lagged. OS/2 sales were far below what had been expected. Most users hadn't moved from MS-DOS to OS/2, as anticipated. And about the only tool available to create SQL Server applications was C. The promised dBASE IV Server Edition from Ashton-Tate was delayed, and although several ISVs had promised front-end development tools for SQL Server, these hadn't materialized yet.

During the preceding six months, Ron had come to really know, respect, and admire SQL Server, and he felt the same about the people at Microsoft with whom he had worked during this period. So in late 1989, Ron accepted a position at Microsoft in the SQL Server group in Redmond, Washington. A few months later, he was running the small but talented and dedicated SQL Server development team.

Kalen's Story

Kalen Delaney saw the first version of Microsoft SQL Server at about the same time that Ron did. She started working for Sybase Corporation's technical support team in 1987. And in 1988, she started working with a team that was testing the new PC-based version of Sybase SQL Server, which a company in the Seattle area was developing for OS/2. Sybase would be providing phone support for customers purchasing this version of the product, and Kalen, along with the rest of the technical support team, wanted to be ready.

Up to that point, she had never actually worked with PC-based systems and had pegged them as being mere toys. Sybase SQL Server was an extremely powerful product, capable of handling hundreds of simultaneous users and hundreds of megabytes of data. Kalen supported customers using Sybase SQL Server databases to manage worldwide financial, inventory, and human resource systems. A serious product was required to handle these kinds of applications, and Kalen thought PCs just didn't fit the bill. However, when she saw a PC sitting on a coworker's desk actually running SQL Server, Kalen's attitude changed in a hurry. Over the next few years, she worked with hundreds of customers in her position in product support and later in her position as Senior Instructor, using Microsoft SQL Server to manage real businesses with more than toy amounts of data, from a PC.

In 1991, Kalen's family left the San Francisco Bay Area to live in the Pacific Northwest, but she continued to work for Sybase as a trainer and course-ware developer. A year later, Sybase dissolved her remote position, and she decided to start her own business. A big decision loomed: should she focus primarily on the Sybase version or the Microsoft version of SQL Server? Because Microsoft SQL Server would run on a PC that she could purchase at her local Sears store with low monthly payments, and because she could buy SQL Server software and the needed operating system in one package, the decision was simple. Microsoft had made it quite easy for the sole proprietor to acquire and develop software and to hone his or her skills on a powerful, real-world, relational database system.

Microsoft SQL Server Ships

By 1990, the co-marketing and distribution arrangement with Ashton-Tate, which was intended to tie SQL Server to the large dBASE community, simply wasn't working. Even the desktop version of dBASE IV was quite late, and it had a reputation of being buggy when it shipped in 1989. The Server Edition, which would ostensibly make it simple to develop higher-performance SQL Server applications using dBASE, was nowhere to be seen.

As many others have painfully realized, developing a single-user, record-oriented application is much different from developing applications for multiple users for which issues of concurrency, consistency, and network latency need to be considered. Initial attempts at marrying the dBASE tools with SQL Server had dBASE treating SQL Server as though it were an Indexed Sequential Access Method (ISAM). A command to request a specific row was issued for each row needed. Although this procedural model was what dBASE users were accustomed to, it wasn't an efficient way to use SQL Server, with which users could gain more power with less overhead by issuing SQL statements to work with sets of information. But at the time, SQL Server lacked the capabilities to make it easy to develop applications that would work in ways dBASE users were accustomed to (such as browsing through data forward and backward, jumping from record to record, and updating records at any time). Scrollable cursors didn't exist yet.

> **NOTE** The effort to get dBASE IV Server Edition working well provided many ideas for how scrollable cursors in a networked client/ server environment should behave. In many ways, it was the prime motivation for including this feature in SQL Server version 6.0 in 1995, six years later.

Only two years earlier, Ashton-Tate had been king of the PC database market. Now it was beginning to fight for its survival and needed to refocus on its core dBASE desktop product. Microsoft would launch OS/2 LAN Manager under the Microsoft name (as opposed to the initial attempts to create only OEM versions), and it needed SQL Server to help provide a foundation for the development of client/server tools that would run on Microsoft LAN Manager and Microsoft OS/2. So Microsoft and Ashton-Tate terminated their co-marketing and distribution arrangements. The product would be repackaged and reintroduced as Microsoft SQL Server.

Microsoft SQL Server version 1.1 shipped in the summer of 1990 as an upgrade to the Ashton-Tate/Microsoft SQL Server version 1.0 that had shipped in 1989. For the first time, SQL Server was a Microsoft-supported, shrink-wrapped product, and it was sold through the newly formed Microsoft Network Specialist channel, whose main charter was to push Microsoft LAN Manager.

> **NOTE** When version 1.1 shipped, Microsoft didn't see SQL Server as a lucrative product in its own right. Within Microsoft, SQL Server was generally thought of as a way to push LAN Manager and OS/2 and wasn't viewed as a strong database product in and of itself. SQL Server would be one of the reasons to buy LAN Manager—that's all.

SQL Server 1.1 had the same features as version 1.0, although it included many bug fixes—the type of maintenance that is understandably necessary for a version 1.0 product of this complexity. But SQL Server 1.1 also supported a significant new client platform, Microsoft Windows 3.0. Windows 3.0 had shipped in May 1990, a watershed event in the computer industry. SQL Server 1.1 provided an interface that enabled Windows 3.0–based applications to be efficiently developed for it. This early and full support for Windows 3.0–based applications proved to be vital to the success of Microsoft SQL Server. The success of the Windows platform would also mean fundamental changes for

Microsoft and SQL Server, although these changes weren't yet clear in the summer of 1990.

With the advent of Windows 3.0 and SQL Server 1.1, many new Windows-based applications showed up and many were, as promised, beginning to support Microsoft SQL Server. By early 1991, suddenly dozens of third-party software products used SQL Server. SQL Server was one of the few database products that provided a Windows 3.0 dynamic link library (DLL) interface practically as soon as Windows 3.0 shipped, which was now paying dividends in the market-place. Quietly but unmistakably, Microsoft SQL Server was leading. Overall sales were still modest, but until tools beyond C existed to build solutions, sales couldn't be expected to be impressive. It was the classic chicken-and-egg situation.

Development Roles Evolve

Microsoft's development role for SQL Server 1.0 was quite limited. As a small porting team at Sybase moved its DataServer engine to OS/2 and moved the DB-Library client interfaces to MS-DOS and OS/2, Microsoft provided test-ing and project management. Microsoft also developed some add-on tools to help make the product easy to install and administer.

Although a number of sites were running OS/2 as an application server with SQL Server or as a file server with LAN Manager, few were using OS/2 for their desktop platforms. Before Windows 3.0, most desktops remained MS-DOS–based, with its well-known limit of 640 KB of addressable real memory. After loading MS-DOS, a network redirector, network card device drivers, and the DB-Library static link libraries that shipped with SQL Server version 1.0, developers trying to write a SQL Server application were lucky to get 50 KB for their own use.

For SQL Server 1.1, rather than ship the DB-Library interface that Sybase had ported from UNIX to MS-DOS, Microsoft wrote its own, from scratch. Instead of 50 KB, developers could get up to 250 KB to write their applications. Although small by today's standards, 250 KB was a huge improvement.

> **NOTE** The same source code used for DB-Library for MS-DOS also produced the Windows and OS/2 DB-Library interfaces. But the MS-DOS RAM cram is what motivated Microsoft to write a new implementation from scratch. The widespread adoption of Windows 3.0 quickly eliminated the MS-DOS memory issue—but this issue was a real problem in 1989 and 1990.

With SQL Server 1.1, Microsoft provided client software and utilities, programming libraries, and administration tools. But the core SQL Server engine was still produced entirely by Sybase; Microsoft didn't even have access to the source code. Any requests for changes, even for bug fixes, had to be made to Sybase.

Microsoft was building a solid support team for SQL Server. It hired some talented and dedicated engineers with database backgrounds. But with no access to source code, the team found it impossible to provide the kind of mission-critical responsiveness that was necessary for customer support. And, again, fixing bugs was problematic because Microsoft depended entirely on Sybase, which had become successful in its own right and was grappling with its explosive growth. Inevitably, some significant differences arose in prioritizing which issues to address, especially when some issues were specific to the Microsoft-labeled product and not to Sybase's product line. Bugs that Microsoft deemed of highest priority sometimes languished because Sybase's priorities were understandably directed elsewhere. The situation was unacceptable.

It was a great day in the SQL Server group at Microsoft when in early 1991, Microsoft's agreement with Sybase was amended to give Microsoft read-only access to the source code for the purpose of customer support. Although they still couldn't fix bugs, at least Microsoft's SQL Server group could read the source code to better understand what might be happening when something went wrong. And they could also read the code to understand how something was expected to work. As anyone with software development experience knows, even the best specification will be ambiguous at times. There's simply no substitute for the source code as the definitive explanation for how something works.

As a small group of developers at Microsoft became adept with the SQL Server source code and internal workings, Microsoft began to do virtual bug fixes. Although they still weren't permitted to alter the source code, they could identify line-by-line the specific modules that needed to be changed to fix a bug. Obviously, when they handed the fix directly to Sybase, high-priority bugs identified by Microsoft were resolved much quicker.

After a few months of working in this way, the extra step was eliminated. By mid-1991, Microsoft could finally fix bugs directly. Because Sybase still controlled the baseline for the source code, all fixes were provided to Sybase for review and inclusion in the code. The developers at Microsoft had to make special efforts to keep the source code highly secured, and the logistics of keeping the source code in sync with Sybase was sometimes a hassle, but all in all, this was *heaven* compared to a year earlier. Microsoft's team of developers was becoming expert in the SQL Server code, and they could now be much more responsive to their customers and responsible for the quality of the product.

OS/2 and Friendly Fire

In 1991, Microsoft released SQL Server 1.11, a maintenance release. SQL Server was slowly but steadily gaining acceptance and momentum—and a long list of independent software vendor (ISV) supporters. Client/server computing wasn't widely deployed yet, but new converts appeared every day. Customer satisfaction and loyalty were high, and press reviews of the product were all favorable. Sales were generally disappointing, but this was hardly a surprise because OS/2 had continued to be a major disappointment. Windows 3.0, however, was a runaway

---

SQL Server's Limitations and the Marketplace

Microsoft SQL Server 1.11 clearly had a scalability limit. It was a 16-bit product because OS/2 could provide only a 16-bit address space for applications. OS/2 lacked some high-performance capabilities, such as asynchronous I/O. Even though an astonishing amount of work could be performed successfully with SQL Server on OS/2, there would come a point at which it would simply run out of gas. No hard limit was established, but in general, SQL Server for OS/2 was used for workgroups of 50 users or less. For larger groups, customers could buy a version of Sybase SQL Server for higher-performance UNIX-based or VMS-based systems.

This was an important selling point for both Microsoft and Sybase. Customers considering the Microsoft product wanted to be sure they wouldn't outgrow it. The large number of ISV tools developed for Microsoft SQL Server worked largely unchanged with Sybase SQL Server, and applications that outgrew OS/2 could be moved quite easily to a bigger, more powerful, more expensive UNIX system. This relationship still made sense for both Microsoft and Sybase.

The need for compatibility and interoperability made it especially important for Microsoft SQL Server to be based on the version 4.2 source code as soon as possible. Furthermore, a major features version hadn't been released since version 1.0 in 1989. In the rapidly moving PC marketplace, the product was in danger of becoming stale. Customers had begun to do serious work with Microsoft SQL Server, and new features were in great demand. Microsoft's version 4.2 would add a long list of significant new features, including server-to-server stored procedures, UNION, online tape backup, and greatly improved international support that would make SQL Server more viable outside the United States.

hit. Rather than move their desktop platforms from MS-DOS to OS/2, huge numbers of PC users moved to Windows 3.0 instead. OS/2 hadn't become a widespread operating system as anticipated, and it was now abundantly clear that it never would be.

At the same time, Microsoft was working on a new SQL Server version that would sync up with the newest Sybase product on UNIX, version 4.2. When Microsoft SQL Server 1.0 shipped, Sybase's product was designated version 3.0. They had added some new features deemed necessary for the PC marketplace, such as *text* and *image* datatypes and browse mode. Sybase subsequently shipped version 4.0 for most platforms and version 4.2 on a more limited basis.

Meanwhile, in May 1991, Microsoft and IBM announced an end to their joint development of OS/2. Clearly, most customers were voting with their dollars for Windows, not OS/2. Microsoft decided to concentrate on future versions of Windows and applications for Windows. The announcement, although not a surprise, rocked the industry nonetheless. Microsoft was well underway in the development of a new microkernel-based operating system that was internally code-named *NT* (new technology). This new system was originally envisioned as a future release of OS/2 and was sometimes referred to as *OS/2 3.0*. After the termination of joint OS/2 development, the NT project was altered to include the Windows user interface and the Win32 application programming interface (API), and it became known henceforth as Microsoft Windows NT.

The first version of Windows NT wasn't expected for two years. Microsoft SQL Server would eventually be moved to Windows NT—that was a no-brainer. But in the meantime, Microsoft had to continue developing SQL Server on OS/2, even though OS/2 was now a competitive product for Microsoft; there was no alternative. For the next couple of years, the SQL Server group got used to getting hit by friendly fire as Microsoft competed vigorously against OS/2.

Version 4.2

Microsoft had been developing SQL Server 4.2 for the forthcoming OS/2 2.0, the first 32-bit version of OS/2. Since SQL Server 4.2 was also planned to be 32-bit, porting the product from its UNIX lineage would be easier because memory segmentation issues wouldn't be a concern. In theory, the 32-bit SQL Server would also perform faster. Many articles comparing 32-bit and 16-bit performance issues appeared in the press, and everyone assumed the 32-bit environment would bring awesome performance gains (although few articles explained correctly why this might or might not be true).

The principal performance gain expected would be due to memory addressing. To address memory in the 16-bit segmented address space of OS/2 1.*x*, basically two instructions were required: one to load the correct segment, and one to load the memory address within that segment. With 32-bit addressing, the instruction to load the segment was unnecessary and memory could be addressed with one instruction, not two. Because addressing memory is so common, some quick calculations showed that the 32-bit version might yield an overall performance increase of perhaps 20 percent or more, if all other operations were of equal speed.

The 32-Bit Platform and Memory Gains

Many people mistakenly believed that SQL Server needed to be a fully 32-bit platform to address more than 16 MB of memory. Under OS/2 1.*x*, an application could access a maximum of 16 MB of real memory; however, an application could access more than 16 MB of *virtual* memory, but paging would result. In OS/2 2.0, an application could access more than 16 MB of real memory and avoid paging. This would allow SQL Server to have a larger cache, and getting data from memory rather than from disk always results in a huge performance gain. However, to the application, all memory in OS/2 is virtual memory—in versions 1.*x* and 2.0. So even the 16-bit version of SQL Server would be able to take advantage of the ability of OS/2 2.0 to access larger real-memory spaces. A 32-bit version was unnecessary for this enhancement.

Unfortunately, the early beta versions of OS/2 2.0 were significantly slower than OS/2 1.*x*, more than offsetting the efficiency in addressing memory. So rather than a performance gain, users saw a significant loss of performance in running Microsoft SQL Server 1.1 and preliminary builds of the 32-bit SQL Server 4.2 on OS/2 2.0.

OS/2 2.0 Release on Hold

Suddenly, the plans for the release of OS/2 2.0 were suspect. Instead of being delivered by the end of 1991, it was unclear whether IBM could deliver version 2.0 at all. At any rate, it appeared doubtful that OS/2 would ship any sooner than the end of 1992. The decision became clear—Microsoft would move SQL Server back to a 16-bit implementation and target it for OS/2 1.3.

Reworking back to 16-bit would cost the Microsoft developers about three months, but they had little choice. In the meantime, another problem appeared. IBM shipped OS/2 1.3, but this version worked only for its brand of PCs. Theoretically, other computer manufacturers could license OS/2 from Microsoft and ship it as part of an OEM agreement. However, the demand for OS/2 had become so small that most OEMs didn't ship it; as a result, buying OS/2 for other PCs was difficult for customers. For the first time, despite the seeming incongruity, Microsoft produced a shrink-wrapped version of OS/2, version 1.3, code named *Tiger*. Tiger shipped in the box with Microsoft SQL Server and Microsoft LAN Manager, lessening the problem that the product was essentially targeted to a dead operating system.

Version 4.2 Released

Microsoft SQL Server version 4.2 entered beta testing in the fall of 1991, and in January 1992, Microsoft CEO Bill Gates (with Sybase's Bob Epstein sharing the stage) formally announced the product at a Microsoft SQL Server developers' conference in San Francisco. Version 4.2 truly had been a joint development between Microsoft and Sybase. The database engine was ported from the UNIX version 4.2 source code, with both Microsoft and Sybase engineers working on the port and fixing bugs. In addition, Microsoft produced the client interface libraries for MS-DOS, Windows, and OS/2, and for the first time it included a Windows GUI tool to simplify administration. Source code for the database engine was merged back at Sybase headquarters, with files exchanged via modem and magnetic tape.

Microsoft SQL Server version 4.2 shipped in March 1992. The reviews were good and customer feedback was positive. As it turned out, the source code for the database engine in this version was the last code that Microsoft received from Sybase (except for a few bug fixes exchanged from time to time).

After Microsoft SQL Server 4.2 shipped, the Big Question for 1992 was, "When will a 32-bit version of Microsoft SQL Server be available?" The issue of 32-bitness became an emotional one. Many people who were the most strident in their demands for it were unclear or confused about what the benefits would be. They assumed that it would automatically have a smaller footprint, run faster, address more memory, and generally be a much higher-performing platform. But the internal work with a 32-bit version for OS/2 2.0 had shown that this wouldn't necessarily be the case.

SQL Server for Windows NT

Contrary to what many people might assume, Microsoft senior management never pressured the SQL Server development team *not* to develop a full 32-bit version for OS/2. One of the joys of working for Microsoft is that senior management empowers the people in charge of projects to make the decisions, and this decision was left with Ron Soukup.

In early 1992, however, the development team faced some uncertainty and *external* pressures. On one hand, the entire customer base was, by definition, using OS/2. Those customers made it quite clear that they wanted—indeed expected—a 32-bit version of SQL Server for OS/2 2.0 as soon as IBM shipped 2.0, and they intended to remain on OS/2 in the foreseeable future. But when OS/2 2.0 would be available was unclear. IBM claimed that OS/2 2.0 would ship by the fall of 1992. Steve Ballmer, Microsoft senior vice president, made a well-known pledge that he'd eat a floppy disk if IBM shipped the product in 1992.

The SQL Server team was now under pressure to have a version of SQL Server running on Windows NT as soon as possible, with prerelease beta versions available when Windows NT was prereleased. The SQL Server team members knew that Windows NT was the future. It would be the high-end operating system solution from Microsoft, and from a developer's perspective, Windows NT would offer many technical advantages over OS/2, including asynchronous I/O, symmetric multiprocessing, and portability to reduced instruction set computing (RISC) architectures. They were champing at the bit to get started.

Although Microsoft had decided in 1991 to fall back to a 16-bit version of SQL Server, Microsoft's developers had continued to work on the 32-bit version. By March 1992, just after shipping version 4.2, they saw that both the 16-bit and 32-bit versions ran slower on the beta versions of OS/2 2.0 than the 16-bit version ran on Tiger (OS/2 1.3). Perhaps by the time OS/2 2.0 actually shipped, it might run faster. But then again, it might not—the beta updates of OS/2 2.0 didn't give any indication that it was getting faster. In fact, it seemed to be getting slower and more unstable.

For a product with the scope of SQL Server, there's no such thing as a small release. There are big releases and bigger releases. Because resources are finite, the developers knew that working on a product geared toward OS/2 2.0 would slow down the progress of Windows NT development and could push back its release. Adding more developers wasn't a good solution. (As many in the industry have come to learn, adding more people is often the cause, and seldom the solution, to software development problems.) Furthermore, if Microsoft chose to develop simultaneously for both OS/2 2.0 and Windows NT, the developers would encounter another set of problems. They would have to add an abstraction layer to hide the differences in the operating systems, or they'd need substantial reengineering for both, or they'd simply take a lowest-common-denominator approach and not use services or features of either system fully.

So Microsoft developers decided to stop work on the 32-bit version of SQL Server for OS/2 2.0. Instead, they moved full-speed ahead in developing SQL Server for Windows NT, an operating system with an installed base of zero. They didn't constrain the architecture to achieve portability back to OS/2 or to any other operating system. They vigorously consumed whatever interfaces and services Windows NT exposed. Windows NT was the only horse, and the development team rode as hard as they could. Except for bug fixing and maintenance, development ceased for SQL Server for OS/2.

Microsoft began to inform customers that future versions, or a 32-bit version, for OS/2 2.0 would depend on the volume of customer demand and that the primary focus was now on Windows NT. Most customers seemed to understand and accept this position, but for customers who had committed their businesses to OS/2, this was understandably not the message that they wanted to hear.

At this time, Sybase was working on a new version of its product, to be named System 10. As was the case when they were working on version 4.2, the developers needed Microsoft SQL Server to be compatible with and have the same version number as the Sybase release on UNIX. OS/2 vs. Windows NT was foremost at Microsoft, but at Sybase, the success of System 10 was foremost.

Although System 10 wasn't even in beta yet, a schedule mismatch existed between the goal of getting a version of Microsoft SQL Server onto Windows NT as soon as possible and getting a version of System 10 onto Windows NT, OS/2 2.0, or both as soon as possible. The development team decided to compromise and specialize. Microsoft would port SQL Server version 4.2 for OS/2 to Windows NT, beginning immediately. Sybase would bring Windows NT into its umbrella of core operating systems for System 10. Windows NT would be among the first operating system platforms on which System 10 would be available. In addition, Microsoft would turn the OS/2 product back over to Sybase so those customers who wanted to stay with OS/2 could do so. Although Microsoft hoped to migrate most of the installed customer base to Windows NT, they knew that this could never be 100 percent. They were honestly pleased to offer those customers a way to continue with their OS/2 plans, via Sybase. The SQL Server development team truly didn't want them to feel abandoned.

This compromise and specialization of development made a lot of sense for both companies. The development team at Microsoft would be working from the stable and mature version 4.2 source code that they had become experts in. Bringing up the product on a brand new operating system was difficult enough, even *without* having to worry about the infant System 10 code line. And Sybase could concentrate on the new System 10 code line, without worrying about the inevitable problems of a prebeta operating system. Ultimately, System 10 and SQL Server for Windows NT would both ship, and the two companies would again move back to joint development. That was the plan, and both sides expected this to be the case in 1992.

The SQL Server team at Microsoft started racing at breakneck speed to build the first version of SQL Server for Windows NT. Time to market was, of course, a prime consideration. Within Microsoft, the team had committed to shipping within 90 days of the release of Windows NT; within the development group, they aimed for 30 days. But time to market wasn't the only, or even chief, goal. They wanted to build the best database server for Windows NT that they could. Because Windows NT was now SQL Server's only platform, the developers didn't need to be concerned about portability issues, and they didn't need to create an abstraction layer that would make all operating systems look alike. All they had to worry about was doing the best job possible with Windows NT. Windows NT was designed to be a portable operating system, and it would be available for many different machine architectures. SQL Server's portability layer would be Windows NT itself.

The development team tied SQL Server into management facilities provided by Windows NT, such as raising events to a common location, installing SQL Server as a Windows NT service, and exporting performance statistics to the Windows NT performance monitor. Because Windows NT allows applications to dynamically load code (using DLLs), an open interface was provided to allow SQL Server to be extended by developers who wanted to write their own DLLs.

This first version of Microsoft SQL Server for Windows NT was far more than a port of the 4.2 product for OS/2. Microsoft essentially rewrote the *kernel* of SQL Server—the portion of the product that interacts with the operating system—directly to the Win32 API.

Another goal of SQL Server for Windows NT was to make it easy to migrate current installations on OS/2 to the new version and operating system. The developers wanted all applications that were written to SQL Server version 4.2 for OS/2 to work unmodified against SQL Server for Windows NT. Because Windows NT could be dual-booted with MS-DOS or OS/2, they decided that SQL Server for Windows NT would directly read from and write to a database created for the OS/2 version. During an evaluation phase, for instance, a customer could work with the OS/2 version, reboot the same machine, work with the Windows NT version, and then go back to OS/2. Although it would be difficult to achieve, the developers wanted 100 percent compatibility.

The developers reworked SQL Server's internals and added many new management, networking, and extensibility features; however, they didn't add new external core database engine features that would compromise compatibility.

The Windows NT–Only Strategy

Many have questioned the Windows NT–only strategy. But in 1992, the UNIX DBMS market was already overcrowded, so Microsoft developers felt they wouldn't bring anything unique to that market. They recognized that SQL Server couldn't even be in the running when UNIX was a customer's only solution. Microsoft's strategy was based on doing the best possible job for Windows NT, being the best product on Windows NT, and helping make Windows NT compelling to customers.

The decision to concentrate on only Windows NT has had far-reaching effects. To be portable to many operating systems, the Sybase code base had to take on or duplicate many operating system services. For example, because threads either didn't exist on many UNIX operating systems or the thread packages differed substantially, Sybase had essentially written its own thread package into SQL Server code. The Windows NT scheduling services, however, were all based on a thread as the schedulable unit. If multiprocessors were available to the system and an application had multiple runnable (not blocked) threads, the application automatically became a multiprocessor application. So the Microsoft SQL Server developers decided to use native Windows NT threads and not the Sybase threading engine.

The development team made similar choices for the use of asynchronous I/O, memory management, network protocol support, user authentication, and exception handling. (In Chapter 3, we'll look at the SQL Server architecture in depth and delve into more of these specifics. The point here is that the goals intrinsic to portability are in conflict with the goal to create the best possible implementation for a single operating system.)

For example, the developers ensured that there were no differences in the SQL dialect or capabilities of the Windows NT and OS/2 versions. The plan was for the future System 10 version to implement many new features. This release would be fundamentally a platform release. To emphasize compatibility with the OS/2-based 4.2 product and with the Sybase product line, Microsoft decided to call the first version of SQL Server for Windows NT *version 4.2*. The product was referred to as simply *Microsoft SQL Server for Windows NT* and often internally as *SQL NT*, a designation that the press and many customers also were beginning to use.

In July 1992, Microsoft hosted a Windows NT developers' conference and distributed a prebeta version of Windows NT to attendees. Even though SQL Server didn't exist yet at a beta level, Microsoft immediately made available via CompuServe the 32-bit programming libraries that developers needed

---

Commitment to Customers

Incidentally, at approximately the same time, Microsoft also shipped a maintenance release for SQL Server for OS/2 (and they shipped another the following year). In porting to Windows NT, the development team found and fixed many bugs that were generic to all platforms. Even though they wouldn't create new SQL Server versions for OS/2, they really meant it when they said that they didn't want to abandon the OS/2 customers.

By March 1993, Microsoft went a step further and made a public beta release; anyone (even competitors) could obtain a SQL Server Client/Server Development Kit (CSDK), the prerelease product, for a nominal charge that essentially covered expenses. Microsoft set up a public support forum on CompuServe and didn't demand that participants sign a nondisclosure agreement. It shipped more than 3000 CSDKs. By May 1993, the volume on the support forum for the prerelease product exceeded that for the shipping OS/2 product. The feedback was highly positive: Microsoft had a winner. The dream of an eventual "client/server for the masses" was being realized.

In July 1993, Microsoft shipped Windows NT 3.1. Within 30 days, achieving their internal goal, the SQL Server development team released the first version of Microsoft SQL Server for Windows NT to manufacturing. Customer and press reaction was terrific. SQL Server for Windows NT was listed in many publications as among the top and most important new products of 1993.

---

for porting their applications from OS/2 or 16-bit Windows to Windows NT. Just as they had enjoyed success back in 1990 by being among the first database products to provide the DLLs necessary for writing Windows 3.0–based applications, Microsoft sought to do the same with Windows NT.

In October 1992, Microsoft shipped the first beta version of SQL Server for Windows NT. The product was essentially feature-complete, provided a full Win32 version of all components, and shipped to more than 100 beta sites. For a database server, having 100 beta sites was unprecedented, as the typical number of beta sites for such a product was approximately 10.

Success Brings Fundamental Change

SQL Server for Windows NT was a success by nearly all measures. The strategy of integrating the product tightly with Windows NT resulted in a product that was substantially easier to use than high-end database products had ever been. Sales were above the internal projections and increased as Windows NT began to win acceptance.

By early December 1993, much of the SQL Server customer base for the OS/2 operating system had already migrated to SQL Server for Windows NT. Surveys showed that most of those who hadn't upgraded to Windows NT yet planned to do so, despite the fact that Sybase had publicly announced its intention to develop System 10 for OS/2.

The upgrade from SQL Server for OS/2 to SQL Server for Windows NT was virtually painless. When applications were moved from one platform to the other, not only did they still work, but they worked better. SQL Server for Windows NT was much faster than SQL Server for OS/2, and most significantly, it was scalable far beyond the limits imposed by OS/2. Within another nine months, Microsoft's SQL Server business had more than doubled, with nearly all sales coming on the Windows NT platform. Although they continued to offer the OS/2 product, it accounted for well below 10 percent of sales.

A Faster SQL Server

Focusing the product on Windows NT had made the product fast. Studies conducted internally at Microsoft, as well as those from private customer benchmarks, all showed similar results: SQL Server for Windows NT (running on low-cost commodity hardware) was competitive in performance with database systems running on UNIX (on much more costly hardware).

In September 1993, Compaq Computer Corporation published the first official, audited Transaction Processing Council (TPC) benchmarks. At that time, on the TPC-B benchmark, well over $1000/TPS (transactions per second) was common, and it was an impressive number that broke the $1000/TPS barrier. Running on a dual-Pentium, 66-MHz machine, SQL Server achieved 226 transactions per second at a cost of $440 per transaction, less than half the cost of the lowest benchmark ever published by any other company. The raw performance number of 226 transactions per second was equally astonishing. At that time, most of the TPC-B numbers on file for UNIX minicomputer systems were still below 100 TPS. Certainly a handful of numbers were higher, but all occurred at a price point of much more than $440/TPS. And looking back perhaps just 18 months from that point, the raw performance of 226 TPS was about as high as any mainframe or minicomputer system had ever achieved.

The implications were clear. SQL Server for Windows NT wasn't simply a low-end or workgroup system. Its performance was competitive with more costly UNIX systems, and the trend toward faster systems running Windows NT was unmistakable. The 66-MHz Pentium processors were the first generation of Pentiums from Intel. Much higher clock speeds were expected to emerge within a few months; hardware with additional processors was anticipated. Furthermore, Microsoft SQL Server for Windows NT would soon be available on RISC processors such as the DEC Alpha-AXP at 250 MHz and the MIPS R4400. The so-called *Moore's Law* (named after Gordon Moore, cofounder of Intel Corporation), which postulates that computing power doubles every 18 months, was clearly being proven true for the type of commodity hardware for which Windows NT and Microsoft SQL Server were designed. Microsoft took a serious look at what would be required to achieve 1000 TPS, definitely putting raw performance in the same league as even the largest systems of the day.

The End of Joint Development

Microsoft's success strained its relationship with Sybase. The competitive landscape of late 1993 was quite different from that of 1987 when Microsoft and Sybase had inked their deal. By 1993, Sybase was a successful software company, by most accounts second only to Oracle in the DBMS market. The credibility and visibility Microsoft brought Sybase was far less important in 1993 than it had been to the upstart company of 1987. Similarly, Microsoft had grown a great deal since 1987. The growth wasn't just in revenues (although that was one of the great success stories of the industry), but in an emphasis on enterprise applications, such as Microsoft SQL Server, that Fortune 1000 companies could use as a platform upon which to run their businesses.

The SQL Server development team had grown as well, from a handful of people in 1990 to more than 50 professionals (not including marketing, support, or field operations), with significant additional growth planned. The first-rate team of engineers knew database and transaction processing and the inner workings of SQL Server, and they were experts in developing for Windows NT. Microsoft now had the talent, size, motivation, and mandate, yet was still constrained in what it could do with the product: the 1987 agreement with Sybase had merely licensed to Microsoft the rights to the Sybase product. Because of this restricted agreement, Microsoft couldn't unilaterally implement new features or changes without Sybase's approval. Contrary to what many people thought, Microsoft had no ownership stake in Sybase and by no means could Microsoft simply call the shots.

Obviously, Sybase had different business needs and therefore different priorities than Microsoft. The development team at Microsoft might, for example, want to integrate SQL Server with messaging by using MAPI (messaging API), but because this feature was specific to the Microsoft operating system, Sybase wouldn't be excited about it. As is always the case in development, many features *could* be done for every feature that *will* actually be done: features specific to Windows NT didn't tend to interest Sybase as much as those that would benefit its UNIX products.

Sybase engineers had to confront the issue of portability to multiple operating systems. In fact, Microsoft's implementation of version 4.2 for Windows NT was already causing friction because Sybase was progressing with System 10 for Windows NT. Sybase was understandably implementing System 10 in a more portable manner than Microsoft had done. This was entirely rational for Sybase's objectives, but from Microsoft's perspective, it meant a looser bond with Windows NT. System 10 would not, *could not,* perform as well on Windows NT as the product that had been designed and written exclusively for Windows NT.

Because of the economics involved, as well as the changing competitive landscape, the Microsoft/Sybase agreement of 1987 was no longer working. Microsoft SQL Server was now a viable competitive alternative to Sybase SQL Server running on UNIX, Novell NetWare, and VMS. Far from seeding the market for Sybase, Microsoft SQL Server was now taking sales away from Sybase. Instead of choosing a UNIX solution, customers could buy Microsoft SQL Server at a fraction of the cost of a UNIX solution, run it on less expensive PC hardware, and install and administer it more easily. Although Sybase earned royalties on sales of Microsoft SQL Server, this amounted to a small fraction of the revenue Sybase would have received if the customer bought Sybase products for UNIX in the first place. Microsoft and Sybase were now often vigorously competing for the same customers. Both companies recognized that a fundamental change in the relationship was needed.

On April 12, 1994, Microsoft and Sybase announced an end to joint development. Each company decided to separately develop its own SQL Server products. Microsoft was free to evolve and change Microsoft SQL Server. Sybase decided to bring its System 10 products (and subsequent versions) to Windows NT—the first time that the Sybase-labeled SQL Server would be available for a Microsoft operating system. (The original agreement gave Microsoft exclusive rights on Microsoft operating systems.) Both companies' products would be backward-compatible for applications that had been developed for the shipping version of Microsoft SQL Server. However, the products would diverge in the future and would have different feature sets and design points. Sybase's product would be fully compatible with its UNIX versions. Microsoft's product would continue to be integrated with Windows NT as much possible. In short, the products would directly compete.

SQL Server Performance: No Secret Formulas

Although Microsoft SQL Server is designed for and optimized for Windows NT, it uses only publicly documented interfaces. From time to time, articles or speakers suggest that Microsoft SQL Server uses private, undocumented APIs in Windows NT to achieve its performance. But this assumption is false, without exception. SQL Server's performance results from using the available and published Windows NT services without any compromise. This is something that other products could also do if developers were willing to dedicate themselves to doing the best possible job for Windows NT, without making compromises for portability to other operating systems.

NOTE Although the Sybase product competed with Microsoft SQL Server, Microsoft encouraged and provided support to get Sybase System 10 shipping on Windows NT as soon as possible, because it was important to the acceptance and success of Windows NT. Such collaboration is typical of many other relationships that are competitive on one level and cooperative on another.

The Charge to SQL95

As late as the beginning of 1994, the SQL Server development team had planned that the next version of the product would pick up the Sybase System 10 source code and new features. But the termination of joint development changed that plan. Sybase contributed no more code, and Microsoft released no System 10 product. Except for a couple of bug fixes, the last code drop received from Sybase was in early 1992, as version 4.2 for OS/2 was shipping.

Time was at a premium. Besides growing sales with new customers, Microsoft had to fight for its significant installed base. Sybase would deliver System 10 on Windows NT later that year. That would be a potentially easy upgrade for Microsoft's installed customer base; so if Microsoft lost customers to System 10, they'd likely lose them forever.

Microsoft quickly planned for an ambitious release that was loaded with new features and performance improvements. It was tagged *SQL95*, borrowing the working moniker from the well-known upcoming Windows 95 release. Because the Big Question of 1994 was "What are your plans for replication?", replication became a keystone of the release. So did scrollable cursors, a feature that the developers had learned (from the ill-fated dBASE IV interface) was necessary to bridge the impedance mismatch between many record-oriented applications and a relational database. No mainstream DBMS product had yet provided a fully functional implementation of scrollable cursors in a client/server environment, and the SQL Server team believed this feature was imperative to add to the database engine. They had also been working on a dramatic new set of management tools, code named *Starfighter* (today's SQL Enterprise Manager), which would also be included in the next release. The new feature list went on and on.

Microsoft's customers were clamoring to hear about the plans for SQL Server post-Sybase. So on June 14, 1994, they put together a briefing event in San Francisco for key customers, analysts, and the press. Jim Allchin, Microsoft senior vice president, walked the attendees through the plans for the future and for the SQL95 release. Attendees were impressed with the plans and direction, but many were openly skeptical of Microsoft's ability to deliver such an impressive product by the end of 1995.

NOTE Some industry press began to sarcastically refer to the planned release as SQL97 and even SQL2000. Internally, the development team was still targeting the first half of 1995. Outside the company, they were more cautious—after all, this is software development, which is still more art than science. Stuff happens, so the SQL Server team said nothing more ambitious than 1995. (Everyone assumed that the planned date was December 31, 1995, and that they'd miss that date too.) The rampant skepticism only served to motivate the SQL Server team even more to show that they could deliver. After all, the team rightly felt that it had *already* delivered an impressive release independent of Sybase. But no one gave them credit for that, so they'd just have to show everyone.

The team worked incredibly hard, even by Microsoft standards, to make this deadline and still deliver a full-featured, high-quality product. The first beta was released at the end of October 1994. Although Starfighter was not feature-complete yet, the database server was complete, and because the server takes the longest lead time for beta sites to really stress it, they went ahead with the beta release. This release was followed with a series of beta updates for the next several months, along with gradual beta-site expansion, eventually surpassing 2000 sites.

For nine months, dinner was delivered each night for late-night workers on the development team—usually a majority. On June 14, 1995, the product was released to manufacturing. Microsoft SQL Server 6.0 (SQL95) had shipped within the original internal target date, much sooner than nearly everyone outside the team expected. It was an immediate hit. Positive reviews appeared in nearly all the trade publications; even more significantly, none were negative or even neutral. Even more important than the press reviews, customer reaction was terrific.

InfoWorld, in its second annual survey of the 100 companies with the most innovative client/server applications in the previous year, showed Microsoft SQL Server as the number two database. SQL Server jumped from 15 percent to 18 percent of those surveyed as the database server of choice—for a virtual tie with Oracle, which dropped from 24 percent to 19 percent. Sybase rose from 12 to 14 percent. Three of the top 10 applications highlighted by *InfoWorld* were built using Microsoft SQL Server.

Of course, the SQL Server development team was happy to see this data, but they took it with a grain of salt. Other data could be interpreted to suggest Microsoft SQL Server's presence was substantially less than the surveys were indicating. And the team recognized that they were still relative newcomers. From a sales perspective, Oracle was clearly king of the hill, and Sybase, Informix, and IBM were also formidable competitors in the DBMS market. Microsoft had not previously been a significant competitive threat. But now it was, and all companies were arming their sales forces with bundles of information for tactics to use to sell against Microsoft SQL Server. Sybase, Informix, and Oracle all promised hot new releases. Although the SQL Server team had been sprinting for nearly four years, now was certainly not the time to get complacent.

Team-Building with Top Talent

Besides working hard on the development of version 6.0, Microsoft was also working to increase the size and strength of the team. It had built a small, crackerjack team that had delivered SQL Server for Windows NT, and this team was the core that delivered SQL95. But the team needed more people, more expertise, and exposure to broader ideas. So they went after top talent in the industry.

Microsoft attracted some industry luminaries—Jim Gray, Dave Lomet, and Phil Bernstein. They also attracted many lesser-known but top development talent from throughout the industry. For example, DEC shopped its Rdb product around, looking to generate cash, and Oracle eventually spent a few hundred million dollars for it. But Microsoft didn't want to buy Rdb. Instead, it hired many of the Rdb project's best developers, augmenting this by hiring several of the best recent Masters' graduates who had specialized in databases.

The Next Version

After shipping version 6.0, many team members took well-deserved vacations after months of working in crunch mode. But within a month, they were actively beginning work on SQL Server version 6.5. With any huge release like version 6.0, some features get deferred due to schedule constraints. And during this ambitious 18-month project, new demands came up that weren't even conceived of as requirements when the project began. For example, the Internet and data warehousing both exploded in importance and demand in 1995. Version 6.5 added capabilities for both. It also included further ease-of-use improvements, gained certification as conforming to the ANSI SQL standard, and provided much richer distributed transactions.

Although version 6.0 was released to manufacturing in June 1995, on December 15, 1995, Microsoft shipped a feature-complete beta version of 6.5

to 150 beta sites. The production version of 6.5 released to manufacturing in April 1996, a scant 10 months after 6.0 was released. The SQL Server team was not about to slow down.

The Secret of the Sphinx

Slowing down was never really an option. Even before SQL Server 6.5 was released, an entirely separate team of developers was hard at work on a brand new vision for Microsoft SQL Server. In 1993, Microsoft had made the decision that databases were to be a core technology in the product line, and in late 1994, it began to hire expertise from DEC and other major vendors to work with Microsoft's Jet and SQL Server teams to start planning components for a whole new generation of database technology. During 1995, the period when SQL Server 6.0 and SQL Server 6.5 were being released, this team was building a new query processor that was being planned as a component for what was to become the Microsoft Data Engine (MSDE).

Development of the component was enhanced by the simultaneous development of OLE DB, which allowed components to be developed independently. Components could then communicate with other components using an OLE DB layer. At the end of 1995, the new query-processing component was integrated into the SQL Server code base, and development of a brand new SQL Server, with the code name *Sphinx,* began in earnest. The team working on the query processor joined the rest of the SQL Server development team.

The development of this new generation of SQL Server had one overriding theme: to re-architect the entire database engine so that the SQL Server product could scale as much as its users wanted it to. This would mean upward growth, to take full advantage of more and faster processors, and as much memory as the operating system could handle. This growth would also have to allow for new techniques to be added to any of the components so that, for example, the query processor code could add an entirely new join algorithm to its repertoire as easily as a new hard drive could be added. In addition to the upward growth, SQL Server would also be expanded outward to support whole new classes of database applications. It would also need to scale downward to run on smaller systems like desktops and laptops.

There were two immediate goals for the first version of this new re-architected system:

- Full row-level locking with an extremely smart lock manager.

- A brand new query processor allowing such techniques as distributed heterogeneous queries, and efficient processing of ad hoc queries. (Ad hoc queries are a fact of life when dealing with data warehousing, Internet-based applications, or both.)

This brand new SQL Server version 7.0 debuted in a limited Beta 1 release in the fall of 1997. Beta 2 was made available to several hundred sites in December 1997. Because of the new architecture, all databases, and the data structures they contained, needed to be completely rebuilt during the upgrade process. Microsoft and the SQL Server development team were absolutely committed to making sure all customers would be successful in moving from SQL Server 6.5 to SQL Server 7.0. A program called the 1K Challenge was instituted, for which 1000 customers were invited to send copies of their databases to the SQL Server development team to be upgraded to version 7.0. A porting lab was set up in the building where the entire development team worked on the Redmond campus. Four or five ISVs every week, from February 1998 through August 1998, sent a team of their own developers to Microsoft to spend an entire week in the lab, making sure their products would work out of the box with the new SQL Server 7.0. The core SQL Server development engineers made themselves available to immediately isolate and fix any bugs encountered, and to spend time talking to the ISVs about the best ways to take advantage of all the new features of SQL Server 7.0 to make their own products even better.

In June 1998, Microsoft publicly released SQL Server 7.0 Beta 3 from its SQL Server Web site, along with a set of exercises demonstrating many of the new features and capabilities of the product. An Internet news server was set up so that any Beta 3 user could report bugs and ask questions of the SQL Server development team. More than 120,000 sites received the Beta 3 version of SQL Server 7.0. This included companies directly requesting the product through the Microsoft Web site, MSDN subscriptions, and Microsoft Beta Program participants (who receive beta versions of all Microsoft products when available). And then at last, after almost four years for some of the earliest team members, SQL Server 7.0 was publicly announced at COMDEX in Las Vegas on November 16, 1998. By the time of the launch, more than a dozen sites were in full production with SQL Server 7.0, including Microsoft's internal Service Advertising Protocol (SAP) implementation and barnesandnoble.com, HarperCollins, CBS Sportsline, Comcast Cellular, and Southwest Securities. The SQL Server 7.0 development team released the product to manufacturing on December 2, 1998, using build 7.00.623.07, with a code freeze date of November 27, 1998. The product became available to the public in January 1999.

The New Future

As expected, most of the team members took well-earned vacations after the December release. But they haven't stopped working on SQL Server. New capabilities are already well past the design stage, ready to be implemented. The development team is using the feedback from the beta forums and from the early users of the released version of SQL Server 7.0 to shape the future of Microsoft SQL Server.

CHAPTER TWO

A TOUR OF SQL SERVER

Microsoft SQL Server 7 is a high-performance, client/server relational database management system (RDBMS). It was designed to support high-volume transaction processing (such as that for online order entry, inventory, accounting, or manufacturing) as well as data warehousing and decision-support applications (such as sales analysis applications). SQL Server runs on Microsoft Windows NT Server–based networks using Intel or DEC Alpha AXP processors and can be installed as a desktop database system on Windows NT Workstation, Windows 95, and Windows 98 machines. Versions of SQL Server for Windows NT Server (on both processor types) and the desktop version ship together on the same CD.

> **NOTE** SQL Server 7 actually has three different editions available on different CDs: Standard edition, Enterprise edition, and Small Business Server edition. Each edition can be installed on either processor type. Each CD also includes the option to install the desktop version on Windows NT, Windows 95, or Windows 98. Chapter 4 will discuss the differences between these editions.

SQL Server 7 also provides many client tools and networking interfaces for other Microsoft operating systems, such as Windows 3.1 and MS-DOS. And because of SQL Server's open architecture, other systems (for example, UNIX-based systems) can interoperate with it as well. SQL Server is part of the core of a family of integrated products, including development tools, systems management tools, distributed system components, and open development interfaces, as shown in Figure 2-1 on the following page. It is also a key part of Microsoft BackOffice.

This book focuses on the capabilities and uses of the SQL Server engine; this chapter provides an overview of the SQL Server family of components and describes the features and benefits of each component. Understanding these features and benefits will prove helpful to you as you develop applications.

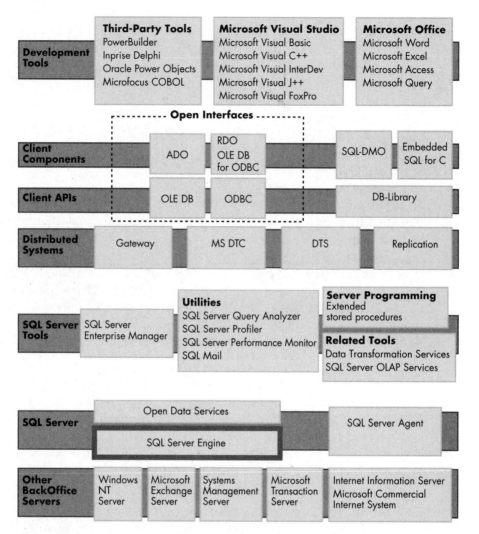

Figure 2-1.
SQL Server and its family of integrated components.

The SQL Server Engine

The SQL Server engine is designed to support a variety of demanding applications, such as online transaction processing (OLTP) and decision-support applications. At the core of its decision-support capabilities is Transact-SQL,

Microsoft's version of Structured Query Language. Beneath this query language are the components that support transaction processing and recoverability.

Transact-SQL

Industrywide, SQL is a well-known and widely used data access language. Every mainstream database management system (DBMS) product implements SQL in some way. Transact-SQL (often referred to as *T-SQL*) is a powerful and unique superset of the SQL standard.

The SQL SELECT statement provides tremendous power and flexibility for retrieving information. Data from multiple tables can be easily projected and the results returned in tabular format with information chosen and correctly combined from the multiple tables. Check out the following two tables from the *pubs* sample database. (The *pubs* database, used for many examples in this book, is installed when SQL Server is installed. For brevity, an abbreviated amount of the data will sometimes be used, as in this example.)

```
publishers Table
pub_id       pub_name              city          state
0736         New Moon Books        Boston        MA
0877         Binnet & Hardley      Washington    DC
1389         Algodata Infosystems  Berkeley      CA


titles Table
title_id    title                                          pub_id
BU1032      The Busy Executive's Database Guide             1389
BU1111      Cooking with Computers: Surreptitious          1389
            Balance Sheets
BU2075      You Can Combat Computer Stress!                0736
BU7832      Straight Talk About Computers                  1389
MC2222      Silicon Valley Gastronomic Treats              0877
MC3021      The Gourmet Microwave                           0877
MC3026      The Psychology of Computer Cooking              0877
```

The following simple SELECT statement logically joins the *titles* and *publishers* tables to project the names of the book titles with the names of the companies publishing each title:

```
SELECT title, pub_name, city, state
FROM titles JOIN publishers
  ON titles.pub_id = publishers.pub_id
```

The result appears on the following page.

title	pub_name	city	state
The Busy Executive's Database Guide	Algodata Infosystems	Berkeley	CA
Cooking with Computers: Surreptitious Balance Sheets	Algodata Infosystems	Berkeley	CA
You Can Combat Computer Stress!	New Moon Books	Boston	MA
Straight Talk About Computers	Algodata Infosystems	Berkeley	CA
Silicon Valley Gastronomic Treats	Binnet & Hardley	Washington	DC
The Gourmet Microwave	Binnet & Hardley	Washington	DC
The Psychology of Computer Cooking	Binnet & Hardley	Washington	DC

This query, a simple SQL statement, shows that standard SQL provides a powerful way to query and manipulate data. (In Chapters 7 and 10, we'll explore SQL queries in much greater depth.)

The National Institute of Standards and Technology (NIST) has certified SQL Server as being compliant with the American National Standards Institute (ANSI) SQL-92 standard. However, considerably more power is available in Transact-SQL because of its unique extensions to the standard.

Standards and Testing

Although the ANSI standard is commonly referred to as *SQL-92*, the official standard is ANSI X3.135-1992 and is entitled *American National Standards Institute Database Language-SQL*. *X3H2* is the designator for the ANSI SQL committee. NIST, a division of the United States Department of Commerce, conducts a suite of tests (which vendors pay the costs of running) to certify compliance with the standard. You can find a summary of products currently certified as compliant at ftp://speckle.ncsl.nist.gov/sql-testing/VPLs.

Transact-SQL Extensions

Transact-SQL provides a number of capabilities that extend beyond typical implementations of SQL. Queries that are difficult to write in standard SQL can be easily and efficiently written using these capabilities. Some favorites include the ability to embed additional SELECT statements in the SELECT list and the ability to drill into a result set by further selecting data directly from a SELECT statement, a feature known as a *derived table*. Transact-SQL provides many system functions for dealing with strings (for finding substrings and so on), for converting datatypes, and for manipulating and formatting date information.

Transact-SQL also provides mathematical operations such as square root. In addition, special operators, such as CUBE and ROLLUP, allow multidimensional analysis to be efficiently projected at the database server, where the analysis can be optimized as part of the execution plan of a query. The CASE expression allows for complex conditional substitutions to be made easily in the SELECT statement. Multidimensional (sometimes referred to as OLAP, or online analytical processing) operators, such as CUBE, and conditional expressions, such as CASE, are especially useful in implementing data warehousing solutions with SQL Server.

The Query Optimizer

In Transact-SQL, a cost-based query optimizer determines the likely best way to access data. This automatic optimization allows you to concentrate on defining your query criteria rather than defining how the query should be executed. For example, this nonprocedural approach eliminates the need for you to know which indexes exist and which, if any, should be used. Would it be more efficient to incur additional I/Os to read index pages in addition to data pages, or would it be better just to scan the data and then sort it? The optimizer automatically, invisibly, and efficiently resolves these types of important questions for you.

The SQL Server optimizer maintains statistics about the volume and dispersion of data, which it then uses to estimate the plan most likely to work best for the operation requested. Because a cost-based optimizer is by definition probability-based, an application might want to override the optimizer in some specialized cases. In your application, you can specify *optimizer hints* that will direct the execution plan chosen. In addition, you can use one of SQL Server's SHOWPLAN options, which explains the execution plan chosen, provides insight into why it was chosen and even allows for tuning of the application and database design.

The Programmable Server

Transact-SQL provides programming constructs—such as variables, conditional operations (IF-THEN-ELSE), and looping—that can dramatically simplify application development by allowing you to use a simple SQL script rather than a third-generation programming language (3GL). These branching and looping constructs can dramatically improve performance in a client/server environment by eliminating the need for network conversations. Minimizing network latency is an important aspect of maximizing client/server application performance. For example, instead of returning a value to the calling application, which requires that the application evaluate and subsequently issue another request, you can build conditional logic directly into the SQL batch file so that the routine is completely evaluated and executed at the server.

You can use Transact-SQL to write complex batches of SQL statements. (A batch of SQL statements in a complex application can potentially be hundreds, or even thousands, of lines long.) An important capability of SQL Server is the SQL Debugging Interface, which allows debuggers such as those available with Microsoft Visual Studio to fully debug Transact-SQL routines, including stepping through the statements, setting breakpoints, and setting watchpoints on Transact-SQL variables.

Stored Procedures

Simply put, stored procedures are collections of SQL statements stored within a SQL Server database. You can code complex queries and transactions into stored procedures and then invoke them directly from the front-end application. Whenever a dynamic SQL command is sent to a database server for processing, the server must parse the command, check its syntax for sense, determine whether the requester has the permissions necessary to execute the command, and formulate an optimal execution plan to process the request. Stored procedures execute faster than batches of dynamic SQL statements, sometimes dramatically faster, because they eliminate the need for reparsing and reoptimizing the requests each time they're executed. SQL Server supports stored procedures that let developers store *groups* of compiled SQL statements on the server for later recall, to limit the overhead when the procedures are subsequently executed.

Stored procedures differ from ordinary SQL statements and from batches of SQL statements in that they're checked for syntax and compiled only the *first time* they're executed. SQL Server stores this compiled version in its memory cache and then uses the cached, compiled version to process subsequent calls, resulting in faster execution times. Stored procedures can also accept parameters, so a single procedure can be used by multiple applications using different input data.

Even if stored procedures provided no performance advantage (which, of course, they do), there would still be a compelling reason to use them: they provide an important layer of insulation from changes in business practices. Suppose, for example, that an application is used to maintain a mailing list for a retailer's catalog distribution. Subsequent to the application being deployed, a change in criteria and logic (that is, the business rules) occurs, thus affecting which customers should automatically receive new catalogs. If the business rules had been programmed directly into the company's applications, every application would need to be modified, likely an expensive and time-consuming operation. Furthermore, if multiple developers worked on the applications, the rules might not have been programmed with the exact same semantics by every programmer.

A stored procedure, on the other hand, can be modified *once,* in seconds, at the server. The applications don't need to be changed or even recompiled. The next time each application executes the stored procedure, the new rules would be in place automatically. In addition to providing a performance advantage, stored procedures can provide an important security function. By granting users access to a stored procedure but not to the underlying tables, you can allow them to access or manipulate data only in the way prescribed by the stored procedure.

Extended Stored Procedures

A unique capability of SQL Server, extended stored procedures allow developers to extend the programming capabilities provided by Transact-SQL and to access resources outside of SQL Server. Messaging integration, security integration, the ability to write Hypertext Markup Language (HTML) files (files formatted for use on the Internet), and much of the power of SQL Server Enterprise Manager (discussed later in this chapter) are all implemented using extended stored procedures. You can create extended stored procedures as external dynamic link libraries (DLLs). (DLLs are typically written in C and C++, although implementation in other languages is also possible.)

For example, you could write a DLL to establish a modem connection, dial the ACME Credit Service, and return a status indicating credit approval or rejection. (The C language more readily lends itself to particular tasks because of such language constructs as arrays, structures, and pointers.) For example, writing a financial function that uses recursion in C (for example, the internal rate of return, or IRR) might be more efficient than writing it as a Transact-SQL stored procedure. Microsoft Open Data Services (ODS) is an API that lets you build extended stored procedures that can return self-describing result sets to the calling client applications, just as a normal procedure would.

Extended stored procedures allow even Microsoft to extend SQL Server. Good engineering practices dictate that where code doesn't benefit from being shared or isn't in common, it should be segregated and isolated. With this principle in mind, Microsoft added integration with messaging via MAPI as a set of extended stored procedures (*xp_sendmail*, *xp_readmail*, and so on) instead of directly modifying the SQL Server engine. Extended stored procedures allow powerful features to be added without any chance of disrupting the core server engine. More features can then be added quickly, with less risk of destabilizing the server. And because the code is loaded dynamically, the DLL is loaded only if a routine is implemented as an extended stored procedure, so the memory footprint of SQL Server doesn't grow for services that aren't being used.

DBMS-Enforced Data Integrity

A database is only as useful as the user's confidence in it. That's why the server must enforce data integrity rules and business policies. SQL Server enforces data integrity within the database itself, guaranteeing that complex business policies are followed and that mandatory relationships between data elements are complied with.

Because SQL Server's client/server architecture allows you to use a variety of front-end applications to manipulate and present the same data from the server, it would be cumbersome to encode all the necessary integrity constraints, security permissions, and business rules into each application. If business policies were all coded in the front-end applications, *every* application would need to be modified *every time* a business policy changed. Even if you attempted to encode business rules into every client application, the danger of an application misbehaving still exists. Most applications can't be fully trusted. Only the server can act as the final arbiter, and the server must not provide a back door for a poorly written or malicious application to subvert its integrity.

SQL Server uses advanced data integrity features, such as stored procedures, declarative referential integrity (DRI), datatypes, constraints, rules, defaults, and triggers, to enforce data integrity. Each of these features has its own use within a database; combining these integrity features can make your database flexible and easy to manage, yet secure.

Declarative Data Integrity

Enforcing data integrity means SQL Server is making sure that all our data is valid. There are several aspects to this concept of data integrity. First is domain integrity. A central tenet of relational database theory is that every *tuple* of every *relation* (more colloquially, every *row* of every *table*) can be uniquely identified. The attribute or combination of attributes (the column or combination of columns) that ensures uniqueness is known as the *primary key*. A table can have only one primary key. SQL Server allows you, when defining a table, to designate the columns that make up the primary key. This is known as a *PRIMARY KEY constraint*. SQL Server uses this PRIMARY KEY constraint to guarantee that the uniqueness of the designated columns is never violated. Domain integrity is enforced for a table by making sure that it has a primary key.

Sometimes multiple columns of a table can uniquely identify a row—for example, an employee table might have an employee ID (*emp_id*) and a Social Security number (*soc_sec_num*) column, and both are considered unique. Such columns are often referred to as *alternate* or *candidate keys*. These keys must also be unique. Although a table can have only one primary key, it can have multiple alternate keys. SQL Server supports the multiple alternate key concept via *UNIQUE constraints*. When a column or combination of columns is declared unique, SQL Server prevents any record from being added or updated that would violate this uniqueness.

Assigning an arbitrary unique number as the primary key when no natural or convenient key exists is often most efficient. For example, businesses commonly use customer numbers or account numbers as unique identifiers or primary keys. SQL Server makes it easy to efficiently generate unique numbers by allowing one column in a table to have the *Identity property*. You use the Identity property to make sure that each value in the column is unique and that the values will increment (or decrement) by the amount you specify from a starting point that you specify. (A column having the Identity property will typically also have a PRIMARY KEY or UNIQUE constraint, but this isn't required.)

The second type of data integrity is referential integrity. SQL Server enforces logical relationships between tables with *FOREIGN KEY constraints*. A *foreign key* in a table is a column or combination of columns that match the primary key (or possibly an alternate key) of another table. The logical relationship between those two tables is the basis of the relational model.

For instance, the simple SELECT example shown on pages 33 and 34 includes a *titles* table and a *publishers* table. The *titles* table column *title_id* (title ID) is its primary key. The *publishers* table column *pub_id* (publisher ID) is its primary key. The *titles* table also includes a *pub_id* column, which isn't the primary key because a publisher can publish multiple titles. Instead, *pub_id* is a foreign key, and it references the primary key of the *publishers* table. After this relationship is declared when the table is defined, SQL Server ensures that a title can't be entered unless a valid publisher for it is in the database, and that a publisher can't be deleted if any titles in the database reference that publisher. Enforcing referential integrity means that the relationship between primary keys and foreign keys is never violated.

The third type of data integrity is domain integrity, which means that individual data values must meet certain criteria. SQL Server makes sure that any data entered matches the type and range of the specified data type and, for example, allows a NULL value to be entered only if the column has been declared as allowing NULLs. SQL Server supports a wide range of datatypes, allowing for great flexibility with efficient storage. This ability to enforce data integrity based on the constraints you define when you create the database tables is known as declarative data integrity.

Datatypes

SQL Server datatypes provide the simplest form of data integrity by restricting the types of information (for example, characters, numbers, or dates) that can be stored in the columns of the database tables. You can also design your own datatypes (*user-defined* datatypes) to supplement those supplied by the system. For example, you could define a *state_code* datatype as two characters (CHAR(2)); SQL Server would then accept only two-character state codes. A user-defined datatype can be used to define columns in *any* table. An advantage of user-defined datatypes is that rules and defaults, which are discussed in the next two sections, can be bound to them for use in multiple tables, eliminating the need to include these types of checks in the front-end application.

CHECK Constraints and Rules

CHECK constraints and rules are integrity constraints that go beyond those implied by a column's datatype. Whenever a user enters a value, SQL Server checks that value against any CHECK constraint or rule created for the specified column to ensure that only values that adhere to the definition of the constraint or rule are accepted.

Although CHECK constraints and rules are essentially equivalent in functionality, CHECK constraints are easier to use and provide more flexibility. A CHECK constraint can be conveniently defined when a column is defined, and constraints can be defined on multiple columns. Rules, however, must be defined and then bound to a column or user-defined datatype separately. While a column or user-defined datatype can have only one rule associated with it, a CHECK constraint can reference multiple columns in the same table, or it can reference one of the built-in functions that SQL Server provides.

Both CHECK constraints and rules can require that a value fall within a particular range, match a particular pattern, or match one of the entries in a specified list. An advantage of CHECK constraints is that they can depend on either the value of another field or fields in the row or on the value returned by one of the system-supplied functions. A rule can't reference other fields. As an example of applying a CHECK constraint or rule, a database containing information on senior citizens could have the CHECK constraint or rule "age field must contain a value between 65 and 120 years." A birth certificate database could require that the date in the *birth_date* field be some date prior to the current date.

Defaults

Defaults allow you to specify a value that SQL Server inserts if no explicit value is entered in a particular field. For example, you could set the current date as the default value for an *order_date* field in a customer order record. Then, if a user or front-end application doesn't make an entry in the *order_date* field, SQL Server automatically inserts the current date. You can also use the keyword DEFAULT as a placeholder in an INSERT or UPDATE statement, instructing SQL Server to set the value to the declared default value.

Triggers

Triggers are a special type of stored procedure. Stored procedures can be executed only when explicitly called; triggers are automatically invoked, or *triggered,* by SQL Server, and this is their main advantage. Triggers are associated with particular pieces of data and are called automatically whenever an attempt to modify that data is made, no matter what causes the modification (a user's entry or an application action).

Conceptually, triggers are similar to a CHECK constraint or rule. SQL Server automatically activates triggers, constraints, and rules whenever an attempt is made to modify the data they protect. CHECK constraints and rules then perform fairly simple types of checks on the data—for example, "make sure the age field has a value between 0 and 120." Triggers, on the other hand, can perform extremely elaborate restrictions on the data, which helps to ensure that the rules by which your business operates can't be subverted. Because triggers are a form of stored procedure, they have the full power of the Transact-SQL language at their disposal, and they can invoke other stored and extended stored procedures. You can write a trigger that enforces complex business rules, such as the following:

Don't accept an order:

If the customer has any past due accounts with us

OR

If the customer has a bad credit rating by ACME Credit Service (with the trigger calling an extended procedure that automatically dials up ACME to get the credit rating)

OR

If the order is for more than $50,000 and the customer has had an account with us for less than six months

This integrity check is quite powerful. Yet the trigger to enforce it is simple to write. Triggers can also enforce *referential integrity,* ensuring that relationships between tables are maintained. For example, a trigger can prohibit a customer record from being deleted if open orders exist for the customer, or it can prohibit any new order for a customer for which no record exists. Triggers can go beyond simply insisting that relationships exist: they can perform *referential actions.* This means that triggers can cause changes to ripple through to other tables. For example, if you want to drop a delinquent customer from your system and delete all of that customer's active orders, a trigger on the *customer* table could automatically delete all entries in the *orders* table.

Triggers automatically execute whenever a specified change to a data object is attempted. A trigger executes once per statement, even if multiple rows are affected. It has access to the before and after images of the data. (These before and after images are reconstructed from the transaction log into pseudotables that can be accessed from within the trigger.) The trigger can then take further action, including rolling back the transaction. Although you can use triggers to enforce referential integrity, it is usually more convenient to establish these relationships when you create the tables by using declarative referential integrity.

Transaction Processing

Transaction processing guarantees the consistency and recoverability of SQL Server databases. A *transaction* is the basic unit of work under SQL Server. Typically, it consists of several SQL commands that read and update the database, but the update is not considered "final" until a COMMIT command is issued. (Note that the example below is pseudocode and that error handling is required to achieve the behavior described.)

Transaction processing in SQL Server assures that all transactions are performed as a single unit of work—even in the presence of a hardware or general system failure. Such transactions are referred to as having the *ACID properties:* atomicity, consistency, isolation, and durability. In addition to the explicit multistatement transactions such as those provided in the DEBIT_CREDIT example below, SQL Server guarantees that a single command that affects multiple rows maintains the ACID properties.

Here's an example in pseudocode of an ACID transaction, followed by an explanation of each of the ACID properties.

```
BEGIN TRANSACTION DEBIT_CREDIT
Debit savings account $1000
Credit checking account $1000
COMMIT TRANSACTION DEBIT_CREDIT
```

Atomicity

SQL Server guarantees the atomicity of its transactions. With atomicity, each transaction is treated as all-or-nothing—it either commits or aborts. If a transaction commits, all of its effects remain. If it aborts, all of its effects are undone. In the previous DEBIT_CREDIT example, if the savings account debit is reflected in the database but the checking account credit isn't, funds will essentially disappear from the database; that is, funds will be debited from the savings account but never credited to the checking account. If the reverse occurred (if the checking account were credited and the savings account were *not* debited), the customer's account would mysteriously increase in value without a corresponding customer cash deposit or account transfer. Because of SQL Server's atomicity feature, both the debit and credit must be completed, or neither event is completed.

Consistency

The consistency property ensures that a transaction won't allow the system to enter an incorrect logical state—the data must always be logically correct. Constraints and rules are honored, even in the event of a system failure. For the DEBIT_CREDIT example, the logical rule is that money can't be created or destroyed—a corresponding, counter-balancing entry must be made for each entry. (Consistency is implied by, and for most situations is redundant to, atomicity, isolation, and durability.)

Isolation

Isolation separates concurrent transactions from the updates of other incomplete transactions. In the DEBIT_CREDIT example, another transaction can't see the work-in-progress while the transaction is being carried out. For example, if another transaction read the balance of the savings account after the debit occurred, and then the DEBIT_CREDIT transaction was aborted, the other transaction would be working from a balance that never logically existed.

Isolation among transactions is accomplished automatically by SQL Server. It locks data to allow multiple concurrent users to work with data, but it prevents side-effects that could distort the results and make them different than would be expected if users serialized their requests (that is, if requests were queued and ran one at a time). This serializability feature is one of the isolation levels that SQL Server supports. SQL Server supports multiple degrees of isolation levels that allow you to make the appropriate tradeoff between how much data to lock and how long locks must be held. This tradeoff is known as *concurrency* vs. *consistency*. Locking reduces concurrency (because locked data is unavailable to other users), but it provides the benefit of higher consistency. (Chapter 13 provides much more detail about locking.)

Durability

After a transaction commits, SQL Server's durability property ensures that the effects of the transaction will persist even if a system failure occurs. Conversely, if a system failure occurs while a transaction is in progress, the transaction will be completely undone, leaving no partial effects on the data. For example, if a power outage occurs in the midst of a transaction before the transaction is committed, the entire transaction will be automatically rolled back when the system is restarted. If the power fails immediately after the acknowledgment of the commit is sent to the calling application, the transaction is guaranteed to exist in the database. Write-ahead logging and automatic rollback and rollforward of transactions during the recovery phase of SQL Server startup assure durability.

Symmetric Server Architecture

SQL Server uses a single-process, multithreaded architecture known as Symmetric Server Architecture that provides scalable high performance with efficient use of system resources. With Symmetric Server Architecture, only one memory address space is provided for the DBMS, eliminating the overhead of having to manage shared memory.

Traditional Process/Thread Model

To understand and contrast the architecture of SQL Server, it's useful for you to first understand the traditional architectures that have been used by UNIX-based DBMS products. UNIX-based DBMS products are usually structured in one of two ways. In the first way, multiple processes (or *shadow processes*) are used, with one process per user, which makes the system quite resource intensive. The second type of architecture employs a single process that tries to simulate an operating system threading facility by moving in a round-robin way among multiple requests, maintaining a stack for each request and switching to that specific stack for whatever unit is being executed.

> **NOTE** A *stack* is a LIFO (last-in, first-out) data structure kept in memory that basically serves as the control block for the executable unit to the operating system (a *thread* on Windows NT, often called a *lightweight process* on other operating systems). A stack stores status data such as function call addresses, passed parameters, and some local variables.

In the first approach, because each process has its own address space, processes must resort to shared memory to communicate with one another. Unfortunately, shared memory is less efficient to use than the private memory of a process's own address space because of the weight of synchronization mechanisms (semaphores, mutexes, and so on) that are needed to avoid collisions while accessing shared memory. In addition, the implementation of stack switching and efficient access to shared memory adds overhead and complexity. Adding complexity to a system is never good. The best way to avoid bugs in software and maximize performance is to keep code simple and, better yet, to write no new code when an existing tried-and-true service exists.

In the second approach—simulated multithreading—the DBMS performs duties usually handled by the operating system. Typically, using such an architecture requires that the executing task be trusted to yield back to the system so another task can be run. If the task doesn't yield (because of software or hardware failure), *all* other tasks will be severely—perhaps fatally—affected.

SQL Server Process/Thread Model

SQL Server 7 uses a scheduling architecture that's somewhere in between the two traditional approaches. Windows NT makes available support for lightweight threads, called *fibers*. Certain high-volume symmetric multiprocessing (SMP) systems can gain considerable performance benefits by using fibers instead of using threads, and Microsoft wanted to make this functionality possible with SQL Server.

> **SEE ALSO** A more complete description of the Windows NT process and thread model is beyond the scope of this book. For more information, refer to *Inside Windows NT*, Second Edition, by David Solomon (Microsoft Press, 1998).

To enable the option of using fibers, SQL Server takes control of its own scheduling of processes. It enables this option by using one or more NT threads as its own schedulers. These threads are called *UMS threads,* or *User Mode Schedulers*. Whether it's running in thread mode or fiber mode, SQL Server uses only one UMS thread per CPU. Each SQL Server process is associated with exactly one UMS thread, and the process will remain with that UMS thread for its lifetime. Windows NT can schedule each of the UMS threads on any of the available processors. Each UMS thread determines which of the SQL Server processes associated with that UMS thread should run at any given time. Chapter 15 examines in detail how to control whether SQL Server processes run on threads or fibers, and the benefits and drawbacks of each option.

SQL Server processes that execute non-SQL Server code aren't scheduled by the UMS. These include processes that run extended stored procedures and processes that run distributed queries. These processes are scheduled on normal operating system threads and managed by Windows NT's own scheduler. In addition, when SQL Server is executing a backup or restore operation, additional UMS threads control the progress of the operation.

Multiuser Performance

The efficiency of the SQL Server threading model is borne out by its multiuser performance. SQL Server is able to efficiently handle hundreds, even thousands, of simultaneous active users. Built-in thread pooling allows workloads of this magnitude to be performed without the need for an external Transaction (TP) Monitor, which adds cost and complexity to a system.

> **NOTE** Of course, questions such as "How many users can SQL Server handle?" or "How big a database can it handle?" never have simple answers. The answers to these questions depend on the application and its design, required response times and throughput, and the hardware on which the system is running.

The majority of systems that just a couple years ago required a mainframe or large minicomputer-based solution can now be efficiently built, deployed, and managed with SQL Server. Such industry-standard benchmarks as TPC-C can be illuminating. Today's SQL Server can perform workloads that surpass those submitted by the largest mainframe systems of a few years ago. As computer resources continue to grow, SQL Server will extend its reach into systems that traditionally would have required a mainframe solution.

Security

SQL Server provides numerous levels of security. At the outermost layer, SQL Server logon security is integrated directly with Windows NT security, allowing a Windows NT server to authenticate users. With this *Windows NT authentication* in place, SQL Server can take advantage of the security features of Windows NT, such as password encryption, password aging, and maximum length restrictions on passwords.

Windows NT authentication relies on *trusted connections,* which make use of the impersonation feature of Windows NT. Through impersonation, SQL Server can take on the security context of the Windows NT user account initiating the connection and test whether the security identifier (SID) has a valid privilege level. Windows NT impersonation and trusted connections are available with any of the available network interfaces (Net-Libraries) when connecting to SQL Server running under Windows NT.

For SQL Server running under Windows 95 or Windows 98, Windows NT authentication isn't available. An administrator must create SQL Server login accounts within SQL Server. Any user connecting to SQL Server must supply a SQL Server login name and password, regardless of whether she has already logged on to the network. This type of validation is what's known as *SQL Server authentication.*

SQL Server can be installed in a *mixed security* model, which means that Windows NT–based clients can connect using Windows NT authentication, and connections that don't come from Windows NT clients, or that come across the Internet, can connect using SQL Server authentication. In addition, when connecting to an instance of SQL Server that has been installed with mixed security, a connection can always supply a SQL Server login name explicitly. This would allow a connection to be made using a login name distinct from the username in Windows NT. However, if you connect to an instance of SQL Server configured for only Windows NT authentication, you won't be able to supply a SQL Server logon name, and your Windows NT username determines your level of access to SQL Server.

Monitoring and Managing Security

SQL Server makes it easy to monitor logon successes and failures. Using SQL Server Enterprise Manager, administrators can simply check the appropriate box in the Security tab of the Properties dialog box for a particular installation of SQL Server. When logon monitoring is enabled in this way, each time a user successfully or unsuccessfully attempts to log on to SQL Server, a message is written to the Windows NT application log, the SQL Server error log, or both, indicating the time, date, and user who tried to log on.

SQL Server has a number of facilities for managing data security. Access privileges (select, insert, update, and delete) can be granted or denied to users or groups of users on objects such as tables and views. Execute privileges can be granted on local and extended stored procedures. For example, to prevent a user from directly updating a specific table, you can write a stored procedure that updates the table and then cascades those updates to other tables as necessary. You can grant the user access to execute the stored procedure, thereby ensuring that all updates will take place through the stored procedure, eliminating the possibility of integrity problems arising from ad hoc updates to the base table.

High Availability

In many mission-critical environments, it's imperative that the application be available at all times—24 hours a day, seven days a week. SQL Server helps availability by providing online backup, online maintenance, automatic recovery, and the ability to install SQL Server on a cluster for failover support.

SQL Server's dynamic online backup allows databases to be backed up while users are actively querying and updating in the database. The SQL Server Agent service provides a built-in scheduling engine that enables backups to occur automatically, without involving the administrator. You can also accomplish other maintenance tasks, such as diagnostics, design changes (for example, adding a column to a table), and integrity changes without having to shut down SQL Server or restrict user access.

Only a few systemwide configuration modifications, such as changing the maximum number of user connections, require that SQL Server be restarted. Although reconfiguration doesn't commonly occur in a well-planned and well-deployed production system, it can typically be completed with less than a minute of system downtime if it's necessary.

In the event of a system failure, such as a power outage, SQL Server ensures rapid database recovery when services are restored. By using the transaction logs associated with each database, SQL Server quickly recovers each database upon startup, rolling back transactions that hadn't completed yet and rolling forward transactions that had committed but weren't written to disk yet. In addition, you can set the SQL Server Agent service to continually monitor the state of SQL Server. If an error occurs that causes SQL Server to stop unexpectedly, the SQL Server Agent service will detect this and can automatically restart SQL Server with minimal interruption.

In cooperation with shared-disk cluster hardware, SQL Server Enterprise Edition provides failover support when installing SQL Server on a node that's part of a Microsoft Cluster Server (MSCS) cluster. The applications communicating with SQL Server don't need to know that the server they're connecting to is actually a virtual server, which can be running on either member of a cluster. If the server on which SQL Server is running fails, the second server in the cluster immediately takes ownership of the disks that hold the SQL Server data and takes over its workload. The second server in the cluster doesn't need to be inactive while the first server is working—it can be running SQL Server while it's performing other activities.

Distributed Data Processing

SQL Server provides features such as linked servers, remote stored procedure calls, and two-phase commit protocol that enable you to easily manage and use data in distributed environments. Microsoft Distributed Transaction Coordinator (MS DTC) was designed to be the vote collector and coordinator of transactions, and it allows many different types of systems to participate, laying the foundation for ACID transactions among heterogeneous systems.

A system participating in a transaction coordinated by MS DTC manages its own work and is called a *resource manager*. This resource manager system communicates with MS DTC, which coordinates all the resource managers participating in the transaction to implement the two-phase commit protocol. Distributed transactions honoring the ACID properties are supported as a whole: the entire distributed transaction at all sites either commits or aborts.

In the first phase of the two-phase commit protocol, all participating resource managers (that is, those that have enlisted in the transaction) *prepare to commit*. This means that they have acquired all the locks and resources they need to complete the transaction. MS DTC then acts as a vote collector. If it gets confirmation that all participants are prepared to commit, it signals to go ahead and commit.

The actual COMMIT is the second phase of the protocol. If one or more participants notify the system that it can't successfully prepare the transaction, MS DTC automatically sends a message to all participants indicating that they must abort the transaction. (In this case, an *abort,* rather than a commit, is the second phase of the protocol.) If one or more participants don't report back to MS DTC in phase one, the resource managers that have indicated they're prepared to commit (but haven't committed because they haven't received the instruction to do so yet) are said to be *in doubt*. Resource managers that have transactions in doubt indefinitely hold the locks and resources necessary to ultimately commit or roll back the transaction, preserving the ACID properties. (SQL Server provides a way to force in-doubt transactions to abort.)

Another important distributed capability allows SQL Server to issue a *remote procedure call (RPC)* to another server running SQL Server. Remote procedure calls are stored procedures that can be invoked from a remote server, allowing server-to-server communication. This communication can be accomplished transparently to the client application, because the client can execute a procedure on one server, and that procedure can then invoke a procedure located on a different server.

Using RPCs can easily extend the capacity of an application without the added cost of reengineering the client application. Remote procedure calls optionally can be coordinated by the MS DTC service to ensure that the transactions maintain their ACID properties. The default behavior is to *not* execute the RPC in the context of a transaction so that if the local transaction is rolled back, work done by the RPC will still be committed. This behavior can be overridden by using the command BEGIN DISTRIBUTED TRANSACTION, or by setting the configuration option *remote proc trans* to 1.

Distributed data can also be managed by defining and accessing *linked servers*. A linked server can be any data source for which an OLE DB provider exists. The most commonly used OLE DB providers are the SQL Server OLE DB provider; the Jet provider, which allows you to connect to Microsoft Access databases; and the Open Database Connectivity (ODBC) provider, which allows you to connect to any ODBC data source.

A linked server is a logical name, defined using the stored procedure *sp_addlinkedserver*. The information you provide when you define the linked server includes the name and location of the datasource to connect to. Once you've defined the name, you can use that name as the first part of a four-part name for any object, such as tables, views, or stored procedures. Objects on the linked server can be queried as well as modified, and they can be used in joins with local objects. The types of queries possible on the linked server depend on the capabilities of the particular OLE DB providers. Some providers, such as the one for SQL Server, allow all data modification operations and full transaction control across linked servers. Others, such as the OLE DB provider for text files, allow only querying of data.

Data Replication

Replication allows you to automatically distribute copies of data from one server to one or more destination servers at one or more remote locations. *Data integrity* is a key design point of SQL Server's replication capabilities. The data at replicating sites might be slightly outdated, but it will accurately reflect the true state of the data at a recent point in time and is guaranteed to reflect any changes made soon after they occur (or soon after a reliable network connection is established).

SQL Server 7 supports three modes of replication, which are detailed on the companion CD in a whitepaper entitled "Understanding SQL Server 7.0 Replication":

- **Transaction-based replication**   In this mode of replication, one site is considered the owner, or publisher, of a published article (a table or a subset of a table), and other sites subscribe to that article. All changes made to the article must be made at the publisher and then replicated to the subscribers.

- **Merge replication**   Although the publisher defines the articles to be published, any participating sites can make changes. System tables keep track of the changes, which are then propagated to all participants, including the original publisher. You can define which type of conflict resolution to use in the event of conflicting updates made by multiple sites.

- **Snapshot replication**   All data from the publishing site is periodically copied to all the subscribing sites. Individual changes aren't propagated. Formerly, this method was called *scheduled table refresh*.

Distributed transactions using the two-phase commit protocol guarantee ACID properties, but replication doesn't. Replication isn't strongly consistent (the *C* in ACID). Instead, replication provides *loosely consistent* data. With the two-phase commit protocol, a transaction is an all-or-nothing proposition, and the data is assured to be *strongly consistent*. But inherent in the two-phase commit algorithm is the fact that a failure at any one site makes the entire transaction fail or can keep the transaction in doubt for long periods of time, during which all participants need to hold locks, crippling concurrency.

At first glance, you might think a system should require that updates be made at all sites in *real time*. In fact, when the costs of two-phase commit are realized (chiefly, the vulnerability that can result from a failure at just one node), the most pragmatic solution might be to make changes in *real enough time*.

For example, suppose you run a car rental agency with 500 rental counters worldwide, and you maintain a customer profile table containing 500,000 renters who belong to your Gold Card program. You want to store this customer profile locally at all 500 rental counters so that even if a communication failure occurs, the profile will be available wherever a Gold Card member might walk up to do business. Although all sites should have up-to-date records of all customers, it would be disastrous to insist that an update of the Gold Card profile must occur as part of a two-phase transaction for all 500 sites or not at all. With this scenario, because of the realities of worldwide communications, or because at one site a storm might have knocked out the power, you probably wouldn't be able to perform a simple update to the customer profile very often.

Replication is a much better solution in such a case. The master customer profile table would be maintained at your corporate headquarters. Replication publishes this data, and the rental counters then subscribe to this information. When customer data is changed, or when a customer is added or removed, these changes (and *only* the changes) are propagated to all the subscribing sites. In a well-connected network, the time delay might be just a few seconds. If a particular site is unavailable, no other sites are affected—they still get their changes. When the unavailable site is back online, the changes are automatically propagated and the subscriber is brought up to date. At any time, a given rental counter might not have exactly the same information as the corporate site—it might be slightly out of date. The data at the rental counter is consistent with the state of the data at the corporate headquarters at some earlier time; it's not necessarily consistent with the current corporate site data. This is considered loosely consistent, as opposed to the strongly consistent model of two-phase commit in which all sites (or none) immediately reflect the change.

Although a time delay can occur in loosely consistent systems, maintaining transactional consistency is one of the chief design points of SQL Server replication. If multiple updates occur as a single atomic transaction to data being replicated, the entire transaction will also be replicated. At the subscribing site, the transaction will either entirely commit or it will again be replicated until it commits.

With SQL Server, data can be replicated continuously or at specified intervals. It can be replicated in its entirety or as filtered subsets (known as *horizontal* and *vertical partitions*). In addition to replication to other SQL Servers, version 7 can replicate to heterogeneous data sources that have an appropriate ODBC driver or OLE DB provider available. These include Access databases, Oracle databases, and other ODBC data sources. Additionally, SQL Server 7 can replicate *from* other data sources, using ODBC drivers or OLE DB providers. These sources include Oracle 8, Microsoft Jet version 4, and IBM DB2.

Unlike SQL Server, some products on the market promote replication as an "Update Anywhere, Anytime, Anyway" model. However, this model has inherently unstable behavior if many nodes participate and update activity is moderate to heavy.[1] Updates made at multiple sites will conflict with one another and must be reconciled. SQL Server 7's merge replication does allow multiple site updates, but it's not a true "Update Anywhere, Anytime, Anyway" solution. Refer to the whitepaper on the companion CD for more details on exactly what SQL Server merge replication can do.

Systems Management

The difficulty of systems management is probably the single biggest obstacle that has inhibited mass deployment of client/server solutions. Far from being a downsized version of the mainframe, today's distributed client/server system can be deployed on dozens or even hundreds of distributed servers, all of which must be controlled to the same exacting standards as mainframe production software systems. The issues here reside both inside and outside the database environment. SQL Server provides a comprehensive architecture and tools for managing the database and related activities.

SQL Server Enterprise Manager

SQL Server Enterprise Manager is a major advancement in making client/server deployments manageable. In SQL Server 7, Enterprise Manager is a snap-in to Microsoft Management Console (MMC). MMC is a tool that provides a common interface for managing various server applications in a Windows network. (Another snap-in that's provided on your SQL Server 7 CD for use with MMC is the Microsoft SQL Server OLAP Services snap-in.)

Easy to use, SQL Server Enterprise Manager supports centralized management of all aspects of multiple installations of SQL Server, including managing security, events, alerts, scheduling, backup, server configuration, tuning, and replication. SQL Server Enterprise Manager allows SQL Server database schemas and objects such as tables, views, and triggers to be created, modified, and

---

1. Gray, Helland, O'Neil, and Shasha, "The Dangers of Replication and a Solution," SIGMOD (1996). SIGMOD (Special Interest Group on Management of Data) is a yearly database-oriented conference for developers. For more information, see http://www.acm.org/sigmod/.

copied. Because multiple installations of SQL Server can be organized into groups and treated as a unit, SQL Server Enterprise Manager can manage hundreds of servers simultaneously.

Although it can run on the same computer as the SQL Server engine, SQL Server Enterprise Manager offers the same management capabilities while running on any Windows NT Workstation or Windows NT Server in the environment. SQL Server Enterprise Manager also runs on Windows 95 and Windows 98, although a few capabilities aren't available in these environments (most notably the ability to use Service Control Manager, a feature of Windows NT, to remotely start and stop SQL Server). In addition, the efficient client/server architecture of SQL Server makes it practical to use the remote access (dial-up networking) capabilities of Windows NT, Windows 95, and Windows 98 for administration and management.

SQL Server Enterprise Manager provides an easy-to-use interface, as shown in Figure 2-2. You can perform even complex tasks with just a few mouse clicks.

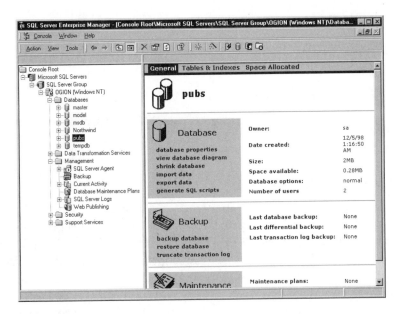

Figure 2-2.
Easy-to-use interface for SQL Server Enterprise Manager.

SQL Server Enterprise Manager relieves you from having to know the specific steps and syntax to complete a job. SQL Server provides over 20 wizards to guide you through the process of setting up and maintaining your installation of SQL Server. A partial list is shown in Figure 2-3.

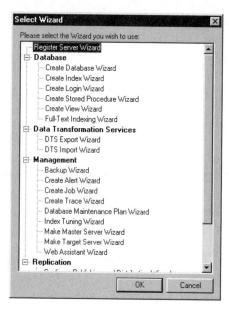

Figure 2-3.
Some of the wizards available for setting up and maintaining your server.

Distributed Management Objects

In the Windows 95, Windows 98, and Windows NT operating systems, Microsoft SQL Server Distributed Management Objects (SQL-DMO) provides 32-bit Automation (formerly known as OLE Automation). These objects, properties, methods, and collections are used to write scripts and programs that can administer multiple servers running SQL Server distributed across a network. SQL Server Enterprise Manager is built entirely with SQL-DMO. You can customize your own specific management needs using SQL-DMO, or you can integrate management of SQL Server into other tools you use or provide.

All SQL Server functions are exposed in the form of objects, methods, and properties. The SQL-DMO model simplifies the management surface of SQL

Server by organizing management functions in terms of the SQL Server object model. The primary object is SQLServer, which contains a collection of Database objects. The Database object contains a collection of Table, View, and StoredProcedure objects. Objects contain properties (*SQLServer.Name = "MARKETING_SVR"*) and methods (SQLServer.Start or SQLServer.Shutdown). Table 2-1 provides some examples of SQL-DMO objects and methods.

Object.Method	Action
SQLServer.Shutdown	Stops SQL Server.
SQLServer.Start	Starts SQL Server.
Database.Dump	Performs a database dump.
Index.UpdateStatistics	Updates optimizer information for indexes.
Database.Tables.Add	Adds a table to a database.

Table 2-1.
SQL-DMO objects and methods.

The SQL-DMO object model is comprehensive, consisting of dozens of distinct objects and hundreds of Component Object Model (COM) interfaces. The organization of these objects, a subset of which is shown in Figure 2-4 on the following page, greatly reduces the task of learning and fully using SQL Server management components.

Any 32-bit Automation–controlling application can harness the power and services of SQL-DMO. Probably the most common such Automation controller is Microsoft Visual Basic.

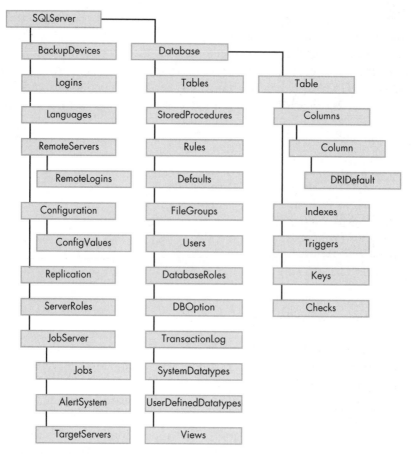

Figure 2-4.
The SQL-DMO model.

Automation and Visual Basic Scripting

The power of using an ActiveX interface (Automation) for SQL Server management becomes clear when you consider the potential of using a robust language such as Visual Basic as a scripting environment for administrative tasks. The following sample code lists the name of and space available on all databases on a server. This code is simple, compact, and easy to write and read, yet powerful. (Traditionally, programming such a task would have required several pages of much more complex C code.)

```
Dim MyServer as New SQLServer      ' Declare the SQL Server object
MyServer.Name = "MARKETING_SVR"
MyServer.Login = "sa"
MyServer.Connect         ' Connect to the SQL Server
' List the name and space available for all databases
For Each MyDB In MyServer.Databases
    Print MyDB.Name, MyDB.SpaceAvailable
Next MyDB
MyServer.Disconnect          ' Disconnect
```

SQL Server Agent

SQL Server Agent is an active, intelligent agent that plays an integral role in the management of the SQL Server environment. It provides a full-function scheduling engine designed to support regular tasks for the management and administration of SQL Server, and it allows you to schedule your own jobs and programs.

SQL Server Agent is a Windows NT–based service that can be started when Windows NT starts. It can also be controlled and configured from within SQL Server Enterprise Manager or SQL Server Service Manager. SQL Server Agent is entirely driven by entries in SQL Server tables that act as its control block. Clients never directly communicate with or connect to SQL Server Agent to add or modify scheduled jobs. Instead, they simply make the appropriate entries in the SQL Server tables (although this typically occurs through SQL Server Enterprise Manager via a simple dialog box that's similar to a typical calendar program). At startup, SQL Server Agent connects to an installation of SQL Server that contains its job table and then loads the list of jobs, the steps that make up each job, and the possible alerts that can be fired.

SQL Server Agent, like the SQL Server engine, is a single multithreaded process. It runs in its own process space and manages the creation of Windows NT threads to execute scheduled jobs. Its discrete managed subsystems (for replication, task management, and event alerting) are responsible for all aspects of processing specific jobs. When jobs are completed (successfully or not), the subsystem returns a result status (with optional messages) to SQL Server Agent. SQL Server Agent then records the completion status in the Windows NT application log and job history table in SQL Server and optionally sends e-mail to the designated administrator reporting the job status.

In SQL Server 7, scheduled jobs can be made up of multiple steps, and each step defines the action to take on success and the action to take on failure. Thus, you can control the execution of subsequent steps when a step fails.

SQL Server 7 allows you to define a server as a *master* server, for the purpose of defining jobs that will be carried out by one or more *target* servers. These target servers periodically poll their master server to determine whether any new jobs have been defined, and if so, the master server downloads the job definitions to the target server. After the jobs are run on the target server, the success or failure status is reported back to the master server. The master server keeps the complete job history for all its target servers.

The event/alert subsystem gives SQL Server its ability to support proactive management. The primary role of the event/alert subsystem is to respond to events by raising alerts and invoking responses. As triggering activities (or user-defined activities) occur in the system, an event is posted to the Windows NT application log. The application log then notifies SQL Server Agent that an event has occurred.

SQL Server Agent determines whether any alerts have been defined for this event by examining the event's error number, severity, database of origin, and message text. If an alert has been defined (in the alert table), the administrator or administrators can be alerted via e-mail, pager, or with a *net send* message. Or a SQL Server Agent task can be invoked when the alert is fired and can take corrective action. (For example, SQL Server Agent might automatically expand a full database.)

If no alerts are defined locally, the event can be forwarded to another server for processing. This feature allows groups of servers to be monitored centrally so that alerts and administrators can be defined once and then applied to multiple servers. Beyond the database environment, Microsoft Systems Management Server (SMS)—a BackOffice component—is available to provide key services to manage the overall software configuration of all the desktops and servers in the environment.

Alerts can also be fired in response to Windows NT Performance Monitor thresholds being crossed. Normally, crossing a threshold isn't considered an error, and no event is written to the Windows NT application log. However, the alert system in SQL Server 7 is integrated with the performance counters available through the Windows NT Performance Monitor (discussed later in this chapter), and SQL Server can take action when a counter rises above or falls below a specified value. The kinds of actions possible are the same actions described above: the administrator or administrators can be alerted via e-mail, pager, or with a *net send* message. Or a SQL Server Agent task can be invoked to take corrective action when the alert is fired.

For example, SQL Server Agent might automatically expand a database that's *almost* full. Note that being almost full is technically not an error: no error number or severity level is associated with this situation. However, because the Windows NT Performance Monitor can detect the condition of a database file reaching a certain percentage of its capacity, an alert can be raised. Figure 2-5 shows the definition of an alert based on a Performance Monitor threshold. This alert will be fired when the log file for the *Northwind* database exceeds 80 percent of its capacity.

Figure 2-5.
Alert definition for an 80 percent full condition in the Northwind *database.*

SQL Server Utilities and Extensions

SQL Server also includes utilities and extensions that provide increased functionality, such as Internet enabling, monitoring capability, easy setup, and easy data importing.

Web Assistant Wizard and Internet Enabling

SQL Server provides dynamic ways for working with the Internet: Web Assistant Wizard and interoperability with Microsoft Internet Information Server (IIS).

Although both Web Assistant Wizard and IIS enable SQL Server data to be used with Web pages, they satisfy different needs.

Web Assistant Wizard generates HTML files from the result sets of SQL Server queries, making it simple to publish SQL Server data on the Internet. Let's say, for example, that a parts supplier keeps its inventory list in SQL Server. The supplier could publish its current parts inventory as a Web page (an HTML file) using Web Assistant Wizard. Web Assistant Wizard allows an ad hoc query or stored procedure to be submitted, provides some simple formatting capabilities, allows for the inclusion of links to other Web pages, and allows a template to be used for more advanced formatting. The output of the query is written as an HTML 2 table, and a Web page is created. The process to create or update the Web page can be automated by Web Assistant Wizard to occur at a regular interval or whenever the data changes (via a trigger).

Web Assistant Wizard is distinct from but complementary to IIS in Back-Office. With Web Assistant Wizard, users browsing the Web page work separately from SQL Server, because the data on the Web page has been extracted. Web Assistant Wizard doesn't use or require IIS, and a page generated by Web Assistant Wizard can be viewed using any Internet browser.

IIS uses SQL Server's high-performance, native ODBC interface to allow SQL queries to be fired from a Web page when a user accesses a particular region on the page. The results are then dynamically retrieved and combined with the HTML file for up-to-date viewing. In addition to Web Assistant Wizard and the dynamic query capabilities enabled with IIS, SQL Server is Internet-enabled in several other important ways. By minimizing network traffic and handshaking, SQL Server is inherently designed for efficient client/server computing. Extremely rich requests can be packaged via stored procedures or Transact-SQL batches for resolution entirely at the server, with only the results sent back to the initiating client application.

This capability has been a hallmark of SQL Server's client/server architecture from the outset, but nowhere is it more important than on the Internet, where network speed and bandwidth are often quite limited. In addition, SQL Server's networking architecture allows for ease of use and security on the Internet, including network name resolution. For example, Internet users can connect via a friendly name such as www.microsoft.com instead of via an arcane IP address such as 200.154.54.678:1433. Secure encryption of data over the Internet is also possible.

SQL Server Profiler

SQL Server Profiler is a graphical utility that allows database administrators and application developers to monitor and record database activity. SQL Server Profiler can display all server activity in real time, or it can create filters that focus on the actions of particular users, applications, or types of commands. SQL Server Profiler can display any SQL statement or stored procedure sent to any instance of SQL Server (assuming your security privileges allow it) as well as the output or response sent back to the initiating client.

SQL Server Profiler allows you to drill down even deeper into SQL Server and see every statement executed as part of a stored procedure, every data modification operation, every lock acquired or released, or every occurrence of a database file growing automatically. And that's just for starters. Dozens of different events can be captured, and dozens of data items can be captured for each event.

The capabilities of SQL Server Profiler provide an important tool for tuning and debugging applications and for auditing and profiling the use of SQL Server. We'll look at SQL Server Profiler in more detail in Chapter 15.

SQL Server Service Manager

SQL Server Service Manager, shown in Figure 2-6 on the following page, manages SQL Server, SQL Server Agent, MS DTC, and Microsoft Search services. It provides a simple way to start, stop, or check the state of any of these services. Once you've used this application after booting Windows NT, the application will place an icon in the taskbar in the area of the taskbar clock. You can right-click this icon to retrieve a menu of all the tasks that SQL Server Service Manager supports.

> **NOTE** On Windows 95 and Windows 98 machines, SQL Server Service Manager looks the same as shown in Figure 2-6. However, the components that can be started aren't services. Windows 95 and Windows 98 don't support services, and SQL Server Service Manager actually starts separate executable programs. (The Search service isn't available at all on Windows 95 and Windows 98.)

Figure 2-6.
SQL Server Service Manager.

Windows NT Performance Monitor Integration

SQL Server provides an extension DLL (SQLCTR70.DLL) that integrates with the Windows NT Performance Monitor and graphically displays important performance statistics, such as memory use, number of users, transactions per second, and CPU use, as well as many others. Integrating with the Windows NT Performance Monitor is advantageous because it allows you to use a single tool to measure all aspects of a system's performance. If SQL Server simply provided its own performance-monitoring tool, you would still have to check the performance of the operating system and network. Integration with the Windows NT Performance Monitor provides one-stop shopping. A Windows NT Performance Monitor graph is shown in Figure 2-7.

Using Windows NT Performance Monitor, you can set an alert on any statistic that's being monitored; when a predefined threshold is reached, Windows NT automatically executes a predefined command. As mentioned above, you can allow SQL Server Agent to respond directly to Windows NT Performance Monitor thresholds being crossed.

Client Network Utility

The Client Network utility is used to configure DB-Library and the Net-Libraries that clients use when connecting to various SQL Servers. If you don't use DB-Library, or if you don't do any customization of network connections, you might not need to use this tool.

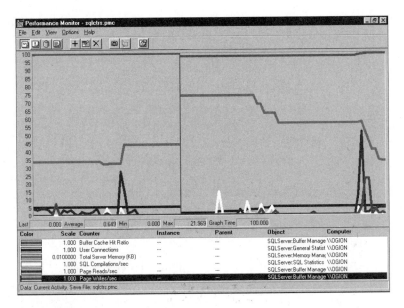

Figure 2-7.
Windows NT Performance Monitor.

Server Network Utility

The Server Network utility is used to manage the Net-Libraries on the server machine. Because the Net-Libraries on which SQL Server will listen for client requests are specified during installation, most administrators will never need to use this utility.

SQL Server Installation

SQL Server's graphical installation program allows you to set up SQL Server with a degree of ease and speed unprecedented for a full-featured DBMS. If you choose the defaults, SQL Server can be installed in 5 to 10 minutes, depending on the speed of the computer. A custom installation typically takes well under 30 minutes. Traditional DBMS products usually require several days for installation and often require that you enroll in training classes before installing the product. SQL Server can even be installed on a remote computer, a particularly useful feature if you manage a large number of servers.

The options for the installation program to use can be easily specified so that it can be fully automated for numerous machines, or you can encapsulate the installation of SQL Server in the rest of an application's installation process. The SQL Server installation program is configured so that it automatically runs when the SQL Server CD is inserted into the CD-ROM drive. If the CD is already in the drive and you want to run the installation program, you can just double-click on Autorun.exe in the root directory of the CD.

After you've installed SQL Server, two command-line utilities are available to change options chosen during the installation process:

- **rebuildm.exe (Rebuild master utility)**   This program allows you to rebuild the *master* database to change the character set, sort order, or Unicode collation. You can also use it to fix a corrupted *master* database.

- **regrebld.exe (Registry rebuild utility)**   This program allows you to restore the SQL Server Registry entries if they become corrupted or lost. You are also given the option to back up the current Registry entries.

ISQL and OSQL

Having a simple interactive window in which to submit basic SQL commands and get results is crucial for a database developer—as a hammer is to a carpenter. Even though other, more sophisticated power tools are useful, the basics are essential. SQL Server provides the basics in two styles: ISQL and OSQL.

Both ISQL (ISQL.EXE) and OSQL (OSQL.EXE) are character-based command-line utilities. ISQL is based on the DB-Library interface, and OSQL is ODBC-based. Many parameters, including the SQL statement or the name of the file containing the statement, can be passed to these character-based utilities. Upon exit, they can return status values to the Windows client that can be checked within a command file (CMD or BAT). Consequently, programs commonly launch scripts of SQL commands by spawning one of these character-based utilities and passing the appropriate parameters and filenames. The SQL Server installation program itself spawns OSQL.EXE numerous times with scripts that install various database objects and permissions.

SQL Server Query Analyzer

For interactive use, SQL Server Query Analyzer (ISQLW.EXE) provides a clean, simple, Windows-based interface for running SQL queries and viewing the results. SQL Server Query Analyzer allows for multiple windows so that simultaneous database connections (to one or more installations of SQL Server) can exist and be separately sized, tiled, or minimized. You can choose to have your query results displayed in a text window or in a grid. SQL Server Query Analyzer provides a graphical representation of SHOWPLAN, the steps chosen by the optimizer for query execution. You can run a tool called Index Analysis from SQL Server Query Analyzer that will recommend useful indexes for any one particular query.

SQL Server Query Analyzer is a wonderfully versatile tool for development and testing of batches and stored procedures that you'll incorporate into your SQL Server applications.

Bulk Copy and Data Transformation Services

SQL Server provides a character-based utility called *bcp*, or bulk copy (BCP.EXE), for flexible importing and exporting of SQL Server data. Similar in format to ISQL and OSQL, *bcp* allows parameters to be passed to it and is often called from command files. A special set of functions exists in ODBC that lets you easily create a custom loader or unloader for your application; the *bcp* utility is a generalized wrapper application that calls these functions.

SQL Server Enterprise Manager provides facilities to simplify the transfer of data into or out of SQL Server, and this functionality is incorporated into the Data Transformation Services (DTS) tool. Unlike the command-line *bcp* utility, DTS allows you to create a new table as you copy data into your SQL Server as well as to easily change column datatypes or formats. DTS goes far beyond just simple import and export of data to or from SQL Server, however. You can also use it to move data to or from any OLE DB data source, applying all kinds of data transformations along the way. Multiple transfers can be defined and stored in a DTS package, which can then be run from a command line with the *dtsrun* utility (DTSRUN.EXE).

SNMP Integration

Support for Simple Network Management Protocol (SNMP, a standard protocol within TCP/IP environments) is provided via SQL Server Management

Information Base (MIB, another standard of the SNMP and TCP/IP environment). A group of database vendors, including Microsoft, cooperated in defining a standard MIB that would report certain status data about a database environment for monitoring purposes.

> **NOTE** This group was a subcommittee of the IETF, the Internet Engineering Task Force, and the draft specification is known as IETF SNMP RDBMS-MIB (RFC 1697). SQL Server MIB is generally based on this proposal but provides additional data beyond that called for in the specification.

For example, status information (such as whether SQL Server is currently running, when it was last started, and how many users are connected) is reported to SNMP via this MIB. A variety of SNMP management and monitoring tools exist and can access this data. If, for example, you use Hewlett-Packard's OpenView or Computer Associate's CA-Unicenter in managing your network, SQL Server MIB enables those tools to also monitor multiple statistics regarding SQL Server.

SQL Server Books Online

In addition to being available in printed form, all SQL Server documentation is available online. A powerful viewer makes it simple to find and search for topics within seconds. Even if you favor printed books, you'll appreciate the speed and convenience of the search capabilities of SQL Server Books Online. In addition, because of the lead time required in the production of the printed manuals that ship with SQL Server, SQL Server Books Online is more complete and accurate than those manuals. Because this book can't hope to and doesn't try to replace the complete documentation set, the SQL Server evaluation CD that accompanies this book also contains the complete SQL Server Books Online documentation. You can view the documentation right from the CD, without installing the SQL Server product. The initial screen displayed when autorun.exe is executed gives you the choice of installing SQL Server or browsing the Books Online.

Client Development Interfaces

SQL Server provides several interfaces supporting client application development. These interfaces—ODBC, Remote Data Objects (RDO), OLE DB, ActiveX Data Objects (ADO), and the legacy interfaces DB-Library and Embedded SQL precompiler—are described in this section. The companion CD included with this book includes a whitepaper entitled "Designing Efficient Applications for SQL Server" that compares all the interfaces described in this section—and a few more besides.

ODBC

ODBC is an API for database access that's both a formal and a de facto industry standard. Besides being one of the most popular database interfaces used by applications today, ODBC has gained status as the formal call-level interface standard by ANSI and ISO. SQL Server provides a high-performance, *native* ODBC interface for all Windows-based programming environments, and it can be distributed royalty-free with any application. The SQL Server ODBC driver implements every function in the ODBC 3 specification. In ODBC-speak, this makes it fully Level 2 (the highest level) conformant.

RDO

RDO is an object interface that's closely tied to ODBC, exposing all the functionality in the ODBC driver and making it easily available to Visual Basic programs. RDO supports building visual controls tied directly to SQL Server data, which greatly reduces the amount of code that must be written to display data on the screen.

OLE DB

OLE DB was first released by Microsoft in 1996 to provide a COM interface to any tabular data source, that is, data that can be represented with rows and columns. This includes data in spreadsheets, and even text files. OLE DB can be viewed as an object version of ODBC but is more powerful in that it can access data from data sources beyond those that ODBC can access. Unlike other object interfaces to SQL Server, such as RDO, OLE DB doesn't make programming a call-level interface like ODBC any easier. In addition, because OLE DB uses pointer data types extensively, it's only accessible from C and C++.

ADO

ADO is a higher-level object interface on top of OLE DB that provides much of the same functionality and performance. Because ADO is pointerless, it can be accessed from scripting languages like JScript, development software like Visual Basic, and C and C++.

ADO is the recommended and supported interface for Internet applications written using Microsoft's Visual InterDev development tool. Applications written with Visual InterDev can call ADO from Active Server Pages (ASP) and incorporate code written in VBScript or JScript.

DB-Library

DB-Library is a SQL Server–specific API that provides all the necessary macros and functions for an application to open connections, format queries, send them to the server, and process the results. You can write custom DB-Library applications using either C, C++, or Visual Basic (or any programming language that's capable of calling a C function).

DB-Library is the original SQL Server programming interface. Libraries are provided for MS-DOS, Windows 3.1, Windows 95, Windows 98, and Windows NT. (The Windows NT library for Intel computers is the same library used for Windows 95 and Windows 98, so you can write a single application that targets both environments.) Developers are granted licensed rights to redistribute the DB-Library runtimes royalty-free. Although DB-Library continues to be officially supported for SQL Server 7, it's not guaranteed to support the full-feature set.

ESQL for C

SQL Server provides an Embedded SQL precompiler (ESQL for C) that allows developers to write SQL Server applications by embedding the SQL queries directly in their C source code. Many minicomputer and mainframe developers are already accustomed to this style of programming, and ESQL might be a natural choice for that reason. In addition, Microsoft has licensed some of the ESQL run-time environment to Microfocus, the leading provider of COBOL compilers and tools. Microfocus offers an embedded SQL interface for SQL Server directly in its COBOL development environment.

Server Development Interface

SQL Server offers an open API for developing server-based applications that work in conjunction with SQL Server. ODS is an event-driven API that is primarily used for developing extended stored procedures. ODS is actually a core part of the SQL Server architecture and benefits from the high-performance architecture. It provides all the network, connection, and thread management that SQL Server uses.

Formerly, ODS was frequently used to develop custom database gateways, data-driven event alerters, external program triggers, and request auditing, in addition to extended stored procedure DLLs. However, with the advent of SQL Server distributed queries and newer technologies such as Windows NT Component Services, the need for ODS in developing applications of this type of gateway has largely been eliminated. It is strongly recommended that you investigate other methods for developing the types of applications just mentioned, and use ODS only for developing extended store procedures.

Summary

The SQL Server component and product family—including SQL Server RDBMS, visual systems management tools, distributed systems components, open client/server interfaces, and visual development tools—provides a complete and robust platform for developing and deploying large-scale applications.

This chapter is intended to only give you an overview of the various tools available. The remainder of this book concentrates on the capabilities and uses of the SQL Server engine, which is the foundation of the product.

585858585 0x5858585

4141 417b000c 015858

585858 5858585

5858585 5858585

43040 3060303030

0xc2b000

xc2b000 pg=0 objid=

indid=0 freeoff=

prevpg=0 objid=4

d=0 freeoff=30

040x17b000c 0158585

858 5858585

858 58585858 585858

P A R T I I

ARCHITECTURAL
OVERVIEW

SQL SERVER ARCHITECTURE

Throughout this book, we'll look at specific features of the Microsoft SQL Server engine. In this chapter, we'll examine what makes up that engine and how it works. If you're interested only in the functional operations of SQL Server and want to consider everything as a black box operation, you can safely skip this chapter. Or if you're new to databases and don't have a clear idea of what makes up an RDBMS, you can come back to this chapter after you become more familiar with SQL Server's external capabilities. This chapter will focus on what happens inside the engine. We'll also point out system behavior that might affect application development and suggest ways to deal with it.

The SQL Server Engine

Figure 3-1 on the next page shows the general architecture of SQL Server. For simplicity, we've made some minor omissions and simplifications and ignored certain "helper" modules.

Now let's look in detail at the major modules.

The Net-Library

The Net-Library (often called Net-Lib, but in this book we'll use Net-Library) abstraction layer enables SQL Server to read from and write to many different network protocols, and each such protocol (such as TCP/IP sockets) can have a specific driver. The Net-Library layer makes it relatively easy to support many different network protocols without having to change the core server code.

A Net-Library is basically a driver that is specific to a particular network interprocess communication (IPC) mechanism. (Be careful not to confuse *driver* with *device driver*.) All code in SQL Server, including Net-Library code, makes calls only to the Microsoft Win32 subsystem. SQL Server uses a common internal interface between Microsoft Open Data Services (ODS), which manages its use of the network, and each Net-Library. If your development project needs to support a new and different network protocol, all network-specific issues can be handled by simply writing a new Net-Library. In addition, you can load multiple Net-Libraries simultaneously, one for each network IPC mechanism in use.

SQL Server uses the Net-Library abstraction layer on both the server and client machines, making it possible to support several clients simultaneously on different networks. Microsoft Windows NT, Windows 95, and Windows 98 allow multiple protocol stacks to be used simultaneously on one system. Net-Libraries are paired. For example, if a client application is using a Named Pipes Net-Library, SQL Server must also be listening on a Named Pipes Net-Library. (You can easily configure multiple Net-Libraries using the SQL Server Network Utility, which is available under Programs\Microsoft SQL Server 7.0 from your Start button.)

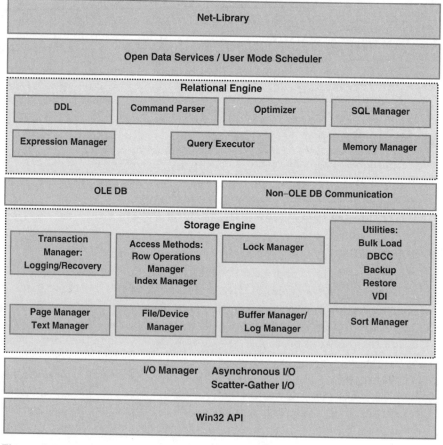

Figure 3-1.
The major components of SQL Server architecture.

It is important to distinguish between the IPC mechanisms and the underlying network protocols. IPC mechanisms used by SQL Server include named pipes, RPC, SPX, and Windows Sockets. Network protocols used include TCP/IP, NetBEUI, NWLink (IPX/SPX), Banyan VINES SPP, and Appletalk ADSP. Two Net-Libraries, Multiprotocol and Named Pipes, can be used simultaneously over multiple network protocols (NetBEUI, NWLink IPX/SPX, and TCP/IP). You can have multiple network protocols in your environment and still use only one Net-Library.

On machines running Windows 95 or Windows 98, you can also use Shared Memory as an IPC mechanism. This is considered both the IPC and the Network protocol and is available only for local connections in which the client is running on the same machine as SQL Server. In addition, SQL Server running on Windows 95 or Windows 98 machines does not support named pipes as an IPC.

The Multiprotocol Net-Library uses the RPC services of Windows NT, Windows 95, or Windows 98. It could just as well have been called the "RPC Net-Library," but "Multiprotocol" better conveys its key benefit. Because the Multiprotocol Net-Library uses the RPC services of the operating system, it can encrypt all traffic (including requests, data, and passwords) between the client application and the SQL Server engine.

Both named pipes and RPC services in Windows NT support impersonation of security contexts to provide an integrated logon capability (also known as Windows NT Authentication). Instead of requiring a separate user ID/password logon each time a connection to SQL Server is requested, SQL Server can impersonate the security context of the user running the application that requests the connection. If that user has sufficient privileges (or is part of a Windows NT domain group that does), the connection is established. Note that Windows NT Authentication is not available when SQL Server is running on Windows 95 or Windows 98. When you connect to SQL Server running on Windows 95 or Windows 98, you must specify a SQL Server logon ID and password.

Some History

If RPCs had been available years ago, Net-Library might never have been invented. When SQL Server ran only on OS/2, it supported only named pipes. The developers wanted to broaden this support to SPX and TCP/IP and potentially other protocols, so they developed Net-Library as an abstraction layer. Now RPC services are available with so many network protocols that RPC alone might have met the need.

Which Net-Library Is Fastest?

Strictly speaking, the TCP/IP Sockets Net-Library is the fastest Net-Library. In a pure network test that does nothing except throw packets back and forth between Net-Library pairs, it is perhaps 30 percent faster than the slowest Net-Library. But for LAN environments and applications, the speed of the Net-Library probably makes little difference because the network interface is generally not a limiting factor in a well-designed application.

On a LAN, however, turning on encryption with the Multiprotocol Net-Library does cause a performance hit—it's the slowest Net-Library option when encryption is turned on. But again, most applications probably wouldn't notice the difference. Your best bet is to choose the Net-Library that matches your network protocols and provides the services you need in terms of unified logon, encryption, and dynamic name resolution. (These choices will be explained further in Chapter 4.)

Open Data Services

Open Data Services (ODS) functions as the client manager for SQL Server; it is basically an interface between server Net-Libraries and server-based applications, including SQL Server. ODS manages the network: it listens for new connections, cleans up failed connections, acknowledges "attentions" (cancellations of commands), coordinates threading services to SQL Server, and returns result sets, messages, and status back to the client.

SQL Server clients and the server speak a private protocol known as *tabular data stream* (*TDS*). TDS is a self-describing data stream. In other words, it contains tokens that describe column names, datatypes, events (such as cancellations), and status values in the "conversation" between client and server. The server notifies the client that it is sending a result set, indicates the number of columns and datatypes of the result set, and so on—all encoded in TDS. Neither clients nor servers write directly to TDS. Instead, the open interfaces of DB-Library and ODBC at the client emit TDS. Both use a client implementation of the Net-Library.

ODS accepts new connections, and if a client unexpectedly disconnects (for example, if a user reboots the client computer instead of cleanly terminating the application), resources such as locks held by that client are automatically freed.

You can use the ODS open interface to help you write a server application, such as a gateway. (MicroDecisionware, subsequently purchased by Sybase, developed its successful database gateway using ODS.) Such applications are called *ODS server applications*. SQL Server is an ODS server application, and it uses the same DLL (OPENDS70.DLL) as all other ODS applications.

ODS Read and Write Buffers

After SQL Server puts result sets into a network output buffer that's equal in size to the configured packet size, the Net-Library dispatches the buffer to the client. The first packet is sent as soon as the network output buffer (the write buffer) is full or, if an entire result set fits in one packet, when the batch is completed. In some exceptional operations (such as one that provides progress information for database dumping or provides DBCC messages), the output buffer is flushed and sent even before it is full or before the batch completes.

SQL Server has two input buffers (read buffers) and one output buffer per client. Double-buffering is needed for the reads because while SQL Server reads a stream of data from the client connection, it must also look for a possible attention. (This allows that "Query That Ate Cleveland" to be canceled directly from the issuer. Although the ability to cancel a request is extremely important, it's relatively unusual among client/server products.) Attentions can be thought of as "out-of-band" data, although they can be sent with network protocols that do not explicitly have an out-of-band channel. The SQL Server development team experimented with double-buffering and asynchronous techniques for the write buffers, but these didn't improve performance substantially. The single network output buffer works very nicely. Even though the writes are not posted asynchronously, SQL Server doesn't need to write through the operating system caching for these as it does for writes to disk.

Because the operating system provides caching of network writes, write operations appear to complete immediately with no significant latency. But if several writes are issued to the same client and the client is not currently reading data from the network, the network cache eventually becomes full and the write blocks. This is essentially a throttle. As long as the client application is processing results, SQL Server has a few buffers queued up and ready for the client connection to process. But if the client's queue is already stacked up with results and is not processing them, SQL Server stalls sending them and the network write operation to that connection has to wait. Since the server has only one output buffer per client, data cannot be sent to that client connection until it reads information off the network to free up room for the write to complete. (Writes to other client connections are not held up, however; only those for the laggard client are affected.)

SQL Server adds rows to the output buffer as it retrieves them. Often, SQL Server can still be gathering additional rows that meet the query's criteria while rows already retrieved are being sent to the client.

Stalled network writes can also affect locks. For example, if READ COM-MITTED isolation is in effect (the default), a share lock can normally be released after SQL Server has completed its scan of that page of data. (Exclusive locks used for changing data must always be held until the end of the transaction to ensure that the changes can be rolled back.) However, if the scan finds more qualifying data and the output buffer is not free, the scan stalls. When the previous network write completes, the output buffer becomes available and the scan resumes. But, as stated above, that write won't complete until the client connection "drains" (reads) some data to free up some room in the pipe (the virtual circuit between the SQL Server and client connection).

If a client connection delays processing results that are sent to it, concurrency issues can result because locks are held longer than they otherwise would be. A sort of chain reaction occurs: if the client connection has not read several outstanding network packets, further writing of the output buffer at the SQL Server side must wait because the pipe is full. Since the output buffer is not available, the scan for data might also be suspended because no space is available to add qualifying rows. Since the scan is held up, any lock on the data cannot be released. In short, if a client application does not process results in a timely manner, database concurrency can suffer.

The size of the network buffer can also affect the speed at which the client receives the first result set. As mentioned earlier, the output buffer is sent when the batch, not simply the command, is done, even if the buffer is not full. (A *batch* is one or more commands sent to SQL Server to be parsed and executed together. For example, if you are using OSQL.EXE, a batch is the collection of all the commands that appear before a specific GO command.) If two queries exist in the same batch and the first query has only a small amount of data, its results are not sent back to the client until the second query is done or has supplied enough data to fill the output buffer. If both queries are fast, this is not a problem. But suppose the first query is fast and the second is slow. And suppose the first query returns 1000 bytes of data. If the network packet size is 4096 bytes, the first result set must wait in the output buffer for the second query to fill it. The obvious solution here is either to make the first command its own batch or to make the network packet size smaller. The first solution is probably the best one in this case, since it is typically difficult to fine-tune your application to determine the best buffer size for each command. But this doesn't mean that each command should be its own batch. Quite the contrary. In fact, under normal circumstances, grouping multiple commands into a single batch is most efficient and recommended because it reduces the amount of hand shaking that must occur between client and server.

ODS Default Net-Libraries

By default, SQL Server on Windows NT always listens on named pipes as well as on TCP/IP and Multiprotocol. SQL Server on Windows 95 and Windows 98 listens on the Shared Memory library instead of on named pipes, but it also has TCP/IP and Multiprotocol available. You can add other Net-Library interfaces. On Windows NT, you can also remove any of the Net-Libraries, but it's best not to remove named pipes. All the other Net-Libraries on Windows NT require an actual network. Because named pipe services exist in Windows NT even when no network is present, using named pipes leaves you a back door into SQL Server even if your network becomes totally nonfunctional. Similarly, SQL Server on Windows 95 and Windows 98 always listens over the Shared Memory IPC by default, so you should avoid removing this option. Even with no network, which is a more likely scenario in Windows 95 and Windows 98 than in Windows NT, Shared Memory is still available for interprocess communication.

Figure 3-2 on the following page shows the path from the SQL Server client application to the SQL Server engine and shows where the Net-Library interface fits in. On the server side, ODS provides functionality that mirrors that of ODBC, OLE DB, or DB-Library at the client. Calls exist for an ODS server application to describe and send result sets, to convert values between datatypes, to assume the security context associated with the specific connection being managed, and to raise errors and messages to the client application.

ODS uses an event-driven programming model. Requests from servers and clients trigger events that your server application must respond to. Using the ODS API, you create a custom routine, called an *event handler,* for each possible type of event. Essentially, the ODS library drives a server application by calling its custom event handlers in response to incoming requests.

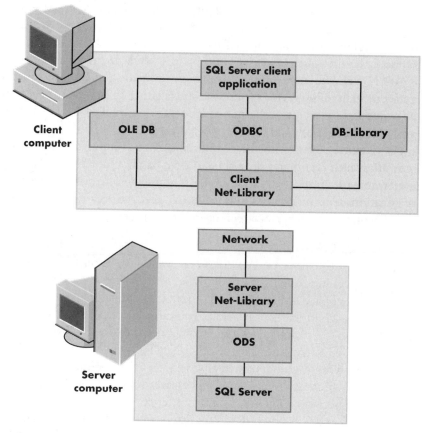

Figure 3-2.
The path from a SQL Server client application to the SQL Server engine.

ODS server applications respond to the following events:

■ **Connect events**   When a connect event occurs, SQL Server initiates a security check to determine whether a connection is allowed. Other ODS applications, such as a gateway to DB/2, have their own logon handlers that determine whether connections are allowed. Events also exist that close a connection, allowing the proper connection cleanup to occur.

■ **Language events**   When a client sends a command string, such as an SQL statement, SQL Server passes this command along to the command parser. A different ODS application, such as a gateway, would install its own handler that accepts and is responsible for execution of the command.

■ **Remote stored procedure events** These events occur each time a client or SQL Server directs a remote stored procedure request to ODS for processing.

ODS also generates events based on certain client activities and application activities. These events allow an ODS server application to respond to changes to the status of the client connection or of the ODS server application.

In addition to handling connections, ODS manages threads (and fibers) for SQL Server. It takes care of thread creation and termination and makes the threads available to the User Mode Scheduler (UMS). Since ODS is an open interface with a full programming API and toolkit, other ISVs writing server applications with ODS get the same benefits that SQL Server derives from this component, including SMP-capable thread management and pooling as well as network handling for multiple simultaneous networks. This multithreaded operation enables ODS server applications to maintain a high level of performance and availability and to transparently use multiple processors under Windows NT because the operating system can schedule any thread on any available processor.

The Relational Engine and the Storage Engine

The SQL Server database engine is made up of two main components, the relational engine and the storage engine. Unlike in earlier versions of SQL Server, these two pieces are clearly separated, and their primary method of communication with each other is through OLE DB. The relational engine comprises all the components necessary to parse and optimize any query. It requests data from the storage engine in terms of OLE DB rowsets and then processes the rowsets returned. The storage engine comprises the components needed to actually access and modify data on disk.

The Command Parser

The command parser handles language events raised by ODS. It checks for proper syntax and translates Transact-SQL commands into an internal format that can be operated on. This internal format is known as a *query tree*. If the parser does not recognize the syntax, a syntax error is immediately raised. Starting with SQL Server 6, syntax error messages identify where the error occurred. However, non–syntax error messages cannot be explicit about the exact source line that was the cause of the error. Because only the parser can access the source of the statement, the statement is no longer available in source format when the command is actually executed. Exceptions to the calling sequence for the command parser are EXECUTE(*"string"*) and cursor operations. Both of these operations can recursively call the parser.

The Optimizer

The optimizer takes the query tree from the command parser and prepares it for execution. This module compiles an entire command batch, optimizes queries, and checks security. The query optimization and compilation result in an execution plan.

The first step in producing such a plan is to *normalize* the query, which potentially breaks down a single query into multiple, fine-grained queries. After the optimizer normalizes the query, it *optimizes* it, which means that the optimizer determines a plan for executing that query. Query optimization is cost-based; the optimizer chooses the plan that it determines would cost the least based on internal metrics that include estimated memory requirements, estimated CPU utilization, and the estimated number of required I/Os. It considers the type of statement requested, checks the amount of data in the various tables affected, looks at the indexes available for each table, and then looks at a sampling of the data values kept for each index or column referenced in the query. The sampling of the data values is called *statistics* and will be discussed in detail in Chapter 14. Based on the available information, the optimizer considers the various access methods and join strategies it could use to resolve a query and chooses the most cost-effective plan. The optimizer also decides which indexes, if any, should be used for each table in the query, and, in the case of a multitable query, the order in which the tables should be accessed and the join strategy to be used.

The optimizer also uses pruning heuristics to ensure that more time isn't spent optimizing a query than it would take to simply choose a plan and execute it. The optimizer does not necessarily do exhaustive optimization. Some products consider every possible plan and then choose the most cost-effective one. The advantage of this exhaustive optimization is that the syntax chosen for a query would theoretically never cause a performance difference, no matter what syntax the user employed. But if you deal with an involved query, it could take much longer to estimate the cost of every conceivable plan than it would to accept a good plan, even if not the best one, and execute it. For example, in one product review, SQL Server (and some other products) consistently executed one complex eight-table join faster than a product whose optimizer produced the same "ideal" execution plan each time, even though SQL Server's execution plan varied somewhat. This was a case in which a pruning technique produced faster results than pure exhaustive optimization. In general, though, you will typically get the same execution plan no matter what equivalent syntax you use to specify the query. Some products have no cost-based optimizer and rely purely on rules to determine the query execution plan. In such cases, the syntax of the query is vitally important. (For example, the execution would start with the first table in the FROM clause.) Such products sometimes claim to have a "rule-based optimizer."

This might simply be a euphemism for "no optimizer"—any optimization was done by the person who wrote the query.

The SQL Server optimizer is cost-based, and with every release it has become "smarter" to handle more special cases and to add more query processing and access method choices. However, by definition, the optimizer relies on probability in choosing its query plan, so sometimes it will be wrong. (Even a 90 percent chance of choosing correctly means that something will be wrong 1 in 10 times.) Recognizing that the optimizer will never be perfect, you can use SQL Server's *query hints* to direct the optimizer to use a certain index—for example, to force the optimizer to follow a specific sequence while working with the tables involved, or to use a particular join strategy.

After normalization and optimization are completed, the normalized tree produced by those processes is compiled into the execution plan, which is actually a data structure. Each command included in it specifies exactly which table will be affected, which indexes will be used (if any), which security checks must be made, and which criteria (such as equality to a specified value) must evaluate to TRUE for selection. This execution plan might be considerably more complex than is immediately apparent. In addition to the actual commands, the execution plan includes all the steps necessary to ensure that constraints are checked. (Steps for calling a trigger are a bit different than those for verifying constraints. If a trigger is included for the action being taken, a call to the procedure that comprises the trigger is appended. A trigger has its own plan that is branched to just before the commit. The specific steps for the trigger are not compiled into the execution plan, like those for constraint verification.)

A simple request to insert one row into a table with multiple constraints can result in an execution plan that requires many other tables to also be accessed or expressions to be evaluated. The existence of a trigger can also cause many additional steps to be executed. The step that carries out the actual INSERT statement might be just a small part of the total execution plan necessary to ensure that all actions and constraints associated with adding a row are carried out.

The SQL Manager

The SQL manager is responsible for everything having to do with managing stored procedures and their plans. It determines when a stored procedure needs recompilation based on changes in the underlying objects' schemas, and it manages the caching of procedure plans so that they can be reused by other processes.

The SQL manager also handles autoparameterization of queries. In SQL Server 7, certain kinds of ad hoc queries are treated as if they were parameterized stored procedures, and query plans are generated and saved for them. This can happen if a query uses a simple equality comparison against a constant, as in the following statement:

```
SELECT * FROM pubs.dbo.titles
WHERE type = 'business'
```

This query can be parameterized as if it were a stored procedure with a parameter for the value of *type*:

```
SELECT * FROM pubs.dbo.titles
WHERE type = @param
```

A subsequent query, differing only in the actual value used for the value of *type*, can use the same query plan that was generated for the original query.

The Expression Manager

The expression manager handles computation, comparison, and data movement. Suppose your query contains an expression like this one:

```
SELECT @myqty = qty * 10 FROM mytable
```

The expression service copies the value of *qty* from the rowset returned by the storage engine, multiplies it by 10, and stores the result in *@myqty*.

The Query Executor

The query executor runs the execution plan that was produced by the optimizer, acting as a dispatcher for all the commands in the execution plan. This module loops through each command step of the execution plan until the batch is complete. Most of the commands require interaction with the storage engine to modify or retrieve data and to manage transactions and locking.

Communication Between the Relational Engine and the Storage Engine

The relational engine uses OLE DB for most of its communication with the storage engine. The following description of that communication is adapted from the section titled "Database Server" in the SQL Server Books Online. It describes how a SELECT statement that processes data from local tables only is processed:

1. The relational engine compiles the SELECT statement into an optimized execution plan. The execution plan defines a series of operations against simple rowsets from the individual tables or indexes referenced in the SELECT statement. (*Rowset* is the OLE DB term for a result set.) The rowsets requested by the relational engine return

the amount of data needed from a table or index to perform one of the operations used to build the SELECT result set. For example, this SELECT statement requires a table scan if it references a table with no indexes:

```
SELECT * FROM ScanTable
```

The relational engine implements the table scan by requesting one rowset containing all the rows from *ScanTable*. This next SELECT statement needs only information available in an index:

```
SELECT DISTINCT LastName
FROM Northwind.dbo.Employees
```

The relational engine implements the index scan by requesting one rowset containing the leaf rows from the index that was built on the *LastName* column. The following SELECT statement needs information from two indexes:

```
SELECT CompanyName, OrderID, ShippedDate
FROM Northwind.dbo.Customers AS Cst
JOIN Northwind.dbo.Orders AS Ord
ON (Cst.CustomerID = Ord.CustomerID)
```

The relational engine requests two rowsets: one for the clustered index on *Customers* and the other for one of the nonclustered indexes on *Orders*.

2. The relational engine then uses the OLE DB API to request that the storage engine open the rowsets.

3. As the relational engine works through the steps of the execution plan and needs data, it uses OLE DB to fetch the individual rows from the rowsets it requested the storage engine to open. The storage engine transfers the data from the data buffers to the relational engine.

4. The relational engine combines the data from the storage engine rowsets into the final result set transmitted back to the user.

Not all communication between the relational engine and the storage engine uses OLE DB. Some commands cannot be expressed in terms of OLE DB rowsets. The most obvious and common example is when the relational engine processes data definition language (DDL) requests to create a table or other SQL Server object.

The Access Methods Manager

When SQL Server needs to locate data, it calls the access methods manager. The access methods manager sets up and requests scans of data pages and index pages and prepares the OLE DB rowsets to return to the relational engine. It contains services to open a table, retrieve qualified data, and update data. The access methods manager doesn't actually retrieve the pages; it makes the request of the Buffer Manager, which ultimately serves up the page already in its cache or reads it to cache from disk. When the scan is started, a look-ahead mechanism qualifies the rows or index entries on a page. Retrieving rows that meet specified criteria is known as a *qualified retrieval*. The access methods manager is employed not only for queries (selects) but also for qualified updates and deletes (for example, UPDATE with a WHERE clause).

A session opens a table, requests and evaluates a range of rows against the conditions in the WHERE clause, and then closes the table. A session descriptor data structure (SDES) keeps track of the current row and the search conditions for the object being operated on (which is identified by the object descriptor data structure, or DES).

The Row Operations Manager and the Index Manager

The row operations manager and the index manager can be considered components of the access methods manager because they carry out the actual method of access. Each is responsible for manipulating and maintaining its respective on-disk data structures, namely rows of data or B-tree indexes. They understand and manipulate information on data and index pages.

The Row Operations Manager

The row operations manager retrieves, modifies, and performs operations on individual rows. (For more information on on-disk structures, see Chapter 5; for more on data page and row format, see Chapter 6.) It performs an operation within a row, such as "retrieve column 2" or "write this value to column 3." As a result of the work performed by the access methods manager, lock manager, and transaction manager, the row will have been found and will be appropriately locked and part of a transaction. After formatting or modifying a row in memory, the row operations manager inserts or deletes a row.

The row operations manager also handles updates. SQL Server 7 offers three methods for handling updates. All three are direct, which means that there is no need for two passes through the transaction log, as was the case with deferred updates in earlier versions of SQL Server. SQL Server 7 has no concept of a deferred data modification operation.

The three update modes in SQL Server 7 are:

- **In-place mode**   This mode is used to update a heap or clustered index when none of the clustering keys change. The update can be done in place, and the new data is written to the same slot on the data page.

- **Split mode**   This mode is used to update nonunique indexes when the index keys change. The update is split into two operations—a delete followed by an insert—and these operations are performed independently of each other.

- **Split with collapse mode**   This mode is used to update a unique index when the index keys change. After the update is rewritten into delete and insert operations, if the same index key is both deleted and then reinserted with a new value, it is "collapsed" into a single update operation.

In Chapter 8, we'll take a look at some actual examples of each of these types of updates.

If you want to reorganize a table—for example, to reestablish a FILL-FACTOR value or to make data more contiguous after a lot of data modification has occurred—you can use a clustered index, which makes the reorganization easy. You simply rebuild the clustered index, which rebuilds the entire table. In the case of a delete, if the row deleted is the last row on a data page, that page is deallocated. (The only exception occurs if that page is the only one remaining in the table. A table always contains at least one page, even if it is empty.)

The Index Manager

The index manager maintains and supports searches on B-trees, which are used for SQL Server indexes. An index is structured as a tree, with a root page and intermediate- and lower-level pages (or branches). A B-tree groups records that have similar index keys, thereby allowing fast access to data by searching on a key value. The B-tree's core feature is its ability to balance the index tree. (*B* stands for *balanced*.) Branches of the index tree are spliced together or split apart as necessary so that the search for any given record always traverses the same number of levels and thus requires the same number of page accesses.

The traverse begins at the root page, progresses to intermediate index levels, and finally moves to bottom-level pages called *leaf pages*. The index is used to find the correct leaf page. On a qualified retrieval or delete, the correct leaf page is the lowest page of the tree at which one or more rows with the specified key or keys reside. SQL Server supports both clustered and nonclustered indexes.

In a nonclustered index, shown in Figure 3-3, the leaf level of the tree (the leaf page of the index) contains every key value in the index along with a row locator for each key value. The row locator is also called a bookmark and indicates where to find the referenced data. A row locator can have one of two forms. If the base table has no clustered index, the table is referred to as a *heap*. The row locators in nonclustered index leaf pages for a heap are pointers to the actual rows in which the data can be found, and these pointers consist of a Row ID (RID), which is a file number, a page number, and a row number on the page. If the base table has a clustered index, the row locators in any nonclustered index leaf pages contain the clustered index key value for the row.

After reaching the leaf level in a nonclustered index, you can find the exact location of the data, although the page on which that data resides must still be separately retrieved. Because you can access the data directly, you don't need to scan all the data pages for a qualifying row. Better yet, in a clustered index, shown in Figure 3-4 on page 92, the leaf level actually contains the data row, not simply the index key. A clustered index keeps the data in a table physically ordered around the key of the clustered index, and the leaf page of a clustered index is in fact the data page itself.

Because data can be physically ordered in only one way, only one clustered index can exist per table. This makes the selection of the appropriate key value on which to cluster data an important performance consideration.

You can also use indexes to ensure the uniqueness of a particular key value. In fact, the PRIMARY KEY and UNIQUE constraints on a column work by creating a unique index on the column's values. The optimizer can use the knowledge that an index is unique in formulating an effective query plan.

Internally, SQL Server always ensures that clustered indexes are unique by adding a 4-byte "uniqueifier" to clustered index key values that occur more than once. This uniqueifier becomes part of the key and is used in all levels of the clustered index and in references to the clustered index key through all nonclustered indexes.

Since SQL Server maintains ordering in index leaf levels, you do not need to unload and reload data to maintain clustering properties as data is added and moved. SQL Server will always insert rows into the correct page in clustered sequence. For a clustered index, the correct leaf page is the data page in which a row will be inserted. For a nonclustered index, the correct leaf page is the one into which SQL Server inserts a row containing the key value (and data row locator) for the newly inserted row. If data is updated and the key values of an index change, or if the row is moved to a different page, SQL Server's transaction control ensures that all affected indexes are modified to reflect these changes. Under transaction control, index operations are performed as atomic operations. The operations are logged and fully recovered in the event of a system failure.

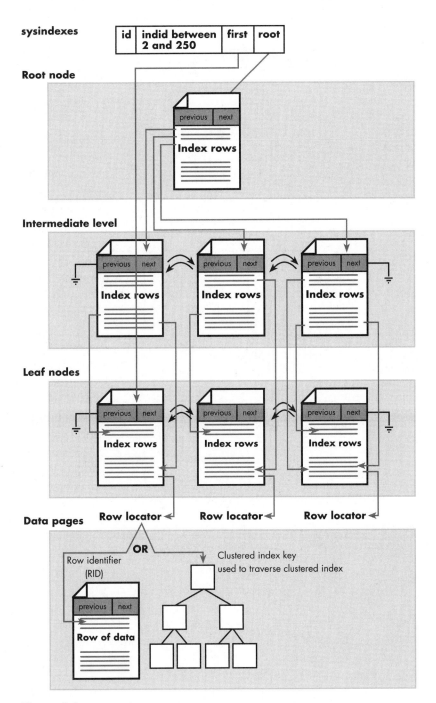

Figure 3-3.
*A nonclustered index with the leaf level containing row locators: either a
RID or a clustered index key value.*

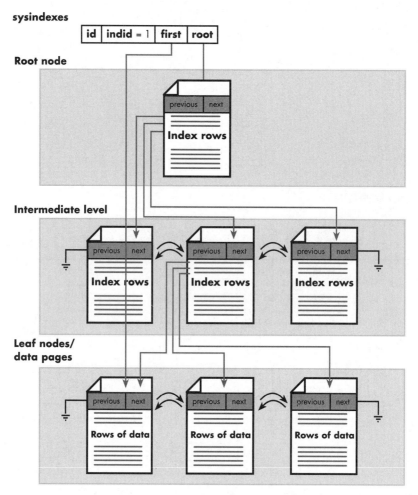

Figure 3-4.
A clustered index with the data located at the leaf level.

Locking and Index Pages

As we'll see in the section on the lock manager, pages of an index use a slightly different locking mechanism than regular data pages. A lightweight lock called a *latch* is used to lock upper levels of indexes. Latches are not involved in deadlock detection because SQL Server 7 uses "deadlock-proof" algorithms for index maintenance.

You can customize the locking strategy for indexes on a table basis or index basis. The system stored procedure s*p_indexoption* lets you enable or disable page or row locks with any particular index or, by specifying a table name, for every index on that table. The setable options are *AllowPageLocks* and *AllowRowLocks*. If both of these options are set to false for a particular index, only table level locks are applied.

The Page Manager and the Text Manager

The page manager and the text manager cooperate to manage a collection of pages as named databases. Each database is a collection of 8 KB disk pages, which are spread across one or more physical files. (In Chapter 5, you'll find more details about the physical organization of databases.)

SQL Server uses six types of disk pages: data pages, text/image pages, index pages, Page Free Space (PFS) pages, Global Allocation Map (GAM and SGAM) pages, and Index Allocation Map (IAM) pages. All user data, except for the *text* and *image* datatypes, are stored on data pages. The *text* and *image* datatypes, which are used for storing large objects (up to 2 GB each of text or binary data), use a separate collection of pages, so the data is not stored on regular data pages with the rest of the rows. A pointer on the regular data page identifies the starting page and offset of the text/image data. Index pages store the B-trees that allow fast access to data. PFS pages keep track of which pages in a database are available to hold new data. Allocation pages (GAMs, SGAMs, and IAMs) keep track of the other pages. They contain no database rows and are used only internally. We'll cover all the types of pages extensively in Chapters 5 and 6.

The page manager allocates and deallocates all types of disk pages, organizing extents of eight pages each. An extent can be either a uniform extent, for which all eight pages are allocated to the same object (table or index), or a mixed extent, which can contain pages from multiple objects. If an object uses less than eight pages, the page manager allocates new pages for that object from mixed extents. When the size of the object exceeds eight pages, the page manager allocates new space for that object in units of entire uniform extents. This optimization prevents the overhead of allocation from being incurred every time a new page is required for a large table; it is incurred only every eighth time. Perhaps most important, this optimization forces data of the same table to be contiguous for the most part. At the same time, the ability to use mixed extents keeps SQL Server from wasting too much space if a database contains many small tables.

To determine how contiguous a table's data is, you use the DBCC SHOWCONTIG command. A table with a lot of allocation and deallocation can get fairly fragmented, and rebuilding the clustered index (which also rebuilds the table) can improve performance, especially when a table is accessed frequently using table scans.

The Transaction Manager

A core feature of SQL Server is its ability to ensure that transactions follow the ACID properties (discussed in Chapter 2). Transactions must be *atomic*—that is, all or nothing. If a transaction has been committed, it must be recoverable by SQL Server no matter what—even if a total system failure occurs one millisecond after the commit was acknowledged. In SQL Server, if work was in progress and a system failure occurred before the transaction was committed, all the work is rolled back to the state that existed before the transaction began. Write-ahead logging makes it possible to always roll back work in progress or roll forward committed work that has not yet been applied to the data pages. Write-ahead logging assures that a transaction's changes—the "before and after" images of data—are captured on disk in the transaction log before a transaction is acknowledged as committed. Writes to the transaction log are always synchronous—that is, SQL Server must wait for them to complete. Writes to the data pages can be asynchronous because all the effects can be reconstructed from the log if necessary. The transaction manager coordinates logging, recovery, and buffer management. These topics are discussed later in this chapter; at this point, we'll just look at transactions themselves.

The transaction manager delineates the boundaries of statements that must be grouped together to form an operation. It handles transactions that cross databases within the same SQL Server, and it allows nested transaction sequences. (However, nested transactions simply execute in the context of the first-level transaction; no special action occurs when they are committed. And a rollback specified in a lower level of a nested transaction undoes the entire transaction.) For a distributed transaction to another SQL Server (or to any other resource manager), the transaction manager coordinates with the Microsoft Distributed

Transaction Coordinator (MS DTC) service using operating system remote procedure calls. The transaction manager marks *savepoints,* which let you designate points within a transaction at which work can be partially rolled back or undone.

The transaction manager also coordinates with the lock manager regarding when locks can be released, based on the isolation level in effect. The isolation level in which your transaction runs determines how sensitive your application is to changes made by others and consequently how long your transaction must hold locks to protect against changes made by others. Four isolation-level semantics are available in SQL Server 7: Uncommitted Read (also called "dirty read"), Committed Read, Repeatable Read, and Serializable.

Your transactions' behavior depends on the isolation level. We'll look at these levels now, but a complete understanding of isolation levels also requires an understanding of locking because the topics are so closely related. The next section gives an overview of locking; more detailed information can be found in Chapter 13.

Uncommitted Read

Uncommitted Read, or dirty read (be careful—do not confuse "dirty read" with "dirty page," which we'll discuss later) lets your transaction read any data that is currently on a data page, whether or not that data has been committed. For example, another user might have a transaction in progress that has updated data, and even though it is holding exclusive locks on the data, your transaction can read it anyway. The other user might then decide to roll back his or her transaction, so logically those changes were never made. If the system is a single-user system and everyone is queued up to access it, the changes would never have been visible to other users. In a multiuser system, however, you read the changes and possibly took action on them. Although this scenario isn't desirable, with Uncommitted Read you won't get stuck waiting for a lock, nor will *your* reads issue share locks (described on page 96) that might affect others.

When using Uncommitted Read, you give up assurances of having strongly consistent data so that you can have the benefit of high concurrency in the system without users locking each other out. So when should you choose Uncommitted Read? Clearly, you don't want to choose it for financial transactions in which every number must balance. But it might be fine for certain decision-support analyses—for example, when you look at sales trends—for which complete precision is not necessary and the tradeoff in higher concurrency makes it worthwhile.

Committed Read

Committed Read is SQL Server's default isolation level. It ensures that an operation will never read data that another application has changed but not yet committed. (That is, it will never read data that logically never existed.) With Committed Read, if a transaction is updating data and consequently has exclusive locks on data rows, your transaction must wait for those locks to be released before you can use that data (whether you are reading or modifying). Also, your transaction must put share locks (at a minimum) on the data that will be visited, which means that data is potentially unavailable to others to use. A share lock doesn't prevent others from reading the data, but it makes them wait to update the data. Share locks can be released after the data has been sent to the calling client—they do not have to be held for the duration of the transaction.

> **NOTE** Although you can never read uncommitted data, if a transaction running with Committed Read isolation subsequently revisits the same data, that data might have changed or new rows might suddenly appear that meet the criteria of the original query. Rows that appear in this way are called *phantoms*.

Repeatable Read

The Repeatable Read isolation level adds to the properties of Committed Read by ensuring that if a transaction revisits data or if a query is reissued, the data will not have changed. In other words, issuing the same query twice within a transaction will not pick up any changes to data values made by another user's transaction.

Preventing nonrepeatable reads from appearing is a desirable safeguard. But there's no free lunch. The cost of this extra safeguard is that all the shared locks in a transaction must be held until the completion (COMMIT or ROLL-BACK) of the transaction. (Exclusive locks must always be held until the end of a transaction, no matter what the isolation level, so that a transaction can be rolled back if necessary. If the locks were released sooner, it might be impossible to undo the work.) No other user can modify the data visited by your transaction as long as your transaction is outstanding. Obviously, this can seriously reduce concurrency and degrade performance. If transactions are not kept short or if applications are not written to be aware of such potential lock contention issues, SQL Server can appear to "hang" when it is simply waiting for locks to be released.

> **NOTE** You can control how long SQL Server waits for a lock to be released by using the session option LOCK_TIMEOUT. We'll discuss this option, as well as many other ways of customizing locking behavior, in Chapter 14.

Serializable

The Serializable isolation level adds to the properties of Repeatable Read by ensuring that if a query is reissued, rows will not have been added in the interim. In other words, phantoms will not appear if the same query is issued twice within a transaction. More precisely, Repeatable Read and Serializable affect sensitivity to another connection's changes, whether or not the user ID of the other connection is the same. Every connection within SQL Server has its own transaction and lock space. We use the term "user" loosely so as to not obscure the central concept.

Preventing phantoms from appearing is another desirable safeguard. But once again, there's no free lunch. The cost of this extra safeguard is similar to that of Repeatable Read—all the shared locks in a transaction must be held until completion of the transaction. In addition, enforcing the Serializable isolation level requires that you not only lock data that has been read, but also lock data *that does not exist!* For example, suppose that within a transaction we issue a SELECT statement to read all the customers whose zip code is between 98000 and 98100, and on first execution no rows satisfy that condition. To enforce the Serializable isolation level, we must lock that "range" of *potential* rows with zip codes between 98000 and 98100 so that if the same query is reissued, there will still be no rows that satisfy the condition. SQL Server handles this by using a special kind of lock called a *range lock,* which we'll discuss in Chapter 13. The Serializable level gets its name from the fact that running multiple serializable transactions at the same time is the equivalent of running them one at a time— that is, serially—without regard to sequence. For example, transactions A, B, and C are serializable only if the result obtained by running all three simultaneously is the same as if they were run one at a time, in any order. Serializable does not imply a known order in which the transactions are to be run. The order is considered a chance event. Even on a single-user system, the order of transactions hitting the queue would be essentially random. If the batch order is important to your application, you should implement it as a pure batch system.

SEE ALSO For an interesting critique of the formal definitions of the ANSI isolation levels, see the companion CD, which contains a technical report called "A Critique of ANSI SQL Isolation Levels," published by the Microsoft Research Center.

The tough part of transaction management, of course, is dealing with rollback/rollforward and recovery operations. We'll return to the topic of transaction management and recovery a bit later. But first we'll further discuss locking and logging.

The Lock Manager

Locking is a crucial function of a multiuser database system such as SQL Server. Recall from Chapter 2 that SQL Server lets you manage multiple users simultaneously and ensures that the transactions observe the properties of the chosen isolation level. At the highest level, Serializable, SQL Server must make the multiuser system perform like a single-user system—as though every user is queued up to use the system alone with no other user activity. Locking guards data and the internal resources that make this possible, and it allows many users to simultaneously access the database and not be severely affected by others' use.

The lock manager acquires and releases various types of locks, such as shared read locks, exclusive locks for writing, intent locks to signal a potential "plan" to perform some operation, extent locks for space allocation, and so on. It manages compatibility between the lock types, resolves deadlocks, and escalates locks if needed. The lock manager controls table, page, and row locks as well as system data locks. (System data, such as page headers and indexes, is private to the database system.)

The lock manager provides two separate locking systems. The first enables row locks, page locks, and table locks for all fully shared data tables, data pages and rows, text pages, and leaf-level index pages and index rows. The second locking system is used internally only for restricted system data; it protects root and intermediate index pages while indexes are being traversed. This internal mechanism uses *latches*, a lightweight, short-term variation of a lock for protecting data that does not need to be locked for the duration of a transaction. Full-blown locks would slow the system down. In addition to protecting upper levels of indexes, latches protect rows while they are being transferred from the storage engine to the relational engine. If you examine locks by using the *sp_lock* stored procedure or a similar mechanism that gets its information from the *syslockinfo* table, you won't see or be aware of latches; you'll see only the locks for fully shared data. However, some counters are available in Performance Monitor to monitor latch requests, acquisitions, and releases. These will be discussed in Chapter 15.

Locking is an important aspect of SQL Server. Many developers are keenly interested in locking because of its potential effect on application performance. Chapter 13 is devoted to the subject, so we won't go into it further here.

Other Managers

Also included in the storage engine are managers for controlling utilities such as bulk load, DBCC commands, backup and restore operations, and the Virtual Device Interface (VDI). VDI allows ISVs to write their own backup and restore utilities and to access the SQL Server data structures directly, without going through the relational engine. There is a manager to control sorting operations and one to physically manage the files and backup devices on disk.

Managing Memory

One of the major goals of SQL Server 7 was to scale easily from a laptop installation on Windows 95 or Windows 98 to an SMP server running on Windows NT Enterprise Edition. This requires a very robust policy for managing memory. By default, SQL Server 7 adjusts it uses of system memory to balance the needs of other applications running on the machine and the needs of its own internal components. SQL Server can also be configured to use a fixed amount of memory. Whether memory allocation is fixed or dynamically adjusted, the total memory space is considered one unified cache and is managed as a collection of various pools with their own policies and purposes. Memory can be requested by and granted to any of several internal components.

The Buffer Manager and Memory Pools

The buffer pool is a memory pool that's the main memory component in the server; all memory not used by another memory component remains in the buffer pool. The Buffer Manager manages disk I/O functions for bringing data and index pages into memory so that data can be shared among users. When other components require memory, they can request a buffer from the buffer pool.

Another memory pool is the operating system itself. Occasionally, SQL Server must request contiguous memory in larger blocks than the 8-KB pages that the buffer pool can provide. Typically, use of large memory blocks is kept to a minimum, so direct calls to the operating system account for a very small fraction of SQL Server's memory usage.

The procedure cache can be considered another memory pool, in which query trees and plans from stored procedures, triggers, or ad hoc queries can be stored. Other pools are used by memory-intensive queries that use sorting or hashing, and by special memory objects that need less than one 8-KB page.

Access to In-Memory Pages

Access to pages in the buffer pool must be fast. Even with real memory, it would be ridiculously inefficient to have to scan the whole cache for a page when you're talking about hundreds of megabytes, or even gigabytes, of data. To avoid this inefficiency, pages in the buffer pool are hashed for fast access. *Hashing* is a technique that uniformly maps a key (in this case, a dbid-fileno-pageno identifier) via a hash function across a set of hash buckets. A *hash bucket* is a page in memory that contains an array of pointers (implemented as a linked list) to the buffer pages. If all the pointers to buffer pages do not fit on a single hash page, a *linked list* chains to additional hash pages.

Given a dbid-fileno-pageno value, the hash function converts that key to the hash bucket that should be checked; in essence, the hash bucket serves as an index to the specific page needed. By using hashing, even when large amounts of memory are present, you can find a specific data page in cache with only a few memory reads (typically one or two).

> **NOTE** Finding a data page might require that multiple hash buckets be accessed via the chain (linked list). The hash function attempts to uniformly distribute the dbid-fileno-pageno values throughout the available hash buckets. The number of hash buckets is set internally by SQL Server and depends on the total size of the buffer pool.

Access to Free Pages (lazywriter)

A data page or an index page can be used only if it exists in memory. Therefore, a buffer in the buffer pool must be available for the page to be read into. Keeping a supply of buffers available for immediate use is an important performance optimization. If a buffer isn't readily available, many memory pages might have to be searched simply to locate a buffer to use as a workspace.

The buffer pool is managed by a process called the lazywriter that uses a clock algorithm to sweep through the buffer pool. Basically, the lazywriter thread maintains a pointer into the buffer pool that "sweeps" sequentially through it (like the hand on a clock). As it visits each buffer, it determines whether that buffer has been referenced since the last sweep by examining a reference count value in the buffer header. If the reference count is not 0, the buffer stays in the pool and its reference count is adjusted in preparation for the next sweep; otherwise, the buffer is made available for reuse: it is written to disk if dirty, removed from the hash lists, and put on a special list of buffers called the free list.

> **NOTE** The set of buffers that the lazywriter sweeps through is sometimes called the LRU (for least recently used list). However, it does not function as a traditional LRU because the buffers do not move within the list according to their use or lack of use; the lazywriter clock hand does all the moving. Also note that the set of buffers that the lazywriter inspects actually include more than pages in the buffer pool. They also include pages from compiled plans for procedures, triggers, or ad hoc queries.

The reference count of a buffer is incremented each time the buffer's contents are accessed by any process. For data or index pages, this is a simple increment by one. But objects that are expensive to create, such as stored procedure plans, get a higher reference count that reflects their "replacement cost." When the lazywriter clock hand sweeps through and checks which pages have been referenced, it does not use a simple decrement. It divides the reference count by 4. This means that frequently referenced pages (those with a high reference count) and those with a high replacement cost are "favored" and their count will not reach 0 any time soon, keeping them in the pool for further use.

The lazywriter hand sweeps through the buffer pool when the number of pages on the free list falls below its minimum size. The minimum size is computed as a percentage of the overall buffer pool size but is always between 128 KB and 4 MB. Currently, the percentage is set at 3 percent, but that could change in future releases.

User threads also perform the same function of searching for pages for the free list. This happens when a user process needs to read a page from disk into a buffer. Once the read has been initiated, the user thread checks to see if the free list is too small. (Note that this process consumes one page of the list for its own read.) If so, the user thread performs the same function as the lazywriter: it advances the clock hand and searches for buffers to free. Currently, it advances the clock hand through 16 buffers, regardless of how many it actually finds to free in that group of 16. The reason for having user threads share in the work of the lazywriter is so that the cost can be distributed across all of the CPUs in an SMP environment.

Keeping Pages in the Cache Permanently

Tables can be specially marked so that their pages are never put on the free list and are therefore kept in memory indefinitely. This process is called *pinning* a table. Any page (data, index, or text) belonging to a pinned table is never marked as free and reused unless it is unpinned. Pinning and unpinning is accomplished using the *pintable* option of the *sp_tableoption* stored procedure. Setting this option to TRUE for a table doesn't cause the table to be brought into cache, nor does it mark pages of the table as "favored" in any way; instead, it avoids the unnecessary overhead and simply doesn't allow any pages belonging to a pinned table to be put on the free list for possible replacement.

Because mechanisms such as write-ahead logging and checkpointing are completely unaffected, such an operation in no way impairs recovery. Still, pinning too many tables can result in few or even no pages being available when a new buffer is needed. In general, you should pin tables only if you have carefully tuned your system, plenty of memory is available, and you have a good feel for which tables constitute hot spots.

Pages that are "very hot" (accessed repeatedly) are never placed on the free list. A page in the buffer pool that has a nonzero use count, such as one that is newly read or newly created, is not added to the free list until its use count falls to 0. Prior to that point, the page is clearly hot and isn't a good candidate for reuse. Very hot pages might never get on the free list, even without their objects being pinned—which is as it should be.

Protection against media failure is achieved using whatever level of RAID (redundant array of independent disks) technology you choose. (We'll look at RAID technology in Chapter 4.) Write-ahead logging in conjunction with RAID protection ensures that you never lose a transaction. (However, a good backup strategy is still essential in case of certain situations, such as when an administrator accidentally clobbers a table.) SQL Server always opens its files by instructing the operating system to write through any other caching that the operating system might be doing. Hence, SQL Server ensures that transactions are atomic—even a sudden interruption of power results in no partial transactions existing in the database, and all completed transactions are guaranteed to be reflected. (It is crucial, however, that a hardware disk-caching controller not "lie" and claim that a write has been completed unless it really has or will be. We'll discuss the use of a hardware caching controller in Chapter 4.)

Checkpoints

Checkpoint operations minimize the amount of work that SQL Server must do when databases are recovered during system startup. Checkpoints are run on a database by database basis. They flush dirty pages from the current database out to disk so that those changes will not have to be redone during database recovery. (A *dirty page* is one that has been modified since it was brought from disk into the buffer pool.) When a checkpoint occurs, SQL Server writes a checkpoint record to the transaction log, which lists all the transactions that are active. This allows the recovery process to build a table containing a list of all the potentially dirty pages.

Checkpoints are triggered when:

- A database owner explicitly issues a checkpoint command to perform a checkpoint in that database.

■ The log is getting full (more than 70 percent of capacity) and the database option *trunc. log on chkpt.* is set. A checkpoint is triggered to truncate the transaction log and free up space.

■ A long recovery time is estimated. When recovery time is predicted to be longer than the *recovery interval* configuration option, a checkpoint is triggered. SQL Server 7 uses a simple metric to predict recovery time because it can recover, or redo, in less time than it took the original operations to run. Thus, if checkpoints are taken at least as often as the recovery interval frequency, recovery will complete within the interval. A recovery interval setting of 1 means checkpoints occur every minute. A minimum amount of work must be done for the automatic checkpoint to fire; this is currently 10 MB of log per minute. In this way, SQL Server doesn't waste time taking checkpoints on idle databases. A default recovery interval of 0 means that SQL Server will choose an appropriate value automatically; for the current version, this is one minute.

Checkpoints and Performance Issues

A checkpoint is issued as part of an orderly shutdown, so a typical recovery upon restart takes only seconds. (An orderly shutdown occurs when you explicitly shut down SQL Server, unless you do so via the SHUTDOWN WITH NOWAIT command. An orderly shutdown also occurs when the SQL Server service is stopped through the Windows NT Service Control Manager or the net stop command from an operating system prompt.) Although a checkpoint speeds up recovery, it does slightly degrade run-time performance.

Unless your system is being pushed with high transactional activity, the run-time impact of a checkpoint probably won't be noticeable. It is minimized via the *fuzzy checkpoint* technique, which reflects the changes to the data pages incrementally. You can also use the recovery interval option of *sp_configure* to influence checkpointing frequency, balancing the time to recover vs. any impact on run-time performance. If you are interested in tracing how often checkpoints actually occur, you can start your SQL Server with trace flag 3502, which writes information to SQL Server's error log every time a checkpoint occurs.

Accessing Pages via the Buffer Manager

The Buffer Manager handles the in-memory version of each physical disk page and provides all other modules access to it (with appropriate safety measures). The memory image in the buffer pool, if one exists, takes precedence over the disk image. That is, the copy of the data page in memory might include updates that have not yet been written to disk. (It might be dirty.) When a page is needed for a process, it must exist in memory (in the buffer pool). If the page is not there, a physical I/O is performed to get it. Obviously, because physical I/Os are expensive, the fewer the better. The more memory there is (the bigger the buffer pool), the more pages can reside there and the more likely a page can be found there.

A database appears as a simple sequence of numbered pages. The database ID (dbid), file number (fileno), and page number (pageno) uniquely specify a page for the entire SQL Server environment. When another module (such as the access methods manager, row manager, index manager, or text manager) needs to access a page, it requests access from the Buffer Manager by specifying the dbid, fileno, and pageno.

The Buffer Manager responds to the calling module with a pointer to the memory buffer holding that page. The response might be immediate if the page is already in the cache, or it might take an instant for a disk I/O to complete and bring the page into memory. Typically, the calling module also requests that the lock manager perform the appropriate level of locking on the page. The calling module notifies the Buffer Manager if and when it is finished dirtying, or making updates to, the page. The Buffer Manager is responsible for writing these updates to disk in a way that coordinates with logging and transaction management.

Large Memory Issues

Systems with hundreds of megabytes of RAM are not uncommon. In fact, for benchmark activities, Microsoft runs with a memory configuration of as much as 2 GB of physical RAM. Using SQL Server on a DEC Alpha processor, or using the Enterprise Edition of SQL Server, allows even more memory to be used. In the future, Windows NT will support a 64-bit address space and memory prices probably will continue to decline, so huge data caches of many gigabytes will not be so unusual. The reason to run with more memory is, of course, to reduce the need for physical I/O by increasing your cache-hit ratio.

Memory: How Much Is Too Much?

Most systems would not benefit from huge amounts of memory. For example, if you have 2 GB of RAM and your entire database is 1 GB, you won't even be able to fill the available memory, let alone benefit from its size. A pretty small portion of most databases is "hot," so a memory size that is only a small percentage of the entire database size can often yield a high cache-hit ratio. If you find that SQL Server is doing a lot of memory-intensive processing, such as internal sorts and hashing, you can add additional memory. Adding additional memory beyond what is needed for a high cache-hit ratio and internal sorts and hashes might bring only marginal improvement.

Read Ahead

SQL Server supports a mechanism called read ahead, whereby the need for data and index pages can be anticipated and pages can be brought into the buffer pool before they are actually read. This performance optimization allows large amounts of data to be processed effectively. Unlike in previous versions of SQL Server, read ahead is managed completely internally, and no configuration adjustments are necessary. In addition, read ahead does not use separate Windows NT threads. This ensures that read ahead stays far enough—but not too far—ahead of the scan of the actual data.

There are two kinds of read ahead: one for table scans and one for index ranges. For table scans, the table's allocation structures are consulted to read the table in disk order. There are up to 32 extents (32 * 8 pages/extent * 8192 bytes/page = 2MB) of read ahead outstanding at a time. The extents are read with a single 64 KB scatter read. (Scatter-gather I/O was introduced in Windows NT 4, Service Pack 2, with the Win32 functions ReadFileScatter and WriteFileScatter. These functions allow SQL Server to issue a single read or write to transfer up to eight pages of data directly to or from SQL Server's buffer pool.) If the table is spread across multiple files in a file group, SQL Server attempts to keep at least eight of the files busy with read ahead instead of sequentially processing the files.

For index ranges, the scan uses level one of the index structure, which is the level immediately above the leaf, to determine which pages to read ahead. It tries to stay a certain number of pages ahead of the scan; that number is currently about 40 plus the configuration value for *max async I/O*. When the index scan starts, read ahead is invoked on the initial descent of the index to minimize the number of reads performed. For instance, for a scan of *WHERE state = 'WA'*, read ahead searches the index for *key = 'WA'*, and it can tell from the level one nodes how many pages have to be examined to satisfy the scan. If the anticipated number of pages is small, all the pages are requested by the initial read ahead; if the pages are contiguous, they are fetched in scatter reads. If the range contains a large number of pages, the initial read ahead is performed and thereafter every time another 16 pages are consumed by the scan, the index is consulted to read in another 16 pages. This has several interesting effects:

- Small ranges can be processed in a single read at the data page level whenever the index is contiguous.

- The scan range (for example, *state = 'WA'*) can be used to prevent reading ahead of pages that will not be used since this information is available in the index.

- Read ahead is not slowed by having to follow page linkages at the data page level. (Read ahead can be done on both clustered indexes and nonclustered indexes.)

NOTE Scatter-gather I/O and asynchronous I/O are available only to SQL Server running on Windows NT. This includes the desktop edition of SQL Server if it has been installed on Windows NT Workstation.

The Log Manager

All changes are "written ahead" by the Buffer Manager to the transaction log. Write-ahead logging ensures that all databases can be recovered to a consistent state even in the event of a complete server failure, as long as the physical medium (hard disk) survives. A process is never given acknowledgment that a transaction has been committed unless it is on disk in the transaction log. For this reason, all writes to the transaction log are synchronous—SQL Server must wait for acknowledgment of completion. Writes to data pages can be made asynchronously, without waiting for acknowledgment, because if a failure occurs the transactions can be undone or redone from the information in the transaction log.

The log manager formats transaction log records in memory before writing them to disk. To format these log records, the log manager maintains regions of contiguous memory called *log caches*. Unlike in previous versions, in SQL Server 7 log records do not share the buffer pool with data and index pages. Log records are maintained only in the log caches.

To achieve maximum throughput, the log manager maintains two or more log caches. One is the current log cache, in which new log records are added. The log manager also has two queues of log caches: a flushQueue, which contains log caches waiting to be flushed, and a freeQueue, which contains log caches that have no data and can be reused.

When a user process requires that a particular log cache be flushed (for example, when a transaction commits), the log cache is placed into the flush-Queue (if it isn't already there). Then the thread (or fiber) is put into the list of connections waiting for the log cache to be flushed. The connection does not do further work until its log records have been flushed.

The *log writer* is a dedicated thread that goes through the flushQueue in order and flushes the log caches out to disk. The log caches are written one at a time. The log writer first checks to see if the log cache is the current log cache. If it is, the log writer pads the log cache to sector alignment and updates some header information. It then issues an I/O event for that log cache. When the flush for a particular log cache is completed, any processes waiting on that log cache are woken up and can resume work.

Transaction Logging and Recovery

The transaction log records all changes made to the database and stores enough information to allow any change to be undone (rolled back) or redone (rolled forward) in the event of a system failure or if it is directed to do so by the application (in the case of a rollback command). Physically, the transaction log is a set of files associated with a database at the time the database is created or altered. Modules that perform database updates write log entries that exactly describe the changes made. Each log entry is labeled with a Log Sequence Number (LSN) that is guaranteed to be unique. All log entries that are part of the same transaction are linked together so that all parts of a transaction can be easily located for both undo activities (as with a rollback) and redo activities (during system recovery).

The Buffer Manager guarantees that the log is written before the changes to the database are written (write-ahead logging). This is possible because SQL Server keeps track of its current position in the log by means of the LSN. Every time a page is changed, the LSN corresponding to the log entry for that change is written into the header of the data page. Dirty pages can be written only when the LSN on the page is less than the LSN for the last page that has been written to the log. The Buffer Manager also guarantees that log pages are written in a specific order, making it clear which log pages must be processed after a system failure, regardless of when the failure occurred. The log records for a transaction are written to disk before the commit acknowledgement is sent to the client process, but the actual changed data might not have been physically written out to the data pages. So although the writes to the log must be synchronous (SQL Server must wait for them to complete so it knows that they are safely on disk), writes to data pages can be asynchronous. That is, writes to the data pages need only be posted to the operating system, and SQL Server can check later to see that they were completed. They don't have to complete immediately because the log contains all the information needed to redo the work, even in the event of a power failure or system crash before the write has completed. The system would be much slower if it had to wait for every I/O request to complete before proceeding.

Logging involves demarcation of the beginning and end of each transaction (and savepoints, if a transaction uses them). Between the beginning and ending demarcations, information exists about the changes made to the data. This information can take the form of the actual "before and after" data values, or it can refer to the operation that was performed so that those values can be derived. The end of a typical transaction is marked with a Commit record, which indicates that the transaction must be reflected in the database or redone if necessary. A transaction aborted during normal runtime (not system restart) due to an explicit rollback or something like a resource error (for example, out of memory) actually undoes the operation by applying changes that undo the original data modifications. The records of these changes are written to the log and marked as "compensation log records." If the system crashes after a transaction commits but before the data is written out to the data pages, the transaction must be recovered. The recovery process runs automatically at system startup. We'll continue to refer to recovery as a system startup function, which is its most common role by far. However, recovery is also run during the final step of restoring a database from backup and can be forced manually.

Recovery performs both redo (rollforward) and undo (rollback) operations. In a redo operation, the log is examined and each change is verified as being already reflected in the database. (After a redo, every change made by the transaction is guaranteed to have been applied.) If the change does not appear in the database, it is again performed from the information in the log. Undo requires the removal of partial changes of a transaction when the transaction had not entirely completed.

During recovery, only changes that occurred or were still open (in progress) since the last checkpoint are redone or undone. There are three phases to the recovery algorithm, and they are centered around the last checkpoint record in the transaction log. The three phases are illustrated in Figure 3-5. The descriptions refer to a crash of SQL Server, but these same recovery plans take place if SQL Server is intentionally stopped.

- **Phase 1: Analysis**   The first phase is a forward pass starting at the last checkpoint record in the transaction log. This pass determines and constructs a dirty page table (DPT) consisting of pages that might have been dirty at the time of the crash (or when SQL Server stopped). An active transaction table is built that consists of uncommitted transactions at the time of the crash.

- **Phase 2: Redo**   This phase repeats history by returning the database to the state it was in at the time of the crash. The starting point for this forward pass is the minimum of all the LSNs in the DPT. The DPT is used to avoid reading pages not needing recovery and to avoid overwriting nonlogged changes.

- **Phase 3: Undo**   This phase moves backward from the end of the log, following the links between entries in the transaction log for each transaction. Any transaction that was not committed at the time of the crash is undone so that none of its changes are actually reflected in the database.

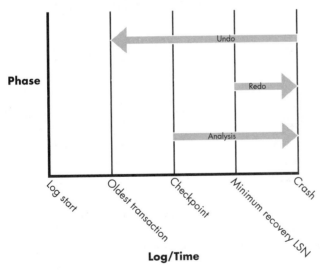

Figure 3-5.
The three phases of the SQL Server recovery process.

Locking and Recovery

Locking, transaction management (rollback and rollforward), and recovery are all closely related. A transaction can be rolled back only if all affected data was locked exclusively so that no other process could have either seen changes in progress (which might still be rolled back) or made changes to resources used by the transaction that would prevent its being rolled back. Only one active transaction can modify a row at a time. This is why exclusive locks must be held until a transaction is either committed or aborted. Until the moment it is committed, the transaction logically does not exist. A transaction operating with Read Uncommitted isolation (dirty read) can sometimes read data that logically never existed because it does not honor the existence of exclusive locks. But any other transaction operating with a higher level of isolation (which occurs by default—operating with Read Uncommitted isolation must be requested) would never allow such a phenomenon.

Page LSNs and Recovery

Every database page has an LSN in the page header that uniquely identifies it, by version, as rows on the page are changed over time. This page LSN reflects the location in the transaction log of the last log entry that modified a row on this page. During a redo operation of transactions, the LSN of each log record is compared to the page LSN of the data page that the log entry modified; if the page LSN is less than the log LSN, the operation indicated in the log entry is redone, as shown in Figure 3-6.

Because recovery finds the last checkpoint record in the log (plus transactions that were still active at the time of the checkpoint) and proceeds from there, recovery time is short and the transaction log can be purged or archived for all changes committed before the checkpoint. Otherwise, recovery could take a long time and transaction logs would become unreasonably large. A transaction log cannot be purged beyond the point of the earliest transaction that is still open, no matter how many checkpoints might have occurred subsequently. If a transaction remains open, the log must be preserved because it is still not clear whether the transaction is done or ever will be done. The transaction might ultimately need to be rolled back or rolled forward.

Some SQL Server administrators have noted that the transaction log seems unable to be purged to free up space, even after the log has been archived. This problem often results from some process having opened a transaction, which it then forgot about. For this reason, from an application development standpoint, you should ensure that transactions are kept short. Another possible reason for this problem relates to a table being replicated using transactional replication when the replication log reader hasn't processed it yet. This situation is less common, though, because typically only a latency of a few seconds occurs while the log reader does its work. You can use DBCC OPENTRAN to look for the earliest open transaction, or oldest replicated transaction not yet processed, and then take corrective measures (such as killing the offending process or running the *sp_repldone* stored procedure to allow the replicated transactions to be purged).

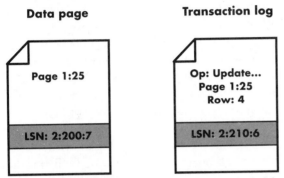

The log record at LSN 2:210:6 refers to page 1:25, which has an LSN value of 2:200:7, which is less than the log LSN. Thus, the update indicated in the log record must be redone.

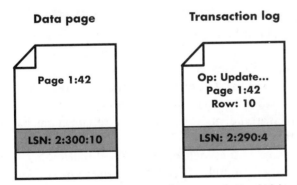

The log record at LSN 2:290:6 refers to page 1:42, which has an LSN value of 2:300:10. The page LSN is greater than the log LSN. Therefore, this page was written to disk after the indicated transaction occurred, and the transaction does not need to be redone.

Figure 3-6.
Comparing LSNs to decide whether to process the log entry.

The SQL Server Kernel and Interaction with the Operating System

The SQL Server kernel is responsible for interacting with the operating system. It's a bit of a simplification to suggest that SQL Server has one module for all operating system calls, but for ease of understanding, you can think of it in this way. All requests to operating system services are made via the Win32 API and C run-time libraries. When SQL Server runs under Windows NT, it runs entirely in the Win32 protected subsystem. Absolutely no calls are made in Windows NT Privileged Mode; they are made in User Mode. This means that SQL Server cannot crash the entire system, it cannot crash another process running in User Mode, and other such processes cannot crash SQL Server. SQL Server has no device driver–level calls, nor does it use any undocumented calls to Windows NT. If the entire system crashes (giving you the so-called "Blue Screen of Death") and SQL Server happens to have been running there, one thing is certain: SQL Server did not crash the system. Such a crash must be the result of faulty or incompatible hardware, a buggy device driver operating in Privileged Mode, or a critical bug in the Windows NT operating system code (which is doubtful).

> **NOTE** The Blue Screen of Death—a blue "bug check" screen with some diagnostic information—appears if a crash of Windows NT occurs. It looks similar to the screen that appears when Windows NT initially boots up.

A key design goal of both SQL Server and Windows NT is scalability. The same binary executable files that run on notebook computer systems run on symmetric multiprocessor super servers with loads of processors. SQL Server includes versions for Intel and RISC hardware architectures on the same CD. Windows NT is an ideal platform for a database server because it provides a fully protected, secure 32-bit environment. The foundations of a great database server platform are preemptive scheduling, virtual paged memory management, symmetric multiprocessing, and asynchronous I/O. Windows NT provides these, and SQL Server uses them fully. The SQL Server engine runs as a single process on Windows NT. Within that process are multiple threads of execution. Windows NT schedules each thread to the next processor available to run one.

Exploiting the Windows NT Platform

Competitors have occasionally, and falsely, claimed that SQL Server must have special, secret hooks into the operating system. Such claims are likely the result of SQL Server's astonishing level of performance. Yes, it is tightly integrated with the Windows NT, Windows 95, and Windows 98 operating systems. But this integration is accomplished via completely public interfaces—there are no secret "hooks" into the operating system. Yes, the product is optimized for Windows NT. That's SQL Server's primary platform. But other products could also achieve this level of optimization and integration if they made it a chief design goal. Instead, they tend to abstract away the differences between operating systems. Of course, there's nothing wrong with that. If Microsoft had to make SQL Server run on 44 different operating systems, it might also take a lowest-common-denominator approach to engineering—to do anything else would be almost impossible. So although such an approach is quite rational, it is in direct conflict with the goal of fully exploiting all services of a given operating system. Since SQL Server runs exclusively on Microsoft operating systems, it intentionally uses every service in the smartest way possible.

Threading and Symmetric Multiprocessing

SQL Server approaches multiprocessor scalability differently than most other symmetric multiprocessing (SMP) database systems. Two characteristics separate this approach from other implementations:

- **Single-process architecture**   SQL Server maintains a single-process, multithreaded architecture that reduces system overhead and memory use. This is called the Symmetric Server Architecture.

- **Native thread-level multiprocessing**   SQL Server supports multiprocessing at the thread level rather than at the process level, which allows for preemptive operation and dynamic load balancing across multiple CPUs. Using multiple threads is significantly more efficient than using multiple processes.

To understand how SQL Server works, it is useful to compare its strategies to strategies generally used by other products. On a nonthreaded operating system such as some UNIX variants, a typical SMP database server has multiple

DBMS processes, each bound to a specific CPU. Some implementations even have one process per user, which results in a high memory cost. These processes communicate using Shared Memory, which maintains the cache, locks, task queues, and user context information. The DBMS must include complex logic that takes on the role of an operating system: it schedules user tasks, simulates threads, coordinates multiple processes, and so on. Because processes are bound to specific CPUs, dynamic load balancing can be difficult or impossible. For the sake of portability, products often take this approach even when they run on an operating system that offers native threading services, such as Windows NT.

SQL Server, on the other hand, uses a clean design of a single process and multiple operating system threads. The threads are scheduled onto a CPU by a User Mode Scheduler, as discussed in Chapter 2. Figure 3-7 shows the difference between SQL Server's threading architecture and that of other typical SMP database systems.

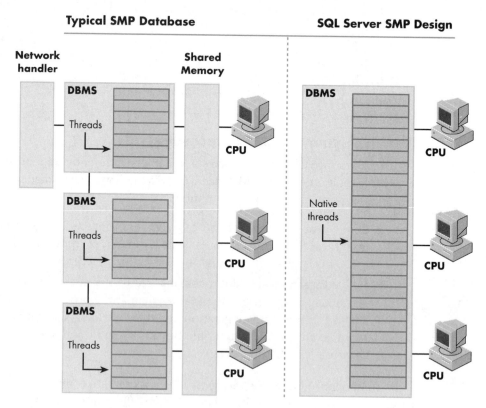

Figure 3-7.
SQL Server's single-process, multiple-thread design.

SQL Server always uses multiple threads, even on a single-processor system. Threads are created and destroyed depending on system activity, so thread count is not constant. Typically, the number of active threads in SQL Server range from 16 to 100, depending on system activity and configuration. A pool of threads handles each of the networks that SQL Server simultaneously supports, another thread handles database checkpoints, another handles the lazywriter process, and another handles the log writer. A separate thread is also available for general database cleanup tasks, such as periodically shrinking a database that is in autoshrink mode. Finally, a pool of threads handles all user commands.

The Worker Thread Pool

Although SQL Server might seem to offer each user a separate operating system thread, the system is actually a bit more sophisticated than that. Because it is inefficient to use hundreds of separate operating system threads to support hundreds of users, SQL Server establishes a pool of worker threads.

When a client issues a command, the SQL Server network handler places the command in a "queue" and the next available thread from the worker thread pool takes the request. Technically, this queue is a Windows NT facility called an IOCompletion port. The SQL Server worker thread waits in the completion queue for incoming network requests to be posted to the IOCompletion port. If no idle worker thread is available to wait for the next incoming request, SQL Server dynamically creates a new thread until the maximum configured worker thread limit has been reached. The client's command must wait for a worker thread to be freed.

Even in a system with thousands of connected users, most are typically idle at any given time. As the workload decreases, SQL Server gradually eliminates idle threads to improve resource and memory use.

The worker thread pool design is efficient for handling thousands of active connections without the need for a transaction monitor. Most competing products, including those on the largest mainframe systems, need to use a transaction monitor to achieve the level of active users that SQL Server can handle without such an extra component. If you support a large number of connections, this is an important capability.

> **NOTE** In many cases, you should allow users to stay connected—even if they will be idle for periods of, say, an hour—rather than have them continually connect and disconnect. Repeatedly incurring the overhead of the logon process is more expensive than simply allowing the connection to remain live but idle.

Active vs. Idle

In the previous context, a user is considered idle from the database perspective. The human end user might be quite active, filling in the data entry screen, getting information from customers, and so forth. But those activities don't require any server interaction until a command is actually sent. So from the SQL Server engine perspective, the connection is idle.

When you think of an active user vs. an idle user, be sure to consider the user in the context of the back-end database server. In practically all types of applications that have many end users, at any given time the number of users who have an active request with the database is relatively small. A system with 1000 active connections might reasonably be configured with 150 or so worker threads. But this doesn't mean that all 150 worker threads are created at the start—they're created only as needed, and 150 is only a high-water mark. In fact, fewer than 100 worker threads might be active at a time, even if end users all think they are actively using the system all the time.

A thread from the worker thread pool services each command to allow multiple processors to be fully utilized as long as multiple user commands are outstanding. In addition, with SQL Server 7, a single user command with no other activity on the system can benefit from multiple processors if the query is complex. SQL Server can break complex queries into component parts that can be executed in parallel on multiple CPUs. Note that this intraquery parallelism occurs only if there are processors to spare—that is, if the number of processors is greater than the number of connections. In addition, intraquery parallelism is not considered if the query is not expensive to run, and the threshold for what constitutes "expensive" can be controlled with a configuration option called *cost threshold for parallelism.*

Under the normal pooling scheme, a worker thread runs each user request to completion. Because each thread has its own stack, stack switching is unnecessary. If a given thread performs an operation that causes a page fault, only that thread, and hence only that one client, is blocked. (A page fault occurs if the thread makes a request for memory and the virtual memory manager of the operating system must swap that page in from disk since it had been paged out. Such a request for memory must wait a long time relative to the normal memory access time because a physical I/O is thousands of times more expensive than reading real memory.)

Now consider something more serious than a page fault. Suppose that while a user request is being carried out, a bug is exposed in SQL Server that results in an illegal operation that causes an access violation (for example, the thread tries to read some memory outside the SQL Server address space). Windows NT immediately terminates the offending thread—an important feature of a truly protected operating system. Because SQL Server makes use of structured exception handling in Windows NT, only the specific SQL Server user who made the request is affected. All other users of SQL Server or other applications on the system are unaffected and the system at large will not crash. Of course, such a bug should never occur and in reality is indeed rare. But this is software, and software is never perfect. Having this important reliability feature is like wearing a seat belt—you hope you never need it, but you're glad it's there in case a crash occurs.

NOTE Since Windows 95 and Windows 98 do not support SMP systems or thread pooling, the previous discussion is relevant only to SQL Server running on Windows NT. The following discussion of disk I/O is also only relevant to SQL Server on Windows NT.

Disk I/O on Windows NT

SQL Server 7 uses two Windows NT features to improve its disk I/O performance: scatter-gather I/O and asynchronous I/O. The descriptions below were adapted from SQL Server's Books Online:

Scatter-gather I/O   As just mentioned, scatter-gather I/O was introduced in Windows NT 4, Service Pack 2. Previously, all the data for a disk read or write on Windows NT had to be in a contiguous area of memory. If a read transferred in 64 KB of data, the read request had to specify the address of a contiguous area of 64 KB of memory. Scatter-gather I/O allows a read or write to transfer data into or out of discontiguous areas of memory.

If SQL Server 7 reads in a 64 KB extent, it does not have to allocate a single 64 KB area and then copy the individual pages to buffer cache pages. It can locate eight buffer pages and then do a single scatter-gather I/O that specifies the address of the eight buffer pages. Windows NT places the eight pages directly into the buffer pages, eliminating the need for SQL Server to do a separate memory copy.

Asynchronous I/O   In an asynchronous I/O, after an application requests a read or write operation, Windows NT immediately returns control to the application. The application can then perform additional work, and it can later test to see if the read or write has completed. By contrast, in a synchronous I/O, the operating system does not return control to the application until the read or write completes. SQL Server supports multiple concurrent asynchronous I/O operations against each file in a database. The maximum number of I/O operations for any file is controlled by the *max async io* configuration option. If *max async io* is left at its default of 32, a maximum of 32 asynchronous I/O operations can be outstanding for each file at any time.

Summary

In this chapter, we've looked at the general workings of the SQL Server engine, including the key modules and functional areas that make up the engine. We've also covered issues dealing with integration with Windows NT. By necessity, we've made some simplifications throughout the chapter, but the information should provide some insight into the roles and responsibilities of the major subsystems in SQL Server, the general flow of the system, and the interrelationships among subsystems.

PART III

USING MICROSOFT SQL SERVER

0x c2b000

xc2b000 pg=0 m_objid=
indid=0 freeoff=
m_revpg=0 m_objid=4
d=0 freeoff=30

0x17b000c 0158585

PLANNING FOR AND INSTALLING SQL SERVER

If you have appropriate hardware that is running Microsoft Windows, installing Microsoft SQL Server is a snap. It requires little more than inserting the CD into the drive and answering a few questions. Even a novice can comfortably install SQL Server in less than 15 minutes. The installation program does not ask a lot of questions about how to configure your system because SQL Server 7 is primarily self-configuring. (We won't spend much time discussing the mechanics of the installation program. You can consult the online Help and the documentation's step-by-step guide if you need to.)

Installing SQL Server is so easy that you might be tempted to dive in a bit too soon. That's OK if you're in "learning mode," but an installation that will be part of a production system deserves some thoughtful planning.

SQL Server Editions

SQL Server is available in three editions, each on its own CD: SBS (Small Business Server) edition, Standard edition, and Enterprise edition. Table 4-1 on the following page, taken from SQL Server Books Online, summarizes the main differences between the editions.

No matter which edition you have, you can install SQL Server on either an Intel-compatible processor or a DEC Alpha–compatible processor. Any edition lets you install the full server and tools suite or just the tools. You can also install the desktop version of SQL Server from any edition if you have chosen to use per-seat licensing, which we'll discuss later in this chapter. You can install SQL Server Desktop on Windows 95, Windows 98, Windows NT Workstation, Windows NT, or Windows NT Enterprise.

Feature	SBS	Standard	Enterprise
Runs on Microsoft BackOffice Small Business Server	Yes	Yes	No
Runs on Microsoft Windows NT Server	No	Yes	No
Runs on Windows NT Server, Enterprise edition	No	Yes	Yes
Extended memory support	No	No	Yes
SQL Server failover support	No	No	Yes
Supports Microsoft Search Service, full-text catalogs, and full-text indexes	Yes	Yes	Yes
Supports Microsoft SQL Server OLAP Services	No	Yes (no user-defined cube partitions)	Yes (includes user-defined cube partitions)
Maximum database size	10 GB	Unlimited	Unlimited
Number of SMP CPUs	4	4	32

Table 4-1.
Features of the three SQL Server editions.

The desktop version does not come with all the SQL Server features, and if you use it on a Windows 95 or Windows 98 machine, you face other restrictions because of the limited capabilities of the operating system.

SQL Server Desktop does not support:

- Parallel queries

- Fiber-mode scheduling

- Failover clusters

- Extended memory addressing

- Defining publications in a transaction-based replication configuration

In addition, if SQL Server Desktop is installed on a Windows 95 or Windows 98 machine, it also does not support:

■ The Named Pipes and Banyan VINES server-side Net-Libraries. (The Windows 95 or Windows 98 computer cannot accept incoming connections using these protocols, but the client tools on such a computer can connect to other SQL Servers on Windows NT using these protocols.)

■ AppleTalk Net-Libraries.

■ Windows NT Authentication for incoming server connections.

■ The server side of using encryption with the Multiprotocol Net-Library.

■ Asynchronous I/O or scatter-gather I/O. (This includes true read ahead scans. SQL Server will issue what it thinks are read ahead requests, but these need to be translated to synchronous calls, because Windows 95 and Windows 98 do not support asynchronous I/O. You will get the benefit of the larger I/Os that read ahead provides, but they will be synchronous.)

■ Any component that corresponds to Windows NT Services. (The SQL Server database engine and SQL Server Agent run as executable programs on Windows 95 and Windows 98.)

■ Event logs. (SQL Server uses a SQL Server Profiler–based mechanism to launch alerts on Windows 95 and Windows 98.)

■ SQL Server Performance Monitor.

■ The SQL Server Version Upgrade utility.

We'll discuss most of these capabilities and tools in more detail later in the book.

NOTE Contrary to the SQL Server online documentation, hash and merge joins are possible with SQL Server Desktop. However, because these join techniques are more memory intensive and the desktop installation is likely to have less memory resources available, the SQL Server query optimizer is much less likely to choose these join techniques. (We'll examine these techniques in Chapter 14 when we look at the SQL Server query optimizer.)

User Connections

SQL Server Desktop and SQL Server SBS impose no hard and fast limits on the number of user connections, unlike earlier versions of SQL Server. SQL Server 7 uses an internal throttling mechanism that is optimized for a workload that corresponds to a certain number of users. SQL Server Desktop is optimized so that the best throughput occurs with about five users. As the number of user connections increases, the total throughput actually starts to decrease, not just for the individual connections but for the entire SQL Server. If you want more throughput, use the Standard, SBS, or Enterprise edition of SQL Server. An SBS installation of SQL Server is also throttled, so its maximum throughput occurs with about 100 user connections.

Embedded SQL Server

If you're looking for a version of SQL Server to embed in your own applications and redistribute, refer to the documentation that comes with Microsoft Access 2000 or Microsoft Office 2000. The installation of either of these products gives you the option of installing the Microsoft Data Engine (MSDE). MSDE is the server component of SQL Server and includes basically the relational engine and the storage engine. None of the usual SQL Server tools are installed; you are expected to use the visual tools that come with Microsoft Visual Studio for creating your objects. Office 2000 and Access 2000 install a tool that lets you do a minimum amount of administration. In addition, you can use all the usual tools that come with a full SQL Server installation (Desktop, SBS, Standard, or Enterprise), such as the SQL Server Enterprise Manager and the SQL Server Query Analyzer, to access the data stored in MSDE. We won't discuss MSDE further in this book; see the documentation for additional Office 2000 or Access 2000 details.

Hardware Guidelines

Because SQL Server runs on any hardware that runs Windows NT, you can choose from among thousands of hardware options. Of course, SQL Server Desktop runs on any hardware that runs Windows 95 or Windows 98; however, since your production applications will be deployed on Windows NT, you must provide the best hardware for the job. Our discussion of hardware will thus focus on the needs of SQL Server running on Windows NT. The following sections offer some guidelines on choosing hardware.

Use Hardware on the Windows Hardware Compatibility List

If you cobble together a system from spare parts, Windows NT will run just fine, but your system might be unreliable. Unless you're a hobbyist and you like to tinker, this method isn't suitable for a production system. Support is another issue. Many people buy motherboards, chassis, processors, hard drives, memory, video cards, and assorted other peripherals separately and put together terrific systems, but the support options are limited.

Keep in mind that even name-brand systems occasionally fail. If you're using hardware that's on the Windows Hardware Compatibility List (HCL) and you get a "blue screen" (Windows NT system crash), you're more likely to be able to identify the problem as a hardware failure or find out, for example, that some known device driver problem occurs with that platform (and that you can get an update for the driver). With a homegrown system, such a problem can be nearly impossible to isolate. If you plan to use SQL Server, data integrity is probably a key concern for you. Most cases of corrupt data in SQL Server can be traced to hardware or device driver failure. (These device drivers are often supplied by the hardware vendor.)

> **NOTE** Over the life of a system, hardware costs are a relatively small portion of the overall cost. Using no-name or homegrown hardware is being penny-wise and pound-foolish. You can definitely get a good and cost-effective HCL-approved system without cutting corners.

Choose a Good Processor

SQL Server 7 runs on only two of the four processor architectures supported by Windows NT: Intel *x*86 and DEC Alpha-AXP. It will not install on Motorola MIPS R4000 and PowerPC processors.

Most SQL Server users have machines with the Intel architecture. Although the SQL Server product versions for both processor architectures are on the same CD, many vendor software components for SQL Server might ship first, or only, for the Intel platform. For example, you might use an accounting software package that is first released or is available only for Intel-based machines. You can run the accounting application on an Intel-based server and use it to communicate via the network with an instance of SQL Server running on a DEC Alpha-AXP–based system as long as the application isn't required to run on the same machine as SQL Server (and you have multiple machines in your environment). In addition, if you ever need to dual-boot your system to MS-DOS, Windows 95, or Windows 98, you should go with Intel. An Intel-based solution is likely to provide all the horsepower your application needs. But the processor is only part of the equation, as we'll see later.

If you're part of a large organization, you probably have a set of standard hardware requirements. SQL Server 7 runs well if you have a RISC platform with Windows NT. SQL Server provides a small amount of processor-specific assembly language for each environment, but otherwise the code is all-common. The SQL Server development group at Microsoft has no "porting" team—versions for both supported processor architectures are built and tested at the same time, and, as mentioned earlier, they are on the same CD. If this is the first time you've used a RISC platform with Windows NT (that is, Alpha-AXP), you'll be surprised at how "normal" it seems compared to the Intel-based systems you probably already use. For example, if you have access to both an Intel and an Alpha machine running Windows NT and SQL Server and they are configured with a switch box that allows them to use the same keyboard, monitor, and mouse, you probably can't tell the systems apart unless you make an effort to find out which one is currently running.

Performance = Fn(Processor Cycles, Memory, I/O Throughput)

System throughput is only as fast as the slowest component. A bottleneck in one area reduces the rest of the system to the speed of the slowest part; the performance of your hardware is a function of the processing power available, the amount of physical memory (RAM) in the system, and the number of I/Os per second that the system can support.

Of course, the most important aspect of performance is the application's design and implementation. You should choose your hardware carefully, but there is no substitute for efficient applications. Although SQL Server can be a brilliantly fast system, you can easily write an application that performs poorly—one that's impossible to "fix" simply by "tuning" the server or by "killing it with hardware." You might double performance by upgrading your hardware or fine-tuning your system; however, application changes can often yield hundredfold increases.

Unfortunately, there's no simple formula for coming up with an appropriately sized system. Many people ask for this, and it is common for minicomputer and mainframe vendors to provide "configuration programs" that claim to do just this. But the goal of those programs often seems to be to sell more hardware.

Once again, your application is the key. In reality, your hardware needs are dependent on your application. How CPU-intensive is it? How much data will you store? How random are the requests for data? Can you expect to get numerous "cache hits" with the most frequently requested data often being found in memory, without having to perform physical I/Os? How many users will simultaneously and actively use the system?

Invest in Benchmarking

If you are planning a large system, it's worthwhile to invest up front in some benchmarking. SQL Server has numerous published benchmarks, most of them Transaction Processing Council (TPC) benchmarks. Although such benchmarks are useful for comparing systems and hardware, they offer only broad guidelines and the benchmark workload is unlikely to compare directly to yours. It's probably best to do some custom benchmarking for your own system.

Benchmarking can be a difficult, never-ending job, so keep the process in perspective. Remember that what counts is how fast your application runs, not how fast your benchmark performs. And sometimes significant benchmarking efforts are unnecessary—the system might perform clearly within parameters or similar enough to other systems. Experience is the best guide. But if you are testing a new application that will be widely deployed, the up-front cost of a benchmark can pay big dividends in terms of a successful system rollout. Benchmarking is the developer's equivalent of the carpenter's adage "Measure twice, cut once."

SEE ALSO For information on TPC benchmarks and a summary of results, see the TPC home page at http://www.tpc.org.

Nothing beats a real-world system test, but that is not always practical. You might need to make hardware decisions before or while the application is being developed. In that case, you should develop a proxy test. Much of the work in benchmarking comes from developing the appropriate *test harness*—the framework used to simultaneously dispatch multiple clients running the test program, to run for exactly an allotted time, and to gather the results.

The companion CD includes a Microsoft benchmark kit that lets you "add water and stir" to produce a benchmark environment within a few hours and simply substitute your own transactions in place of the kit's transactions. The kit includes the source code and executables used in previous TPC-B benchmarks. Although TPC-B might not be directly relevant to your system, the real value is in the kit's test harness—the framework that drives "virtual clients" and synchronizes start and stop times, records results, and so on. Before you use the kit, you should first try to run the TPC-B test without modification. Try to achieve results roughly comparable to those listed in the kit. (Allow for hardware differences—you're looking only for a "reasonableness quotient.") Then you can easily modify the tests with your own custom transaction to better simulate your actual system. Other products, such as Dynameasure by Bluecurve, Inc. (http://www.bluecurve.com), aid in benchmarking for SQL Server performance.

Hardware Components

The following general guidelines are no substitute for your own experience with your application because of the many variables that might exist, but they can help you at the outset. For simplicity, the following sections assume that your server is basically dedicated to running SQL Server, with little else going on. (You can certainly combine SQL Server with other applications on the same machine, and you can administer SQL Server on the same machine as SQL Server Enterprise Manager. Or you can support multiple databases from one SQL Server machine.)

The Processor

SQL Server is CPU intensive, more so than you might think if you assume that it is mostly I/O constrained. Plenty of processing capacity is a good investment. Your system uses a lot of processing cycles to manage many connections, manage the data cache effectively, optimize and execute queries, check constraints, execute stored procedures, lock tables and indexes, and enforce security. Because SQL Server typically performs few floating-point operations, a processor that is fabulous with such operations but mediocre with integer operations is not the ideal choice. Before you choose a processor, you should check benchmarks such as SPECInt (integer)—not SPECfp (floating-point) or any benchmark that is a combination of floating-point and integer performance. Performance on SPECInt correlates to the relative performance of SQL Server among different processor architectures, given sufficient memory and I/O capacity. The correlation is a bit loose, of course, because other factors (the size of the processor cache, the system bus efficiency, the efficiency of the optimizing compiler used to build the system when comparing processor architectures, and many other variables) also play an important role. But integer-processing performance is a key metric for SQL Server.

Figure 4-1 shows SPECInt95 ratings for various processors running Windows NT. These figures are based on the processor vendors' data as stated in August 1998 on their Web pages. To highlight the tremendous increases in the performance of mainstream hardware, we have included figures for some older Pentium processors, even though you clearly would not go out and buy these today. Future processors will offer even better performance. In early 2000, both the Intel Merced processor and the Alpha EV68 processor are expected to ship. The Merced is expected to have a SPECInt95 rating of between 30 and 60, and the EV68 might have a rating as high as 75.

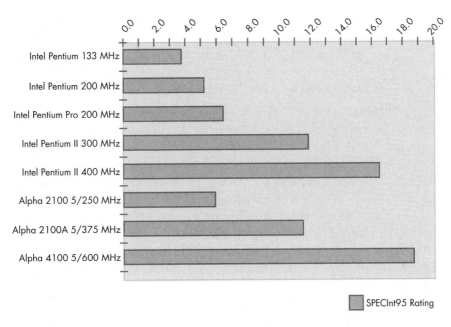

Figure 4-1.
SPECInt95 benchmarks.

SQL Server is built for SMP, but if your system is dedicated to SQL Server and supports fewer than 100 simultaneous users, a single CPU system will likely meet your needs. If you are working with large data warehousing applications, you can use an SMP system effectively with a small number of users. SQL Server 7 can run complex queries in parallel, which means that the same query is processed simultaneously by multiple processors, each doing a subset of the computations. SQL Server executes queries on multiple processors only if the number of processors is greater than the number of active connections. If you are uncertain about your needs or you expect them to grow, get a single-processor system that can be upgraded to a dual (or even quad) system.

Since Moore's Law—which states that processing power doubles every 18 months—has held true, you should buy the fastest single-processor system in its class. Buy tomorrow's technology, not yesterday's. With many other applications, the extra processing power doesn't make much difference, but SQL Server is CPU intensive. The 62 percent difference in SPECInt95 performance between a 133 MHz Pentium and a 200 MHz Pentium Pro can yield a similar difference in SQL Server performance.

TIP Remember that the processor's cache affects its performance. A big L2 (level 2, or secondary) cache is a good investment. You might see a difference of 20 percent or better simply by using a 512-KB L2 cache instead of a 256-KB L2 cache in a given system. The cost difference is perhaps $100, so this is money well spent.

If your application is already available or you can conduct a fairly realistic system test, you can be much more exacting in evaluating your hardware needs. Using the Windows NT Performance Monitor, simply profile the CPU usage of your system during a specified period of time. (Use the Processor object and the *% Processor Time* counter.) Watch all processors if you're using an SMP system. If your system is consistently above 70 percent usage or can be expected to grow to that level soon, or if it frequently spikes to greater than 90 percent for 10 seconds or more, you should consider getting a faster processor or an additional processor. You can use the SPECInt95 guidelines to determine the relative additional processing power that would be available by upgrading to a different or an additional processor.

NOTE Adding an additional processor does not double your processing power. For a system with up to four processors, adding another processor on an efficient SMP hardware platform usually yields at most an additional 80 to 90 percent of the processing power of the first CPU. Gains above 70 percent can be achieved in the four-to-eight CPU range if your system is really CPU hungry. But most systems today would be bottlenecked somewhere else before they would demand the amount of processing power that a modern four-way CPU system delivers. If your system already has plenty of CPU cycles to spare, adding a processor contributes little.

Memory

SQL Server uses memory for two broad purposes: for its own code and internal data structures and for its buffer cache. SQL Server uses only about 3.5 MB of real memory for its code and internal structures. (People are often surprised at this small number.) User connections consume about 24 KB of memory each at the time they are initiated. Memory is used for many purposes in SQL Server 7; we looked at some of them in Chapter 3 and will discuss additional details regarding memory usage in Chapter 15. By default, SQL Server 7 automatically configures the amount of memory it uses based on its needs and the needs of the operating system and other running applications.

If the SQL Server Buffer Manager can find data in the cache (memory), it can avoid physical I/Os. As discussed earlier, retrieving data from memory is tens of thousands of times faster than the mechanical operation of performing a physical I/O. (Performing physical I/O operations also consumes thousands more CPU clock cycles than simply addressing real memory.) As a rule, you should add physical memory to the system until you stop getting significant increases in cache hits—or until you run out of money. You can easily monitor cache hits with Performance Monitor. (For more information, see Chapter 15.) Using the SQLServer:Buffer Manager object, watch the *Buffer Cache Hit Ratio* counter. If adding additional physical memory makes *Buffer Cache Hit Ratio* increase significantly, the memory is a good investment.

As mentioned earlier, by default SQL Server automatically adjusts its memory use to meet its needs and the needs of the rest of the system. However, an administrator can override this and configure SQL Server to use a fixed amount of memory. You should be extremely cautious if you decide to do this. Configuring memory appropriately is crucial to good performance; configuring too much or too little memory can drastically impair performance. Too little memory gives you a poor buffer cache-hit ratio. Too much memory means that the aggregate working sets of the operating system and all applications (including SQL Server) will exceed the amount of real memory, requiring memory to be paged to and from disk. You can monitor paging in Performance Monitor using statistics such as the Memory object's counter for Pages/Sec.

Fortunately, adding physical memory to systems is usually quite simple (you pop in some SIMMs) and economical. You should start conservatively and add memory based on empirical evidence as you test your application. SQL Server needs no single correct amount of memory, so it's pointless to try to establish a uniform memory configuration for all SQL Server applications that you might ever deploy.

SQL Server can run with a minimum 32-MB system (64 MB for SQL Server Enterprise edition), but as is typically the case with a minimum requirement, this is not ideal. If your budget isn't constrained, you should consider starting with at least 64 MB of RAM. (If your budget is flexible or you have reason to believe that your application will be more demanding, you might want to bump up memory to 128 MB. But it's probably best not to go higher than this initially without some evidence that your SQL Server application will use it.)

NOTE The code sizes of both SQL Server and Windows NT system executables are larger for RISC architectures than for Intel architectures. SQL Server data structures are essentially the same size for both Intel and RISC, but the starting "tax" is higher for RISC. If you are running on a RISC platform, we recommend starting with an additional 24 MB of memory.

When you buy your initial system, give some consideration to the configuration of the memory SIMMs, not only to the total number of megabytes, so that you can later expand in the most effective way. If you're not careful, you can get a memory configuration that makes it difficult to upgrade. For example, suppose that your machine allows four memory banks for SIMMs and you want 64 MB of memory that you might upgrade in the future. If your initial configuration of 64 MB was done with four 16-MB SIMMs, you're in trouble. If you want to upgrade, you have to remove the 16-MB SIMMs and buy all new memory. But if you configure your 64 MB as two 32-MB SIMMs, you can add another one or two such SIMMs to get to 96 MB or 128 MB without replacing any of the initial memory. Starting with one 64-MB SIMM gives you even more flexibility in upgrading.

When deciding on the initial amount of memory, you should also consider whether your system will be more query intensive or more transaction intensive. Although more memory can help either way, it typically benefits query intensive systems most, especially if part of the data is "hot" and often queried. That data tends to remain cached, and more memory allows more of the data to be accessed from the cache instead of necessitating physical I/Os. If you have a query-intensive system, you might want to start with more memory than 64 MB. In contrast, a transaction-intensive system might get relatively few cache hits, especially if the transactions are randomly dispersed or don't rely much on pre-existing data. In such a system, the amount of memory needed might be low, and adding a faster I/O subsystem might make more sense than adding more memory.

Disk Drives, Controllers, and Disk Arrays

Obviously, you need to acquire enough disk space to store all your data, plus more for working space and system files. But you should not simply buy storage capacity—you should buy I/O throughput and fault tolerance as well. A single 8-GB drive stores as much as eight 1-GB drives, but its maximum I/O throughput is likely to be only about one-eighth as much as the combined power of eight smaller drives (assuming that the drives have the same speed). Even relatively small SQL Server installations should have at least two or three physical disk drives rather than a single large drive. Microsoft has benchmarked systems that can do, say, 1000 tps (in a Debit-Credit scenario) using more than 40 physical disk drives and multiple controllers to achieve the I/O rates necessary to sustain that level of throughput.

If you know your transaction level or can perform a system test to determine it, you might be able to produce a good estimate of the number of I/Os per second you need to support during peak use. Then you should procure a combination of drives and controllers that can deliver that number.

Typically, you should buy a system with SCSI drives, not IDE or EIDE drives. An IDE channel supports only two devices. An EIDE setup consists of two IDE channels and can support four (2×2) devices. But more important, an IDE channel can work with only a single device at a time—and even relatively small SQL Server installations usually have at least 2 or 3 disk drives. If multiple disks are connected on an IDE channel, only one disk at a time can do I/O. (This is especially problematic if the channel also supports a slow device such as a CD-ROM drive. With an average access time of 200 milliseconds (ms), your disk I/O would be held up for 0.2 seconds, on average, while the CD is accessed. A hard drive today usually has access times of 6 to 8 ms, which is about 30 times faster.)

SCSI is also a lot smarter than IDE or EIDE. A SCSI controller hands off commands to a SCSI drive and then logically disconnects and issues commands to other drives. If multiple commands are outstanding, the SCSI controller queues the commands inside the associated device (if the device supports command queuing) so that the device can start on the next request as soon as the current request finishes. When a request finishes, the device notifies the controller. A SCSI channel can support multiple fast drives and allow them to work at full speed. Slow devices such as CD-ROM drives and tape drives do not hog the SCSI channel because the controller logically disconnects. A single SCSI channel can support many drives, but from a practical standpoint, we recommend about a 5:1 ratio if you need to push the drives close to capacity. (That is, you should add an additional channel for every 5 drives or so.) If you are not pushing the drives to capacity, you might be able to use as many as 8 to 10 drives per channel—even more with some high-end controllers or random I/O patterns.

In TPC benchmarks (which are I/O intensive, and in which the I/O is deliberately random), Microsoft generally follows a 6:1 ratio of drives per SCSI channel. (Since TPC-C measures both performance and cost, Microsoft must balance the cost and benefits, just as they would for a real application.) Most real applications don't have such perfectly random I/O characteristics, however. When the I/O is perfectly random, a significant amount of the I/O time is spent with the disk drives seeking (that is, with the disk arm positioning itself to the right spot) rather than transferring data, which consumes the SCSI channel. Seeking is taxing only on the drive itself, not on the SCSI channel, so the ratio of drives per channel can be higher in the benchmark.

Note that we're speaking in terms of channels, not controllers. Most controllers have a single SCSI channel, so you can think of the two terms as synonymous. Some high-end cards (typically RAID controllers, not just standard SCSI) are dual-channel cards. For example, the Compaq Smart-2DH Array controller is a dual-channel controller that can efficiently push 14 drives (7 per channel).

Some History

The original acronym *RAID* apparently stood for "redundant array of *inexpensive* disks," as evidenced in the paper presented to the 1988 ACM SIGMOD by Patterson, Gibson, and Katz called "A Case for Redundant Arrays of Inexpensive Disks (RAID)." However, the current *RAID*book, published by the RAID Advisory Board, uses *independent,* which seems like a better description because the key function of RAID is to make separate, physically independent drives function logically as one drive.

RAID Solutions

Simply put, RAID solutions are usually the best choice for SQL Server for these reasons:

- RAID makes multiple physical disk drives appear logically as one drive.

- Different levels of RAID provide different performance and redundancy features.

- RAID provides different ways of distributing physical data across multiple disk drives.

■ RAID can be provided as a hardware solution (with a special RAID disk controller card), but it does not necessarily imply special hardware. RAID can also be implemented via software.

■ Windows NT Server provides RAID levels 0 (striping), 1 (mirroring), and 5 (striping with parity) for implementation with SQL Server.

Some RAID levels provide increased I/O bandwidth (striping), and others provide fault-tolerant storage (mirroring or parity). With a hardware RAID controller, you can employ a combination of striping and mirroring, often referred to as RAID-1&0 (and sometimes as RAID-10 or RAID-1+0). RAID solutions vary in how much additional disk space is required to protect the data and how long it takes to recover from a system outage. The type and level of RAID you choose depends on your I/O throughput and fault tolerance needs.

RAID-0
RAID-0, or striping, offers pure performance but no fault tolerance. I/O is done in "stripes" and is distributed among all drives in the array. Instead of the I/O capacity of one drive, you get the benefit of all the drives. A table's hot spots are dissipated, and the data transfer rates go up cumulatively with the number of drives in the array. So although an 18-GB disk might do 80 to 90 random I/Os per second, an array of eight 2.1-GB disks striped with Windows NT Server's RAID-0 might in aggregate perform more than 400 I/Os per second, which is a lot.

Choose an Appropriate Backup Strategy

Although you can use RAID for fault tolerance, it is no substitute for regular backups. RAID solutions can protect against a pure disk-drive failure, such as a head crash, but that's far from the only case in which you need a backup. If the controller fails, garbage data might appear on both your primary and redundant disks. Even more likely, an administrator could accidentally clobber a table; a disaster at the site, such as a fire, flood, or earthquake, could occur; or a simple software failure (in a device driver, the operating system, or SQL Server) could threaten your data. RAID does not protect your data against any of those problems, but backups do.

NOTE You could argue that RAID-0 shouldn't be considered RAID at all because there is no redundancy. That might be why it's classified as level 0.

Windows NT Server provides RAID-0; a hardware RAID controller can also provide it. RAID-0 requires little processing overhead, so a hardware implementation of RAID-0 offers at best a marginal performance advantage over the built-in Windows NT capability. One possible advantage is that RAID-0 in hardware often lets you adjust the stripe size, while the size is fixed at 64 KB in Windows NT and cannot be changed.

RAID-1

RAID-1, or mirroring, is conceptually simple: a mirror copy exists for every disk drive. Writes are made to the primary disk drive and to the mirrored copy. Because writes can be made concurrently, the elapsed time for a write is usually not much greater than it would be for a single, unmirrored device. The write I/O performance to a given logical drive is only as fast as a single physical drive is able to go.

Hardware-Based vs. Software-Based RAID

If price and performance are your only criteria, you might find that software-based RAID is perfectly adequate. If you have a fixed budget, the money you save on hardware RAID controllers might be better spent elsewhere, such as on a faster processor, more disks, more memory, or an uninterruptible power supply.

While in pure performance terms it might not be better to spend extra on low-end hardware RAID (as long as you have sufficient CPU capacity in the server), mid-level to high-end RAID offers many other benefits, including hot swappability of drives and intelligent controllers that are well worth the extra money—especially for systems that need to run 24 hours a day, 7 days a week.

You might also combine hardware-based and software-based RAID to great advantage. For example, if you have three hardware-based RAID units, each with 7-GB to 9-GB disks, with RAID-5 you would have 6 x 9 = 54 GB in each, and Windows NT would see three 54-GB disks. You can then use software-based RAID on Windows NT to define a RAID-0 stripe set to get a single 162-GB partition on which to create SQL Server databases.

Therefore, you can at best get I/O rates of perhaps 80 to 90 I/Os per second to a given logical RAID-1 drive, as opposed to the much higher I/O rates to a logical drive that can be achieved with RAID-0. You can, of course, use multiple RAID-1 drives. But if a single table is the hot spot in your database, even multiple RAID-1 drives will not be of much help from a performance perspective. (SQL Server 7 lets you create filegroups within a database for, among other purposes, placing a table on a specific drive or drives. But no range partitioning capability is available for data within a table, so this option doesn't really give you the control you need to eliminate hot spots.) If you need fault tolerance, RAID-1 is normally the best choice for the transaction log. Because transaction log writes are synchronous and sequential, unlike writes to the data pages, they are ideally suited to RAID-1.

Read performance with RAID-1 can be significantly increased because a read can be obtained from either the primary device or the mirror device. (A single read is not performed faster, but multiple reads are faster in aggregate because they can be performed simultaneously.) If one of the drives fails, the other continues and SQL Server uses the surviving drive. Until the failed drive is replaced, fault tolerance is not available unless multiple mirror copies were used.

NOTE The Windows NT RAID software does not allow you to keep multiple mirror copies; it allows only one copy. But some RAID hardware controllers offer this feature. You can keep one or more mirror copies of a drive to ensure that even if a drive fails, a mirror still exists. If a crucial system is difficult to access in a timely way to replace a failed drive, this option might make sense.

Windows NT Server provides RAID-1, and some hardware RAID controllers also provide it. RAID-1 requires little processing overhead, so a hardware implementation of RAID-1 offers at best a marginal performance advantage over the built-in Windows NT capability (although the hardware solution might provide the ability to mirror more than one copy of the drive).

RAID-5

RAID-5, or striping with parity, is a common choice for SQL Server use. RAID-5 not only logically combines multiple disks to act like one disk, but it also records extra parity information on every drive in the array (thereby requiring only one extra drive). If any drive fails, the others can reconstruct the data and continue without any data loss or immediate down time. By doing an Exclusive OR (XOR) between the surviving drives and the parity information, the bit patterns for a failed drive can be derived on the fly.

RAID-5 is less costly to implement than mirroring all the drives, since only one additional drive is needed rather than the double drives that mirroring requires. Although RAID-5 is commonly used, it is often not the best choice for SQL Server because it imposes a significant I/O hit on write performance because both the data and the parity information must be written. RAID-5 can turn one write into two reads and two writes to keep the parity information updated. This doesn't mean that a single write takes four or five times as long, because the operations are done in parallel. It does mean, however, that many more I/Os occur in the system, so many more drives and controllers are required to reach the I/O levels that RAID-0 can achieve. So although RAID-5 certainly is less costly than mirroring all the drives, the performance overhead for writes is significant. Read performance, on the other hand, is excellent—essentially equivalent to that of RAID-0.

RAID-5 makes sense, then, for the data portion of a database that needs fault tolerance, that is heavily read, and that does not demand high write performance. Typically, you should not place the transaction log on a RAID-5 device unless the system has a low rate of changes to the data. (As mentioned before, RAID-1 is a better choice for the transaction log because of the sequential nature of I/O to the log.)

RAID-5 requires more overhead for writes than RAID-0 or RAID-1, so the incremental advantage provided by a hardware RAID-5 solution over the Windows NT software solution can be somewhat higher because more work must be offloaded to the hardware. However, such a difference would be noticeable only if the system were nearly at I/O capacity. If this is the case in your system, you probably shouldn't use RAID-5 in the first place because of the write performance penalty. You're probably better served by the combination of RAID-0 and RAID-1, known as RAID-1&0.

RAID-1&0

RAID-1&0, or mirroring and striping, is the ultimate choice for performance and recoverability. (This capability is sometimes also referred to as RAID-1+0 or RAID-10.) A set of disks is striped to provide the performance advantages of RAID-0, and the stripe is mirrored to provide the fault-tolerance features and increased read performance of RAID-1. Performance for both writes and reads is excellent.

The most serious drawback to RAID-1&0 is cost. Like RAID-1, it demands duplicate drives. In addition, the built-in RAID software of Windows NT does not provide this solution, so RAID-1&0 requires a hardware RAID controller. Some hardware RAID controllers explicitly support RAID-1&0. But you can achieve this support using virtually any RAID controller by combining its capabilities with those of Windows NT. For example, you can set up two stripe sets of the same size and number of disks using hardware RAID. Then you can use Windows NT mirroring on the two stripe sets, which Windows NT sees as two drives of equal size. If you need high read and write performance and fault tolerance and you cannot afford an outage or decreased performance if a drive fails, RAID-1&0 is the best choice.

A separate RAID-1&0 array usually is not an appropriate choice for the transaction log. Because the write activity tends to be sequential and is synchronous, the benefits of multiple spindles are not realized. A RAID-1 mirroring of the transaction log is preferable and cheaper. With internal Debit-Credit benchmarks, Microsoft has shown that the transaction log on a simple RAID-1 device is sufficient to sustain thousands of transactions per second—which is likely more than you need. Log records are packed, and a single log write can commit multiple transactions (known as *group commit*). In the Debit-Credit benchmarks, 40 transactions can be packed into a log record. At a rate of 100 writes per second (writes/second), the log on a RAID-1 mirror would not become a bottleneck until around 4000 tps.

NOTE Practically speaking, this threshold is probably even higher than 4000 tps. For pure sequential I/O, 100 writes/second is a conservative estimate. Although a typical disk drive is capable of doing 80 to 90 random I/Os per second, the rate for pure sequential I/O—largely eliminating the seek time of the I/Os—is probably better than 100 writes/second.

In a few cases, a physically separate RAID-1&0 array for the log might make sense—for example, if your system requires high OLTP (online transaction processing—write) performance but you also used replication of transactions. Besides performing sequential writes to the log, the system also does many simultaneous reads of the log for replication and might benefit from having the multiple spindles available. (In most cases, however, the log pages are in cache, so RAID-1&0 probably won't provide a significant benefit. However, if replication is in a "catch-up" mode because the distribution database is not available or for some other reason, some significant benefit might exist.)

Choosing the Best RAID Solution

Table 4-2 on the following page summarizes the characteristics of various RAID configurations commonly used with SQL Server. Obviously, innumerable configurations are possible, but this chart will help you predict the characteristics for additional configurations as well as typical ones. You should reject

Option	Description	Relative read performance	Relative write performance	Eases I/O hot spots and does not require handcrafting physical layout	Relative cost	Up-to-the-minute data protection (for failure of one drive)	Any single drive failure does not cause immediate outage of SQL Server	Can sustain multiple drive failures without an outage of SQL Server	Supported with Windows NT Server software, without need for special hardware controller
1	1 physical drive	Very low	Very low	No	Very low	No	No	No	Yes
2	2 physical drives: DATA: Separate LOG: Separate No RAID	Low	Low	No	Low	No	No	No	Yes
3	Multiple drives: (3+) DATA: RAID-0 LOG: Separate, physical non-RAID drive	High[1]	High	Yes	Low-Moderate	No	No	No	Yes
4	Multiple drives: DATA: RAID-0 LOG: Separate, physical mirrored, RAID-1 devices	High	High	Yes	Moderate	Yes	No[2]	No	Yes
5	Multiple drives: DATA: RAID-1 LOG: Separate, physical RAID-1 devices	Varies widely[3]	Varies widely[3]	No	High	Yes	Yes	Partial[4]	Yes
6	Multiple drives: DATA: RAID-5 LOG: Separate, physical RAID-1 devices	High	Low-Moderate	Yes	Moderate	Yes	Yes	No	Yes
7	Multiple drives: DATA: RAID-1&0 LOG: Separate, physical RAID-1 devices	Very high	High	Yes	High	Yes	Yes	Partial[4]	No
8	Multiple drives: DATA: RAID-1&0 with multiple, mirrored copies LOG: Separate, physical RAID-1 devices with multiple, mirrored copies	Very high	High	Yes	Very high	Yes	Yes	Yes	No

[1] For all "high" read/write performance classifications noted here, understand that the performance will increase as more drives are added. For example, with a RAID-0 array of two drives, you might not yet classify read/write performance as high, but you can add more drives until you reach the I/O rates you require.

[2] Except that a failure to the log drive, which is mirrored, can be sustained without an immediate outage.

[3] This is case-by-case dependent. The degree to which I/Os can be balanced by carefully laying out the database will determine if this is a good performing option. This is a difficult proposition to get right and one we typically try to avoid.

[4] If a primary is lost, and then its mirror is also lost, drive failures cannot be sustained. With the loss of two different primaries (or mirrors), drive failures can be sustained.

Table 4-2.

Characteristics of RAID configurations used with SQL Server.

Option 1 for all but the smallest environments because with this option the entire system runs with one disk drive. This is not efficient even for a low-end system, unless you have little write performance and enough memory to get a high cache-hit ratio. Unless you're running SQL Server on a laptop, there's little excuse for using only one drive.

Option 2, two physical drives and no use of RAID, represents an entry-level or development system. It offers far-from-ideal performance and no fault tolerance. But it is significantly better than having only a single drive. RAID is unnecessary with just two drives, and separating your log from your data on the drives is the best you can do.

If you don't need fault tolerance and limited recovery ability is sufficient, Option 3, using RAID-0 for the data and placing the transaction log on a separate physical device (without mirroring), is an excellent configuration. It offers peak performance and low cost. One significant downside, however, is that if a drive fails, you can recover the data only to the point of your last transaction log or database backup. Because of this, Option 3 is not appropriate for many environments.

Option 4 is the entry level for environments in which it is essential that no data be lost if a drive fails. This option uses RAID-0 (striping, without parity) for the devices holding the data and RAID-1 (mirroring) for the transaction log, so data can always be recovered from the log. However, any failed drive in the RAID-0 array renders SQL Server unable to continue operation on that database until the drive is replaced. You can recover all the data from the transaction logs, but you experience an outage while you replace the drive and load your transaction logs. If a drive fails on either a transaction log or its mirrored copy, the system continues unaffected, using the surviving drive for the log. However, until the failed log drive is replaced, fault tolerance is disabled and you are back to the equivalent of Option 3. If that surviving drive also fails, you must revert to your last backup, and you'll lose changes that occurred since the last transaction log or database backup.

Option 4 offers excellent performance—almost as good as Option 3. This might come as a surprise to those concerned with the mirroring of the log. RAID-1, of course, turns a single write into two. However, since the writes are done in parallel, the elapsed time for the I/O is about the same as it would be for a single drive, assuming that both the primary and mirrored drives are physically separate and are used only for log operations. If you need to protect all data but recovery time is not a major concern and an outage while you recover is acceptable (that is, if loading transaction logs or database backups is acceptable), Option 4 is ideal.

Data Placement Using Filegroups

Are you better off simply putting all your data on one big RAID-0 striped set or should you use filegroups to carefully place your data on specific disk drives? Unless you are an expert at performance tuning and really understand your data access patterns, we don't recommend using filegroups as an alternative to RAID. To use filegroups to handcraft your physical layout, you must understand and identify the hot spots in the database. And although filegroups do allow you to place tables on certain drives, doing so is tricky. It's currently not possible to partition certain ranges of a table to different disks, so hot spots often occur no matter how cleverly you designed your data distribution. If you have three or more physical disk drives, you probably should use some level of RAID, not filegroups.

If you cannot tolerate an interruption of operations because of a failed drive, you should consider some form of RAID-1 or RAID-5 for your database (as well as for the *master* database and *tempdb*, the internal workspace area), as described in Options 5 through 8.

Option 5 uses basic RAID-1, a one-for-one mirroring of drives for the data as well as the log. We don't recommend this because RAID-1 does not provide the performance characteristics of RAID-0. Recall that RAID-0 enables multiple drive spindles to operate logically as one, with additive I/O performance capabilities. Although RAID-1 can theoretically work well if you handcraft your data layout, in practice this has the same drawbacks as using filegroups instead of RAID-0. (See the sidebar on the top of this page.) This high-cost option is usually not a high-performing option, at least if the database has significant hot spots. It is appropriate only for specialized purposes in which I/O patterns can be carefully balanced.

Option 6, using RAID-5 for the data and RAID-1 for the log, is appropriate if the write activity for the data is moderate at most and the update activity can be sustained. Remember that RAID-5 imposes a significant penalty on writes because it must maintain parity information so that the data of a reconstructed drive can be regenerated on the fly. Although the system does remain usable while operating with a failed drive, I/O performance is terrible: each read of the failed disk becomes four reads of the other disks, and each write becomes four reads plus a write, so throughput drops precipitously when a drive fails. With RAID-5, if you lose another drive in the system before you replace the first failed drive, you can't recover because the parity information can't continue to be maintained after the first drive is lost. Until the failed drive is replaced and regenerated, continued fault-tolerance capability is lost. RAID-5 uses fewer bytes for storage overhead than are used by mirroring all drives, but with the low price of disk drives and because disks are rarely full, the performance tradeoff is often simply not worth it. Finally, RAID-5 has more exposure to operational error than mirroring. If the person replacing the failed drive in a RAID-5 set makes a mistake and pulls a good drive instead of the failed drive, the failed drive might be unrecoverable.

If you need high read and write performance, cannot lose any data, and cannot suffer an unplanned system outage when a drive fails, Option 7— RAID-1&0 and a simple RAID-1 mirror for your log—is the way to go. As mentioned earlier, RAID-1&0 offers the ultimate combination of performance and fault tolerance. Its obvious disadvantage is cost. Option 7 requires not only a doubling of disk drives but also special hardware array controllers, which command a premium price.

Options 7 and 8 differ in whether additional mirrored copies are kept. Option 7 presents the typical case, with one-for-one mirroring of every physical drive in the system. If the primary drive fails, the mirror continues seamlessly. If the mirror fails, the primary drive continues, of course. Other drives in a different primary-mirror pair might also conceivably fail and the system can still continue. However, if one drive in a pair fails, the system cannot continue if its mirror also fails. (This is really bad luck, but it happens.) Option 7, using the combined capabilities of striping and mirroring (RAID-1&0), is probably a better choice for many sites that currently use RAID-5. The performance and fault-tolerance capabilities are significantly better, and today's low-priced hardware does not make the cost prohibitive.

If you need the utmost in fault tolerance to drive failures and your application is extremely mission critical, you can consider more than a single mirrored copy of the data and log. Option 8 is overkill for most environments, but today's cost of hard drives doesn't necessarily make this option prohibitive. If you have a server in a remote offsite location and it's difficult to get a technician to the site in a timely manner, building in expensive fault-tolerance capabilities might make sense.

The Bottom Line: Buy the Right System

By now, you should know there is no one correct answer to the RAID-level question. The appropriate decision depends on your performance characteristics and fault tolerance needs. A complete discussion of RAID and storage systems is beyond the scope of this book. But the most important point is that you shouldn't simply buy storage space—you should buy the system that gives you the appropriate level of redundancy and fault tolerance for your data.

> **SEE ALSO** You'll find a good general discussion of RAID in the SQL Server Books Online documentation (in the volume entitled "Optimizing Database Performance"). The documentation is runnable from the SQL Server evaluation CD included with this book. For a detailed, authoritative discussion, consult the *RAID* book produced by the RAID Advisory Board. (For more information about the RAID Advisory Board, see its home page at http://www.raid-advisory.com.)

Hardware or Software RAID?

After choosing a RAID level, you must decide whether to use the RAID capabilities of your operating system or those of a hardware controller. If you decide to use RAID-1&0, the choice is simple. Windows NT Server RAID does not currently offer the ability to keep more than one mirror copy of a drive, so you must use hardware array controllers. In addition, Windows 95 and Windows 98 do not support software-based RAID at all, and Windows NT Workstation provides only RAID-0 support. As for solutions using RAID-0 and RAID-1, there might not be much performance advantage of a hardware array controller over the capabilities of Windows NT Server. If price and performance are your main criteria, you can use standard fast-wide SCSI controllers and use the money you save to buy more drives or more memory. Several of the formal TPC benchmarks submitted using SQL Server used only the Windows NT versions of RAID-0 and RAID-1 solutions (Option 4) and standard SCSI controllers and drives, with no special hardware RAID support. Hardware RAID solutions provide the largest relative performance difference over the equivalent Windows NT software solution if you use RAID-5, but even in this case, the difference is usually marginal at best. Each hardware RAID controller can cost thousands of dollars, and a big system still needs multiple controllers. Using hardware controllers makes the most sense when you need the additional capabilities they provide, such as hot swappability, discussed in the following section.

More About Drives and Controllers

No matter what RAID level you use, you should replace a failed drive as soon as possible. For this reason, you should consider a system that offers *hot swappable drives*. These drives let you quickly replace the faulty drive without shutting down the system. If the drive is part of a RAID-1 or RAID-5 set, SQL Server can continue to run without error or interruption when the drive fails and even when it is physically replaced. If you use the Windows NT version of RAID-1 or RAID-5, SQL Server must be shut down only briefly to regenerate the drive because that process requires an exclusive lock on the disk drive by the operating system. When you restart SQL Server, the server computer won't even need to be rebooted. (Some hardware RAID solutions might also be able to regenerate or remirror the drive "below" the level of the operating system and hence not require SQL Server to be shut down.) Some systems also offer *hot standby drives*, which are simply extra drives that are already installed, waiting to take over. Either of these approaches can get you back in business quickly.

Your disk controller must guarantee that any write operation reported to the operating system as successful will actually be completed. Write-back caching controllers that "lie" (that report a write as completed but do not guarantee to actually perform the write) can result in corrupt databases and must never be used. In a write-back cache scheme, performance is increased because the bits are simply written to the cache (memory) and the I/O completion is immediately acknowledged. The controller writes the bits to the actual media a moment later. This introduces a timing window that makes the system vulnerable unless the controller designer has protected the cache (with a battery backup and so on) and has provided correct recovery logic.

Let's say, for example, that a power failure occurs immediately after the controller reports that a write operation has completed but before the cache is actually written to disk. With write-ahead logging, SQL Server assumes that any change is physically written to its transaction log before acknowledging the commit to the client. If the controller has just cached the write and then fails and never completes it, the system's integrity is broken. If a controller provides write-back caching as a feature, it must also guarantee that the writes will be completed and that they will be properly sequenced if they are reported to the operating system as successful. To be reliable, the caching controller also must guarantee that once it reports that an I/O has completed, the I/O will actually be carried out, no matter what. For example, a good solution is the Compaq SMART-2DH Array Controller, which uses write-back caching. It employs a built-in battery backup and has solutions that guarantee that any write reported as completed will in fact be completed. If the system fails before a write operation has been completed, the operation is maintained in the controller's memory and is performed immediately after the system restarts, before any other I/O operations occur.

If a controller cannot guarantee that the write will ultimately be completed, you should disable the write-back caching feature of the controller or use a different controller. Disabling write-back caching in an I/O-intensive environ-ment (more than 250 I/Os per second) might result in a SQL Server perfor-mance penalty of less than 5 percent. (After all, those writes must be performed eventually. The caching reduces the latency, but ultimately just as much I/O must be carried out.) In a less I/O-intensive test, the effect would likely be negligible. Realistically, the amount of the penalty doesn't matter much if the write isn't guaranteed to complete. Write-back caching must be disabled or you eventually get corrupt data.

This point warrants repeating: to be reliable, the caching controller must assure that no matter what, once an I/O is reported as complete, the I/O will be carried out. The caching controller must intercept the IOCHCK (I/O Channel Check) and RESET bus signal and not reset the controller logic, dis-carding any cached writes. If a motherboard glitch causes an abrupt system halt (such as a single-bit parity error), the controller must preserve the cached data and must know how to flush it upon startup. Also, an uninterruptible power supply (UPS) can fail if its batteries run down or if it wasn't properly config-ured and doesn't engage on power failure. The cost of any of these problems is a potentially corrupted database. Either don't use a write-caching controller or buy one that can handle these issues (such as the Compaq SMART-2DH).

Uninterruptible Power Supply

If you are not using a write-back caching controller, you do not need UPS hardware to protect the integrity of your data from a power outage. SQL Server recovers your system to a consistent state after any sudden loss of power. How-ever, you should definitely consider using a UPS; support for UPS hardware is built into Windows NT Server. Most hardware failures, such as memory fail-ures and hardware crashes, result from power spikes that a UPS would prevent. Adding a UPS (a $200 to $500 proposition) is probably the single most important thing you can do from a hardware perspective to maximize the availability and reliability of your system.

Without a UPS, after a power flicker or power spike the machine reboots and perhaps does a CHKDSK of the file system, which can take several minutes. During this time, your SQL Server is unavailable. A UPS can prevent these interruptions. Even if a power outage lasts longer than the life of your UPS, you have time to do an orderly shutdown of SQL Server and checkpoint all the databases. The subsequent restart will be much faster because no transactions need to be rolled back or rolled forward.

Battery Backup, UPS, and Caching

A UPS is not the same as the battery backup of the on-board controller RAM. The job of a UPS is to bridge power failures and to give you time to do an orderly shutdown of the system. The computer continues to run for a while from the power supplied by the UPS, and it can be shut down in an orderly way (which the UPS software will do) if power doesn't get restored within the expected battery life.

The battery backup on a caching controller card ensures that the contents of the controller's volatile memory survive—the memory is not lost, so when the system restarts the write completes. But it doesn't provide the power to actually make sure that a write succeeds. Some cards even allow the battery backed-up RAM to be moved to a different controller if the initial controller fails. Some provide two sets of batteries so that one can be replaced while the other maintains the RAM's contents, theoretically allowing you to keep adding new batteries indefinitely.

You might expect that using a caching controller that doesn't have a battery backup in combination with a UPS is generally OK if you do an orderly shutdown of SQL Server during the life of the UPS's power. However, this is not always the case. SQL Server support engineers who get customers' servers back up and running can tell horror stories about customers who use write-caching controllers that were not designed around transactional integrity. The caching controller must take into account issues besides power. For example, how does the controller respond to the user pressing the Reset button on the computer? A well-known caching controller of a couple years ago would dump its cache if you hit the Reset button—those writes were never carried out even though the calling application (SQL Server) was notified that they had been carried out. This situation often led to corrupt databases.

The Disk Subsystem

The reliability of the disk subsystem (including device drivers) is vitally important to the integrity of your SQL Server data. To help you uncover faulty disk systems, the SQL Server support team created a stand-alone, I/O-intensive, multithreaded file system stress test application. It exercises the Win32 overlapped (asynchronous) I/O services, opens its files with the same write-through cache flags used by SQL Server, and does similar types of I/O patterns. But the test is totally distinct from SQL Server. If this non–SQL Server I/O test cannot run without I/O errors, you do not have a reliable platform on which to run SQL Server, period. Of course, like any diagnostic program, the test might miss some subtle errors. But your confidence should certainly be higher than it would be without testing. You can download the test program for free from the Microsoft Support site at http://support.microsoft.com; select the Drivers And Other Downloads option from the list at the left of the screen. Next select BackOffice, and then SQL Server. You can then choose SQLHDTST.EXE: SQL Server File System Stress Utility from the list of downloadable files. SQLHDTST.EXE is also included on the companion CD.

Fallback Server Capability

Older versions of SQL Server had a *fallback* (*failover* or *hot-standby*) server in place, ready to take over the workload of a failed server. This capability required specialized hardware and used a set of stored procedures to set up the fallback server and to notify it when failover needed to take place. Applications had to know the fallback server name and attach to that server if the original server was unavailable. These procedures are no longer supported in SQL Server 7. Instead, SQL Server Enterprise edition can take advantage of Microsoft Cluster Server (MSCS), which is available on Windows NT Enterprise edition. You can install SQL Server 7 on multiple nodes in a cluster, and all nodes are seen as having a single name on the network. Applications do not have to be aware that SQL Server is installed on a cluster, and MSCS handles the failover completely invisibly to users of SQL Server. For more details, see the documentation for Windows NT Enterprise edition.

MSCS (and the older fallback capability) requires specialized hardware. By using various RAID options, you can protect your data without clustering. But without clustering, you are not protected against an application outage if the machine fails. MSCS can automatically shift the control of a "switchable" hard-drive array from a damaged node in the cluster to another node. For example, hardware can be configured with one separately housed hard-drive array connected to two computers. Only one of the connections to the hard-drive array is active at any time. The other hard-drive connection becomes active only if the system detects that the computer currently in control of the hard drive has shut down because of a hardware failure.

The instance of SQL Server on the second node in the cluster can itself perform useful work while the first instance of SQL Server operates normally. The second server can run SQL Server (using different databases than those used by the primary server), or it can act as a file and print server, or it can run some other application. If the second server needs to take over the work of the first server, the second server must have enough resources to add the primary server's workload to its existing workload. (Alternatively, you can decide that the first server's existing workload should take a back seat and that the second server's previous applications should be shut down when it takes over.)

NOTE Keep in mind that even with clustering, you need RAID to protect against media failure. The log, at least, must be mirrored to protect against a disk failure. The second server can run the disk drives of the failed first server, but those drives must also be protected against media failure.

Most applications probably do not need clustering because today's hardware is highly reliable. The most common hardware failure occurs in a disk drive, which can be protected without clustering by using RAID. As with RAID, clustering does not reduce the need for comprehensive and rigorous backup procedures. You'll probably need backups to recover from an occasional administrator mistake (human error), a catastrophe such as a fire or flood at the site, or a software anomaly. But some applications are so critical that the redundancy of clustering is necessary.

Other Hardware Considerations

If the server is mostly a "lights-out" operation and you will not be administering it locally or running other applications from the actual server machine, it doesn't make much sense to buy a first-class monitor or video card. Consider using an electronic switch box and sharing a monitor, keyboard, and mouse among multiple servers. If you do not use multiple servers, use a basic VGA monitor and video card.

From a performance perspective, a single high-quality network card is sufficient to handle virtually every SQL Server installation. Windows NT Server can support multiple network cards simultaneously, and sometimes your network topology will compel you to use this configuration with SQL Server as well. (Perhaps you are supporting both Ethernet and Token Ring clients on the same server.) One of the largest SQL Server installations at Microsoft supports more than 4000 concurrent physical workstations, and it does so using a single 100-megabit FDDI card. Some sites support hundreds or thousands of users with a single 10-megabit Ethernet card. From a performance perspective, you should never need multiple network cards.

When you plan your hardware configuration, be sure to plan for your backup needs. You can back up to either tape or disk devices. As with regular I/O, you will frequently need multiple backup devices to sustain the I/O rates required for backup. SQL Server can stripe its backup to multiple devices, including tape devices, for higher performance. For the reasons mentioned earlier when we discussed disk devices, a SCSI tape device is typically preferable to an IDE/EIDE device.

NOTE Not long ago, backup meant tape. Today, with disks costing less than $0.30 per megabyte, many sites configure their hardware with additional disk devices purely for backup use because they prefer the extra speed and ease that backup to disk offers over tape backup. Some sites even use hot swappable drives for their backup; they rotate between a few sets of such drives, keeping a set off site in case of disaster.

The Operating System

The SQL Server engine runs best on Windows NT Server, and your production applications are meant to run on SQL Server on Windows NT Server or Windows NT Enterprise. Although you can install the desktop version of SQL Server on Windows NT Workstation, Windows 95, or Windows 98, many SQL Server capabilities are not supported on the desktop version. (We discussed these limitations earlier in the chapter.) Memory management and the process scheduling behavior on Windows NT Server are better tailored to services such as SQL Server than is Windows NT Workstation, Windows 95, or Windows 98, which focus on desktop applications. The simple fact is that SQL Server runs better with medium to large workloads on Windows NT Server than on any other platform.

Support for SQL Server on a particular platform or version of Windows NT does not necessarily mean that it won't work with other configurations. But you should stick with the supported platforms for the following reasons:

- Only supported platforms get significant test coverage. An unsupported platform might seem to work, but a subtle problem might occur later.

■ Authorized SQL Server support providers and Microsoft SQL Server Enterprise Technical Support (ETS) focus on the supported platforms; if your problem is specific to the unsupported platform, you might not be able to get enough help.

■ Typically, a new release of SQL Server is targeted at the most recent (or sometimes an impending) release of Windows NT Server and also supports the prior major release. As of this writing, Windows 2000 is already in Beta 2 release, so SQL Server 7 runs on Windows NT 4 (with Service Pack 4) and Windows 2000 (formerly called Windows NT 5). It is not supported on Windows NT Server 3.51 or earlier. If you try to run Setup on a Windows NT version earlier than version 4 with Service Pack 4, you will get an error and be prevented from continuing.

You can install SQL Server on any Windows NT Server in your domain, but for the best performance do not install it on your primary or backup domain controllers (PDCs or BDCs). Although SQL Server will run fine on a PDC or BDC, the controller's tasks of maintaining and replicating the Windows NT user database take up processing cycles and memory. In less resource-intensive environments, this usually doesn't make much of a difference, but if your system is part of a large domain, it is better to separate SQL Server processing from those activities.

The File System

The performance difference between running SQL Server on the two major file systems of Windows NT—NTFS and FAT—is minimal. This isn't surprising, because SQL Server manages the structures within its database files without much use of the operating system.

We recommend NTFS as the file system of choice for SQL Server. It's more robust than FAT, and it's better able to recover fully and quickly from an ungraceful system shutdown. The integrity of the file system is vital to the integrity of your data, so this fact alone should drive most SQL Server users to NTFS. And the security features of NTFS are vital if security is important to you. Unlike FAT, NTFS allows security and auditing on all files; these are important ways to protect your data when SQL Server is not running. (SQL Server provides its own robust security.) When SQL Server is not running, the operating system is your prime protection. If you have a legitimate need to dual-boot your system to MS-DOS, Windows 95, or Windows 98 or if you need to use some disk utilities that work only with FAT, you might choose FAT. (You can, of course, make the boot partition FAT and format the other partitions with NTFS.)

You can safely use NTFS file compression, but you will see a substantial decrease in performance—perhaps as much as 50 percent if your system is I/O intensive. So typically, file compression is not an appropriate choice for SQL Server.

With previous versions, you could run SQL Server on a new partition that was not formatted with any file system. Such a partition is commonly referred to as a *raw partition*. Although you cannot run SQL Server 7 from a raw partition, you still have the option of creating database files on raw partitions. Storing data on raw partitions is common for UNIX database products, and users who have UNIX DBMS backgrounds sometimes do this with SQL Server as well. Under heavy workloads, raw partitions can provide a small (a couple of percent) performance benefit. If the I/O system is not at capacity, you will probably notice no performance difference at all.

For most installations, using raw partitions is not appropriate. Even if you gain some performance benefits by forgoing a file system, you forgo benefits such as basic file operations and utilities (copy, delete, rename, dir) and important operations such as detecting and resolving bad disk sectors that a file system provides. If there's no file system to perform bad sector operations, you must be sure that your hardware will take care of this. (This type of hardware is available but costly.)

Running on raw partitions was common in UNIX environments because the UNIX file system could not always be counted on to write through its cache and hence could not be trusted (for the same reasons discussed earlier with write-back caching controllers). The UNIX file system was also sometimes avoided because it caused a significant performance penalty in SQL Server. Neither case is true with Windows NT. SQL Server opens its files with the FILE_FLAG_WRITE_THROUGH flag set in the Win32 API call to CreateFile. This flag instructs Windows NT to acknowledge the operation as completed only when hardware reports that the bits are actually on disk.

Security and the User Context

To install SQL Server on a machine, you need not be an administrator of the domain, but you must have administrator privileges on the machine. Users can install most of the SQL Server client utilities without administrator privileges.

Before you set up your system, give some thought to the user context in which SQL Server and SQL Server Agent will run. A new SQL Server environment can set up the SQL Server engine to run in the context of the special system (LocalSystem) account. This account is typically used to run services, but it has no privileges on other machines, nor can it be granted such privileges. Because LocalSystem is always present, Setup can reliably use it. However, the default is to have the SQL Server service and the SQL Server Agent service run in the context of the domain Administrator account. This allows SQL Server to more easily perform tasks that require an external security context, such as backing up to another machine or using replication. If you don't have access to the domain Administrator account, you might want to set up SQL Server to run in the context of a local Administrator. This will still give SQL Server sufficient privileges to run on the local machine.

If you're not going to use the LocalSystem account, it's a good idea to change the account under which SQL Server runs to a user account that you have created just for this purpose, rather than use the actual local or domain Administrator account. The account must be in the local Administrators group if you are installing on Windows NT. You can create this account before you begin installing SQL Server, or you can change the account under which SQL Server runs at a later time. Changing the account is easy: you use the Services applet in the Windows NT Control Panel. When you choose or create a user account for running SQL Server, choose the Password Never Expires option for that account in Windows NT User Manager; if the password expires, SQL Server won't start until the information in the Services applet is updated. (This is why we don't recommend using the real Administrator account for SQL Server; that account will probably have its password changed regularly.)

If you will use the mail integration features (SQLMail), you should be aware of one additional issue: if you are using Microsoft Exchange on the same machine as SQL Server, you should run SQL Server in the context of the user account for which your Exchange client is configured. SQL Server can then pick up the Exchange configuration for that user automatically.

By default, the installation program chooses to use the same account for both the SQL Server and the SQL Server Agent services. However, you can override this account sharing during or after installation using the Services applet in Control Panel. SQL Server Agent needs a domain-level security context to connect to other computers in more situations than does SQL Server. For example, if you plan to publish data for replication, SQL Server Agent needs a security context to connect to the subscribing machines. If you will not publish data for replication or schedule tasks on SQL Server that require access to other computers, you can have SQL Server Agent run in the LocalSystem account. If you specify a domain account but the domain controller cannot validate the account (perhaps because the domain controller is temporarily unavailable), go ahead and install using the LocalSystem account and change it later using the Services applet or from SQL Server Enterprise Manager.

Licensing

When you install SQL Server, you'll see a dialog box asking which licensing choice you want to use: Per-Server or Per-Seat. A special licensing option, the Internet Connector, is available for using SQL Server on the Internet.

> **NOTE** The license agreement in the SQL Server box is a legal document that you should read and understand. This section explains the licensing schemes but does not represent the official licensing policy of the product. Packaging and licensing periodically change. Consult the licensing agreement to be sure you are in compliance and have chosen the best options for your needs.

Per-server licensing lets you support a stated maximum number of simultaneous users for a specific installation of SQL Server. This is probably the simplest option, although it might not be the best choice for you. Choose per-server if you have only one or two instances of SQL Server in your environment or if you use SQL Server with a large number of occasional users, with a minority of them being connected to the specific instance of SQL Server at any time. Per-server licensing is considered unlimited for more than 250 users with SQL Server Enterprise edition.

Per-seat licensing lets you economically deploy multiple instances of SQL Server to serve a given population of users. A user with a per-seat license can access any instance of SQL Server in the environment. You can deploy additional instances of SQL Server with minimal expense and you don't have to buy additional client licenses. You simply acquire as many additional server licenses as you need, and your users are already licensed to use them.

The two licensing options also require you to buy user licenses (also referred to as CALs, or client access licenses). But you (the administrator) must decide whether to aggregate the count of user licenses and use the per-server option to support a maximum number of simultaneous users or to designate each license to a specific user, who can then access any number of SQL Server instances in the environment. If need be, you can start with per-server licensing and later convert to per-seat licensing. The conversion is done on the honor system; you don't have to notify Microsoft. It is, however, intended to be a one-time, one-way conversion.

Table 4-3 shows the estimated retail prices (ERP) for each license type as of January 1999.

License Type	ERP U.S.
Server license + 5 CALs	$1399
Server license + 10 CALs	$1999
Server license + 25 CALs	$3999
5 CALs	$739
20 CALs	$2369
Internet Connector licensing option	$2999 per processor on each machine on which SQL Server will be running on the Internet

Table 4-3.
Prices of SQL Server license types.

Licensing Scenarios

To better understand these licensing options, consider a couple of scenarios involving the ACME Company, which is deploying its first installation of SQL Server. All 100 employees will access the application from time to time, but ACME is confident that no more than 25 users will do so simultaneously. ACME chooses per-server licensing and a SQL Server license that includes 25 CALs. This choice is the most economical for ACME. Its 100 users do not each need to have a license to access any installation of SQL Server (especially since ACME will initially have only one installation of SQL Server).

Scenario #1

After three months, the popularity of the application grows and periodically someone trying to connect to SQL Server gets error message 18458, which states that all licensed connections are in use. ACME calculates that it now needs to support 35 simultaneous users. It buys a 10-pack of user licenses to add to the 25 that it purchased with SQL Server. Using the Licensing applet in the Windows NT Control Panel, ACME updates the per-server licensing option for SQL Server to indicate its new status of supporting 35 simultaneous connections.

Scenario #2

ACME decides to expand its use of SQL Server. It plans to deploy seven new SQL Server machines and possibly more later. All 100 employees will never access any single installation of SQL Server simultaneously, but they all will use one or more applications that use SQL Server as a regular part of their jobs. ACME decides to move to per-seat licensing. It converts its 35 user licenses to specific users and buys seven more SQL Server packages, each with 10 CALS, and installs each of them with the per-seat option. It then converts the existing SQL Server installation from the per-server to the per-seat option. Later in the year, ACME grows even more and decides to roll out two more SQL Server installations, for a total of 10. But because its user base has only grown by a few employees, ACME needs to procure only two new SQL Server packages, with the minimum of 5 CALs with each. All of its employees are already licensed to use any and all SQL Server installations deployed, and the cost of each new SQL Server, even if accessed by every employee in the company, is only $1399.

> **NOTE** SQL Server Desktop can only be installed on a machine that has a per-seat CAL.

Internet Licensing

Neither of the first two licensing options makes sense when you use SQL Server on the Internet. The per-seat choice makes no sense because potentially millions of "users" can access your Web site and behind the scenes cause a query to get executed that extracts data from SQL Server. It is impossible, not to mention prohibitively expensive, to determine whether the users are licensed for SQL Server use. Similarly, the per-server option isn't practical because Internet access is usually stateless. Unlike in a typical client/server environment, a client on the Internet rarely stays connected to SQL Server. With a product such as Microsoft Internet Information Server (IIS) with the Internet Connector feature, users on the Internet cause commands and queries to be dynamically dispatched to SQL Server. For example, a user might click on a region of a Web page that shows current seat availability for a concert, resulting in a query to SQL Server. A connection is established on behalf of the user, the query is processed, the user disconnects, and the result set of the query is dynamically merged into the Web page that the user is viewing. All this happens in perhaps a second or two. When the user makes another request a moment later, the same process occurs.

In a normal LAN-based client/server application, a client remains connected at least for several minutes, even while the client has no active query processing. On the Internet, it is impractical to count distinct SQL Server users— at least in the same way that the per-server license option was intended to support. For this reason, Microsoft offers the SQL Server Internet Connector licensing option, which you can use instead of or in addition to user licenses. SQL Server can be accessed through your Web server software (such as IIS) on an unlimited basis in a cost-effective way. If you use SQL Server only for publishing data on your Web server, the Internet Connector license is essentially all you need. But remember that if you are also supporting a number of more traditional client/server users, you must have the appropriate user licenses.

Note that you do not need the Internet Connector license if users are simply accessing an HTML file that was statically built with the Web Assistant Wizard. Unlike the situation in which Internet users cause queries to be dispatched dynamically to SQL Server, in this case users do not cause statements to be issued to SQL Server; they simply read an HTML file created and periodically updated with SQL Server data. Therefore, the file is essentially static. Reading the file does not cause work to be performed at the SQL Server. (The user running the Web Assistant Wizard must be a licensed user, of course.)

Licensing Limits

Strict enforcement is not the goal of SQL Server licensing. The licenses let honest users be honest and make it easier for users to manage their environment and remain in compliance. The standard Windows NT Server licensing dialog box appears during installation. The user chooses the appropriate licensing option and, in the case of the per-server option, enters the number of user licenses purchased specifically for that server.

For per-server licensing, SQL Server keeps a list of all workstations currently connected. Each workstation represents one user. In this respect, a *user* is different from a SQL Server *connection,* since an application often has several connections open to the same instance of SQL Server. In addition, one workstation can use multiple applications that access the same installation of SQL Server. The user count for per-server licensing is based on a unique value for each workstation. Typically, this value reflects the identifier for the first Network Interface Card (NIC) found in the system. (Network software relies on a unique signature that is included on each NIC upon its manufacture.) The SQL Server client interfaces grab the NIC's identifier and pass it as part of the login handshake between client and server. The count is incremented if the NIC signature is not included in SQL Server's list of connected workstations. If the signature does exist in the list, SQL Server recognizes that the connection is from a workstation that is already connected and the count does not change. When all connections having a given NIC ID disconnect, the count decreases. Even if multiple application types from a given workstation connect to the server, they all contain the same NIC ID and are recognized as one user. For example, a Windows NT Workstation might be simultaneously running an old MS-DOS–based application, a Windows 3.11 DB-Library application, a 32-bit Windows DB-Library application, a 32-bit ODBC application, and an OLE DB application. Although these all access SQL Server and some might use multiple connections, the SQL Server per-server counting mechanism recognizes all of them as the same user and the count for all of them is one.

A client without a network card can access SQL Server using Remote Access Services (RAS). When no NIC ID is available, the client creates a random number and uses it for all connections from that workstation. (If a machine has a NIC, the NIC ID is used even when the connection is via RAS rather than the network card.) Although this random number could theoretically collide with another random number, the chances of this happening are less than those for winning the lottery. Even if it did happen, the collision would reduce the count and would never cause the count to inaccurately exceed the stated limit.

To change the per-server count, you simply use the Licensing applet and adjust the count accordingly. The next time SQL Server starts, the new value takes effect. Obviously, this does not enforce license compliance—it is completely up to you to enter and keep the correct value. But the applet provides a way for you to monitor your compliance and fulfills the goal of letting honest people stay honest. You should also be aware that a small overhead in static memory structures exists at the server to keep the count for each user licensed. If a reasonable value is entered, overhead should never be an issue.

With per-seat licensing, SQL Server simply calls the Windows NT APIs that are used for integration with the License Manager and the Licensing applet (sometimes referred to as the "honesty" API) and reports each user who logged on. SQL Server cannot know that a workstation that just connected actually has a user license to access the server. But by providing the information to the Windows NT services, you can use the Windows NT Server License Manager (contained in the Administrative Tools program group) to monitor compliance. Both the per-server and per-seat licensing options call the Windows NT "honesty" services.

One final point about licensing: in a three-tier architecture, clients sometimes connect to an application server, which in turn connects to SQL Server. In effect, the application server multiplexes the client connections to SQL Server. The application as a whole might service a large number of clients, but only the single, middle-tier application server directly connects to SQL Server. However, the licensing policies of SQL Server are based on the clients who access SQL Server services, albeit by a proxy. So even though the physical connection in this case is from the single application server machine, if 50 users make use of SQL Server by proxy, SQL Server must be licensed for all 50 users.

Network Protocols

If you accept the default installation option during setup, SQL Server on Windows NT installs named pipes, TCP/IP Sockets, and multiprotocol as its interprocess communication (IPC) mechanism for communication with its clients. SQL Server can simultaneously use many IPC mechanisms and networking protocols (but any specific client connection uses only one for its connection). As you learned in Chapter 3, each SQL Server networking interface is known as a Net-Library and represents a specific IPC mechanism. In addition to the above three, you can install one or more of the following Net-Libraries shown in Figure 4-2.

- NWLink IPX/SPX
- Appletalk ADSP
- DECNet Sockets
- Banyan VINES

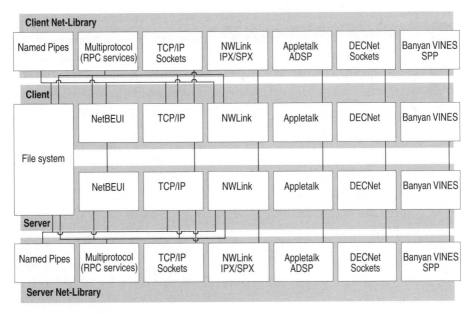

Figure 4-2.
SQL Server Net-Library interface options.

Both the Named Pipes and Multiprotocol Net-Libraries use protocol-independent IPC mechanisms (named pipes and RPC services). This means that you can use either interface with multiple underlying network protocols, including TCP/IP, NetBEUI, and NWLink IPX/SPX. All of the other choices imply not only the IPC mechanism but the specific network protocol that both the client and the server must use.

Although the Named Pipes Net-Library remains a good choice, its use as a default is mostly historical. Named pipes was the first, and for a while the only, IPC mechanism used by the early versions of SQL Server. Later, even when TCP/IP sockets and IPX/SPX were supported, those protocols were more difficult to configure than named pipes, requiring configuration at each client. For example, using TCP/IP required that the administrator configure an arcane IP address at every client workstation for every instance of SQL Server it might access. Now, with the sophisticated network naming services provided by Windows NT (for example, WINS, DHCP, and DNS), other Net-Libraries such as Multiprotocol and TCP/IP Sockets are almost as easy to use as Named Pipes.

Unless you have a compelling reason to choose a different network interface (the most compelling, of course, is if your existing network or network standards dictate some other network choice), use the defaults because they provide the most functionality. They are protocol independent and allow the use of Windows NT Authentication when you connect to SQL Server, which lets you provide a single logon name to your users so they don't have to log on to both the Windows NT domain and the SQL Server. Windows NT Authentication for SQL Server uses the Windows NT impersonation features, which are available only with these default networking choices. Windows NT Authentication is an important feature for convenience and ease of administration as well as for making your system more secure. Windows NT Authentication is also assumed with SQL Server replication services and when Performance Monitor connects to SQL Server.

The Multiprotocol interface is built using Windows NT RPC services. It offers one important feature that none of the other networks offers—encryption. All conversation between the client and server can be encrypted using the encryption services provided by Windows NT. (A 40-bit key is the maximum currently allowed for export by the U.S. government, so this is the key size used for Windows NT versions sold outside the United States. Windows NT 4, sold in the United States, uses a 128-bit key for tighter security.) Your data is secure even from someone using a hardware device such as a "network sniffer" to intercept network packets right off the wire. The encryption services work across the Internet as well.

The Cost of Encryption

Encryption services impose about a 25 percent performance overhead for network traffic. However, with use on a LAN, the network is rarely the performance bottleneck in a well-designed application and the actual performance difference is usually much less noticeable. But network performance is a bigger concern with a slow WAN or Internet application. In those cases, it can become a bottleneck. Even with slow networks, however, the performance issues usually relate to how often you make requests to the server (that is, how many network "round-trips" you make) rather than the speed of the Net-Library.

When you use the Multiprotocol interface and provide multiple underlying network protocols for it to choose from, you can explicitly choose the default binding. For example, by default the Multiprotocol network interface might, behind the scenes, use named pipes over NWLink. However, you can configure the interface to choose TCP/IP sockets instead if this is important in your network. (For more details, see the name resolution information under the Multiprotocol Clients topic in the "Administering SQL Server" section of SQL Server Books Online.) The ability to dynamically enumerate network computers that run SQL Server is not available with the Multiprotocol network interface.

Microsoft internal testing has found the TCP/IP Sockets Net-Library to be the fastest networking choice. (As stated in the above sidebar, in a typical LAN you rarely see the network as a performance bottleneck. In a low-speed WAN, however, this can be an important issue.) Some network administrators have also been concerned about potentially routing NetBIOS traffic across their LANs and WANs. However, if SQL Server is not using the Named Pipes Net-Library and the Multiprotocol Net-Library is not using named pipes under the covers for IPC, SQL Server is not using NetBIOS at all and this is not a concern.

The NWLink IPX/SPX Net-Library is of most interest to those running Novell networking software on their clients accessing SQL Server. If you are using a Novell NetWare–based network and file server but your SQL Server clients use Windows 95, Windows 98, or Windows NT, using the NWLink IPX/SPX Net-Library is unnecessary. Either Named Pipes or Multiprotocol over the underlying NWLink network protocol is probably a better choice because Windows NT Authentication is not available with the NWLink IPX/SPX Net-Library. If your clients use networking software provided by Novell, NWLink IPX/SPX is probably your best choice. Server enumeration is available with NWLink IPX/SPX using the NetWare Bindery services.

Choose Banyan VINES and DECNet Sockets if you interoperate with those environments. The Banyan VINES Net-Library uses StreetTalk naming services for server enumeration and name resolution. There is no support for dynamic SQL Server enumeration on DECNet. Windows NT Authentication is not an option with either of these Net-Libraries.

Use Appletalk ADSP Net-Library if you will support Apple Macintosh clients (using the Inprise—formerly Visigenic—ODBC driver for Macintosh) running only Appletalk, not TCP/IP.

During installation, you must supply additional information for any of the network options you have selected—for example, the port number or network name on which the server running SQL Server will "listen" for new connections or broadcast its existence to a network naming service. In most cases, you should accept the default unless you have a compelling reason not to. In the case of TCP/IP Sockets, you should accept the default port number of 1433. This number is reserved for use with SQL Server by the Internet Assigned Numbers Authority (IANA), and as such it should not conflict with a port used by any other server application on your computer. (This assumes that the developers of other applications also followed the proper protocol of getting assigned numbers.)

Even if you will primarily use another Net-Library for SQL Server use, we recommend that you do not remove Named Pipes. If your network fails entirely, you can still access your SQL Server machine locally using named pipes as the IPC mechanism, because it is an intrinsic service of Windows NT even when the computer is not part of a network. Named pipes can provide a convenient "last chance" way to access SQL Server if, for example, your network card has failed and network access is currently unavailable. If you decide not to use the Named Pipes Net-Library, remove it after installation is complete. The installation program assumes the existence of named pipes services so that it can operate if the computer is not in a network environment.

SQL Server on Windows 95 and Windows 98 does not support the server Named Pipes, Banyan VINES, and AppleTalk Net-Libraries. SQL Server does support the client side of Named Pipes and Banyan VINES Net-Libraries on Windows 95 and Windows 98, so Windows 95 and Windows 98 clients can use them to connect to SQL Server installations on Windows NT.

TIP If you are new to networking and don't know your IP from your DHCP, don't fret. Accept the defaults and configure your networking later as your understanding improves (or get your network administrator to help you). Although it's a good idea to understand your networking choices before installing SQL Server, you can easily change the networking options later without disturbing your SQL Server environment.

Character Sets and Sort Orders

During installation, you must decide which character set and sort order to use. A SQL Server installation defines a single character set in addition to supporting Unicode (2-byte character) data. It also defines two sort orders, one for non-Unicode data and one for Unicode data. If you decide later that you want a different character set or sort order, you must rebuild all databases, including SQL Server's *master* database. Most of the discussion below concerns non-Unicode data. Unicode data is discussed later in a separate section.

Character Sets

A single (non-Unicode) character is stored in SQL Server as 1 byte (8 bits), which means that 256 (2^8) different characters can be represented. But all the world's languages in aggregate have many more than 256 characters. Hence, if you don't want to store all your data as Unicode, which takes twice as much storage space, you must choose a character set that contains all the characters (referred to as the *repertoire*) you need to work with. For installations in the Western Hemisphere and Western Europe, the ISO character set (also often referred to as Windows Characters, ISO 8859-1, Latin-1, or ANSI) is the default and is compatible with the character set used by all versions of Windows in those regions. (Technically, there is a slight difference between the Windows character set and ISO 8859-1.) If you choose ISO, you might want to skip the rest of this section on character sets, but you should still familiarize yourself with sort order issues.

You should also ensure that all your client workstations use a character set that is consistent with the characters used by your installation of SQL Server. SQL Server stores a byte value for a character. If, for example, the character ¥, the symbol for the Japanese yen, is entered by a client application using the standard Windows character set, its byte value (known as the *code point*) of 165 (0xA5) is stored in SQL Server. If an MS-DOS–based application using code page 437 retrieves that value, that application displays the character Ñ. (MS-DOS uses the term *code pages* to mean character sets. You can think of them as interchangeable terms.) In both cases, the byte value of 165 is stored, but the Windows character set and the MS-DOS code page 437 render it differently. You must consider whether the ordering of characters is what is semantically expected (discussed later in the "Sort Orders" section) and whether the character is rendered on the application monitor (or other output device) as expected. SQL Server provides services in the OLE DB provider, the ODBC driver, and

The ASCII Character Set

It is worth pointing out that the first 128 characters are the same for the character sets ISO, code page 437, and code page 850. These 128 characters make up the ASCII character set. (Standard ASCII is only a 7-bit character set. ASCII was simple and efficient to use in telecommunications because the character and a "stop bit" for synchronization could all be expressed in a single byte.) If your application uses ASCII characters but not the so-called *extended characters* (typically characters with diacritical marks, such as à, Å, ä) that differentiate the upper 128 characters between these three character sets, it probably doesn't matter which character set you choose. In this situation (only), whether you choose any of these three character sets or use different character sets on your client and server machines doesn't matter because the rendering and sorting of every important character uses the same byte value in all cases.

DB-Library that use Windows services to perform character set conversions. Conversions cannot always be exact, however, because by definition each character set has a somewhat different repertoire of characters. For example, there is no exact match in code page 437 for the Windows character Ō, so the conversion must give a close, but different, character.

Windows NT and SQL Server 7 also support 2-byte characters that allow representation of virtually every character used in any language. This is known as Unicode, and it provides many benefits—with some costs. The principal cost is that 2 bytes instead of 1 are needed to store a character. SQL Server allows storage of Unicode data by using three new datatypes: *nchar*, *nvarchar*, and *ntext*. We'll discuss these when we talk about datatypes in Chapter 6. The use of Unicode characters for certain data does not affect the character set chosen to store the non-Unicode data.

Earlier versions of SQL Server did not support Unicode, but they did support double-byte character sets (DBCS). DBCS is a hybrid approach and is the most common way for applications to support Asian languages such as Japanese and Chinese. With DBCS encoding, some characters are 1 byte and others are 2 bytes. The first bit in the character indicates whether the character is a 1-byte or a 2-byte character. (In Unicode, every character is 2 bytes.) However, for non-Unicode datatypes, each character is considered 1 byte for storage.

To store two DBCS characters, a field would need to be declared as *char(4)* instead of *char(2)*. But SQL Server correctly parses and understands DBCS characters in its string functions.

Table 4-4 lists the character sets available in SQL Server and notes DBCSs. The DBCSs are still available for backward compatibility, but for new applications that need more flexibility in character representation than the default ISO code page provides, you should consider using the Unicode datatypes exclusively. As mentioned earlier, most sites in countries of the Western Hemisphere and in Western Europe are best served by the default ISO character set. The choices for code page 437 and code page 850 might be of interest if you are supporting many older MS-DOS–based applications that use those code pages or for other backward compatibility reasons. The other character sets are mostly locale specific.

Code Page	Character Set
1252 (ISO)	Default, multilingual
850	Multilingual
437	U.S. English
874	Thai (DBCS)
932	Japanese (DBCS)
936	Chinese—simplified (DBCS)
949	Korean (DBCS)
950	Chinese—traditional (DBCS)
1250	Central European
1251	Cyrillic
1253	Greek
1254	Turkish
1255	Hebrew
1256	Arabic
1257	Baltic

Table 4-4.
SQL Server character sets.

Sort Orders

Character sets are not important in many sites, but in nearly every site, whether you realize it or not, the basics of sort order (more properly called *collating sequence*) is important. Sort order determines how characters compare and assign their values. It determines whether your SQL Server installation is case sensitive. (For example, is an uppercase *A* considered identical to a lowercase *a*?) If you use only ASCII characters and no extended characters, you should simply decide your case-sensitivity preference and choose accordingly. By default, SQL Server installs a case-insensitive sort order. (That is, *A* and *a* are considered equivalent.) To change the default, you simply choose an option during installation that provides case sensitivity, such as Binary Order or Dictionary Order, Case-Sensitive.

Sort order affects not only the ordering of a result set but also which rows of data qualify for that result set. If a query's criterion is

```
WHERE name='SMITH',
```

the case sensitivity installed determines whether a row with the name *Smith* qualifies.

Character matching, string functions, and aggregate functions (MIN(), MAX(), COUNT (DISTINCT), GROUP BY, UNION, CUBE, LIKE, and ORDER BY) all behave differently with character data depending on the sort order specified.

Sort Order Semantics

The sort order also determines more subtle semantic differences. The following lengthy discussion principally applies to use of extended characters. If you plan to work with only 7-bit ASCII characters, you can skip this section.

A given sort order option is specific to a character set. Not every sorting option is available in every character set. For example, you will find the option for Croatian Dictionary Order, Case-Sensitive, only with the 1250, Central European character set. The DBCS character sets (Japanese, Chinese, and Korean) each provide two sort options. The first is Binary, which means that characters are sorted on the basis of their internal byte values, without regard to cultural correctness. The other choice makes use of Windows NT National Language Support (NLS) capabilities and provides a Case-Insensitive, Dictionary option consistent with the Windows NT character sorting in the respective localized version of the operating system. Hence, the English version of SQL Server can be used on the Chinese version of Windows NT, and it can work properly with double-byte Chinese characters and can sort them in a culturally correct manner.

For non-DBCS character sets, SQL Server provides more sorting options (which we'll explain in a moment). In addition, Unicode data has its own sort order, referred to as the Unicode collation sequence.

Figure 4-3 shows the sort-order definition for the default sort order and character set. You can obtain similar information for whatever sort order you are using by running the procedure *sp_helpsort*. For example, the output shows that the letter *A* is defined for the current sort order definition file as having this collating sequence:

A=a À=à Á=á Â=â Ã=ã Ä=ä Å=å Æ=*

This definition states that *A* should be treated identically to *a*, as should all uppercase characters and their lowercase equivalents in this sort order. Both *A* and *a* have a value before *À* and *à* (*a*-grave) followed by *Á* and *á* (*a*-acute) and then *Â* and *â* (*a*-circumflex). Next is *Ã* and *ã* followed by *Ä* and *ä*, *Å* and *å*, and finally *Æ* and *æ*.

```
Unicode data sorting
--------------------
Locale ID = 1033

 case insensitive, kana type insensitive, width insensitive


Sort Order Description
------------------------------------------------------------------
Character Set = 1, iso_1
    ISO 8859-1 (Latin-1) - Western European 8-bit character set.
Sort Order = 52, nocase_iso
    Case-insensitive dictionary sort order for use with several
    Western European languages including English, French, and
    German.  Uses the ISO 8859-1 character set.


Characters, in Order
------------------------------------------------------------------
!"#$%&'()*+,-./:;<=>?@[\]^_`{|}~ ¡¢£¤¥¦§¨©ª«¬-®¯°±²³´µ
¶·¸¹º»¼½¾¿×÷0123456789A=a À=à Á=á Â=â Ã=ã Ä=ä Å=å Æ=æ B=b
C =c Ç=ç D=d E=e È=è É=é Ê=ê Ë=ë F=f G=g H=h I=i Ì=ì Í=í Î=î Ï=ï J =j K=k L=l M=m
N=n Ñ=ñ O=o Ò=ò Ó=ó Ô=ô Õ=õ Ö=ö Ø=ø P=p Q=q R=r S =s ß T=t U=u Ù=ù Ú=ú
Û=û Ü=ü V=v W=w X=x Y=y Ý=ý ÿ Z=z Ð=ð Þ=þ
```

Figure 4-3.
The definition for the default character set and sort order.

The default sort order is case insensitive, for both comparison and sorting purposes. You must use a variation of this sort order, which is called *case insensitivity with preference*, when you work with multilingual characters. In a sort order "with preference," even though *A* is defined as equal to *a* for the purposes of string comparison (affecting character searches, including the constructs DISTINCT, UNION, LIKE, and so on), the *preference* option causes all collating (order by) to present the *A* before the *a*. In general terms, the semantics are "For the search process, treat *A* and *a* as identical, but show it to me with the *A* results preceding *a*." You might prefer this behavior, for example, when you want to print a list of both uppercase and lowercase entries, without regard to case but with names in uppercase printing before those in lowercase rather than their being randomly intermixed.

You can actually think of characters as having primary, secondary, and tertiary sort values, which are different for different sort order choices. To be more precise, the above sort order defines all *A*-like values as having the same primary sort value. *A* and *a* not only have the same primary sort value, they also have the same secondary sort value because they are defined as equal. The character *à* has the same primary value as *A* and *a* but is not declared equal to them, so *à* has a different secondary value. And although *A* and *a* have the same primary and secondary sort values, with an uppercase preference sort order each has a different tertiary sort value, which allows it to compare identically but sort differently. If your sort order does not have uppercase preference, *A* and *a* have the same primary, secondary, and tertiary sort values.

A character's primary sort value is used to distinguish it from other characters, without regard to case and diacritical marks. It is essentially an optimization: if two characters do not have the same primary sort value, they cannot be considered identical for either comparison or sorting and there is no reason to look further. The secondary sort value distinguishes two characters that share the same primary value. If the characters share the same primary and secondary values (for example *A = a*), they are treated as identical for comparisons. The tertiary value allows the characters to compare identically but sort differently. Hence, based on *A = a*, apple and Apple are considered equal. However, *Apple* sorts before *apple* when a sort order with uppercase preference is used. If there is no uppercase preference, whether *Apple* or *apple* sorts first is simply a random event based on the order in which the data is encountered when retrieved.

Some sort order choices allow for accent insensitivity. This means that extended characters with diacritics are defined with primary and secondary values equivalent to those without. If you want a search of *name = 'Jose'* to find both

Jose and *José*, you should choose accent insensitivity. Such a sort order defines all *E*-like characters as equal and has the following in the *sp_helpsort* output:

E=e=è=É=é=ê=ë

All the accent-insensitive sort orders provided by SQL Server also have uppercase preference enabled, which means that in an ORDER BY, the *E*-like characters above, although considered equivalent for character matching, sort as *E, e, è, É, é, ê, ë*, with each uppercase letter paired with its lowercase equivalent and distinguished from the other *E*-like characters. Technically, there is no reason that you can't have a sort order of Accent Insensitive Without Preference. But because the large number of existing sort orders are confusing to most people, not every conceivable variation is offered.

> **NOTE** When deciding on the case sensitivity for your SQL Server installation, you should be aware that the case sensitivity applies to object names as well as your user data because object names (the metadata) are stored in tables just like user data. So if you have a case-insensitive sort order, the table *CustomerList* is seen as identical to a table called *CUSTOMERLIST* and to one called *customerlist*. If your server is case sensitive and you have a table called *CustomerList*, SQL Server will not find the table if you refer to it as *customerlist*.

Binary Sorting

Each character set offers a binary sorting option. With binary sorting, you do not have to specify each character's sort position. Characters are sorted based on their internal byte representation. If you look at a chart for the character set, you see the characters ordered by this numeric value. In a binary sort, the characters sort according to their position by value, just as they are in the chart. Hence, by definition, a binary sort is always case sensitive and accent sensitive and every character has a unique byte value.

Binary sorting is the fastest sorting option because all that is required internally is a simple byte-by-byte comparison of the values. But if you use extended characters, binary sorting is not semantically desirable. Characters that are *A*-like, such as *Ä, ä, Å*, and *å*, all sort after *Z* because the extended character *A*'s are in the top 128 characters and *Z* is a standard ASCII character in the lower 128. If you deal with only ASCII characters (or otherwise don't care about the sort order of extended characters), you want case sensitivity, and you don't care about "dictionary" sorting, binary sorting is an ideal choice. (In case-sensitive dictionary sorting, the letters *ABCXYZabcxyz* sort as *AaBbCcXxYyZz*.

In binary sorting, all uppercase letters appear before any lowercase letters: for example, *ABCXYZabcxyz*.)

Performance Considerations

Binary sorting uses significantly fewer CPU instructions than sort orders with defined sort values. So binary sorting is ideal if it fulfills your semantic needs. However, you won't pay a noticeable penalty for using either a simple case-insensitive sort order (for example, Dictionary Order, Case-Insensitive) or a case-sensitive choice that offers better support than binary sorting for extended characters. Most large sorts in SQL Server tend to be I/O bound, not CPU bound, so the fact that there are fewer CPU instructions used by binary sorting doesn't typically translate to a significant performance difference. When you sort a small amount of data that is not I/O bound, even though binary sorting is faster, the difference is minimal; the sort will be fast in both cases.

A more significant performance difference results if you choose a sort order that is Case-Insensitive, Uppercase Preference. Recall that this choice considers all values as equal from the comparison standpoint, which also includes indexing. Characters retain a unique tertiary sort order, so they might be treated differently by an ORDER BY clause. Uppercase Preference can often require an additional sort operation in queries, more than with simple case insensitivity.

Consider a query that specifies *WHERE LAST_NAME >= 'Jackson' ORDER BY LAST_NAME*. If an index exists on the *last_name* field, the query optimizer will likely use it to find rows whose *last_name* value is greater than or equal to *Jackson*. If there is no need to use Uppercase Preference, the optimizer knows that because it is retrieving records based on the order of *last_name*, there is also no need to physically sort the rows because they were extracted in that order already. *Jackson, jackson*, and *JACKSON* are all qualifying rows. All are indexed and treated identically, and they simply appear in the results set in the order in which they were encountered. If Uppercase Preference is required for sorting, a subsequent sort of the qualifying rows is required to differentiate the rows, even though the index can still be used for selecting qualifying rows. If many qualifying rows are present, the performance difference between the two cases (one needs an additional sort operation) can be dramatic. This doesn't mean that you shouldn't choose Uppercase Preference. If you require those semantics, the performance aspect might well be a secondary concern. But you should be aware of the trade-off and decide which is most important to you. Determine whether your application can simply be made to input character data in all lowercase or uppercase consistently.

Installing SQL Server

Now that you understand all the preliminary considerations of installing and using SQL Server, you're ready to install the software. The actual mechanics of installation are simple—the installation program starts automatically when you insert the CD into the drive; if it doesn't, you can initiate the installation by executing the autorun.exe program at the root of the SQL Server CD.

SQL Server 7 is installed using the InstallShield program, which is common to many Microsoft products. One advantage of using InstallShield instead of a specific SQL Server Setup program is that you can use the Add/Remove Programs options in the Control Panel to add or remove SQL Server components. In addition, InstallShield makes the process of running an unattended installation much easier than in previous versions. The lengthiest part of installation, along with the mechanics of copying the files, is building and configuring SQL Server's *master* database, in which SQL Server stores configuration information and information about all other databases, as well as many system stored procedures. If you accept the default character set and sort order, the installation program simply copies a mostly prebuilt *master* database from the files master.mdf and mastlog.ldf from the CD. These files are in a subfolder called Data, in the folder for the particular architecture of the machine you are installing on, either alpha or x86. After copying these files, the installation program does a small amount of additional configuration. A new installation using the default character set can typically take less than 15 minutes from start to finish (sometimes as little as 5 minutes, depending on the speed of your hardware and how much "think time" you need for the questions). If you do not accept the default character set or sort order, the installation program must reindex the entire *master* database. This reindexing is a totally automatic operation, but it can add 5 to 10 minutes to the installation time. The total installation time is still usually under 30 minutes.

When the installation program runs and upgrades a previous installation, it rebuilds all the system stored procedures to ensure that the most recent versions are installed. By default, installation does not actually visit or modify the data pages of user databases. When you upgrade from a prior version of SQL Server to SQL Server 7, you must perform an upgrade on any user databases you want to use with SQL Server 7. You can do this during the installation process, or you can upgrade databases one at a time after the installation is complete.

For more details on the installation, see the online documentation and the whitepaper entitled "Installing Microsoft SQL Server 7.0"on the companion CD.

Basic Configuration After Installation

After the installation, you should verify the basic operation of SQL Server. SQL Server 7 is mostly self-configuring. Many options are available to fine-tune the configuration, but these are necessary only for specialized purposes. We'll discuss configuration in Chapter 15. Initially, you should leave the default configuration alone until you have a particular reason to change it.

Starting the SQL Server Service

After a successful installation, start SQL Server. The most common way to do this is by using the SQL Server Service Manager (from the Start menu). Choose Programs, Microsoft SQL Server 7.0, and then Service Manager. (The installation program also puts the SQL Server Service Manager in the startup group for the operating system, so after rebooting your machine, an icon for the SQL Server Service Manager appears on the taskbar, in the corner near the clock. You can also use the Services applet of the Windows NT Control Panel or SQL Server Enterprise Manager or issue a NET START MSSQLSERVER command from a Windows NT console (DOS prompt). You can also configure SQL Server to start automatically, either through the Services applet of the Windows NT Control Panel or by editing the properties of SQL Server in the Enterprise Manager.

After SQL Server is running (the icon on the taskbar will have a green arrow), use one of the most basic applications, SQL Server Query Analyzer, to ensure that you can connect. Initially, the only available SQL Server login name (sa) has a null password, so you can leave *sa* in the Login Name box and leave the password field blank. Or you can select the Use Windows NT Authentication option so that no Login Name or Password is required. Then change your database to the *pubs* sample database and run a couple of simple queries (for example, *SELECT * FROM authors ORDER BY au_lname*) to be sure that SQL Server is running correctly.

Changing the System Administrator Password

After you verify that SQL Server is running and responding to queries, you should change the password for the System Administrator (sa) account. From the Query Analyzer, use *sp_password* to change the *sa* password. As mentioned earlier, initially the password is null (no password). Be sure to pick a password you'll remember, because by design there is no way to read a password (it is stored encrypted)—it can only be changed to something else. Using Query Analyzer from the *master* database to change the password to *Banks_14*, you'd issue the following command:

```
sp_password NULL, 'Banks_14', sa
```

Using SQL Server Enterprise Manager, you can change the password from the server's Security folder. Select Logins, and then double-click *sa* in the right pane.

Note that the actual password is stored in a table as SQL Server data. So if you've chosen a case-sensitive sort order, passwords will also be case sensitive and must be entered exactly as defined.

SQL Server Enterprise Manager vs. SQL Statements

You can do nearly any task with SQL Server. At the lowest level, you can issue an SQL statement or a stored procedure. However, it's usually simpler to use SQL Server Enterprise Manager, which provides a front end for these commands and frees you from needing to know exact steps and syntax. Administrators who are proficient with Microsoft Visual Basic for Applications (VBA) might choose to use simple VBA scripts that use the SQL Server database administration object model, known as SQL-DMO (SQL Distributed Management Objects).

Since this book is geared toward database developers and administrators, we'll typically show the SQL statements and stored procedures that are used to accomplish a task and simply reference the easier methods, assuming that this will provide the best explanation of what's going on. We'll also tell you what to do without providing step-by-step directions. You can consult the SQL Server documentation for exact syntax of all options and so on. This book is meant to complement, but not replace, the product documentation.

Configuring SQL Server's Error Log

A new error log is created each time the SQL Server service is started. (The online documentation says you have to stop and start the computer running SQL Server to start a new error log, but this is not true.) If you want to start a new error log without stopping and restarting SQL Server, you can use the *sp_cycle_errorlog* system stored procedure. Keep in mind that the new error log created when you execute this procedure will not contain all the normal boot messages that are put in the error log when SQL Server starts up. You'll have to refer to an older copy of the error log to see these messages. However, if you execute *sp_cycle_errorlog* too many times, you might not have any copies that contain the boot messages. By default, SQL Server retains copies of the previous six error logs and gives the most recent copy (prior to the currently active error log) the extension .1, the second most recent copy the extension .2, and so on.

The current error log has no extension. You can change the number of error logs maintained by editing the registry. Find the key HKEY_LOCAL_MACHINE\ SOFTWARE\Microsoft\MSSQLServer\MSSQLServer, and edit that key by adding a new value. Define the value with the name *NumErrorLogs* and the type REG_DWORD. Supply any initial value desired, but keep in mind that the value you enter when editing the registry will be in hexadecimal.

Remote and Unattended Installation

SQL Server can be installed on a remote computer, and it can be totally scripted, requiring no user intervention. With SQL Server 7, the InstallShield-based installation, remote setup, and unattended setup are almost the same thing. The remote installation option can be useful when you are responsible for many SQL Server installations. In fact, the feature was added (in the days predating Microsoft Systems Management Server) at the behest of Microsoft's own MIS organization, which manages more than 200 machines running SQL Server (and thousands of databases). Installing and upgrading on any of those 200 servers from one computer greatly simplified MIS's work.

Other sites script their installations by using the unattended installation feature to deploy many servers instead of using the remote installation option, which is still an interactive process. Microsoft Systems Management Server uses this capability and can be used to install SQL Server at multiple sites. (In fact, unattended installation scripts and a PDF file, used by Systems Management Server, are provided on the root directory of the SQL Server CD.)

The unattended installation option is also useful if you are embedding SQL Server into a turnkey solution and want to provide a single, unified installation. As should be apparent by now, the SQL Server installation program makes multiple entries to the Registry, changes system paths and various system settings, creates program groups and user accounts, and performs basic initial configuration for its operation. The installation program is far from a glorified file-copy program. It would not be realistic for solution providers to create their own programs to install SQL Server as part of their services or products. But they can easily achieve the same results by simply creating a script that can drive the SQL Server installation program without any user intervention.

Remote Installation

Remote installation is similar to a normal, local installation. After you choose the remote installation option (by clicking Remote in the first dialog box of the installation program), you are prompted to answer a few questions in addition to those a local installation needs. Along with providing the machine name of the anticipated SQL Server, you must do the following:

■ Run the installation program from an account with Administrator privileges on the remote (target) server.

■ Be aware that drive paths should be relative to the remote server.

After specifying that you want a Remote installation, the information that you provide in the rest of the dialog boxes is collected into a file called setup.iss. Once the information is collected, a program is started on the remote computer, and then the local installation program exits. The remote program (remsetup.exe) copies files to the \admin$ share directory and runs an unattended installation on the remote computer, using the options specified in the setup.iss file.

Unattended Installation

Unattended installation creates a file using the options you selected in the SQL Server installation program. To invoke an unattended installation, you must first generate an InstallShield ISS file using one of three methods, described in the following list. All the methods require that you run the SQL Server installation program from a command prompt instead of using the autorun.exe program. The program is in either the alpha\Setup or x86\Setup folders on the SQL Server installation CD.

■ **Normal installation** The normal installation creates a file called setup.iss (which it saves in the Mssql7\Install folder) containing your answers to all the questions in the installation dialog boxes.

■ **Deferred installation** You start the SQL Server installation program (Setupsql.exe) with the *k=Rc* switch and proceed through the dialog boxes to install SQL Server as usual. This causes Setup to create the setup.iss file and save it in your Windows directory—this will not actually install SQL Server on the local computer.

■ **Manual file creation** The installation CD contains a sample setup file called sql70ins.iss. You can use a text editor to modify this file to correspond to the installation options you want. For details of the format of this file, see the online documentation.

After the setup ISS file is created, you can move or copy it to another location for use on other servers. For subsequent automated installations, start Setupsql and specify a previously generated setup ISS file as input by using the *-f1* command-line option. The syntax for this command is:

```
Setupsql.exe -f1 <full path to iss file> -SMS -s
```

175

The *-s* switch causes setup to run in a silent mode with no user interface. If the *-SMS* switch is not specified, the setup program will launch InstallShield to perform the installation, and then exit, with control immediately returning to the user. If the *-SMS* switch is specified, the setup program will wait until the installation is complete before terminating. This allows an automated process, or a user-created batch file, to launch the setup program, wait for setup to complete, and then perform additional actions. Without the *-SMS* switch, the additional actions might be initiated before the installation of SQL Server completes.

> **NOTE** For remote or unattended installation, you might choose to copy all the necessary files from the CD to a network share. (For example, if you're installing on an Intel processor, you copy everything but the \alpha folder; for a DEC Alpha installation, you copy everything but the \x86 folder.) Normally, you should not notice any difference between network installation and installation from the CD. However, note that the InstallShield program will fail if the full pathname of any of the source files is more than 255 characters long.

Changing Installation Options

With the exception of character set and sort order, all the decisions you make during installation can be changed at a later time. As mentioned earlier, you can change your decisions about the account under which the SQL Server services should run and whether SQL Server should start automatically when the system starts. You do this either through Control Panel's Services applet or by editing the properties of your SQL Server through SQL Server Enterprise Manager. You can also change the Security options for SQL Server using SQL Server Enterprise Manager to specify whether SQL Server should use Windows NT authentication only or whether it should also use Standard SQL Server authentication. You can change the network interface options using the Server Network Utility. The character set and sort order cannot be changed on an existing SQL Server installation without rebuilding your master database and recreating all your user databases. (Restoring backups is not sufficient. A restore maintains the character set and sort order that were in effect at the time the backup was made.)

Prior versions of SQL Server allowed you to run the setup program with special flags to carry out special operations. Because SQL Server 7 installation uses the generic InstallShield, no SQL Server–specific flags are allowed on the setup command line. Instead, SQL Server 7 provides additional utilities to carry out these special operations:

■ **Rebuilding the master database** The Rebuild master utility rebuildm.exe in the \mssql7\binn directory rebuilds the *master* database completely. You might have to restore backups of *msdb* and *model* system databases after you rebuild the *master* database. If any user databases are to be restored or attached after *master* is rebuilt, you must specify the same sort order, code page, and Unicode collation when you rebuild *master* as used by those databases.

■ **Rebuilding the Registry entries** You can use the regrebld.exe program in \mssql7\binn to restore the SQL Server registry entries if they become corrupted. You can also run the *regrebld* program using the *–Backup* option to back up the Registry at any time. You can also use the *–Restore* option, which is equivalent to running *regrebld* with no parameters. The SQL Server installation program runs *regrebld –Backup* at the end of the installation process to create an initial set of Registry backup files. You might have to rebuild the Registry if the Windows NT Registry was partially corrupted (for example, if it was inadvertently deleted using the REGEDT32.EXE program) or if Windows NT was reinstalled (not upgraded) on a machine and the new Registry is not aware of the previous SQL Server installation.

Adding Additional Components

If you want to add components, you can rerun the SQL Server installation program from the original CD. The program will detect and display components you already have installed and let you select additional components. The main dialog box is very specific about the actions it will perform: "Selecting components already installed will not reinstall them and unselecting components already installed will not remove them." The components you might want to install in this way, after the initial installation, include:

■ **Server components** You can install the upgrade tools (to upgrade databases from version 6.*x* to SQL Server 7), replication support, and full-text search capabilities.

■ **Management tools** You can install the SQL Server Enterprise Manager, the SQL Server Query Analyzer, the SQL Server Profiler, and DTC Client Support.

Two other tools are available with SQL Server 7 that are not part of the standard installation. The initial installation screen gives you the choice of installing SQL Server (Desktop or full server edition), SQL Server 7.0 OLAP Services, or English Query. If you choose either of the latter two options, SQL Server itself is not installed and an existing SQL Server 7 installation will not be affected.

Summary

SQL Server offers unprecedented ease of installation for a database server of its caliber. But you should understand your choices in terms of hardware, licensing, and sort orders before you proceed too far down the path of a major application rollout. Installing SQL Server is also fast and reliable. You need to do very little custom configuration because SQL Server 7 automatically configures itself as needed.

The SQL Server installation offers options for unattended and remote installation, for installing a Desktop version, and for client-tools–only installation. Utilities are provided for changing many of the options chosen during the initial installation, but to add new components you must keep your original CD handy. (That is, if you haven't copied its contents to a network share.)

CHAPTER FIVE

DATABASES AND DATABASE FILES

Simply put, a Microsoft SQL Server database is a collection of objects that hold and manipulate data. A typical SQL Server installation has only a handful of databases, but it's not unusual for a single installation to contain several dozen databases. (Theoretically, one SQL Server can have as many as 32,767 databases. But practically speaking, this limit would never be reached.)

A SQL Server database:

- Is a collection of many *objects*, such as tables, views, stored procedures, and constraints. The theoretic limit is 2^{31} (or more than 2 billion) objects. Typically, the number of objects ranges from hundreds to tens of thousands.

- Is owned by a single user account but can contain objects owned by other users.

- Has its own set of system tables that catalog the definition of the database.

- Maintains its own set of user accounts and security.

- Is the primary unit of recovery and maintains logical consistency among objects in the database. (For example, primary and foreign key relationships always refer to other tables within the same database, not to other databases.)

- Has its own transaction log and manages the transactions within the database.

- Can participate in two-phase commit transactions with other SQL Server databases on the same server or different servers.

- Can span multiple disk drives and operating system files.

- Can range in size from 1 MB through a theoretical limit of 1 TB (1,048,576 MB) in size.
- Can grow and shrink, either automatically or by command.
- Can have objects joined in queries with objects from other databases in the same SQL Server installation.
- Can have specific options set or disabled. (For example, you can set a database to be read-only or to be a source of published data in replication.)
- Is conceptually similar to but richer than the ANSI SQL-schema concept (discussed later in this chapter).

A SQL Server database is *not*:

- Synonymous with an entire SQL Server installation.
- A single SQL Server table.
- A specific operating system file.

A database itself isn't synonymous with an operating system file, but a database always exists in two or more such files. These files are known as SQL Server *database files* and are specified either at the time the database is created, using the CREATE DATABASE command, or afterwards, using the ALTER DATABASE command.

Special System Databases

A new SQL Server installation will automatically include several databases: *master*, *model*, *tempdb*, *pubs*, *Northwind*, and *msdb*.

master

The *master* database is composed of system tables that keep track of the server installation as a whole and all other databases that are subsequently created. Although every database has a set of system catalogs that maintain information about objects it contains, the *master* database has system catalogs that keep information about disk space, file allocations, usage, systemwide configuration settings, login accounts, the existence of other databases, and the existence of other SQL servers (for distributed operations). The *master* database is absolutely critical to your system, so be sure that you always keep a current backup copy of it. Operations such as creating another database, changing configuration values, or modifying login accounts all make modifications to *master*, so after performing such activities, make sure you back up *master*.

model

The *model* database is simply a template database. Every time you create a new database, SQL Server makes a copy of *model*. If you'd like every new database to start out with certain objects or permissions, you can put them in *model*, and all new databases will inherit them.

tempdb

The temporary database, *tempdb*, is a workspace. SQL Server's *tempdb* database is unique among all other databases because it's re-created—not recovered—every time SQL Server is restarted. It's used for temporary tables explicitly created by users, for worktables to hold intermediate results created internally by SQL Server during query processing and sorting, and for the materialization of static cursors and the keys of keyset cursors. Operations within *tempdb* are logged so that transactions on temporary tables can be rolled back, but the records in the log contain only enough information to roll back a transaction, not to recover (or redo) it. No recovery information is needed because every time SQL Server is started, *tempdb* is completely re-created; any previous user-created objects (that is, all your tables and data) will be gone. Logging only enough information for rolling back transactions in *tempdb* is a new feature in SQL Server 7 and can potentially increase the performance of INSERT statements to make them up to four times faster than inserts in other (fully logged) databases.

All users have the privileges to create and use private and global temporary tables that reside in *tempdb*. (Private and global table names have # and ## prefixes, respectively, which will be discussed in more detail in Chapter 6.) However, by default, users don't have the privileges to use *tempdb* and then create a table there (unless the table name is prefaced with # or ##). But you can easily add such privileges to *model*, from which *tempdb* is copied every time the SQL Server is restarted, or you can grant the privileges in an autostart procedure that runs each time SQL Server is restarted. If you do choose to add those privileges to the *model* database, you must remember to revoke those privileges on any other new databases you subsequently create if you don't want them to appear there as well.

pubs

The *pubs* database is a sample database used extensively by much of the SQL Server documentation and in this book. You can safely delete it if you like, although it consumes only 2 MB of space. So if you're not scrounging for a few more megabytes of disk space, we recommend leaving *pubs* there. This database is admittedly fairly simple, but that's a feature, not a bug. The *pubs* database provides good examples, without a lot of peripheral issues obscuring their central points. Another nice feature of *pubs* is that it's pretty ubiquitous in the SQL Server community, which makes it easy to use to illustrate examples without requiring the audience to try to understand the underlying tables. As you become more skilled with SQL Server, chances are you'll find yourself also using it to illustrate examples with your developer or user community.

Northwind

The *Northwind* database is another sample database that was originally developed for use with Microsoft Access. Much of the documentation dealing with application programming interfaces (APIs) uses *Northwind*, as do some of the newer examples in the SQL Server documentation. It's a bit more complex than *pubs*, and at almost 4 MB, slightly larger. We'll be using it to illustrate some concepts that aren't easily demonstrated using *pubs*. As with *pubs*, you can safely delete *Northwind* if you like, although the disk space needed is still extremely small compared to what you'll be using for your real data. We recommend leaving *Northwind* there.

msdb

The *msdb* database is used by the SQL Server Agent service, which performs scheduled activities such as backups and replication tasks. In general, other than performing backups and maintenance on this database, you should ignore *msdb*. (But you might take a peek at the backup history and other information kept there.) All the information in *msdb* is accessible from the SQL Server Enterprise Manager tools, so you usually don't need to access these tables directly. Think of the *msdb* tables as another form of system tables: just as you should never directly modify system tables, you shouldn't directly add data to or delete data from tables in *msdb* unless you really know what you're doing or are instructed to do so by a Microsoft SQL Server technical support engineer.

Database Files

A database file is nothing more than an operating system file. (In addition to database files, SQL Server also has *backup devices,* which are logical devices that map to operating system files, to physical devices such as tape drives, or even to named pipes.) A database spans at least two, and possibly several, database files, and these files are specified when a database is created or altered. Every database must span at least two files, one for the data (as well as indexes and allocation pages), and one for the transaction log. SQL Server 7 allows the following three types of database files:

■ **Primary data files**   Every database has one primary data file that keeps track of all the rest of the files in the database, in addition to storing data. By convention, the name of a primary data file has the extension MDF.

■ **Secondary data files**   A database might have zero or more secondary data files. By convention, the name of a secondary data file has the extension NDF.

■ **Log files**   Every database will have at least one log file that contains the information necessary to recover all transactions in a database. By convention, a log file will have the suffix LDF.

Database files each have several properties. These include a logical filename, a physical filename, an initial size, a maximum size, and a growth increment. The properties of each file are noted in the *sysfiles* table (depicted in Table 5-1), which contains one row for each file used by a database.

Column Name	Description
fileid	The file identification number (unique for each database).
groupid	The filegroup identification number.
size	The size of the file (in 8-KB pages).
maxsize	The maximum file size (in 8-KB pages). A value of 0 indicates no growth, and a value of −1 indicates that the file should grow until the disk is full.
growth	The growth size of the database. A value of 0 indicates no growth. Can be either number of pages or percentage of file size, depending on value of status.
status	0x2 = Disk file. 0x40 = Log device. 0x80 = File has been written to since last backup. 0x100000 = Growth is in percentage, not pages.
name	The logical name of the file.
filename	The name of the physical device, including the full path of the file.

Table 5-1.
The sysfiles *table.*

Creating Databases

The easiest way to create a database is to use SQL Server Enterprise Manager, which provides a graphical front end to Transact-SQL commands and stored procedures that accomplish those tasks. Figure 5-1 shows SQL Enterprise Manager's Database Properties dialog box, which represents the CREATE DATABASE Transact-SQL command.

Only someone with the *sysadmin* role or a user who's been granted CREATE DATABASE permission by someone with the *sysadmin* role can issue the CREATE DATABASE command. The command is used to create a new user database.

When you create a new user database, SQL Server copies the *model* database, which—as you just learned—is simply a template database. For example, if you have an object that you would like created in every subsequent user database, create that object in *model* first. (You can also use *model* to set default database options in all subsequent databases.) In addition to objects you might create in *model*, 18 system tables and 20 system views are included in *model*, which means that every new database also includes these 38 system objects. SQL Server uses these objects for the definition and maintenance of each database.

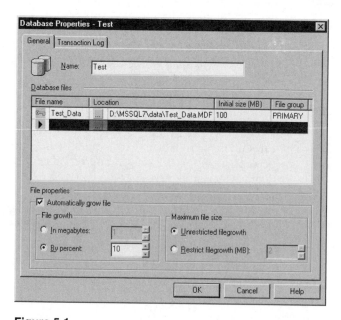

Figure 5-1.
The Database Properties dialog box, which creates a new database that is called Test.

(Three of the system views are provided for backward compatibility and have no current functionality. They mimic information that was available in earlier versions of SQL Server.) The system objects are the ones whose names start with *sys*. If you haven't added any other objects to *model*, these 38 system objects will be the entire contents of a newly created database. Every Transact-SQL command or system stored procedure that creates, alters, or drops a SQL Server object will result in entries being made to system tables.

> **WARNING** Do not directly modify the system tables. You might render your database unusable by doing so. Direct modification is prevented by default: a system administrator must take deliberate action via the *sp_configure* stored procedure to allow system tables to be modified directly.

A new user database must be 1 MB or greater in size, and the primary data file size must be at least as large as the primary data file of the *model* database. Almost all the possible arguments to the CREATE DATABASE command have default values so that it's possible to create a database using a simple form of CREATE DATABASE, such as this:

```
CREATE DATABASE testdb
```

This would create the *testdb* database, with a default size, on two files whose logical names—*testdb* and *testdb_log*—are derived from the name of the database. The corresponding physical files would be testdb.mdf and testdb_log.ldf. They would be created in the default data directory, as determined at the time SQL Server was installed.

> **NOTE** If you use the SQL Server Enterprise Manager to create a database called *testdb*, the default logical and physical names will be different than if you use the CREATE DATABASE command. The Enterprise Manager will give the data file the logical name of *testdb_Data* (instead of just *test*), and the physical file will have the name testdb_data.mdf.

The SQL Server login account that created the database is known as the *database owner*, or DBO, and will always have the username DBO when using this database. The default size of the data file is the size of the primary data file of the *model* database, and the default size of the log file is half a megabyte. Whether the database name, *testdb*, is case sensitive depends on the sort order you choose during setup. If you accepted the default, the name is case insensitive. (Note that the actual command CREATE DATABASE is case insensitive, regardless of the case sensitivity chosen for data.)

Other default values apply to the new database and its files. If the LOG ON clause is not specified, but data files are specified, a log file will be automatically created with a size that is 25 percent of the sum of the sizes of all data files.

For the files, if the MAXSIZE clause isn't specified, the file will grow until the disk is full. (In other words, the file size is considered unlimited.) Both SIZE and MAXSIZE can be specified in units of MB (the default) or KB. A value of 0 for FILEGROWTH indicates no growth. The default value is 10 percent, and the minimum value is 64 KB.

CREATE DATABASE Example

The following is a complete example of the CREATE DATABASE command, specifying three files and all the properties of each file:

```
CREATE DATABASE Archive
ON
PRIMARY ( NAME = Arch1,
          FILENAME = 'c:\mssql7\data\archdat1.mdf',
          SIZE = 100MB,
          MAXSIZE = 200,
          FILEGROWTH = 20),
       ( NAME = Arch2,
          FILENAME = 'c:\mssql7\data\archdat2.ndf',
          SIZE = 100MB,
          MAXSIZE = 200,
          FILEGROWTH = 20),
LOG ON
       ( NAME = Archlog1,
          FILENAME = 'c:\mssql7\data\archlog1.ldf',
          SIZE = 100MB,
          MAXSIZE = 200,
          FILEGROWTH = 20)
```

Expanding and Shrinking Databases

Databases can be expanded and shrunk either automatically or manually. The mechanism for automatic expansion is completely different from the mechanism for automatic shrinkage. Manual expansion is also handled differently than manual shrinkage. Log files have their own rules for growing and shrinking, so we'll discuss changes in log file size in a separate section.

Automatic File Expansion

Expansion of a database can happen automatically to any one of the database's files when that particular file becomes full. The file property FILEGROWTH determines how that automatic expansion will happen. The FILEGROWTH specified when the file is first defined can be qualified using the suffix MB, KB, or % and will always be rounded up to the nearest 64 KB. If the value is specified as a percent, the growth increment is the specified percentage of the size of the file when the expansion occurs. The file property MAXSIZE sets an upper limit on the size to which a file can grow.

Manual File Expansion

Manual expansion of a database file is accomplished using the ALTER DATABASE command to change the SIZE property of one or more of the files. When altering a database, the new size of a file must be larger than the current size. To decrease the size of files, you must use other commands.

Automatic File Shrinkage

The database option *autoshrink* allows a database to shrink automatically. The effect is the same as doing a DBCC SHRINKDATABASE *(dbname, 25)*. This option leaves 25 percent free space in a database after the shrink, and any free space beyond that 25 percent is returned to the operating system. The thread that performs autoshrink, which will always have server process ID (spid) 6, will shrink databases at 30-minute intervals. The DBCC SHRINKDATABASE command will be discussed in more detail momentarily.

Manual File Shrinkage

You can manually shrink a database using the following two DBCC commands:

```
DBCC SHRINKFILE ( {file_name | file_id }
[, target_size][, {NOTRUNCATE | TRUNCATEONLY} ]  )

DBCC SHRINKDATABASE (database_name [, target_percent]
[, {NOTRUNCATE | TRUNCATEONLY} ]  )
```

DBCC SHRINKFILE

DBCC SHRINKFILE allows you to shrink files in the current database. When *target_size* is specified, DBCC SHRINKFILE attempts to shrink the specified file to the specified size in megabytes. Used pages in the part of the file to be freed are relocated to available free space in the part of the file retained.

For example, for a 10-MB data file, a DBCC SHRINKFILE with a *target_size* of 8 causes all used pages in the last 2 MB of the file to be reallocated into any free slots in the first 8 MB of the file. DBCC SHRINKFILE doesn't shrink a file past the size needed to store the data. For example, if 70 percent of the pages in a 10-MB data file are used, a DBCC SHRINKFILE statement with a *target_size* of 6 shrinks the file to only 7 MB, not 6 MB.

DBCC SHRINKDATABASE

The DBCC SHRINKDATABASE command shrinks all files in a database. The database can't be made smaller than the *model* database. In addition, the DBCC SHRINKDATABASE command will not allow any file to be shrunk to a size smaller than its minimum size. The minimum size of a database file is the initial size of the file (specified when the database was created) or the size to which the file has been explicitly extended or reduced, using either the ALTER DATABASE or DBCC SHRINKFILE command. If you need to shrink a database smaller than this minimum size, you should use the DBCC SHRINKFILE command to shrink individual database files to a specific size. The size to which a file is shrunk will then become the new minimum size.

The numeric argument given to the DBCC SHRINKDATABASE command is a percentage of free space to leave in each file of the database. For example, if we have used 60 MB of a 100-MB database file, we can specify a shrink percentage of 25 percent. SQL Server will shrink the file to a size of 80 MB, since 25 percent of 80 is 20, meaning we'll have 20 MB of free space in addition to the original 60 MB of data. In other words, the 80 MB file will have 25 percent of its space free. On the other hand, if we have used 80 MB or more of a 100-MB database file, there is no way SQL Server can shrink this file to leave 25 percent free space. In that case, the file size remains unchanged.

Because DBCC SHRINKDATABASE is shrinking the database on a file-by-file basis, the mechanism used to perform the actual shrinking is the same as that used with DBCC SHRINKFILE. SQL Server will first move pages to the front of files to free up space at the end and then will release the appropriate number of freed pages to the operating system. Two options for the DBCC SHRINKDATABASE and DBCC SHRINKFILE commands can force SQL Server to do either one or the other of the two steps just mentioned:

- The NOTRUNCATE option causes all the freed file space to be retained in the database files. SQL Server only compacts the data by moving it to the front of the file. The default is to release the freed file space to the operating system.

■ The TRUNCATEONLY option causes any unused space in the data files to be released to the operating system. No attempt is made to relocate rows to unallocated pages. When TRUNCATEONLY is used, *target_size* and *target_percent* are ignored.

NOTE DBCC SHRINKFILE specifies a target *size* in megabytes. DBCC SHRINK DATABASE specifies a target *percentage* of free space to leave in the database.

Changes in Log Size

No matter how many physical files have been defined for the transaction log, SQL Server always treats the log as one contiguous file. For example, when the DBCC SHRINKDATABASE command determines how much the log can be shrunk, it does not consider the log files separately but determines the shrinkable size based on the entire file.

The transaction log for any database is managed as a set of Virtual Log Files (VLFs) whose size is determined internally by SQL Server, based on the total size of all the log files and the growth increment used when enlarging the log. A log always grows in units of entire VLFs and can only be shrunk to a VLF boundary. (Figure 5-2 on the following page illustrates a physical log file along with several VLFs.) A VLF can exist in one of the following three states:

■ **Active** The active portion of the log begins at the minimum log sequence number (LSN) representing an active (uncommitted) transaction. The active portion of the log ends at the last LSN written. Any VLFs that contain any part of the active log are considered active VLFs. (Unused space in the physical log is not part of any VLF.)

■ **Recoverable** The portion of the log preceding the oldest active transaction is only needed to maintain a sequence of log backups for recovery purposes.

■ **Reusable** If transaction log backups are not being maintained, or if you have already backed up the log, VLFs prior to the oldest active transaction are not needed and can be reused.

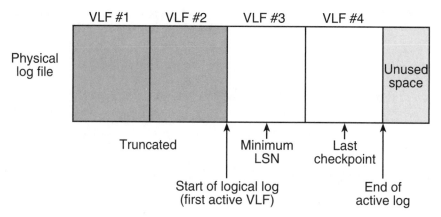

Figure 5-2.
The multiple virtual log files that make up a physical log file.

SQL Server will assume you're not maintaining a sequence of log backups if any of the following are true:

- You have truncated the log using BACKUP LOG WITH NO_LOG or BACKUP LOG WITH TRUNCATE_ONLY.

- You have set the database to truncate the log automatically on a regular basis with the database option *trunc. log on chkpt.*

- You have performed an unlogged operation (like fast BCP) since the last full database backup.

- You have never taken a full database backup.

In any of the situations just described, when SQL Server reaches the end of the physical log file, it will start reusing that space in the physical file by circling back to the file's beginning. In effect, SQL Server will recycle the space in the log file that is no longer needed for recovery or backup purposes. If a log backup sequence *is* being maintained, the part of the log before the minimum LSN cannot be overwritten until those log records have actually been backed up. Once you have performed the log backup, SQL Server can circle back to the beginning of the file. Once SQL Server has circled back to start writing log records earlier in the log file, the reusable portion of the log is then between the end of the logical log and active portion of the log. Figure 5-3 on the following page depicts this cycle.

You can actually observe this behavior in one of the sample databases, such as *pubs*, assuming you have never made a full backup of the database. If you have

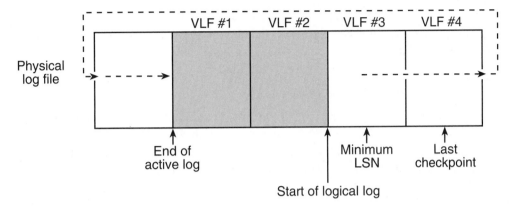

Figure 5-3.
The active portion of the log circling back to the beginning of the physical log file.

never made any modifications to *pubs*, the size of its transaction log file will be just about 0.75 MB. This next script creates a new table in the *pubs* database, inserts three records, and then updates those records 1000 times. Each update is an individual transaction, and each one is written to the transaction log. However, you should note that the log has not grown at all, even after 3000 update records are written. (If you have already taken a backup of *pubs*, you might want to re-create the database before trying this example. You can do that by running the script *instpubs.sql* in the folder \mssql7\install.)

```
CREATE TABLE newtable ( a int)
GO
INSERT INTO newtable VALUES (10)
INSERT INTO newtable VALUES (20)
INSERT INTO newtable VALUES (30)
GO
DECLARE @counter int
SET @counter = 1
WHILE @counter < 1000 BEGIN
    UPDATE newtable SET a = a + 1
    SET @counter = @counter + 1
END
```

Now make a backup of the *pubs* database after making sure that the option *trunc. log on chkpt.* is not set. (We'll look at database options later in this chapter.) You can use this statement to make the backup, substituting for c: whatever drive your SQL Server is installed on:

```
BACKUP DATABASE pubs to disk = 'c:\mssql7\backup\pubs.bak'
```

Run the update script again, starting with the DECLARE statement. You should see that the physical log file has now grown to accommodate the log records added. The initial space in the log could not be reused because SQL Server assumed that you were saving that information for backups.

Now you can try to shrink the log back down again. If you issue the following command:

```
DBCC SHRINKDATABASE (pubs)
```

Or if you issue the DBCC SHRINKFILE command for the log file, SQL Server will mark a shrinkpoint in the log, but no actual shrinking will take place until log records are freed by either backing up or truncating the log. You can truncate the log with this statement:

```
BACKUP LOG pubs WITH TRUNCATE_ONLY
```

At this point, you should notice the physical size of the log file has been reduced. If a log is truncated without any prior shrink command issued, SQL Server will mark the space used by the truncated records as available for reuse, but it does not change the size of the physical file.

In certain circumstances, you might notice that running the above commands exactly as specified still does not shrink the physical log file. This can happen when the active part of the log is located at the end of the physical file. Physical shrinking can only take place from the end of the log, and the active portion is never shrinkable. To remedy this situation, you can carry out the following four steps:

1. Make sure earlier VLFs are reusable by backing up or truncating the log.

2. Execute a few dozen update statements so that the active VLF moves to an earlier physical location.

3. Execute DBCC SHRINKDATABASE to mark a shrinkpoint.

4. Truncate or backup the log a second time to force the physical shrinkage.

NOTE If a database log backup sequence is not being maintained for a database, the database can be set into log truncate mode by setting the *trunc. log on chkpt.* database option to TRUE. In conjunction with the *autoshrink* option, this means that the log will be physically shrunk at regular intervals. Contrary to the SQL Server 7 documentation, a database does not come out of log truncate mode by backing up the full database.

If a database has the *autoshrink* option on, an *autoshrink* process kicks in once every 30 minutes and determines the size to which the log should be shrunk. The log manager accumulates statistics on the maximum amount of log space used in the 30-minute interval between shrinks. The *autoshrink* process marks the *shrinkpoint* of the log as 125 percent of the maximum log space used or as the minimum size of the log, whichever is larger. (Minimum size is the creation size of the log or the size to which it has been manually increased or decreased.) The log will then shrink to that size whenever it gets the chance, which will be when either the log gets truncated or backed up. It's possible to have *autoshrink* without having *trunc. log on chkpt.*, although there's no way to guarantee that the log will actually shrink. (If, for example, the log is never backed up, it will never be cleared.)

Database Filegroups

You can group data files for a database together into filegroups for allocation and administration purposes. In some cases, you can improve performance by controlling the placement of data and indexes into specific filegroups on specific disk drives. Three types of filegroups in a SQL Server database are possible:

- **Primary filegroup** This filegroup contains the primary data file and any files not put into another specific filegroup. All pages from system tables are always allocated from files in the primary filegroup.

- **User-defined filegroup** You can create user-defined filegroups by using the FILEGROUP keyword in the CREATE DATABASE or ALTER DATABASE statement.

- **Default filegroup** This filegroup contains the pages for all tables and indexes that aren't placed in a specific filegroup. Only one filegroup in each database can be the default filegroup. A database owner can change which filegroup is the default by using the ALTER DATABASE statement. If no default filegroup was specified, the primary filegroup is also the default filegroup.

Most SQL Server databases will have a single data file in one (default) filegroup. In fact, most users will probably never know enough about how SQL Server works to know what a filegroup is. As a user steps up the level of database sophistication, she might decide to use multiple devices to spread out the I/O for a database. The easiest way to accomplish this is to create a database file on a RAID (redundant array of independent disks) device. Still, there would be no need to use filegroups. Move another level up the sophistication and complexity scale, where she decides that she really wants multiple files. Perhaps she wants to add disk space on another drive, or perhaps she just wants to create a database that uses more space than is available on a single drive. She still doesn't need filegroups and can accomplish her goals using CREATE DATABASE with a list of files on separate drives.

Why Use Multiple Files?

You might wonder what would be the reason for creating a database on multiple files located on one physical drive. There's no performance benefit in doing so. However, it does give you added flexibility in two important ways.

First, if you need to restore a database from a backup because of a disk crash, you should be aware that the new database must contain the same number of files as the original. For example, if your original database consisted of one large 12-GB file, you would need to restore it into a database with one file of that size. If you don't have another 12-GB drive immediately available, you won't be able to restore the database! If, however, you originally created the database on several smaller files, you have added flexibility during a restoration. You might be more likely to have several 4-GB drives available than one large 12-GB drive.

Second, spreading the database onto multiple files, even onto the same drive, gives you the flexibility of easily moving the database onto separate drives if you modify your hardware configuration in the future. Microsoft's internal SAP system uses a SQL Server 7 database created on 12 files. Microsoft thought this would give it the ultimate flexibility. They could separate the files into two groups of six, six groups of two, four groups of three, and so on. This allows them to experiment with performance enhancements gained as files are spread over different numbers of physical drives.

More sophisticated DBAs might decide that they want to have different tables assigned to different drives. Only then will they need to use filegroups. The easiest way to accomplish this goal is to use SQL Server Enterprise Manager to create the database, still without having to learn anything about filegroup syntax. Only the most sophisticated users who want to write scripts that set up databases with multiple filegroups will need to know the underlying details.

You can also use filegroups to allow a DBA to back up only parts of the database at one time. However, if you create an index in a filegroup that's different from the one the table resides in, you must back up both filegroups (the filegroup containing the table and the filegroup containing the index). If you create more than one index in a filegroup that's different from the filegroup in which the table resides, you must immediately back up all filegroups to accommodate these differing filegroups. The BACKUP statement detects all these filegroup situations and communicates to the user the minimum filegroups that must be backed up.

When adding space to objects stored in a particular filegroup, the data is stored in a *proportional fill* manner, which means that if you have one file in a filegroup with twice as much free space as another, the first file will have two extents (or units of space) allocated from it for each extent allocated from the second file. We'll discuss extents in more detail later in this chapter.

FILEGROUP CREATION Example

This example creates a database named *sales* with three filegroups:

- The primary filegroup with the files Spri1_dat and Spri2_dat. The FILEGROWTH increment for these files is specified as 15 percent.

- A filegroup named SalesGroup1 with the files SGrp1Fi1 and SGrp1Fi2.

- A filegroup named SalesGroup2 with the files SGrp2Fi1 and SGrp2Fi2.

```
CREATE DATABASE Sales
ON PRIMARY
( NAME = SPri1_dat,
FILENAME = 'c:\mssql7\data\SPri1dat.mdf',
SIZE = 10,
MAXSIZE = 50,
FILEGROWTH = 15% ),
( NAME = SPri2_dat,
FILENAME = 'c:\mssql7\data\SPri2dat.mdf',
```

(continued)

```
    SIZE = 10,
    MAXSIZE = 50,
    FILEGROWTH = 15% ),
    FILEGROUP SalesGroup1
    ( NAME = SGrp1Fi1_dat,
    FILENAME = 'c:\mssql7\data\SG1Fi1dt.mdf',
    SIZE = 10,
    MAXSIZE = 50,
    FILEGROWTH = 5 ),
    ( NAME = SGrp1Fi2_dat,
    FILENAME = 'c:\mssql7\data\SG1Fi2dt.mdf',
    SIZE = 10,
    MAXSIZE = 50,
    FILEGROWTH = 5 ),
    FILEGROUP SalesGroup2
    ( NAME = SGrp2Fi1_dat,
    FILENAME = 'c:\mssql7\data\SG2Fi1dt.mdf',
    SIZE = 10,
    MAXSIZE = 50,
    FILEGROWTH = 5 ),
    ( NAME = SGrp2Fi2_dat,
    FILENAME = 'c:\mssql7\data\SG2Fi2dt.mdf',
    SIZE = 10,
    MAXSIZE = 50,
    FILEGROWTH = 5 )
    LOG ON
    ( NAME = 'Sales_log',
    FILENAME = 'c:\mssql7\data\saleslog.ldf',
    SIZE = 5MB,
    MAXSIZE = 25MB,
    FILEGROWTH = 5MB )
```

Altering a Database

You can use the ALTER DATABASE statement to change a database's definition in one of the following ways:

- Add one or more new data files to the database, which you can optionally put in a user-defined filegroup. You must put all files added in a single ALTER DATABASE statement in the same filegroup.

- Add one or more new log files to the database.

- Remove a file or a filegroup from the database. You can do this only if the file or filegroup is completely empty. Removing a filegroup will remove all the files in the filegroup.

- Add a new filegroup to a database.

- Modify an existing file in one of the following ways:

  ❑ Increase the value of the SIZE property.

  ❑ Change the MAXSIZE or FILEGROWTH properties.

  ❑ Change the NAME property for files only in the *tempdb* database; this change doesn't go into effect until you stop and restart SQL Server.

- Modify an existing filegroup in one of the following ways:

  ❑ Mark the filegroup as READONLY so that updates to objects in the filegroup aren't allowed. The primary filegroup cannot be made READONLY.

  ❑ Mark the filegroup as READWRITE, which reverses the READONLY property.

  ❑ Mark the filegroup as the default filegroup for the database.

The ALTER DATABASE statement can make only one of the changes just described each time it is executed. Note that it's impossible to move a file from one filegroup to another.

ALTER DATABASE Examples

The following examples demonstrate what you can do with ALTER DATA-BASE. This first example increases the size of a database file:

```
USE master
GO
ALTER DATABASE Test1
MODIFY FILE
(NAME = 'test1dat3',
SIZE = 20MB)
```

This next example creates a new filegroup in a database, adds two 5-MB files to the filegroup, and makes the new filegroup the default filegroup. Three ALTER DATABASE statements are needed:

```
ALTER DATABASE Test1
ADD FILEGROUP Test1FG1
GO
ALTER DATABASE Test1
ADD FILE
```

(continued)

197

```
( NAME = 'test1dat3',
FILENAME = 'c:\mssql7\data\t1dat3.ndf',
SIZE = 5MB,
MAXSIZE = 100MB,
FILEGROWTH = 5MB),
( NAME = 'test1dat4',
FILENAME = 'c:\mssql7\data\t1dat4.ndf',
SIZE = 5MB,
MAXSIZE = 100MB,
FILEGROWTH = 5MB)
TO FILEGROUP Test1FG1
GO
ALTER DATABASE Test1
MODIFY FILEGROUP Test1FG1 DEFAULT
GO
```

Databases Under the Hood

A database consists of user-defined space for the permanent storage of user objects such as tables and indexes. This space is allocated in one or more operating system files.

Databases are divided into logical pages (of 8 KB each), and within each file the pages are numbered contiguously from 0 to *x*, with the upper value *x* being defined by the size of the file. You can then refer to any page by specifying a database ID, a file ID, and a page number. When you use the ALTER DATABASE command to enlarge a file, the new space is added to the end of the file. That is, the first page of the newly allocated space is page *x* + 1 on the file you're enlarging. When you shrink a database by using either the DBCC SHRINKDATABASE or DBCC SHRINKFILE command, pages are removed starting at the highest page in the database (at the end) and moving toward lower-numbered pages. This ensures that page numbers within a file are always contiguous.

The *master* database contains 49 system tables: the same 18 tables found in user databases, plus 31 tables that are found only in *master*. Ten of these tables—including *syslockinfo, sysperfinfo, syscurconfigs,* and *sysprocesses*—don't physically exist in the *master* database; rather, they're built dynamically each time a user queries them. Twelve of these tables contain information about remote servers; they won't contain any data until you define other servers with which you'll be communicating. The *master* database also contains 23 system views: the same 20 found in all user databases, plus 3 additional views. All these system objects, in both the *master* and *user* databases, have names that begin with *spt_*. To see a list of the system tables and views that are found in only the *master* database, you can execute the following query:

```
SELECT type, name FROM master..sysobjects
WHERE type IN ('s', 'v') AND name NOT IN
    (SELECT name FROM model..sysobjects)
GO
```

The *master* database also contains 10 tables that can be referred to as *pseudo-system tables*. These table names begin with *spt_* and are used as storage areas for various system procedures, but they aren't true system tables. You should never modify them directly because that could break some of the system procedures. However, deleting them wouldn't invalidate the basic integrity of the database, which is the case if true system tables are altered.

When you create a new database using the CREATE DATABASE statement, it's given a unique database ID, or *dbid*, and a new row is inserted in the *master..sysdatabases* table for that database. Only the *master* database contains a *sysdatabases* table. Figure 5-4 depicts a sample *sysdatabases* table, and Table 5-2 on the following page shows its columns.

The rows in *sysdatabases* are updated when a database's ownership or name is changed or when database options are changed. (Later in the chapter, we'll discuss this in more detail.)

```
name        dbid   suid    mode    status   crdate       cmptlevel   filename
---------   -----  -----   -----   ------   ----------   ---------   ------------------------------
credit      8      1       0       0        1998-12-12   70          d:\mssql7\data\pto_data.mdf
master      1      1       0       8        1998-09-26   70          D:\MSSQL7\DATA\MASTER.MDF
model       3      1       0       0        1998-10-21   70          D:\MSSQL7\DATA\model.mdf
msdb        4      1       0       8        1998-10-21   70          D:\MSSQL7\DATA\msdbdata.mdf
newdb       7      NULL    0       12       1998-12-08   70          D:\MSSQL7\DATA\newdb.mdf
Northwind   6      1       0       12       1998-12-17   70          D:\MSSQL7\DATA\northwnd.mdf
pubs        5      1       0       0        1998-12-17   70          D:\MSSQL7\data\pubs.mdf
tempdb      2      1       0       12       1998-12-18   70          D:\MSSQL7\DATA\TEMPDB.MDF
test        9      1       0       0        1998-12-18   70          D:\MSSQL7\data\test.mdf
```

Figure 5-4.
Partial listing of a sysdatabases *table.*

Column	Information
name	Name of the database.
dbid	Unique database ID; can be reused when the database is dropped.
sid	System ID of the database creator.
mode	Locking mode, used internally while a database is being created.
status	Bit mask that shows whether a database is read only, off line, designated for use by a single user only, and so on. Some of the settings can be selected by the user with the *sp_dboption* stored procedure; others are internally set. (The SQL Server product documentation shows all the bit-mask values.)
status2	Another bit-mask–like status, with bits indicating additional database options. (Not shown in Figure 5-4.)
crdate	For user databases, this is the date when the database was created. For *tempdb*, this is the date and time SQL Server was last started. For other system databases, this date is not really useful. Depending on decisions made during installation, this could be the date Microsoft originally created the database prior to shipping the code, or it could be the date that you installed SQL Server.
reserved	Reserved for future use.
category	Another bit-mask–like status. Contains information about whether the database is involved with replication. (Not shown in Figure 5-4.)
cmptlevel	Compatibility level for the database. This concept is briefly discussed at the end of this chapter.
filename	Operating system path and name for the primary file.
suid	ID of SQL Server login that owns the database. (Note that the *sid* column (above) contains the ID of the creator of the database, which might or might not be the owner.) The column *suid* always refers to the current owner.
version	Internal version of SQL Server with which the database was created. (Not shown in Figure 5-4.)

Table 5-2.

Columns of the sysdatabases *table.*

Space Allocation

The space in a database is used for storing tables and indexes. As mentioned earlier in the chapter, space is managed in units called *extents*. An extent is made up of eight logically contiguous pages (or 64 KB of space). To make its space allocation more efficient, SQL Server 7 doesn't allocate entire extents to tables with small amounts of data. SQL Server 7 has two types of extents:

- **Uniform extents**   These extents are owned by a single object; all eight pages in the extent can be used by the owning object only.

- **Mixed extents**   These are shared by up to eight objects.

A new table or index is allocated pages from mixed extents. When the table or index grows to eight pages, all future allocations use uniform extents.

When a table or index needs more space, SQL Server needs to find some space that's available to be allocated. If the table or index is still less than eight pages total, SQL Server needs to find a mixed extent with space available. If the table or index is already eight pages or larger, SQL Server needs to find a free uniform extent. SQL Server uses two special types of pages to record which extents have been allocated and which type of use (mixed or uniform) the extent is available for:

- **Global Allocation Map (GAM) pages**   These pages record which extents have been allocated for any type of use. Each GAM covers 64,000 extents, or almost 4 GB of data. This means one GAM page exists for every 4 GB of size. A GAM has one bit for each extent in the interval it covers. If the bit is 1, the corresponding extent is in use; if the bit is 0, the extent is free.

- **Secondary Global Allocation Map (SGAM) pages**   These pages record which extents are currently used as mixed extents and have at least one unused page. Just like a GAM, each SGAM covers 64,000 extents, or almost 4 GB of data. The SGAM has 1 bit for each extent in the interval it covers. If the bit is 1, the extent is being used as a mixed extent and has free pages; if the bit is 0, the extent isn't being used as a mixed extent, or it's a mixed extent whose pages are all in use.

The following page shows the bit patterns each extent will have set in the GAM and SGAM based on its current use.

Current Use of Extent	GAM Bit Setting	SGAM Bit Setting
Free, not in use	0	0
Uniform extent, or full mixed extent	1	0
Mixed extent with free pages	1	1

If SQL Server needs to find a new, completely unused extent, it can use any extent with a corresponding bit value of 1 in the GAM page. If SQL Server needs to find a mixed extent with available space (one or more free pages), it finds an extent with a value in the GAM of 0 and a value in the SGAM of 1.

SQL Server can quickly locate the GAMs in a file, because a GAM is always the third page in any database file (page 2). And an SGAM is the fourth page (page 3). Another GAM appears every 64,000 extents (512,000 pages) after the first GAM on page 2, and another SGAM every 64,000 extents (512,000 pages) after the first SGAM on page 3. Page 0 in any file is the File Header page, and only one exists per file. Page 1 is a Page Free Space (PFS) page, which will be discussed shortly.

In Chapter 6, we'll continue to explore how individual pages within a table look, but because we're talking about space allocation here, we'll examine how to keep track of which pages belong to which tables. Index Allocation Map (IAM) pages map the extents in a database file used by a heap or index. Remember from Chapter 3 that a heap is a table without a clustered index. Each heap or index has one or more IAM pages recording all the extents allocated to the object. A heap or index has at least one IAM for each file on which it has extents. A heap or index can have more than one IAM on a file if the range of the extents exceeds the range that an IAM can record.

An IAM contains a small header, eight page-pointer slots, and a set of bits mapping a range of extents onto a file. The header has the address of the first extent in the range mapped by the IAM. The eight page-pointer slots might contain pointers to pages belonging to the relevant objects that are contained in mixed extents; only the first IAM for an object will have values in these pointers. Once an object takes up more than eight pages, all its extents are uniform extents—which means an object will never need more than eight pointers to pages in mixed extents. If rows have been deleted from a table, it can actually use fewer than eight of these pointers. Each bit of the bitmap represents an extent in the range, regardless of whether the extent is allocated to the object owning the IAM. If a bit is on, the relative extent in the range is allocated to the object owning the IAM; if a bit is off, the relative extent isn't allocated to the object owning the IAM.

For example, if the bit pattern in the first byte of the IAM is 1100 0000, it means that the first and second extents in the range covered by the IAM are allocated to the object owning the IAM and that extents 3 through 8 aren't allocated to the object owning the IAM.

IAM pages are allocated as needed for each object and are located randomly in the database file. Each IAM covers a possible range of 512,000 pages. *Sysindexes.FirstIAM* points to the first IAM page for an object. All the IAM pages for that object are linked in a chain.

> **NOTE**   In a heap, the data pages and the rows within them aren't in any specific order and aren't linked together. The only logical connection between data pages is recorded in the IAM pages.

Once extents have been allocated to an object, SQL Server can use pages in those extents to insert new data. If the data is to be inserted into a B-tree, the location of the new data is based on the ordering within the B-tree. If the data is to be inserted into a heap, the data can be inserted into any available space. PFS pages within a file record whether an individual page has been allocated and the amount of space free on each page. Each PFS page covers 8000 contiguous pages (almost 64 MB). For each page, the PFS has 1 byte recording whether the page is empty, 1–25 percent full, 26–50 percent full, 51–75 percent full, or more than 75 percent full. This information is used when SQL Server needs to find a page with free space available to hold a newly inserted row. The second page (page 1) of a file is a PFS page, as is every 8000th page thereafter.

Database Options

Twenty-two options exist at the database level to control certain behavior within that database. By default, all options are FALSE unless they were set to TRUE in the *model* database, in which case all databases created after the option was changed in *model* will have the same values. You can easily set some of these options by using SQL Server Enterprise Manager. You can set all of them directly by using the *sp_dboption* system stored procedure. All options correspond to bits in the *status* and *status2* columns of *sysdatabases*, although those bits can also show states that can't be set directly by the database owner (such as when the database is in the process of being recovered).

Some of the database options have corresponding SET options that you can turn on or off for a particular connection. Be aware that the ODBC or OLE DB drivers will turn a number of these SET options on by default, so applications will act as though the corresponding database option had already been set. Chapter 6 goes into more detail about the SET options that are set by the ODBC and OLE DB drivers.

Executing *sp_dboption* with no parameters shows all options that can be set:

```
> EXEC sp_dboption

Settable database options:
-------------------------------------
ANSI null default
ANSI nulls
ANSI warnings
auto create statistics
auto update statistics
autoclose
autoshrink
concat null yields null
cursor close on commit
dbo use only
default to local cursor
merge publish
offline
published
quoted identifier
read only
recursive triggers
select into/bulkcopy
single user
subscribed
torn page detection
trunc. log on chkpt.
```

Three of the options deal with the behavior of NULLs; these will be covered in much more detail in Chapter 6. The following list describes the meaning of each of the options:

ANSI warnings   When TRUE, errors or warnings are issued when conditions such as "division by zero" or "arithmetic overflow" occur.

auto create statistics   When TRUE, statistics are automatically created by the SQL Server optimizer on columns referenced in a query's WHERE clause. Adding statistics improves query performance because the SQL Server optimizer can better determine how to evaluate a query. By default, *auto create statistics* is true.

auto update statistics   When TRUE, existing statistics are automatically updated if the data in the tables has changed. SQL Server keeps a counter of the number of modifications that have been made to a table and uses it to determine when statistics are outdated. When FALSE, existing statistics are not automatically updated; instead, they can be updated manually. By default, *auto update statistics* is true. We'll discuss statistics in much more detail in Chapter 14.

autoclose   When TRUE, the database is closed and shut down cleanly when the last user of the database exits, thereby freeing any resources. By default, this option is automatically set to TRUE for all databases when SQL Server runs on Microsoft Windows 95 or Windows 98. When a user tries to use the database again, it automatically reopens. If the database was shut down cleanly, the database isn't initialized (reopened) until a user tries to use the database the next time SQL Server is restarted. The *autoclose* option is handy for desktop databases because it allows you to manage database files as normal files. You can move them, copy them to make backups, or even e-mail them to other users. However, you shouldn't use the *autoclose* option for databases accessed by an application that repeatedly makes and breaks connections to SQL Server. The overhead of closing and reopening the database between each connection will negatively affect performance.

autoshrink   When TRUE, the database files are candidates for periodic shrinking. Both data files and log files can be automatically shrunk by SQL Server. The only way to free space in the log files so that they can be shrunk is to back up the transaction log, or set *trunc. log on chkpt.* to TRUE. The log files shrink at the point the log is backed up or truncated.

cursor close on commit   When TRUE, any open cursors are automatically closed (in compliance with SQL-92) when a transaction is committed. By default, when this setting is FALSE, cursors remain open across transaction boundaries and close only when the connection is closed or when they are explicitly closed. This setting has no effect on ROLLBACK.

dbo use only   When TRUE, this option prevents all users except the database owner from subsequently using the database. Usually, this option is used only temporarily, during times when you want to make the database inaccessible to other users—for example, when you want to change table structures and need to keep users out until finished. (If you *never* want some other user to access the database, you simply wouldn't add that user to the *sysusers* table of that database. You wouldn't use *dbo use only*.)

default to local cursor   When TRUE, and cursors aren't specified as GLOBAL when created, the scope of the cursor is local to the batch, stored procedure, or trigger in which the cursor was created. The cursor name is valid only within this scope. The cursor can be referenced by local cursor variables in the batch, stored procedure, or trigger, or by a stored procedure output parameter. When FALSE, and cursors aren't specified as LOCAL when created, the scope of the cursor is global to the connection. The cursor name can be referenced in any stored procedure or batch executed by the connection. We'll discuss cursors in much greater detail in Chapter 11.

merge publish When TRUE, the database can be used for merge replication publications. The option is usually set automatically when using the replication wizards to set up a database for replication.

offline This option is typically used for databases on removable media such as CDs. Placing databases on line and off line allows them to be mounted and dismounted while SQL Server is running.

published This option permits the tables of a database to be published for replication. Like *merge publish*, *published* is not normally set by a database owner, but rather by the replication wizards.

quoted identifier When TRUE, identifiers can be delimited by double quotation marks, and literals must be delimited by single quotation marks. All strings that are delimited by double quotation marks are interpreted as object identifiers. Quoted identifiers don't have to follow the Transact-SQL rules for identifiers. They can be keywords and can include characters not normally allowed in Transact-SQL identifiers. You can't use double quotation marks to delimit literal string expressions; you must use single quotation marks to enclose literal strings. If a single quotation mark (') is part of the literal string, it can be represented by two single quotation marks ("). This setting must be TRUE if reserved keywords are used for object names in the database. When FALSE (default), identifiers can't be in quotation marks and must follow all Transact-SQL rules for identifiers. Literals can be delimited by either single or double quotation marks. Literal strings in expressions can be delimited by single or double quotation marks. If a literal string is delimited by double quotation marks, the string can contain embedded single quotation marks, such as apostrophes.

read only Use this option to prevent any operation in the database that would modify, insert, or delete data; create or drop database objects; or change database configuration settings. The data can be read but can't be changed in any way.

recursive triggers When TRUE, this option allows triggers to fire recursively. Indirect recursion occurs when a trigger fires and performs an action that causes a trigger on another table to fire, thereby causing an update to occur on the original table, which causes the original trigger to fire again. For example, an application updates table *T1*, which causes trigger *Trig1* to fire. *Trig1* updates table *T2*, which causes trigger *Trig2* to fire. *Trig2* in turn updates table *T1*, which causes *Trig1* to fire again. Direct recursion occurs when a trigger fires and performs an action that causes the same trigger to fire again. For example, an application updates table *T3*, which causes trigger *Trig3* to fire. *Trig3* updates table *T3* again, which causes trigger *Trig3* to fire again. When FALSE (default), triggers can't be fired recursively.

select into/bulkcopy This option allows certain nonlogged operations—such as using the UPDATETEXT or WRITETEXT commands without logging, using SELECT INTO with a permanent table, using fast bulk copy (bcp), or performing a table load. Using nonlogged operations obviously prevents subsequent recovery from a transaction log backup. After a nonlogged operation is performed, further BACKUP LOG commands are prohibited. Instead, you can use BACKUP DATABASE to back up the entire database. (Setting this option to TRUE does not prevent transaction log backups. You must have this option on and then actually perform an unlogged operation for SQL Server to prohibit the BACKUP LOG command.)

single user This option restricts the database's use to one active SQL Server connection.

subscribed This option permits a database to subscribe to a published (replicated) database.

torn page detection When TRUE, this option causes a bit to be flipped for each 512-byte sector in a database page (8 KB) whenever the page is written to disk. This option allows SQL Server to detect incomplete I/O operations caused by power failures or other system outages. If a bit is in the wrong state when the page is later read by SQL Server, this means the page was written incorrectly; a torn page has been detected. Although SQL Server database pages are 8 KB, disks perform I/O operations using 512-byte sectors. Therefore, 16 sectors are written per database page. A torn page can occur if the system crashes (for example, because of power failure) between the time the operating system writes the first 512-byte sector to disk and the completion of the 8-KB I/O operation. If the first sector of a database page is successfully written before the crash, it will appear that the database page on disk was updated, although it might not have succeeded. Using battery-backed disk caches can ensure that data is successfully written to disk or not written at all. In this case, don't set *torn page detection* to TRUE, as it isn't needed. If a torn page is detected, the database will need to be restored from backup because it will be physically inconsistent.

trunc. log on chkpt. When this option is set, every time a checkpoint occurs (when data pages in the cache that were modified since the last checkpoint are written to disk), transactions that have already been committed—and the log records flushed to disk—are purged from the log. After the log is purged, you can perform BACKUP/RESTORE operations only at the database level, not at the transaction log level. But setting this option does relieve you of having to worry about truncating the transaction log to keep it from filling up. You can't disable logging, because if an operation weren't logged, it couldn't be recovered or rolled back. Most of the time, when someone wants to disable logging, the real question is, "How can I make logging invisible and not demand any administration?" The *trunc. log on chkpt.* option usually accomplishes this: the log simply wraps and never requires intervention. Note that the log must be large enough to accommodate the single largest transaction so that it can be recovered or rolled back. This option is often used during application development; you can also use it if your backup strategy can rely solely on database backups, not transaction log backups.

The *trunc. log on chkpt.* option causes the transaction log to be truncated (committed transactions are removed) every time the CHECKPOINT process occurs. When *trunc. log on chkpt.* is set, a checkpoint occurs for the database every time the log becomes 70 percent full. SQL Server doesn't, however, issue the checkpoint if the log can't be truncated because of an outstanding transaction. When *trunc. log on chkpt.* is set, SQL Server also attempts a checkpoint when a "log full" error occurs. It can be useful to select this option while doing development work to prevent the log from growing. While the *trunc. log on chkpt.* option is set, the transaction log can't be backed up because the truncated transaction logs in the backups can't be used to recover from media failure. Issuing the BACKUP LOG statement produces an error message that instructs you to use the BACKUP DATABASE statement. The *tempdb* database is always truncated by the checkpoint process even if the *trunc. log on chkpt.* option is set to FALSE.

NOTE The only options that you can set for the *master* database are *autoclose, torn page detection,* and *trunc. log on chkpt.* The *tempdb* database can't be set to *read only, single user,* or *dbo use only.*

Changing Database Options

Only someone with the *sysadmin* or *dbowner* role can change an option. To change an option, you must specify the database name, option, and TRUE or FALSE. You need to specify only enough of the option name to ensure its recognition (even just a single letter in the case of, say, *published*). For example, to turn on *published, select into/bulkcopy,* and *ANSI null default,* you would type the following:

```
> EXEC sp_dboption 'testdb', 'pub', TRUE
> EXEC sp_dboption 'testdb', 'select into', TRUE
> EXEC sp_dboption 'testdb', 'null default', TRUE
```

To check that the options are set, you would type

```
> EXEC sp_dboption 'testdb'
```

and the following would appear:

```
The following options are set:
---------------------------------
select into/bulkcopy
ANSI null default
published
```

Executing the *sp_helpdb* stored procedure for a database shows some of the options that have been set to TRUE, but not all. (It shows only those options whose status bit is in *sysdatabase.status* and not those in *sysdatabases.status2*). However, *sp_helpdb* provides other useful information, such as database size, creation date, and database owner. Executing *sp_helpdb* with no parameters shows information about all the databases in that installation. The following databases exist on a new default installation of SQL Server, and *sp_helpdb* produces this output (though the created dates and sizes can vary):

```
> EXEC sp_helpdb
name        db_size owner dbid  created      status
--------    ------- ----- ----  -----------  ----------------------
master      8.25 MB sa    1     Jun 19 1998  trunc. log on chkpt.
model       1.50 MB sa    3     Jul  7 1998  no options set
msdb        9.75 MB sa    4     Jul  7 1998  trunc. log on chkpt.
Northwind   3.94 MB sa    6     Jul  7 1998  select into/bulkcopy,
                                             trunc. log on chkpt.
pubs        2.00 MB sa    5     Jul  7 1998  trunc. log on chkpt.
tempdb      8.50 MB sa    2     Jun 19 1998  select into/bulkcopy
```

Other Database Considerations

Keep these additional points in mind about databases on SQL Server.

Database Doesn't Equal Schema

The ANSI SQL-92 standard includes the notion of a *schema*, or more precisely, an *SQL-schema*, which in many ways is similar to SQL Server's database concept. Per the ANSI standard, an SQL-schema is a collection of *descriptors*, each of which is described in the documentation as "a coded description of an SQL object." Basically, a schema is a collection of SQL objects, such as tables, views, and constraints. ANSI SQL-schemas are similar to SQL Server databases.

SQL Server 6.5 introduced support for the ANSI SQL-schema. However, the notion of a database within SQL Server is long standing and much richer than its concept of a schema. SQL Server provides more extensive facilities for working with a database than for working with a schema. SQL Server includes commands, stored procedures, and powerful tools such as SQL Server Enterprise Manager that are designed around the fundamental SQL Server concept of a database. These tools control backup, loading, security, enumeration of objects, and configuration; counterparts don't exist for schemas. The SQL Server implementation of schema is essentially a check box feature providing conformance with the ANSI standard; it's not the preferred choice. Generally speaking, you'll want to use databases, not schemas.

Removable Media

After you've created a database, you can package it so that it can be distributed via removable media such as CD. This can be useful for distributing large datasets. For example, perhaps you want to put a detailed sales history on a CD database and send a copy to each of your branch offices. Typically, such a database would be read-only (because CDs are read-only), although that isn't absolutely required.

To create a removable media database, you create the database using the stored procedure *sp_create_removable* instead of the CREATE DATABASE statement. When calling the procedure, you must specify three or more files (one for the system catalog tables, one for the transaction log, and one or more for the user data tables). You must have a separate file for the system tables because when the removable media database is distributed and installed, the system tables will be installed to a writable device (so that users can be added, permissions can be granted, and so on), even though the data itself is likely to remain on a read-only device.

Because removable media devices such as CDs are typically slower than hard drives, it's also possible to distribute on removable media a database that will then be moved to a hard disk. If you're using a writable removable device, such as an optical drive, be sure that the device and controller are both on the Hardware Compatibility List (HCL). We also recommend that you run the hard-disk test discussed in Chapter 4 on any such device. The failure rates of removable media devices are typically higher than those for standard hard disks.

A database can use multiple CDs or removable media devices. However, all media must be available simultaneously. For example, if a database uses three CDs, the system needs to have three CD drives so that all discs can be available when the database is used.

You can use the *sp_certify_removable* stored procedure to ensure that a database created with the intention of being burned onto a CD or other removable media meets the restrictions just noted. Use the *sp_dbinstall* stored procedure the first time someone at a site wants to use a database sent on removable media. Subsequently, to use a removable media database, use the *offline* option of the *sp_dboption* stored procedure to toggle its availability. This book's companion CD contains an example script that creates a database, ensures that it's appropriate for removable media use, and then installs it on your system. However, a database with no tables or data is pretty useless, so in the next chapter you'll learn how to create tables.

Compatibility Level

SQL Server 7 includes a tremendous amount of new functionality and changes certain behaviors that existed prior to version 7. To provide the most complete level of backward compatibility, Microsoft allows you set the compatibility level of a database to one of three modes: 70, 65, or 60. A database that has been upgraded (using the Upgrade Wizard) will have its compatibility level set to the SQL Server version under which the database was last used (either 65 or 60).

All the examples and explanations in this book assume that you're using a database that's in 70 compatibility mode, unless otherwise mentioned. If you find that your SQL statements behave differently than the ones in the book, you should first verify that your database is in 70 compatibility mode by executing this procedure:

```
exec sp_dbcmptlevel 'database name'
```

To change to a different compatibility level, run the procedure using a second argument of one of the three modes:

```
exec sp_dbcmptlevel 'database name', compatibility mode
```

NOTE Not all changes in behavior from older versions of SQL Server can be duplicated by changing the compatibility level. For a complete list of the behavioral differences in the three modes, please see the online documentation for the *sp_dbcmptlevel* procedure.

The compatibility-level options are meant to only allow a transition period while you're upgrading a database and application to SQL Server 7. We strongly suggest that you carefully consider your use of this option and make every effort to change your applications so that compatibility options are no longer needed. Microsoft doesn't guarantee that these options will continue to work in future versions of SQL Server.

Summary

A database is a collection of objects, such as tables, views, and stored procedures. Although a typical SQL Server installation will have many databases, it will always include the following three: *master*, *model*, and *tempdb*. (An installation will usually also include *pubs*, *Northwind*, and *msdb*.) Every database has its own transaction log; integrity constraints among objects keep a database logically consistent.

Databases are stored in operating system files in a one-to-many relationship. Each database has at least one file for the data and one file for the transaction log. You can easily increase and decrease the size of databases and their files. Databases and their files can grow and shrink either manually or automatically.

Now that you understand database basics, it's time to move on to tables, the fundamental data structures with which you work.

CHAPTER SIX

TABLES

In this chapter, we'll look at some in-depth implementation examples. But let's start with a basic introduction to tables. Simply put, a *table* is a collection of data about a specific *entity* (person, place, or thing) that has a discrete number of named *attributes* (for example, quantity or type). Tables are at the heart of Microsoft SQL Server and the relational model in general. Tables are easy to understand—they're just like the everyday lists you make for yourself. In SQL Server, a table is often referred to as a *base table* to emphasize where data is stored. Calling it a base table also distinguishes the table from a *view,* a virtual table that's an internal query referencing one or more base tables.

Attributes of a table's data (such as color, size, quantity, order date, and supplier's name) take the form of named *columns* in the table. Each instance of data in a table is represented as a single entry, or *row* (formally called a *tuple*). In a true relational database, every row in a table is unique, and each row has a unique identifier called the *primary key.* (SQL Server, in accordance with the ANSI SQL standard, doesn't require that you make a row unique or declare a primary key. However, because both of these concepts are central to the relational model, you should always implement them.)

Most tables will have some relationship to other tables. For example, in an order-entry system, the *orders* table likely has a *customer_number* column in which it keeps track of the customer number for an order; *customer_number* also appears in the *customer* table. Assuming that *customer_number* is a unique identifier, or the primary key, of the *customer* table, a foreign key relationship is established by which the *orders* and *customer* tables can subsequently be joined.

So much for the 30-second database design primer. You can find plenty of books that discuss logical database and table design, but this isn't one of them. We assume that you understand basic database theory and design and that you generally know what your tables will look like. The rest of this chapter discusses the internals of tables in SQL Server and implementation considerations.

Creating Tables

SQL Server uses the ANSI SQL standard CREATE TABLE syntax. SQL Server Enterprise Manager provides a front-end, fill-in-the-blanks table designer, which might make your job easier. Ultimately, the SQL syntax is always sent to SQL Server to create a table. You can create a table directly using a tool such as OSQL, ISQL, or the Query Analyzer; from SQL Server Enterprise Manager; or using a third-party data modeling tool (such as ER*win* or Microsoft Visual InterDev) that transmits the SQL syntax under the cover of a friendly interface.

In this chapter, we emphasize direct use of the data definition language (DDL) rather than discussing the interface tools. You should keep all DDL commands in a script so that you can run them easily at a later time to re-create the table. (Even if you use one of the friendly front-end tools, it's critical that you can later re-create the table.) SQL Server Enterprise Manager and other front-end tools can create and save operating system files with the SQL DDL commands necessary to create the object. This DDL is essentially source code, and you should treat it as such. Keep a backup copy. You should also consider keeping these files under version control using a source control product such as Microsoft Visual SourceSafe or PVCS from Micro Focus (formerly INTERSOLV).

At the basic level, creating a table requires little more than knowing what you want to name it, what columns it will contain, and what range of values (domain) each column will be able to store. Here's the basic syntax for creating the *customer* table, with three fixed-length character (*char*) columns. (Note that this table definition isn't necessarily the most efficient way to store data because it always requires 46 bytes per entry plus a few bytes of overhead regardless of the actual length of the data.)

```
CREATE TABLE customer
(
name        char(30),
phone       char(12),
emp_id      char(4)
)
```

This example shows each column on a separate line for readability. As far as the SQL Server parser is concerned, whitespaces created by tabs, carriage returns, and the Spacebar are identical. From the system's standpoint, the following CREATE TABLE example is identical to the one above; but it's harder to read from a user's standpoint:

```
CREATE TABLE customer (name char(30), phone char(12), emp_id char(4))
```

This simple example shows just the basics of creating a table. We'll see many more detailed examples later in this chapter.

Naming Tables and Columns

A table is always created within a database and is owned by one particular user. Normally, the owner is the user who created the table, but anyone with the *sysadmin* or *db_owner* role can create a table owned by another user. A database can contain multiple tables with the same name, as long as the tables have different owners. The full name of a table has three parts, in this form:

database.owner.tablename

For example, say that a user (with the username *Kalen*) created a sample *customer* table in the *pubs* sample database. This user's table would have the *pubs.kalen.customer* three-part name. (If this user is also the database owner, *pubs.dbo.customer* would be her table's name because *dbo* is the special username for the database owner in every database.)

The first two parts of the three-part name specification have default values. The default for the name of the database is whatever database context you're currently working in. The table owner actually has two possible defaults. If no table owner name is specified when referencing a table, SQL Server will assume that either you or the owner of the database owns the table. For example, if our hypothetical user owns the *customer* table and her database context is the *pubs*, she can refer to the table simply as *customer*.

NOTE To access a table owned by anyone other than yourself or the database owner, you must include the owner name along with the table name.

Column names should be descriptive, and because you'll use them repeatedly, you should avoid wordiness. The name of the column (or any object in SQL Server, such as a table or a view) can be whatever you choose, as long as the name conforms to the SQL Server rules for identifiers: it must consist of a combination of 1 through 128 letters, digits, or the symbols #, $, @, or _. (For more specific identifier rules, see "Using Identifiers" in SQL Server Books Online. The discussions there and in the *Microsoft SQL Server Transact-SQL and Utilities Reference* are true for all SQL Server object names, not just for column names.)

Reserved Keywords

Certain reserved keywords, such as *table*, *create*, *select*, and *update*, have special meaning to the SQL Server parser, and collectively they make up the SQL language implementation. If at all possible, you shouldn't use reserved keywords for your object names. In addition to the SQL Server reserved keywords, the SQL-92 standard has its own list of reserved keywords. In some cases, this list is more restrictive than SQL Server's list; in other cases, it's less restrictive.

SQL Server Books Online has a complete list of both SQL Server's reserved keywords and the SQL-92 standard's list.

Watch out for SQL-92's reserved keywords. They aren't reserved keywords in SQL Server yet, but they could become reserved keywords in a future SQL Server version. Using a SQL-92 reserved keyword might require that you alter your application before upgrading it if the word has become a SQL Server reserved keyword.

Delimited Identifiers

You can't use keywords in your object names unless you use a delimited identifier. In fact, if you use a delimited identifier, not only can you use keywords as identifiers, but you can use any other string—whether it follows the rules for identifiers or not—as an object name. This includes spaces and other nonalphanumeric characters normally not allowed. Two types of delimited identifiers exist:

- Bracketed identifiers are delimited by square brackets ([*object name*]).

- Quoted identifiers are delimited by double quotation marks ("*object name*").

You can use bracketed identifiers in any environment, but to use quoted identifiers, you must enable a special option using SET QUOTED_IDENTIFIER ON. Once you have turned on QUOTED_IDENTIFIER, double quotes will always be interpreted as referencing an object. To delimit string or date constants, you have to use single quotes. Let's look at some examples. Because *column* is a reserved keyword, the first statement that follows would be illegal in all circumstances, and the second one would be illegal unless QUOTED_IDENTIFIER was on. The third statement would be legal in any circumstances.

```
CREATE TABLE customer (name char(30), column char(12), emp_id char(4))
```

```
CREATE TABLE customer (name char(30), "column" char(12), emp_id char(4))
```

```
CREATE TABLE customer (name char(30), [column] char(12), emp_id char(4))
```

The ODBC driver that comes with SQL Server sets the option QUOTED_IDENTIFIER to ON by default, but some of the SQL Server–specific tools will set it to OFF. You can determine whether this option is on or off for your session by executing the following command:

```
DBCC useroptions
```

Some History

Prior to version 7.0 of SQL Server, the documentation discussed two categories of special words, which were called *keywords* and *reserved words*. The keywords were already part of the product, and reserved words were listed as having a good chance of becoming a part of the product in a future version.

The rationale behind reserved words was that for version 6.0, the developers needed to add a lot of new keywords to support the latest functionality. In general, these words hadn't been reserved in version 4.21. Adding so many new keywords made it tough for many sites, because they had to modify their applications by changing these keywords in order to upgrade. Although it probably seemed capricious and unwarranted to add keywords that simply *might* be used in the future, the developers knew that *some* new functionality would be added in future versions.

Through version 6.5, the documentation continued to designate reserved words for future use. Now in version 7.0, SQL Server is following the ANSI SQL guidelines much more closely. So instead of documenting separate lists of reserved words and keywords, the documentation can just rely on what ANSI has already specified.

If you're using the Query Analyzer, you can check your setting by either running the command on the previous page or choosing the Configure command from the File menu and examining the Connection tab.

Theoretically, you could always use delimited identifiers with all object and column names, and then you'd never have to worry about reserved keywords. However, we don't recommend this. Many third-party tools for SQL Server don't handle quoted identifiers well. Using quoted identifiers might make upgrading to future versions of SQL Server more difficult. During the upgrade process to SQL Server 7, objects such as views and stored procedures are automatically dropped and re-created so that they include the structures of the latest version.

When you use quoted identifiers, upgrading can't be fully automated and you must tell the Upgrade Wizard whether it should assume that QUOTED_IDENTIFIER is on. If you don't know, or if you have a mixture of objects, you can tell the wizard to use a mixed mode. This means that the Upgrade Wizard will first try interpreting all objects with double quotation marks as though the option is on, and only if that's unsuccessful will it assume that the option is off for that object. This interpretation might not always result in the stored procedure or view having the same meaning as was intended.

Rather than using delimited identifiers to protect against reserved keyword problems, you should simply adopt some simple naming conventions. For example, you can precede column names with the first few letters of the table name and an underscore (_). Not only does this naming style make the column or object name more readable, but it also greatly reduces your chances of encountering a keyword or reserved word conflict.

Naming Conventions

Many organizations and multiuser development projects adopt standard naming conventions, which is generally good practice. For example, assigning a standard moniker of *cust_id* to represent a customer number in every table clearly shows that all the tables share common data. On the other hand, if an organization used several monikers in the tables to represent a customer number, such as *cust_id*, *cust_num*, *customer_number*, and *customer_#*, it wouldn't be as obvious that these monikers represented common data.

One naming convention is the Hungarian-style notation for column names. Hungarian-style notation is a widely used practice in C programming, whereby variable names include information about their datatypes. Hungarian-style notation uses names such as *sint_nn_custnum* to indicate that the *custnum* column is a small integer (*smallint* of 2 bytes) and is NOT NULL (doesn't allow nulls). Although this practice makes good sense in C programming, it defeats the datatype independence that SQL Server provides; therefore, we recommend *against* using it.

Suppose, for example, that after the table is built and applications have been written, you discover that the *custnum* column requires a 4-byte integer (*int*) instead of a 2-byte small integer. You can re-create the table relatively easily and define the column as an *int* instead of a *smallint*. (Alternatively, you can use the ALTER TABLE command to modify the datatype of the existing table.) SQL Server stored procedures will handle the different datatype automatically. Applications using ODBC, OLE DB, or DB-Library that bind the retrieved column to a character or integer datatype will be unaffected. The applications would need to change if they bound the column to a small integer variable because the variable's type would need to be larger. Therefore, you should try not to be overly conservative with variable datatypes, especially in your client applications. You should be most concerned with the type on the server side; the type in the application can be larger and will automatically accommodate smaller values. By overloading the column name with datatype information, which is readily available from the system catalogs, the insulation from the underlying datatype is compromised. (You could, of course, change the datatype from a *smallint* to an *int*, but then the Hungarian-style name would no longer accurately reflect the column definition. Changing the column name would then result in the need to change application code, stored procedures, or both.)

Datatypes

SQL Server provides many datatypes, as shown in Table 6-1 on the following page. Choosing the appropriate datatype is simply a matter of mapping the domain of values you need to store to the corresponding datatype. In choosing datatypes, you want to avoid wasting storage space while allowing enough space for a sufficient range of possible values over the life of your application.

Datatype Synonyms

SQL Server syntactically accepts as datatypes both the words listed as synonyms and the base datatypes shown in Table 6-1, but it uses only the type listed as the datatype. For example, you can define a column as *character(1)*, *character*, or *char(1)*, and SQL Server will accept them all as valid syntax. Internally, however, the expression is considered *char(1)*, and subsequent querying of the SQL Server system catalogs for the datatype will show it as *char(1)*, regardless of the syntax that you used when you created it.

Globally Unique Identifiers

Most available datatypes in SQL Server are well documented, so we'll leave it up to you to find additional details in the product documentation. However, one special datatype merits a bit more discussion.

Using a globally unique identifier (GUID)—also called a universal unique identifier (UUID)—is becoming an important way to identify data, objects, software applications, and applets in distributed systems. A GUID is a 128-bit (16-byte) value generated in a way that, for all practical purposes, guarantees uniqueness worldwide, even among disconnected computers. SQL Server 7 supports a datatype called *uniqueidentifier* for storing a globally unique identifier. The Transact-SQL language supports the system function NEWID(), which can be used to generate a *uniqueidentifier* value. A column or variable of datatype *uniqueidentifier* can be initialized to a value in one of the following two ways:

- Using the system-supplied function NEWID()
- Using a string constant in the following form (32 hexadecimal digits separated by hyphens as shown): xxxxxxxx-xxxx-xxxx-xxxx-xxxxxxxxxxxx (Each *x* is a hexadecimal digit in the range 0 through 9 or *a* through *f*.)

Type of Data	Base Datatype	Synonyms	Range/Domain	Storage Size
Integer	int	integer	Whole numbers from −2,147,483,648 to 2,147,483,647	4 bytes
	smallint		Whole numbers from −32,768 to 32,767	2 bytes
	tinyint		Whole numbers from 0 to 255	1 byte
	bit		0 or 1	Bit datatypes share a byte with other bit columns of the same table. Hence, 8-bit columns of the same table use 1 byte of storage. If the table has only 1-bit columns, it still uses 1 byte, although 7 more such columns could be added "for free."
Packed decimal (exact numeric)	decimal (p,s)	dec numeric	Whole or fractional numbers from −10^{38} to 10^{38}	2–17 bytes, depending on specified precision, p, which can range to 38 digits. On average, 1 byte of storage is required per every 2 digits of precision.
Floating point (approx numeric)	float (15-digit precision)	float(n), where n is between 8 and 15 Double precision	Approximations of numbers from −1.79E^{308} to 1.79E^{308} Positive range: 2.23E$^{−308}$ to 1.79E^{308} Negative range: −2.23E$^{−308}$ to −1.79E^{308}	8 bytes
	real (7-digit precision)	float(n), where n is between 1 and 7	Approximations of numbers from −3.40E^{38} to 3.40E^{38} Positive range: 1.18E$^{−38}$ to 3.40E^{38} Negative range: −1.18E$^{−38}$ to −3.40E^{38}	4 bytes
Character (fixed length)	char(n)	character (n) character [character without a specific size is synonymous to a 1-character field, char(1)].	Up to 8000 characters, as designated by n, of the installed character set	1 byte per character n declared, even if partially unused.
Character (variable length)	varchar(n)	character varying (n), char varying (n)	Up to 8000 characters, as designated by n, of the installed character set	1 byte per character stored. Declared but unused characters do not consume storage.
Unicode character strings	nchar(n)	national character (n), national char(n)	Up to 4000 characters	2 bytes per character declared.
	nvarchar(n)	national character varying (n), national char varying (n)	Up to 4000 characters	2 bytes per character declared. Declared but unused do not use storage.
	ntext	national text	Up to 2^30-1 (1,073,741,823) characters	See text for description.

Table 6-1.

SQL Server datatypes.

Type of Data	Base Datatype	Synonyms	Range/Domain	Storage Size
Monetary	money		Numbers with accuracy to one ten-thousandth of a unit (four decimal places), typically used to store currency values. From −922,337,203,685,477.5808 to 922,337,203,685,477.5807	8 bytes
	smallmoney		Numbers with accuracy to one ten-thousandth of a unit (four decimal places), typically used to store currency values. From −214,748.3648 to 214,748.3647	4 bytes
Date and Time	datetime		Combined date and time representation. (SQL Server does not have separate DATE and TIME datatypes.) Date part: 01-JAN-1753 to 31-DEC-9999. Time part: Number of milliseconds since midnight of the given date	8 bytes
	smalldatetime		Combined date and time representation. Date part: 01-JAN-1900 to 06-JUN-2079. Time part: Number of minutes since midnight of the given date	4 bytes
Binary (fixed length)	binary[n]		Any binary representation (bit patterns) up to 255 bytes	n bytes, even if n is partially unused.
Binary (variable length)	varbinary[n]	binary varying	Any binary representation (bit patterns) up to 255 bytes	The number of bytes actually stored. No storage for space declared but not used.
Long text/BLOB	text and image		Text: Character data up to $2^{31}-1$ ($2,147,483,647$) characters. Image: Binary data up to $2^{31}-1$ ($2,147,483,647$) characters. The text and image datatypes are always variable length.	If not null, a 16-byte pointer is used on the data page, plus however many 8-KB pages are required to store the actual length. Text and image pages can be shared with other text and image data from the same table.
Numerics	cursor		A reference to a cursor, can be used for variables only, not table definitions.	
	timestamp		A database-wide unique number.	8 bytes
	uniqueidentifier		A globally unique identifier.	16 bytes

This datatype can be quite cumbersome to work with, and the only operations that are allowed against a *uniqueidentifier* value are comparisons (=, <>, <, >, <=, >=) and checking for NULL. (The online product documentation states that only the equality and inequality operators, = and <>, are allowed for *uniqueidentifier* columns, but this is incorrect. In fact, you can even sort by a *uniqueidentifier* column.) However, using this datatype internally can have several advantages.

One advantage is that the values are guaranteed to be globally unique for any machine on a network, because the last six bits of a *uniqueidentifier* value make up the node number for the machine. On a machine with a network interface card (NIC), the node is the unique IEEE 802 identifier of that card. On a machine without a NIC (for example, a home computer that connects to the Internet via modem), the node is a pseudo-random, 48-bit value that isn't guaranteed to be unique now but is highly likely to be unique for the near future.

Another advantage is that the list of *uniqueidentifier* values can't be exhausted. This is *not* the case with other datatypes frequently used as unique identifiers. In fact, this datatype is used internally by SQL Server for row-level merge replication. A *uniqueidentifier* column can have a special property called the ROWGUIDCOL property; at most, one *uniqueidentifier* column can have this property per table. The ROWGUIDCOL property can be specified as part of the column definition in CREATE TABLE and ALTER TABLE ADD *column* or added or dropped for an existing column through ALTER TABLE ALTER COLUMN.

A *uniqueidentifier* column with the ROWGUIDCOL property can be referenced using the keyword ROWGUIDCOL in a query. This is similar to referencing an identity column through the IDENTITYCOL keyword. The ROWGUIDCOL property does *not* imply any automatic value generation, and if automatic value generation is needed, the NEWID() function should be defined as the default value of the column. You can have multiple *uniqueidentifier* columns per table, but only one of them can have the ROWGUIDCOL property. You can use the *uniqueidentifier* datatype for whatever reason you come up with, but if you're using one to identify the current row, an application must have a generic way to ask for it without needing to know the column name. That's what the ROWGUIDCOL property does.

Variable-Length vs. Fixed-Length Datatypes

Deciding to use a variable-length or a fixed-length datatype isn't always straightforward or obvious. As a general rule, variable-length datatypes are most appropriate when you expect significant variance in the size of the data for a column and when the data in the column won't be frequently changed.

Using variable-length datatypes can yield important storage savings. Choosing them can sometimes result in a minor performance loss and at other times can result in improved performance. A row with variable-length columns requires special offset entries to be internally maintained. These entries keep track of the actual length of the column. Calculating and maintaining the offsets requires slightly more overhead than a pure fixed-length row, which needs no such offsets at all. This task requires a few addition and subtraction operations to maintain the offset value. However, the extra overhead of maintaining these offsets is generally inconsequential, and this alone would not make a significant difference on most, if not all, systems.

On the other hand, using variable-length columns can sometimes improve performance because they can allow more rows to fit on a page. But the efficiency results from more than simply requiring less disk space. A data page for SQL Server is 8 KB (8192 bytes), of which 8096 bytes are available to store data. (The rest is for internal use to keep track of structural information about the page and the object to which it belongs.) One I/O operation brings back the entire page. If you can fit 80 rows on a page, a single I/O operation brings back 80 rows. But if you can fit 160 rows on a page, one I/O operation is essentially twice as efficient. In operations that scan for data and return lots of adjacent rows, this can amount to a significant performance improvement. The more rows you can fit per page, the better your I/O and cache-hit efficiency will be.

For example, consider a simple customer table. Suppose you could define it in two ways, fixed-length and variable-length, as shown in Figure 6-1 and in Figure 6-2 on the following page.

```
CREATE TABLE customer
(
cust_id        smallint   NOT NULL,
cust_name      char(50)   NOT NULL,
cust_addr1     char(50)   NOT NULL,
cust_addr2     char(50)   NOT NULL,
cust_city      char(50)   NOT NULL,
cust_state     char(2)    NOT NULL,
cust_zip       char(10)   NOT NULL,
cust_phone     char(20)   NOT NULL,
cust_fax       char(20)   NOT NULL,
cust_email     char(30)   NOT NULL,
cust_web_url   char(20)   NOT NULL
)
```

Figure 6-1.
A customer table with fixed-length columns.

```
CREATE TABLE customer
(
cust_id        smallint      NOT NULL,
cust_name      varchar(50)   NOT NULL,
cust_addr1     varchar(50)   NOT NULL,
cust_addr2     varchar(50)   NOT NULL,
cust_city      varchar(50)   NOT NULL,
cust_state     char(2)       NOT NULL,
cust_zip       varchar(10)   NOT NULL,
cust_phone     varchar(20)   NOT NULL,
cust_fax       varchar(20)   NOT NULL,
cust_email     varchar(30)   NOT NULL,
cust_web_url   varchar(20)   NOT NULL
)
```

Figure 6-2.
A customer table with variable-length columns.

Columns that contain addresses, names, or Internet URLs all have data that varies significantly in length. Let's look at the differences between choosing fixed-length columns vs. choosing variable-length columns. In Figure 6-1, using all fixed-length columns, every row uses 304 bytes for data, regardless of the number of characters actually inserted into the row. Furthermore, SQL Server needs an additional 10 bytes of overhead for every row in this table, so the rows will need a total of 314 bytes for storage. But assume that even though the table must accommodate addresses and names up to the specified size, on average, the actual entries are only half the maximum size.

In Figure 6-2, assume that for all the variable-length (*varchar*) columns, the average entry is actually only about half the maximum. Instead of a row length of 304 bytes, the average length is 184 bytes. This length is computed as follows: the *smallint* and *char(2)* columns total 4 bytes. The *varchar* columns' maximum total length is 300, half of which is 150 bytes. And a 2-byte overhead exists for each of nine *varchar* columns, for 18 bytes. Add 2 more bytes for any row that has one or more variable-length columns. In addition, this row requires another 10 bytes of overhead, regardless of the presence of variable-length fields. (This is the same 10 bytes of overhead needed in the case of all fixed-length columns; in other words, all rows have these same 10 bytes of constant overhead.) So the total is 4 + 150 + 18 + 2 + 10, or 184. (The actual meaning of each of these bytes of overhead will be discussed later in this chapter.)

In the fixed-length example in Figure 6-1, you always fit 25 rows on a data page (8096/314, discarding the remainder). In the variable-length example in Figure 6-2, you can fit an average of 44 rows per page (8096/184). The table using variable-length columns will consume about half as many pages in storage, a single I/O operation will retrieve almost twice as many rows, and a page cached in memory is twice as likely to contain the row you're looking for.

When choosing lengths for columns, don't be wasteful—but don't be cheap, either. Allow for future needs, and realize that if the additional length doesn't change how many rows will fit on a page, the additional size is free anyway. Consider again the examples in Figures 6-1 and 6-2. The *cust_id* was declared as a *smallint*, meaning that its maximum positive value is 32,767 (unfortunately, SQL Server doesn't provide any unsigned *int* or unsigned *smallint* datatypes), and it consumes 2 bytes of storage. Although 32,767 customers might seem like a lot to a new company, the company might be surprised by its own success and, in a couple of years, find out that 32,767 is too limited.

The database designers might regret that they tried to save 2 bytes and didn't simply make the datatype an *int*, using 4 bytes but with a maximum positive value of 2,147,483,647. They'll be especially disappointed if they realize they didn't really save any space. If you compute the rows-per-page calculations just discussed, increasing the row size by 2 bytes, you'll see that the same number of rows still fit on a page. The additional 2 bytes are free—they were simply wasted space before. They never cause fewer rows per page in the fixed-length example, and they'll rarely cause fewer rows per page even in the variable-length case.

So which strategy wins? Potentially better update performance, or more rows per page? Like most questions of this nature, no one answer is right. It depends on your application. If you understand the tradeoffs, you'll be able to make the best choice. Now that you know the issues, this general rule merits repeating: variable-length datatypes are most appropriate when you expect significant variance in the size of the data for that column and when the column won't be updated frequently.

Much Ado About NULL

The issue of whether to allow NULL has become an almost religious one for many in the industry, and no doubt the discussion here will outrage a few people. However, our intention isn't to engage the philosophical debate. Pragmatically, dealing with NULL brings added complexity to the storage engine, because SQL Server keeps a special bitmap in every row to indicate which nullable columns actually *are* NULL. If NULLs are allowed, SQL Server must decode this bitmap for every row accessed. Allowing NULL also adds complexity in application code, which can often lead to bugs. You must always add special logic to account for the case of NULL.

You, as the database designer, might understand the nuances of NULL and three-valued logic when used in aggregate functions, when doing joins, and when searching by values. However, you need to consider whether your development staff understands as well. We recommend, if possible, that you use all NOT NULL columns and define *default* values (discussed later in this chapter) for missing or unknown entries (and possibly make such character columns *varchar* if the default value is significantly different in size from the typical entered value).

In any case, it's good practice to explicitly declare NOT NULL or NULL when creating a table. If no such declaration exists, SQL Server assumes NOT NULL. (In other words, no NULLs will be allowed.) However, you can set the default to allow NULLs by using a session setting or a database option. The ANSI SQL standard says that if neither is specified, NULL should be assumed, but as mentioned, this isn't SQL Server's default. If you script your DDL and then run it against another server that has a different default setting, you'll get different results if you don't explicitly declare NULL or NOT NULL in the column definition.

Several database options and session settings can control SQL Server's behavior regarding NULL values. You set database options using the system procedure *sp_dboption*. And you enable session settings for one connection at a time using the SET command.

The database option *ANSI null default* corresponds to the two session settings ANSI_NULL_DFLT_ON or ANSI_NULL_DFLT_OFF. When the *ANSI null default* database option is false (the default setting for SQL Server), new columns created with the ALTER TABLE and CREATE TABLE statements are, by default, NOT NULL if the nullability status of the column isn't explicitly specified. SET ANSI_NULL_DFLT_OFF and SET ANSI_NULL_DFLT_ON are mutually exclusive options, yet both options exist to determine whether the database option should be overridden. When on, each option forces the opposite option off. Neither option, when set off, turns the opposite option on. Instead, turning an option off only discontinues the current on setting.

Use the function GETANSINULL() to determine the default nullability for your current session. This function returns 1 when new columns will allow null values and the column or datatype nullability isn't explicitly defined when the table is created or altered. We strongly recommend declaring NULL or NOT NULL explicitly when you create a column. This removes all ambiguity and ensures that you're in control of how the table will be built regardless of the default nullability setting.

The database option *concat null yields null* corresponds to the session setting SET CONCAT_NULL_YIELDS_NULL. When CONCAT_NULL_YIELDS_NULL is on, concatenating a NULL value with a string yields a NULL result. For example, SELECT 'abc' + NULL yields NULL. When SET CONCAT_NULL_YIELDS_NULL is off, concatenating a NULL value with a string yields the string itself. (The NULL value is treated as an empty string.) For example, SELECT 'abc' + NULL yields *abc*. If the session level setting isn't specified, the value of the database option *concat null yields null* applies. Also, if SET CONCAT_NULL_YIELDS_NULL is off, SQL Server uses the *concat null yields null* setting of *sp_dboption*.

The database option *ANSI nulls* corresponds to the session setting SET ANSI_NULLS. When true, all comparisons to a null value evaluate to NULL (unknown). When false, comparisons of non-Unicode values to a null value evaluate to TRUE if both values are NULL. In addition, when this value is TRUE, your code must use the condition IS NULL to determine whether a column has a NULL value. When this value is FALSE, SQL Server allows "= NULL" as a synonym for "IS NULL" and "<> NULL" as a synonym for "IS NOT NULL." You can see this behavior yourself by looking at the *titles* table in the *pubs* database. The *titles* table has two rows with a NULL price. The first batch of statements that follows, when executed from the Query Analyzer, should return two rows, and the second batch should return no rows:

```
-- First batch will return 2 rows
use pubs
set ansi_nulls off
go
select * from titles where price = null
go

--Second batch will return no rows
use pubs
set ansi_nulls on
go
select * from titles where price = null
go
```

A fourth session setting is ANSI_DEFAULTS. Setting this to ON is a shortcut for enabling both ANSI_NULLS and ANSI_NULL_DEFAULT_ON, as well as other session settings not related to NULL handling. SQL Server's ODBC driver and the SQL Server OLE DB provider automatically set ANSI_DEFAULTS to ON. You can change the ANSI_NULLS setting when defining your DSN. Two of the client tools supplied with SQL Server (Query Analyzer and the text-based *osql*) use the SQL Server ODBC driver but then internally turn off some of these options. To see which options are enabled for the tool you're using, you can run the following command:

```
DBCC USEROPTIONS
```

Here's a sample of the output it might return:

```
Set Option                    Value
-------------------------     ------------------------
textsize                      64512
language                      us english
dateformat                    mdy
datefirst                     7
ansi_null_dflt_on             SET
ansi_warnings                 SET
ansi_padding                  SET
ansi_nulls                    SET
concat_null_yields_null       SET
```

WARNING Although internally SQL Server's default behavior is to *not* allow NULLs unless specifically declared in the CREATE TABLE statement, you might never see this behavior in action. Because SQL Server Query Analyzer, the basic tool for submitting SQL code to SQL Server, is ODBC-based, it automatically turns on the ANSI_NULL_DEFAULT_ON option. This setting means that all your new columns will allow NULLs by default. We can't overemphasize that you're best bet for avoiding confusion is to *always* state explicitly in your table definition whether NULLs should be allowed.

The database compatibility level controls two additional aspects of how SQL Server handles NULL values, as determined by the system procedure *sp_dbcmptlevel*. If the compatibility level is set to 70, the nullability of *bit* columns without explicit nullability is determined by either the session setting of SET ANSI_NULL_DFLT_ON or SET ANSI_NULL_DFLT_OFF or the database setting of *ANSI null default*. In 60 or 65 compatibility mode, *bit* columns created without an explicit NULL or NOT NULL option in CREATE TABLE or ALTER TABLE are created as NOT NULL.

The database compatibility level also controls whether SQL Server interprets an empty string (two single quotes with nothing between them) as either a single space or as a true empty string. In compatibility level 60 or 65, SQL Server interprets empty strings as single spaces. If the compatibility level is 70, SQL Server interprets empty strings as truly empty, that is, a character string with no characters in it. Sometimes this empty space is referred to as a NULL, but SQL Server doesn't treat it like a NULL. SQL Server marks NULLs internally as NULLS, but an empty string is actually stored as a variable-length character field of 0 length.

In 60 or 65 compatibility mode, the empty string ('') is interpreted as a single space in INSERT or assignment statements on *varchar* data. In concatenating *varchar*, *char*, or *text* data, the empty string is interpreted as a single space. This means that you can never have a truly empty string. The only alternative in 60 or 65 compatibility mode would be to define the field as allowing NULLs, and use a NULL in place of an empty string.

As you can see, you can configure and control the treatment and behavior of NULL values several ways, and you might think it would be impossible to keep track of all the variations. If you try to control every aspect of NULL handling separately within each individual session, you can cause immeasurable confusion and even grief. However, you'll notice that most of the issues become moot if you follow a few basic recommendations:

- Never allow NULL values inside your tables.
- Include a specific NOT NULL qualification in your table definitions.
- Make sure all your databases are running in 70 compatibility mode.

If you must use NULLs in some cases, you can minimize problems by always following the same rules, and the easiest rules to follow are the ones that ANSI already specifies.

Internal Storage—The Details

This section covers system catalogs and the internal data storage of tables. Although you can use SQL Server effectively without understanding the internals, understanding the details of how SQL Server stores data will help you develop efficient applications. (If you don't need this in-depth information, you can skip this discussion and proceed to the section on indexes on p. 246.)

When you create a table, one or more rows are inserted into a number of system catalogs to manage that table. At a minimum, rows are added to the *sysobjects*, *sysindexes*, and *syscolumns* system catalogs (tables). When you define the new table with one or more constraints, rows are added to the *sysreferences* and *sysconstraints* system tables.

For every table created, a single row that contains—among other things—the name, object ID, and owner of the new table is added to the *sysobjects* table. The *sysindexes* table will gain a single row that contains pointers to the first data page that the new table uses and information regarding the table's size, including the number of pages and rows currently being used. The *syscolumns* table will gain one row for each column in the new table, and each row will contain information such as the column name, datatype, and length. Each column receives a column ID, which directly corresponds to the order in which you specified the columns when you created the table. That is, the first column listed in the CREATE TABLE statement will have a column ID of 1, the second column will have a column ID of 2, and so on. Figure 6-3 shows the rows added to the *sysobjects*, *sysindexes*, and *syscolumns* system tables when you create a table. (Not all columns are shown for each table.)

Notice in the *syscolumns* output in the figure that the *xoffset* column contains negative numbers in some rows. (Ignore the *offset* column. It's used only to store row structure information for older versions of SQL Server.) Any column that contains variable-length data will have a negative *xoffset* value in *syscolumns*. The negative numbers are assigned to the variable-length columns in decreasing order ($-1, -2, -3$, and so on) in the order in which the column is specified in the CREATE TABLE statement. You can see in Figure 6-3 that the employee last name (*emp_lname*) is the first variable-length column in the table.

```
CREATE TABLE employee    (
                         emp_lname       varchar(15)    NOT NULL,
                         emp_fname       varchar(10)    NOT NULL,
                         address         varchar(30)    NOT NULL,
                         phone           char(12)       NULL,
                         job_level       smallint       NOT NULL
                         )
```

sysobjects	id		name		uid	xtype			
	165575628		employee		1	U			

sysindexes	id		indid	dpages		reserved		rows	first
	165575628		0	1		2		0	0x560000000100

syscolumns	id		colid	name		xtype	length	xoffset	
	165575628		1	emp_lname		167	15	-1	
	165575628		2	emp_fname		167	10	-2	
	165575628		3	address		167	30	-3	
	165575628		4	phone		175	12	4	
	165575628		5	job_level		52	2	16	

Figure 6-3.
Catalog information stored after creating a table.

Data Pages

Data pages are the structures that contain all of a table's nontext and image data. As with all other types of pages in SQL Server, data pages have a fixed size of 8 KB, or 8192 bytes. Data pages consist of three major components: the page header, data rows, and the row offset array, as shown in Figure 6-4.

Page Header

As you can see in Figure 6-4, the page header occupies the first 96 bytes of each data page (leaving 8096 bytes for data and row offsets). Table 6-2 on the following page shows the information contained in the page header.

Data Rows

Following the page header is the area in which the table's actual data rows are stored. The maximum size of a single data row is 8096 bytes. A data row can't span multiple pages (except for nontext and image columns, which are stored in their own separate pages). The number of rows stored on a given page will vary depending on the structure of the table and on the data being stored. A table that has all fixed-length columns will always store the same number of rows per page; variable-length rows will store as many rows as will fit based on the actual length of the data entered. Keeping row length compact allows more rows to fit on a page, thus reducing I/O and improving the cache-hit ratio.

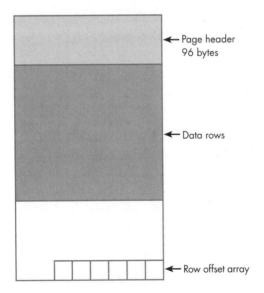

← Page header
96 bytes

← Data rows

← Row offset array

Figure 6-4.
The structure of a data page.

Field	Contains
pageID	File number and page number of this page in the database.
nextPage	File number and page number of the next page, if this page is in a page chain.
prevPage	File number and page number of the previous page, if this page is in a page chain.
objID	ID of the object to which this page belongs.
lsn	Log sequence number (LSN) value used for changes and updates to this page.
slotCnt	Total number of slots used on this page.
level	Level of this page in an index (always 0 for leaf pages).
indexId	Index ID of this page (always 0 for data pages).
freeData	Byte offset of the first free space on this page.
pminlen	Number of bytes in fixed-length portion of rows.
freeCnt	Number of free bytes on page.
reservedCnt	Number of bytes reserved by all transactions.
xactreserved	Number of bytes reserved by the most recently started transaction.
tornBits	1 bit per sector for detecting torn page writes (discussed in Chapter 5).
flagBits	2-byte bitmap that contains additional information about the page.

Table 6-2.

Information contained in the page header.

Row Offset Array

The row offset array is a block of 2-byte entries, each of which indicates the offset on the page on which the corresponding data row begins. Every row has a 2-byte entry in this array, and these 2 bytes were included in the discussion on page 224 in which we mentioned the 10 overhead bytes needed by every row. Although these bytes aren't stored in the row with the data, they do impact the number of rows that will fit on a page.

The row offset array indicates the logical order of rows on a page. For example, if a table has a clustered index, SQL Server will store the rows in the order of the clustered index key. This doesn't mean that the rows will be physically stored on the page in the order of the clustered index key, but that slot 0 in the offset array will refer to the first row in the order, slot 1 will refer to the second row, and so forth. As we'll see shortly when we examine an actual page, the offset of these rows can be anywhere on the page.

There's no internal global row number for every row in a table. You can use the combination of page number and slot number on the page to uniquely identify each row in a table.

Examining Data Pages

You can view the contents of a data page by using the DBCC PAGE statement, which allows you to view the page header, data rows, and row offset table for any given data page in a database. (Only a system administrator can use DBCC PAGE.) But because you typically won't need to view the content of a data page, you won't find much about DBCC PAGE in the SQL Server documentation. Nevertheless, in case you want to use it, here's the syntax:

```
DBCC PAGE ( {dbid | dbname}, filenum, pagenum [, printopt] [, cache] )
```

The DBCC PAGE command includes the parameters shown in Table 6-3. Figure 6-5 on the following page shows sample output from DBCC PAGE. Note that DBCC TRACEON (3604) instructs SQL Server to return the results to the client instead of to the error log, as is the default for many of the DBCC commands that deal with internals issues.

Parameter	Description
dbid	ID of the database containing the page.
dbname	Name of the database containing the page.
filenum	File number containing the page.
pagenum	Page number within the file.
printopt	Optional print option; takes one of these values:
	0 Default; print the buffer header and page header.
	1 Print the buffer header, page header, each row separately, and the row offset table.
	2 Print the buffer and page headers, page as a whole, and the offset table.
cache	Optional; location of page; takes one of these values:
	0 Print the page as found on disk.
	1 Default; print the page as found in cache (if it resides in cache); otherwise, retrieve and print the page from disk.

Table 6-3.
Parameters of the DBCC PAGE command.

```
dbcc traceon(3604)
go
dbcc page(pubs, 1,96, 1,1)
go
PAGE:

BUFFER:

BUF @0x11DB5AC0
---------------
bpage = 0x12116000        bhash = 0x00000000        bpageno = (1:96)
bdbid = 5                 breferences = 0           bkeep = 1
bstat = 0x9               bspin = 0                 bnext = 0x00000000

PAGE HEADER:

Page @0x12116000
---------------
m_pageId = (1:96)         m_headerVersion = 1       m_type = 1
m_typeFlagBits = 0x0      m_level = 0               m_flagBits = 0x0
m_objId = 117575457       m_indexId = 0             m_prevPage = (0:0)
m_nextPage = (0:0)        pminlen = 24              m_slotCnt = 23
m_freeCnt = 6010          m_freeData = 2136         m_reservedCnt = 0
m_lsn = (6:213:17)        m_xactReserved = 0        m_xactId = (0:0)
m_ghostRecCnt = 0         m_tornBits = 0
GAM (1:2) ALLOCATED, SGAM (1:3) NOT ALLOCATED, PFS (1:1) 0x60 MIXED_EXT
ALLOCATED 0_PCT_FULL

DATA:

Slot = 0                        Offset = 0x631
Record Type = PRIMARY_RECORD
Record Attributes =  NULL_BITMAP VARIABLE_COLUMNS
12116631:   00180030   20383034   2d363934   33323237 0...408 496-7223
12116641:   34394143   01353230   00000009   00330005 CA94025.......3.
12116651:   003f0038   0058004e   2d323731   312d3233 8.?.N.X.172-32-1
12116661:   57363731   65746968   6e686f4a   316e6f73 176WhiteJohnson1
12116671:   32333930   67694220   52206567   654d2e64 0932 Bigge Rd.Me
12116681:   206f6c6e   6b726150            nlo Park

Slot = 1                        Offset = 0xb8
Record Type = PRIMARY_RECORD
Record Attributes =  NULL_BITMAP VARIABLE_COLUMNS
121160b8:   00180030   20353134   2d363839   30323037 0...415 986-7020
121160c8:   34394143   01383136   00000009   00330005 CA94618.......3.
121160d8:   00400038   00580051   2d333132   382d3634 8.@.Q.X.213-46-8
121160e8:   47353139   6e656572   6a72614d   6569726f 915GreenMarjorie
121160f8:   20393033   64723336   2e745320   31342320 309 63rd St. #41
12116108:   6b614f31   646e616c            10akland

Slot = 2                        Offset = 0x110
Record Type = PRIMARY_RECORD
Record Attributes =  NULL_BITMAP VARIABLE_COLUMNS
12116110:   00180030   20353134   2d383435   33323737 0...415 548-7723
12116120:   34394143   01353037   00000009   00330005 CA94705.......3.
12116130:   003f0039   0055004d   2d383332   372d3539 9.?.M.U.238-95-7
12116140:   43363637   6f737261   6568436e   356c7972 766CarsonCheryl5
12116150:   44203938   69777261   6e4c206e   7265422e 89 Darwin Ln.Ber
12116160:   656c656b         79            keley

/* Data for slots 3 through 20 not shown */
```

Figure 6-5.
Sample output from DBCC PAGE.

```
Slot = 20                    Offset = 0x2c7
Record Type = PRIMARY_RECORD
Record Attributes =  NULL_BITMAP VARIABLE_COLUMNS
121162c7:  00180030  20373037  2d383434  32383934  0...707 448-4982
121162d7:  35394143  00383836  00000009  00330005  CA95688.......3.
121162e7:  0042003b  0055004c  2d333938  312d3237  ;.B.L.U.893-72-1
121162f7:  4d383531  64614263  486e6564  68746165  158McBaddenHeath
12116307:  30337265  75502031  6d616e74  61636156  er301 PutnamVaca
12116317:  6c6c6976            65                   ville
Slot = 21                    Offset = 0x1c0
Record Type = PRIMARY_RECORD
Record Attributes =  NULL_BITMAP VARIABLE_COLUMNS
121161c0:  00180030  20313038  2d363238  32353730  0...801 826-0752
121161d0:  34385455  00323531  00000009  00330005  UT84152.......3.
121161e0:  003d0039  0059004b  2d393938  322d3634  9.=.K.Y.899-46-2
121161f0:  52353330  65676e69  6e6e4172  20373665  035RingerAnne67
12116200:  65766553  2068746e  532e7641  20746c61  Seventh Av.Salt
12116210:  656b614c  74694320            79         Lake City
Slot = 22                    Offset = 0x165
Record Type = PRIMARY_RECORD
Record Attributes =  NULL_BITMAP VARIABLE_COLUMNS
12116165:  00180030  20313038  2d363238  32353730  0...801 826-0752
12116175:  34385455  00323531  00000009  00330005  UT84152.......3.
12116185:  003f0039  005b004d  2d383939  332d3237  9.?.M.[.998-72-3
12116195:  52373635  65676e69  626c4172  36747265  567RingerAlbert6
121161a5:  65532037  746e6576  76412068  6c61532e  7 Seventh Av.Sal
121161b5:  614c2074  4320656b            797469     t Lake City


OFFSET TABLE:
Row - Offset
22 (0x16) -  357 (0x165)
21 (0x15) -  448 (0x1c0)
20 (0x14) -  711 (0x2c7)
19 (0x13) - 1767 (0x6e7)
18 (0x12) -  619 (0x26b)
17 (0x11) -  970 (0x3ca)
16 (0x10) - 1055 (0x41f)
15 (0xf)  -  796 (0x31c)
14 (0xe)  -  537 (0x219)
13 (0xd)  - 1673 (0x689)
12 (0xc)  - 1226 (0x4ca)
11 (0xb)  - 1949 (0x79d)
10 (0xa)  - 1488 (0x5d0)
9 (0x9)   - 1854 (0x73e)
8 (0x8)   - 1407 (0x57f)
7 (0x7)   - 1144 (0x478)
6 (0x6)   -   96 (0x60)
5 (0x5)   - 2047 (0x7ff)
4 (0x4)   -  884 (0x374)
3 (0x3)   - 1314 (0x522)
2 (0x2)   -  272 (0x110)
1 (0x1)   -  184 (0xb8)
0 (0x0)   - 1585 (0x631)
```

As you can see, the output from DBCC PAGE is divided into four main sections: Buffer, Page Header, Data, and Offset Table (really the Offset Array). The Buffer section shows information about the buffer for the given page. (A *buffer* in this context is an in-memory structure that manages a page.)

The Page Header section in Figure 6-5 displays the data for all the header fields on the page. (Table 6-2 shows the meaning of most of these fields.) The Data section contains information for each row. For each row, DBCC PAGE indicates the slot position of the row and the offset of the row on the page. The page data is then divided into three parts. The left column indicates the byte position within the row where the displayed data occurs. The next four columns contain the actual data stored on the page, displayed in hexadecimal. The right column contains a character representation of the data. Only character data will be readable in this column, although some of the other data might be displayed.

The Offset Table section shows the contents of the row offset array at the end of the page. In the figure, you can see that this page contains 23 rows, with the first row (indicated by slot 0) beginning at offset 1585 (0x631). The first row physically stored on the page is actually row 6, with an offset in the row offset array of 96. DBCC PAGE displays the rows in slot number order, even though, as you can see by the offset of each of the slots, that isn't the order in which the rows physically exist on the page.

Structure of Data Rows

A table's data rows have the general structure shown in Figure 6-6. The data for all fixed-length columns is stored first, followed by the data for all variable-length columns. Table 6-4 on page 238 shows the information stored in each row.

Status Bits A contains a bitmap indicating properties of the row. The bits have the following meaning:

- **Bit 0** Versioning information; in SQL Server 7, it's always 0.

- **Bits 1 through 3** Taken as a 3-bit value, 0 indicates a primary record, 1 indicates a forwarded record, 2 indicates a forwarded stub, 3 indicates an index record, 4 indicates a blob fragment, 5 indicates a ghost index record, and 6 indicates a ghost data record. (We'll discuss forwarding and ghost records in Chapter 8.)

- **Bit 4** Indicates that a NULL bitmap exists; in SQL Server 7, a NULL bitmap is always present, even if no NULLs are allowed in any column.

- **Bit 5** Indicates that variable-length columns exist in the row.

- **Bits 6 and 7** Not used in SQL Server 7.

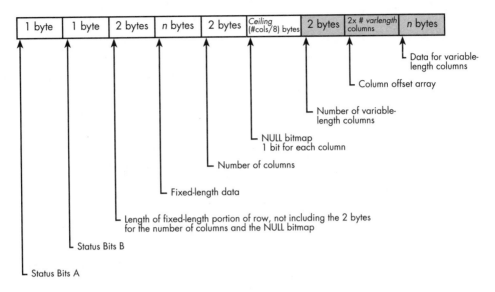

Figure 6-6.
The structure of data rows.

Within each block of fixed-length or variable-length data, the data is stored in the column order in which the table was created. For example, suppose a table is created with the following statement:

```
CREATE TABLE Test1    (Col1 int NOT NULL,
                       Col2 char(25) NOT NULL,
                       Col3 varchar(60) NULL,
                       Col4 money NOT NULL,
                       Col5 varchar(20) NOT NULL)
```

The fixed-length data portion of this row would contain the data for *Col1*, followed by the data for *Col2*, followed by the data for *Col4*. The variable-length data portion would contain the data for *Col3*, followed by the data for *Col5*. For rows that contain only fixed-length data, the following is true:

■ The first hexadecimal digit of the first byte of the data row will be 1, indicating that no variable-length columns exist. (The first hexadecimal digit is comprised of bits 4 through 7; bits 6 and 7 are *always* 0, and if no variable-length columns exist, bit 5 is also 0. Bit 4 is *always* 1, so the value of the four bits is displayed as 1.)

■ The data row ends after the NULL bitmap, which follows the fixed-length data. (That is, the shaded portion shown in Figure 6-6 won't exist in rows with only fixed-length data.)

■ The total length of every data row will be the same.

Information	Mnemonic	Size
Status Bits A	TagA	1 byte
Status Bits B (not used in SQL Server 7)	TagB	1 byte
Fixed-length size	Fsize	2 bytes
Fixed-length data	Fdata	Fsize − 4
Number of columns	Ncol	2 bytes
NULL bitmap (1 byte for each column in table; a 1 indicates that the corresponding column is NULL)	Nullbits	Ceiling (Ncol / 8)
Number of variable-length columns	VarCount	2 bytes
Variable column offset array	VarOffset	2 * VarCount
Variable-length data	VarData	VarOff[VarCount] − (fsize + 4 + Ceiling (Ncol / 8) + 2 * VarCount)

Table 6-4.
Information stored in a table's data rows.

Column Offset Array

A data row that has all fixed-length columns has no *variable column count* or *column offset array*. A data row that has variable-length columns has a column offset array in the data row with a 2-byte entry for each variable-length column, indicating the position within the row where each column ends. (The terms *offset* and *position* aren't exactly interchangeable. *Offset* is 0-based, and *position* is 1-based. A byte at an offset of 7 is in the eighth byte position in the row.)

Storage of Fixed-Length and Variable-Length Rows

Two examples follow that illustrate how fixed-length and variable-length data rows are stored. First, the simpler case of an all fixed-length row:

```
CREATE TABLE Fixed
    (Col1 char(5)      NOT NULL,
     Col2 int          NOT NULL,
     Col3 char(3)      NULL,
     Col4 char(6)      NOT NULL,
     Col5 float        NOT NULL)
```

When this table is created, the following row (or one very much like it) is inserted into the *sysindexes* system table:

```
id            name   indid  first           minlen
-----------   -----  ------ --------------- ------
1797581442    Fixed  0      0xC70000000100  30
```

And these rows are inserted into the *syscolumns* system table:

```
name  colid  xtype  length  xoffset
----  -----  -----  ------  -------
Col1  1      175    5       4
Col2  2      56     4       9
Col3  3      175    3       13
Col4  4      175    6       16
Col5  5      62     8       22
```

For tables containing only fixed-length columns, the *minlen* value in *sysindexes* will be equal to the sum of the column lengths (from *syscolumns.length*), plus 4 bytes. It won't include the 2 bytes for the number of columns, or the bytes for the null bitmap.

To look at a specific data row in this table, first insert a new row:

```
INSERT Fixed VALUES ('ABCDE', 123, null, 'CCCC', 4567.8)
```

Figure 6-7 on the following page shows this row's actual contents on the data page. To run the DBCC PAGE command, we had to take the value of *first* from the *syindexes* output above (0xC70000000100) and convert it to a file and page address. In hexadecimal notation, each set of two characters represents a byte. We first had to swap the bytes to get 00 01 00 00 00 C7. The first two groups represent the 2-byte file number, and the last four groups represent the page number. So the file is 0x0001, which is 1, and the page number is 0x000000C7, which is 199 in decimal.

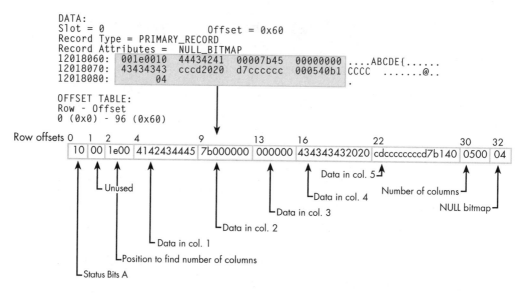

```
DATA:
Slot = 0                        Offset = 0x60
Record Type = PRIMARY_RECORD
Record Attributes =   NULL_BITMAP
12018060:  001e0010  44434241  00007b45  00000000  ....ABCDE{......
12018070:  43434343  cccd2020  d7cccccc  000540b1  CCCC  .......@..
12018080:       04                                     .

OFFSET TABLE:
Row - Offset
0 (0x0) - 96 (0x60)
```

Figure 6-7.

A data row containing all fixed-length columns (header not shown).

NOTE The *sysindexes* table contains three columns that represent page numbers within a database: *first*, *firstIAM*, and *root*. Each is stored in a byte-swapped format. To convert to a decimal file number and page number, you must first swap the bytes and then convert the values from hexadecimal to decimal. You could use the Windows calculator to do the conversion. However, a script has been provided on the companion CD to create a stored procedure called *ConvertPageNums*, which will convert all these columns in the *sysindexes* table for you.

WARNING Version 7 of SQL Server does not guarantee that the *sysindexes.first* column will also indicate the first page of a table. We have found that *first* is reliable until you begin to perform deletes and updates on the data in the table.

Reading the output takes a bit of practice. DBCC PAGE displays the data rows in groups of 4 bytes at a time. Within each group of four, the bytes are listed in reverse order. So the first group of four bytes is byte 3, byte 2, byte 1, and byte 0. The shaded area in the figure has been expanded to show the bytes in the actual byte-number sequence.

The first byte is Status Bits A, and its value (0x10) indicates that only bit 4 is on, so the row has no variable-length columns. The second byte in the row remains unused. The third and fourth bytes (1e00) indicate the length of the fixed-length fields, which is also the column offset in which the *Ncol* value can be found. (The byte-swapped value is 0x001e, which translates to 30.) You can identify the data in the row for each column simply by using the offset value in the *syscolumns* table: the data for column *Col1* begins at offset 4, the data for column *Col2* begins at offset 9, and so on. As an *int*, the data in Col2 (7b000000) must be byte-swapped to give us the value 0x0000007b, which is equivalent to 123 in decimal.

Note that the 3 bytes of data for *Col3* are all zeros, representing an actual NULL in the column. Because the row has no variable-length columns, the row ends 3 bytes after the data for column *Col5*. The 2 bytes starting right after the fixed-length data at offset 30 (0500, which is byte-swapped to yield 0x0005) indicate that five columns are in the row. The last byte is the NULL bitmap. The value of 4 means that only the third bit is on, because in our row, the third column was indeed a NULL.

> **WARNING** Fixed-length columns always use the full number of bytes defined for the table, even if the column holds a NULL value. If you've used previous versions of SQL Server, this might take you by surprise. We know of at least one large database at a manufacturing company that expanded to three or four times its size when upgraded to version 7. This is because they had fields in many tables defined as *char(255)* and allowing NULLs. Some tables had 10 or more such columns, and the vast majority of the data was actually NULL. However, in SQL Server 7, every one of these columns needed a full 255 bytes of storage and the database ballooned in size!

Here's the somewhat more complex case of a table with variable-length data. Each row has three *varchar* columns:

```
CREATE TABLE Variable
    (Col1 char(3)      NOT NULL,
     Col2 varchar(250) NOT NULL,
     Col3 varchar(5)   NULL,
     Col4 varchar(20)  NOT NULL,
     Col5 smallint NULL)
```

When you create this table, the following row is inserted into the *sysindexes* system table:

```
id          name      indid  first          minlen
----------- --------- ------ -------------- ------
1333579789  Variable  0      0xC90000000100 9
```

And these rows are inserted into the *syscolumns* system table:

```
name colid  xtype length xoffset
---- ------ ----- ------ -------

Col1 1      175   3      4
Col2 2      167   250    -1
Col3 3      167   5      -2
Col4 4      167   20     -3
Col5 5      52    2      7
```

Now insert a row into the table:

```
INSERT Variable VALUES
    ('AAA', REPLICATE('X',250), NULL, 'ABC', 123)
```

The REPLICATE function is used here to simplify populating a column; this function builds a string of 250 *X*s to be inserted into *Col2*.

As shown in Figure 6-8, the data for the fixed-length columns is located using the offset value in *syscolumns*. In this case, *Col1* begins at offset 4, and *Col5* begins at offset 7.

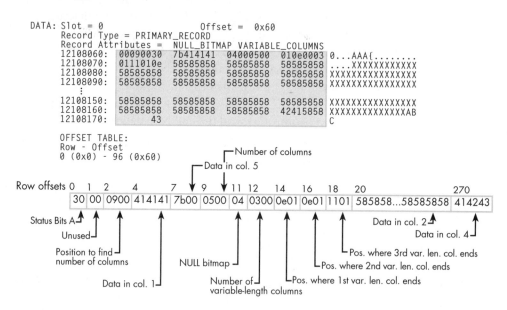

Figure 6-8.
A data row with variable-length columns (header not shown).

To find the variable-length columns, first locate the column offset tables in the row. Right after the 2-byte field indicating the total number of columns (0500), and the NULL bitmap with the value 0x04, a 2-byte field exists with the value 0x0300 (or 3, decimal) indicating that three variable-length fields exist.

Next comes the column offset array. Three 2-byte values indicate the ending position of each of the three variable-length columns: 0e01 is byte-swapped to 0x010e, so the first variable byte column ends at position 270. The next 2-byte offset is also 0e01, so that column has no length and has nothing stored in the variable data area. (Unlike fixed-length fields, if a variable-length field has a NULL value, it takes no room in the data row. SQL Server distinguishes between a *varchar* containing NULL and an empty string by determining whether the bit for the field is 0 or 1 in the NULL bitmap.) The third 2-byte offset is 1101, which, when byte-swapped, gives us 0x0111. This means the row ends at position 273 (and is a total of 273 bytes in length).

The total storage space needed for a row depends on a number of factors. Variable-length fields add additional overhead to a row, and their actual size is probably unpredictable. Even for fixed-length fields, the number of bytes of overhead can change depending on the number of columns in the table. In the earlier example pertaining to Figure 6-1, we mentioned that 10 bytes of overhead existed if a row contained all fixed-length columns. For that row, 10 is the correct number. The size of the NULL bitmap needs to be long enough to store a bit for every column in the row. In the Figure 6-1 example, the table had 11 columns, so the NULL bitmap needed to be 2 bytes. In the examples illustrated by Figures 6-7 and 6-8, the table had only 5 columns, so the NULL bitmaps needs only a single byte. Don't forget that the total row overhead also needs to include the 2 bytes for each row in the offset table at the bottom of the page.

Page Linkage

Unlike earlier versions of SQL Server, SQL Server 7 doesn't connect the individual data pages of a table in a doubly linked list unless the table has a clustered index. All levels of indexes are linked together, and since the data is considered the leaf level of a clustered index, SQL Server does maintain the linkage. However, for a heap, there is no such linked list connecting the pages to each other. The only way that SQL Server determines which pages belong to a table is by inspecting the IAMs for the table.

If the table has a clustered index, you can use the *M_nextPage* and *M_prevPage* values in the page header information to determine the ordering of pages in the list. Alternatively, you can use the DBCC EXTENTINFO command to get a list of all the extents that belong to an object. This example uses the *Orders* table in the *Northwind* database:

```
dbcc extentinfo ('Northwind', 'Orders', 1 )
```

The last argument indicates only extents for index 1, which is the clustered index (and includes the data). Here is the output:

file_id	page_id	pg_alloc	ext_size	obj_id	index_id	avg_used
1	143	1	1	357576312	1	25
1	145	1	1	357576312	1	25
1	291	1	1	357576312	1	25
1	292	1	1	357576312	1	25
1	293	1	1	357576312	1	25
1	294	1	1	357576312	1	25
1	295	1	1	357576312	1	25
1	296	1	1	357576312	1	25
1	304	8	8	357576312	1	25
1	328	5	8	357576312	1	25

Notice that the first eight rows indicate an extent size (*ext_size*) of 1. As discussed in Chapter 5, the first eight pages of a table are allocated from mixed extents. Only after the table has reached eight pages does SQL Server allocate uniform extents of eight pages each. The last two rows in the table show this situation, and the page number (*page_id*) column gives the page number of the first page of the extent. Note that the last extent (starting on page 328) has used only five of its pages at this time.

Text and Image Data

As mentioned earlier, if a table contains text or image data, the actual data isn't stored on the data pages with the rest of the data for a row. Instead, SQL Server stores a 16-byte pointer in the data row that indicates where the actual data can be found. In SQL Server 7, individual *text*, *ntext*, and *image* pages aren't limited to holding data for only one occurrence of a *text*, *ntext*, or *image* column. A *text*, *ntext*, or *image* page can hold data from multiple columns and from multiple rows; the page can even have a mix of *text*, *ntext*, and *image* data. One text or image page can hold only text or image data from a single table.

Text or image data is stored in a collection of 8-KB pages that aren't necessarily located next to each other. In SQL Server 7, the pages are logically organized in a B-tree structure, while in earlier versions of SQL Server, pages were linked together in a page chain. The advantage of the SQL Server 7 method is that operations starting in the middle of the string are more efficient. SQL Server 7 can quickly navigate the tree, while earlier versions of SQL Server had to scan through the page chain. The structure of the B-tree differs slightly depending on whether the amount of data is less than or more than 32 KB. (See Figure 6-9 for the general structure.) We'll discuss B-trees in more detail in the next section of the chapter.

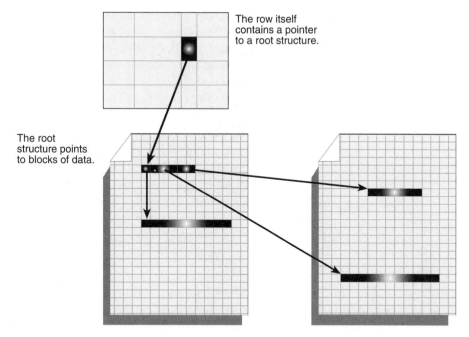

The row itself contains a pointer to a root structure.

The root structure points to blocks of data.

Figure 6-9.
A text column pointing to a B-tree that contains the blocks of data.

If the amount of data is less than 32 KB, the text pointer in the data row points to an 84-byte text root structure. This forms the root node of the B-tree structure. The root node points to the blocks of text or image data. While the data for *text*, *ntext*, and *image* columns is arranged logically in a B-tree, physically both the root node and the individual blocks of data are spread throughout the *text*, *ntext*, and *image* pages for the table. They're placed wherever space is available. The size of each block of data is determined by the size written by an application. Small blocks of data will be combined to fill a page. If the amount of data is less than 64 bytes, it's all stored in the root structure.

If the amount of data for one occurrence of a *text* or *image* column exceeds 32 KB, SQL Server starts building intermediate nodes between the data blocks and the root node. The root structure and the data blocks are interleaved throughout the text and image pages in the same manner as described earlier. The intermediate nodes, however, are stored in pages that aren't shared between occurrences of text or image columns. Each page storing intermediate nodes contains only intermediate nodes for one *text* or *image* column in one data row.

Indexes

Indexes are the other significant user-defined, on-disk data structure (in addition to tables). An index provides fast access to data when the data can be searched by the value that is the index key. We discussed indexes in Chapter 3, but some of that information bears repeating and elaboration here in our discussion of tables. (If indexing is a topic of interest to you, make sure you read "The Index Manager" section of Chapter 3. Indexing is also discussed in the context of query tuning in Chapter 14.) Think of indexes in your everyday life. You're reading a SQL Server book, and you want to find entries for the word *SELECT*. You have two basic choices for doing this: you can open the book and scan through it page by page, or you can look in the index in the back, find the word *SELECT*, and then turn to the page numbers listed. That is exactly how an index works in SQL Server. SQL Server supports clustered and nonclustered indexes (discussed further in the next two sections). Both types use standard B-trees, as shown in Figure 6-10.

A B-tree provides fast access to data by searching on a key value of the index. B-trees cluster records with similar keys. The *B* stands for *balanced,* and balancing the tree is a core feature of a B-tree's usefulness. The trees are managed, and branches are grafted as necessary so that navigating down the tree to find a value and locate a specific record always takes only a few page accesses. Because the trees are balanced, finding any record requires about the same amount of resources, and retrieval speed will be consistent because the index has the same depth throughout.

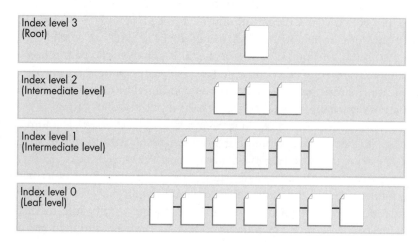

Figure 6-10.
A standard B-tree for a SQL Server index.

An index consists of a tree with a root from which the navigation begins, possible intermediate index levels, and bottom-level leaf pages. The index is used to find the correct leaf page. The number of levels in an index will vary depending on the number of rows in the table and the size of the key column or columns for the index. If you create an index using a large key, fewer entries will fit on a page, so more pages (and possibly more levels) will be needed for the index. On a qualified retrieval or delete, the correct leaf page will be the lowest page of the tree in which one or more rows with the specified key or keys reside. In any index, the leaf level contains every key value, in key sequence.

Clustered Indexes

The leaf level of a clustered index contains the data pages, not just the index keys. A clustered index keeps the data in a table physically ordered around the key. Deciding which key to cluster on is an important performance consideration. When the index is traversed to the leaf level, the data itself has been *retrieved*, not simply *pointed to*.

Because data can be physically ordered in only one way, a table can have only one clustered index. The query optimizer strongly favors a clustered index because it allows the data to be found directly at the leaf level. Because it defines the actual order of the data, a clustered index allows especially fast access for queries looking for a range of values. The query optimizer detects that only a certain range of data pages must be scanned. Most tables should have a clustered index. If your table will have only one index, it generally should be clustered.

In SQL Server 7, all clustered indexes are unique. If a clustered index is built without specifying the unique keyword, SQL Server will force uniqueness by adding a *uniqueifier* to the rows when necessary. This *uniqueifier* is a 4-byte value added as a secondary sort key to only the rows that have duplicates of their primary sort key.

Nonclustered Indexes

In a nonclustered index, the lowest level of the tree (the leaf level) contains a bookmark that tells SQL Server where to find the data row corresponding to the key in the index. As we saw in Chapter 3, a bookmark can have one of two forms. If the table has a clustered index, the bookmark is the clustered index key. If the table is a heap (in other words, it has no clustered index), the bookmark will be a RID, which is an actual row locator in the form File#:Page#:Slot#. (In contrast, in a clustered index, the leaf page *is* the data page.)

The presence or absence of a nonclustered index doesn't affect how the data pages are organized, so you're not restricted to having only one nonclustered index per table, as is the case with clustered indexes. Each table can include as many as 249 nonclustered indexes, but you'll usually want to have far less than this number.

> **NOTE** If you're using an index to enforce uniqueness, there's a better way. PRIMARY KEY and UNIQUE constraints make use of indexing for enforcement. We'll discuss these constraints shortly.

Searching for data using a nonclustered index requires first that the index is traversed and then that the record pointed to is retrieved. For example, to get to a data page using an index with a depth of three—a root page, one intermediate page, and the leaf page—all three index pages must be traversed. If the leaf level contains a clustered index key, all the levels of the clustered index will be traversed to locate the specific row. The clustered index will probably have two levels because in most cases, the clustered index is one level shallower than a nonclustered index. The data page still must be retrieved, although it has been exactly identified, so there's no need to scan the entire table. Still, it takes six logical I/O operations to get one data page. You can see that a nonclustered index is a win only if it's highly selective.

Structure of Index Pages

Index pages are structured much like data pages. As with all other types of pages in SQL Server, index pages have a fixed size of 8 KB, or 8192 bytes. Index pages also have a 96-byte header but, unlike data pages, no offset array appears at the end of the page. Each index has a row in the *sysindexes* table, with an *indid* value of either 1, for a clustered index, or a number between 2 and 250, indicating a nonclustered index. (An *indid* value of 255 indicates *text* or *image* information.) The *root* column value contains a file number and page number where the root of the index can be found. You can then use DBCC PAGE to examine index pages, just as you do for data pages.

Creating Indexes

The typical syntax for creating an index is straightforward:

```
CREATE [UNIQUE] [CLUSTERED | NONCLUSTERED] INDEX index_name
    ON table_name (column_name [,
    column_name]...)
```

CREATE INDEX has some additional options available for specialized purposes:

```
[WITH
[PAD_INDEX]
[[,] FILLFACTOR = fillfactor]
```

```
[[,] IGNORE_DUP_KEY]
[[,] DROP_EXISTING]
[[,] STATISTICS_NORECOMPUTE]
]
[ON filegroup]
```

FILLFACTOR is probably the most commonly used of these options. FILLFACTOR lets you reserve some space on each leaf page of an index. (In a clustered index, this equals the data page.) By reserving some free space with FILLFACTOR, you can later avoid the need to split pages to make room for an entry. (Refer to the discussion of index management and page splitting in Chapter 3.) But remember that FILLFACTOR is not maintained; it indicates only how much space is reserved with the existing data. If you need to, you can use the DBCC DBREINDEX command to rebuild the index and to reestablish the original FILLFACTOR specified.

> **TIP** If you'll be rebuilding all of a table's indexes, simply specify the clustered index with DBCC DBREINDEX. Doing so internally rebuilds the entire table and all nonclustered indexes.

FILLFACTOR isn't usually specified on an index-by-index basis, but you can specify it this way for fine-tuning. If FILLFACTOR isn't specified, the serverwide default is used. The value is set for the server via *sp_configure, fillfactor*. This value is 0 by default, which means that leaf pages of indexes are made as full as possible. FILLFACTOR generally applies only to the index's leaf page (the data page for a clustered index). In specialized and high-use situations, you might want to reserve space in the intermediate index pages to avoid page splits there, too. You can do this by using the PAD_INDEX option, which uses the same value as FILLFACTOR.

The DROP_EXISTING option is valid only when creating a clustered index and specifies that the given table's clustered index should be dropped and rebuilt. Then all existing nonclustered indexes are updated. Because nonclustered indexes must go through the clustered index to gain access to rows in a table, the DROP_EXISTING option prevents the nonclustered indexes from having to be rebuilt twice. Normally, when a clustered index is dropped, every nonclustered index has to be rebuilt to change its bookmarks to RIDs instead of the clustering keys. Then, if a clustered index is built (or rebuilt), all the nonclustered indexes must be rebuilt again to update the bookmarks. The DROP_EXISTING option to the CREATE INDEX command allows a clustered index to be rebuilt without affecting any nonclustered indexes on the table.

You can ensure the uniqueness of a key by using the PRIMARY KEY and UNIQUE constraints, which we'll discuss beginning on page 255. These constraints work by making a unique index on the key value or values. If an UPDATE or INSERT statement would affect multiple rows, and if even one row is found that would cause duplicate keys in the table, the entire statement is aborted and no rows are affected. With a unique index, you can use the IGNORE_DUP_KEY option so that a nonunique error on a multiple-row UPDATE or INSERT won't cause the entire statement to be rolled back. The nonunique row will be discarded, and all other rows will be inserted or updated. IGNORE_DUP_KEY doesn't allow the uniqueness of the index to be violated; instead, it makes a violation in a multiple-row data modification nonfatal to all the nonviolating rows.

The STATISTICS_NORECOMPUTE option will be discussed in Chapter 14 of the book, when we discuss statistics maintenance.

User-Defined Datatypes

A user-defined datatype (UDDT) provides a convenient way for you to guarantee consistent use of underlying native datatypes for columns known to have the same domain of possible values. For example, perhaps your database will store various phone numbers in many tables. Although no single, definitive way exists to store phone numbers, in this database consistency is important. You can create a *phone_number* UDDT and use it consistently for any column in any table that keeps track of phone numbers to ensure that they all use the same datatype. Here's how to create this UDDT:

```
EXEC sp_addtype phone_number, 'varchar(20)', 'not null'
```

And here's how to use the new UDDT when creating a table:

```
CREATE TABLE customer
(
cust_id        smallint       NOT NULL,
cust_name      varchar(50)    NOT NULL,
cust_addr1     varchar(50)    NOT NULL,
cust_addr2     varchar(50)    NOT NULL,
cust_city      varchar(50)    NOT NULL,
cust_state     char(2)        NOT NULL,
cust_zip       varchar(10)    NOT NULL,
cust_phone     phone_number,
cust_fax       varchar(20)    NOT NULL,
cust_email     varchar(30)    NOT NULL,
cust_web_url   varchar(20)    NOT NULL)
```

When the table is created, internally the datatype of *cust_phone* is known to be *varchar(20)*. Notice that both *cust_phone* and *cust_fax* are *varchar(20)*, although *cust_phone* has that declaration through its definition as a UDDT.

Here's how the *customer* table appears in the entries in the *syscolumns* table for this table:

```
SELECT colid, name, xtype, length, xusertype, offset
FROM syscolumns WHERE id=object_id('customer')
```

colid	name	xtype	length	xusertype	offset
1	cust_id	52	2	52	2
2	cust_name	167	50	167	-1
3	cust_addr1	167	50	167	-2
4	cust_addr2	167	50	167	-3
5	cust_city	167	50	167	-4
6	cust_state	175	2	175	4
7	cust_zip	167	10	167	-5
8	cust_phone	167	20	261	-6
9	cust_fax	167	20	167	-7
10	cust_email	167	30	167	-8
11	cust_web_u	167	20	167	-9

You can see that both the *cust_phone* and *cust_fax* columns have the same *xtype* (datatype), although the *cust_phone* column shows that the datatype is a UDDT (*xusertype* = 261). The type is resolved when the table is created, and the UDDT can't be dropped or changed as long as one or more tables are currently using it. Once declared, a UDDT is static and immutable, so no inherent performance penalty occurs in using a UDDT instead of the native datatype.

The use of UDDTs can make your database more consistent and clear. SQL Server implicitly converts between compatible columns of different types (either native types or UDDTs of different types).

Currently, UDDTs don't support the notion of subtyping or inheritance, nor do they allow a DEFAULT value or CHECK constraint to be declared as part of the UDDT itself. These powerful object-oriented concepts will likely make their way into future versions of SQL Server. These limitations not withstanding, UDDT functionality is a dynamic and often underused feature of SQL Server.

Identity Property

It is common to provide simple counter-type values for tables that don't have a natural or efficient primary key. Columns such as *customer_number* are usually simple counter fields. SQL Server provides the Identity property that makes generating unique numeric values easy. Identity isn't a datatype; it's a *column property* that you can declare on a whole-number datatype such as *tinyint, smallint, int,* and *numeric/decimal* (having a scale of zero). Each table can have only one column with the Identity property. The table's creator can specify the starting number (seed) and the amount that value increments or decrements. If not otherwise specified, the seed value starts at 1 and increments by 1, as shown in this example:

```
CREATE TABLE customer
(
cust_id        smallint        IDENTITY  NOT NULL,
cust_name      varchar(50)     NOT NULL,
)
```

To find out which seed and increment values were defined for a table, you can use the IDENT_SEED(*tablename*) and IDENT_INCR(*tablename*) functions. The statement

```
SELECT IDENT_SEED('CUSTOMER'), IDENT_INCR('CUSTOMER')
```

produces

```
1    1
```

for the *customer* table because values weren't explicitly declared and the default values were used.

This next example explicitly starts the numbering at 100 (seed) and increments the value by 20:

```
CREATE TABLE customer
(
cust_id        smallint        IDENTITY(100,20)  NULL,
cust_name      varchar(50)     NOT NULL,
)
```

The value automatically produced with the Identity property will normally be unique, but it isn't guaranteed by the Identity property itself, nor is it guaranteed to be consecutive. For efficiency, a value is considered used as soon as it is presented to a client doing an INSERT operation. If that client doesn't ultimately commit the INSERT, the value will never appear, so a break will occur in the consecutive numbers. An unacceptable level of serialization would exist if the next number couldn't be parceled out until the previous one was actually committed or rolled back. (And even then, as soon as a row was deleted, the values would no longer be consecutive. Gaps are inevitable.)

NOTE If you need exact sequential values without gaps, Identity isn't the appropriate feature to use. Instead, you should implement a *next_number*-type table in which you can make the operation of bumping the number contained there part of the larger transaction (and incur the serialization of queuing for this value).

To temporarily disable the automatic generation of values in an *identity* column, use the SET IDENTITY_INSERT *tablename* ON option. In addition to filling in gaps in the identity sequence, this option is useful for tasks such as bulk loading data in which the previous values already exist. For example, perhaps you're loading a new database with customer data from your previous system. You might want to preserve the previous customer numbers but have new ones automatically assigned using Identity. The SET option was created exactly for cases like this.

Because of the SET option's ability to override values, the Identity property alone doesn't enforce uniqueness of a value within the table. Although Identity will generate a unique number, it can be overridden with the SET option. To enforce uniqueness (which you'll almost always want to do when using Identity), you should also declare a UNIQUE or PRIMARY KEY constraint on the column. If you insert your own values for an *identity* column (using SET IDENTITY_INSERT), when automatic generation resumes, the next value will be the next incremented value (or decremented value) of the highest value that exists in the table, whether it was generated previously or explicitly inserted.

> **TIP** If you're using the *bcp* utility for bulk loading data, be aware of the /E (uppercase) parameter if your data already has assigned values that you want to keep for a column having the Identity property. You can also use the Transact-SQL BULK INSERT command with the KEEPIDENTITY option. For more information, see the SQL Server documentation for *bcp* and BULK INSERT.

The keyword IDENTITYCOL automatically refers to the specific column in a table, whatever its name, that has the Identity property. If *cust_id* is that column, you can refer to the column as IDENTITYCOL without knowing or using the column name, or you can refer to it explicitly as *cust_id*. For example, the following two statements work identically and return the same data:

```
SELECT IDENTITYCOL FROM customer
SELECT cust_id FROM customer
```

The column name returned to the caller is *cust_id*, not IDENTITYCOL, in both of these cases.

When inserting rows, you must omit an *identity* column from the column list and VALUES section. (The only exception is when the IDENTITY_INSERT option is on.) If you do supply a column list, you must omit the column for which the value will be automatically supplied. Here are two valid INSERT statements for the *customer* table shown earlier:

```
INSERT customer VALUES ('ACME Widgets')
INSERT customer (cust_name) VALUES ('AAA Gadgets')
```

Selecting these two rows produces this output:

```
cust_id    cust_name
-------    ---------
1          ACME Widgets
2          AAA Gadgets
```

(2 row(s) affected)

Sometimes in applications, it's desirable to immediately know the value produced by Identity for subsequent use. For example, a transaction might first add a new customer and then add an order for that customer. To add the order, you probably need to use the *cust_id*. Rather than select the value from the *customer* table, you can simply select the special system function @@IDENTITY, which contains the last identity value used by that connection. It doesn't necessarily provide the last value inserted into the table, however, because another user might have subsequently inserted data. If multiple INSERT statements are carried out in a batch to the same or different tables, the variable has the value for the last statement only.

You can't define the Identity property as part of a UDDT, but you can declare the Identity property on a column that uses a UDDT. A column having the Identity property must always be declared NOT NULL (either explicitly or implicitly), or error message number 8147 will result from the CREATE TABLE statement, and CREATE won't succeed. Likewise, you can't declare the Identity property and a DEFAULT on the same column. To check that the current identity value is valid based on the current maximum values in the table, and to reset it if an invalid value is found (which should never be the case), use the DBCC CHECKIDENT (*tablename*) statement.

Identity values are fully recoverable. If a system outage occurs while insert activity is taking place with tables that have *identity* columns, the correct value will be recovered when SQL Server is restarted. This is accomplished during the SQL Server checkpoint processing by flushing the current identity value for all tables. For activity beyond the last checkpoint, subsequent values are reconstructed from the transaction log during the standard database recovery process. Any inserts into a table having the Identity property are known to have changed the value, and the current value is retrieved from the last INSERT statement (post-checkpoint) for each table in the transaction log. The net result is that when the database is recovered, the correct current identity value is also recovered.

SQL Server, unlike some other products, doesn't require that you maintain a large safety buffer or burning set. After a system failure, products that don't recover their autosequencing values sometimes add a large number to the last known value on recovery to ensure that a number isn't reused. This can result in odd and probably undesirable values. For example, values might be progressing nicely as 101, 102, 103, 104, 105, and so on. Then a system outage occurs. Because the next value isn't recovered, these products don't detect exactly where to resume (104? 105? 106? 107?). To avoid reusing a number, these products simply add a safety buffer; the number after 105 might be 1106, with a safety buffer of 1000. This can result in some odd patterns for what are loosely thought of as sequential numbers (for example, 102, 103, 104, 105, 1106, 1107, 2108, 2109, 3110). Because SQL Server recovers the exact value, large gaps like this never occur.

In rare cases, the identity value can get out of sync. If this happens, you can use the DBCC CHECKINDENT command to reset the identity value to the appropriate number. In addition, the RESEED option to this command allows you to set a new starting value for the identity sequence. Take a look in the online documentation for complete details.

Constraints

Constraints provide a powerful yet easy way for you to enforce relationships between tables (*referential integrity*) by declaring primary, foreign, and alternate keys. CHECK constraints enforce *domain integrity*. Domain integrity enforces valid entries for a given column by restricting the type (through datatypes), the format (through CHECK constraints and rules), or the range of possible values (through REFERENCES to foreign keys, CHECK constraints, and rules). The declaration of a column as either NULL or NOT NULL can be thought of as a type of constraint. And you can declare default values for use when a value isn't known at insert or update time.

PRIMARY KEY and UNIQUE Constraints

A central tenet of the relational model is that every tuple (row) in a relation (table) is in some way unique and can be distinguished in some way from every other row in the table. The combination of all columns in a table could be used as this unique identifier, but in practice, the identifier is usually at most the combination of a handful of columns, and often it's just one column: the primary key. Although some tables might have multiple unique identifiers, each table can have only one primary key. For example, perhaps the *employee* table maintains both an *Emp_ID* column and an *SSN* (Social Security number) column, both of which can be considered unique. Such column pairs are often referred to as *alternate keys* or *candidate keys,* although both terms are design terms and aren't used by the ANSI SQL standard or by SQL Server. In practice, one of the two columns is logically promoted to primary key with the PRIMARY KEY constraint, and the other will usually be declared by a UNIQUE constraint. Although neither the ANSI SQL standard nor SQL Server require it, it's good practice to always declare a PRIMARY KEY constraint on every table. Furthermore, you must designate a primary key for a table that will be published for transaction-based replication.

Internally, PRIMARY KEY and UNIQUE constraints are handled almost identically, so we'll discuss them together here. Declaring a PRIMARY KEY or UNIQUE constraint simply results in a unique index being created on the specified column or columns, and this index enforces the column's uniqueness, in the same way that a unique index created manually on a column would. The query optimizer makes decisions based on the presence of the unique index rather than on the fact that a column was declared as a primary key. How the index got there in the first place is irrelevant to the optimizer.

Nullability

All columns that are part of a primary key must be declared (either explicitly or implicitly) as NOT NULL. Columns that are part of a UNIQUE constraint can be declared to allow NULL. However, for the purposes of unique indexes, all NULLs are considered equal. So if the unique index is on a single column, only one NULL value can be stored (another good reason to try to avoid NULL whenever possible). If the unique index is on a composite key, one of the columns can have many NULLs, as long as the value in the other column is unique.

Index Attributes

The index attributes of CLUSTERED or NONCLUSTERED can be explicitly specified when declaring the constraint. If not specified, the index for a UNIQUE constraint will be nonclustered, and the index for a PRIMARY KEY constraint will be clustered (unless CLUSTERED has already been explicitly stated for a unique index, because only one clustered index can exist per table). The index FILLFACTOR attribute can be specified if a PRIMARY KEY or UNIQUE constraint is added to an existing table using the ALTER TABLE command. FILLFACTOR doesn't make sense in a CREATE TABLE statement because the table has no existing data, and FILLFACTOR on an index affects how full pages are only when the index is initially created. FILLFACTOR isn't maintained when data is added.

Choosing Keys

Try to keep the key lengths as compact as possible. Columns that are the primary key or that are unique are most likely to be joined and frequently queried.

Compact key lengths allow more index entries to fit on a given 8-KB page, reducing I/O, increasing cache hits, and speeding character matching. When no naturally efficient compact key exists, it's often useful to manufacture a surrogate key using the Identity property on an *int* column. (If *int* doesn't provide enough range, a good second choice is a *numeric* column with the required precision and with scale 0.) You might use this surrogate as the primary key, use it for most join and retrieval operations, and declare a UNIQUE constraint on the natural but inefficient columns that provide the logical unique identifier in your data. (Or you might dispense with creating the UNIQUE constraint altogether if you don't need to have SQL Server enforce the uniqueness. Indexes slow performance of data modification statements because the index, as well as the data, must be maintained.)

Another reason for keeping your primary key short is relevant when the primary key has a clustered index on it (the default). Because clustered index keys are used as the locators for all nonclustered indexes, the clustered key will occur over and over again. A large key for your clustered index will mean your nonclustered indexes will end up large.

Although it's permissible to do so, don't create a PRIMARY KEY constraint on a column of type *float* or *real*. Because these are approximate datatypes, the uniqueness of such columns is also approximate, and the results can sometimes be unexpected.

Removing Constraints

You can't directly drop a unique index created as a result of a PRIMARY KEY or UNIQUE constraint by using the DROP INDEX statement. Instead, you must drop the constraint by using ALTER TABLE DROP CONSTRAINT (or you have to drop the table itself). This feature was designed so that a constraint can't be compromised accidentally by someone who doesn't realize that the index is being used to enforce the constraint. There is no way to temporarily disable a PRIMARY KEY or UNIQUE constraint. If disabling is required, use ALTER TABLE DROP CONSTRAINT, and then later restore the constraint by using ALTER TABLE ADD CONSTRAINT. If the index you use to enforce uniqueness is clustered, when you add the constraint to an existing table, the entire table and all nonclustered indexes are internally rebuilt to establish the cluster order. This can be a time-consuming task, and it requires about 1.2 times the existing table space as a temporary work area in the database would require (2.2 times in total, counting the permanent space needed) so that the operation can be rolled back if necessary.

Creating Constraints

Typically, you declare PRIMARY KEY and UNIQUE constraints when you create the table (CREATE TABLE). However, you can add or drop both by subsequently using the ALTER TABLE command. To simplify matters, you can declare a PRIMARY KEY or UNIQUE constraint that includes only a single column on the same line where you define that column in the CREATE TABLE statement. Such a constraint is known as a *column-level constraint.* Or you can declare the constraint after all columns have been defined; this constraint is known as a *table-level constraint.* Which approach you use is largely a matter of personal preference. We find the column-level syntax more readable and clear. You can use abbreviated syntax with a column-level constraint, in which case SQL Server will generate the name for the constraint, or you can use a slightly more verbose syntax that uses the clause CONSTRAINT *name.* A table-level constraint must always be named by its creator. If you'll be creating the same database structure across multiple servers, it's probably wise to explicitly name column-level constraints so that the same name will be used on all servers.

Following are examples of three different ways to declare a PRIMARY KEY constraint on a single column. All methods cause a unique, clustered index to be created. Note the (abridged) output of the *sp_helpconstraint* procedure for each—especially the constraint name.

EXAMPLE 1

```
CREATE TABLE customer
(
cust_id       int            IDENTITY  NOT NULL  PRIMARY KEY,
cust_name     varchar(30)    NOT NULL
)
GO

EXEC sp_helpconstraint customer
GO

>>>>

Object Name
-----------
customer

constraint_type          constraint_name
----------------------   -------------------------------
PRIMARY KEY (clustered)  PK__customer__68E79C55
```

EXAMPLE 2

```
CREATE TABLE customer
(
cust_id      int          IDENTITY   NOT NULL
                          CONSTRAINT cust_pk PRIMARY KEY,
cust_name    varchar(30)  NOT NULL
)
GO

EXEC sp_helpconstraint customer
GO
```

>>>>

```
Object Name
-----------
customer

constraint_type              constraint_name
-----------------------      ---------------
PRIMARY KEY (clustered)      cust_pk
```

No foreign keys reference this table.

EXAMPLE 3

```
CREATE TABLE customer
(
cust_id      int          IDENTITY   NOT NULL,
cust_name    varchar(30)  NOT NULL,
CONSTRAINT customer_PK PRIMARY KEY (cust_id)
)
GO

EXEC sp_helpconstraint customer
GO
```

>>>>

```
Object Name
-----------
customer

constraint_type              constraint_name
---------------              ---------------
PRIMARY KEY (clustered)      customer_PK
```

No foreign keys reference this table.

In Example 1, the constraint name bears the seemingly cryptic name of *PK__customer__68E79C55*. There is some method to this apparent madness—all types of column-level constraints use this naming scheme (which we'll discuss later in this chapter). Whether you choose a more intuitive name of your own, such as *customer_PK* in Example 3, or the less intuitive (but information-packed), system-generated name produced with the abbreviated column-level syntax is up to you. However, when a constraint involves multiple columns, as is often the case for PRIMARY KEY, UNIQUE, and FOREIGN KEY constraints, the only way to syntactically declare them is with a table-level declaration. The syntax for creating constraints is quite broad and has many variations. A given column could have the Identity property, be part of a primary key, be a foreign key, and be declared NOT NULL. The order of these specifications isn't mandated and can be interchanged. Here's an example of creating a table-level, UNIQUE constraint on the combination of multiple columns. (The primary key case is essentially identical.)

```
CREATE TABLE customer_location
(
cust_id                 int     NOT NULL,
cust_location_number    int     NOT NULL,
CONSTRAINT customer_location_unique UNIQUE
    (cust_id, cust_location_number)
)
GO

EXEC sp_helpconstraint customer_location
GO

>>>
Object Name
----------------
customer_location


constraint_type   constraint_name            constraint_keys
--------------    -----------------------    ---------------
UNIQUE            customer_location_unique   cust_id,
(non-clustered)                              cust_location_number

No foreign keys reference this table.
```

As noted earlier, a unique index is created to enforce either a PRIMARY KEY or a UNIQUE constraint. The name of the index is based on the constraint name, whether it was explicitly named or system generated. The index used to enforce the CUSTOMER_LOCATION_UNIQUE constraint in the above example is also named *customer_location_unique*. The index used to enforce the column-level, PRIMARY KEY constraint of the *customer* table in Example 1 is named *PK__customer__68E79C55*, which is the system-generated name of the constraint. You can use the *sp_helpindex* stored procedure to see information for all indexes of a given table. For example:

```
EXEC sp_helpindex customer
```

```
>>>
index_name                       index_description    index_keys
-----------------------------    -----------------    ----------
PK__customer__68E79C55           clustered, unique,   cust_id
                                 primary key
                                 located on default
```

You can't directly drop an index created to enforce a PRIMARY KEY or UNIQUE constraint. However, you can rebuild the index by using DBCC DBREINDEX, which is useful when you want to reestablish a given FILLFACTOR for the index or to reorganize the table, in the case of a clustered index.

FOREIGN KEY Constraints

As the term implies, logical relationships between tables is a fundamental concept of the relational model. In most databases, certain relationships must exist (that is, the data must have referential integrity), or the data will be logically corrupt.

SQL Server automatically enforces referential integrity through the use of FOREIGN KEY constraints. (This feature is sometimes referred to as declarative referential integrity, or DRI, to distinguish it from other features, such as triggers, that you can also use to enforce the existence of the relationships.)

A foreign key is one or more columns of a table whose values must be equal to a value in another column having a PRIMARY KEY or UNIQUE constraint in another table (or the same table when it references itself). After the foreign key is declared in a CREATE TABLE or ALTER TABLE statement, SQL Server restricts a row from being inserted or updated in a table that *references* another table if the relationship wouldn't be established. SQL Server also restricts the rows in the table being referenced from being deleted or changed in a way that would destroy the relationship.

Here's a simple way to declare a primary key/foreign key relationship:

```
CREATE TABLE customer
(
cust_id      int          NOT NULL  IDENTITY  PRIMARY KEY,
cust_name    varchar(50)  NOT NULL
)
```

(continued)

261

```
CREATE TABLE orders
(
order_id    int         NOT NULL  IDENTITY  PRIMARY KEY,
cust_id     int         NOT NULL  REFERENCES customer(cust_id)
)
```

The *orders* table contains the column *cust_id*, which references the primary key of the *customer* table. An order (*order_id*) must not exist unless it relates to an existing customer (*cust_id*). You can't delete a row from the *customer* table if a row that references it currently exists in the *orders* table, and you can't modify the *cust_id* column in a way that would destroy the relationship.

The previous example shows the syntax for a column-level constraint, which you can declare only if the foreign key is a single column. This syntax uses the keyword REFERENCES, and the term "foreign key" is implied but not explicitly stated. The name of the FOREIGN KEY constraint is generated internally, following the same general form described earlier for PRIMARY KEY and UNIQUE constraints. Here's a portion of the output of *sp_helpconstraint* for both the *customer* and *orders* tables. (The tables were created in the *pubs* sample database.)

```
EXEC sp_helpconstraint customer
>>>

Object Name
-----------
customer

constraint_type     constraint_name           constraint_keys
----------------    ----------------------    ----------------
PRIMARY KEY         PK__customer__07F6335A    cust_id
(clustered)

Table is referenced by
-----------------------------------------------------
pubs.dbo.orders: FK__orders__cust_id__0AD2A005


EXEC sp_helpconstraint orders
>>>

Object Name
-----------
orders
```

```
constraint_type      constraint_name                constraint_keys
----------------     ---------------------------    ---------------
FOREIGN KEY          FK__orders__cust_id__0AD2A005  cust_id
                                                    REFERENCES
                                                    pubs.dbo.
                                                    customer(cust_id)

PRIMARY KEY          PK__orders__09DE7BCC           order_id
(clustered)
```

No foreign keys reference this table.

As with PRIMARY KEY and UNIQUE constraints, you can declare FOREIGN KEY constraints at the column and table levels. If the foreign key is a combination of multiple columns, you must declare FOREIGN KEY constraints at the table level. The following example shows a table-level, multiple-column FOREIGN KEY constraint:

```
CREATE TABLE customer
(
cust_id         int          NOT NULL,
location_num    smallint     NULL,
cust_name       varchar(50)  NOT NULL,
CONSTRAINT CUSTOMER_UNQ UNIQUE CLUSTERED (location_num, cust_id)
)

CREATE TABLE orders
(
order_id    int        NOT NULL   IDENTITY CONSTRAINT ORDER_PK
                                  PRIMARY KEY NONCLUSTERED,
cust_num    int        NOT NULL,
cust_loc    smallint   NULL,
CONSTRAINT FK_ORDER_CUSTOMER FOREIGN KEY (cust_loc, cust_num)
REFERENCES customer (location_num, cust_id)
)

GO

EXEC sp_helpconstraint customer
EXEC sp_helpconstraint orders
GO

>>>
Object Name
-----------
customer
```

(continued)

```
constraint_type        constraint_name      constraint_keys
-----------------      ----------------     --------------------
UNIQUE (clustered)     CUSTOMER_UNQ         location_num, cust_id


Table is referenced by
--------------------------
pubs.dbo.orders: FK_ORDER_CUSTOMER


Object Name
-----------
orders

constraint_type        constraint_name      constraint_keys
-----------------      ----------------     ------------------
FOREIGN KEY            FK_ORDER_CUSTOMER    cust_loc, cust_num
                                           REFERENCES pubs.dbo.customer
                                           (location_num, cust_id)

PRIMARY KEY           ORDER_PK              order_id
(non-clustered)
No foreign keys reference this table.
```

The previous example also shows the following variations of how you can create constraints:

FOREIGN KEY constraints You can use a FOREIGN KEY constraint to reference a UNIQUE constraint (an alternate key) instead of a PRIMARY KEY constraint. (Note, however, that referencing a PRIMARY KEY is much more typical and is generally better practice.)

Matching column names and datatypes You don't have to use identical column names in tables involved in a foreign key reference, but it's often good practice. The *cust_id* and *location_num* column names are defined in the *customer* table. The *orders* table, which references the *customer* table, uses the names *cust_num* and *cust_loc*. Although the column names of related columns can differ, the datatypes of the related columns must be identical, except for nullability and variable-length attributes. (For example, a column of *char(10) NOT NULL* can reference one of *varchar(10) NULL*, but it can't reference a column of *char(12) NOT NULL*. A column of type *smallint* can't reference a column of type *int*.) Notice in the preceding example that *cust_id* and *cust_num* are both *int NOT NULL* and that *location_num* and *cust_loc* are both *smallint NULL*.

UNIQUE columns and NULL values You can declare a UNIQUE constraint on a column that allows NULL, but only one entirely NULL UNIQUE column is allowed when multiple columns make up the constraint. More precisely, the UNIQUE constraint would allow one entry for each combination of values that includes a NULL, as though NULL were a value in itself. For example, if the constraint contained two *int* columns, exactly one row of each of these combinations (and so on) would be allowed:

NULL	NULL
0	NULL
NULL	0
1	NULL
NULL	1

This case is questionable: NULL represents an unknown, yet using it this way clearly implies that NULL is equal to NULL. (As you'll recall, we recommend that you avoid using NULLs, especially in key columns.)

Index attributes You can specify the CLUSTERED and NONCLUSTERED index attributes for a PRIMARY KEY or UNIQUE constraint. (You can also specify FILLFACTOR when using ALTER TABLE to add a constraint.) The index keys will be created in the order in which you declare columns. In the preceding example, we specified *location_num* as the first column of the UNIQUE constraint, even though it follows *cust_id* in the table declaration, because we want the clustered index to be created with *location_num* as the lead column of the B-tree and, consequently, to keep the data clustered around the location values.

CONSTRAINT syntax You can explicitly name a column-level constraint by declaring it with the more verbose CONSTRAINT syntax on the same line or section as a column definition. You can see this syntax for the PRIMARY KEY constraint in the *orders* table. There's no difference in the semantics or run-time performance of a column-level or table-level constraint, and it doesn't matter to the system whether the constraint name is user specified or system generated. (A slight added efficiency occurs when you initially create a column-level constraint rather than a table-level constraint on only one column, but typically, only run-time performance matters.) However, the real advantage of explicitly naming your constraint rather than using the system-generated name is improved understandability. The constraint name is used in the error message for any constraint violation, so creating a name such as CUSTOMER_PK will probably make more sense to users than a name such as *PK__customer__cust_i__0677FF3C*. You should choose your own constraint names if such error messages are visible to your users.

Unlike a PRIMARY KEY or UNIQUE constraint, an index isn't automatically built for the column or columns declared as FOREIGN KEY. However, in many cases, you'll want to build indexes on these columns because they're often used for joining to other tables. To enforce foreign key relationships, SQL Server must add additional steps to the execution plan of every insert, delete, and update (if the update affects columns that are part of the relationship) that affects either the table referencing another table or the table being referenced itself. The execution plan, determined by the SQL Server optimizer, is simply the collection of steps that carries out the operation. (In Chapter 14, you'll see the actual execution plan by using the SET SHOWPLAN ON statement.)

If no FOREIGN KEY constraints exist, a statement specifying the update of a single row of the *orders* table might have an execution plan like the following:

1. Find a qualifying *order* record using a clustered index.

2. Update the *order* record.

When a FOREIGN KEY constraint exists on the *orders* table, the same operation would have additional steps in the execution plan:

1. Check for the existence of a related record in the *customer* table (based on the updated *order* record) using a clustered index.

2. If no related record is found, raise an exception and terminate the operation.

3. Find a qualifying *order* record using a clustered index.

4. Update the *order* record.

The execution plan is more complex if the *orders* table has many FOREIGN KEY constraints declared. Internally, a simple update or insert operation might no longer be possible. Any such operation requires checking many other tables for matching entries. Because a seemingly simple operation could require checking as many as 253 other tables (see the next paragraph) and possibly creating multiple worktables, the operation might be much more complicated than it looks and much slower than expected.

A table can have a maximum of 253 FOREIGN KEY references. This limit is derived from the internal limit of 256 tables in a single query. In practice, an operation on a table with 253 or fewer FOREIGN KEY constraints might still fail with an error because of the 256-table query limit if worktables are required for the operation.

A database designed for excellent performance doesn't reach anything close to this limit of 253 FOREIGN KEY references. For best performance results, use FOREIGN KEY constraints judiciously. Some sites use many FOREIGN KEY constraints because the constraints they declare are logically redundant. Take the case in the following example. The *orders* table declares a FOREIGN KEY constraint to both the *master_customer* and *customer_location* tables:

```
CREATE TABLE master_customer
(
cust_id       int          NOT NULL  IDENTITY  PRIMARY KEY,
cust_name     varchar(50)  NOT NULL
)

CREATE TABLE customer_location
(
cust_id     int        NOT NULL,
cust_loc    smallint   NOT NULL,
CONSTRAINT PK_CUSTOMER_LOCATION PRIMARY KEY (cust_id,cust_loc),
CONSTRAINT FK_CUSTOMER_LOCATION FOREIGN KEY (cust_id)
    REFERENCES master_customer (cust_id)
)

CREATE TABLE orders
(
order_id    int        NOT NULL  IDENTITY  PRIMARY KEY,
cust_id     int        NOT NULL,
cust_loc    smallint   NOT NULL,
CONSTRAINT FK_ORDER_MASTER_CUST FOREIGN KEY (cust_id)
    REFERENCES master_customer (cust_id),
CONSTRAINT FK_ORDER_CUST_LOC FOREIGN KEY (cust_id, cust_loc)
    REFERENCES customer_location (cust_id, cust_loc)
)
```

Although logically, the relationship between the *orders* and *master_customer* tables exists, the relationship is redundant to and subsumed by the fact that *orders* is related to *customer_location*, which has its own FOREIGN KEY constraint to *master_customer*. Declaring a foreign key for *master_customer* adds unnecessary overhead without adding any further integrity protection.

NOTE In the case just described, perhaps declaring a foreign key adds readability to the table definition, but you can achieve this readability by simply adding comments to the CREATE TABLE command. It's perfectly legal to add a comment practically anywhere—even in the middle of a CREATE TABLE statement. A more subtle way to achieve this readability is to declare the constraint so that it appears in *sp_helpconstraint* and in the system catalogs, but to then disable the constraint by using the ALTER TABLE NOCHECK option. Because the constraint would then be unenforced, an additional table wouldn't be added to the execution plan.

The CREATE TABLE statement that is shown in the following example for the *orders* table omits the redundant foreign key and, for illustrative purposes, includes a comment. Despite the lack of a FOREIGN KEY constraint in the *master_customer* table, you still couldn't insert a *cust_id* that didn't exist in the *master_customer* table, because the reference to the *customer_location* table would prevent it.

```
CREATE TABLE orders
(
order_id     int        NOT NULL  IDENTITY  PRIMARY KEY,
cust_id      int        NOT NULL,
cust_loc     smallint   NOT NULL,
--- Implied Foreign Key Reference of:
--- (cust_id) REFERENCES master_customer (cust_id)
CONSTRAINT FK_ORDER_CUST_LOC FOREIGN KEY (cust_id, cust_loc)
    REFERENCES customer_location (cust_id, cust_loc)
)
```

Note that the table on which the foreign key is declared (the referencing table, which in this example is *orders*) isn't the only table that requires additional execution steps. When being updated, the table being referenced (in this case *customer_location*) also must have additional steps in its execution plan to ensure that an update of the columns being referenced won't break a relationship and create an orphan entry in the *orders* table. Without making any changes directly to the *customer_location* table, you can see a significant decrease in update or delete performance because of foreign key references added to other tables.

Practical Considerations for FOREIGN KEY Constraints

When using constraints, you should consider triggers, performance, and indexing. Let's take a look at the ramifications of each.

Constraints and triggers Triggers won't be discussed in detail until Chapter 10, but for now, you should simply note that constraints are enforced before a triggered action is performed. If the constraint is violated, the statement will abort before the trigger fires.

NOTE The owner of a table isn't allowed to declare a foreign key reference to another table unless the owner of the other table has granted REFERENCES permission to the first table owner. Even if the owner of the first table is allowed to select from the table to be referenced, that owner must have REFERENCES permission. This prevents another user from changing the performance of operations on your table without your knowledge or consent. You can grant any user REFERENCES permission even if you don't also grant SELECT permission, and vice versa. The only exception is that the DBO, or any user who is a member of the *db_owner* role, has full default permissions on all objects in the database.

Performance considerations In deciding on the use of foreign key relationships, you must balance the protection provided with the corresponding performance overhead. Be careful not to add constraints that form logically redundant relationships. Excessive use of FOREIGN KEY constraints can severely degrade the performance of seemingly simple operations.

Constraints and indexing The columns specified in FOREIGN KEY constraints are often strong candidates for index creation. You should build the index with the same key order used in the PRIMARY KEY or UNIQUE constraint of the table it references so that joins can be performed efficiently. Also be aware that a foreign key is often a subset of the table's primary key. In the *customer_location* table used in the preceding two examples, *cust_id* is part of the primary key as well as a foreign key in its own right. Given that *cust_id* is part of a primary key, it's already part of an index. In this example, *cust_id* is the lead column of the index, and building a separate index on it alone probably isn't warranted. However, if *cust_id* were *not* the lead column of the index B-tree, it might make sense to build an index on it.

Constraint Checking Solutions

Sometimes two tables reference one another, which creates a bootstrap problem. Suppose *Table1* has a foreign key reference to *Table2*, but *Table2* has a foreign key reference to *Table1*. Even before either table contains any data, you'll be prevented from inserting a row into *Table1* because the reference to *Table2* will fail. Similarly, you can't insert a row into *Table2* because the reference to *Table1* will fail.

ANSI SQL has a solution: *deferred constraints*, in which you can instruct the system to postpone constraint checking until the entire transaction is committed. Using this elegant remedy puts both INSERT statements into a single transaction that results in the two tables having correct references by the time COMMIT occurs. Unfortunately, no mainstream product currently provides the deferred option for constraints. The deferred option is part of the complete SQL-92 specification, which no product has yet fully implemented. It's not required for NIST certification as ANSI SQL-92 compliant, a certification that Microsoft SQL Server has achieved.

SQL Server 7 provides *immediate* constraint checking; it has no deferred option. SQL Server offers three options for dealing with constraint checking: it allows you to add constraints after adding data, it lets you temporarily disable checking of foreign key references, and it allows you to use the *bcp* (bulk copy) program or BULK INSERT command to initially load data and avoid checking FOREIGN KEY constraints. (You can override this default option with *bcp* or the BULK INSERT command and force FOREIGN KEY constraints to be validated.) To add constraints after adding data, don't create constraints via the CREATE TABLE command. After adding the initial data, you can add constraints by using the ALTER TABLE command.

With the second option, the table owner can temporarily disable checking of foreign key references by using the ALTER TABLE *table* NOCHECK CONSTRAINT statement. Once data exists, you can reestablish the FOREIGN KEY constraint by using ALTER TABLE *table* CHECK CONSTRAINT. Note that when an existing constraint is reenabled using this method, SQL Server doesn't automatically check to see that all rows still satisfy the constraint. To do this, you can simply issue a *dummy update* by setting a column to itself for all rows, determining whether any constraint violations are raised, and then fixing them. (For example, you could issue UPDATE ORDERS SET *cust_id = cust_id*.)

Finally you can use the *bcp* program or the BULK INSERT command to initially load data. The BULK INSERT command and the *bcp* program don't check any FOREIGN KEY constraints, by default. You can use the CHECK_CONSTRAINTS option to override this behavior. BULK INSERT and *bcp* are faster than regular INSERT commands because they usually bypass normal integrity checks and most logging.

When using ALTER TABLE to add (instead of reenable) a new FOREIGN KEY constraint for a table in which data already exists, the existing data is checked by default. If constraint violations occur, the constraint won't be added. With large tables, such a check can be quite time-consuming. You do have an alternative—you can add a FOREIGN KEY constraint and omit the check. To do this, specify the WITH NOCHECK option with ALTER TABLE. All subsequent operations will be checked, but existing data won't be checked. As in the case for reenabling a constraint, you could then perform a dummy update to flag any violations in the existing data. If you use this option, you should do the dummy update as soon as possible to ensure that all the data is clean. Otherwise, your users might see constraint error messages when they perform update operations on the preexisting data, even if they haven't changed any values.

Restrictions on Dropping Tables

If you're dropping tables, you must drop all the referencing tables, or drop the referencing FOREIGN KEY constraints before dropping the referenced table. For example, in the preceding example's *orders, customer_location,* and *master_customer* tables, the following sequence of DROP statements fails because a table being dropped is referenced by a table that still exists—that is, *customer_location* can't be dropped because the *orders* table references it, and *orders* isn't dropped until later:

```
DROP TABLE customer_location
DROP TABLE master_customer
DROP TABLE orders
```

Changing the sequence to the following works fine because *orders* is dropped first:

```
DROP TABLE orders
DROP TABLE customer_location
DROP TABLE master_customer
```

When two tables reference each other, you must first drop the constraints or set them to NOCHECK (both operations use ALTER TABLE) before the tables can be dropped. Similarly, a table that's being referenced can't be part of a TRUNCATE TABLE command. You must drop or disable the constraint, or you must simply drop and rebuild the table.

Self-Referencing Tables

A table can be self-referencing—that is, the foreign key can reference one or more columns in the same table. The following example shows an employee table, in which a column for manager references another *employee* entry:

```
CREATE TABLE employee
(
emp_id      int          NOT NULL PRIMARY KEY,
emp_name    varchar(30)  NOT NULL,
mgr_id      int          NOT NULL REFERENCES employee(emp_id)
)
```

The *employee* table is a perfectly reasonable table. It illustrates most of the issues we've discussed. However, in this case, a single INSERT command that satisfies the reference is legal. For example, if the CEO of the company has an *emp_id* of 1 and is also his own manager, the following INSERT will be allowed and can be a useful way to insert the first row in a self-referencing table:

```
INSERT employee VALUES (1,'Chris Smith',1)
```

Although SQL Server doesn't currently provide a deferred option for constraints, self-referencing tables add a twist that sometimes makes SQL Server use deferred operations internally. Consider the case of a nonqualified DELETE statement that deletes many rows in the table. After all rows are ultimately deleted, you can assume that no constraint violation would occur. However, while some rows are deleted internally and others remain during the delete operation, violations would occur because some of the referencing rows would be orphaned before they were actually deleted. SQL Server handles such *interim violations* automatically and without any user intervention. As long as the self-referencing constraints are valid at the *end* of the data modification statement, no errors are raised during processing.

To gracefully handle these interim violations, however, additional processing and worktables are required to hold the work-in-progress. This adds substantial overhead and can also limit the actual number of foreign keys that can be used. An UPDATE statement can also cause an interim violation. For example, if all employee numbers are to be changed by multiplying each by 1000, the following UPDATE statement would require worktables to avoid the possibility of raising an error on an interim violation:

```
UPDATE employee SET emp_id=emp_id * 1000, mgr_id=mgr_id * 1000
```

The additional worktables and the processing needed to handle the worktables are made part of the execution plan. Therefore, if the optimizer sees that a data modification statement *could* cause an interim violation, the additional temporary worktables will be created, even if no such interim violations ever actually occur. These extra steps are needed only in the following situations:

- A table is self-referencing (it has a FOREIGN KEY constraint that refers back to itself).

- A single data modification statement (UPDATE, DELETE, or INSERT based on a SELECT) is performed and can affect more than one row. (The optimizer can't determine *a priori*, based on the WHERE clause and unique indexes, whether more than one row could be affected.) Multiple data modification statements within the transaction don't apply—this condition must be a single statement that affects multiple rows.

■ Both the referencing and referenced columns are affected (which is always the case for DELETE and INSERT operations, but might or might not be the case for UPDATE).

If a data modification statement in your application meets the above criteria, you can be sure that SQL Server is automatically using a limited and special-purpose form of deferred constraints to protect against interim violations.

Referential Actions

The full ANSI SQL-92 standard contains the notion of the *referential action*, sometimes (incompletely) referred to as a *cascading delete*. SQL Server 7 doesn't provide this feature as part of FOREIGN KEY constraints, but this notion warrants some discussion here because the capability exists via triggers.

The idea behind referential actions is this: sometimes, instead of just preventing an update of data that would violate a foreign key reference, you might be able to perform an additional, compensating action that would still enable the constraint to be honored. For example, if you were to delete a *customer* table, which had references to *orders*, it would be possible to have SQL Server automatically delete all those related *order* records (that is, cascade the delete to *orders*), in which case the constraint wouldn't be violated and the *customer* table could be deleted. This feature is intended for both UPDATE and DELETE statements, and four possible actions are defined: NO ACTION, CASCADE, SET DEFAULT, and SET NULL.

■ **NO ACTION**   The delete is prevented. This default mode, per the ANSI standard, occurs if no other action is specified. SQL Server constraints provide this action (without the NO ACTION syntax). NO ACTION is often referred to as RESTRICT, but this usage is slightly incorrect in terms of how ANSI defines RESTRICT and NO ACTION. ANSI uses RESTRICT in DDL statements such as DROP TABLE, and it uses NO ACTION for FOREIGN KEY constraints. (The difference is subtle and unimportant. It's common to refer to the FOREIGN KEY constraint as having an action of RESTRICT.)

■ **CASCADE**   A delete of all matching rows in the referenced table occurs.

■ **SET DEFAULT**   The delete is performed, and all foreign key values in the referencing table are set to a default value.

■ **SET NULL**   The delete is performed, and all foreign key values in the referencing table are set to NULL.

Implementation of referential actions isn't required for NIST certification as ANSI SQL-92 conformant. SQL Server will provide referential actions in a future release. Until then, the program performs these actions via triggers, as discussed in Chapter 10. Creating triggers for such actions or for constraint enforcement is easy. Practically speaking, performance is usually equivalent to that of a FOREIGN KEY constraint, because both need to do the same type of operations to check the constraint.

> **NOTE** Because a constraint is checked before a trigger fires, you can't have both a constraint to enforce the relationship when a new key is inserted into the referencing table and a trigger that performs an operation such as a cascade delete from the referenced table. Triggers need to perform *both* the enforcement (an INSERT trigger on the referencing table) and the referential action (a DELETE trigger on the referenced table). If you do have both a constraint and a trigger, the constraint will fail and the statement will be aborted before the trigger to cascade the delete fires.
>
> You might still want to declare the foreign key relationship largely for readability so that the relationship between the tables is clear. Simply use the NOCHECK option of ALTER TABLE to ensure that the constraint won't be enforced, and then the trigger will fire. (The trigger must also take on the enforcement of the constraint.)

SQL Server users often request support for referential actions, and it will surely be implemented in a future version. However, using application logic for such actions and SQL Server constraints (without referential actions other than NO ACTION) to safeguard the relationship is more often applicable. Although referential actions are intuitive, how many applications could really avail themselves of this feature? How many real-world examples exist in which the application is so simplistic that you would go ahead and unconditionally delete (or set to the default or to NULL) all matching rows in a related table? Probably not many. Most applications would perform some additional processing, such as asking a user if she *really* intends to delete a customer who has open orders. The declarative nature of referential actions doesn't provide a way to hook in application logic to handle cases like these. Probably the most useful course, then, is to use SQL Server's constraints to restrict breaking relationships and have the application deal with updates that would produce constraint violations. This method will probably continue to be the most useful even after referential actions are added.

CHECK Constraints

Enforcing *domain integrity* (that is, ensuring that only entries of expected types, values, or ranges can exist for a given column) is also important. SQL Server provides two ways to enforce domain integrity: CHECK constraints and rules. CHECK constraints allow you to define an expression for a table that must not evaluate to FALSE for a data modification statement to succeed. (Note that we didn't say that the constraint must evaluate to TRUE. The constraint will allow the row if it evaluates to TRUE or to unknown. The constraint evaluates to unknown when NULL values are present, and this introduces three-value logic. The issues of NULLs and three-value logic are discussed in depth in Chapter 7.) Rules perform almost the same function as CHECK constraints, but they use different syntax and have fewer capabilities. Rules have existed in SQL Server since its initial release in 1989, well before CHECK constraints, which are part of the ANSI SQL-92 standard and were added in version 6 in 1995.

CHECK constraints make a table's definition more readable by including the domain checks in the DDL. Rules have a potential advantage in that they can be defined once and then bound to multiple columns and tables (using *sp_bindrule* each time), while you must respecify a CHECK constraint for each column and table. But the extra binding step can also be a hassle, so this capability for rules is beneficial only if a rule will be used in many places. Although performance between the two approaches is identical, CHECK constraints are generally preferred over rules because they're a direct part of the table's DDL, they're ANSI-standard SQL, they provide a few more capabilities than rules (such as the ability to reference other columns in the same row or to call a system function), and perhaps most importantly, they're more likely than rules to be further enhanced in future releases of SQL Server. For these reasons, we're going to concentrate on CHECK constraints.

CHECK constraints (and rules) add additional steps to the execution plan to ensure that the expression doesn't evaluate to FALSE (which would result in the operation being aborted). Although steps are added to the execution plan for data modifications, these are typically much less expensive than the extra steps discussed earlier for FOREIGN KEY constraints. For foreign key checking, another table must be searched, requiring additional I/O. CHECK constraints deal only with some logical expression for the specific row already being operated on, so no additional I/O is required. Because additional processing cycles are used to evaluate the expressions, the system requires more CPU use. But if there's plenty of CPU power to spare, the effect might well be negligible. (You can watch this by using Performance Monitor.)

Like other constraint types, you can declare CHECK constraints at the column or table level. For a constraint on one column, the run-time performance is the same for the two methods. You must declare a CHECK constraint that refers to more than one column as a table-level constraint. Only a single column-level CHECK constraint is allowed for a specific column, although the constraint can have multiple logical expressions that can be AND'ed or OR'ed together. And a specific column can have or be part of many table-level expressions.

Some CHECK constraint features have often been underutilized by SQL Server database designers, including the ability to reference other columns in the same row, use system and niladic functions (which are evaluated at runtime), and use AND/OR expressions. The following example shows a table with multiple CHECK constraints (as well as a PRIMARY KEY constraint and a FOREIGN KEY constraint) and showcases some of these features:

```
CREATE TABLE employee
(
emp_id          int         NOT NULL PRIMARY KEY
                            CHECK (emp_id BETWEEN 0 AND 1000),

emp_name        varchar(30) NOT NULL CONSTRAINT no_nums
                            CHECK (emp_name NOT LIKE '%[0-9]%'),

mgr_id          int         NOT NULL REFERENCES employee(emp_id),

entered_date    datetime    NULL CHECK (entered_date >=
                            CURRENT_TIMESTAMP),

entered_by      int         CHECK (entered_by IS NOT NULL),
                            CONSTRAINT valid_entered_by CHECK
                            (entered_by = SUSER_ID(NULL) AND
                            entered_by <> emp_id),

CONSTRAINT valid_mgr CHECK (mgr_id <> emp_id OR emp_id=1),

CONSTRAINT end_of_month CHECK (DATEPART(DAY, GETDATE()) < 28)
)
GO

EXEC sp_helpconstraint employee
GO
>>>>

Object Name
---------------
employee
```

constraint_type	constraint_name	constraint_keys
CHECK on column emp_id	CK__employee__emp_id__2C3393D0	([emp_id] >= 0 [emp_id] <= 1000)
CHECK on column entered_by	CK__employee__entered_by__300424B4	(((not([entered_by] is null))))
CHECK on column entered_date	CK__employee__entered_date__2F10007B	([entered_date] >= getdate())
CHECK Table Level	end_of_month	(datepart(day, getdate()) < 28)
FOREIGN KEY	FK__employee__mgr_id__2E1BDC42	mgr_id
CHECK on column emp_name	no_nums	([emp_name] not like '%[0-9]%')
PRIMARY KEY (clustered)	PK__employee__2B3F6F97	emp_id
CHECK Table Level	valid_entered_by	([entered_by] = suser_id(null) and [entered_by] <> [emp_id])
CHECK Table Level	valid_mgr	([mgr_id] <> [emp_id] or [emp_id] = 1)

```
Table is referenced by
--------------------------------
pubs.dbo.employee: FK__employee__mgr_id__2E1BDC42
```

This example illustrates the following points:

Constraint syntax   CHECK constraints can be expressed at the column level with abbreviated syntax (leaving naming to SQL Server), such as the check on *entered_date*; at the column level with an explicit name, such as the NO_NUMS constraint on *emp_name*; or as a table-level constraint, such as the VALID_MGR constraint.

Regular expressions   CHECK constraints can use regular expressions—for example, NO_NUMS ensures that a digit can never be entered as a character in a person's name.

AND/OR   Expressions can be AND'ed and OR'ed together to represent more complex situations—for example, VALID_MGR. However, SQL Server won't check for logical correctness at the time a constraint is added to the table. Suppose you wanted to restrict the values in a *department_id* column to either negative numbers or values greater than 100. (Perhaps numbers between 0 and 100 are reserved.) You could add this column and constraint to the table using ALTER TABLE.

```
ALTER TABLE employee
add department_no int CHECK(department_no < 100 AND department_no > 100)
```

However, once the above command has been executed successfully and the new column and constraint have been added to the table, we'll never be able to put another row into the table. We accidentally typed *AND* in the ALTER TABLE statement instead of *OR*, but that isn't considered an illegal CHECK constraint. Each time we tried to insert a row, SQL Server tried to validate that the value in the *department_no* column was both less than 0 and more than 100! Any value for *department_no* that doesn't meet that requirement will cause the insert to fail. It could take a long time to come up with a value to satisfy this constraint. In this case, we'd have to drop the constraint and add a new one with the correct definition before we could insert any rows.

Constraint reference   Table-level CHECK constraints can refer to more than one column in the same row. For example, VALID_MGR insists that no employee can be his own boss, except employee number 1, who is assumed to be the CEO. SQL Server currently has no provision that allows you to check a value from another row or from a different table.

NULL prevention   You can make a CHECK constraint prevent NULL values—for example, CHECK (*entered_by* IS NOT NULL). Generally, you would simply declare the column NOT NULL.

Unknown expressions   A NULL column might make the expression logically unknown. For example, a NULL value for *entered_date* gives CHECK *entered_date* >= CURRENT_TIMESTAMP an unknown value. This doesn't reject the row, however. The constraint rejects the row only when the expression is clearly false, even if it isn't necessarily true.

System functions   System functions, such as GETDATE(), APP_NAME(), DATALENGTH(), and SUSER_ID(), as well as niladic functions, such as SYSTEM_USER, CURRENT_TIMESTAMP, and USER, can be used in CHECK constraints. This subtle feature is powerful and can be useful, for example, for assuring that a user can change only records that she has entered by comparing *entered_by* to the user's system ID, as generated by SUSER_ID() (or by comparing *emp_name* to SYSTEM_USER). Note that niladic functions such as CURRENT_TIMESTAMP are provided for ANSI SQL conformance and simply map to an underlying SQL Server function, in this case GETDATE(). So while the DDL to create the constraint on *entered_date* uses CURRENT_TIMESTAMP, *sp_helpconstraint* shows it as GETDATE(), which is the underlying function. Either expression is valid and equivalent in the CHECK constraint. The VALID_ENTERED_BY constraint ensures that the *entered_by* column can be set only to the currently connected user's ID, and it ensures that users can't update their own records.

System functions and column references A table-level constraint can call a system function without referencing a column in the table. In the example preceding this list, the END_OF_MONTH CHECK constraint calls two date functions, DATEPART() and GETDATE(), to ensure that updates can't be made after day 28 of the month (when the business's payroll is assumed to be processed). The constraint never references a column in the table. Similarly, a CHECK constraint might call the APP_NAME() function to ensure that updates can be made only from an application of a certain name, instead of from an ad hoc tool such as the Query Analyzer.

As with FOREIGN KEY constraints, you can add or drop CHECK constraints by using ALTER TABLE. When adding a constraint, by default the existing data is checked for compliance; you can override this default by using the NOCHECK syntax. You can later do a dummy update to check for any violations. The table or database owner can also temporarily disable CHECK constraints by using WITH NOCHECK in the ALTER TABLE statement.

Default Constraints

A default allows you to specify a constant value, NULL, or the run-time value of a system function if no known value exists or if the column is missing in an INSERT statement. Although you could argue that a default isn't truly a constraint (because a default doesn't enforce anything), you can create defaults in a CREATE TABLE statement using the CONSTRAINT keyword; therefore, defaults will be referred to as constraints. Defaults add little overhead, and you can use them liberally without too much concern about performance degradation.

SQL Server provides two ways of creating defaults. Since the original SQL Server release in 1989, you can create a default (CREATE DEFAULT) and then bind the default to a column (*sp_bindefault*). Default constraints were introduced in 1995 with SQL Server 6.0 as part of the CREATE TABLE and ALTER TABLE statements, and they're based on the ANSI SQL standard (which includes such niceties as being able to use system functions). Using defaults is pretty intuitive. The type of default you use is a matter of preference; both perform the same function internally. Future enhancements are likely to be made to the ANSI-style implementation. Having the default within the table DDL seems a cleaner approach. We recommend that you use defaults within CREATE TABLE and ALTER TABLE rather than within CREATE DEFAULT, so we'll focus on that style here.

Here's the example from the previous CHECK constraint discussion, now modified to include several defaults:

```
CREATE TABLE employee
(
emp_id        int         NOT NULL  PRIMARY KEY  DEFAULT 1000
                          CHECK (emp_id BETWEEN 0 AND 1000),

emp_name      varchar(30) NULL  DEFAULT NULL  CONSTRAINT no_nums
                          CHECK (emp_name NOT LIKE '%[0-9]%'),

mgr_id        int         NOT NULL  DEFAULT (1)  REFERENCES
                          employee(emp_id),

entered_date  datetime    NOT NULL  CHECK (entered_date >=
                          CONVERT(char(10), CURRENT_TIMESTAMP, 102))
                          CONSTRAINT def_today DEFAULT
                          (CONVERT(char(10), GETDATE(), 102)),

entered_by    int         NOT NULL  DEFAULT SUSER_ID()
                          CHECK (entered_by IS NOT NULL),

CONSTRAINT valid_entered_by CHECK (entered_by=SUSER_ID() AND
entered_by <> emp_id),

CONSTRAINT valid_mgr CHECK (mgr_id <> emp_id OR emp_id=1),

CONSTRAINT end_of_month CHECK (DATEPART(DAY, GETDATE()) < 28)
)
GO
```

```
EXEC sp_helpconstraint employee
GO

>>>
```

```
Object Name
---------------
employee
```

constraint_type	constraint_name	constraint_keys
CHECK on column emp_id	CK__employee__emp_id__2C3393D0	([emp_id] >= 0 [emp_id] <= 1000)
CHECK on column entered_by	CK__employee__entered_by__300424B4	(((not([entered_by] is null))))
DEFAULT on column entered_date	def_today	convert(char(10), getdate(),102))
DEFAULT on column emp_id	DF__employee__emp_id__35BCFE0A	(1000)
DEFAULT on column emp_name	DF__employee__emp_name__37A5467C	(null)
DEFAULT on column entered_by	DF__employee__entered_by__3D5E1FD2	(suser_id())
DEFAULT on column mgr_id	DF__employee__mgr_id__398D8EEE	(1)
CHECK on column entered_date	CK__employee__entered_date__2F10007B	([entered_date] >= getdate())
CHECK Table Level	end_of_month	(datepart(day, getdate()) < 28)
FOREIGN KEY	FK__employee__mgr_id__2E1BDC42	mgr_id
CHECK on column emp_name	no_nums	([emp_name] not like '%[0-9]%')

(continued)

```
PRIMARY KEY              PK__employee__2B3F6F97                    emp_id
(clustered)

CHECK Table Level        valid_entered_by                         ([entered_by] =
                                                                  suser_id(null)
                                                                  and [entered_by]
                                                                  <> [emp_id])

CHECK Table Level        valid_mgr                                ([mgr_id] <>
                                                                  [emp_id] or
                                                                  [emp_id] = 1)

Table is referenced by
----------------------------------
pubs.dbo.employee: FK__employee__mgr_id__2E1BDC42
```

The preceding code demonstrates the following about defaults:

Column-level constraint   A default constraint is always a column-level constraint because it pertains to only one column. You can use the abbreviated syntax that omits the keyword CONSTRAINT and the specified name, letting SQL Server generate the name, or you can specify the name by using the more verbose CONSTRAINT *name* DEFAULT syntax.

Clashes with CHECK constraint   A default value can clash with a CHECK constraint. This problem appears only at runtime, not when you create the table or when you add the default via ALTER TABLE. For example, a column with a default of 0 and a CHECK constraint that states that the value must be greater than 0 would never be able to insert or update the default value.

PRIMARY KEY or UNIQUE constraint   You can assign a default to a column having a PRIMARY KEY or a UNIQUE constraint. Such columns must have unique values, so only one row could exist with the default value in that column. The preceding example sets a DEFAULT on a primary key column for illustration, but in general, this practice is unwise.

Parentheses and quotation marks   You can write a constant value within parentheses, as in DEFAULT (1), or without them, as in DEFAULT 1. A character or date constant must be enclosed in either single or double quotation marks.

NULL vs. default value   A tricky concept is knowing when a NULL is inserted into a column vs. when a default value is entered. A column declared NOT NULL with a default defined uses the default only under one of the following conditions:

- The INSERT statement specifies its column list and omits the column with the default.

- The INSERT statement specifies the keyword DEFAULT in the values list (whether the column is explicitly specified as part of the column list or implicitly specified in the values list and the column list is omitted, meaning "All columns in the order in which they were created"). If the values list explicitly specifies NULL, an error is raised and the statement fails; the default value isn't used. If the INSERT statement omits the column entirely, the default is used and no error occurs. (This behavior is in accordance with ANSI SQL.) The keyword DEFAULT can be used in the values list, and this is the only way the default value will be used if a NOT NULL column is specified in the column list of an INSERT statement (either, as in the following example, by omitting the column list—which means all columns—or by explicitly including the NOT NULL column in the columns list).

```
INSERT EMPLOYEE VALUES (1, 'The Big Guy', 1, DEFAULT, DEFAULT)
```

Table 6-5 summarizes the behavior of INSERT statements based on whether a column is declared NULL or NOT NULL and whether it has a default specified. It shows the result for the column for three cases:

- Omitting the column entirely (no entry).

- Having the INSERT statement use NULL in the values list.

- Specifying the column and using DEFAULT in the values list.

	No Entry		Enter NULL		Enter DEFAULT	
	No Default	*Default*	*No Default*	*Default*	*No Default*	*Default*
NULL	NULL	default	NULL	NULL	NULL	default
NOT NULL	error	default	error	error	error	default

Table 6-5.
INSERT behavior with defaults.

NOTE Although you can declare DEFAULT NULL on a column allowing NULL, SQL Server does this without declaring a default at all, even when using the DEFAULT keyword in an INSERT or UPDATE statement.

Declaring a default on a column that has the Identity property wouldn't make sense, and SQL Server will raise an error if you try it. The Identity property acts as a default for the column. But the DEFAULT keyword cannot be used as a placeholder for an *identity* column in the values list of an INSERT statement. You can use a special form of INSERT statement if a table has a default value for every column (an *identity* column does meet this criteria) or allows NULL. The following statement uses the DEFAULT VALUES clause instead of a column list and values list:

```
INSERT EMPLOYEE DEFAULT VALUES
```

TIP You can generate some test data by putting the Identity property on a primary key column and declaring default values for all other columns and then repeatedly issuing an INSERT statement of this form within a Transact-SQL loop.

More About Constraints

This section covers some tips and considerations that you should know about when working with constraints. We'll look at constraint names and system catalog entries, the *status* field, constraint failures, multiple-row data modifications, and integrity checks.

Constraint Names and System Catalog Entries

Earlier in this chapter, you learned about the cryptic-looking constraint names that SQL Server generates. Now we'll explain the naming. Consider again the following simple CREATE TABLE statement:

```
CREATE TABLE customer
(
cust_id      int          IDENTITY  NOT NULL  PRIMARY KEY,
cust_name    varchar(30)  NOT NULL
)
```

The constraint produced from this simple statement bears the nonintuitive name *PK__customer__59FA5E80*. All types of column-level constraints use this naming scheme. (Note that although the NULL/NOT NULL designation is often thought of as a constraint, it's not quite the same. Instead, this designation is treated as a column attribute and has no name or representation in the *sysobjects* system table.)

The first two characters (PK) show the constraint type—PK for PRIMARY KEY, UN for UNIQUE, FK for FOREIGN KEY, and DF for DEFAULT. Next are two underscore characters (__) used as a separator. (You might be tempted to use one underscore as a separator, to conserve characters and to avoid having to truncate as much. However, it's common to use an underscore in a table name or a column name, both of which appear in the constraint name. Using two underscore characters distinguishes which kind of a name this is and where the separation occurs.)

Next comes the table name (*customer*), which is limited to 116 characters for a PRIMARY KEY constraint and slightly fewer characters for all other constraint names. For all constraints other than PRIMARY KEY, there are then two more underscore characters for separation followed by the next sequence of characters, which is the column name. The column name is truncated to five characters, if necessary. If the column name has fewer than five characters in it, the length of the table name portion can be slightly longer.

And finally, the hexadecimal representation of the object ID for the constraint (*59FA5E80*) comes after another separator. (This value is used as the *id* column of the *sysobjects* system table and the *constid* column of the *sysconstraints* system table.) Object names are limited to 128 characters in SQL Server 7, so the total length of all portions of the constraint name must also be less than or equal to 128.

Note the queries and output using this value that are shown in Figure 6-11.

```
Query:
SELECT OBJECT_NAME(0x59FA5E80), OBJECT_ID('customer')

Results:
PK__customer__59FA5E80      1493580359


Query:
SELECT * FROM sysconstraints WHERE constid = 0x59FA5E80

Results:
constid      id          colid sparel status  actions error
----------   ----------  ----- ------ ------- ------- -----
1509580416   1493580359  0     0      133665  4096    0


Query:
SELECT name, id, type FROM sysobjects WHERE id = 0x59FA5E80

Results:
name                          id          type
----------------------------  ----------  ----
PK__customer__59FA5E80        1509580416  K
```

Figure 6-11.
Querying the system tables using the hexadecimal ID value.

TIP The hexadecimal value 0x59FA5E80 is equal to the decimal value 1509580416, which is the value of *constid* in *sysconstraints* and of *id* in *sysobjects*.

These sample queries of system tables show the following:

- **A constraint is an object** A constraint has an entry in the *sysobjects* table in the *xtype* column of C, D, F, PK, or UQ for CHECK, DEFAULT, FOREIGN KEY, PRIMARY KEY, and UNIQUE, respectively.

- *Sysconstraints* **relates to** *sysobjects* The *sysconstraints* table is really just a view of the *sysobjects* system table. The *constid* column in the view is the object ID of the constraint, and the *id* column of *sys-constraints* is the object ID of the base table on which the constraint is declared.

- *Colid* **values** If the constraint is a column-level CHECK, FOR-EIGN KEY, or DEFAULT, the *colid* has the *colid* of the column. This *colid* is related to the *colid* of *syscolumns* for the base table represented by *id*. A table-level constraint, or any PRIMARY KEY/UNIQUE constraint (even if column level), always has 0 in this column.

TIP To see the names and order of the columns in a PRIMARY KEY or UNIQUE constraint, you can query the *sysindexes* and *syscolumns* tables for the index being used to enforce the constraint. The name of the constraint and that of the index enforcing the con-straint are the same, whether the name was user specified or system generated. The columns in the index key are somewhat cryptically encoded in the *keys1* and *keys2* fields of *sysindexes*. The easiest way to decode these values is to simply use the *sp_helpindex* system stored procedure, or you can use the code of that procedure as a template if you need to decode them in your own procedure.

Decoding the *status* Field

The *status* field of the *sysconstraints* view is a pseudo–bit-mask field packed with information. If you know how to crack this column, you can essentially write your own *sp_helpconstraint*-like procedure. Note that the documentation is incomplete regarding the values of this column. One way to start decoding this column is to look at the definition of the *sysconstraints* view using the *sp_helptext* system procedure.

The lowest four bits, obtained by AND'ing *status* with 0xF (*status & 0xF*), contain the constraint type. A value of 1 is PRIMARY KEY, 2 is UNIQUE, 3 is FOREIGN KEY, 4 is CHECK, and 5 is Default. The fifth bit is on (*status & 0x10 <> 0*) when the constraint was created at the column level. The sixth bit is on (*status & 0x20 <> 0*) when the constraint was created at the table level.

Some of the higher bits are used for internal status purposes, such as noting whether a nonclustered index is being rebuilt and for other internal states. Table 6-6 shows some of the other bit-mask values you might be interested in:

Bit-Mask Value	Description
512	The constraint creates a clustered index.
1024	The constraint creates a nonclustered index.
16384	The constraint has been disabled.
32767	The constraint has been enabled.
131072	SQL Server generates a name for the constraint.

Table 6-6.
Bit-mask values.

Using this information, and not worrying about the higher bits used for internal status, you could use the following query to show constraint information for the *employee* table:

```
SELECT
    OBJECT_NAME(constid) 'Constraint Name',
    constid 'Constraint ID',
    CASE (status & 0xF)
        WHEN 1 THEN 'Primary Key'
        WHEN 2 THEN 'Unique'
        WHEN 3 THEN 'Foreign Key'
        WHEN 4 THEN 'Check'
        WHEN 5 THEN 'Default'
        ELSE 'Undefined'
    END 'Constraint Type',
    CASE (status & 0x30)
        WHEN 0x10 THEN 'Column'
        WHEN 0x20 THEN 'Table'
        ELSE 'NA'
    END 'Level'
FROM sysconstraints
WHERE id=OBJECT_ID('employee')

>>>
```

(continued)

Constraint Name	Constraint ID	Constraint Type	Level
PK__employee__49C3F6B7	1237579447	Primary Key	Table
DF__employee__emp_id__4AB81AF0	1253579504	Default	Column
CK__employee__emp_id__4BAC3F29	1269579561	Check	Column
DF__employee__emp_name__4CA06362	1285579618	Default	Column
no_nums	1301579675	Check	Column
DF__employee__mgr_id__4E88ABD4	1317579732	Default	Column
FK__employee__mgr_id__4F7CD00D	1333579789	Foreign Key	Column
CK__employee__entered_date__5070F446	1349579846	Check	Column
def_today	1365579903	Default	Column
DF__employee__entered_by__52593CB8	1381579960	Default	Column
CK__employee__entered_by__534D60F1	1397580017	Check	Column
valid_entered_by	1413580074	Check	Table
valid_mgr	1429580131	Check	Table
end_of_month	1445580188	Check	Table

Constraint Failures in
Transactions and Multiple-Row Data Modifications

Many bugs occur in application code because the developers don't understand how failure of a constraint affects a multiple-statement transaction declared by the user. The biggest misconception is that any error, such as a constraint failure, automatically aborts and rolls back the entire transaction. Rather, after an error is raised, it's up to the transaction to either proceed and ultimately commit, or to roll back. This feature provides the developer with the flexibility to decide how to handle errors. (The semantics are also in accordance with the ANSI SQL-92 standard for COMMIT behavior.)

Following is an example of a simple transaction that tries to insert three rows of data. The second row contains a duplicate key and violates the PRIMARY KEY constraint. Some developers believe that this example wouldn't insert *any* rows because of the error that occurred in one of the statements; they think that this error causes the *entire* transaction to be aborted. However, this isn't what happens—instead, the statement inserts two rows and then commits that change. Although the second INSERT fails, the third INSERT is processed because no error checking occurred between the statements, and then the transaction does a COMMIT. Because no instructions were provided to take some other action after the error other than to proceed, proceed is exactly what SQL Server does. It adds the first and third INSERT statements to the table and ignores the second statement.

```
IF EXISTS (SELECT * FROM sysobjects WHERE name='show_error' AND
    type='U')
    DROP TABLE show_error
GO

CREATE TABLE show_error
(
col1    smallint NOT NULL PRIMARY KEY,
col2    smallint NOT NULL
)
GO

BEGIN TRANSACTION

INSERT show_error VALUES (1, 1)
INSERT show_error VALUES (1, 2)
INSERT show_error VALUES (2, 2)

COMMIT TRANSACTION
GO

SELECT * FROM show_error
GO

Server: Msg 2627, Level 14, State 1
[Microsoft][ODBC SQL Server Driver][SQL Server]Violation of PRIMARY KEY
constraint 'PK__show_error__6754599E'. Cannot insert duplicate key in
object 'show_error'.
The statement has been aborted.
col1    col2
----    ----
1       1
2       2
```

Here's a modified version of the transaction. This example does some simple error checking using the system function @@ERROR and rolls back the transaction if any statement results in an error. In this example, no rows are inserted because the transaction is rolled back:

```
IF EXISTS (SELECT * FROM sysobjects WHERE name='show_error'
    AND type='U')
    DROP TABLE show_error
GO

CREATE TABLE show_error
(
```

(continued)

```
col1     smallint NOT NULL PRIMARY KEY,
col2     smallint NOT NULL
)
GO

BEGIN TRANSACTION
INSERT show_error VALUES (1, 1)
IF @@ERROR <> 0 GOTO TRAN_ABORT
INSERT show_error VALUES (1, 2)
if @@ERROR <> 0 GOTO TRAN_ABORT
INSERT show_error VALUES (2, 2)
if @@ERROR <> 0 GOTO TRAN_ABORT
COMMIT TRANSACTION
GOTO FINISH

TRAN_ABORT:
ROLLBACK TRANSACTION

FINISH:
GO

SELECT * FROM show_error
GO

Server: Msg 2627, Level 14, State 1
[Microsoft][ODBC SQL Server Driver][SQL Server]Violation of PRIMARY KEY
constraint 'PK__show_error__6B24EA82'. Cannot insert duplicate key in
object 'show_error'.
The statement has been aborted.
col1   col2
----   ----
```

Because many developers have handled transaction errors incorrectly, and because it can be tedious to add an error check after every command, SQL Server includes a SET statement that aborts a transaction if it encounters any error during the transaction. (Transact-SQL has no WHENEVER statement, although such a feature would be useful for situations like this.) Using SET XACT_ABORT ON causes the entire transaction to be aborted and rolled back if any error is encountered. The default setting is OFF, which is consistent with semantics prior to version 6.5 (when this SET option was introduced) as well as with ANSI-standard behavior. By setting the option XACT_ABORT ON, we can now rerun the example that does no error checking, and no rows will be inserted:

```
IF EXISTS (SELECT * FROM sysobjects WHERE name='show_error'
    AND type='U')
    DROP TABLE show_error
GO

CREATE TABLE show_error
(
col1    smallint NOT NULL PRIMARY KEY,
col2    smallint NOT NULL
)
GO

SET XACT_ABORT ON
BEGIN TRANSACTION

INSERT show_error VALUES (1, 1)
INSERT show_error VALUES (1, 2)
INSERT show_error VALUES (2, 2)

COMMIT TRANSACTION
GO

SELECT * FROM show_error
GO

Server: Msg 2627, Level 14, State 1
[Microsoft][ODBC SQL Server Driver][SQL Server]Violation of PRIMARY KEY
constraint 'PK__show_error__6D0D32F4'. Cannot insert duplicate key in
object 'show_error'.

col1    col2
----    ----
```

A final comment about constraint errors and transactions: A single data modification statement (such as an UPDATE statement) that affects multiple rows is automatically an atomic operation, even if it's not part of an explicit transaction. If such an UPDATE statement finds 100 rows that meet the criteria of the WHERE clause but one row fails because of a constraint violation, no rows will be updated.

The Order of Integrity Checks

The modification of a given row will fail if any constraint is violated or if a trigger aborts the operation. As soon as a failure in a constraint occurs, the operation is aborted, subsequent checks for that row aren't performed, and no trigger fires for the row. Hence, the order of these checks can be important, as the list on the following page shows.

1. Defaults are applied as appropriate.

2. NOT NULL violations are raised.

3. CHECK constraints are evaluated.

4. FOREIGN KEY checks of *referencing* tables are applied.

5. FOREIGN KEY checks of *referenced* tables are applied.

6. UNIQUE/PRIMARY KEY is checked for correctness.

7. Triggers fire.

Altering a Table

SQL Server 7 allows existing tables to be modified in several ways, and we've seen some of these methods already. You can use ALTER TABLE to add or drop constraints from a table. We've seen that some types of constraints have the option of not being applied to existing data by using the WITH NOCHECK option. Using the ALTER table command, you can make the following types of changes to an existing table:

- Change the datatype or NULL property of a single column.

- Add one or more new columns, with or without defining constraints for those columns.

- Add one or more constraints.

- Drop one or more constraints.

- Drop one or more columns.

- Enable or disable one or more constraints (only applies to CHECK and FOREIGN KEY constraints).

- Enable or disable one or more triggers.

Changing a Datatype

By using the ALTER COLUMN clause of ALTER TABLE, you can modify the datatype or NULL property of an existing column. But be aware of the following restrictions:

- The modified column can't be a *text*, *image*, *ntext*, or *timestamp* column.

- If the modified column is the ROWGUIDCOL for the table, only DROP ROWGUIDCOL is allowed; no datatype changes are allowed.

- The modified column can't be a computed or replicated column.

- The modified column can't have a CHECK or FOREIGN KEY constraint defined on it. '

- The modified column can't be referenced in a computed column.

- The modified column can't have the type changed to *timestamp*.

- If the modified column participates in an index, the only type changes that are allowed are increasing the length of a variable-length type, changing nullability of the column (for example, VARCHAR(10) to VARCHAR(20)), or both.

- If the modified column has a default defined on it, the only changes that are allowed are increasing or decreasing the length of a variable-length type, changing nullability, or both.

- The old type of the column should have an allowed implicit conversion to the new type.

- The new type always has ANSI_PADDING semantics if applicable, regardless of the current setting.

- If conversion of old type to new type causes an overflow (arithmetic or size), the ALTER TABLE statement is aborted.

Here's the syntax and an example of using the ALTER COLUMN clause of the ALTER TABLE statement:

SYNTAX

```
ALTER TABLE table-name ALTER COLUMN column-name
        { type_name [ ( prec [, scale] ) ] [ NULL | NOT NULL ]
        | {ADD | DROP} ROWGUIDCOL }
```

EXAMPLE

```
/* Change the length of the emp_name column in the employee
   table from varchar(30) to varchar(50) */
ALTER TABLE employee
ALTER COLUMN emp_name (varchar(50)
```

Adding a New Column

You can add a new column, with or without specifying column-level constraints. You can add only one column for each ALTER TABLE statement. If the new column doesn't allow NULLs and isn't an identity column, the new column must have a default constraint defined. SQL Server populates the new column in every row with a NULL, the appropriate identity value, or the specified default. If the newly added column is nullable and has a default constraint, the existing rows of the table are *not* filled with the default value, but rather with NULL values. You can override this restriction by using the WITH VALUES clause so that the existing rows of the table are filled with the specified default value.

Adding, Dropping, Disabling, or Enabling a Constraint

Constraint modifications were covered earlier in the discussion about constraints. The trickiest part of using ALTER TABLE to manipulate constraints is that the word CHECK can be used in three different ways:

- To specify a CHECK constraint.

- To defer checking of a newly added constraint. In the following example, we're adding a constraint to validate that *cust_id* in *orders* matches a *cust_id* in *customer*, but we don't want the constraint applied to existing data:

```
ALTER TABLE orders
WITH NOCHECK
ADD FOREIGN KEY (cust_id) REFERENCES customer (cust_id)
```

NOTE We could also use WITH CHECK to force the constraint to be applied to existing data, but that's unnecessary because it's the default behavior.

- To enable or disable a constraint. In the next example, we're enabling all the constraints on the employee table:

```
ALTER TABLE EMPLOYEE
CHECK ALL
```

One more commonly misunderstood aspect of using ALTER TABLE to drop constraints is that dropping a PRIMARY KEY or UNIQUE constraint will automatically drop the associated index. In fact, the only way to drop those indexes is by altering the table to remove the constraint.

Dropping a Column

You can use ALTER TABLE to remove one or more columns from a table. However, you can't drop the following columns:

- A replicated column.

- A column used in an index.

- A column used in a CHECK, FOREIGN KEY, UNIQUE, or PRIMARY KEY constraint.

- A column associated with a default defined with the DEFAULT keyword or bound to a default object.

- A column bound to a rule, accomplished via the following syntax:

```
ALTER TABLE table-name
      DROP COLUMN column-name [,next-column-name]...
```

NOTE Notice the syntax difference between adding a new column and dropping a column: when adding a new column to a table, the word COLUMN isn't used, but when dropping a column, the word COLUMN is required.

Enabling or Disabling a Trigger

You can enable or disable one or more (or *all*) triggers on a table using the ALTER TABLE command. We'll look at this topic in more detail when we discuss triggers in Chapter 10.

Note that not all the ALTER TABLE variations require SQL Server to change every row when the ALTER TABLE is issued. In many cases, SQL Server can just change the metadata (in *syscolumns*) to reflect the new structure. In particular, the data isn't touched when a column is dropped, when a new column is added and NULL is assumed as the new value for all rows, when the length of a variable-length column is changed, or when a non-nullable column is changed to allow NULLs. All other changes to a table's structure require SQL Server to physically update every row and to write the appropriate records to the transaction log.

Temporary Tables

Temporary tables are useful workspaces, like scratch pads, that you can use to try out intermediate data processing or to share work-in-progress with other connections. You can create temporary tables from within any database, but they exist in only the *tempdb* database, which is created every time the server is restarted. Don't assume that temporary tables aren't logged: temporary tables, and actions on those tables, are logged in *tempdb* so that transactions can be rolled back as necessary. However, the log isn't used for recovery of the database at system restart because the database is entirely re-created. Likewise, *tempdb* is never restored from a backup, so the log in *tempdb* is never needed for restoring the database. Unlike earlier versions of SQL Server, SQL Server 7 can log just enough information to allow rollback of transactions, without logging the additional information that would be necessary to recover those transactions, either at system startup or when recovering from a backup. This reduced logging means that data modification operations on tables in *tempdb* can be up to four times faster than the same operations in other databases. You can use temporary tables in three ways in SQL Server: privately, globally, and directly.

Private Temporary Tables (#)

By prefixing a table name with a single pound sign (#)—for example, CREATE TABLE #*my_table*—the table can be created from within any database as a private temporary table. Only the connection that created the table can access the table, making it truly private. Privileges can't be granted to another connection. As a temporary table, it exists for the life of that connection only; that connection can drop the table via DROP TABLE. Because the scoping of a private temporary table is specific to the connection that created it, you won't encounter a name collision should you choose a table name that's used in another connection. Private temporary tables are analogous to local variables—each connection has its own private version, and private temporary tables that are held by other connections are irrelevant. (However, temporary tables do differ from local variables in one crucial way: temporary tables exist for the life of the session, while local variables exist only for a single batch.)

Global Temporary Tables (##)

By prefixing the table name with double pound signs (##)—for example, CREATE TABLE ##*our_table*—a global temporary table can be created from within any database and any connection. Any connection can subsequently access the table for retrieval or data modification, even without specific permission. Unlike private temporary tables, all connections can use the single copy of a global temporary table. Therefore, you can encounter a name collision if another connection has created a global temporary table of the same name, and the CREATE TABLE statement will fail.

A global temporary table exists until the creating connection terminates and all current use of the table completes. After the creating connection terminates, however, only those connections already accessing it are allowed to finish, and no further use of the table is allowed. If you want a global temporary table to exist permanently, you can create the table in a stored procedure that's marked to autostart whenever SQL Server is started. That procedure can be put to sleep using WAITFOR and it will never terminate, so the table will never be dropped. Or you can choose to use *tempdb* directly, which is discussed next.

Direct Use of *tempdb*

Realizing that *tempdb* is re-created every time SQL Server is started, you can use *tempdb* to create a table or you can fully qualify the table name to include the database name *tempdb* in the CREATE TABLE statement issued from another database. To do this, you need to establish *create table* privileges in *tempdb*. You can set up privileges in *tempdb* in one of two ways every time SQL Server starts: you can set the privileges in *model* (the template database) so that they are copied to *tempdb* when it's created at system restart, or you can have an *autostart* procedure set the *tempdb* privileges every time SQL Server is started. One reason to consider *not* setting the privileges for *tempdb* in the *model* database is because *tempdb* isn't the only database that will be affected. Any new database you create will inherit those permissions too.

Tables directly created in *tempdb* can exist even after the creating connection is terminated, and the creator can specifically grant and revoke access permissions to specific users:

```
-- Creating a table in tempdb from pubs. Another method would be
-- to first do a 'use tempdb' instead of fully qualifying
-- the name.
CREATE TABLE tempdb.dbo.testtemp
(col1 int)
```

Constraints on Temporary Tables

A few articles about SQL Server erroneously state that constraints don't work on temporary tables. However, all constraints work on temporary tables explicitly built in *tempdb* (not using the # or ## prefixes). All constraints except FOREIGN KEY constraints work with tables using the # (private) and ## (global) prefixes. FOREIGN KEY references on private and global temporary tables are designed not to be enforced, because such a reference could prevent the temporary table from being dropped at close-connection time (for private temporary tables) or when a table goes out of scope (for global temporary tables) if the referencing table wasn't dropped first.

Summary

Tables are the heart of relational databases in general and of SQL Server in particular. In this chapter, we've looked at datatype issues, including size and performance tradeoffs. SQL Server provides a datatype for almost every use. We've looked at variable-length datatype issues and seen that it's simplistic to think that variable-length datatypes are either always good or always bad to use. We've also seen how data is physically stored in data pages and discussed some of the system table entries that are made to support tables.

SQL Server provides user-defined datatypes for support of domains, and it provides the Identity property to make a column produce autosequenced numeric values. SQL Server also provides constraints offering a powerful way to ensure your data's logical integrity. In addition to the NULL/NOT NULL designation, SQL Server provides PRIMARY KEY, UNIQUE, FOREIGN KEY, CHECK, and DEFAULT constraints. The discussion of these features also touched on a number of pragmatic issues, such as performance implications, conflicts between different constraints and triggers, and transaction semantics when a constraint fails.

To get the most out of SQL Server, you must understand tables, datatypes, and constraints. This chapter has provided some insight into subtleties that you might not have gleaned from the reference documentation of these features.

CHAPTER SEVEN

QUERYING DATA

You wouldn't have any reason to store data if you didn't want to retrieve it. Relational databases gained wide acceptance principally because they enabled users to query, or access, data easily, without using predefined, rigid navigational paths. Indeed, the acronym *SQL* stands for Structured *Query* Language. Microsoft SQL Server provides rich and powerful query capabilities.

In this chapter, we'll examine the SELECT statement and concentrate on features beyond the basics, including NULL, OUTER JOIN, correlated subqueries, aggregates, UNION, and the special CUBE operator. In Chapter 8, we'll see how to modify data. Then in Chapters 9 and 10, we'll build on these topics and explore the constructs and techniques that make Transact-SQL more than simply a query language.

The SELECT Statement

The SELECT statement is the most frequently used SQL command and is the fundamental way to query data. The syntax is intuitive—at least in its simplest forms—and resembles how you might state a request in English. As its name implies, however, SQL is not only intuitive but also *structured* and precise. But even though a SELECT statement can be intuitive, it can also be obscure or even tricky. Brainteasers showing how to write a SELECT statement to perform some tricky task often appear in database publications, and as long as the query represented is syntactically correct, you'll get a result. However, it might *not* be the result you really want—you might get the answer to a different question than the one you thought you posed! Incorrectly stated queries (queries with incorrect semantics) commonly cause bugs in applications, so you should understand proper query formulation.

The basic form of SELECT, using brackets ([ ]) to identify optional items, appears on the following page.

```
SELECT [DISTINCT][TOP n] <columns to be chosen, optionally eliminating
                          duplicate rows from result set or limiting
                          number of rows to be returned>
[FROM] <table names>
[WHERE] <criteria that must be true for a row to be chosen>
[GROUP BY] <columns for grouping aggregate functions>
[HAVING] <criteria that must be met for aggregate functions>
[ORDER BY] <optional specification of how the results should be
            sorted>
```

Note that the only clause that must always be present is the verb SELECT; the other clauses are optional. For example, if the entire table is needed, data doesn't need to be restricted to certain criteria, so the WHERE clause isn't needed.

Here's a simple query that retrieves all columns of all rows from the *authors* table in the *pubs* sample database:

```
select * from authors
```

Figure 7-1 shows the output.

Using tools such as OSQL and Query Analyzer, you can issue queries interactively. You can also, of course, build queries into applications. The calling application determines the formatting of the data output. SQL Server returns the data back to the calling application, which then works with the data. In the case of an ad hoc query tool, it displays the output on a monitor.

```
au_id       au_lname        au_fname    phone        address                   city           state zip   contract
----------- --------------- ----------- ------------ ------------------------- -------------- ----- ----- --------
172-32-1176 White           Johnson     408 496-7223 10932 Bigge Rd.           Menlo Park     CA    94025 1
213-46-8915 Green           Marjorie    415 986-7020 309 63rd St. #411         Oakland        CA    94618 1
238-95-7766 Carson          Cheryl      415 548-7723 589 Darwin Ln.            Berkeley       CA    94705 1
267-41-2394 O'Leary         Michael     408 286-2428 22 Cleveland Av. #14      San Jose       CA    95128 1
274-80-9391 Straight        Dean        415 834-2919 5420 College Av.          Oakland        CA    94609 1
341-22-1782 Smith           Meander     913 843-0462 10 Mississippi Dr.        Lawrence       KS    66044 0
409-56-7008 Bennet          Abraham     415 658-9932 6223 Bateman St.          Berkeley       CA    94705 1
427-17-2319 Dull            Ann         415 836-7128 3410 Blonde St.           Palo Alto      CA    94301 1
472-27-2349 Gringlesby      Burt        707 938-6445 PO Box 792                Covelo         CA    95428 1
486-29-1786 Locksley        Charlene    415 585-4620 18 Broadway Av.           San Francisc   CA    94130 1
527-72-3246 Greene          Morningstar 615 297-2723 22 Graybar House Rd.      Nashville      TN    37215 0
648-92-1872 Blotchet-Halls  Reginald    503 745-6402 55 Hillsdale Bl.          Corvallis      OR    97330 1
672-71-3249 Yokomoto        Akiko       415 935-4228 3 Silver Ct.              Walnut Creek   CA    94595 1
712-45-1867 del Castillo    Innes       615 996-8275 2286 Cram Pl. #86         Ann Arbor      MI    48105 1
722-51-5454 DeFrance        Michel      219 547-9982 3 Balding Pl.             Gary           IN    46403 1
724-08-9931 Stringer        Dirk        415 843-2991 5420 Telegraph Av.        Oakland        CA    94609 0
724-80-9391 MacFeather      Stearns     415 354-7128 44 Upland Hts.            Oakland        CA    94612 1
756-30-7391 Karsen          Livia       415 534-9219 5720 McAuley St.          Oakland        CA    94609 1
807-91-6654 Panteley        Sylvia      301 946-8853 1956 Arlington Pl.        Rockville      MD    20853 1
846-92-7186 Hunter          Sheryl      415 836-7128 3410 Blonde St.           Palo Alto      CA    94301 1
893-72-1158 McBadden        Heather     707 448-4982 301 Putnam                Vacaville      CA    95688 0
899-46-2035 Ringer          Anne        801 826-0752 67 Seventh Av.            Salt Lake Ci   UT    84152 1
998-72-3567 Ringer          Albert      801 826-0752 67 Seventh Av.            Salt Lake Ci   UT    84152 1
```

Figure 7-1.
The authors *table in the* pubs *sample database.*

More Information About the SQL Language

In general, this book concentrates on topics specific to Microsoft SQL Server, but it wouldn't be complete without some discussion of the SQL language. Because the treatment of generic SQL in this book is, by design, far from complete, here's a list of some of our favorite books about SQL. (For complete publication details and more references, see the "Suggested Reading" section at the end of this book.)

Using SQL, by James Groff and Paul Weinberg, is excellent for new SQL users looking for a good primer. Experienced users will probably want to use one of the other books mentioned here instead.

Understanding the New SQL: A Complete Guide, by Jim Melton and Alan R. Simon, is an excellent reference for ANSI SQL-92 semantics and conformance issues. (Jim Melton is an active participant in the SQL standards work and editor of the ANSI SQL-92 standard.) Although you can get the ANSI SQL-92 specification directly from ANSI, this book translates the standard into understandable English.

A Guide to the SQL Standard, by C. J. Date with Hugh Darwin, is similar in purpose and focus to the Melton and Simon book; however, this book's coverage is more compact, gives some additional insight into why something is the way it is, and provides more discussion of semantics. It's an especially good reference for issues about the use of NULL. You can use this book hand-in-hand with the Melton and Simon book, and you'll find that their differences complement each other well.

SQL for Smarties, by Joe Celko, is the book to consult for insight into subtle but powerful ways to write queries that are nonintuitive. In places, this one is truly the SQL book for the Mensa crowd—it has many mind-bending puzzles about how to write an SQL query to perform some obscure task. It's loaded with examples, and you can often find a solution to a problem similar in scope to one you might face. (Note that the answers to the problems are nearly all formulated using only ANSI-standard SQL. In some cases, a SQL Server–specific extension would provide a more intuitive or more efficient solution.) Although it focuses on advanced topics, Celko's book also provides a comprehensive treatment of many query topics in an easy-to-read, conversational style. This book is underrated, but it's well worth a spot on the shelf of any SQL database developer.

The power of the SQL language begins to reveal itself when you limit the information to be returned to specified ranges. For example, you could specify that a query from one table return only certain columns or rows that meet your stated criteria. In the select list, you would specify the exact columns you want, and then in the WHERE clause, you would specify the criteria that determine whether a row should be included in the answer set. Still using the *pubs* sample database, suppose that we want to find the first name and the city, state, and zip code of residence for authors whose last name is *Ringer*:

```
SELECT au_lname, au_fname, city, state, zip
FROM authors
WHERE au_lname='Ringer'
```

Here's the output:

```
au_lname    au_fname    city              state    zip
--------    --------    --------------    -----    -----
Ringer      Albert      Salt Lake City    UT       84152
Ringer      Anne        Salt Lake City    UT       84152
```

The results of this query tell us that two authors are named Ringer. But we're interested only in Anne. Retrieving only Anne Ringer's data requires an additional expression that is combined (AND'ed) with the original. In addition, we'd like the output to have more intuitive names for some columns, so we respecify the query:

```
SELECT 'Last Name'=au_lname, 'First'=au_fname, city, state, zip
FROM authors
WHERE au_lname='Ringer' and au_fname='Anne'
```

Here's the output, just as we wanted it:

```
Last Name    First    city              state    zip
---------    -----    --------------    -----    -----
Ringer       Anne     Salt Lake City    UT       84152
```

Joins

You gain much more power when you join tables, which typically results in combining columns of matching rows to project and return a *virtual table*. Usually, joins are based on the primary and foreign keys of the tables involved, although the tables aren't required to explicitly declare keys. The *pubs* sample database contains a table of authors (*authors*) and a table of book titles (*titles*).

An obvious query would be, "Show me the titles that each author has written, and sort the results alphabetically by author. I'm interested only in authors who live outside California." Neither the *authors* table nor the *titles* table alone has all this information. Furthermore, a many-to-many relationship exists between authors and titles; an author might have written several books, and a book might have been written by multiple authors. So an intermediate table, *titleauthor*, exists expressly to associate authors and titles, and this table is necessary to correctly join the information from *authors* and *titles*. To join these tables, you must include all three tables in the FROM clause of the SELECT statement, specifying that the columns that make up the keys have the same values. Figure 7-2 shows you how.

```
SELECT
'Author'=RTRIM(au_lname) + ', ' + au_fname,
'Title'=title
FROM authors AS A JOIN titleauthor AS TA
    ON A.au_id=TA.au_id          -- JOIN CONDITION
JOIN titles AS T
    ON T.title_id=TA.title_id    -- JOIN CONDITION
WHERE A.state <> 'CA'
ORDER BY 1
```

Figure 7-2.
Joining two tables via a third, intermediate table.

Here's the output:

```
Author                        Title
----------------------        ------------------------------------
Blotchet-Halls, Reginald      Fifty Years in Buckingham Palace
                              Kitchens
DeFrance, Michel              The Gourmet Microwave
del Castillo, Innes           Silicon Valley Gastronomic Treats
Panteley, Sylvia              Onions, Leeks, and Garlic: Cooking
                              Secrets of the Mediterranean
Ringer, Albert               Is Anger the Enemy?
Ringer, Albert               Life Without Fear
Ringer, Anne                 The Gourmet Microwave
Ringer, Anne                 Is Anger the Enemy?
```

Before discussing join operations further, let's study the example in Figure 7-2. The author's last and first names have been concatenated into one field. The RTRIM (right trim) function is used to strip off any trailing whitespace from the *au_lname* column. Then we add a comma and a space and concatenate on the *au_fname* column. This column is then *aliased* as simply *Author* and is returned to the calling application as a single column.

NOTE The RTRIM function isn't needed for this example. Because the column is of type *varchar*, trailing blanks wouldn't be present. RTRIM is shown for illustration purposes only.

Another important point is that the ORDER BY 1 clause indicates that the results should be sorted by the first column in the result set. It's more typical to use the column name rather than its number, but using the column number provides a convenient shorthand when the column is derived and hence, isn't present in the base table or view (virtual table) being queried.

We could have specified the same expression of the column using *ORDER BY RTRIM(au_lname) + ', ' + au_fname* instead. SQL Server provides an extension to the ANSI standard that allows sorting by columns that aren't included in the select list. So even though we don't individually select the columns *au_lname*, *au_fname*, or *state*, we could nonetheless choose to order the query based on these columns by specifying columns *ORDER BY au_lname, au_fname, state*. We'll see this in the next example (Figure 7-3). Notice also that the query contains comments (*-- JOIN CONDITION*). A double hyphen (--) signifies that the rest of the line is a comment (similar to *//* in C++). You can also use the C-style */* comment block */*, which allows blocks of comment lines.

TIP Comments can be nested, but you should generally try to avoid this. You can easily introduce a bug by not realizing that a comment is nested within another comment and misreading the code.

Now let's examine the join in Figure 7-2: The ON clauses specify how the tables relate and set the join criteria, stating that *au_id* in *authors* must equal *au_id* in *titleauthor*, and *title_id* in *titles* must equal *title_id* in *titleauthor*. This type of join is referred to as an *equijoin*, and it's the most common join operation. To remove ambiguity, you must qualify the columns. You can do this by specifying the columns in the form *table.column*, such as *authors.au_id = title_author.au_id*. The more compact and common way to do this, however, is by specifying a *table alias* in the FROM clause, as was done in this figure. By following the *titles* table with the word *AS* and the letter *T*, the *titles* table will be referred to as *T* from that point on. Typically, such an alias consists of one or two letters, although it can be much longer (following the same rules as identifiers).

After a table is aliased, it *must* be referred to by the alias, so now we can't refer to *authors.au_id* because the *authors* table has been aliased as *A*. We must use *A.au_id*. Note also that we refer to the *state* column of *authors* as *A.state*. The other two tables don't contain a *state* column, so qualifying it with the *A.* prefix isn't necessary; however, doing so makes the query more readable—and less prone to subsequent bugs.

The join in Figure 7-2 is accomplished using the ANSI JOIN SQL syntax, introduced in SQL Server version 6.5. Many examples and applications still continue to use an old-style JOIN syntax, which is shown below. (The term "old-style JOIN" is actually used by the SQL-92 specification.) The ANSI JOIN syntax is based on ANSI SQL-92. The main differences between the two types of join formulations are:

- The ANSI JOIN actually uses the keyword JOIN.

- The ANSI JOIN segregates join conditions from search conditions.

The ANSI JOIN syntax specifies the JOIN conditions in the ON clauses (one for each pair of tables), and the search conditions are specified in the WHERE clause—for example, WHERE *state <> 'CA'*. Although slightly more verbose, the explicit JOIN syntax is more readable. There's no difference in performance; behind the scenes, the operations are the same. Figure 7-3 shows how the query in Figure 7-2 can be equivalently respecified using the old-style JOIN syntax.

```
SELECT
'Author'=RTRIM(au_lname) + ', ' + au_fname,
'Title'=title
FROM authors A, titles T, titleauthor TA
WHERE
A.au_id=TA.au_id AND T.title_id=TA.title_id   -- JOIN CONDITIONS
AND A.state <> 'CA'
ORDER BY 1
```

Figure 7-3.
Explicit JOIN syntax that produces the same result yielded by Figure 7-2.

The query in Figure 7-3 produces the same output and the same execution plan as the query in Figure 7-2.

One of the most common errors new SQL users make when using the old-style JOIN syntax is not specifying the join condition. Omitting the WHERE clause is still a valid SQL request and causes an answer set to be returned. However, that result set is likely not what the user wanted. In Figure 7-3, omitting the WHERE clause would return the *Cartesian product* of the three tables: it would generate every possible combination of rows between them. Although in a few unusual cases you might want all permutations, usually this is just a user error. The number of rows returned is huge and typically doesn't represent anything meaningful. For example, the Cartesian product of the three small tables here (*authors*, *titles*, and *titleauthor* each have less than 26 rows) generates 10,350 rows of (probably) meaningless output.

Using the ANSI JOIN syntax, it's impossible to accidentally return a Cartesian product of the tables—one reason to use ANSI JOINs almost exclusively. The ANSI JOIN syntax requires an ON clause for specifying how the tables are related. In cases where you actually do want a Cartesian product, the ANSI JOIN syntax allows a CROSS JOIN operator to be used, which we'll see in more detail later in this chapter.

> **NOTE** In other examples throughout this book, we'll use the ANSI JOIN syntax almost exclusively. You might want to try translating some of them into queries using old-style JOIN syntax, because you should be able to recognize both forms. If you have to read SQL code written earlier than version 7, you're bound to come across queries using this older syntax.

The most common form of joins is an *equijoin*, sometimes also referred to as an *inner join* to differentiate it from an *outer join*, which we'll discuss shortly. Strictly speaking, an inner join isn't quite the same as an equijoin, which by definition means that the condition is based on equality; an inner join can use an operator such as less than (>) or greater than (<), although this is relatively unusual and esoteric. To make this distinction clear, you can use the INNER JOIN syntax in place of JOIN, as in this example:

```
INNER JOIN titleauthor TA ON A.au_id=TA.au_id
```

Other than making the syntax more explicit, there's no difference in the semantics or the execution. By convention, the modifier INNER generally isn't used.

NOTE ANSI SQL-92 also specifies the natural join operation, in which you don't have to specify the tables' column names. By specifying syntax such as *FROM authors NATURAL JOIN titleauthor*, the system automatically knows how to join the tables without your specifying the column names to match. SQL Server doesn't yet support this feature.

The ANSI specification calls for the natural join to be resolved based on identical column names between the tables. Perhaps a better way to do this would be based on a declared primary key–foreign key relationship, *if it exists*. Admittedly, declared key relationships have issues, too, because there's no restriction that only one such foreign key relationship is set up. Also, if the natural join were limited to only such relationships, all joins would have to be known in advance—as in the old CODASYL days.

The FROM clause in Figure 7-3 shows an alternative way to specify a table alias, by omitting the word "AS". The use of the word "AS" preceding the table alias, as used in Figure 7-2, conforms to ANSI SQL-92. From SQL Server's standpoint, the two methods are equivalent (stating *FROM authors AS A* is identical to stating *FROM authors A*). Commonly, the AS formulation is used when doing ANSI SQL-92 join operations, and the formulation that omits AS is used with the old-style join formulation. However, you can use either alias formulation—it's strictly a matter of preference.

Outer Joins

Equijoins choose only rows from the respective tables that match the equality condition. In other words, if a row in the first table doesn't match any rows in the second table, that row won't be returned in the result set. In contrast, outer joins preserve some or all of the unmatched rows. To illustrate how easily subtle semantic errors can be introduced, let's refer back to the queries in Figures 7-2 and 7-3, in which we wanted to see the titles written by all authors not living in California. The result omitted two writers who do not, in fact, live in California. *Was the query wrong?* No! The query performed exactly as written—we didn't specify that authors who currently have no titles in the database should be included. The results of the query were as we requested. In fact, the *authors* table has four rows that have no related row in the *titleauthor* table, which means these "authors" actually haven't written any books. Two of these authors don't contain the value CA in the *state* column, as the code on the following page shows.

```
au_id         Author                 state
----------    --------------------   -----
341-22-1782   Smith, Meander         KS
527-72-3246   Greene, Morningstar    TN
724-08-9931   Stringer, Dirk         CA
893-72-1158   McBadden, Heather      CA
```

The *titles* table has one row for which there is no author in our database, as shown below. (Later in this chapter, you'll see the types of queries used to produce these two result sets.)

```
title_id    title
--------    -----------------------------------
MC3026      The Psychology of Computer Cooking
```

If the queries in Figures 7-2 and 7-3 were meant to be "Show me the titles that each author has written; include authors even if there's no title by that author currently in our database; if there's a title for which there is no author, show me that as well; sort the results alphabetically by the author; I'm interested only in authors who live outside of California," the query would use an outer join so that authors with no matching titles would be selected. Figure 7-4 shows this outer-join query.

```
SELECT
'Author'=RTRIM(au_lname) + ', ' + au_fname,
'Title'=title
FROM
    (                      -- JOIN CONDITIONS
    -- FIRST join authors and titleauthor
        (authors AS A
        FULL OUTER JOIN titleauthor AS TA ON A.au_id=TA.au_id
        )
    -- The result of the previous join is then joined to titles
        FULL OUTER JOIN titles AS T ON TA.title_id=T.title_id
    )
WHERE
state <> 'CA' OR state IS NULL
ORDER BY 1
```

Figure 7-4.
An outer-join query, which preserves rows with no matches.

Here's the output:

Author	Title
NULL	The Psychology of Computer Cooking
Blotchet-Halls, Reginald	Fifty Years in Buckingham Palace Kitchens
DeFrance, Michel	The Gourmet Microwave
del Castillo, Innes	Silicon Valley Gastronomic Treats
Greene, Morningstar	NULL
Panteley, Sylvia	Onions, Leeks, and Garlic: Cooking Secrets of the Mediterranean
Ringer, Albert	Is Anger the Enemy?
Ringer, Albert	Life Without Fear
Ringer, Anne	The Gourmet Microwave
Ringer, Anne	Is Anger the Enemy?
Smith, Meander	NULL

The query in Figure 7-4 demonstrates a *full outer join*. Rows in the *authors* and *titles* tables that don't have a corresponding entry in *titleauthor* are still presented, but with a NULL entry for the *title* or *author* column. (The data from the *authors* table is requested as a comma between the last names and the first names. Because we have the option CONCAT_NULL_YIELDS_NULL set to ON, the result is NULL for the *author* column. If we didn't have that option set to ON, SQL Server would have returned the single comma between the nonexistent last and first names.) A full outer join preserves nonmatching rows from both the lefthand and righthand tables. In Figure 7-4, the *authors* table is presented first, so it is the lefthand table when joining to *titleauthor*. The result of that join is the lefthand table when joining to *titles*.

ANSI Outer Joins

At the beginning of this chapter, we promised not to go into much detail about generic SQL operations. The outer join formulations here are standard ANSI SQL-92. However, this area is one in which there aren't enough good examples; using OUTER JOIN with more than two tables introduces some obscure issues. Few products provide support for full outer joins, and frankly, the current SQL Server documentation is thin in its discussion of outer joins. Because you must understand outer joins thoroughly if you are to use OUTER JOIN, we'll go into a bit more detail in this section.

You can generate missing rows from one or more of the tables by using either a *left outer join* or a *right outer join*. So if we want to preserve all authors and generate a row for all authors who have a missing title, but we don't want to preserve titles that have no author, we can reformulate the query using LEFT OUTER JOIN, as shown in Figure 7-5. This join preserves entries only on the lefthand side of the join. Note that the left outer join of the *authors* and *titleauthor* columns generates two such rows (for Greene and Smith). The result of the join in Figure 7-5 is the lefthand side of the join to *titles*; therefore, the LEFT OUTER JOIN must be specified again to preserve these rows with no matching *titles* rows.

```
⋮
FROM
    (
        (authors as A
        LEFT OUTER JOIN titleauthor AS TA ON A.au_id=TA.au_id
        )
        LEFT OUTER JOIN titles AS T ON TA.title_id=T.title_id
    )
⋮
```

Figure 7-5.
Using LEFT OUTER JOIN to preserve rows on only the lefthand side of the joins.

Here's the output:

```
Author                      Title
--------------------------  ---------------------------------------
Blotchet-Halls, Reginald    Fifty Years in Buckingham Palace
                            Kitchens
DeFrance, Michel            The Gourmet Microwave
del Castillo, Innes         Silicon Valley Gastronomic Treats
Greene, Morningstar         NULL
Panteley, Sylvia            Onions, Leeks, and Garlic: Cooking
                            Secrets of the Mediterranean
Ringer, Albert              Is Anger the Enemy?
Ringer, Albert              Life Without Fear
Ringer, Anne                The Gourmet Microwave
Ringer, Anne                Is Anger the Enemy?
Smith, Meander              NULL
```

The query in Figure 7-5 produces the same rows as the full outer join, except for the row for *The Psychology of Computer Cooking*. Because only LEFT OUTER JOIN was specified, there was no request to preserve *titles* (righthand) rows that have no matching rows in the result of the join of *authors* and *titleauthor*.

You must use care with OUTER JOIN operations, because the order in which tables are joined affects which rows are preserved and which aren't. In an equijoin, the associative property holds (if A equals B, then B equals A) and no difference results, whether something is on the left or the right side of the equation, and no difference results in the order in which joins are specified. This is definitely *not* the case for OUTER JOIN operations. For example, consider the following two queries and their results:

QUERY 1

```
SELECT
'Author'= RTRIM(au_lname) + ', ' + au_fname,
'Title'=title
FROM (titleauthor AS TA
RIGHT OUTER JOIN authors AS A ON (A.au_id=TA.au_id))
FULL OUTER JOIN titles AS T ON (TA.title_id=T.title_id)
WHERE
A.state <> 'CA' or A.state is NULL
ORDER BY 1
Author                          Title
----------------------          ------------------------------------
NULL                            The Psychology of Computer Cooking
Blotchet-Halls, Reginald        Fifty Years in Buckingham Palace
                                Kitchens
DeFrance, Michel                The Gourmet Microwave
del Castillo, Innes             Silicon Valley Gastronomic Treats
Greene, Morningstar             NULL
Panteley, Sylvia                Onions, Leeks, and Garlic: Cooking
                                Secrets of the Mediterranean
Ringer, Albert                  Is Anger the Enemy?
Ringer, Albert                  Life Without Fear
Ringer, Anne                    The Gourmet Microwave
Ringer, Anne                    Is Anger the Enemy?
Smith, Meander                  NULL
```

This query produces results semantically equivalent to the previous FULL OUTER JOIN formulation in Figure 7-4, although we've switched the order of the *authors* and *titleauthor* tables. This query and the previous one preserve both authors with no matching titles and titles with no matching authors. This might not be obvious, because RIGHT OUTER JOIN is clearly different than FULL OUTER JOIN. However, in this case we know it's true because FOREIGN KEY and NOT NULL constraints exist on the *titleauthor* table to ensure that there can never be a row in the *titleauthor* table that doesn't match a row in the *authors* table. So we can be confident that the *titleauthor* RIGHT OUTER JOIN to *authors* can't produce any fewer rows than would a FULL OUTER JOIN.

But if we modify the query ever so slightly by changing the join order again, look what happens:

QUERY 2

```
SELECT
'Author'=RTRIM(au_lname) + ', ' + au_fname,
'Title'=title
FROM (titleauthor AS TA
FULL OUTER JOIN titles AS T ON TA.title_id=T.title_id)
RIGHT OUTER JOIN authors AS A ON A.au_id=TA.au_id
WHERE
A.state <> 'CA' or A.state is NULL
ORDER BY 1
```

Author	Title
Blotchet-Halls, Reginald	Fifty Years in Buckingham Palace Kitchens
DeFrance, Michel	The Gourmet Microwave
del Castillo, Innes	Silicon Valley Gastronomic Treats
Greene, Morningstar	NULL
Panteley, Sylvia	Onions, Leeks, and Garlic: Cooking Secrets of the Mediterranean
Ringer, Albert	Is Anger the Enemy?
Ringer, Albert	Life Without Fear
Ringer, Anne	The Gourmet Microwave
Ringer, Anne	Is Anger the Enemy?
Smith, Meander	NULL

At a glance, Query 2 looks equivalent to Query 1, although the join order is slightly different. But notice how the results differ. This query didn't achieve the goal of preserving the *titles* rows without corresponding *authors*, and the row for *The Psychology of Computer Cooking* is again excluded. This row would have been preserved in the first join operation:

```
FULL OUTER JOIN titles AS T ON TA.title_id=T.title_id
```

But then this row is discarded, because the second join operation,

```
RIGHT OUTER JOIN authors AS A ON A.au_id=TA.au_id
```

preserves only authors without matching titles. Because the title row for *The Psychology of Computer Cooking* is on the lefthand side of this join operation and only a RIGHT OUTER JOIN operation is specified, this title is discarded.

NOTE Just as INNER is an optional modifier, so is OUTER. Hence, LEFT OUTER JOIN can be equivalently specified as LEFT JOIN, and FULL OUTER JOIN can be equivalently expressed as FULL JOIN. However, although INNER is seldom used by convention and is usually only implied, OUTER is almost always used by convention when specifying any type of outer join.

Because join order matters, we urge you to use parentheses and indentation carefully when specifying OUTER JOIN operations. Indentation, of course, is always optional, and use of parentheses is often optional. But as this example shows, it's easy to make mistakes that result in your queries returning the wrong answers. As is true with almost all programming, simply getting into the habit of using comments, parentheses, and indentation often results in such bugs being noticed and fixed by a developer or database administrator before they make their way into your applications.

Who's Writing the Queries?

Notice that the terms "developer" or "database administrator" are used on the preceding page, not "end user." SQL is often regarded as a language suitable for end users as well as database professionals. To an extent, such as with straightforward single table queries, this is true. But if you expect end users to understand the semantics of outer joins or to deal correctly with NULL, you might as well just give them a random data generator. These concepts are tricky, and it's your job to insulate your users from them. Later in this chapter, you'll see how you can use views to help accomplish this.

The Obsolete *= OUTER JOIN Operator

Prior to version 6.5, SQL Server had limited outer-join support in the form of the special operators *= and =*. Many people assume that the LEFT OUTER JOIN syntax is simply a synonym for *=, but this isn't the case. LEFT OUTER JOIN is semantically different from and superior to *=.

For equijoins, the associative property holds, so the issues with old-style JOIN syntax don't exist. You can use either new-style or old-style syntax with equijoins. For outer joins, you should consider the *= operator obsolete and move to the OUTER JOIN syntax as quickly as possible—the *= operator might be dropped entirely in future releases of SQL Server.

ANSI's OUTER JOIN syntax, which was adopted in SQL Server version 6.5, recognizes that for outer joins, the conditions of the join must be evaluated separately from the criteria applied to the rows that are joined. ANSI gets it right by separating the JOIN criteria from the WHERE criteria. The old SQL Server *= and =* operators are prone to ambiguities, especially when three or more tables, views, or subqueries are involved. Often the results aren't what you'd expect, even though you might be able to explain them. But sometimes you simply can't get the result you want. These aren't implementation bugs; more accurately, these are inherent limitations in trying to apply the outer-join criteria in the WHERE clause.

When *= was introduced, no ANSI specification existed for OUTER JOIN, or even for INNER JOIN. Just the old-style join existed, with operators like =* in the WHERE clause. So the designers quite reasonably tried to fit an outer-join operator into the WHERE clause, which was the only place that joins were ever stated. Other products, notably Oracle with its plus (+) syntax, also followed this approach; consequently, these products suffer from similar ambiguities and limitations. However, efforts to resolve this situation helped spur the specification for proper OUTER JOIN syntax and semantics within the ANSI SQL committee. Using outer joins correctly is difficult, and SQL Server is one of the few mainstream products that has done so.

To illustrate the semantic differences and problems with the old *= syntax, we'll walk through a series of examples using both new and old outer-join syntax. The following is essentially the same outer-join query shown in Figure 7-4, but this one returns only a count. It correctly finds the 11 rows, preserving both authors with no titles and titles with no authors.

```
-- New style OUTER JOIN correctly finds 11 rows
SELECT COUNT(*)
FROM
    (
    -- FIRST join authors and titleauthor
        (authors AS A
        LEFT OUTER JOIN titleauthor AS TA ON A.au_id=TA.au_id
        )
```

```
    -- The result of the previous join is then joined to titles
        FULL OUTER JOIN titles AS T ON TA.title_id=T.title_id
    )
WHERE
state <> 'CA' OR state IS NULL
ORDER BY 1
```

There's really no way to write this query—which does a full outer join—using the old syntax, because the old syntax simply isn't expressive enough. Here's what looks to be a reasonable try—but it generates several rows that you wouldn't expect.

```
-- Attempt with old-style join. Really no way to do FULL OUTER
-- JOIN. This query finds 144 rows--WRONG!!
SELECT COUNT(*)
FROM
    authors A, titleauthor TA, titles T
WHERE
A.au_id *= TA.au_id
AND
TA.title_id =* T.title_id
AND
(state <> 'CA' OR state IS NULL)
ORDER BY 1
```

Now let's examine some issues with the old-style outer join using a simple example of only two tables, *customers* and *orders*:

```
CREATE TABLE Customers
(
Cust_ID      int  PRIMARY KEY,
Cust_Name    char(20)
)

CREATE TABLE Orders
(
OrderID     int    PRIMARY KEY,
Cust_ID     int    REFERENCES Customers(Cust_ID)
)
GO

INSERT Customers VALUES (1, 'Cust 1')
INSERT Customers VALUES (2, 'Cust 2')
INSERT Customers VALUES (3, 'Cust 3')
INSERT Orders VALUES (10001, 1)
INSERT Orders VALUES (20001, 2)
GO
```

At a glance, in the simplest case, the new-style and old-style syntax appear to work the same. Here's the new syntax:

```
SELECT
'Customers.Cust_ID'=Customers.Cust_ID, Customers.Cust_Name,
    'Orders.Cust_ID'=Orders.Cust_ID
FROM Customers LEFT JOIN Orders
    ON Customers.Cust_ID=Orders.Cust_ID
```

Here's the output:

Customers.Cust_ID	Cust_Name	Orders.Cust_ID
1	Cust 1	1
2	Cust 2	2
3	Cust 3	NULL

And here's the old-style syntax:

```
SELECT 'Customers.Cust_ID'=Customers.Cust_ID, Customers.Cust_Name,
    'Orders.Cust_ID'=Orders.Cust_ID
FROM Customers, Orders WHERE Customers.Cust_ID *= Orders.Cust_ID
```

Here's the output:

Customers.Cust_ID	Cust_Name	Orders.Cust_ID
1	Cust 1	1
2	Cust 2	2
3	Cust 3	NULL

But as soon as you begin to add restrictions, things get tricky. What if you want to filter out *Cust 2*? With the new syntax it's easy, but remember not to filter out the row with NULL that the outer join just preserved!

```
SELECT 'Customers.Cust_ID'=Customers.Cust_ID, Customers.Cust_Name,
'Orders.Cust_ID'=Orders.Cust_ID
FROM Customers LEFT JOIN Orders
    ON Customers.Cust_ID=Orders.Cust_ID
WHERE Orders.Cust_ID <> 2 OR Orders.Cust_ID IS NULL
```

Here's the output:

Customers.Cust_ID	Cust_Name	Orders.Cust_ID
1	Cust 1	1
3	Cust 3	NULL

Now try to do this query using the old-style syntax and filter out *Cust 2*:

```
SELECT 'Customers.Cust_ID'=Customers.Cust_ID, Customers.Cust_Name,
'Orders.Cust_ID'=Orders.Cust_ID
FROM Customers, Orders
WHERE Customers.Cust_ID *= Orders.Cust_ID
AND (Orders.Cust_ID <> 2 OR Orders.Cust_ID IS NULL)
```

Here's the output:

Customers.Cust_ID	Cust_Name	Orders.Cust_ID
1	Cust 1	1
2	Cust 2	NULL
3	Cust 3	NULL

Notice that this time, we don't get rid of *Cust 2*. The check for NULL occurs before the JOIN, so the outer-join operation puts *Cust 2* back. This result might be less than intuitive, but at least we can explain and defend it. That's not always the case, as you'll see in a moment.

If you look at the preceding query, you might think that we should have filtered out *Customers.Cust_ID* rather than *Orders.Cust_ID*. How did we miss that? Surely this query will fix the problem:

```
SELECT 'Customers.Cust_ID'=Customers.Cust_ID, Customers.Cust_Name,
'Orders.Cust_ID'=Orders.Cust_ID
FROM Customers, Orders
WHERE Customers.Cust_ID *= Orders.Cust_ID
AND (Customers.Cust_ID <> 2 OR Orders.Cust_ID IS NULL)
```

Here's the output:

Customers.Cust_ID	Cust_Name	Orders.Cust_ID
1	Cust 1	1
2	Cust 2	NULL
3	Cust 3	NULL

Oops! Same result. The problem here is that *Orders.Cust_ID IS NULL* is now being applied *after* the outer join, so the row is presented again. If we're careful and understand exactly how the old outer join is processed, we can get the results we want with the old-style syntax for this query. We need to understand that the *OR Orders.Cust_ID IS NULL* puts back *Cust_ID 2*, so just take that out. The code appears on the next page.

```
SELECT 'Customers.Cust_ID'=Customers.Cust_ID, Customers.Cust_Name,
    'Orders.Cust_ID'=Orders.Cust_ID
FROM Customers, Orders
WHERE Customers.Cust_ID *= Orders.Cust_ID
AND Customers.Cust_ID <> 2
```

Here's the output:

```
Customers.Cust_ID          Cust_Name          Orders.Cust_ID
-----------------          ---------          --------------
1                          Cust 1             1
3                          Cust 3             NULL
```

Finally! This result is what we want. And if we really think about it, the semantics are even understandable (although different from the new style). So maybe this is much ado about nothing; all we have to do is understand how it works, right? Wrong. Besides the issues of joins with more than two tables and the lack of a full outer join, we also can't effectively deal with subqueries and views (virtual tables). For example, let's try creating a view with the old-style outer join:

```
CREATE VIEW Cust_old_OJ AS
(SELECT Orders.Cust_ID, Customers.Cust_Name
FROM Customers, Orders
WHERE Customers.Cust_ID *= Orders.Cust_ID)
```

A simple select from the view looks fine:

```
SELECT * FROM Cust_old_OJ
```

And it gives this output:

```
Cust_ID          Cust_Name
-------          ---------
1                Cust 1
2                Cust 2
NULL             Cust 3
```

But restricting from this view doesn't seem to make sense:

```
SELECT * FROM Cust_old_OJ WHERE Cust_ID <> 2
    AND Cust_ID IS NOT NULL
```

The output shows NULLs in the *Cust_ID* column, even though we tried to filter them out:

```
Cust_ID          Cust_Name
-------          ---------
1                Cust 1
NULL             Cust 2
NULL             Cust 3
```

If we expand the view to the full select and we realize that *Cust_ID* is *Orders.Cust_ID*, not *Customers.Cust_ID*, perhaps we can understand why this happened. But we still can't filter out those rows!

In contrast, if we create the view with the new syntax and correct semantics, it works exactly as expected:

```
CREATE VIEW Cust_new_OJ AS
(SELECT Orders.Cust_ID, Customers.Cust_Name
FROM Customers LEFT JOIN Orders
    ON Customers.Cust_ID=Orders.Cust_ID )
GO

SELECT * FROM Cust_new_OJ WHERE Cust_ID <> 2 AND Cust_ID IS NOT NULL
```

Here's what was expected:

```
Cust_ID          Cust_Name
-------          ---------
1                Cust 1
```

In these examples, the new syntax performed the outer join and then applied the restrictions in the WHERE clause to the result. In contrast, the old style applied the WHERE clause to the tables being joined and then performed the outer join, which can reintroduce NULL rows. This is why the results often seemed bizarre. However, if that behavior is what you want, you could apply the criteria in the JOIN clause instead of in the WHERE clause.

The following example uses the new syntax to mimic the old behavior. The WHERE clause is shown here simply as a placeholder to make it clear that the statement *Cust_ID <> 2* is in the JOIN section, not in the WHERE section.

```
SELECT 'Customers.Cust_ID'=Customers.Cust_ID, Customers.Cust_Name,
    'Orders.Cust_ID'=Orders.Cust_ID
FROM Customers LEFT JOIN Orders
    ON Customers.Cust_ID=Orders.Cust_ID
    AND Orders.Cust_ID <> 2
WHERE 1=1
```

Here's the output:

```
Customers.Cust_ID        Cust_Name        Orders.Cust_ID
-----------------        ---------        --------------
1                        Cust 1           1
2                        Cust 2           NULL
3                        Cust 3           NULL
```

As you can see, the row for *Cust 2* was filtered out from the *Orders* table before the join, but because it was NULL, it was reintroduced by the OUTER JOIN operation.

With the improvements in outer-join support, you can now use outer joins where you couldn't previously. A bit later, you'll see how to use an outer join instead of a correlated subquery in a common type of query.

Cross Joins

In addition to INNER JOIN, OUTER JOIN, and FULL JOIN, the ANSI JOIN syntax allows a CROSS JOIN. Earlier, you saw that the advantage of using the ANSI JOIN syntax was that you wouldn't *accidentally* create a Cartesian product. However, in some cases, this behavior might be exactly what you want. SQL Server allows you to specify a CROSS JOIN with no ON clause to produce a Cartesian product. So when would you really *want* to get a Cartesian product?

One possible use for CROSS JOINs is to generate sample or test data. For example, to generate 10,000 names for a sample *employees* table, you don't have to come up with 10,000 individual INSERT statements. All you need to do is build a *first_names* table and a *last_names* table with 26 names each (perhaps one starting with each letter of the English alphabet), and a *middle_initials* table with the 26 letters. When these three small tables are joined using the CROSS JOIN operator, the result will be well over 10,000 unique names to insert into the *employee* table. The SELECT statement used to generate these names would look like this:

```
SELECT first_name, middle_initial, last_name
FROM first_names CROSS JOIN middle_initials
    CROSS JOIN last_names
```

To summarize the five types of ANSI JOIN operations, consider two tables, *TableA* and *TableB*:

INNER JOIN (default)

```
TableA INNER JOIN TableB ON join_condition
```

The INNER JOIN returns rows from either table only if they have a corresponding row in the other table. In other words, the INNER JOIN disregards any rows in which the specific join condition, as specified in the ON clause, isn't met.

LEFT OUTER JOIN

```
TableA LEFT OUTER JOIN TableB ON join_condition
```

The LEFT OUTER JOIN returns all rows for a connection that exists between *TableA* and *TableB*; in addition, it returns all rows from *TableA* for which no corresponding row exists in *TableB*. In other words, it preserves unmatched rows from *TableA*. *TableA* is sometimes called the *preserved* table. When returning the unmatched rows from *TableA*, any columns selected from *TableB* are returned as NULL.

RIGHT OUTER JOIN

```
TableA RIGHT OUTER JOIN TableB ON join_condition
```

The RIGHT OUTER JOIN returns all rows for which a connection exists between *TableA* and *TableB*; in addition, it returns all rows from *TableB* for which no corresponding row exists in *TableA*. In other words, it preserves unmatched rows from *TableB*, and in this case, *TableB* is the preserved table. When returning the unmatched rows from *TableB*, any columns selected from *TableA* are returned as NULL.

FULL OUTER JOIN

```
TableA FULL OUTER JOIN TableB ON join_condition
```

The FULL OUTER JOIN returns all rows for which a connection exists between *TableA* and *TableB*. In addition, it returns all rows from *TableA* for which no corresponding row exists in *TableB*, with any values selected from *TableB* returned as NULL. In addition, it returns all rows from *TableB* for which no corresponding row exists in *TableA*, with any values selected from *TableA* returned as NULL. In other words, FULL OUTER JOIN acts as a combination of LEFT OUTER JOIN and RIGHT OUTER JOIN.

CROSS JOIN

```
TableA CROSS JOIN TableB
```

The CROSS JOIN returns all rows from *TableA* combined with all rows from *TableB*. No ON clause exists to indicate any connecting column between the tables. A CROSS JOIN returns a Cartesian product of the two tables.

Dealing with NULL

The FULL OUTER JOIN example shown in Figure 7-4 has a necessary twist because of the NULL value that's generated for the missing author *state* column. Note the WHERE clause:

```
WHERE state <> 'CA' OR state IS NULL
```

Without

```
OR state IS NULL
```

our favorite row, which contains the title *The Psychology of Computer Cooking*, wouldn't have been selected. Because this title is missing its corresponding author, the *state* column for the query is NULL.

The expression

```
state <> 'CA'
```

doesn't evaluate to TRUE for a NULL value. NULL is considered unknown. If you were to omit the expression

```
OR state IS NULL
```

and execute the query once with the predicate

```
state = 'CA'
```

and once with the predicate

```
state <> 'CA'
```

it might seem intuitive that, between the two queries, all rows must have been selected. But this isn't the case. A NULL *state* satisfies neither condition, and the row with the title *The Psychology of Computer Cooking* wouldn't be part of either result.

This example illustrates the essence of *three-valued logic*, so named because a comparison can evaluate to one of three conditions: TRUE, FALSE, or

Unknown. Dealing with NULL entries requires three-valued logic. If you allow NULL entries or have cases in which outer joins are necessary, correctly applying three-valued logic is necessary to avoid introducing bugs into your application.

Assume that the table *Truth_Table* has columns X and Y. We have only one row in the table, as follows, with X being *NULL* and Y being *1*:

```
X      Y
----   -
NULL   1
```

Without looking ahead, test yourself to see which of the following queries returns *1*:

```
SELECT 1 FROM Truth_Table WHERE X <> Y -- NOT EQUAL
SELECT 1 FROM Truth_Table WHERE X = Y  -- EQUAL
SELECT 1 FROM Truth_Table WHERE X != Y -- NOT EQUAL
                                       -- (alternative formulation)
SELECT 1 FROM Truth_Table WHERE X < Y  -- LESS THAN
SELECT 1 FROM Truth_Table WHERE X !< Y -- NOT LESS THAN
SELECT 1 FROM Truth_Table WHERE X > Y  -- GREATER THAN
SELECT 1 FROM Truth_Table WHERE X !> Y -- NOT GREATER THAN
```

In fact, none of the previous SELECT statements returns *1*, because none of the comparison operations against X, which is NULL, evaluate to TRUE. All evaluate to Unknown. Did you score 100 percent? If so, are you confident that all your developers would also score 100? If you allow NULL, your answer had better be yes.

Further complexity arises when you use expressions that can be Unknown with the logical operations of AND, OR, and NOT. Given that an expression can be TRUE, FALSE, or Unknown, the truth tables in Table 7-1 on the following page summarize the result of logically combining expressions.

These truth tables can reveal some situations that otherwise might not be obvious. For example, you might assume that the condition *(X >= 0 OR X <= 0)* must be TRUE, because X for any number always evaluates to TRUE; it must be either 0 or greater, or 0 or less. However, if X is NULL, then $X >= 0$ is Unknown, and $X <= 0$ is also Unknown. Therefore, the expression evaluates as *Unknown OR Unknown*. As the OR truth table shows, this evaluates to Unknown. To further illustrate, the following SELECT statement doesn't return a *1*:

```
SELECT 1 FROM Truth_Table WHERE (X >= 0 OR X <= 0)
```

AND with Value	True	Unknown	False
TRUE	TRUE	Unknown	FALSE
Unknown	Unknown	Unknown	FALSE
FALSE	FALSE	FALSE	FALSE

OR with Value	True	Unknown	False
TRUE	TRUE	TRUE	TRUE
Unknown	TRUE	Unknown	Unknown
FALSE	TRUE	Unknown	FALSE

NOT	Evaluates to
TRUE	FALSE
Unknown	Unknown
FALSE	TRUE

Table 7-1.
Truth tables showing results of logically combining expressions.

And because *(X >= 0 OR X <= 0)* is Unknown, the condition:

```
WHERE NOT(X >= 0 OR X <= 0)
```

is equivalent (in pseudocode) to:

```
WHERE NOT (Unknown)
```

The NOT truth table shows that *NOT (Unknown)* is Unknown, so the following negation of the previous SELECT statement also returns nothing:

```
SELECT 1 FROM Truth_Table WHERE NOT(X >= 0 OR X <= 0)
```

And, at the possible risk of belaboring this point, since neither expression evaluates to TRUE, OR'ing them makes no difference either; consequently, this SELECT also returns nothing:

```
SELECT 1 FROM TRUTH_TABLE
    WHERE (X >= 0 OR X <= 0) OR NOT(X >= 0 OR X <= 0)
```

The fact that none of these SELECT statements evaluates to TRUE, even when negating the expression, illustrates that *not* evaluating to TRUE doesn't imply evaluating to FALSE. Rather, it means either evaluating to FALSE or evaluating to Unknown.

Two special operators, IS NULL and IS NOT NULL, exist to deal with NULL. Checking an expression with one of these operators always evaluates to either TRUE or FALSE. No Unknown condition is produced when using IS NULL or IS NOT NULL, as shown in Table 7-2.

IS NULL	Evaluates to	IS NOT NULL	Evaluates to
TRUE	FALSE	TRUE	TRUE
NULL	TRUE	NULL	FALSE
FALSE	FALSE	FALSE	TRUE

Table 7-2.
Truth tables for IS NULL and IS NOT NULL.

In the full outer-join query example, the search criteria was

```
WHERE state <> 'CA' OR state IS NULL
```

For the row with the title *The Psychology of Computer Cooking* (which was produced from the outer-join operation preserving the *titles* row with an unmatched *authors* entry), the *authors.state* column is NULL. Hence, the expression

```
state <> 'CA'
```

is Unknown for that row, but the expression

```
state IS NULL
```

is TRUE for that row. The full expression evaluates to *(Unknown OR TRUE)*, which is TRUE, and the row qualifies. Without

```
OR state IS NULL
```

the expression is only *(Unknown)*, so the row doesn't qualify.

NULL in the Real World

As you know, we strongly recommend that you minimize the use of NULL. In outer-join operations, you should carefully account for NULL values that are generated to preserve rows that don't have a match in the table being joined. And even if you're comfortable with three-valued logic, your developers and anyone querying the data using the SQL language typically won't be; therefore, introducing NULL will be a source of bugs just waiting to happen. You can, of course, make all column definitions NOT NULL and declare default values if no value is specified.

You can often avoid problems of having no matching rows—without the need for outer-join operations—by providing *placeholder*, or *dummy*, rows. For example, you could easily create a dummy *titles* row and a dummy *authors* row. By using constraints or triggers, you could insist that every row in *authors* must have a matching entry in *titleauthor*, even if the ultimate matching row in *titles* is simply the dummy row. Likewise, every row in *titles* could be made to reference *titleauthor*, even if the matching row in *authors* is just the dummy row. Having done this, a standard equijoin returns all rows because no unmatched rows exist. There's no outer join or NULL complication.

Here's an example: After adding a dummy row for *authors*, one for *titles*, and one for each unmatched row into the *titleauthor* table, a standard inner join (with INNER specified purely to emphasize the point) is used to produce essentially the same results as the FULL OUTER JOIN. The only difference in the results is that the placeholder values ***No Current Author*** and ***No Current Title*** are returned instead of NULL.

```
BEGIN TRAN -- Transaction will be rolled back so as to avoid
           -- permanent changes

-- Dummy authors row
INSERT authors
(au_id, au_lname, au_fname, phone, address, city, state, zip, contract)
VALUES
('000-00-0000', '***No Current Author***',
', 'NONE', 'NONE', 'NONE', 'XX', '99999', 0)


-- Dummy titles row
INSERT titles
(title_id, title, type, pub_id, price, advance, royalty, ytd_sales,
notes, pubdate)
VALUES
('ZZ9999', '***No Current Title***',
'NONE', '9999', 0.00, 0, 0, 0, 'NONE', '1900.01.01')
```

```
-- Associate authors with no current titles to dummy title
INSERT titleauthor VALUES ('341-22-1782', 'ZZ9999', 0, 0)
INSERT titleauthor VALUES ('527-72-3246', 'ZZ9999', 0, 0)
INSERT titleauthor VALUES ('724-08-9931', 'ZZ9999', 0, 0)
INSERT titleauthor VALUES ('893-72-1158', 'ZZ9999', 0, 0)

-- Associate titles with no current author to dummy author
INSERT titleauthor VALUES ('000-00-0000', 'MC3026', 0, 0)

-- Now do a standard INNER JOIN
SELECT
'Author'=RTRIM(au_lname) + ', ' + au_fname,
'Title'=title
FROM
        authors AS A                 -- JOIN conditions
        INNER JOIN titleauthor AS TA ON A.au_id=TA.au_id
        INNER JOIN titles AS T ON t.title_id=TA.title_id
WHERE
A.state <> 'CA'
ORDER BY 1

ROLLBACK TRAN     -- Undo changes
```

This is the result:

```
Author                      Title
-------------               ------------------
***No Current Author***,    The Psychology of Computer Cooking
Blotchet-Halls, Reginald    Fifty Years in Buckingham Palace
                            Kitchens

DeFrance, Michel            The Gourmet Microwave
del Castillo, Innes         Silicon Valley Gastronomic Treats
Greene, Morningstar         ***No Current Title***
Panteley, Sylvia            Onions, Leeks, and Garlic: Cooking
                            Secrets of the Mediterranean

Ringer, Albert             Is Anger the Enemy?
Ringer, Albert             Life Without Fear
Ringer, Anne               The Gourmet Microwave
Ringer, Anne               Is Anger the Enemy?
Smith, Meander             ***No Current Title***
```

Earlier, you saw how OUTER JOIN became complicated and prone to mistakes. It's comforting to know that, regardless of the order in which we specify the tables for the join operation using dummy rows, the semantics and results are the same because now this operation is simply an equijoin.

However, dummy values won't solve all the woes created by using NULL. First, using dummy values demands more work in your application to ensure that relationships to the placeholder values are maintained. Even more important, many queries still need to be able to discern that the placeholders are special values, or the results of the query could be suspect. For example, if you used the placeholder value of 0 (zero) instead of NULL for a *salary* field in an *employee* table, you'd have to be careful not to use such a value in a query looking for average values or minimum salaries, because a salary of 0 would alter your average or minimum calculations inappropriately. If the placeholder is simply another designation for "unknown," you must write your queries with that in mind. Placeholder values usually solve the issues that arise in joining tables, and they can be an effective alternative to using OUTER JOIN. With placeholder values, developers are less likely to write incorrect queries, especially those who have only basic SQL knowledge.

In the previous example, the naïve query returns the same result set as the query with an OUTER JOIN and the criteria *OR state IS NULL*. It took careful work to construct the placeholder data and maintain the relationships for this to be the case. But the group database expert (probably you!) can do that work, and once done, individuals with less SQL or database knowledge won't be as likely to introduce bugs in their queries simply because they're unfamiliar with the issues of OUTER JOINS and three-valued logic. Sometimes you might feel you have to use NULL values; however, if you can minimize or avoid these cases, you're wise to do so.

If dummy entries aren't practical for you to use, try a few other tricks. A handy and underused function is ISNULL. Using ISNULL(*expression, value*) substitutes the specified value for the expression when the expression evaluates to NULL. In the earlier outer-join example, the WHERE clause was specified as

```
WHERE state <> 'CA' OR state IS NULL
```

By using the ISNULL function, a special value (in this case, *XX*) can be assigned to any NULL *state* values. Then the expression <> *'CA'* always evaluates to TRUE or FALSE rather than to Unknown. The clause *OR state IS NULL* isn't needed.

The following query produces the full outer-join result, without using IS NULL:

```
SELECT
'Author'=RTRIM(au_lname) + ', ' + au_fname,
'Title'=title
FROM
    authors AS A              -- JOIN CONDITIONS
    FULL OUTER JOIN titleauthor AS TA ON A.au_id=TA.au_id
    FULL OUTER JOIN titles AS T ON t.title_id=TA.title_id
WHERE
ISNULL(state, 'XX') <> 'CA'
ORDER BY 1
```

IS NULL and = NULL

You've seen how the IS NULL operator exists to handle the special case of looking for NULL. Because NULL is considered Unknown, ANSI-standard SQL doesn't provide for an equality expression of NULL—that is, there's no *WHERE value = NULL*. Instead, you must use the IS NULL operator *WHERE value IS NULL*. This can make queries more awkward to write and less intuitive to non-SQL experts. One of my favorite SQL gurus at Microsoft, Rick Vicik, says tongue-in-cheek that this is because "NULLs are evil and you should experience extra pain every time you use one." And it's somewhat curious, or at least nonorthogonal, that ANSI SQL doesn't force an UPDATE statement to set a value TO NULL but instead uses the = NULL formulation. (Table 7-3 on the following page summarizes this state of affairs.)

> **NOTE** *Orthogonal* is an adjective, somewhat jargonish, that's often applied to programming languages and APIs. It's a mathematical term meaning that the sum of the products of corresponding elements in a system equals 0. This implies that a system is orthogonal if all of its primitive operations fully describe the base capabilities of the system and those primitives are independent and mutually exclusive of one another. In broader use, the term also denotes a certain symmetry and consistency. For example, an API that has a *GetData* call would also have a *PutData* call, each taking arguments that are as consistent as possible between the two. The two APIs make up a mutually exclusive domain of operations that you can perform on data, and they are named and invoked in a consistent manner. Such a pair of APIs would be considered orthogonal. SQL Server 7 has a BULK INSERT command but no BULK EXPORT command, so this is another example of *nonorthogonal* behavior.

ANSI SQL Doesn't Provide for This	And Provides Only for This
SELECT... WHERE salary = NULL	SELECT... WHERE salary IS NULL

Yet ANSI SQL Uses Only This	And Not Something Like This
UPDATE employee SET salary = NULL	UPDATE employee SET salary TO NULL

Table 7-3.
ANSI SQL's treatment of NULLs.

SQL Server provides an extension to ANSI SQL that allows queries to use = NULL as an alternative to IS NULL. (The SET ANSI_NULLS option has an oblique reference to this extension, but it's never been thoroughly explained.)

Note that the formulation is not = *"NULL"*—the quotation marks would have the effect of searching for a character string containing the word *NULL*, as opposed to searching for the special meaning of NULL. This way of specifying = NULL is simply a shorthand for IS NULL and provides a more convenient formulation of queries, especially by allowing NULL within an IN clause. The IN clause is a standard SQL shorthand notation for an expression that checks multiple values, as illustrated below:

Multiple OR Conditions	**Equivalent Shorthand Formulation**
WHERE state = 'CA' OR state = 'WA' OR state ='IL'	WHERE state IN ('CA', 'WA', 'IL')

If you wanted to find states that are either one of the three values depicted in the previous example or NULL, ANSI SQL prescribes that the condition be stated using both an IN clause and an *OR state IS NULL* expression; SQL Server also allows all the conditions to be specified with the IN clause, as shown here:

ANSI SQL Prescribes	**SQL Server also Allows**
WHERE state IN ('CA', 'WA', 'IL') OR state IS NULL	WHERE state IN ('CA', 'WA', 'IL', NULL)

The = NULL shorthand can be particularly handy to use when you're dealing with parameters passed to a stored procedure, and this is the main reason it exists. Here's an example:

```
CREATE PROCEDURE get_employees (@dept char(8), @class char(5))
AS
    SELECT * FROM employee WHERE employee.dept=@dept
        AND employee.class=@class
```

By default, we can pass NULL to this procedure for either parameter; no special treatment is necessary. But without the = NULL shorthand, we need to put in extensive special handling even for this simple procedure:

```
CREATE PROCEDURE get_employees (@dept char(8), @class char(5))
AS
    IF (@dept IS NULL AND @class IS NOT NULL)
        SELECT * FROM employee WHERE employee.dept IS NULL
        AND employee.class=@class
    ELSE IF (@dept IS NULL AND @class IS NULL)
        SELECT * FROM employee WHERE employee.dept IS NULL
        AND employee.class IS NULL
    ELSE IF (@dept IS NOT NULL AND @class IS NULL)
        SELECT * FROM employee WHERE employee.dept=@dept
        AND employee.class IS NULL
    ELSE
        SELECT * FROM employee WHERE employee.dept=@dept
        AND employee.class=@class
```

This example is pretty trivial, and the situation becomes much more complex if you have multiple parameters and any one of them might be NULL. You then need a SELECT statement for every combination of parameters that might be NULL or NOT NULL. It can get ugly quickly.

> **WARNING**   The = NULL syntax is only possible when you have the ANSI_NULLS and ANSI_DEFAULTS options set to OFF, and if you have the database option ANSI NULLS set to FALSE. Since the ODBC driver and OLE DB provider can set these options on, you need to verify what is in effect for your connection.

As mentioned earlier, dealing with NULL becomes an issue of nearly religious fervor to some in the database industry. No doubt, a few people will find the SQL Server extension that allows an expression to be checked for = NULL to be a grave and serious deviation from three-valued logic (which is the primary reason this extension hasn't been well-documented, although many users have discovered it). As long as you realize that = NULL is purely a convenient shorthand for IS NULL, it should be clear to you that no violation of three-valued logic has occurred. Those of you who are vehemently opposed to such formulations don't have to use these extensions, of course. You can also prevent this extension from working by enabling the SET ANSI_NULLS option.

Subqueries

SQL Server has an extremely powerful capability to nest queries, which provides a natural and efficient way to express WHERE clause criteria in terms of the results of other queries. You can express most joins as *subqueries,* although this method is often less efficient than performing the join operation. For example, using the *pubs* database to find all employees of the New Moon Books publishing company, we can write the query as either a join (using ANSI join syntax) or as a subquery.

Here's the query as a join (equijoin, or inner join):

```
SELECT emp_id, lname
FROM employee JOIN publishers ON employee.pub_id=publishers.pub_id
WHERE pub_name='New Moon Books'
```

This is the query as a subquery:

```
SELECT emp_id, lname
FROM employee
WHERE employee.pub_id IN
    (SELECT publishers.pub_id
    FROM publishers WHERE pub_name='New Moon Books')
```

You can write a join (equijoin) as a subquery (subselect), but the converse isn't necessarily true. The equijoin has the advantage in that the two sides of the equation equal each other and the order doesn't matter. Clearly, in a subquery, it does matter which query is the nested query. This difference is why a join can often be evaluated more quickly than an apparently equivalent subquery (subselect). A join gives the optimizer more options to choose from.

Performing relatively complex operations is simple when you use subqueries. For example, earlier we saw that the *pubs* sample database has four rows in the *authors* table that have no related row in the *titleauthor* table (which prompted our outer-join discussion). The following simple subquery returns those four *author* rows:

```
SELECT 'Author ID'=A.au_id,
    'Author'=CONVERT(varchar(20), RTRIM(au_lname) +', '
    + RTRIM(au_fname)), state
FROM authors A
WHERE A.au_id NOT IN
    (SELECT B.au_id FROM titleauthor B)
```

Here's the output:

Author ID	Author	state
341-22-1782	Smith, Meander	KS
527-72-3246	Greene, Morningstar	TN
724-08-9931	Stringer, Dirk	CA
893-72-1158	McBadden, Heather	CA

The IN operation is commonly used for subqueries, either to find matching values (similar to a join) or to find nonmatching values by negating it (NOT IN), as shown above. Using the IN predicate is actually equivalent to saying = ANY. If we wanted to find every row in *authors* that had at least one entry in the *titleauthor* table, we could use either of these queries.

Here's the query using IN:

```
SELECT 'Author ID'=A.au_id,
    'Author'=CONVERT(varchar(20), RTRIM(au_lname) + ', '
    + RTRIM(au_fname)), state
FROM authors A
WHERE A.au_id IN
    (SELECT B.au_id FROM titleauthor B)
```

This is the query using equivalent formulation with = ANY:

```
SELECT 'Author ID'=A.au_id,
    'Author'=CONVERT(varchar(20), RTRIM(au_lname) + , '
    + RTRIM(au_fname)), state
FROM authors A
WHERE A.au_id=ANY
    (SELECT B.au_id FROM titleauthor B)
```

Here's the output:

Author ID	Author	state
172-32-1176	White, Johnson	CA
213-46-8915	Green, Marjorie	CA
238-95-7766	Carson, Cheryl	CA
267-41-2394	O'Leary, Michael	CA
274-80-9391	Straight, Dean	CA
409-56-7008	Bennet, Abraham	CA

(continued)

333

427-17-2319	Dull, Ann	CA
472-27-2349	Gringlesby, Burt	CA
486-29-1786	Locksley, Charlene	CA
648-92-1872	Blotchet-Halls, Regi	OR
672-71-3249	Yokomoto, Akiko	CA
712-45-1867	del Castillo, Innes	MI
722-51-5454	DeFrance, Michel	IN
724-80-9391	MacFeather, Stearns	CA
756-30-7391	Karsen, Livia	CA
807-91-6654	Panteley, Sylvia	MD
846-92-7186	Hunter, Sheryl	CA
899-46-2035	Ringer, Anne	UT
998-72-3567	Ringer, Albert	UT

Each of these formulations is equivalent to testing the value of *au_id* in the *titles* table to the *au_id* value in the first row in the *titleauthor* table, and then OR'ing it to a test of the *au_id* value of the second row, and then OR'ing it to a test of the value of the third row, and so on. As soon as one row evaluates to TRUE, the expression is TRUE, and further checking can stop because the row in *titles* qualifies. However, it's an easy mistake to conclude that NOT IN must be equivalent to <> ANY, and some otherwise good discussions of the SQL language have made this exact mistake. And, more significantly, some products have also erroneously implemented it as such. Although IN is equivalent to = ANY, NOT IN is instead equivalent to <> ALL, not to <> ANY.

NOTE Careful reading of the ANSI SQL-92 specifications also reveals that NOT IN is equivalent to <> ALL but is not equivalent to <> ANY. Section 8.4 of the specifications shows that R NOT IN T is equivalent to NOT (R = ANY T). Furthermore, careful study of section 8.7 <quantified comparison predicate> reveals that NOT (R = ANY T) is TRUE if and only if R <> ALL T is TRUE. In other words, NOT IN is equivalent to <> ALL.

By using NOT IN, you're stating that *none* of the corresponding values can match. In other words, *all* of the values must not match (<> ALL), and if even one does match, it's FALSE. With <> ANY, as soon as one value is found to be not equivalent, the expression is TRUE. This, of course, is also the case for every row of *authors*—rows in *titleauthor* will always exist for other *au_id* values, and hence all *authors* rows will have at least one nonmatching row in *titleauthor*. That is, every row in *authors* will evaluate to TRUE for a test of <> ANY row in *titleauthor*.

The following query using <> ALL returns the same four rows as the earlier one that used NOT IN:

```
SELECT 'Author ID'=A.au_id,
    'Author'=CONVERT(varchar(20), RTRIM(au_lname) + ', '
    + RTRIM(au_fname)), state
FROM authors A
WHERE A.au_id <> ALL
    (SELECT B.au_id FROM titleauthor B)
```

The output follows:

Author ID	Author	state
341-22-1782	Smith, Meander	KS
527-72-3246	Greene, Morningstar	TN
724-08-9931	Stringer, Dirk	CA
893-72-1158	McBadden, Heather	CA

If we made the mistake of thinking that because IN is equivalent to = ANY, then NOT IN is equivalent to <> ANY, we would write the query as follows. This returns all **23** rows in the *authors* table!

```
SELECT 'Author ID'=A.au_id,
    'Author'=CONVERT(varchar(20), RTRIM(au_lname) + ', '
    + RTRIM(au_fname)), state
FROM authors A
WHERE A.au_id <> ANY
    (SELECT B.au_id FROM titleauthor B)
```

Here's the output:

Author ID	Author	state
172-32-1176	White, Johnson	CA
213-46-8915	Green, Marjorie	CA
238-95-7766	Carson, Cheryl	CA
267-41-2394	O'Leary, Michael	CA
274-80-9391	Straight, Dean	CA
341-22-1782	Smith, Meander	KS
409-56-7008	Bennet, Abraham	CA
427-17-2319	Dull, Ann	CA
472-27-2349	Gringlesby, Burt	CA
486-29-1786	Locksley, Charlene	CA
527-72-3246	Greene, Morningstar	TN
648-92-1872	Blotchet-Halls, Regi	OR
672-71-3249	Yokomoto, Akiko	CA

(continued)

712-45-1867	del Castillo, Innes	MI
722-51-5454	DeFrance, Michel	IN
724-08-9931	Stringer, Dirk	CA
724-80-9391	MacFeather, Stearns	CA
756-30-7391	Karsen, Livia	CA
807-91-6654	Panteley, Sylvia	MD
846-92-7186	Hunter, Sheryl	CA
893-72-1158	McBadden, Heather	CA
899-46-2035	Ringer, Anne	UT
998-72-3567	Ringer, Albert	UT

The examples just shown use IN, NOT IN, ANY, and ALL to compare values to a set of values from a subquery. This is common. However, it's also common to use expressions and compare a set of values to a single, scalar value. For example, to find *titles* whose royalties exceed the average of all royalty values in the *roysched* table by 25 percent or more, you could use this simple query:

```
SELECT titles.title_id, title, royalty
FROM titles
WHERE titles.royalty >=
    (SELECT 1.25 * AVG(roysched.royalty) FROM roysched)
```

This query is perfectly good, because the aggregate function AVG (*expression*) stipulates that the subquery must return exactly one value and no more. Without using IN, ANY, or ALL (or their negations), a subquery that returned more than one row would result in an error. If we incorrectly rewrote the query as follows, without the AVG function, we'd get run-time error 512:

```
SELECT titles.title_id, title, royalty
FROM titles
WHERE titles.royalty >=
    (SELECT 1.25 * roysched.royalty FROM roysched)
```

This returns the following output:

```
Msg 512, Level 16, State 1
Subquery returned more than 1 value. This is illegal when the
subquery follows =, !=, <, <=, >, >=, or when the subquery is used as
an expression.
```

It is significant that this error is a run-time error and not a syntax error, meaning that in the SQL Server implementation, if that subquery didn't produce more than one row, the query would be considered valid and would execute. For example, with the knowledge that the subquery here would return only one row, this query is valid and returns six rows:

```
SELECT titles.title_id, title, royalty
FROM titles
WHERE titles.royalty >=
    (SELECT 1.25*roysched.royalty FROM roysched
    WHERE roysched.title_id='MC3021' AND lorange=0)
```

The output follows:

```
title_id    title
--------    ----------------------------------------
BU2075      You Can Combat Computer Stress!
MC2222      Silicon Valley Gastronomic Treats
MC3021      The Gourmet Microwave
PC1035      But Is It User Friendly?
PS2091      Is Anger the Enemy?
TC4203      Fifty Years in Buckingham Palace Kitchens
```

However, this sort of query can be dangerous, and you should avoid it or use it only when you know a PRIMARY KEY or UNIQUE constraint will ensure that the subquery returns only one value. The query here appears to work, but it's a bug waiting to happen. As soon as another row is added to the *roysched* table, say with *title_id* of MC3021 and a *lorange* of 0, the query returns an error—and no constraint exists to prevent such a row from being added.

You might argue that SQL Server should determine whether a query formation could conceivably return more than one row regardless of the data at the time and then disallow such a subquery formulation. The decision to allow this stemmed from the philosophy that such a query might be quite valid when the database relationships are properly understood, so the power shouldn't be limited to try to protect naïve users. Whether you agree with this philosophy or not, it's consistent with SQL in general—and you should know by now that you can easily write a perfectly legal, syntactically correct query that answers a question entirely different from the one you thought you were asking!

Correlated Subqueries

You can use powerful correlated subqueries to compare specific rows of one table to a condition in a matching table. For each row otherwise qualifying in the main (or top) query, the subquery is evaluated. Conceptually, a correlated subquery is similar to a loop in programming, although it's entirely without procedural constructs such as *do-while* or *for*. The results of each execution of the subquery must be correlated to a row of the main query. In the next example, for every row in the *titles* table that has a price of $19.99 or less, the row is compared with sales in stores in California, for which the revenue (*price* × *qty*) is greater than $250. In other words, "Show me titles with prices of under $20 that have sales of more than $250 in California."

```
SELECT T.title_id,title
FROM titles T
WHERE price <= 19.99
AND T.title_id IN (
    SELECT S.title_id FROM sales S, stores ST
    WHERE S.stor_id=ST.stor_id
    AND ST.state='CA' AND S.qty*T.price > 250
    AND T.title_id=S.title_id)
```

Here's the result:

```
title_id        title
--------        ----------------------------
BU7832          Straight Talk About Computers
PS2091          Is Anger the Enemy?
TC7777          Sushi, Anyone?
```

Notice that this correlated subquery, like many subqueries, could have been written as a join (here using the old-style JOIN syntax):

```
SELECT T.title_id, T.title
FROM sales S, stores ST, titles T
WHERE S.stor_id=ST.stor_id
AND T.title_id=S.title_id
AND ST.state='CA'
AND T.price <= 19.99
AND S.qty*T.price > 250
```

It becomes nearly impossible to create alternative joins when the subquery isn't doing a simple IN or when it uses aggregate functions. For example, suppose that we want to find titles that lag in sales for each store. This could be defined as "Find any title for every store in which the title's sales in that store are below 80 percent of the average of sales for all stores that carry that title, and ignore titles that have no price established (that is, the price is NULL)." An intuitive way to do this is to first think of the main query that will give us the gross sales for each title and store, and then for each such result, do a subquery that finds the average gross sales for the title for all stores. Then we correlate the subquery and the main query, keeping only rows that fall below the 80 percent standard.

Such an example follows. For clarity, notice the two distinct queries, each of which answers a separate question. Then notice how they can be combined into a single correlated query to answer the specific question posed here. All three queries use the old-style JOIN syntax.

```
-- This query computes gross revenues by
-- title for every title and store
SELECT T.title_id, S.stor_id, ST.stor_name, city, state,
    T.price*S.qty
FROM titles AS T, sales AS S, stores AS ST
WHERE T.title_id=S.title_id AND S.stor_id=ST.stor_id

-- This query computes 80% of the average gross revenue for each
-- title for all stores carrying that title:
SELECT T2.title_id, .80*AVG(price*qty)
FROM titles AS T2, sales AS S2
WHERE T2.title_id=S2.title_id
GROUP BY T2.title_id

-- Correlated subquery that finds store-title combinations whose
-- revenues are less than 80% of the average of revenues for that
-- title for all stores selling that title
SELECT T.title_id, S.stor_id, ST.stor_name, city, state,
    Revenue=T.price*S.qty
FROM titles AS T, sales AS S, stores AS ST
WHERE T.title_id=S.title_id AND S.stor_id=ST.stor_id
AND T.price*S.qty <
    (SELECT 0.80*AVG(price*qty)
    FROM titles T2, sales S2
    WHERE T2.title_id=S2.title_id
    AND T.title_id=T2.title_id )
```

And the answer is (from the third query):

title_id	stor_id	stor_name	city	state	Revenue
BU1032	6380	Eric the Read Books	Seattle	WA	99.95
MC3021	8042	Bookbeat	Portland	OR	44.85
PS2091	6380	Eric the Read Books	Seattle	WA	32.85
PS2091	7067	News & Brews	Los Gatos	CA	109.50
PS2091	7131	Doc-U-Mat: Quality Laundry and Books	Remulade	WA	219.00

When the newer ANSI JOIN syntax was first introduced, it wasn't obvious how to use it to write a correlated subquery. And it could be that the creators of the syntax forgot about the correlated subquery case, because using the syntax seems like a hybrid of the old and the new: the correlation is still done in the WHERE clause, rather than in the JOIN clause. For illustration, examine the two equivalent formulations of the above query using the ANSI JOIN syntax shown on the following page.

```
SELECT T.title_id, S.stor_id, ST.stor_name, city, state,
    Revenue=T.price*S.qty
FROM titles AS T JOIN sales AS S ON T.title_id=S.title_id
    JOIN stores AS ST ON S.stor_id=ST.stor_id
WHERE T.price*S.qty <
    (SELECT 0.80*AVG(price*qty)
    FROM titles T2 JOIN sales S2 ON T2.title_id=S2.title_id
    WHERE T.title_id=T2.title_id )

SELECT T.title_id, S.stor_id, ST.stor_name, city, state,
    Revenue=T.price*S.qty
FROM titles AS T JOIN sales AS S
    ON T.title_id=S.title_id
    AND T.price*S.qty <
        (SELECT 0.80*AVG(T2.price*S2.qty)
        FROM sales AS S2 JOIN titles AS T2
            ON T2.title_id=S2.title_id
        WHERE T.title_id=T2.title_id)
    JOIN stores AS ST ON S.stor_id=ST.stor_id
```

Often, correlated subqueries use the EXISTS statement, which is the most convenient syntax to use when multiple fields of the main query are to be correlated to the subquery. (In practice, EXISTS is seldom used other than with correlated subqueries.) EXISTS simply checks for a nonempty set. It returns (internally) either TRUE or NOT TRUE, which we won't refer to as FALSE, given the issues of three-valued logic and NULL. Because no column value is returned, TRUE or NOT TRUE, convention dictates that a column list isn't specified and also dictates that the asterisk (*) character is used instead.

A common use for EXISTS is to answer a query such as "Show me the titles for which no stores have sales."

```
SELECT T1.title_id, title FROM titles T1
WHERE NOT EXISTS
(SELECT *
FROM titles T2 JOIN sales S ON (T2.title_id=S.title_id)
WHERE T2.title_id=T1.title_id )
```

```
title_id    title
--------    -----------------------------------
MC3026      The Psychology of Computer Cooking
PC9999      Net Etiquette
```

Conceptually, this query is pretty straightforward. The subquery, a simple equijoin, finds all matches of *titles* and *sales*. Then NOT EXISTS correlates *titles* to those matches, looking for *titles* that don't have even a single row returned in the subquery.

Another common use of EXISTS determines whether a table is empty. The optimizer knows that as soon as it gets a single hit using EXISTS, the operation is TRUE, and further processing is unnecessary. For example, here's how you determine whether the *authors* table is empty:

```
SELECT 'Not Empty' WHERE EXISTS (SELECT * FROM authors)
```

Earlier, when discussing outer join, we mentioned that it's now possible to use an outer-join formulation to address what was traditionally a problem in need of a correlated subquery solution. Here's an outer-join formulation for the problem described earlier, "Show me the titles for which no stores have sales."

```
SELECT T1.title_id, title FROM titles T1
    LEFT OUTER JOIN sales S ON T1.title_id=S.title_id
WHERE S.title_id IS NULL
```

> **TIP** Depending on your data and indexes, the outer-join formulation might be faster or slower than a correlated subquery. But before automatically deciding to write your query one way or the other, you might want to come up with a couple of alternative formulations, and choose the one that's fastest in your situation.
>
> In this example, for which little data exists, both solutions run in subsecond elapsed time. But the outer-join query requires fewer than half the number of logical I/Os than does the correlated subquery. With more data, that difference would be significant.

This query works by joining the *stores* and *title* tables and by preserving the titles for which no store exists. Then, in the WHERE clause, it specifically chooses *only* the rows that it preserved in the outer join. Those rows are the ones for which a title had no matching store.

Other times, a correlated subquery might be preferable to a join, especially if it's a self-join back to the same table or some other exotic join. Here's an example. Given the following table (and assuming that the *row_num* column is guaranteed unique), suppose that we want to identify the rows for which *col2* and *col3* are duplicates of another row:

row_num	col2	col3
1	C	D
2	A	A

(continued)

```
3               A               D
4               C               B
5               C               C
6               B               C
7               C               A
8               C               B
9               C               D
10              D               D
```

We can do this in two standard ways. The first uses a self-join. In a self-join, the table (or view) is used multiple times in the FROM clause and aliased at least once. Then it can be treated as an entirely different table, comparing columns, and so on. A self-join to find the rows having duplicate values for *col2* and *col3* is easy to understand:

```
SELECT DISTINCT A.row_num, A.col2, A.col3
FROM match_cols AS A, match_cols AS B
WHERE A.col2=B.col2 AND A.col3=B.col3 AND A.row_num <> B.row_num
ORDER BY A.col2, A.col3
```

```
row_num         col2            col3
-------         ----            ----
4               C               B
8               C               B
1               C               D
9               C               D
```

But in this case, a correlated subquery using aggregate functions provides a considerably more efficient solution, especially if many duplicates exist:

```
SELECT A.row_num, A.col2, A.col3 FROM match_cols AS A
WHERE EXISTS (SELECT B.col2, B.col3 FROM match_cols AS B
                 WHERE B.col2=A.col2
                 AND B.col3=A.col3
                 GROUP BY B.col2, B.col3 HAVING COUNT(*) > 1)
ORDER BY A.col2, A.col3
```

This correlated subquery has another advantage over the self-join example—the *row_num* column doesn't need to be unique to solve the problem at hand.

You can take a correlated subquery a step further to ask a seemingly simple question that's surprisingly tricky to answer in SQL: "Show me the stores that have sold every title." Ron Soukup uses a variation of this question when interviewing testing candidates who profess strong SQL knowledge. Even though it seems reasonable, relatively few candidates can answer this request, especially if we throw in the restrictions that they aren't allowed to use an aggregate function like COUNT(*) and that the solution must be a single SELECT statement (that is, creating temporary tables or the like isn't allowed).

The previous query already revealed two titles that no store has sold, so we know that with the existing dataset, no stores can have sales for all titles. For illustrative purposes, let's add sales records for a hypothetical store that does, in fact, have sales for every title. Following that, we'll see the query that finds all stores that have sold every title (which we know ahead of time is only the phony one we're entering here):

```
-- The phony store
INSERT stores (stor_id, stor_name, stor_address, city, state, zip)
VALUES ('9999', 'WE SUPPLY IT ALL', 'One Main St', 'Poulsbo',
    'WA','98370')

-- By using a combination of hard-coded values and selecting every
-- title, generate a sales row for every title
INSERT sales (stor_id, title_id, ord_num, ord_date, qty, payterms)
SELECT '9999', title_id, 'PHONY1', GETDATE(), 10, 'Net 60'
FROM titles

-- Find stores that supply every title
SELECT ST.stor_id, ST.stor_name, ST.city, ST.state
FROM stores ST
WHERE NOT EXISTS
    (SELECT * FROM titles T1
    WHERE NOT EXISTS
        (SELECT *
        FROM titles T2 JOIN sales S ON (T2.title_id=S.title_id)
        WHERE T2.title_id=T1.title_id AND ST.stor_id=S.stor_id)
    )
```

Here's the result:

stor_id	stor_name	city	state
9999	WE SUPPLY IT ALL	Poulsbo	WA

Although this query might be difficult to think of immediately, you can easily understand why it works. In English, it says "Show me the store(s) such that no titles exist that the store doesn't sell." This query consists of the two subqueries that are applied to each store. The bottommost subquery produces all the titles that the store has sold. The upper subquery is then correlated to that bottom one to look for any titles that are *not* in the list of those that the store has sold. The top query returns any stores that aren't in this list. This type of query is known as a *relational division,* and unfortunately, it isn't as easy to express as we'd like. Although the query shown on the previous page is quite understandable, once you have a solid foundation in SQL, it's hardly intuitive. As is almost always the case, you could probably use other formulations to write this query.

We've already alluded to doing this query without using an aggregate function like COUNT. There's nothing wrong with using an aggregate function— Ron imposes the restriction only to make his test more of a brainteaser. If you think of the query in English as "Find the stores that have sold as many unique titles as there are total unique titles," you'll find the following formulation somewhat more intuitive. Of those who get this brainteaser right, this formulation (or a slight variation) is probably the most popular (if we don't have the restriction of not using the COUNT function). It actually runs slightly faster in SQL Server 7 than the NOT EXISTS formulation mentioned earlier.

```
SELECT ST.stor_id, ST.stor_name
FROM stores ST, sales SA, titles T
WHERE SA.stor_id=ST.stor_id AND SA.title_id=T.title_id
GROUP BY ST.stor_id,ST.stor_name
HAVING COUNT(DISTINCT SA.title_id)=(SELECT COUNT(*) FROM titles T1)
```

The following formulation runs much more efficiently than either of the previous two. The syntax is similar to the one above but still novel in its approach because it's just a standard subquery, not a join or a correlated subquery. You might think it's an illegal query, since it does a GROUP BY and a HAVING without an aggregate in the select list of the first subquery. But that's OK, both in terms of what SQL Server allows and in terms of the ANSI specification. What isn't allowed is having an item in the select list that isn't an aggregate function but then omitting it from the GROUP BY clause, if there is a GROUP BY clause.

```
-- Find stores that have sold every title
SELECT stor_id, stor_name FROM stores WHERE stores.stor_id IN
(SELECT stor_id FROM sales GROUP BY stor_id
    HAVING COUNT(DISTINCT title_id)=(SELECT COUNT(*) FROM titles)
)
```

And as a lead-in to the next topic, here's a formulation that uses a derived table, a feature that allows you to use a subquery in a FROM clause. This capability takes a SELECT statement and aliases it as though it were a table, and then it allows you to select from the select list. This query also runs efficiently.

```
SELECT ST.stor_id, ST.stor_name
FROM stores ST,
    (SELECT stor_id, COUNT(DISTINCT title_id) AS title_count
        FROM sales
        GROUP BY stor_id
    ) as SA
WHERE ST.stor_id=SA.stor_id AND SA.title_count=
    (SELECT COUNT(*) FROM titles)
```

Views and Derived Tables

Think of a view as a virtual table. Simply put, a view is a named SELECT statement that dynamically produces a result set that you can further operate on. A view doesn't actually store any data. It acts as a filter to underlying tables in which the data is stored. The SELECT statement that defines the view can be from one or more underlying tables or from other views. To relieve users of the complexity of having to know how to write an outer join properly, we can turn the prior outer-join query into a view:

```
CREATE VIEW outer_view AS
(
SELECT
    'Author'=RTRIM(au_lname) + ', ' + au_fname, 'Title'=title
FROM (titleauthor AS TA
FULL OUTER JOIN titles AS T ON (TA.title_id=T.title_id))
RIGHT OUTER JOIN authors AS A ON (A.au_id=TA.au_id)
WHERE
A.state <> 'CA' OR A.state IS NULL
)
```

Now, instead of formulating the outer join, we can simply query the outer-join view, *outer_view*. Then we can do a search for author names starting with *Ri*.

```
SELECT * FROM outer_view WHERE Author LIKE 'Ri%' ORDER BY Author
```

Here's the output:

```
Author            Title
---------------   ----------------------
Ringer, Albert    Is Anger the Enemy?
Ringer, Albert    Life Without Fear
Ringer, Anne      The Gourmet Microwave
Ringer, Anne      Is Anger the Enemy?
```

345

Notice that the view defines the set of rows that are included, but it doesn't define the rows' ordering. If we want a specific order, we must specify the ORDER BY clause in the SELECT statement on the view rather than on the SELECT statement that defines the view.

A *derived table* is a fancy name for the result of using another SELECT statement in the FROM clause of a SELECT statement. This fits the relational model nicely, because the result of a SELECT statement should be a table—so that it's nicely orthogonal and we can subsequently select from it. You can think of a view as a named derived table. A view is named, and its definition is persistent and reusable; a derived table is a completely dynamic, temporal concept. To show the difference, here's an equivalent *LIKE 'Ri%'* query using a derived table instead of a view:

```
SELECT *
FROM
    (SELECT
    'Author'=RTRIM(au_lname) + ', ' + au_fname, 'Title'=title
    FROM (titleauthor AS TA
    FULL OUTER JOIN titles AS T ON (TA.title_id=T.title_id))
    RIGHT OUTER JOIN authors AS A ON (A.au_id=TA.au_id)
    WHERE A.state <> 'CA' OR A.state IS NULL
    ) AS T
WHERE T.Author LIKE 'Ri%'
```

You can insert, update, and delete rows in a view but not in a derived table. Keep in mind that you're always modifying rows in the tables on which a view is based, because the view has no data of its own. Think of it as modifying data *through* a view rather than modifying data *in* a view. Some limitations to modifying data through a view exist; although the SQL Server documentation explains them, they bear repeating here with a bit more comment:

Modifications restricted to one base table   Data modification statements (INSERT and UPDATE only) are allowed on multiple-table views if the data modification statement affects only one base table. DELETE statements are never allowed on multiple-table views, because you can't use data modification statements on more than one underlying table in a single statement. You can never modify through a view that's based on a UNION.

INSERT statements and NOT NULL columns   INSERT statements aren't accepted unless all the NOT NULL columns without defaults in the underlying table or view are included in the view through which you're inserting new rows, and values for those columns are included in the INSERT statement. (SQL Server has no way to supply values for NOT

NULL columns in the underlying table or view if no default value has been defined.)

Data restrictions   All columns being modified must adhere to all restrictions for the data modification statement as if they were executed directly against the base table. This applies to column nullability, con-straints, identity columns, and columns with rules and/or defaults and base table triggers.

Limitations on INSERT and UPDATE statements   INSERT and UPDATE statements can't add or change any column in a view that's a computation, nor can they change a view that includes aggregate functions, built-in functions, UNION, a GROUP BY clause, or DISTINCT.

READTEXT or WRITETEXT   You can't use READTEXT or WRITETEXT on text or image columns in views.

Modifications and view criteria   By default, data modification statements through views aren't checked to determine whether the rows affected are within the scope of the view. For example, you can issue an INSERT statement for a view that adds a row to the underlying base table, but that doesn't add the row to the view. This behavior occurs because the column values are all valid to the table, so they can be added; however, if the column values don't meet the view's criteria, they aren't represented in the selection for the view. Similarly, you can issue an UPDATE statement that changes a row in a way that the row no longer meets the criteria for the view. If you want all modifications to be checked, use the WITH CHECK OPTION option when creating the view.

For the most part, these restrictions are logical and understandable, except for WITH CHECK OPTION. For instance, if you use a view that defines some select criteria and allows the rows produced by the view to be modified, you must use WITH CHECK OPTION or you might experience the bizarre results of inserting a row that you can never see or updating rows in such a way that they disappear from the view.

Here's an example:

```
CREATE VIEW CA_authors AS
(
SELECT * FROM authors
WHERE state='CA'
)
GO
```

(continued)

```
BEGIN TRAN -- So we can roll back this nonsense
SELECT * FROM CA_authors

-- (returns 15 rows)

UPDATE CA_authors SET state='IL'
SELECT * FROM CA_authors

-- (returns 0 rows)

ROLLBACK TRAN
```

Should we be able to update rows in a way that causes them to disappear from the view or add rows and never see them again? It's a matter of opinion. But because the SQL Server behavior is as ANSI SQL specifies, and such disappearing rows are as specified, you should consider *always* using WITH CHECK OPTION if a view is to be updated and the criteria are such that WITH CHECK OPTION might be violated.

If we rewrite the view, as follows

```
CREATE VIEW CA_authors AS
(
SELECT * FROM authors
WHERE state='CA'
)
WITH CHECK OPTION
```

when we attempt to update the state column to *IL*, the command fails and we get this error message:

```
Msg 550, Level 16, State 2
The attempted insert or update failed because the target view either
specifies WITH CHECK OPTION or spans a view which specifies WITH CHECK
OPTION and one or more rows resulting from the operation did not qualify
under the CHECK OPTION constraint. Command has been aborted.
```

Views also have an often overlooked ability to use a system function in the view definition, making it dynamic for the connection. For example, suppose that we keep a personnel table that has a column called *sqldb_name*, which is the person's login name to SQL Server. The function SUSER_NAME (*server_user_id*) returns the login name for the current connection. We can create a view using the SUSER_NAME system function to limit that user to only his or her specific row in the table:

```
CREATE VIEW My_personnel AS
(
SELECT * FROM personnel WHERE sqldb_name = SUSER_NAME()
)
WITH CHECK OPTION
```

SQL Server provides system functions that return the application name, database username (which might be different from the server login name), and workstation name, and these functions can be used in similar ways. You can see from the previous example that a view can also be important in dealing with security. For details on the system functions, see the SQL Server documentation.

Altering Views

SQL Server 7 allows you to alter the definition of a view. The syntax is almost identical to the syntax for creating the view initially:

```
ALTER VIEW view_name [(column [,…n])]
[WITH ENCRYPTION]
AS
select_statement
[WITH CHECK OPTION]
```

The big difference is that *view_name* must already exist, and the definition specified replaces whatever definition the view had before ALTER VIEW was executed. You might wonder why this is a useful command, since the entire definition must be reentered in the ALTER VIEW. Why don't we just drop the view and recreate it? The benefit comes from the fact that the view's *object_id* won't change, meaning all the internal references to this view remain intact. If other views reference this one, they'll be unaffected. If stored procedures access this view, they won't need to be recompiled. If you've assigned permissions on this view to various users and roles, dropping the view would lose all permission information. Altering the view keeps the permissions intact.

There is one gotcha when dealing with permissions on views, if the permissions have been assigned on individual columns. Internally, SQL Server keeps track of permissions by the column ID number. If you alter a view and change the order of the columns, the permissions might no longer be what you expect. Suppose you've created a view on the *authors* table to select the authors' names and phone numbers. You want all users to be able to see the authors' names, but you want the phone numbers to be unavailable.

```
CREATE VIEW authorlist (first, last, phone)
AS
SELECT au_lname, au_fname, phone
FROM authors
GO
GRANT SELECT ON authorlist (first, last) TO PUBLIC
GO
```

All users in the *pubs* database can now execute this command:

```
SELECT first, last FROM authorlist
```

We now alter the view to put the phone number column in the first position:

```
ALTER VIEW authorlist (phone, first, last)
AS
SELECT phone, au_lname, au_fname
FROM authors
```

Because the permissions have been granted on the first two columns, users will get an error message when they run this same query:

```
Server: Msg 230, Level 14, State 1
SELECT permission denied on column 'last' of object 'authorlist',
database 'pubs', owner 'dbo'.
```

However, all users can now select the values in the *phone* column, which we were trying to keep hidden.

Other Search Expressions

In addition to the SELECT statement and joins, SQL Server provides other useful search expressions that enable you to tailor your queries. These expressions include LIKE and BETWEEN, along with aggregate functions such as AVG, COUNT, and MAX.

LIKE

In an earlier example, we used LIKE to find authors whose names start with *Ri*. LIKE allows you to search using the simple pattern matching that is standard with ANSI SQL, but SQL Server adds capability by introducing wildcard characters that allow the use of regular expressions. Table 7-4 shows how wildcard characters are used in searches:

Wildcard	Searches for
%	Any string of zero or more characters.
-	Any single character.
[ ]	Any single character within the specified range (for example, [a-f]) or the specified set (for example, [abcdef]).
[^]	Any single character not within the specified range (for example, [^a-f]) or the specified set (for example, [^abcdef]).

Table 7-4.
Wildcard characters recognized by SQL Server for use in regular expressions.

The following examples from the SQL Server documentation show how LIKE can be used (Table 7-5).

Form	Searches for
LIKE 'Mc%'	All names that begin with the letters *Mc* (McBadden).
LIKE '%inger'	All names that end with *inger* (Ringer, Stringer).
LIKE '%en%'	All names that include the letters *en* (Bennet, Green, McBadden).
LIKE '-heryl'	All six-letter names ending with *heryl* (Cheryl, Sheryl).
LIKE '[CK]ars[eo]n'	All names that begin with *C* or *K*, then *ars*, then *e* or *o*, and then end with *n* (Carsen, Karsen, Carson, and Karson).
LIKE '[M-Z]inger'	All names ending with *inger* that begin with any single letter from *M* through *Z* (Ringer).
LIKE 'M[^c]%'	All names beginning with the letter *M* that don't have the letter *c* as the second letter (MacFeather).

Table 7-5.
Use of LIKE in searches.

Trailing Blanks

Trailing blanks (blank spaces) can cause considerable confusion and errors. In SQL Server, using trailing blanks requires that you be aware of differences in how *varchar* and *char* data is stored and of how the SET ANSI_PADDING option is used.

Suppose that we create a table with five columns and insert data as follows:

```
SET ANSI_PADDING OFF   -- OFF is the default if nothing is set

DROP TABLE checkpad
GO

CREATE TABLE checkpad
(
rowid        smallint      NOT NULL PRIMARY KEY,
c10not       char(10)      NOT NULL,
c10nul       char(10)      NULL,
v10not       varchar(10)   NOT NULL,
v10nul       varchar(10)   NULL
)

-- Row 1 has names with no trailing blanks
INSERT checkpad VALUES (1, 'John', 'John', 'John', 'John')

-- Row 2 has each name inserted with three trailing blanks
INSERT checkpad VALUES
    (2, 'John   ', 'John   ', 'John   ', 'Jo hn   ')

-- Row 3 has each name inserted with a full six trailing blanks
INSERT checkpad VALUES
    (3, 'John      ', 'John      ', 'John      ', 'John      ')

-- Row 4 has each name inserted with seven trailing blanks too many
INSERT checkpad VALUES
    (4, 'John       ', 'John       ', 'John       ', 'John       ')
```

We can then use the following query to analyze the contents of the table. We use the DATALENGTH(*expression*) function to determine the actual length of the data, and then convert to VARBINARY() to display the hexadecimal values of the characters stored. (For those who don't have the ASCII chart memorized, a blank space is 0x20.) We then use a LIKE to try to match each column, once with one trailing blank and once with six trailing blanks.

```
SELECT ROWID,
"0xC10NOT"=CONVERT(VARBINARY(10), c10not), L1=DATALENGTH(c10not),
"LIKE 'John %'"=CASE WHEN (c10not LIKE 'John %') THEN 1 ELSE 0 END,
"LIKE 'John      %'"=CASE WHEN (c10not LIKE 'John      %')
```

```
        THEN 1 ELSE 0 END,
"0xC10NUL"=CONVERT(VARBINARY(10), c10nul), L2=DATALENGTH(c10nul),
"LIKE 'John %'"=CASE WHEN (c10nul LIKE 'John %') THEN 1 ELSE 0 END,
"LIKE 'John      %'"=CASE WHEN (c10nul LIKE 'John      %')
        THEN 1 ELSE 0 END,
"0xV10NOT"=CONVERT(VARBINARY(10), v10not), L3=DATALENGTH(v10not),
"LIKE 'John %'"=CASE WHEN (v10not LIKE 'John %') THEN 1 ELSE 0 END,
"LIKE 'John      %'"=CASE WHEN (v10not LIKE 'John      %')
        THEN 1 ELSE 0 END,
"0xV10NUL"=CONVERT(VARBINARY(10), v10nul), L4=DATALENGTH(v10nul),
"LIKE 'John %'"=CASE WHEN (v10nul LIKE 'John %') THEN 1 ELSE 0 END,
"LIKE 'John      %'"=CASE WHEN (v10nul LIKE 'John      %')
        THEN 1 ELSE 0 END
FROM checkpad
```

Figure 7-6 shows the results of this query from the *checkpad* table.

ROWID	0xC10NOT	L1	LIKE 'John %'	LIKE 'John %'	0xC10NUL	L2	LIKE 'John %'	LIKE 'John %'	0xV10NOT	L3	LIKE 'John %'	LIKE 'John %'	0xV10NUL	L4	LIKE 'John %'	LIKE 'John %'
1	0x4A6F686E202020 202020	10	1	1	0x4A6F686E	4	0	0	0x4A6F686E	4	0	0	0x4A6F686E	4	0	0
2	0x4A6F686E202020 202020	10	1	1	0x4A6F686E	4	0	0	0x4A6F686E	4	0	0	0x4A6F686E	4	0	0
3	0x4A6F686E202020 202020	10	1	1	0x4A6F686E	4	0	0	0x4A6F686E	4	0	0	0x4A6F686E	4	0	0
4	0x4A6F686E202020 202020	10	1	1	0x4A6F686E	4	0	0	0x4A6F686E	4	0	0	0x4A6F686E	4	0	0

Figure 7-6.
Results with SET ANSI_PADDING OFF.

Without enabling SET ANSI_PADDING ON, SQL Server trims trailing blanks for variable-length columns and for fixed-length columns that allow NULLs. Notice that only column *c10not* has a length of 10. The other three columns are treated identically and end up with a length of 4 and no padding. For these columns, even trailing blanks explicitly entered within the quotation marks are trimmed. All the variable-length columns as well as the fixed-length column that allows NULLs have only the 4 bytes J-O-H-N (4a-6f-68-6e) stored. The true fixed-length column, *c10not*, is automatically padded with six blank spaces (0x20) to fill the entire 10 bytes.

All four columns would match *LIKE 'John%'* (no trailing blanks), but only the fixed-length column *c10not* matches *LIKE 'John %'* (one trailing blank) and *LIKE 'JOHN   %'* (six trailing blanks). The reason for this should be apparent when you realize that those trailing blanks are truncated and aren't part of the stored values for the other columns. A column query will get a hit with LIKE and trailing blanks only when the trailing blanks are stored. In this example, only the *c10not* column stores trailing blanks, so that's where the hit occurs.

SQL Server has dealt with trailing blanks in this way for a long time. However, when the developers began work to pass the National Institute of Standards and Technology (NIST) test suite for ANSI SQL conformance, they realized that this behavior was inconsistent with the ANSI specification. The specification requires that you always pad *char* datatypes and that you don't truncate trailing blanks entered by the user, even for *varchar*. We can argue for either side—both the long-standing SQL Server behavior and the ANSI specification behavior can be desirable, depending on the circumstances. However, if SQL Server changed its behavior to conform to ANSI, it would break many deployed SQL Server applications. So, to satisfy both sides, the ANSI_ PADDING option was added in version 6.5. If we enable SET ANSI_ PADDING ON, re-create the table, reinsert the rows, and then issue the same query, we get different results from those shown in Figure 7-6. Figure 7-7 shows these results.

By setting ANSI_PADDING ON, the *char(10)* columns *c10not* and *c10nul*, whether declared NOT NULL or NULL, are always padded out to 10 characters regardless of how many trailing blanks were entered. In addition, the variable-length columns *v10not* and *v10nul* contain the number of trailing blanks that were inserted. Trailing blanks are not truncated. Because the variable-length columns now store any trailing blanks that were part of the INSERT (or UPDATE) statement, the columns get hits in queries with LIKE and trailing blanks if the query finds that number of trailing blanks (or more) in the columns' contents. Notice that no error occurs by inserting a column with seven (instead of six) trailing blanks. The final trailing blank simply gets truncated. If you want a warning message to appear in such cases, you can use SET ANSI_WARNING ON.

ROWID	0xC10NOT	L1	LIKE 'John %'	LIKE 'John' %'	0xC10NUL	L2	LIKE 'John %'	LIKE 'John' %'	0xV10NOT	L3	LIKE 'John %'	LIKE 'John' %'	0xV10NUL	L4	LIKE 'John %'	LIKE 'John' %'
1	0x4A6F686E2020 20202020	10	1	1	0x4A6F686E20 2020202020	10	1	1	0x4A6F686E	4	0	0	0x4A6F686E	4	0	0
2	0x4A6F686E2020 20202020	10	1	1	0x4A6F686E20 2020202020	10	1	1	0x4A6F686E 202020	7	1	0	0x4A6F686E 202020	7	1	0
3	0x4A6F686E2020 20202020	10	1	1	0x4A6F686E20 2020202020	10	1	1	0x4A6F686E 2020202020 20	10	1	1	0x4A6F686E 2020202020 20	10	1	1
4	0x4A6F686E2020 20202020	10	1	1	0x4A6F686E20 2020202020	10	1	1	0x4A6F686E 2020202020 20	10	1	1	0x4A6F686E 2020202020 20	10	1	1

Figure 7-7.
Results with SET ANSI_PADDING ON.

Note that the SET ANSI_PADDING ON option applies to a table only if the option was enabled at the time the table was created (or to the column if it was added via ALTER TABLE). Enabling this option for an existing table does nothing. To determine whether a column has ANSI_PADDING set to ON, examine the status field of the *syscolumns* table and do a bitwise AND 20 (decimal). If the bit is on, you know the column was created with the option enabled. For example:

```
SELECT name, 'Padding On'=CASE WHEN status & 20 <> 0
    THEN 'YES' ELSE 'NO' END
FROM syscolumns WHERE id=OBJECT_ID('checkpad') AND name='v10not'
GO
```

SET ANSI_PADDING ON also affects the behavior of *binary* and *varbinary* fields, but the padding is done with zeros instead of spaces. Table 7-6 on the following page shows the effects of the SET ANSI_PADDING setting when values are inserted into columns with *char*, *varchar*, *binary*, and *varbinary* data types.

Note than when a fixed-length column allows NULLs, it mimics the behavior of variable-length columns if ANSI_PADDING is off, and it mimics the behavior of fixed-length columns if ANSI_PADDING is on.

The SQL Server ODBC driver and OLE DB Provider for SQL Server automatically set ANSI_PADDING to ON when connecting. This can be configured in ODBC data sources, in ODBC connection attributes, or OLE DB connection properties set in the application before connecting.

Setting of ANSI_PADDING	char(n) NOT NULL or binary(n) NOT NULL	char(n) NULL or binary(n) NULL	varchar(n) or varbinary(n)
ON	Pad original value to the length of the column.	Follows same rules as for *char(n)* or *binary(n)* NOT NULL.	Trailing blanks (for *varchar*) or zeros (for *varbinary*) in values inserted aren't trimmed. Values are not padded to the length of the column.
OFF	Pad original value to the length of the column.	Follows same rules as for *varchar* or *varbinary*.	Trailing blanks (for *varchar*) or trailing zeros (for *varbinary*) are trimmed.

Table 7-6.

The effects of the ANSI_PADDING setting.

Regardless of how the column was created, SQL Server provides functions that can help you deal effectively with trailing blanks. The RTRIM(*char_expression*) function removes trailing blanks if they exist. You can add trailing blanks to your output by concatenating with the SPACE(*integer_expression*) function. An easier way is to use the CONVERT function to convert to a fixed-length *char()* of whatever length you want. Then variable-length columns will be returned as fully padded, regardless of the ANSI_PADDING setting and regardless of the columns' actual storage, by converting them to *char(10)* or whatever size you want. The following SELECT statement against the *checkpad* table illustrates this:

```
SELECT CONVERT(VARBINARY(10), CONVERT(char(10), v10nul))
    FROM checkpad
```

Here's the result:

```
0x4a6f686e202020202020
0x4a6f686e202020202020
0x4a6f686e202020202020
0x4a6f686e202020202020
```

BETWEEN

BETWEEN is shorthand for greater-than-or-equal-to AND less-than-or-equal-to. The clause *WHERE C BETWEEN B AND D* is equivalent to writing *WHERE C >= B AND C <= D*. This one's not too tricky, but the order of the values to be checked is important when you use BETWEEN. If *B, C,* and *D* are increasing values, you can see that *WHERE C BETWEEN D AND B* wouldn't be true because it would evaluate to *WHERE C >= D AND C <= B*. Some early versions of SQL Server let you reverse the order, such that the meaning was equivalent to *WHERE (C >= B AND C <= D) OR (C >= D AND C <= B)*. However, that behavior was considered to be a bug and it was corrected in 1993.

Aggregate Functions

Aggregate functions (sometimes referred to as *set functions*) allow you to summarize a column of output. SQL Server provides six general aggregate functions that are standard ANSI SQL-92 fare. (Therefore, we won't go into much depth about their general use; instead, we'll focus on some aspects specific to SQL Server.) Table 7-7 on the following page summarizes SQL Server's aggregate functions.

Consider the following table, *automobile_sales_detail*. We'll use this table to demonstrate how aggregate functions simplify finding the answers to complex questions:

rowid	model	year	color	units_sold
1	Chevy	1990	Red	5
2	Chevy	1990	White	87
3	Chevy	1990	Blue	62
4	Chevy	1991	Red	54
5	Chevy	1991	White	95
6	Chevy	1991	Blue	49
7	Chevy	1992	Red	31
8	Chevy	1992	White	54
9	Chevy	1992	Blue	71
10	Ford	1990	Red	64
11	Ford	1990	White	62
12	Ford	1990	Blue	63
13	Ford	1991	Red	52
14	Ford	1991	White	9
15	Ford	1991	Blue	55
16	Ford	1992	Red	27
17	Ford	1992	White	62
18	Ford	1992	Blue	39

Aggregate Function	Description
AVG(*expression*)	Returns the average (mean) of all the values, or only the DISTINCT values, in the expression. You can use AVG with numeric* columns only. Null values are ignored.
COUNT(*expression*)	Returns the number of non-null values in the expression. When DISTINCT is specified, COUNT finds the number of unique non-null values. You can use COUNT with both numeric and character columns. Null values are ignored.
COUNT(*)	Returns the number of rows. COUNT(*) takes no parameters and can't be used with DISTINCT. All rows are counted, even those with null values.
MAX(*expression*)	Returns the maximum value in the expression. You can use MAX with numeric, character, and datetime columns but not with *bit* columns. With character columns, MAX finds the highest value in the collating sequence. MAX ignores any null values. DISTINCT is available for ANSI compatibility, but it's not meaningful with MAX.
MIN(*expression*)	Returns the minimum value in the expression. You can use MIN with numeric, character, and datetime columns, but not with *bit* columns. With character columns, MIN finds the value that is lowest in the sort sequence. MIN ignores any null values. DISTINCT is alvailable for ANSI compatibility, but it's not meaningful with MIN.
SUM(*expression*)	Returns the sum of all the values, or only the DISTINCT values, in the expression. You can use SUM with numeric columns only. Null values are ignored.

* As used here, *numeric columns* refers to *decimal, float, int, money, numeric, real, smallint, smallmoney,* and *tinyint* datatypes.

Table 7-7.
SQL Server's aggregate functions.

You can increase the power of aggregate functions by allowing them to be grouped and by allowing the groups to have criteria established for inclusion via the HAVING clause. The following queries provide some examples.

EXAMPLE 1

Show the oldest and newest model years for sale, and show the average sales of all the entries in the table:

```
SELECT 'Oldest'=MIN(year), 'Newest'=MAX(year),
    'Avg Sales'=AVG(units_sold)
FROM automobile_sales_detail
```

Here's the output:

```
Oldest    Newest    Avg Sales
------    ------    ---------
1990      1992      52
```

EXAMPLE 2

Do the Example 1 query, but show the values for autos that are Chevys only:

```
SELECT 'Oldest'=MIN(year), 'Newest'=MAX(year),
    'Avg Sales'=AVG(units_sold)
FROM automobile_sales_detail
WHERE model='Chevy'
```

And the result:

```
Oldest    Newest    Avg Sales
------    ------    ---------
1990      1992      56
```

EXAMPLE 3

Show the same values as in Example 1, but group them based on the model and color of the cars:

```
SELECT model, color, 'Oldest'=MIN(year), 'Newest'=MAX(year),
    'Avg Sales'=AVG(units_sold)
FROM automobile_sales_detail
GROUP BY model, color
ORDER BY model, color
```

The output appears on the following page.

model	color	Oldest	Newest	Avg Sales
Chevy	Blue	1990	1992	60
Chevy	Red	1990	1992	30
Chevy	White	1990	1992	78
Ford	Blue	1990	1992	52
Ford	Red	1990	1992	47
Ford	White	1990	1992	44

EXAMPLE 4

Show the same values for only those model-year rows with average sales of 65 or less. Also, order and group the output first by color and then by model, but keep the columns in the same order:

```
SELECT model, color, 'Oldest'=MIN(year), 'Newest'=MAX(year),
    'Avg Sales'=AVG(units_sold)
FROM automobile_sales_detail
GROUP BY color, model HAVING AVG(units_sold) <= 65
ORDER BY color, model
```

Here's the output:

model	color	Oldest	Newest	Avg Sales
Chevy	Blue	1990	1992	60
Ford	Blue	1990	1992	52
Chevy	Red	1990	1992	30
Ford	Red	1990	1992	47
Ford	White	1990	1992	44

NOTE We include an ORDER BY clause in these queries, even though we specify the criteria of the ORDER BY to be the same criteria that the GROUP BY clause uses. In earlier releases of SQL Server, this wasn't necessary, because GROUP BY always returned the rows in the order of the grouping columns. SQL Server 7 has several alternative strategies for handling GROUP BY that don't require sorting of the results, so it's unpredictable which order the results will be returned in. If you want the results in a particular order, you must specify ORDER BY.

An Alternative to Using COUNT(*)

You can use COUNT(*) to find the count of all the rows in the table, but a considerably faster way exists. The *rows* column in the *sysindexes* table keeps the current rowcount dynamically for the clustered index. If one exists, *indid* = 1. If no clustered index exits, *sysindexes* keeps the count for the table (*indid* = 0). A quicker query than using COUNT(*) to find the count of all rows in the table looks something like this:

```
SELECT rows
    FROM sysindexes
    WHERE id=OBJECT_ID ("authors")
    AND indid < 2
```

This query works only for base tables, not views, and it works only if you apply no selection criteria via a WHERE clause. If you want to respond to a query such as "Show me the count of all rows for which the author lives in California," you'd still need to use COUNT(*). In addition, there's no guarantee that this number will be accurate 100 percent of the time. In previous versions of SQL Server, certain operations (such as SELECT INTO), didn't always correctly update the *rows* column in *sysindexes*. SQL Server 7 is much more likely to keep *sysindexes* up to date, but there's still no guarantee. If you absolutely must know exactly how many rows are in a table in your application, use the COUNT(*) aggregate.

Aggregate Functions and NULLs

As usual, you must understand the effect of using NULLs to use them appropriately with aggregate functions. Unfortunately, these effects aren't necessarily intuitive or even consistent. Because NULL is considered Unknown, one could certainly argue that using SUM(), MAX(), MIN(), or AVG() on a table containing one or more NULL values should also produce NULL. Obviously, if we have three employees and we don't know the salaries of two of them, it's totally inaccurate to state that the SUM() of the salaries for the three employees is equal to the one known salary. Yet this is exactly how SUM(), MIN(), MAX(), AVG(), and COUNT() work (but not COUNT(*)). Implicitly, these functions seem to tack on the criterion of "for only those values that are not NULL."

You will likely want these operations to work this way most of the time, and pragmatically, it's good that they work like this because they're simpler to use for common cases. But if you don't understand exactly how these functions will affect your code, you might introduce some bugs. For example, if you were to divide SUM() by the result of COUNT(*) as a way to compute the mean value, the result probably wouldn't be what you intended—SUM() disregards the NULL values, but COUNT(*) counts the rows that include those NULL values.

We've suggested a few times that using default or dummy values can be a good alternative to using NULL. But we've also tried to make clear that while these alternatives solve some issues, they introduce other problems. You must account for aggregates, and you might want to get back to exactly the semantics that aggregates such as SUM() use with defaults, ignoring the default or dummy values. Aggregating on only one column is pretty straightforward, and your WHERE clause could simply exclude those values you want to disregard. But if you're aggregating on multiple columns, eliminating rows in the WHERE clause might be a poor solution.

For example, suppose that in our *employee* table, we have both an *emp_age* column and an *emp_salary* column. To avoid using NULL, we use 0.00 when we don't know the actual value. We want one query to do aggregations of each column. Yet we don't want to disregard a row's value for *emp_age* if we don't have an actual value for *emp_salary*, or vice versa.

Here's our *employee* table:

```
emp_id    emp_name    emp_age    emp_salary
------    --------    -------    ----------
1         Smith       34         26000.00
2         Doe         30         35000.00
3         Jones       45         0.00
4         Clark       0          65000.00
5         Kent        63         0.00
```

Now suppose we want to write a simple query to get the count of all employees, the average and lowest salaries, and the average and lowest ages. Here's our first simplistic query:

```
SELECT
'Num Employees'=COUNT(*),
'Avg Salary'=AVG(emp_salary),
'Low Salary'=MIN(emp_salary),
'Avg Age'=AVG(emp_age),
'Youngest'=MIN(emp_age)
FROM employee
```

Here's the result:

```
Num Employees    Avg Salary    Low Salary    Avg Age    Youngest
-------------    ----------    ----------    -------    --------
5                25200.00      0.00          34         0
```

Obviously, this query doesn't correctly answer our question, because the dummy values of 0 have distorted the results for the AVG() and MIN() columns. So we decide to exclude those rows by stating in the WHERE clause that the salary should not be the default value:

```
SELECT
'Num Employees'=COUNT(*),
'Avg Salary'=AVG(emp_salary),
'Low Salary'=MIN(emp_salary),
'Avg Age'=AVG(emp_age),
'Youngest'=MIN(emp_age)
FROM employee
WHERE emp_salary > 0 AND emp_age > 0
```

Here's what we get:

Num Employees	Avg Salary	Low Salary	Avg Age	Youngest
2	30500.00	26000.00	32	30

This query is marginally better because at least the average salary is no longer lower than any actually known salary. The values are based on only the first two employees, Smith and Doe—we have *five* employees, not just *two*, as this result claims. Two other employees, Jones and Kent, are significantly older than the two who were used to compute the average age. And had Clark's salary been considered, the average salary would be much higher. We are seemingly stuck and can't write a single query to answer the question; we might have to write separate queries to get the count, the salary information, as well as the age information.

Fortunately, the NULLIF() function comes to the rescue. This function is one of many handy Transact-SQL functions. NULLIF() takes two expressions, NULLIF(*expression1, expression2*), and returns NULL if the two expressions are equivalent, and *expression1* if they aren't equivalent. The NULLIF() function is roughly the mirror image of another function, ISNULL(), which produces a value if a NULL is encountered (discussed earlier in this chapter). The NULLIF() function is actually a special-purpose shorthand of the ANSI SQL-92 CASE expression (discussed in detail in Chapter 9). Using NULLIF() is equivalent to the following:

```
CASE
    WHEN expression1=expression2 THEN NULL
    ELSE expression1
END
```

Hence, NULLIF *(emp_salary, 0)* produces NULL for those rows in which the salary equals 0. By converting the 0 values to NULL, we can use the aggregate functions just as we'd use them with NULL so that SUM() and MIN() will disregard the NULL entries.

```
SELECT
'Num Employees'=COUNT(*),
'Avg Salary'=AVG(NULLIF(emp_salary, 0)),
'Low Salary'=MIN(NULLIF(emp_salary, 0)),
'Avg Age'=AVG(NULLIF(emp_age, 0)),
'Youngest''=MIN(NULLIF(emp_age, 0))
FROM employee
```

Here's the more accurate result:

Num Employees	Avg Salary	Low Salary	Avg Age	Youngest
5	42000.00	26000.00	43	30

Finally! This result is exactly what we wanted, and all five employees are represented. Of the three whose salaries we know, the average salary is $42,000.00 and the low salary is $26,000.00. Of the four whose ages we know, the average age is 43 and the youngest is 30.

Datacube—Aggregate Variations

The previous aggregate examples in this chapter, all using standard SQL-92 syntax, show that by formulating a specific query on the sample table with one of the aggregate functions, we can answer almost any question regarding aggregate sales for some combination of model, year, and color of car. However, answering any of these questions requires a separate, specific query. Of course, it's common to look at data and keep formulating and posing new and different questions. Such questions are the hallmark of data mining, decision-support systems (DSS), online analytic processing (OLAP), or whatever name is being used these days for this age-old need to examine data.

To address this inherent weakness in standard SQL, developers have created several front-end tools that maintain a set of data that allows changes in aggregation to be easily queried, avoiding the need to sweep through data for every new aggregation request. One such tool is Microsoft OLAP Services, which you can install from the same CD that contains your SQL Server 7 software. OLAP tools can add a lot of value, and they make it easy to slice and dice the values pertaining to any "cut" of the data groupings. But even these tools can perform better with help from the database engine.

> ## Some History
>
> The motivation for inventing CUBE came from a paper written by Jim Gray, and others, soon after Jim joined Microsoft as a researcher. After reading his paper, a few of the developers got excited about adding the feature to the 6.5 release, and Don Reichart did a masterful job of implementing this important feature in record time. Subsequently, this feature was submitted to the ANSI SQL committee as a proposed addition to the standard. For more details about CUBE, you can read the paper that Jim Gray submitted to the ACM on the companion CD.

SQL Server has two extensions to GROUP BY—CUBE and ROLLUP—that allow SQL Server to optionally generate all the aggregate groupings in a single query.

CUBE

CUBE explodes data to produce a result set containing a superset of groups, with a cross-tabulation of every column to the value of every other column, as well as a special super-aggregate value that can be thought of as meaning ALL VALUES. Here's the CUBE for the 18 rows of the *automobile_sales_detail* table. Notice that these 18 rows generate 48 rows in the datacube.

units	model	year	color
62	Chevy	1990	Blue
5	Chevy	1990	Red
87	Chevy	1990	White
154	Chevy	1990	ALL
49	Chevy	1991	Blue
54	Chevy	1991	Red
95	Chevy	1991	White
198	Chevy	1991	ALL
71	Chevy	1992	Blue
31	Chevy	1992	Red
54	Chevy	1992	White
156	Chevy	1992	ALL
508	Chevy	ALL	ALL
63	Ford	1990	Blue
64	Ford	1990	Red
62	Ford	1990	White
189	Ford	1990	ALL

(continued)

55	Ford	1991	Blue
52	Ford	1991	Red
9	Ford	1991	White
116	Ford	1991	ALL
39	Ford	1992	Blue
27	Ford	1992	Red
62	Ford	1992	White
128	Ford	1992	ALL
433	Ford	ALL	ALL
941	ALL	ALL	ALL
125	ALL	1990	Blue
69	ALL	1990	Red
149	ALL	1990	White
343	ALL	1990	ALL
104	ALL	1991	Blue
106	ALL	1991	Red
104	ALL	1991	White
314	ALL	1991	ALL
110	ALL	1992	Blue
58	ALL	1992	Red
116	ALL	1992	White
284	ALL	1992	ALL
182	Chevy	ALL	Blue
157	Ford	ALL	Blue
339	ALL	ALL	Blue
90	Chevy	ALL	Red
143	Ford	ALL	Red
233	ALL	ALL	Red
236	Chevy	ALL	White
133	Ford	ALL	White
369	ALL	ALL	White

The results of the CUBE make it simple to answer just about any sales aggregation question that we can think of. If we want to get sales information for all 1992 automobiles, regardless of model or color, we can find the corresponding row and see that 284 cars were sold. To find all Chevy sales for all years and colors, it's equally easy to find 508. Such a result set might be used as is for a reference chart or in coordination with an OLAP tool.

The number of rows exploded by a CUBE operation can be surprisingly large. In the example above, 18 rows generated 48 rows of output. However, the result of a CUBE operation won't necessarily produce more rows of output than what appears in the underlying data. The number of rows generated will depend on the number of attributes being grouped and on the actual combinations in your data. Without detailed knowledge of your data, the number of rows produced by a CUBE operation can't be predicted. However, the upper bound can be easily predicted. The upper bound will be equal to the cross-product of the *(number of distinct values + 1)* value for each attribute. The addition of 1 is for the case of "ALL." The *automobile_sales_detail* example has three attributes: model, year, and color.

> Upper bound of number of rows
> = (Number of models + 1) * (Number of years + 1) *
>   (Number of colors + 1)
> = (2 + 1) * (3 + 1) * (3 + 1)
> = 48

This example should make it clear that the upper bound of the number of rows depends not on the number of data rows, but rather on the number of attributes being grouped and the number of distinct values for each attribute. For example, if the table had 18 million instead of 18 data rows but still had no more than two models, three years, and three colors (there's no stated UNIQUE or PRIMARY KEY constraint on the model, year, or color fields), the CUBE operation will again return only 48 rows.

The actual number of rows might be considerably less than the upper bound, however, because CUBE doesn't try to force a 0 or a NULL aggregate for combinations for which no values exist. In the carefully constructed example you just saw, there's complete coverage across every attribute. Each of the two models has an entry for each of the three years and for each of the three colors. But suppose that no sales data appears for the 1990 Chevy and that no red Fords exist for any year. The raw data would look like this:

Rowid	Model	Year	Color	Units_Sold
1	Chevy	1991	Red	54
2	Chevy	1991	White	95
3	Chevy	1991	Blue	49
4	Chevy	1992	Red	31
5	Chevy	1992	White	54
6	Chevy	1992	Blue	71
7	Ford	1990	White	62
8	Ford	1990	Blue	63
9	Ford	1991	White	9
10	Ford	1991	Blue	55
11	Ford	1992	White	62
12	Ford	1992	Blue	39

367

Here's the new cube:

Units	Model	Year	Color
49	Chevy	1991	Blue
54	Chevy	1991	Red
95	Chevy	1991	White
198	Chevy	1991	ALL
71	Chevy	1992	Blue
31	Chevy	1992	Red
54	Chevy	1992	White
156	Chevy	1992	ALL
354	Chevy	ALL	ALL
63	Ford	1990	Blue
62	Ford	1990	White
125	Ford	1990	ALL
55	Ford	1991	Blue
9	Ford	1991	White
64	Ford	1991	ALL
39	Ford	1992	Blue
62	Ford	1992	White
101	Ford	1992	ALL
290	Ford	ALL	ALL
644	ALL	ALL	ALL
63	ALL	1990	Blue
62	ALL	1990	White
125	ALL	1990	ALL
104	ALL	1991	Blue
54	ALL	1991	Red
104	ALL	1991	White
262	ALL	1991	ALL
110	ALL	1992	Blue
31	ALL	1992	Red
116	ALL	1992	White
257	ALL	1992	ALL
120	Chevy	ALL	Blue
157	Ford	ALL	Blue
277	ALL	ALL	Blue
85	Chevy	ALL	Red
85	ALL	ALL	Red
149	Chevy	ALL	White
133	Ford	ALL	White
282	ALL	ALL	White

We now have 12 data rows but still three attributes and the same number of distinct values for each attribute. But instead of 48 rows for the result of the CUBE, the result contains only 39 rows because some combinations of attributes have no data. For example, no row exists for all models of red cars for 1990 because no data met that specific criterion.

If you would benefit from always having the full cube populated when you use CUBE, you might want to add a placeholder row with dummy values for the columns being aggregated so that every combination is represented. Or you could run a query that produces the cross-product of all combinations not existing, and then UNION the result with the cube. (We'll see an example of this later when discussing UNION.) Be careful: as the number of attributes and the cardinality between the values increases, the cube can quickly get large. The full cube based on five attributes, each having 50 distinct values, with at least one matching entry for each combination, generates $(50 + 1)^5$, or 345,025,251, rows in the cube. If coverage of all these combinations is nowhere near full, the cube might otherwise have generated "only" a few thousand rows instead of more than 345 million!

So far, we haven't seen the actual query used to produce the cube because you need to understand the basic concepts before yet again dealing with issues of NULL. A simple GROUP BY *column* WITH CUBE will not, by default, produce super-aggregate rows having a value that outputs as "ALL." The ALL value is really a nonvalue, like NULL (gasp!). In fact, the ALL column is represented by (gulp!) a special kind of NULL, referred to as a *grouping NULL*.

While implementing this new feature, the developers debated whether to use NULL or invent a new marker value similar in some ways to NULL but clearly still separate from data. The decision wasn't easy. A new data value would be more theoretically pure. The meaning of "ALL" is really different from "unknown" or "missing"—that is, it's different from NULL. However, had they introduced another special-meaning marker, it would require the same level of complexity necessary to work with as NULL—with special operators like IS ALL—and the truth tables would become all the more difficult to work with in expressions such as =, <, IN, and so on. And they did have some precedents that they wanted to avoid.

In many ways, the longtime SQL Server feature COMPUTE BY is quite similar to CUBE. (Actually, it's more similar to the derivative of CUBE—ROLLUP—which we'll see shortly.) COMPUTE BY, although helpful, is a rarely used feature, largely because COMPUTE BY doesn't generate a standard row format for the result set but rather returns a special *alternate result set*.

Applications must go to significant lengths to handle this special-purpose result, which is nonrelational in that the output itself isn't a table. Most applications didn't or couldn't go the distance; hence, most applications don't support COMPUTE BY. Because of this, the SQL Server development team chose to overload NULL, which applications must already deal with to some extent. (This presents a few wrinkles of its own, which we'll come back to.)

Following is the basic query and a discussion of how "ALL" is produced in the results:

```
SELECT SUM(units_sold), model, year, color
FROM automobile_sales_detail
GROUP BY model, year, color WITH CUBE
```

Here's the output:

	model	year	color
62	Chevy	1990	Blue
5	Chevy	1990	Red
87	Chevy	1990	White
154	Chevy	1990	NULL
49	Chevy	1991	Blue
54	Chevy	1991	Red
95	Chevy	1991	White
198	Chevy	1991	NULL
71	Chevy	1992	Blue
31	Chevy	1992	Red
54	Chevy	1992	White
156	Chevy	1992	NULL
508	Chevy	NULL	NULL
63	Ford	1990	Blue
64	Ford	1990	Red
62	Ford	1990	White
189	Ford	1990	NULL
55	Ford	1991	Blue
52	Ford	1991	Red
9	Ford	1991	White
116	Ford	1991	NULL
39	Ford	1992	Blue
27	Ford	1992	Red
62	Ford	1992	White
128	Ford	1992	NULL
433	Ford	NULL	NULL
941	NULL	NULL	NULL

125	NULL	1990	Blue
69	NULL	1990	Red
149	NULL	1990	White
343	NULL	1990	NULL
104	NULL	1991	Blue
106	NULL	1991	Red
104	NULL	1991	White
314	NULL	1991	NULL
110	NULL	1992	Blue
58	NULL	1992	Red
116	NULL	1992	White
284	NULL	1992	NULL
182	Chevy	NULL	Blue
157	Ford	NULL	Blue
339	NULL	NULL	Blue
90	Chevy	NULL	Red
143	Ford	NULL	Red
233	NULL	NULL	Red
236	Chevy	NULL	White
133	Ford	NULL	White
369	NULL	NULL	White

Notice that rather than ALL, which we had constructed earlier to be a placeholder, the super-aggregate values are represented by NULL—here formatted as *NULL* as in the SQL Server Query Analyzer, although this is application specific. The data in this case had no NULL values, so we could easily tell the difference between NULL meaning "unknown" and NULL meaning "ALL."

If your data uses some NULL values, however, you won't be so lucky. Suppose that we add one row of data that has NULL for both model and year (assuming these columns allow NULL):

```
INSERT automobile_sales_detail values (NULL, NULL, 'White', 10)
```

The last row in the CUBE above (having 369 as total sales for all white cars) would be seemingly indistinguishable from this actual data row. Fortunately, the GROUPING() function comes to the rescue to differentiate the two. It returns 1 (TRUE) if the element is an ALL value and 0 (FALSE) otherwise. Here is a modified query to show the CUBE with the inclusion of the row having NULL values and with the addition of the GROUPING() function to designate ALL values:

```
SELECT 'Units Sold'=SUM(units_sold),
model, 'ALL Models'=GROUPING(model),
year, 'ALL Years'=GROUPING(year),
```

(continued)

371

```
color, 'ALL Colors'=GROUPING(color)
FROM automobile_sales_detail
GROUP BY model, year, color WITH CUBE
```

Here's the result set:

Units Sold	model	ALL Models	year	ALL Years	color	ALL Colors
10	NULL	0	NULL	0	White	0
10	NULL	0	NULL	0	NULL	1
10	NULL	0	NULL	1	NULL	1
62	Chevy	0	1990	0	Blue	0
5	Chevy	0	1990	0	Red	0
87	Chevy	0	1990	0	White	0
154	Chevy	0	1990	0	NULL	1
49	Chevy	0	1991	0	Blue	0
54	Chevy	0	1991	0	Red	0
95	Chevy	0	1991	0	White	0
198	Chevy	0	1991	0	NULL	1
71	Chevy	0	1992	0	Blue	0
31	Chevy	0	1992	0	Red	0
54	Chevy	0	1992	0	White	0
156	Chevy	0	1992	0	NULL	1
508	Chevy	0	NULL	1	NULL	1
63	Ford	0	1990	0	Blue	0
64	Ford	0	1990	0	Red	0
62	Ford	0	1990	0	White	0
189	Ford	0	1990	0	NULL	1
55	Ford	0	1991	0	Blue	0
52	Ford	0	1991	0	Red	0
9	Ford	0	1991	0	White	0
116	Ford	0	1991	0	NULL	1
39	Ford	0	1992	0	Blue	0
27	Ford	0	1992	0	Red	0
62	Ford	0	1992	0	White	0
128	Ford	0	1992	0	NULL	1
433	Ford	0	NULL	1	NULL	1
951	NULL	1	NULL	1	NULL	1
10	NULL	1	NULL	0	White	0
10	NULL	1	NULL	0	NULL	1
125	NULL	1	1990	0	Blue	0
69	NULL	1	1990	0	Red	0
149	NULL	1	1990	0	White	0
343	NULL	1	1990	0	NULL	1
104	NULL	1	1991	0	Blue	0

106	NULL	1	1991	0	Red	0
104	NULL	1	1991	0	White	0
314	NULL	1	1991	0	NULL	1
110	NULL	1	1992	0	Blue	0
58	NULL	1	1992	0	Red	0
116	NULL	1	1992	0	White	0
284	NULL	1	1992	0	NULL	1
182	Chevy	0	NULL	1	Blue	0
157	Ford	0	NULL	1	Blue	0
339	NULL	1	NULL	1	Blue	0
90	Chevy	0	NULL	1	Red	0
143	Ford	0	NULL	1	Red	0
233	NULL	1	NULL	1	Red	0
10	NULL	0	NULL	1	White	0
236	Chevy	0	NULL	1	White	0
133	Ford	0	NULL	1	White	0
379	NULL	1	NULL	1	White	0

Note that the GROUPING() function takes a column name as an argument. A 0 returned for GROUPING(*column_name*) means the value returned for that column is a *real* value. A 1 returned for GROUPING(*column_name*) means that the value returned for that column is not real—it was returned only because of the use of the CUBE or ROLLUP option.

The GROUPING() function enables you to differentiate between a GROUPING NULL value and a NULL value, but hardly makes reading and analyzing it as intuitive as using ALL. An alternative would be to write a view that outputs a grouping value as ALL. You might be more comfortable turning your programmers and power users loose on such a view rather than relying on them to understand GROUPING NULL vs. NULL value. This example uses the CASE expression, which is discussed in detail in Chapter 9:

```
CREATE VIEW auto_cube (units, model, year, color) AS
SELECT SUM(units_sold),
CASE    WHEN (GROUPING(model)=1) THEN 'ALL'
    ELSE ISNULL(model, '????')
    END,
CASE    WHEN (GROUPING(year)=1) THEN 'ALL'
    ELSE ISNULL(CONVERT(char(6), year), '????')
    END,
CASE    WHEN (GROUPING(color)=1) THEN 'ALL'
    ELSE ISNULL(color, '????')
    END
FROM automobile_sales_detail
GROUP BY model, year, color WITH CUBE
```

Having constructed this view, it's simple for someone to work with, to understand the difference between grouping values (represented by 'ALL') and NULL data values (represented by ' ????'), and to easily further refine the query if necessary to look for certain data. This example shows a simple query:

```
SELECT * FROM auto_cube
```

And the results:

units	model	year	color
10	????	????	White
10	????	????	ALL
10	????	ALL	ALL
62	Chevy	1990	Blue
5	Chevy	1990	Red
87	Chevy	1990	White
154	Chevy	1990	ALL
49	Chevy	1991	Blue
54	Chevy	1991	Red
95	Chevy	1991	White
198	Chevy	1991	ALL
71	Chevy	1992	Blue
31	Chevy	1992	Red
54	Chevy	1992	White
156	Chevy	1992	ALL
508	Chevy	ALL	ALL
63	Ford	1990	Blue
64	Ford	1990	Red
62	Ford	1990	White
189	Ford	1990	ALL
55	Ford	1991	Blue
52	Ford	1991	Red
9	Ford	1991	White
116	Ford	1991	ALL
39	Ford	1992	Blue
27	Ford	1992	Red
62	Ford	1992	White
128	Ford	1992	ALL
433	Ford	ALL	ALL
951	ALL	ALL	ALL
10	ALL	????	White
10	ALL	????	ALL
125	ALL	1990	Blue
69	ALL	1990	Red

149	ALL	1990	White
343	ALL	1990	ALL
104	ALL	1991	Blue
106	ALL	1991	Red
104	ALL	1991	White
314	ALL	1991	ALL
110	ALL	1992	Blue
58	ALL	1992	Red
116	ALL	1992	White
284	ALL	1992	ALL
182	Chevy	ALL	Blue
157	Ford	ALL	Blue
339	ALL	ALL	Blue
90	Chevy	ALL	Red
143	Ford	ALL	Red
233	ALL	ALL	Red
10	????	ALL	White
236	Chevy	ALL	White
133	Ford	ALL	White
379	ALL	ALL	White

Working with this view is easy. Grouping values appear as "ALL." Actual NULL values are represented by question marks, appropriate because they're unknown. We can easily further select from the view to drill into any dimension of the cube that we like. For example, to find all Chevy sales, regardless of the year and color:

```
SELECT * FROM auto_cube
WHERE model='Chevy' AND year='ALL' AND color='ALL'
```

Here are the results:

units	model	year	color
-----	-----	----	-----
508	Chevy	ALL	ALL

In this view, we elected to output everything as character data; thus, "ALL" was a reasonable choice. If keeping the data numeric had been important, we would've chosen some special value, such as –999999.

ROLLUP

If you're looking for a hierarchy or a *drill-down report* (what you might know as a *control-break report* if you've ever programmed in COBOL), CUBE can be overkill. It generates many more result rows than you want, and it obscures the requested information with more data. (Don't be confused by thinking that data and information are equivalent.) Using CUBE, you'll get all permutations, including super-aggregates, for all attributes for which corresponding data exists. SQL Server provides the ROLLUP operator to extract statistics and summary information from result sets. ROLLUP returns only the values for a hierarchy of the attributes that you specify.

This behavior is best explained with an example. If we change the CUBE query to use ROLLUP instead, the results are more compact and easier to interpret when we drill into progressive levels of details for sales by model. However, with ROLLUP, we don't get one-stop shopping to answer a question like "How many white cars of any model were sold?"

```
SELECT 'units sold'=SUM(units_sold),
'model'=CASE WHEN (GROUPING(model)=1) THEN 'ALL'
    ELSE ISNULL(model, '????')
    END,
'year'=CASE WHEN (GROUPING(year)=1) THEN 'ALL'
    ELSE ISNULL(CONVERT(char(6), year), '????')
    END,
'color'=CASE WHEN (GROUPING(color)=1) THEN 'ALL'
    ELSE ISNULL(color, '????')
    END
FROM automobile_sales_detail
GROUP BY model, year, color WITH ROLLUP
```

The results:

units sold	model	year	color
10	????	????	White
10	????	????	ALL
10	????	ALL	ALL
62	Chevy	1990	Blue
5	Chevy	1990	Red
87	Chevy	1990	White
154	Chevy	1990	ALL
49	Chevy	1991	Blue
54	Chevy	1991	Red
95	Chevy	1991	White
198	Chevy	1991	ALL
71	Chevy	1992	Blue
31	Chevy	1992	Red
54	Chevy	1992	White
156	Chevy	1992	ALL
508	Chevy	ALL	ALL

63	Ford	1990	Blue
64	Ford	1990	Red
62	Ford	1990	White
189	Ford	1990	ALL
55	Ford	1991	Blue
52	Ford	1991	Red
9	Ford	1991	White
116	Ford	1991	ALL
39	Ford	1992	Blue
27	Ford	1992	Red
62	Ford	1992	White
128	Ford	1992	ALL
433	Ford	ALL	ALL
951	ALL	ALL	ALL

ROLLUP is similar to COMPUTE BY, which has nice functionality. However, COMPUTE BY is not as relational as ROLLUP—it doesn't simply produce results as an ordinary table of values. COMPUTE BY always requires special application programming to deal with its alternate result sets, which are essentially equivalent to super-aggregates. Recall that CUBE and ROLLUP simply use ordinary result sets and that the super-aggregates are represented as a GROUPING NULL. Generally speaking, CUBE and ROLLUP are more preferable than COMPUTE BY because they're easier to fit into applications; you can use them with views, CASE, subselects, and column aliases; and they're internally better optimized. But for completeness, here's an example using COMPUTE BY as functionally equivalent to ROLLUP:

```
SELECT units_sold, model, year, color
FROM automobile_sales_detail
ORDER BY model, year, color
COMPUTE SUM(units_sold) BY model, year
COMPUTE SUM(units_sold) BY model
COMPUTE SUM(units_sold)
```

And the results:

```
units_sold   model   year   color
----------   -----   ----   -----
10           NULL    NULL   White

Sum
===========
10
Sum
===========
10
```

(continued)

units_sold	model	year	color
62	Chevy	1990	Blue
5	Chevy	1990	Red
87	Chevy	1990	White

Sum
===========
154

units_sold	model	year	color
49	Chevy	1991	Blue
54	Chevy	1991	Red
95	Chevy	1991	White

Sum
===========
198

units_sold	model	year	color
71	Chevy	1992	Blue
31	Chevy	1992	Red
54	Chevy	1992	White

Sum
===========
156
Sum
===========
508

units_sold	model	year	color
63	Ford	1990	Blue
64	Ford	1990	Red
62	Ford	1990	White

Sum
===========
189

```
units_sold    model    year    color
----------    -----    ----    -----
55            Ford     1991    Blue
52            Ford     1991    Red
9             Ford     1991    White

Sum
===========
116


units_sold    model    year    color
----------    -----    ----    -----
39            Ford     1992    Blue
27            Ford     1992    Red
62            Ford     1992    White

Sum
===========
128
Sum
===========
433
Sum
===========
951
```

Statistical Aggregates

SQL Server 7 introduces four new aggregate functions, in addition to the standard six described earlier. These functions are used for statistical applications and are considered aggregate functions because they operate on a set of values instead of on one single value. Table 7-8 on the following page describes the four statistical aggregate functions.

You could find the standard deviation and variance of the prices in the *titles* table with this query:

```
SELECT stdev(price), var(price)
FROM titles
```

Alternatively, you could calculate the standard deviation and variance of the prices for each different type of book:

```
SELECT type, stdev(price), var(price)
FROM titles
GROUP BY type
```

Aggregate Function	Description
STDEV(*expression*)	Returns the statistical standard deviation of all values in the given expression.
STDEVP(*expression*)	Returns the statistical standard deviation for the population for all values in the given expression.
VAR(*expression*)	Returns the statistical variance of all values in the given expression.
VARP(*expression*)	Returns the statistical variance for the population for all values in the given expression.

Table 7-8.
Statistical aggregate functions.

TOP

We've already seen that the WHERE clause allows us to limit the number of rows that a SELECT statement will return, but using a WHERE clause assumes we have knowledge of the actual data values present. What if we wanted to see only a screenful of rows from a table but had no idea which range of values were present in the table? Prior to SQL Server version 7, we could use the option SET ROWCOUNT *n* to limit SQL Server to sending only *n* rows to the client. Every SELECT statement would just stop sending rows back to the client after *n* rows had been sent.

For example, the following will return only 10 rows from the *authors* table:

```
SET ROWCOUNT 10
GO
SELECT * FROM authors
GO
```

This is useful in some situations, but it's quite limited in functionality. The TOP keyword used in the SELECT list allows much greater control over the quantity of data we'd like to see. Here's the syntax for using TOP:

```
SELECT [ TOP n [PERCENT] [ WITH TIES] ] select_list
FROM table_list
WHERE conditions
...rest of query
```

When the query includes an ORDER BY clause, TOP causes the first *n* rows ordered by the ORDER BY clause to be output. When the query has no ORDER

BY clause, we can't predict which rows will be returned. Compare the output of the following two queries:

QUERY 1

```
SELECT TOP 5 title_id, price, type
FROM titles

title_id price                 type
-------- --------------------- ------------
BU1032   19.9900               business
BU1111   11.9500               business
BU2075   2.9900                business
BU7832   19.9900               business
MC2222   19.9900               mod_cook
```

QUERY 2

```
SELECT TOP 5 title_id, price, type
FROM titles
ORDER BY price DESC

title_id price                 type
-------- --------------------- ------------
PC1035   22.9500               popular_comp
PS1372   21.5900               psychology
TC3218   20.9500               trad_cook
PC8888   20.0000               popular_comp
BU1032   19.9900               business
```

Notice that simply including TOP 5 in the SELECT list is equivalent to setting ROWCOUNT to 5. SQL Server just stops returning rows after the first five. In the example above, however, you should note that other books exist with a price of $19.99, but because we wanted only five, we didn't see them. Does this output really answer the question, "What are the five highest priced books?" If you answered no and really want to see all the books with the same price as the ones listed, you can use the WITH TIES option. This option is only allowable if your SELECT statement includes an ORDER BY:

```
SELECT TOP 5 WITH TIES title_id, price, type
FROM titles
ORDER BY price DESC
```

This returns the following eight rows:

```
title_id price                            type
-------- ----------------------           ------------
PC1035   22.9500                          popular_comp
PS1372   21.5900                          psychology
TC3218   20.9500                          trad_cook
PC8888   20.0000                          popular_comp
BU1032   19.9900                          business
BU7832   19.9900                          business
MC2222   19.9900                          mod_cook
PS3333   19.9900                          psychology
```

If we want to see a certain fraction of the rows, we can use TOP with PERCENT, which will round up to the nearest integer number of rows:

```
SELECT TOP 30 Percent title_id, price, type
FROM titles
ORDER BY price DESC
```

You can think of SQL Server carrying out this operation by first counting out the number of rows specified by TOP—in this case, five. Only after the first five are returned will SQL Server check to see if any other rows have a value equivalent to the last one returned.

This won't necessarily give you books with the five highest prices. If we changed TOP 5 to TOP 8, you'd get the same eight rows back as above, which represent only five different prices.

If we really wanted to see the eight highest prices, we could use DISTINCT with TOP. We couldn't select *title_id* at the same time, because DISTINCT applies to the whole result row, and every *title_id* and *price* combination is distinct in itself. However, we could use a subquery to determine which rows have one of the eight highest prices:

```
SELECT title_id, price, type
FROM titles
WHERE price in (SELECT DISTINCT TOP 8 price
    FROM titles
    ORDER BY price DESC)
```

In this case, the rows wouldn't come back in descending order of price, because the order is controlled by the outer query. You'd have to add another ORDER BY at the end.

The *titles* table contains 18 rows, and 30 percent of 18 is 5.6. This is rounded up to return these six rows:

```
title_id price                   type
-------- --------------------    ------------
PC1035   22.9500                 popular_comp
PS1372   21.5900                 psychology
TC3218   20.9500                 trad_cook
PC8888   20.0000                 popular_comp
BU1032   19.9900                 business
BU7832   19.9900                 business
```

We can also use the WITH TIES option with PERCENT. If used in the above query, we'd then get the additional two rows that also have a price of $19.99.

UNION

UNION is a conceptually easy topic. Given the same number of columns and compatible datatypes, UNION combines two or more result sets into a single result set. By default, duplicate rows are eliminated, although you can include them by specifying UNION ALL. The datatypes of the result sets to be combined with UNION don't need to be identical, but they must be able to be *implicitly* converted. If this isn't the case, you can *explicitly* convert them to identical or compatible types using the handy CONVERT() function.

The following example shows UNION at its most basic level. It also demonstrates that a SELECT statement in SQL Server doesn't need to be from a table or a view but can be a constant or a variable:

```
SELECT col1=2, col2=1
UNION
SELECT xxx=1, yyy=2
UNION
SELECT '3','0'
UNION
SELECT TAN(0), 3*1000/10/100   -- Tangent of 0 is 0.
                               -- So this row produces 0.0, 3
UNION
SELECT 1, 2
```

The output follows:

```
col1    col2
----    ----
0.0     3
3.0     0
1.0     2
2.0     1
```

Earlier versions of SQL Server always returned the result of a UNION in sorted order, unless you specified UNION ALL. This occurred because UNION eliminated duplicate rows using a sorting strategy. The ordering was simply a by-product of the sorting to eliminate duplicates. However, SQL Server 7 has several alternative strategies available for removing duplicates, so there's no guarantee of any particular order when using UNION. If order is important to you, you should explicitly use ORDER BY at the end of the last SELECT statement.

In the example above, the datatypes are compatible but not identical. Because TAN(0) returns a numeric datatype, *col1* is automatically cast to numeric (since using an integer would lose precision), and the other values are implicitly converted. In addition, the one duplicate row (1.0, 2) is eliminated, and the columns take their monikers from the first result set.

If you used UNION ALL instead of UNION, the duplicate row wouldn't be eliminated and no extra work would be needed to determine which rows were distinct. If there's no need to eliminate duplicates, or if you know that there won't be any duplicates, you can achieve a noticeable performance improvement by using UNION ALL. The following query illustrates the use of UNION ALL and uses ORDER BY to present the results in a particular order. It also converts the result of the tangent operation to a *tinyint* so that *col1* is then implicitly converted to an *int*.

```
SELECT col1=2, col2=1
UNION ALL
SELECT xxx=1, yyy=2
UNION ALL
SELECT '3', '0'
UNION ALL
SELECT CONVERT(smallint, TAN(0)), 3*1000/10/100
-- Tangent of 0 is 0. So this row produces 0.0, 3
UNION ALL
SELECT 1, 2
ORDER BY col2
```

Here's the output:

```
col1    col2
----    ----
3       0
2       1
1       2
1       2
0       3
```

Earlier, we saw that the CUBE operation wouldn't generate missing rows with the value 0. However, you might occasionally want the full cube, with 0 as the SUM() value for missing combinations. We promised you an example of how this could be accomplished using UNION, so here's the example. And here's the key—the table can be cross-joined to itself to produce a 0 row for every combination possible given the non-NULL data. This query will use the existing data to produce a list of every possible combination of model, color, and year:

```
SELECT DISTINCT units_sold=0, A.model, B.color, C.year
FROM
automobile_sales_detail A
CROSS JOIN
automobile_sales_detail B
CROSS JOIN
automobile_sales_detail C
```

Here's the output:

```
units_sold    model    color    year
----------    -----    -----    ----
0             Chevy    Blue     1990
0             Chevy    Blue     1991
0             Chevy    Blue     1992
0             Chevy    Red      1990
0             Chevy    Red      1991
0             Chevy    Red      1992
0             Chevy    White    1990
0             Chevy    White    1991
0             Chevy    White    1992
0             Ford     Blue     1990
0             Ford     Blue     1991
0             Ford     Blue     1992
0             Ford     Red      1990
0             Ford     Red      1991
0             Ford     Red      1992
0             Ford     White    1990
0             Ford     White    1991
0             Ford     White    1992
```

The real underlying data is the set of 12 rows shown earlier and shown again here. Recall that six combinations have no value—that is, there are no Chevys for 1990 and no red Fords:

model	year	color	units_sold
Chevy	1991	Red	54
Chevy	1991	White	95
Chevy	1991	Blue	49
Chevy	1992	Red	31
Chevy	1992	White	54
Chevy	1992	Blue	71
Ford	1990	White	62
Ford	1990	Blue	63
Ford	1991	White	9
Ford	1991	Blue	55
Ford	1992	White	62
Ford	1992	Blue	39

Having generated all the dummy rows as such, we can then easily UNION the cross-joined dummy results with the output of the CUBE. But that still wouldn't do because we'd get both a real row and a dummy row whenever a real combination exists. SQL Server gives you several good ways to solve this dilemma. You can use NOT EXISTS to produce the dummy rows only for combinations that don't exist. Another approach, and perhaps the most intuitive one, is to make a view of the cross-joined dummy rows and the actual data, and then perform the CUBE on the view. The 0 values, of course, don't affect the SUM, so this works nicely:

```
CREATE VIEW fullcube
    (
    units_sold,
    model,
    year,
    color
    )
    AS
    (
    SELECT D.units_sold, D.model, D.year, D.color
    FROM automobile_sales_detail D
    UNION ALL
    SELECT DISTINCT 0,
    A.model, C.year, B.color
    FROM
```

```
automobile_sales_detail A
CROSS JOIN
automobile_sales_detail B
CROSS JOIN
automobile_sales_detail C
)
```

Having constructed the view, we can then issue our CUBE query against it, just as we did previously against the base table:

```
SELECT units_sold=SUM(units_sold), model, year, color
FROM fullcube
GROUP BY model, year, color WITH CUBE
```

Here's the output:

units_sold	model	year	color
0	Chevy	1990	Blue
0	Chevy	1990	Red
0	Chevy	1990	White
0	Chevy	1990	NULL
49	Chevy	1991	Blue
54	Chevy	1991	Red
95	Chevy	1991	White
198	Chevy	1991	NULL
71	Chevy	1992	Blue
31	Chevy	1992	Red
54	Chevy	1992	White
156	Chevy	1992	NULL
354	Chevy	NULL	NULL
63	Ford	1990	Blue
0	Ford	1990	Red
62	Ford	1990	White
125	Ford	1990	NULL
55	Ford	1991	Blue
0	Ford	1991	Red
9	Ford	1991	White
64	Ford	1991	NULL
39	Ford	1992	Blue
0	Ford	1992	Red
62	Ford	1992	White
101	Ford	1992	NULL
290	Ford	NULL	NULL
644	NULL	NULL	NULL
63	NULL	1990	Blue

(continued)

```
0        NULL    1990    Red
62       NULL    1990    White
125      NULL    1990    NULL
104      NULL    1991    Blue
54       NULL    1991    Red
104      NULL    1991    White
262      NULL    1991    NULL
110      NULL    1992    Blue
31       NULL    1992    Red
116      NULL    1992    White
257      NULL    1992    NULL
120      Chevy   NULL    Blue
157      Ford    NULL    Blue
277      NULL    NULL    Blue
85       Chevy   NULL    Red
0        Ford    NULL    Red
85       NULL    NULL    Red
149      Chevy   NULL    White
133      Ford    NULL    White
282      NULL    NULL    White
```

Then we can define yet another view on top to generate the "ALL" and "????" placeholders. No NULL data exists in this example, so we'll look at only the "ALL" case:

```
CREATE VIEW auto_cube (units, model, year, color) AS
SELECT SUM(units_sold),
ISNULL(model, 'ALL'), ISNULL(CONVERT(char(4), year), 'ALL'),
ISNULL(color, 'ALL')
FROM fullcube
GROUP BY model, year, color WITH CUBE
```

One advantage of filling out the cube with placeholder rows is that no matter what combination we formulate, we'll get an answer. There are no unknowns and no need to include the GROUPING() function. Had we not constructed the cube, this query would return no rows found instead of a row with 0 units:

```
SELECT * FROM auto_cube WHERE model='Chevy' AND color='ALL'
AND year='1990'
```

units	model	year	color
0	Chevy	1990	ALL

Just for fun, here's the equivalent of the *fullcube* view as a derived table:

```
SELECT units_sold=SUM(T1.units_sold), T1.model, T1.year, T1.color
FROM (
    SELECT D.units_sold, D.model, D.year, D.color
    FROM automobile_sales_detail D
    UNION ALL
    SELECT DISTINCT 0,
    A.model, C.year, B.color
    FROM
    automobile_sales_detail A
    CROSS JOIN
    automobile_sales_detail B
    CROSS JOIN
    automobile_sales_detail C
    )
        AS T1
GROUP BY T1.model, T1.year, T1.color WITH CUBE
GO
```

Now that you've seen these somewhat exotic uses of CROSS JOIN and views to fill out the cube, be aware that if you had wanted the whole cube to be generated, you might have inserted some placeholder rows with a value of 0 in the base table itself (assuming you had access to do so). That way, every combination is accounted for in the base table itself.

Summary

This chapter examined the SELECT statement, the hallmark of the SQL language. Although we presented a fairly well-rounded treatment of SELECT, instead of focusing on basic queries, we looked at more subtle issues and SQL Server–specific capabilities.

We saw the issues of NULL and three-valued logic and learned why you must always consider these issues while you're properly formulating queries. In three-valued logic, an answer is TRUE, FALSE, or Unknown. If you must work with NULL values but you don't understand three-valued logic, you'll introduce bugs. You must fully understand three-valued logic or structure the database to avoid the use of NULL.

You must also understand NULL when doing JOIN operations, and we discussed issues concerning OUTER JOIN with several examples. Unlike a JOIN based on equality, the JOIN order for an OUTER JOIN is vitally important. We looked at search expressions such as LIKE and the issues of trailing blanks.

We examined aggregate functions, again with a discussion of how you must understand NULL for proper use of these functions.

Finally, we looked at the CUBE and ROLLUP OLAP extensions to the standard GROUP BY clause for use with aggregate functions and considered some pragmatic tips and techniques for using these capabilities.

Although this chapter is far from a complete treatise on the SQL language, or on all SQL Server's capabilities, it demonstrates how to use SQL Server facilities and extensions to help you solve real-world problems and write better applications.

MODIFYING DATA

In Chapter 7, we looked at how to query data. In this chapter, we'll look at inserting, updating, and deleting data in tables. We'll see the basic SQL commands for these operations but focus on Microsoft SQL Server–specific behaviors. This chapter considers each statement as an independent, atomic operation. The ability to group multiple statements into an all-or-nothing atomic operation (that is, a *transaction*) is presented in Chapter 10. Chapter 6 examined various types of constraints. Although using constraints is closely related to discussions about modifying data, this chapter's information and examples of modifying data assume that the modifications being performed satisfy any constraints on a table.

Basic Modification Operations

SQL has three basic data modification statements: INSERT, UPDATE, and DELETE. In previous chapters, we used some of these in examples without comment, assuming that you're already familiar with them. Here, we'll quickly review the most typical operations. Along with SELECT, the INSERT, UPDATE, and DELETE statements are referred to as *DML*, or *data manipulation language*. (DML is sometimes mistakenly referred to as *data modification language*, in which case SELECT couldn't be included, because it doesn't modify anything.) SELECT can manipulate data as it's being returned by using functions, aggregates, grouping, and so forth. (Create operations such as CREATE TABLE are *DDL—data definition language—*whereas security operations such as GRANT/DENY/REVOKE are *DCL—data control language*.)

INSERT

You generally use INSERT to add one row to a table. Here's the most common form of INSERT:

```
INSERT [INTO] {table_name|view_name} [(column_list)]
VALUES value_list
```

In SQL Server, the use of INTO is always optional. ANSI SQL specifies using INTO, however. If you're providing a value for every column in the table, and the values appear in the exact order in which the columns were defined, the column list is optional. (The one exception to this is when the table has an *identity* column, which you must not include in the list of values. You'll learn more about inserting into a table that contains an *identity* column a bit later in this chapter.) If you omit a value for one or more columns or if the order of your values differs from the order in which the columns were defined for the table, you must use a named columns list. If you don't provide a value for a particular column, that column must allow NULL, or it must have a default declared for it. (You can use the keyword DEFAULT as a placeholder.) You can *explicitly enter* NULL for a column, or SQL Server will *implicitly enter* NULL for an omitted column for which no default value exists.

You can issue an INSERT statement for a view, but the row is always added to only one underlying table. (Remember that views don't store any data of their own.) You can insert data into a view, as long as values (or defaults) are provided for all the columns of the underlying table into which the new row is added. Following are some simple examples of using INSERT statements in a table that is similar to *publishers* in the *pubs* sample database. The CREATE TABLE statement is shown so that you can easily see column order and so that you can see which columns allow NULL and which have defaults declared.

```
CREATE TABLE publishers2
(
    pub_id        int            NOT NULL PRIMARY KEY IDENTITY,
    pub_name      varchar(40)    NULL DEFAULT ('Anonymous'),
    city          varchar(20)    NULL,
    state         char(2)        NULL,
    country       varchar(30)    NOT NULL DEFAULT('USA')
)
GO

INSERT publishers2 VALUES ('AAA Publishing', 'Vancouver', 'BC',
'Canada')

INSERT INTO publishers2 VALUES ('Best Publishing', 'Mexico City',
NULL, 'Mexico')

INSERT INTO publishers2 (pub_name, city, state, country)
VALUES ('Complete Publishing', 'Washington', 'DC', 'United States')

INSERT publishers2 (state, city) VALUES ('WA', 'Poulsbo')
```

```
INSERT publishers2 VALUES (NULL, NULL, NULL, DEFAULT)

INSERT publishers2 VALUES (DEFAULT, NULL, 'WA', DEFAULT)

INSERT publishers2 VALUES (NULL, DEFAULT, DEFAULT, DEFAULT)

INSERT publishers2 DEFAULT VALUES
GO
```

The table has these values:

pub_id	pub_name	city	state	country
0001	AAA Publishing	Vancouver	BC	Canada
0002	Best Publishing	Mexico City	NULL	Mexico
0003	Complete Publishing	Washington	DC	United States
0004	Anonymous	Poulsbo	WA	USA
0005	NULL	NULL	NULL	USA
0006	Anonymous	NULL	WA	USA
0007	NULL	NULL	NULL	USA
0008	Anonymous	NULL	NULL	USA

These INSERT examples are pretty self-explanatory, but you should be careful of the following:

- If a column is declared to allow NULL and it also has a default bound to it, omitting the column entirely from the INSERT statement results in the default value being inserted, not the NULL value. (This is also true if the column is declared NOT NULL.)

- Other than for quick-and-dirty, one-time use, you're better off providing the column list to explicitly name the columns. Your INSERT statement will still work even if you add a column via ALTER TABLE.

- If one of the INSERT statements in this example had failed, the others would have continued and succeeded. Even if we wrapped multiple INSERT statements in a BEGIN TRAN/COMMIT TRAN block (and did nothing more than that), a failure of one INSERT (because of an error such as a constraint violation or duplicate value) wouldn't cause the others to fail. This behavior is expected and proper. If you want all the statements to fail when one statement fails, you must add error handling. (Chapter 13 covers error handling in more detail.)

■ The special form of the INSERT statement that uses DEFAULT VALUES and no column list is a shorthand method that enables you to avoid supplying the keyword DEFAULT for each column.

■ You can't specify the column name for a column that has the Identity property, and you can't use the DEFAULT placeholder for a column with the Identity property. (This would be nice, but SQL Server doesn't currently work this way.) You must completely omit a reference to the identity column. To explicitly provide a value for the column, you must use SET IDENTITY_INSERT ON. You can use the DEFAULT VALUES clause, however.

Behavior of DEFAULT and NULL

You should understand the general behavior of INSERT in relationship to NULL and DEFAULT precedence. If you omit a column from the column list and the values list, the column takes on the default value, if one exists. If a default value doesn't exist, SQL Server tries a NULL value. An error results if the column has been declared NOT NULL. If NULL is explicitly specified in the values list, a column is set to NULL (assuming it allows NULL), even if a default exists. When you use the DEFAULT placeholder on a column allowing NULL and no default has been declared, NULL is inserted for that column. An error results in a column declared NOT NULL without a default if you specify NULL or DEFAULT, or if you omit the value entirely.

Table 8-1 summarizes the results of an INSERT statement that omits columns, specifies NULL, or specifies DEFAULT, depending on whether the column is declared NULL or NOT NULL and whether it has a default declared.

Expressions in the VALUES Clause

So far, the INSERT examples have demonstrated only constant values in the VALUES clause of INSERT. In fact, you can use a scalar expression such as a function or a local variable in the VALUES clause. (We'll see functions and variables in Chapter 9. Hopefully, the basics are clear. If not, you can take a quick look ahead and then return to this chapter.) You can't use an entire SELECT statement as a scalar value even if you're certain that it returns only one row and one column. However, you can take the result of that SELECT statement and assign it to a variable, and then you can use that variable in the VALUES clause. In the next section, we'll see how a SELECT statement can completely replace the VALUES clause.

	Column Default Status			
	Default Exists		No Default Exists	
	Nullability of Column			
Entry Description	Null	Not Null	Null	Not Null
Value entered for column satisfies all constraints	Value entered	Value entered	Value entered	Value entered
Value entered for column fails some constraint on table	ERROR Default not used even if it exists	ERROR Default not used even if it exists	ERROR Default not used even if it exists	ERROR Default not used even if it exists
Column omitted	DEFAULT	DEFAULT	NULL	ERROR
Explicitly entered NULL	NULL	ERROR	NULL	ERROR
Explicitly entered DEFAULT	DEFAULT	DEFAULT	NULL	ERROR

Table 8-1.
The effects of an INSERT statement that omits columns, specifies NULL, or specifies DEFAULT.

Here's a contrived example that demonstrates how functions, expressions, arithmetic operations, string concatenation, and local variables are used within the VALUES clause of an INSERT statement:

```
CREATE TABLE mytable
(
int_val        int,
smallint_val   smallint,
numeric_val    numeric(8,2),
tiny_const     tinyint,
float_val      float,
date_val       datetime,
char_strng     char(10)
)
GO

DECLARE @myvar1 numeric(8, 2)
SELECT @myvar1=65.45
```

(continued)

```
INSERT mytable (int_val, smallint_val, numeric_val, tiny_const,
    float_val, date_val, char_strng)
VALUES
(OBJECT_ID('mytable'), @@spid, @myvar1 / 10.0, 5,
SQRT(144), GETDATE(), REPLICATE('A', 3) + REPLICATE('B', 3))
GO
SELECT * FROM mytable
GO
```

Your results should look something like this:

```
int_val       smallint_val    Numeric_val    tiny_const    float_val
-----------   -------------   ------------   ----------   ---------
162099618     12              6.55           5            12.0

date_val      char_string
-----------   -----------
1999-08-19    AAABBB
13:09:38.790
```

If you run this query, your values will be slightly different because your table will have a different *object_id* value, your process ID (*spid*) might be different, and you'll certainly be executing this query at a different date and time.

Multiple-Row INSERT Statements

The most typical use of INSERT is to add one row to a table. However, two special forms of INSERT (INSERT/SELECT and INSERT/EXEC) and a special SELECT statement (SELECT INTO) allow you to add multiple rows of data at once. Note that you can use the system function @@ROWCOUNT after all these statements to find out the number of rows affected.

INSERT/SELECT   As mentioned earlier, you can use a SELECT statement instead of a VALUES clause with INSERT. You get the full power of SELECT, including joins, subqueries, UNION, and all the other goodies. The table you're inserting into must already exist; the table can be a permanent table or a temporary table. The operation is atomic, so a failure of one row, such as from a constraint violation, causes all rows chosen by the SELECT statement to be thrown away. An exception to this occurs if a duplicate key is found on a unique index created with the IGNORE_DUP_KEY option. In this case, the duplicate row is thrown out but the entire statement continues and isn't aborted. You can, of course, also use expressions in the SELECT statement, and using the CONVERT function is common if the target table has a datatype that's different from that of the source table.

Here's an example: Suppose we want to copy the *authors* table (in the *pubs* sample database) to a temporary table. But rather than show the author ID as a *char* field in Social Security–number format with hyphens, we want to strip those hyphens out and store the ID as an *int*. We want to use a single name field with the concatenation of the last and first name. We also want to record the current date but strip off the time so that the internal time is considered midnight. (If you're working only with dates, this is a good idea because it avoids issues that occur when the time portions of columns aren't equal.) We'll also record each author's area code—the first three digits of her phone number. We need the author's state, but if it's NULL, we'll use WA instead.

```
CREATE TABLE #authors
(
    au_id           int             PRIMARY KEY,
    au_fullname     varchar(60)     NOT NULL,
    date_entered    smalldatetime   NOT NULL,
    area_code       char(3)         NOT NULL,
    state           char(2)         NOT NULL
)
GO

INSERT INTO #authors
SELECT
CONVERT(int, SUBSTRING(au_id, 1, 3) + SUBSTRING(au_id, 5, 2)
    + SUBSTRING(au_id, 8, 4)),
au_lname + ', ' + au_fname,
CONVERT(varchar, GETDATE(), 102),
CONVERT(char(3), phone),
ISNULL(state, 'WA')
FROM authors

SELECT * FROM #authors
```

Here's the result:

au_id	au_fullname	date_entered	area_code	state
172321176	White, Johnson	1998-08-19 00:00:00	408	CA
213468915	Green, Marjorie	1998-08-19 00:00:00	415	CA
238957766	Carson, Cheryl	1998-08-19 00:00:00	415	CA
267412394	O'Leary, Michael	1998-08-19 00:00:00	408	CA
274809391	Straight, Dean	1998-08-19 00:00:00	415	CA
341221782	Smith, Meander	1998-08-19 00:00:00	913	KS

(continued)

409567008	Bennet, Abraham	1998-08-19 00:00:00	415	CA
427172319	Dull, Ann	1998-08-19 00:00:00	415	CA
472272349	Gringlesby, Burt	1998-08-19 00:00:00	707	CA
486291786	Locksley, Charlene	1998-08-19 00:00:00	415	CA
527723246	Greene, Morningstar	1998-08-19 00:00:00	615	TN
648921872	Blotchet-Halls, Reginald	1998-08-19 00:00:00	503	OR
672713249	Yokomoto, Akiko	1998-08-19 00:00:00	415	CA
712451867	del Castillo, Innes	1998-08-19 00:00:00	615	MI
722515454	DeFrance, Michel	1998-08-19 00:00:00	219	IN
724089931	Stringer, Dirk	1998-08-19 00:00:00	415	CA
724809391	MacFeather, Stearns	1998-08-19 00:00:00	415	CA
756307391	Karsen, Livia	1998-08-19 00:00:00	415	CA
807916654	Panteley, Sylvia	1998-08-19 00:00:00	301	MD
846927186	Hunter, Sheryl	1998-08-19 00:00:00	415	CA
893721158	McBadden, Heather	1998-08-19 00:00:00	707	CA
899462035	Ringer, Anne	1998-08-19 00:00:00	801	UT
998723567	Ringer, Albert	1998-08-19 00:00:00	801	UT

INSERT/EXEC   You can use INSERT with the results of a stored procedure or a dynamic EXECUTE statement taking the place of the VALUES clause. This procedure is similar to the INSERT/SELECT form, except that EXEC is used instead. The EXEC should return exactly one result set with types that match the table you've set up for it. You can pass parameters if executing a stored procedure, use EXEC('*string*'), or even call out to extended procedures (your own custom DLLs) or to remote procedures on other servers. By calling to a remote procedure on another server, putting the data into a temporary table, and then joining on it, you get the capabilities of a distributed join.

An example explains this better: Suppose that we want to store the results of executing the *sp_configure* stored procedure in a temporary table. (You can also do this with a permanent table.)

```
CREATE TABLE #config_out
(
name_col    varchar(50),
minval      int,
maxval      int,
configval   int,
runval      int
)

INSERT #config_out
    EXEC sp_configure

SELECT * FROM #config_out
```

Here's the result:

name_col	minval	maxval	configval	runval
allow updates	0	1	0	0
default language	0	9999	0	0
fill factor (%)	0	100	0	0
language in cache	3	100	3	3
max async IO	1	255	32	32
max text repl size (B)	0	2147483647	65536	65536
max worker threads	10	1024	255	255
nested triggers	0	1	1	1
network packet size(B)	512	65535	4096	4096
recovery interval(min)	0	32767	0	0
remote access	0	1	1	1
remote proc trans	0	1	0	0
show advanced options	0	1	0	0
user options	0	4095	0	0

If we want to execute the procedure against the remote server named *dogfood*, that's almost as easy. Assuming the same table *#config_out* exists:

```
INSERT #config_out
    EXEC dogfood.master.dbo.sp_configure
```

NOTE Before executing a procedure on another server, you must perform several administrative steps to enable the servers to communicate with each other. Refer to the SQL Server documentation for the details. Once you carry out these few simple steps, procedures can be executed on the remote server by just including the name of the server as part of the procedure name, as shown in the previous example.

SELECT INTO SELECT INTO is in many ways similar to INSERT/SELECT, but it directly builds the table rather than requiring that the table already exist. In addition, SELECT INTO operates with a special nonlogged mode, which makes it faster. To use SELECT INTO to populate a permanent table, the database must have the *select into/bulkcopy* option enabled (for example, *EXEC sp_dboption pubs, 'select into/bulkcopy', true*). Note that if you use SELECT INTO with a permanent table, your next backup must be a full database backup because the transaction log won't have the records for these operations. In fact, you'll get an error message if you try to back up the transaction log after running an unlogged operation.

NOTE Always use nonlogged operations with care. Think about their effects on your backup and restore plans before you launch such an operation.

You can also use SELECT INTO with temporary tables (# and ## prefixed) without enabling the *select into/bulkcopy* option. Because temporary tables don't have to be recovered, not logging the data inserted into them isn't a problem. (A user executing SELECT INTO must have permission to select from the target table and also have CREATE TABLE permission, because this statement does both actions.)

SELECT INTO is handy. It's commonly used to easily copy a table or perhaps to drop a column that's no longer needed. In the latter case, you'd simply omit the unnecessary column from the select list. Or you can change the datatypes of columns by using CONVERT in the select list.

To illustrate the SELECT INTO statement, here's an equivalent operation to the earlier INSERT/SELECT example. The results, including the column names of the new temporary table, appear identical to those produced using INSERT/SELECT.

```
SELECT
CONVERT(int, SUBSTRING(au_id, 1, 3) + SUBSTRING(au_id, 5, 2)
+ SUBSTRING(au_id, 8, 4)) AS au_id,
au_lname + ', ' + au_fname AS au_fullname,
CONVERT(varchar, GETDATE(), 102) AS date_entered,
CONVERT(char(3), phone) AS area_code,
ISNULL(state, 'WA') AS state

INTO #authors
FROM authors
```

There's one important difference between the two procedures: the datatypes of the table created automatically are slightly different from the datatypes declared explicitly using INSERT/SELECT. If the exact datatypes were important, you could use CONVERT to cast them to the types you want in all cases, or you could create the table separately and then use INSERT/SELECT.

BULK INSERT

SQL Server 7 provides a command to load a flat file of data into a SQL Server table. However, no corresponding command exists to copy data *out* to a file. The file to be copied in must be either a local file or one available via a UNC name. Here's the general syntax for the command, called BULK INSERT:

```
BULK INSERT [['database_name'.]['owner'].]{'table_name' FROM data_file}
    [WITH
        (
            [ BATCHSIZE [ = batch_size]]
```

```
[[,] CODEPAGE [ = ACP | OEM | RAW | code_page]]
[[,] DATAFILETYPE [ =
    {'char' | 'native'| 'widechar' | 'widenative'}]]
[[,] FIELDTERMINATOR [ = 'field_terminator']]
[[,] FIRSTROW [ = first_row]]
[[,] FORMATFILE [ = 'format_file_path']]
[[,] KEEPIDENTITY]
[[,] KEEPNULLS
[[,] LASTROW [ = last_row]]
[[,] MAXERRORS [ = max_errors]]
[[,] CHECK_CONSTRAINTS]
[[,] ORDER ({column [ASC | DESC]} [, ...n])]
[[,] ROWTERMINATOR [ = 'row_terminator']]
[[,] TABLOCK]
)
```

To use the BULK INSERT command, the table must already exist. The number and datatypes of the columns must be compatible with the data in the file that you plan to copy in.

Here's a simple example to give you a feel for what this command can do:

1. Create a simple table in the *pubs* database, using the following batch:

```
USE pubs
CREATE TABLE mybcp
(col1 char(3),
col2 INT)
```

2. Use your favorite editor (for example, *notepad*). Save a text file named *mydata.txt* to the root directory of drive C. Include the following text:

```
abc,1;def,2;ghi,3;
```

3. Finally, load the file into the table with the following Transact-SQL statement:

```
BULK INSERT pubs.dbo.mybcp
FROM 'c:\mydata.txt'
WITH
(DATAFILETYPE = 'char',
FIELDTERMINATOR = ',', ROWTERMINATOR = ';')
```

NOTE The BULK INSERT command will work only if SQL Server is running on the machine local to the specified logical disk, in this case, C.

As the syntax specification shows, the BULK INSERT command has quite a few possible arguments. These arguments appear in the online documentation, but some of the arguments might be unclear, so it's worth mentioning the highlights. (See Table 8-2.)

Argument	Description
BATCHSIZE	Each batch is copied to the server as a single transaction. If an entire batch is successfully loaded, the data is immediately written to disk. If a server failure occurs in the middle of a batch, all rows in that batch will be lost, but all rows up to the end of the previous batch will still be available. By default, all data in the specified data file is one batch.
ORDER (*column_list*) where *column_list* = {*column* [ASC | DESC] [,...*n*]}	The data file is already sorted by the same columns in *column_list* as the destination table. A clustered index on the same columns, in the same order as the columns in *column_list*, must already exist in the table. Using a sorted data file can improve the performance of the BULK INSERT command. By default, BULK INSERT assumes the data file is unordered.
TABLOCK	A table-level lock is acquired for the duration of the bulk copy. It improves performance because of reduced lock contention on the table. This special kind of Bulk-Update lock is primarily compatible only with other BulkUpdate locks, so a table can be loaded quickly using multiple clients running BULK INSERT in parallel. By default, no table-level lock is acquired. You can still run parallel BULK INSERTS, but their performance will be much slower, similar to running individual INSERT statements. (Chapter 13 covers locking in detail.)

Table 8-2.
BULK INSERT command arguments.

Argument	Description
CHECK_CONSTRAINTS	Any constraints on the table are applied during the bulk copy. By default, constraints aren't enforced. Applying constraints can have several benefits and is the recommended approach. By checking the constraints on the data, you know that the data you load will be valid. In addition, SQL Server might be able to better optimize the entire operation, because it has advance knowledge of the kind of data that will be loaded.

Unlike for previous versions of SQL Server, we don't always recommend that you drop all your indexes before running the BULK INSERT operation (or the BCP command, described in the next section). In many cases, the copy operation doesn't perform noticeably better if a table has no indexes, so you should usually leave your indexes on a table while copying data into it. The only exception is when you want to have multiple clients load data into the same table simultaneously; then you should drop indexes before loading the data.

When SQL Server executes a BULK INSERT operation, the rows of data go straight into the server as an OLE DB row set. The functionality of a BULK INSERT operation is quite similar to that of the command-line utility BCP, which is discussed in the next section. In contrast to the BULK INSERT operation, BCP data is sent to SQL Server as a Tabular Data Stream (TDS) result set and flows through network protocols and ODS. This can generate a lot of additional overhead, and you might find that BULK INSERT is up to twice as fast as BCP for copying data into a table from a local file.

Tools and Utilities Related to Multiple-Row Insert

INSERT and BULK INSERT aren't the only ways to get data into SQL Server tables. SQL Server also provides some tools and utilities for loading tables from external sources. Because the focus of this book isn't on the utilities and tools, we won't discuss the details; however, you should at least be aware of the options available.

Bulk copy libraries, SQL-DMO objects, and BCP.EXE   The ODBC standard doesn't directly support SQL Server bulk copy operations. When running against SQL Server version 7, however, the SQL Server 7 ODBC driver supports a set of older DB-Library functions that perform SQL Server bulk copy operations. The specialized bulk copy support requires that the following files be available: *odbcss.h*, *odbcbcp.lib*, and *odbcbcp.dll*.

The BCP.EXE command-line utility for SQL Server 7 is written using the ODBC bulk copy interface. This utility has little code other than that accepting various command-line parameters and then invoking the functions of the *bcp* library. We won't go into all the details of BCP.EXE here, except to say that it was built for function, not form. It's totally command-line driven. If you're a fan of UNIX utilities, you'll love it! The possible arguments are similar to those for the BULK INSERT command, and you can find a complete description in the online documentation.

The SQL-DMO BulkCopy object ultimately invokes these same *bcp* functions, but it provides some higher-level methods and ease of use within the world of COM (Component Object Model) objects. The BulkCopy object represents the parameters of a single bulk-copy command issued against SQL Server.

The BulkCopy object doesn't have a place in the SQL-DMO object tree. Instead, BulkCopy is used as a parameter to the ImportData method of the Table object and the ExportData method of the Table and View objects.

Data Transformation Services   One of the most exciting tools available with SQL Server 7 is *Data Transformation Services (DTS)*. Using this tool, you can import and export data to and from any OLE DB or ODBC data source. You can do a straight copy of the data, or you can transform the data using simple SQL statements or procedures. Alternatively, you can execute a Microsoft ActiveX script that modifies (transforms) the data when copied from the source to the destination, or you can perform any operation supported by the Microsoft JScript, PerlScript, or Microsoft Visual Basic Script (VBScript) languages.

Unlike the BCP and BULK INSERT operations just described, DTS creates the destination table for you as part of the copying operation and allows you to specify the exact column names and datatypes (depending on what the destination data store allows). DTS is installed by default with a standard SQL Server setup, and complete documentation is available in Books Online.

Transfer SQL Server Objects   SQL Server Enterprise Manager puts an easy-to-use graphical interface on top of the SQL-DMO BulkCopy object to make it easy to transfer data between two SQL Server installations. This provides the same functionality as the SQL Transfer Manager utility or the transfer management interface in earlier versions of SQL Server. The tool allows you to transfer all objects—not just data, but stored procedures, rules, constraints, and so on—but only when moving from one SQL Server database to another SQL Server database. The Transfer Objects tool is accessible from the DTS Package Designer by specifying the task *Transfer SQL Server Objects*.

Whether you use the *bcp* libraries through the BCP.EXE utility, SQLDMO, BULK INSERT, or the transfer functions of SQL Enterprise Manager, be aware of a few bulk copy specifics:

- When used to copy data into a SQL Server table, bulk copy has two main forms: logged and nonlogged. (Previous versions of SQL Server called the two forms *fast* bulk copy and *slow* bulk copy. In SQL Server 7, both forms are very fast, so these terms are no longer used.) Nonlogged bulk copy is faster than logged bulk copy for several reasons. For one, the nonlogged copy moves data in units of extents at a time, instead of as single-row operations.

- Because nonlogged bulk copy doesn't allow any indexes on a table, there's no overhead of maintaining those indexes.

- Nonlogged bulk copy doesn't log the individual data rows inserted. (It does log page and extent allocations, however, so your transaction log will grow during a large copy operation.) As is true with any nonlogged operation, you must deal with any failures manually while the load is in progress. If that's not possible, use logged bulk copy, in which all activity is logged and therefore recoverable. If you can start everything over, including the table creation, use nonlogged bulk copy. With nonlogged bulk copy, the table must not have any indexes (which also means that it can't have a PRIMARY KEY or UNIQUE constraint). And the database must have the *select into/ bulk copy* option enabled.

- If the table is marked for replication, the copy will be done using logged bulk copy. The flowchart in Figure 8-1 on the following page summarizes the conditions that determine whether a logged or nonlogged bulk copy operation will be performed.

If you can't use nonlogged bulk copy, you should use logged bulk copy. (Logged bulk copy is still faster than a standard INSERT statement because it comes in at a lower level within SQL Server.)

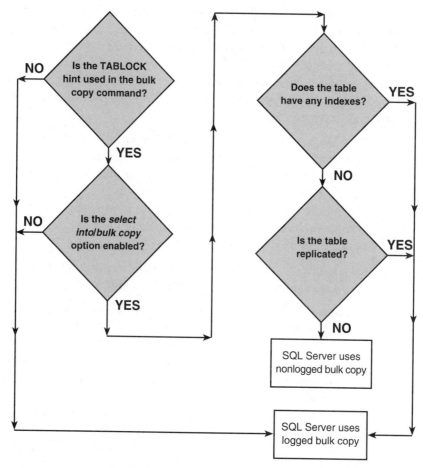

Figure 8-1.
How SQL Server determines whether to execute a bulk copy operation in logged or nonlogged mode.

UPDATE

UPDATE, the next data modification statement, is used to change existing rows. Usually, UPDATE contains a WHERE clause that limits the update to only a subset of rows in the table. (The subset could be a single row, which would generally be accomplished by testing for equality to the primary key values in the WHERE clause.) If no WHERE clause is provided, every row in the table is changed by UPDATE. You can use the @@ROWCOUNT system function to determine the number of rows that were updated.

Here's the basic UPDATE syntax:

```
UPDATE {table_name|view_name}
SET column_name1 = {expression1|NULL|DEFAULT|(SELECT)}
    [, column_name2 = {expression2|NULL|DEFAULT|(SELECT)}
WHERE {search_conditions}
```

Columns are set to an expression. The expression can be almost anything that returns a scalar value—a constant, another column, an arithmetic expression, a bunch of nested functions that end up returning one value, a local variable, or a system function. You can set a column to a value conditionally determined using the CASE expression or to a value returned from a subquery. You can also set columns to NULL (if the column allows it) or to DEFAULT (if a default is declared or if the column allows NULL), much like with the INSERT statement.

You can set multiple columns in a single UPDATE statement. Like a multiple-row INSERT, an UPDATE that affects multiple rows is an atomic operation—if a single UPDATE statement affects multiple rows and one row fails a constraint, all the changes made by that statement are rolled back.

The following simple UPDATE statements should be self-explanatory. Later in this chapter, we'll show you some that aren't this simple and intuitive.

```
-- Change a specific employee's last name after his marriage
UPDATE employee
    SET lname='Thomas-Kemper'
WHERE emp_id='GHT50241M'

-- Raise the price of every title by 12%
-- No WHERE clause so it affects every row in the table
UPDATE titles
    SET price=price * 1.12

-- Publisher 1389 was sold, changing its name and location.
-- All the data in other tables relating to pub_id 1389 is
-- still valid; only the name of the publisher and its
-- location have changed.
UPDATE publishers
    SET pub_name='O Canada Publications',
        city='Victoria',
        state='BC',
```

(continued)

```
            country='Canada'
WHERE pub_id='1389'

-- Change the phone number of authors living in Gary, IN,
-- back to the DEFAULT value
UPDATE authors
    SET phone=DEFAULT
WHERE city='Gary' AND state='IN'
```

Forcing the Use of Defaults

Notice the use of the keyword DEFAULT in the last example. Sometimes you'll want to stamp a table with the name of the user who last modified the row or with the time it was last modified. You could use system functions, such as SUSER_NAME() or GETDATE(), as the DEFAULT value, and then restrict all data modification to be done via stored procedures that explicitly update such columns to the DEFAULT keyword. Or you could make it policy that such columns must always be set to the DEFAULT keyword in the UPDATE statement, and then you could monitor this by also having a CHECK constraint on the same column that insists that the value be equal to that which the function returns. (If you use GETDATE(), you'll probably want to use it in conjunction with other string and date functions to strip off the milliseconds and avoid the possibility that the value from the DEFAULT might be slightly different than that in the CHECK.) Here's a sample using SUSER_NAME():

```
CREATE TABLE update_def
(
up_id       int          PRIMARY KEY,
up_byname   varchar(30)  NOT NULL DEFAULT SUSER_NAME()
    CHECK (up_byname=SUSER_NAME())
-- Assume other columns would be here
)
GO


UPDATE update_def
SET
-- SET other columns to their value here, and then append the
-- following
up_byname=DEFAULT
WHERE up_id=1
GO
```

More Advanced UPDATE Examples

You can go well beyond these UPDATE examples, however, and use subqueries, the CASE statement, and even joins in specifying search criteria. (Chapter 9 covers CASE in depth.) For example, the following UPDATE statement is like a correlated subquery. It sets the *ytd_sales* field of the *titles* table to the sum of all *qty* fields for matching titles:

```
UPDATE titles
SET titles.ytd_sales=(SELECT SUM(sales.qty) FROM sales
    WHERE titles.title_id=sales.title_id)
```

In the next example, you can use the CASE expression with UPDATE to selectively give pay raises based on an employee's review rating. Assume that reviews have been turned in and big salary adjustments are due. A review rating of 4 doubles the employee's salary. A rating of 3 increases the salary by 60 percent. A rating of 2 increases the salary by 20 percent, and a rating lower than 2 doesn't change the salary.

```
UPDATE employee_salaries
    SET salary =
        CASE review
            WHEN 4 THEN salary * 2.0
            WHEN 3 THEN salary * 1.6
            WHEN 2 THEN salary * 1.2
            ELSE salary
        END
```

DELETE

DELETE, the last data manipulation statement, removes rows from a table. Once the action is committed, no undelete action is available. (If it's not wrapped in a BEGIN TRAN/COMMIT TRAN block, the COMMIT, of course, occurs by default as soon as the statement completes.) Because you delete only rows, not columns, you never specify column names in a DELETE statement as you do with INSERT or UPDATE. But in many other ways, DELETE acts much like UPDATE—you specify a WHERE clause to limit the delete to certain rows. If you omit the WHERE clause, every row in the table will be deleted. The system function @@ROWCOUNT keeps track of the number of rows deleted. You can delete through a view but only if the view is based on a single table (because there's no way to specify to delete only certain rows in a multiple-table view). If you delete through a view, all the underlying FOREIGN KEY constraints on the table must still be satisfied for the delete to succeed.

Here's the general form of DELETE:

```
DELETE [FROM] {table_name | view_name} [WHERE clause]
```

The FROM preposition is ANSI standard, but its inclusion is always optional in SQL Server (similar to INTO with INSERT). The preposition must be specified per ANSI SQL. If the preposition is always needed, it is logically redundant, which is why SQL Server doesn't require it.

Here are some simple examples:

```
DELETE discounts
-- Deletes every row from the discounts table but does not
-- delete the table itself. An empty table remains.

DELETE FROM sales WHERE qty > 5
-- Deletes those rows from the sales table that have a value for
-- qty of 6 or more

DELETE FROM WA_stores
-- Attempts to delete all rows qualified by the WA_stores view,
-- which would delete those rows from the stores table that have
-- state of WA. This delete is correctly stated but would fail
-- because of a foreign key reference.
```

TRUNCATE TABLE

In the first example, *DELETE discounts* deletes every row of that table. Every row is fully logged. SQL Server provides a much faster way to purge all the rows from the table: using TRUNCATE TABLE empties the whole table by deallocating all the table's data pages and index pages. TRUNCATE TABLE is orders-of-magnitude faster than an unqualified DELETE against the whole table. Delete triggers on the table won't fire (because the rows deleted aren't individually logged), and TRUNCATE TABLE will still work. If a foreign key references the table to be truncated, however, TRUNCATE TABLE won't work. And if the table is publishing data for replication, which requires the log records, TRUNCATE TABLE won't work.

Despite contrary information, TRUNCATE TABLE isn't really an unlogged operation. The deletions of rows aren't logged because they don't really occur. Rather, entire pages are deallocated. But the page deallocations *are* logged. If TRUNCATE TABLE weren't logged, it couldn't be used inside transactions, which must have the capacity to be rolled back. A simple example demonstrates that the action can indeed be rolled back:

```
BEGIN TRAN
-- Get the initial count of rows
SELECT COUNT(*) FROM titleauthor
     25

TRUNCATE TABLE titleauthor

-- Verify that all rows are now gone
SELECT COUNT(*) FROM titleauthor
      0

-- Undo the truncate operation
ROLLBACK TRAN

-- Verify that rows are still there after the undo
SELECT COUNT(*) FROM titleauthor
     25
```

Modifying Data Through Views

You can specify INSERT, UPDATE, and DELETE statements on views as well as on tables, although you should be aware of some restrictions and other issues. Modifications through a view end up modifying the data in an underlying base table (and only one such table) because views don't store data. All three types of data modifications work easily for single-table views, especially in the simplest case in which the view exposes all the columns of the base table. But a single-table view doesn't necessarily have to expose every column of the base table—it could restrict the view to a subset of columns only.

For any modification, all the underlying constraints of the base table must still be satisfied. For example, if a column in the base table is defined as NOT NULL and doesn't have a DEFAULT declared for it, the column must be visible to the view, and the insert must supply a value for it. If the column weren't part of the view, an insert through that view could never work because the NOT NULL constraint could never be satisfied. And, of course, you can't modify or insert a value for a column that's derived by the view, such as an arithmetic calculation or concatenation of two strings of the base table. (You can still modify the nonderived columns in the view, however.)

Basing a view on multiple tables is far less straightforward. You can issue an UPDATE statement against a view that is a join of multiple tables, but only if all columns being modified (that is, the columns in the SET clause) are part of the same base table. An INSERT statement can also be performed against a view that does a join only if columns from a single table are specified in the INSERT statement's column list. Only the table whose columns are specified will have a row inserted: any other tables in the view will be unaffected. A DELETE statement can't be executed against a view that's a join, because entire rows are deleted and modifications through a view can affect only one base table. (Because no columns are specified in a delete, from which table would the rows be deleted?)

In the real world, you would probably have little use for an INSERT statement against a view with a join because all but one table in the underlying query would be totally ignored. But the insert is possible. The following simple example illustrates this:

```
CREATE TABLE one
(
col11    int    NOT NULL,
col12    int    NOT NULL
)

CREATE TABLE two
(
col21    int    NOT NULL,
col22    int    NOT NULL
)
GO

CREATE VIEW one_two
AS
(SELECT col11, col12, col21, col22
FROM one LEFT JOIN two ON (col11=col21))
GO

INSERT one_two (col11, col12)
VALUES (1, 2)

SELECT * FROM one_two
```

Here's the result set:

```
col11    col12    col21    col22
-----    -----    -----    -----
1        2        NULL     NULL
```

Notice that this insert specifies values only for columns from table *one*, and only table *one* gets a new row. Selecting from the view produces the row only because LEFT OUTER JOIN is specified in the view. Because table *two* contains no actual rows, a simple equijoin would have found no matches. Although the row would still have been inserted into table *one,* it would have seemingly vanished from the view. You could specify the view as an equijoin and use WITH CHECK OPTION to prevent an insert that wouldn't find a match. But the insert must still affect only one of the tables, so matching rows would already need to exist in the other table. We'll come back to WITH CHECK OPTION in the next section; for now, we'll simply see how this would be specified:

```
CREATE VIEW one_two_equijoin
AS
(SELECT col11, col12, col21, col22
FROM one JOIN two ON (col11=col21))
WITH CHECK OPTION
GO
```

If we try to specify all columns with either view formulation, even if we simply try to insert NULL values into the columns of table *two,* an error results because the single INSERT operation can't be performed on both tables. (Admittedly, the error message is slightly misleading.)

```
INSERT one_two (col11, col12, col21, col22)
VALUES (1, 2, NULL, NULL)
Msg 4405, Level 16, State 2
View 'one_two' is not updatable because the FROM clause names
multiple tables.
```

Similarly, a DELETE against this view with a join will be disallowed and results in the same message:

```
DELETE one_two
Msg 4405, Level 16, State 2
View 'one_two' is not updatable because the FROM clause names
multiple tables.
```

The UPDATE case isn't common, but it's somewhat more realistic. You'll probably want to avoid allowing updates through views that do joins, and the next example shows why.

Given the following view,

```
CREATE VIEW titles_and_authors
AS
(
SELECT A.au_id, A.au_lname, T.title_id, T.title
FROM
```

(continued)

```
authors AS A
FULL OUTER JOIN titleauthor AS TA ON (A.au_id=TA.au_id)
FULL OUTER JOIN titles AS T ON (TA.title_id=T.title_id)
)
```

selecting from the view

```
SELECT * FROM titles_and_authors
```

yields this:

au_id	au_lname	title_id	title
172-32-1176	White	PS3333	Prolonged Data Deprivation: Four Case Studies
213-46-8915	Green	BU1032	The Busy Executive's Database Guide
213-46-8915	Green	BU2075	You Can Combat Computer Stress!
238-95-7766	Carson	PC1035	But Is It User Friendly?
267-41-2394	O'Leary	BU1111	Cooking with Computers: Surreptitious Balance Sheets
267-41-2394	O'Leary	TC7777	Sushi, Anyone?
274-80-9391	Straight	BU7832	Straight Talk About Computers
409-56-7008	Bennet	BU1032	The Busy Executive's Database Guide
427-17-2319	Dull	PC8888	Secrets of Silicon Valley
472-27-2349	Gringlesby	TC7777	Sushi, Anyone?
486-29-1786	Locksley	PC9999	Net Etiquette
486-29-1786	Locksley	PS7777	Emotional Security: A New Algorithm
648-92-1872	Blotchet-Halls	TC4203	Fifty Years in Buckingham Palace Kitchens
672-71-3249	Yokomoto	TC7777	Sushi, Anyone?
712-45-1867	del Castillo	MC2222	Silicon Valley Gastronomic Treats
722-51-5454	DeFrance	MC3021	The Gourmet Microwave
724-80-9391	MacFeather	BU1111	Cooking with Computers: Surreptitious Balance Sheets
724-80-9391	MacFeather	PS1372	Computer Phobic AND Non-Phobic Individuals: Behavior Variations
756-30-7391	Karsen	PS1372	Computer Phobic AND Non-Phobic Individuals: Behavior Variations
807-91-6654	Panteley	TC3218	Onions, Leeks, and Garlic: Cooking Secrets of the Mediterranean
846-92-7186	Hunter	PC8888	Secrets of Silicon Valley
899-46-2035	Ringer	MC3021	The Gourmet Microwave
899-46-2035	Ringer	PS2091	Is Anger the Enemy?
998-72-3567	Ringer	PS2091	Is Anger the Enemy?

```
998-72-3567   Ringer      PS2106   Life Without Fear
341-22-1782   Smith       NULL     NULL
527-72-3246   Greene      NULL     NULL
724-08-9931   Stringer    NULL     NULL
893-72-1158   McBadden    NULL     NULL
NULL          NULL        MC3026   The Psychology of Computer
                                   Cooking
```

```
(30 rows affected)
```

The following UPDATE statement works fine because only one underlying table, *authors,* is affected. This example changes the author's name from *DeFrance* to *DeFrance-Macy.*

```
UPDATE TITLES_AND_AUTHORS
SET au_lname='DeFrance-Macy'
WHERE au_id='722-51-5454'
(1 row(s) affected)
```

This UPDATE statement yields an error, however, because two tables from a view can't be updated in the same statement:

```
UPDATE TITLES_AND_AUTHORS
SET au_lname='DeFrance-Macy', title='The Gourmet Microwave Cookbook'
WHERE au_id='722-51-5454' and title_id='MC3021'

Msg 4405, Level 16, State 2
View 'TITLES_AND_AUTHORS' is not updatable because the FROM clause
names multiple tables.
```

If you created the view, it might seem obvious that the UPDATE statement above won't be allowed. But if the person doing the update isn't aware of the underlying tables, which a view does a great job of hiding, it will *not* be obvious why one UPDATE statement works and the other one doesn't.

In general, it's a good idea to avoid allowing updates (and inserts) through views that do joins. Such views are extremely useful for querying and are wonderful constructs that make querying simpler and less prone to bugs from misstating joins. But modifications against them are problematic. If you do allow an update through a view that's a join, be sure that the relationships are properly protected via FOREIGN KEY constraints or triggers, or you'll run into bigger problems.

Suppose, for example, that we wanted to change only the *au_id* column in the example view above. If the existing value in the underlying *authors* table is referenced by a row in *titleauthor,* such an update won't be allowed because it would orphan the row in *titleauthor.* The FOREIGN KEY constraint protects against the modification. But here, we'll temporarily disable the FOREIGN KEY constraint between *titleauthor* and *titles*:

```
ALTER TABLE titleauthor     -- This disables the constraint
    NOCHECK CONSTRAINT ALL
```

Notice that although we'll be updating the *authors* table, the constraint we're disabling (the constraint that would otherwise be violated) is on the *titleauthor* table. New users often forget that a FOREIGN KEY constraint on one table is essentially a constraint on *both* the referencing table (here, *titleauthors*) and on the referenced table (here, *titles*). With the constraint now disabled, we change the value of *au_id* through the view for the author Anne Ringer:

```
-- With constraint now disabled, the following update succeeds:
UPDATE titles_and_authors
SET au_id='111-22-3333'
WHERE au_id='899-46-2035'
```

But look at the effect on the same SELECT of all rows in the view:

au_id	au_lname	title_id	title
172-32-1176	White	PS3333	Prolonged Data Deprivation: Four Case Studies
213-46-8915	Green	BU1032	The Busy Executive's Database Guide
213-46-8915	Green	BU2075	You Can Combat Computer Stress!
238-95-7766	Carson	PC1035	But Is It User Friendly?
267-41-2394	O'Leary	BU1111	Cooking with Computers: Surreptitious Balance Sheets
267-41-2394	O'Leary	TC7777	Sushi, Anyone?
274-80-9391	Straight	BU7832	Straight Talk About Computers
409-56-7008	Bennet	BU1032	The Busy Executive's Database Guide
427-17-2319	Dull	PC8888	Secrets of Silicon Valley
472-27-2349	Gringlesby	TC7777	Sushi, Anyone?
486-29-1786	Locksley	PC9999	Net Etiquette
486-29-1786	Locksley	PS7777	Emotional Security: A New Algorithm
648-92-1872	Blotchet-Halls	TC4203	Fifty Years in Buckingham Palace Kitchens
672-71-3249	Yokomoto	TC7777	Sushi, Anyone?
712-45-1867	del Castillo	MC2222	Silicon Valley Gastronomic Treats
722-51-5454	DeFrance-Macy	MC3021	The Gourmet Microwave
724-80-9391	MacFeather	BU1111	Cooking with Computers: Surreptitious Balance Sheets
724-80-9391	MacFeather	PS1372	Computer Phobic AND Non-Phobic Individuals: Behavior Variations

756-30-7391	Karsen	PS1372	Computer Phobic AND Non-Phobic Individuals: Behavior Variations
807-91-6654	Panteley	TC3218	Onions, Leeks, and Garlic: Cooking Secrets of the Mediterranean
846-92-7186	Hunter	PC8888	Secrets of Silicon Valley
NULL	NULL	MC3021	The Gourmet Microwave
NULL	NULL	PS2091	Is Anger the Enemy?
998-72-3567	Ringer	PS2091	Is Anger the Enemy?
998-72-3567	Ringer	PS2106	Life Without Fear
111-22-3333	Ringer	NULL	NULL
341-22-1782	Smith	NULL	NULL
527-72-3246	Greene	NULL	NULL
724-08-9931	Stringer	NULL	NULL
893-72-1158	McBadden	NULL	NULL
NULL	NULL	MC3026	The Psychology of Computer Cooking

(31 rows affected)

Although we haven't added or deleted any rows, instead of producing 30 rows total from the view, as was the case earlier, the view now produces 31 rows. This is because the outer join fabricates a row for the new *au_id* that has no match in the *titles* table. (It appears with NULL title fields.) Also notice that the two titles that matched the old *au_id* now have NULLs in their author fields. This might be comprehensible to someone who has a detailed understanding of the tables, but if the view is the only window that exists for updating the table, it will be extremely confusing.

If in future releases, referential actions are added that allow updates to cascade, you might reconsider whether to use updates against views based on joins; you'd still have the problem of affecting columns from more than one table without being able to know which is which. (Chapter 10 covers the implementation of referential actions via triggers.) Theoretically, it's possible to update many more views—such as joins—than SQL Server currently allows. But until these additional algorithms for updatability of views make their way into a future release, it's simply best to avoid the problem.

WITH CHECK OPTION

Earlier, we saw that modifying data with views based on one table is pretty straightforward—but there's one "gotcha" to think about: disappearing rows. By default, a view can allow an UPDATE or an INSERT, even if the result is that the row no longer qualifies for the view. Consider the view on the following page that qualifies only stores in the state of Washington.

```
CREATE VIEW WA_stores AS
SELECT * FROM stores
WHERE state='WA'
GO

SELECT stor_id, stor_name, state
FROM WA_stores
```

Here's the result:

```
stor_id    stor_name                                      state
-------    ------------------------------------          -----
6380       Eric the Read Books                            WA
7131       Doc-U-Mat: Quality Laundry and Books           WA
(2 rows affected)
```

The following UPDATE statement changes both qualifying rows so that they no longer qualify from the view and have seemingly disappeared.

```
UPDATE WA_stores
SET state='CA'
SELECT stor_id, stor_name, state
FROM WA_stores
```

And the result:

```
stor_id    stor_name      state
-------    ---------      -----

(0 rows affected)
```

Modifications you make against a view without WITH CHECK OPTION can result in rows being added or modified in the base table, but the rows can't be selected from the view because they don't meet the view's criteria. The rows seem to disappear, as the example above illustrates.

If you allow data to be modified through a view that uses a WHERE clause, consider using WITH CHECK OPTION when defining the view. In fact, it would be better if WITH CHECK OPTION were the default behavior. But the behavior described above is in accordance with the ANSI and ISO SQL standards, and the expected result is that the disappearing row phenomenon can occur unless WITH CHECK OPTION is specified. Of course, any modifications you make through the view must also satisfy the constraints of the underlying table, or the statement will be aborted. This is true whether WITH CHECK OPTION is declared or not.

The following example shows how WITH CHECK OPTION protects against the disappearing rows phenomenon:

```
CREATE VIEW WA_stores AS
SELECT * FROM stores
WHERE state='WA'
WITH CHECK OPTION
GO

UPDATE WA_stores
SET state='CA'
```

Here's the result:

```
Msg 550, Level 16, State 2
The attempted insert or update failed because the target view either
specifies WITH CHECK OPTION or spans a view which specifies WITH
CHECK OPTION and one or more rows resulting from the operation did
not qualify under the CHECK OPTION constraint.
Command has been aborted.

SELECT stor_id, stor_name, state
FROM WA_stores
```

And the final result:

```
stor_id    stor_name                                 state
-------    ------------------------------------      -----
6380       Eric the Read Books                       WA
7131       Doc-U-Mat: Quality Laundry and Books      WA
(2 rows affected)
```

Reenabling Integrity Constraints

To demonstrate a point in the preceding section, we disabled foreign key checks on the *titleauthor* table. When you're reenabling constraints, make sure that no rows violate the constraints. By default, when you add a new constraint, SQL Server automatically checks for violations, and the constraint won't be added until the data is cleaned up and such violations are eliminated. You can suppress this check by using the NOCHECK option. With this option, when you reenable an existing constraint that has just been disabled, SQL Server doesn't recheck the constraint's relationships.

After reenabling a disabled constraint, adding a new constraint with the NOCHECK option, or performing a bulk load operation without specifying the CHECK CONSTRAINTS option, you should check to see that constraints have been satisfied. Otherwise, the next time a row is updated, you might get an error suggesting that the constraint has been violated, even if the update at that time seems to have nothing to do with that specific constraint.

419

You can query for constraint violations using subqueries of the type discussed in Chapter 7. You must formulate a separate query to check for every constraint, which can be tedious if you have many constraints. It's sometimes easier to issue a dummy update, setting the columns equal to themselves, to be sure that all constraints are valid. If the table has many constraints and you think that none are likely to have been violated, doing the dummy update can be a convenient way to confirm, in one fell swoop, that all constraints are satisfied. If no errors result, you know that *all* constraints are satisfied.

Note that if FOREIGN KEY constraints exist, the dummy update actually resets the values. This update is performed as a delete/insert operation (which we'll see a bit later in this chapter). Although a dummy update can be a convenient way to test all constraints, it might be inappropriate for your environment because a lengthy operation could fill up the transaction log. If a violation occurs, you'll still need to do queries to pinpoint the violation. The dummy update doesn't isolate the offending rows—it only tells you that a constraint was violated.

In an earlier example, we disabled the constraints on the *titleauthor* table and updated one row in such a way that the FOREIGN KEY constraint was violated. Here's an example in which we reenable the constraints on *titleauthor* and then do a dummy update, which reveals the constraint failure:

```
-- Reenable constraints. Note this does not check the validity
-- of the constraints.
ALTER TABLE titleauthor
    CHECK CONSTRAINT ALL
GO

-- Do a dummy update to check the constraints
UPDATE titleauthor
SET au_id=au_id, title_id=title_id

 Msg 547, Level 16, State 2
UPDATE statement conflicted with COLUMN FOREIGN KEY constraint
'FK__titleauth__au_id__1312E04B'. The conflict occurred in database
'pubs', table 'authors', column 'au_id'
Command has been aborted.
```

The constraint failure occurred because of the foreign key reference to the *authors* table. We know that it must be a case of an *au_id* value in the *titleauthor* table that has no match in *authors,* but we don't know which are the offending rows. Chapter 7 shows you a few approaches for finding such nonmatching rows. One of the most useful approaches is to use an outer join and then restrict the results to show only the rows that had to be fabricated for preservation on the outer-join side. These rows are the nonmatching rows—exactly the ones we're interested in:

```
SELECT A.au_id, TA.au_id
FROM authors AS A RIGHT OUTER JOIN titleauthor
    AS TA ON (A.au_id=TA.au_id)
WHERE A.au_id IS NULL
```

```
au_id     au_id
-----     -----
NULL      899-46-2035
NULL      899-46-2035
```

Data Modification Internals

In Chapter 6, we examined how SQL Server stores data. Now we'll look at what SQL Server actually does internally when data is modified. We've already discussed (in Chapters 3 and 6) clustered indexes and how they control space usage within SQL Server. As a rule of thumb, you should *always* have a clustered index on a table. Only a couple of cases exist in which you would *not* have one. In Chapter 14, when we look at the query optimizer, we'll examine the benefits and tradeoffs of clustered and nonclustered indexes and establish some guidelines for their use. In this chapter, we'll look only at how SQL Server deals with the existence of indexes when processing data modification statements.

Inserting Rows

When inserting new rows into a table, SQL Server must determine where to put that row. When a table has no clustered index (we'll refer to this kind of table as a *heap*), a new row is always inserted wherever room is available in the table. In Chapter 5, we looked at how IAMs and the PFS pages keep track of which extents in a file already belong to a table, and which of the pages in those extents have space available. Even without a clustered index, space management is quite efficient. If no pages with space are available, SQL Server must allocate a whole new extent to the table. Chapter 5 also discussed how the GAMs and SGAMs were used to find extents available to be allocated to an object.

A clustered index directs an insert to a specific page, determined by which value the new row has for the clustered index key columns. This insert occurs when the new row is the direct result of an INSERT statement or when it's the result of an UPDATE statement executed via a delete-followed-by-insert

(delete/insert) strategy. New rows are inserted into their clustered position, splic-
ing in a page via a page split if the current page has no room. We saw in Chapters 3 and 6 that if a clustered index isn't declared as unique, and duplicate values
are inserted for a key, an automatic uniqueifier is generated for all subsequent
rows with the same key. Earlier versions of SQL Server allowed duplicates of a
clustered index key value, and if all the rows with the same key values wouldn't
fit on the same page, SQL Server used a special kind of page called an *overflow
page*. In SQL Server 7, overflow pages aren't needed because all clustered index keys are forced to be unique.

Because the clustered index dictates a particular ordering for the rows in
a table, every new row has a specific location where it belongs. If there's no room
for the new row on the page where it belongs, you must allocate a new page
and link it into the list of pages. If possible, this new page will be allocated from
the same extent as the other pages to which it will be linked. If the extent is full,
a new extent (eight pages, or 64 KB) is allocated to the object. As described in
Chapter 5, SQL Server uses the GAM pages to find an available extent.

Splitting Pages

After SQL Server finds the new page, the original page must be split; half the
rows are left on the original page and half are moved to the new page. In some
cases, SQL Server finds that even after the split, there's no room for the new
row, which, because of variable-length fields, could potentially be much larger
than any of the existing rows on the pages. After the split, one or two rows are
promoted to the parent page.

An index tree is always searched from the root down, so during an insert
operation, it is split on the way down. This means that while the index is being
searched on an insert, the index is being protected in anticipation of possibly
being updated. A parent node (not a leaf node) is latched until the child node is
known to be available for its own latch. Then the parent latch can be released safely.

Before the latch on a parent node is released, SQL Server determines
whether the page will accommodate another two rows and splits it if not. This
occurs only if the page is being searched with the objective of adding a row to
the index. The goal is to ensure that the parent page always has room for the
row or rows that result from a child page splitting. (Occasionally, this results in
pages being split that don't need to be—at least not yet. In the long run, it's a
performance optimization.) Three types of splits can occur, depending on the
type of page being split: root page of an index, intermediate index page, and
data page.

Splitting the Root Page of an Index

If the root page of an index needs to split in order to insert a new index row, two new pages are allocated to the index. All the rows from the root are split between these two new pages, and the new index row is inserted into the appropriate place on one of these pages. The original root page is still the root, but now it has only two rows on it, pointing to each of the newly allocated pages. A root page split creates a new level in the index. Because indexes are usually only a few levels deep, this type of split doesn't occur often.

Splitting the Intermediate Index Page

An intermediate index page split is accomplished simply by locating the midpoint of the index keys on the page, allocating a new page, and then copying the lower half of the old index page into the new page. Again, this doesn't occur often, although it's more common than splitting the root page.

Splitting the Data Page

A data page split is the most interesting and potentially common case, and it's probably the only split that you, as a developer, should be concerned with. Data pages split only under insert activity and only when a clustered index exists on the table. If no clustered index exists, the insert goes on any page where there's room for the new row, according to the PFS pages. Although splits are caused only by insert activity, that activity can be a result of an UPDATE statement, not just an INSERT statement. As you're about to learn in detail, if the row can't be updated in place or at least on the same page, the update is performed as a delete of the original row followed by an insert of the new version of the row. The insertion of the new row can, of course, cause a page split.

Splitting a data page is a complicated operation. Much like an intermediate index page split, it's accomplished by locating the midpoint of the index keys on the data page, allocating a new page, and then copying half of the old page into the new page. It requires that the index manager determine the page on which to locate the new row and then handle large rows that don't fit on either the old page or the new page. When a data page is split, the clustered index key values don't change, so the nonclustered indexes aren't affected.

Let's look at what happens to a page when it splits. The following script creates a table with large rows, so big, in fact, that only five rows will fit on a page. Once the table is created and populated with five rows, we'll find its first page by looking at the *sysindexes.first* column. As discussed in Chapter 6, we'll convert the address of the first page of the table to a decimal value and then use DBCC PAGE to look at the contents of the page. Because we don't need to see all 8000 bytes of data on the page, we'll look at only the row offset array at the end of the page, and then see what happens to those rows when we insert a sixth row.

```
/* First create the table */
use pubs
go
drop table bigrows
go
create table bigrows
(a int  primary key,
 b varchar(1600))
go
/* Insert five rows into the table */
insert into bigrows
 values (5, replicate('a', 1600))

insert into bigrows
 values (10, replicate('b', 1600))

insert into bigrows
 values (15, replicate('c', 1600))

insert into bigrows
 values (20, replicate('d', 1600))

insert into bigrows
 values (25, replicate('e', 1600))

go
select first from sysindexes where id = object_id ('bigrows')
go
/* Convert the value returned to a decimal by byte-swapping
   and then doing a hex-to-decimal conversion on the last four
   bytes. See Chapter 6 for details. For our example,
   we'll assume the converted value is decimal 249. */

dbcc traceon(3604)
go
dbcc page(pubs, 1, 249, 1, 1)
go
```

Here is the row offset array from the results:

```
Row - Offset
4 (0x4) - 6556 (0x199c)
3 (0x3) - 4941 (0x134d)
2 (0x2) - 3326 (0xcfe)
```

```
1 (0x1) - 1711 (0x6af)
0 (0x0) - 96 (0x60)
```

Now insert one more row, and look at the row offset array again.

```
insert into bigrows
 values (22, replicate('x', 1600))
go
dbcc page(pubs, 1, 249,1,1)
go
```

When inspecting the original page after the split, you might find it contains either the first half of the rows from the original page or the second half. SQL Server will normally move the rows so that the new row to be inserted goes on the new page. Since the rows are moving anyway, it makes more sense to adjust their positions to accommodate the new inserted row. In this example, the new row, with a clustered key value of 22, would have been inserted in the second half of the page. So when the page split appears, the first three rows stay on the original page 249. You need to inspect the page header to find the location of the next page, which contains the new row.

The page number is indicated by the field called *m_nextPage*. This value is expressed as a *file number:page number* pair, in decimal, so we can easily use it with the DBCC PAGE command. When we ran this query, we got an *m_nextPage* of 1:179, so we ran the following command:

```
dbcc page(pubs, 1, 179, 1, 1)
```

Here is the row offset array after the insert, for the second page:

```
Row - Offset
2 (0x2) - 1711 (0x6af)
1 (0x1) - 3326 (0xcfe)
0 (0x0) - 96 (0x60)
```

Note a few important points from this output. After the page split, there are three rows on the page: the last two original rows with keys of 20 and 25, and the new row with a key of 22.

If you examine the actual data on the page, you'll notice that the new row with the key of 22 is at slot position 1, even though the row itself is the last one on the page. Slot 1 (with value 22) starts at offset 3326, and slot 2 (with value 25) starts at offset 1711. The clustered key ordering of the rows is indicated by the slot number of the row, not by the physical position on the page. If a clustered index is on the table, the row at slot 1 will always have a key value less than the row at slot 2 and greater than the row at slot 0.

You can also run DBCC PAGE on the first page and see the first three rows in the same position as they were originally.

Although the typical page split isn't too expensive, you'll want to minimize the frequency of page splits in your production system, at least during peak usage times. You can avoid system disruption during busy times by reserving some space on pages using the FILLFACTOR clause when you're creating the clustered index on existing data. You can use this clause to your advantage during your least-busy operational hours by periodically re-creating the clustered index with the desired FILLFACTOR. That way, the extra space is available during your peak usage times, and you'll save the overhead of splitting then. (Using SQL Server Agent, you can easily schedule the rebuilding of indexes to occur at times when activity is lowest.)

NOTE Using the FILLFACTOR setting is helpful only when you're creating the index on existing data; the FILLFACTOR value isn't maintained when inserting new data. Trying to maintain extra space on the page would actually defeat the purpose because you'd need to split pages anyway to keep that amount of space available.

Deleting Rows

When deleting rows from a table, we need to consider what happens both to the data pages and the index pages. Remember that the data is actually the leaf level of a clustered index, and deleting rows from a table with a clustered index happens the same way as deleting rows from the leaf level of a nonclustered index. Deleting rows from a heap table is managed in a different way, as is deleting from node pages of an index.

Deleting Rows from a Heap

Unlike earlier versions of SQL Server, SQL Server 7 doesn't automatically compress space on a page when a row is deleted. As a performance optimization, the compaction doesn't occur until a page needs additional contiguous space for inserting a new row. We can see this in the following example, which deletes a row from the middle of a page and then inspects that page using DBCC PAGE. Figure 8-2 shows the output from DBCC PAGE.

```
use pubs
go
drop table smallrows
go
create table smallrows
(a int identity,
 b char(10))
go
insert into smallrows
 values ('row 1')
```

```
insert into smallrows
 values ( 'row 2')
insert into smallrows
 values ( 'row 3')
insert into smallrows
 values ( 'row 4')
insert into smallrows
 values ( 'row 5')
go
select first from sysindexes where id = object_id ('smallrows ')
go
dbcc traceon(3604)
go
dbcc page(pubs, 1, 248,1,1)
go
```

```
DATA:
Slot = 0                        Offset = 0x60
Record Type = PRIMARY_RECORD
Record Attributes =   NULL_BITMAP
120ec060:  00120010  00000001  20776f72  20202031 ........row 1
120ec070:  00022020         00                    ...
Slot = 1                        Offset = 0x75
Record Type = PRIMARY_RECORD
Record Attributes =   NULL_BITMAP
120ec075:  00120010  00000002  20776f72  20202032 ........row 2
120ec085:  00022020         00                    ...
Slot = 2                        Offset = 0x8a
Record Type = PRIMARY_RECORD
Record Attributes =   NULL_BITMAP
120ec08a:  00120010  00000003  20776f72  20202033 ........row 3
120ec09a:  00022020         00                    ...
Slot = 3                        Offset = 0x9f
Record Type = PRIMARY_RECORD
Record Attributes =   NULL_BITMAP
120ec09f:  00120010  00000004  20776f72  20202034 ........row 4
120ec0af:  00022020         00                    ...
Slot = 4                        Offset = 0xb4
Record Type = PRIMARY_RECORD
Record Attributes =   NULL_BITMAP
120ec0b4:  00120010  00000005  20776f72  20202035 ........row 5
120ec0c4:  00022020         00                    ...

OFFSET TABLE:
Row - Offset
4 (0x4) - 180 (0xb4)
3 (0x3) - 159 (0x9f)
2 (0x2) - 138 (0x8a)
1 (0x1) - 117 (0x75)
0 (0x0) - 96 (0x60)
```

Figure 8-2.
Page contents before a delete.

Now we'll delete the middle row (WHERE a = 3) and look at the page again. Figure 8-3 on the following page contains the output from the second execution of DBCC PAGE.

```
delete from smallrows
where a = 3
go
dbcc page(pubs, 1, 248,1,1)
go
```

```
DATA:
Slot = 0                    Offset = 0x60
Record Type = PRIMARY_RECORD
Record Attributes =   NULL_BITMAP
120ec060:  00120010   00000001  20776f72  20202031 ........row 1
120ec070:  00022020      00                         ...
Slot = 1                    Offset = 0x75
Record Type = PRIMARY_RECORD
Record Attributes =   NULL_BITMAP
120ec075:  00120010   00000002  20776f72  20202032 ........row 2
120ec085:  00022020      00                         ...
Slot = 3                    Offset = 0x9f
Record Type = PRIMARY_RECORD
Record Attributes =   NULL_BITMAP
120ec09f:  00120010   00000004  20776f72  20202034 ........row 4
120ec0af:  00022020      00                         ...
Slot = 4                    Offset = 0xb4
Record Type = PRIMARY_RECORD
Record Attributes =   NULL_BITMAP
120ec0b4:  00120010   00000005  20776f72  20202035 ........row 5
120ec0c4:  00022020      00                         ...

OFFSET TABLE:
Row - Offset
4 (0x4) - 180 (0xb4)
3 (0x3) - 159 (0x9f)
2 (0x2) - 0 (0x0)
1 (0x1) - 117 (0x75)
0 (0x0) - 96 (0x60)
```

Figure 8-3.
Page contents after the delete from a heap.

Note that in the heap table in Figure 8-3, the row doesn't show up in the page itself. The row offset array at the bottom of the page shows that row 3 (at slot 2) is now at offset 0 (which means there really is no row using slot 2), and the row using slot 3 is at its same offset as before the delete. The data on the page is *not* compressed.

Deleting from a B-Tree

In the leaf level of an index, when rows are deleted, they're marked as *ghost* records. This means that the row stays on the page, but a bit is changed in the row header to indicate that the row is really a ghost. The page header also reflects the number of ghost records on a page. Ghost records are primarily a concurrency optimization for key-range locking. The details of key-range locking, as well as all other locking modes, are discussed in Chapter 13, but a short explanation is in order here, just for completeness.

Ghost records are present only in the index leafs. If ghost records weren't used, the entire range surrounding a deleted key would have to be locked. So suppose you had a unique index on an integer and the index contained the values 1, 30, and 100. If you deleted 30, SQL Server would need to lock (and prevent inserts into) the entire range between 1 and 100. With ghosted records, the 30 is still visible to be used as an endpoint of a key-range lock so that during the delete transaction, SQL Server can allow inserts for any other value, other than 30 itself, to proceed. Even after the delete of 30 is committed, the ghost record will still be available for key-range locks to use, providing greater concurrency.

SQL Server provides a special housekeeping thread that periodically checks B-trees for the existence of ghosted records and asynchronously removes them from the leaf level of the index. (This same thread carries out the automatic shrinking of databases if you have that option set. When this thread is active, the Current Activity window in SQL Server Enterprise Manager, or the *sp_who* command, will show you an active process with a *spid* value of 6.)

The following example builds the same table used in the previous DELETE example, but this time the table has a primary key declared, which means a clustered index will be built. The data is the leaf level of the clustered index, so when the row is removed, it will be marked as a ghost. (Figure 8-4 on page 431 shows the output from DBCC PAGE.)

```
use pubs
go
drop table smallrows
go
create table smallrows
(a int identity primary key,
 b char(10))
go
insert into smallrows
 values ('row 1')
insert into smallrows
 values ( 'row 2')
insert into smallrows
 values ( 'row 3')
insert into smallrows
 values ( 'row 4')
insert into smallrows
 values ( 'row 5')
go
select first from sysindexes where id = object_id ('smallrows ')
go
```

(continued)

```
delete from smallrows
where a = 3
go
dbcc page(pubs, 1, 253,1,1)
go
```

Note that in Figure 8-4, because the table has a clustered index, the row still shows up in the page itself. The header information for the row shows that this is really a ghosted record. The row offset array at the bottom of the page shows that the row at slot 2 is still at the same offset and that all rows are in the same location as before the deletion. In addition, the page header gives us a value (*m_ghostRecCnt*) for the number of ghosted records in the page. To see the total count of ghost records in a table, you can enable trace flag 2514. If you then execute the DBCC CHECKTABLE command, you'll see the number of ghost records in that table.

```
DBCC TRACEON (2514)
GO
DBCC CHECKTABLE (smallrows)
```

You'll see results that look like this:

```
DBCC results for 'smallrows'.
There are 4 rows in 1 page for object 'smallrows'.
Ghost Record count = 1
DBCC execution completed. If DBCC printed error messages, contact your
system administrator.
```

Note that the trace flag setting applies only to the current connection. You can force the setting to apply to all connections by enabling the trace flag along with a –1:

```
DBCC TRACEON (2514, -1)
```

Deleting in the Node Levels of an Index

When you delete a row from a table, all nonclustered indexes need to be maintained, because every nonclustered index had a pointer to the row that's now gone. Rows in index node pages aren't ghosted when deleted, but just like heap pages, the space isn't compressed until new index rows need space in that page.

Reclaiming Pages

When the last row is deleted from a data page, the entire page is deallocated. (If the page is the only one remaining in the table, it isn't deallocated. A table always contains at least one page, even if it's empty.) This also results in the deletion of the row in the index page that pointed to the old data page. Index pages are deallocated if an index row is deleted (which again might occur as part of a delete/insert update strategy), leaving only one entry in the index page. That entry is moved to its neighboring page, and then the empty page is deallocated.

The discussion so far has focused on the page manipulation necessary for deleting a single row. If multiple rows are deleted in a single deletion operation, you need to be aware of some other issues. Because the issues of modifying multiple rows in a single query are the same for inserts, updates, and deletes, we'll discuss this issue near the end of the chapter.

```
PAGE HEADER:

Page @0x12048000
----------------
m_pageId = (1:253)         m_headerVersion = 1        m_type = 1
m_typeFlagBits = 0x0       m_level = 0                m_flagBits = 0x8000
m_objId = 18099105         m_indexId = 0              m_prevPage = (0:0)
m_nextPage = (0:0)         pminlen = 18               m_slotCnt = 5
m_freeCnt = 7981           m_freeData = 201           m_reservedCnt = 0
m_lsn = (15:132:2)         m_xactReserved = 0         m_xactId = (0:1083)
m_ghostRecCnt = 1          m_tornBits = 0
GAM (1:2) ALLOCATED, SGAM (1:3) ALLOCATED, PFS (1:1) 0x68 MIXED_EXT
ALLOCATED 0_PCT_FULL

DATA:
Slot = 0                        Offset = 0x60
Record Type = PRIMARY_RECORD
Record Attributes =  NULL_BITMAP
12048060:  00120010  00000001 20776f72  20202031 ........row 1
12048070:  00022020           00                  ...
Slot = 1                        Offset = 0x75
Record Type = PRIMARY_RECORD
Record Attributes =  NULL_BITMAP
12048075:  00120010  00000002 20776f72  20202032 ........row 2
12048085:  00022020           00                  ...
Slot = 2                        Offset = 0x8a
Record Type = GHOST_DATA_RECORD
Record Attributes =  NULL_BITMAP
1204808a:  0012001c  00000003 20776f72  20202033 ........row 3
1204809a:  00022020           00                  ...
Slot = 3                        Offset = 0x9f
Record Type = PRIMARY_RECORD
Record Attributes =  NULL_BITMAP
1204809f:  00120010  00000004 20776f72  20202034 ........row 4
120480af:  00022020           00                  ...
Slot = 4                        Offset = 0xb4
Record Type = PRIMARY_RECORD
Record Attributes =  NULL_BITMAP
120480b4:  00120010  00000005 20776f72  20202035 ........row 5
120480c4:  00022020           00                  ...

OFFSET TABLE:
Row - Offset
4 (0x4) - 180 (0xb4)
3 (0x3) - 159 (0x9f)
2 (0x2) - 138 (0x8a)
1 (0x1) - 117 (0x75)
0 (0x0) - 96 (0x60)
```

Figure 8-4.
Page contents after the delete from a table with a clustered index.

Updating Rows

SQL Server updates rows in multiple ways, automatically and invisibly choosing the fastest update strategy that can be applied for the specific operation. In determining the strategy, SQL Server evaluates the number of rows affected, how the rows will be accessed (via a scan or an index retrieval, and via which index), and whether changes to the index keys will occur. Updates can happen either in place or as a delete followed by an insert. In addition, updates can be managed by the query processor or by the storage engine. In this section, we'll examine only whether the update happens in place. The decision of whether the update is controlled by the query processor or the storage engine is actually relevant to all data modification operations (not just updates), so we'll look at that in a separate section.

Earlier versions of SQL Server could perform either a direct or a deferred update. Deferred meant that the update occurred in two complete passes. The first pass used the transaction log as a holding area, in which SQL Server recorded *all* the changes that were going to be made and marked them as NO-OP (because they weren't actually executed at that time). The second pass would then reread the log and apply the changes. Because all changes—including changes to every nonclustered index—must be recorded twice, this was log intensive. In addition, in earlier versions of SQL Server, any time a row moved, every nonclustered index had to be updated to hold the new location of the row. Deferred updates were by far the slowest kind of update.

In SQL Server 7, no deferred updates exist. All updates are done in a direct mode, without using the transaction log as an intermediate holding area. In addition, because of the way SQL Server 7 maintains nonclustered indexes, the overhead of moving rows, even if the table has multiple nonclustered indexes, is an inexpensive operation.

Moving Rows

What happens if a table row has to move to a new location? In SQL Server 7, this can happen because a row with variable-length columns is updated to a new, larger size so that it no longer fits on the original page. It can also happen when the clustered index column is changing, because rows are stored in order of the clustering key. For example, if we have a clustered index on *lastname*, a row with a *lastname* value of *Abbot* will be stored near the beginning of the table. If the *lastname* value is then updated to *Zappa*, this row will have to move to be near the end of the table.

In Chapter 3, we looked at the structure of indexes and saw that the leaf level of nonclustered indexes contains a row locator for every single row in the table. If the table has a clustered index, that row locator is the clustering key for that row. So if—and only if—the clustered index key is being updated, modifications are required in every nonclustered index. Keep this fact in mind when deciding which columns to build your clustered index on. It's a great idea to cluster on a nonvolatile column.

If a row moves because it no longer fits on the original page, it will still have the same row locator (in other words, the clustering key for the row stays the same), and no nonclustered indexes will have to be modified.

In Chapter 3, we also saw that if a table has no clustered index (in other words, it's a heap), then the row locator stored in the nonclustered index is actually the physical location of the row. In SQL Server 7, if a row in a heap moves to a new page, the row will leave a forwarding pointer in the original location. The nonclustered indexes won't need to be changed; they'll still refer to the original location, and from there they'll be directed to the new location.

Let's look at an example. We'll create a table a lot like the one we created for doing inserts, but this table will have a third column of variable length. After we populate the table with five rows, which will fill the page, we'll update one of the rows to make its third column much longer. The row will no longer fit on the original page and will have to move. Remember that we need to select the *first* column from *sysindexes* to know the address of the page. The value you actually supply to DBCC PAGE depends on the value that *first* returns.

```
use pubs
go
drop table bigrows
go
create table bigrows
(a int identity ,
 b varchar(1600),
 c varchar(1600))
go
insert into bigrows
  values (replicate('a', 1600), '')
insert into bigrows
  values (replicate('b', 1600),'')
insert into bigrows
  values (replicate('c', 1600),'')
insert into bigrows
  values (replicate('d', 1600),'')
```

(continued)

```
insert into bigrows
 values (replicate('e', 1600),'')
go
select first from sysindexes where id = object_id ('bigrows')
go
update bigrows
set c = replicate('x', 1600)
where a = 3
go
dbcc traceon(3604)
go
dbcc page(pubs, 1, 266,1,1)
go
```

We won't show you the entire output from the DBCC PAGE command, but we'll show you what appears in the slot where the row with *a = 3* used to appear:

```
Slot = 2                       Offset = 0x1feb
Record Type = FORWARDING_STUB                      Record Attributes =
11ef3feb:  0000f904  00000100       00          .........
```

The value of 4 in the first byte means this is just a forwarding stub. The 0000f9 in the next 3 bytes is the page number to which the row has been moved. Because this is a hexadecimal value, we need to convert it to 249 decimal. The next group of four bytes tells us the page is at slot 0, file 1. If you then use DBCC PAGE to look at that page 249, you can see what the forwarded record looks like.

Managing Forward Pointers

Forward pointers allow us to modify data in a heap without worrying about having to make drastic changes to the nonclustered indexes. If a row that has been forwarded must move again, the original forwarding pointer is updated to point to the new location. We'll never end up with a forwarding pointer pointing to another forwarding pointer. In addition, if the forwarded row shrinks enough to fit in its original place, the forward pointer is eliminated, and the record moves back to its place.

In a future version of SQL Server, some mechanism might be invented for performing a physical reorganization of the data in a heap, which will get rid of forward pointers. Currently, when a forward pointer is created, it stays there forever—with only two exceptions. The first exception is the case just discussed, when a row shrinks enough to return to its original location. The second exception is when the entire database shrinks. The RIDs (used as the row locators) are actually reassigned when a file is shrunk. The shrink process *never* generates forwarded rows. For those pages removed because of the shrinking process, any forwarded rows or stubs they contain will be effectively "unforwarded."

Updating in Place

Unlike earlier versions of SQL Server, updating a row right in place is the rule rather than the exception in SQL Server 7. This means that the row stays in exactly the same location on the same page, and only the bytes affected are changed. In addition, in most cases of updating in place, the log will contain a single record for each such updated row. The exceptions occur when the table has an update trigger on it or when the table is marked for replication. In these cases, the update still happens in place, but the log contains a delete record followed by an insert record.

In cases where a row can't be updated in place, the cost of a not-in-place update is minimal because of the way the nonclustered indexes are stored and because of the use of forwarding pointers. Updates will happen in place if a heap is being updated or if a table with a clustered index is updated without changing any of the clustering keys.

To see the total count of forwarded records in a table, enable trace flag 2509 and then execute the DBCC CHECKTABLE command:

```
DBCC TRACEON (2509)
GO
DBCC CHECKTABLE (bigrows)
```

You'll see results like this:

```
DBCC results for 'bigrows'.
There are 5 rows in 2 pages for object 'bigrows'.
Forwarded Record count = 1
DBCC execution completed. If DBCC printed error messages, contact
your system administrator.
```

Updating *Not* in Place

If your update can't happen in place because you're updating clustering keys, it will occur as a delete followed by an insert. In some cases, you'll get a hybrid update: some of the rows are updated in place and some aren't. If you're updating index keys, SQL Server will build a list of all the rows that need to change as both a delete and an insert operation. This list is stored in memory, if it's small enough, and is written to *tempdb* if necessary.

This list is then sorted by key value and operator (delete or insert). If the index whose keys are changing isn't unique, the delete and insert steps are then applied to the table. If the index is unique, an additional step is carried out to collapse delete and insert operations on the same key into a single update operation. Let's look at a simple example. The code at the top of the following page builds a table with a unique clustered index on column X and then updates that column in both rows.

```
use pubs
GO
DROP TABLE T1
GO
CREATE TABLE T1(X int primary key, Y int)
INSERT T1 VALUES(1, 10)
INSERT T1 VALUES(2, 20)
GO
UPDATE T1 SET X = 3 - X
GO
```

Table 8-3 shows the operations that SQL Server generates internally for the above update statement. This list of operations is called the *input stream* and consists of both the old and new values of every column and an identifier for each row that is to be changed.

Operation	Original X	Original Y	New X	New Y	Row ID
update	1	10	2	10	ROW1
update	2	20	1	20	ROW2

Table 8-3.
A SQL Server input stream for an update operation.

However, in this case the updates must be split into delete and insert operations. If they aren't, the update to the first row, changing *X* from 1 to 2, will fail with a duplicate-key violation. So a converted input stream is generated and looks like Table 8-4.

Operation	Original X	Original Y	Row ID
delete	1	10	ROW1
insert	2	10	<null>
delete	2	20	ROW2
insert	1	20	<null>

Table 8-4.
Converted input stream for an update operation.

Note that for insert operations, the RID isn't relevant in the input stream of operations to be performed. Before a row is inserted, it has no RID. This input stream is then sorted by index key and operation, as in Table 8-5.

Operation	X	Y	Row ID
delete	1	10	ROW1
insert	1	20	<null>
delete	2	20	ROW2
insert	2	10	<null>

Table 8-5.
Input stream sorted by index key and operation.

Finally, if the same key value has both a delete and an insert, the two rows in the input stream are collapsed into an update operation. So the final input stream looks like Table 8-6.

Operation	Original X	Original Y	New X	New Y	Row ID
update	1	10	1	20	ROW1
update	2	20	2	10	ROW2

Table 8-6.
The final output stream for an update operation.

Note that, although the original query was an update to column X, after the split, sort, and collapse of the input stream the final set of actions looks like we're updating column Y! This method of actually carrying out the update ensures that no intermediate violations of the index's unique key occur.

Part of the graphical query plan for this update (Figure 8-5 on the following page) shows you the split, sort, and collapse phases. We'll be looking at query plans and the mechanisms for examining query plans in Chapter 14.

Updates to any nonclustered index keys also affect the leaf level of the index by splitting the operation into deletes and inserts. Think of the leaf level of a nonclustered index as a mini–clustered index, so any modification of the key could potentially affect the sequence of values in the leaf level. Just like for the data in a clustered index, the actual type of update is determined by whether the index is unique or not. If the nonclustered index is nonunique, the update is split into delete and insert operators. If the nonclustered index is unique, the split is followed by a sort and an attempt to collapse any deletes and inserts on the same key back into an update operation.

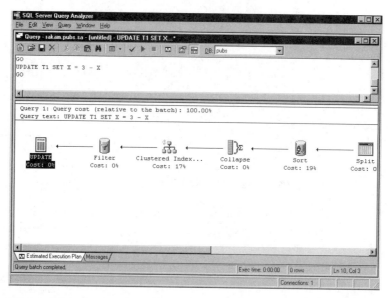

Figure 8-5.
The update query plan displayed graphically.

Table-Level vs. Index-Level Data Modification

We've just considered the placement and index manipulation necessary for modifying either a single row or only a few rows with no more than a single index. If you are modifying multiple rows in a single insertion operation (insert, update, or delete) or by using BCP or the BULK INSERT command, and the table has multiple indexes, you must be aware of some other issues. In SQL Server 7, two different strategies exist to maintain all the indexes that belong to a table. The query optimizer chooses between them based on its estimate of the anticipated execution costs for each strategy.

The two strategies are called table-level modification and index-level modification. Table level is sometimes called *row at a time,* and index level is sometimes called *index at a time.* In a table-level modification, all indexes are maintained for each row as that row is modified. If the update stream isn't sorted in any way, SQL Server will have to do a lot of random index accesses, one access per index per update row. If the update stream is sorted, it can't be sorted in more than one order; therefore, there might be nonrandom index accesses for at most, one index.

In index-level modifications, SQL Server gathers all the rows to be modified and sorts them for each index. In other words, there are as many sort operations as there are indexes. Then, for each index, the updates are merged into the index, and each index page will never be accessed more than once, even if multiple updates pertain to a single index leaf page.

438

Clearly, if the update is small, say less than a handful of rows, and the table and its indexes are sizable, then the query optimizer usually considers table level the best choice. Most OLTP operations will use table-level modifications. On the other hand, if the update is relatively large, table-level modifications require a lot of random I/O operations and might even read and write each leaf page in each index multiple times. In that case, index-level modification performs much better. The amount of logging required is the same for both strategies.

Let's look at a specific example with some actual numbers. Suppose you use BULK INSERT to increase the size of a table by 1 percent (which could correspond to one week in a two-year sales history table). The table is stored in a heap (no clustered index), and the rows are simply appended at the end because there is not much available space on other pages in the table. There's nothing to sort on for insertion into the heap, and the rows (and the required new heap pages and extents) are simply appended at the end of the heap. Assume also that there are two nonclustered indexes on columns a and b. The insert stream is sorted on column a and merged into the index on a.

If an index entry is 20 bytes long, an 8 KB page filled at 70 percent (which is the natural, self-stabilizing value in a B-tree after lots of random insertions and deletions) would contain 8 KB * 70% / 20 bytes = 280 entries. Eight pages (one extent) would then contain 2240 entries, presuming leaf pages are nicely laid out in extents. A 1 percent table growth implies, on average, 2.8 new entries per page, or 22.4 new entries per extent.

Table-level (row-at-a-time) insertion would touch each page, on average, 2.8 times. Unless the buffer pool is large, row-at-a-time insertion reads, updates, and writes each page 2.8 times. That is 5.6 I/O operations per page, or 44.8 I/O operations per extent. Index-at-a-time reads, updates, and writes each page (and extent, again presuming a nice contiguous layout) exactly once. In the best case, about 45 page I/O operations have been replaced by 2 extent I/O operations, for each extent. Of course, the cost of doing the insert this way also includes the cost of sorting the inputs for each index. But the much-reduced cost of the index-level strategy can easily dwarf the cost of sorting.

NOTE Earlier versions of SQL Server always recommended that you drop all your indexes if you were going to import a lot of rows into a table using a bulkcopy interface, because no index-level strategy existed for maintaining all the indexes.

You can determine whether your updates were done at the table level or the index level by inspecting the SHOWPLAN output. (Query plans and SHOWPLAN will be discussed in more detail in Chapter 14.) If SQL Server performs the update at the index level, you'll see a plan produced that contains an update operator for each of the affected indexes. If SQL Server performs the update at the table level, you'll see only a single update operator in the plan.

Logging

Standard INSERT, UPDATE, and DELETE statements are always logged to ensure atomicity, and you can't disable logging of these operations. The modification must be known to be safely on disk in the transaction log (write-ahead logging) before the commit of the statement or transaction can be acknowledged to the calling application. Page allocations and deallocations, including those done by TRUNCATE TABLE, are also logged. You can specify a few unlogged operations by enabling the *select into/bulkcopy* option. These unlogged operations are available for faster bulk loading of data.

Locking

Any data modification must always be protected with some form of exclusive lock. For the most part, SQL Server makes all the locking decisions internally; a user or programmer doesn't need to request a particular kind of lock. Chapter 13 explains the different types of locks and their compatibility. Chapter 14 discusses techniques for overriding SQL Server's default locking behavior. However, because locking is closely tied to data modification, you should always be aware of the following:

- Every type of data modification performed in SQL Server requires some form of exclusive lock. For most data modification operations, SQL Server considers row locking as the default, but if many locks are required, this could escalate to page locks or even a full table lock.

- Update locks can be used to signal the intention to do an update and are important to avoiding deadlock conditions. But ultimately, the UPDATE operation requires that an exclusive lock be performed. The update lock serializes access to ensure that an exclusive lock will be able to be acquired, but the update lock isn't sufficient by itself.

- Exclusive locks must always be held until the end of a transaction in case the transaction needs to be undone (unlike shared locks, which can be released as soon as the scan moves off the page, assuming READ COMMITTED isolation is in effect).

- If a full table scan must be employed to find qualifying rows for an update or a delete, SQL Server has to inspect every row to determine the row to modify. Other processes that need to find individual rows will be blocked even if they are ultimately going to modify different rows. Without inspecting the row, SQL Server has no way of knowing whether the row qualifies for the modification or not. If you're modifying only a subset of rows in the table, as determined by a WHERE clause, make sure that you have indexes available to allow SQL Server to access the needed rows directly and not have to scan every row in the table. (We'll talk about how to choose the best indexes for your tables in Chapter 14.) Doing full table scans to modify rows isn't going to result in a high-concurrency environment.

Summary

This chapter covered data modification within SQL Server. You modify most data using the three SQL DML statements: INSERT, UPDATE, and DELETE. Although you can typically think of INSERT as affecting only one row, SQL Server provides several forms of INSERT that can insert an entire result set at once. In addition, SQL Server offers utilities and interfaces for fast bulk loading of data. UPDATE and DELETE operations can be searched operations, bringing to bear all the power of the SQL query language to specify which rows are to be modified.

We also looked at some internal considerations, including the placement of rows in tables, logging, locking, and space usage. We discussed several possible update methods, along with examples illustrating the various update strategies.

Next we'll study Transact-SQL extensions, which offer the kind of power normally associated with programming languages.

PROGRAMMING WITH TRANSACT-SQL

Microsoft Transact-SQL allows you to use standard SQL as a programming language to write logic that can execute within the database engine. This extremely powerful capability is one of the keys to the success and growth of Microsoft SQL Server. Transact-SQL simplifies application development and reduces the amount of conversation necessary between the client application and the server by allowing more code to be processed at the server.

In this book, we won't delve into all the available syntax of the Transact-SQL language. We'll leave that to the SQL Server documentation. Instead, we'll see the significant programming constructs available, along with some comments and examples. In Chapter 7, "Querying Data," we examined the SELECT statement, which is the foundation for effective use of Transact-SQL. Before reading any further, be sure you have a good understanding of the concepts presented in that chapter.

This chapter focuses on the Transact-SQL programming extensions, such as control of flow, looping, error handling, and environment-specific options. These extensions allow you to easily write complex routines entirely in SQL, and they provide the basis for the additional power of Transact-SQL over standard SQL. In Chapter 10, we'll look at cover batches, transactions, stored procedures, and triggers. Chapter 11 deals with cursors, which bridge the set-based world of SQL with sequential processing. In Chapter 12, we'll look at some extensive Transact-SQL examples that sometimes use Transact-SQL in nonintuitive ways. For those of you interested in developing applications using SQL Server, all of these chapters provide important information.

Transact-SQL as a Programming Language

Is Transact-SQL really a programming language? On the one hand, Microsoft doesn't claim that Transact-SQL is an alternative to C, C++, Microsoft Visual Basic, COBOL, Fortran, or such 4GL development environments as

PowerBuilder or Delphi. You'd be hard-pressed to think of a substantial application that you could write entirely in Transact-SQL, and every one of those other languages or tools exists to do exactly that. Also, Transact-SQL offers no user interface and no file or device I/O, and the programming constructs are simple and limited.

On the other hand, you can still argue that, yes, Transact-SQL *is* a specialized language, which is best used in addition to one of those other languages or tools. It allows SQL Server to be programmed to execute complex tasks requiring branching and looping without the need for code to be written in another language. Transact-SQL provides the services to declare and set variables, to branch, to loop, and to check errors. You can write reusable routines that you subsequently invoke and pass variables to. You can introduce bugs if you make an error in logic or syntax. Your Transact-SQL code can quickly get so complicated that you will be glad you can use the same debugger you use for C, C++, and Java development to debug Transact-SQL routines.

With Transact-SQL routines, conditional logic executes within the SQL Server engine and even within an executing SQL statement. This can greatly improve performance—the alternative would be message-passing between the client process and the server. In today's increasingly networked world, reducing round-trip conversations is key to developing and deploying efficient applications. Some might claim that the emergence of the Internet makes client/server computing irrelevant. But in fact, the typically slow network conditions found in Internet applications make client/server computing *more important*—operations should be written so that the client/server conversation is minimized. The best way to do this is to use the programming aspects of Transact-SQL to let whole routines execute remotely, without the need for intermediate processing at the client. The corresponding performance gains are phenomenal.

In addition, by having SQL Server (rather than the application) handle the database logic, applications can often better insulate themselves from change. An application can execute a procedure simply by calling it and passing some parameters, and then the database structure or the procedure can change radically while the application remains entirely unaffected. As long as the inputs and outputs of the procedure are unchanged, the application is shielded from underlying changes to the database. Being able to encapsulate the database routines can result in a more efficient development environment for large projects in which the application programmers are often distinct from the database experts.

Programming at Multiple Levels

In the early days of database management systems, a single computer handled all processing—what we now call the *one-tier model*. The advent of client/server computing introduced the classic *two-tier model*: a server that receives requests from and provides data to a separate client. The newest approach, the *three-tier model*, places an intermediate layer between the database server and the client application.

The three-tier model has gained supporters who view the model as preferable—for some applications—to the more traditional two-tier client/server model. Figures 9-1 and 9-2 show both models.

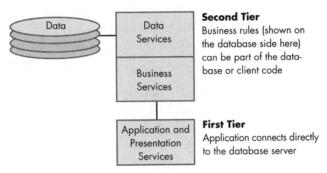

Figure 9-1.
The two-tier model.

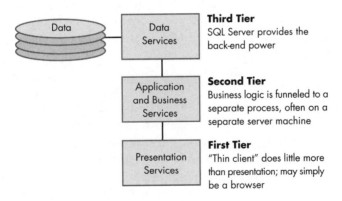

Figure 9-2.
The three-tier model.

The two-tier model has a client (first tier) and a server (second tier); the client handles application and presentation logic, and the server handles data services and business services. The two-tier model uses the so-called *fat client*—the client does a large amount of application processing locally. Many solutions deployed use this topology; certainly the lion's share of today's non-Internet client/server solutions are two-tier.

In the three-tier model, a *thin client* handles mostly presentation tasks. Supporters of the three-tier approach point out that this model allows the client computer to be less powerful; allows a variety of different client operating environments (obviously the case with Internet browsers); and reduces the complexity of installing, configuring, and maintaining software at the client. The client connects to an application server that handles the application process. The application server then connects to the database server, handling data services. The application server is typically a more powerful machine than the client, and it has all the issues of application code maintenance, configuration, operations, and so on.

Presumably, far fewer application servers exist than clients; therefore, server costs and issues should be reduced in the three-tier model. (The three tiers are logical concepts; the actual number of computers involved might be more or less than three.) Typically, you're part of a three-tier model when you use the Internet with a browser and access a Web page residing on an Internet server that performs database work. An example of a three-tier application is a mail-order company's Web page that checks current availability by using ODBC calls to access its inventory in SQL Server.

Both two-tier and three-tier solutions have advantages and disadvantages, and each can be viewed as a potential solution to a given problem. The specifics of the problem and the constraints imposed by the environment (including costs, hardware, and expertise of both the development staff and the user community) should drive the solution's overall design. However, some people claim that a three-tier solution means that such capabilities as stored procedures, rules, constraints, or triggers are no longer important or shouldn't be used. In a three-tier solution, the middle tier doing application logic is still a client from the perspective of the database services (that is, SQL Server). Consequently, for that tier, it's still preferable that remote work be done close to the data. If the data can be accessed by servers other than the application server, integrity checking must be done at the database server as well as in the application. (Otherwise, you've left a gaping hole through which the integrity checks in the application can be circumvented.)

> ### A Three-Tier Solution That Works
>
> Perhaps the single most successful three-tier solution available today
> is R/3 from SAP. The financial and operations capabilities that R/3
> provides use a three-tier model, with a terminal-like interface connected
> to the R/3 application server that then accesses Microsoft SQL Server.
> (R/3 supports several different database systems, but here we're em-
> phasizing the solution's topology when using SQL Server.) The R/3
> application server wisely and heavily uses stored procedures that pro-
> vide both performance gains and development efficiency.

Throughout the remainder of this book, unless otherwise noted, we'll use
the term *client* from the perspective of SQL Server. The client sends the commands
and processes the results, and it makes no difference to SQL Server whether an
application server process does this or whether the process that the end user is
running directly does it. The benefits of the programmable server provide much
more efficient network use and better abstraction of data services from the
application and application server.

Transact-SQL Programming Constructs—The Basics

Transact-SQL extends standard SQL by adding many useful programming
constructs. These constructs will look familiar to developers experienced with
C/C++, Basic/Microsoft Visual Basic, Fortran, Java, Pascal, and similar languages. The Transact-SQL extensions are wonderful additions to the original
SQL standard. Before the extensions were available, requests to the database
were always simple, single statements. Any conditional logic had to be provided
by the calling application. With a slow network or via the Internet, this would
be disastrous, requiring many trips across the network—more than are needed
by simply letting conditions be evaluated at the server and allowing subsequent
branching of execution.

Variables

Without variables, a programming language wouldn't be particularly useful;
Transact-SQL is no exception. Variables that you declare are *local variables,*
having scope and visibility only within the batch or stored procedure in which

you declare them. (The next chapter discusses the details of batches and stored procedures.) In code, the single @ character designates a local variable.

Transact-SQL has no true global variables. Older documentation refers to certain parameterless system functions as *global variables* because they're designated by @@, which is similar to the designation for local variables. We'll look at these in a little more detail at the end of the chapter, in the section on system functions.

User-declared global variables would be a nice enhancement that we might see in a future release. Until then, temporary tables provide a decent alternative for sharing values among connections.

Local Variables

You declare local variables at the beginning of a batch or a stored procedure. (The batch or stored procedure can be part of a transaction as well.) You can subsequently assign values to local variables either with the SELECT statement or the SET statement, using an equal (=) operator. The values you assign using the SET statement can be constants, other variables, or expressions. When assigning to a variable using a SELECT statement, the values to be assigned are typically selected from a column in a table. The syntax for declaring and using the variables is identical, regardless of the method you use to assign the values to the variable. In the following example, we declare a variable, assign it a value using the SET statement, and then use that variable in a WHERE clause:

```
DECLARE @limit money
SET @limit = $10
SELECT * FROM titles
WHERE price <= @limit
```

We could have written the same code using the SELECT statement instead of the SET statement. However, you typically use SELECT when the values to be assigned are found in a column of a table. A SELECT statement used to assign values to one or more variables is called an *assignment SELECT*. You can't combine the functionality of the assignment SELECT and a "regular" SELECT in the same statement. That is, if a SELECT statement is used to assign values to variables, it can't also return values to the client as a result set. In the following simple example, we declare two variables, assign values to them from the *roysched* table, and then select their values as a result set.

```
DECLARE @min_range int, @hi_range int        -- Variables declared
SELECT  @min_range=MIN(lorange),
        @hi_range=MAX(hirange) FROM roysched  -- Variables assigned
SELECT  @min_range, @hi_range                 -- Variables returned
```

Note that a single DECLARE statement can declare multiple variables. When using a SELECT statement for assigning values, we can assign more than one value at a time. When using SET to assign values to variables, we must use a separate SET statement for each variable. For example, the following SET statement will return an error:

```
SET @min_range = 0, @hi_range = 100
```

Be careful when assigning variables by selecting a value from the database— you want to ensure that the SELECT statement will return only one row. It's perfectly legal to assign a variable to a SELECT statement that will return multiple rows, but the variable's value probably isn't what you expect: no error message is returned, and the variable has the value of the last row returned.

For example, suppose that the following *stor_name* values exist in the *stores* table of the *pubs* database:

```
stor_name
---------
Eric the Read Books
Barnum's
News & Brews
Doc-U-Mat: Quality Laundry and Books
Fricative Bookshop
Bookbeat
```

The following assignment runs without error but is probably a mistake:

```
DECLARE @stor_name varchar(30)
SELECT @stor_name=stor_name FROM stores
```

The resulting value of *@stor_name* is the last row, *Bookbeat*. But consider the order returned, without an ORDER BY clause, as a chance occurrence. Assigning a variable to a SELECT statement that returns more than one row usually wouldn't be intended, and it's probably a bug introduced by the developer. To avoid this situation, you should qualify the SELECT statement with an appropriate WHERE clause to limit the result set to the one row that meets your criteria.

Alternatively, you can use an aggregate function, such as MAX(), MIN(), or SUM(), to limit the number of rows returned. Then you can select only the value you want. If you want the assignment to be to only one row of a SELECT statement that might return many rows (and it's not important which row that is), you should at least use SET ROWCOUNT 1 or SELECT TOP 1 to avoid the effort of gathering many rows, with all but one row thrown out. (In this case, the first row would be returned, not the last. You could use ORDER BY to explicitly indicate which row should be first.) You might also consider checking the value of @@ROWCOUNT immediately after the assignment and, if it's greater than 1, branch off to an error routine.

Also be aware that if the SELECT statement assigning a value to a variable doesn't return any rows, nothing will be assigned. The variable will keep whatever value it had before the assignment SELECT statement was run. For example, suppose we use the same variable twice to find the first names of authors with a particular last name:

```
DECLARE @firstname varchar(20)
SELECT @firstname = au_fname
FROM authors
WHERE au_lname = 'Greene'
SELECT @firstname  -- return the first name as a result
SELECT @firstname = au_fname
FROM authors
WHERE au_lname = 'Delaney'
SELECT @firstname  -- return the first name as a result
```

If you run the previous code, you'll see the same first name returned both times, because no authors with the last name of Delaney exist, at least not in the *pubs* database!

You can also assign a value to a variable in an UPDATE statement. This approach can be useful and more efficient than using separate statements to swap values. For example, suppose that in the *jobs* table, we realize the *min* and *max* columns have accidentally been reversed. The following UPDATE statement efficiently swaps all the values. (To run this example, you must disable the CHECK constraints on the *min_lvl* and *max_lvl* columns.)

```
DECLARE @tmp_val tinyint
BEGIN TRAN
UPDATE jobs SET @tmp_val=min_lvl, min_lvl=max_lvl,
    max_lvl=@tmp_val
```

Control-of-Flow Tools

Like any programming language worth its salt, Transact-SQL provides a decent set of control-of-flow tools. (True, Transact-SQL has only a handful of tools, perhaps not as many as you'd like, but they're enough to make it dramatically more powerful than standard SQL.) The control-of-flow tools include conditional logic (IF...ELSE and CASE), loops (only WHILE, but it comes with CONTINUE and BREAK options), unconditional branching (GOTO), and the ability to return a status value to a calling routine (RETURN). Table 9-1 presents a quick summary of these control-of-flow constructs, which you'll see used at various times in this book.

Construct	Description
BEGIN...END	Defines a statement block. Using BEGIN...END allows a group of statements to be executed. Typically, BEGIN immediately follows IF, ELSE, or WHILE. (Otherwise, only the next statement will be executed.) For C programmers, BEGIN...END is similar to using a {..} block after IF.
GOTO label	Continues processing at the statement following the specified label.
IF...ELSE	Defines conditional and, optionally, alternate execution when a condition is false.
RETURN [n]	Exits unconditionally. Typically used in a stored procedure or trigger (although it can also be used in a batch). Optionally, a whole number n (positive or negative) can be set as the return status, which can be assigned to a variable when executing the stored procedure.
WAITFOR	Sets a time for statement execution. The time can be a delay interval (up to 24 hours) or a specific time of day. The time can be supplied as a literal or with a variable.
WHILE	The basic looping construct for SQL Server. Repeats a statement (or block) while a specific condition is true.
...BREAK	Exits the innermost WHILE loop.
...CONTINUE	Restarts a WHILE loop.

Table 9-1.

Control-of-flow constructs in Transact-SQL.

CASE

The CASE expression is enormously powerful. Although CASE is part of the ANSI SQL-92 specification, it's not required for ANSI compliance certification, and few products other than Microsoft SQL Server have implemented it. If you have experience with an SQL database system other than Microsoft SQL Server, chances are you haven't used CASE. If that's the case (pun intended), you should get familiar with it now. It's time well spent. CASE was added in version 6.0, and once you get used to using it, you'll wonder how SQL programmers ever managed without it.

CASE is a conceptually simpler way to do IF-ELSE IF-ELSE IF-ELSE IF-ELSE–type operations. It's roughly equivalent to a *switch* statement in C. However, CASE is far more than a shorthand for IF—in fact, it's not really even that. CASE is an expression, not a control-of-flow keyword, which means that it can be used *only* inside other statements. You can use CASE in a SELECT statement in the SELECT list, in a GROUP BY clause, or in an ORDER BY clause. You can use it in the SET clause of an UPDATE statement. You can include CASE in the values list for an INSERT statement. You can also use CASE in a WHERE clause in any SELECT, UPDATE, or DELETE statement. Anywhere that T-SQL expects an expression, you can use CASE to determine the value of that expression.

Here's a simple example of CASE. Suppose that we want to classify books in the *pubs* database by price. We want to segregate them as low priced, moderately priced, or expensive. And we'd like to do this with a single SELECT statement and not use UNION. Without CASE, we can't do it. With CASE, it's a snap:

```
SELECT
title,
price,
'classification'=CASE
    WHEN price < 10.00 THEN 'Low Priced'
    WHEN price BETWEEN 10.00 AND 20.00 THEN 'Moderately Priced'
    WHEN price > 20.00 THEN 'Expensive'
    ELSE 'Unknown'
    END
FROM titles
```

Notice that even in this example, we need to worry about NULL, because a NULL price won't fit into any of the category buckets.

Following are the abbreviated results.

```
title                                      price   classification
-------------------------------------      ------  -----------------
The Busy Executive's Database Guide         19.99   Moderately Priced
Cooking with Computers: Surreptitious       11.95   Moderately Priced
Balance Sheets
You Can Combat Computer Stress!              2.99   Low Priced
Straight Talk About Computers               19.99   Moderately Priced
Silicon Valley Gastronomic Treats           19.99   Moderately Priced
The Gourmet Microwave                        2.99   Low Priced
The Psychology of Computer Cooking          NULL    Unknown
But Is It User Friendly?                    22.95   Expensive
```

If all the conditions after your WHEN clauses are equality comparisons against the same value, you can use an even simpler form so that you don't have to keep repeating the expression. Suppose we want to print the type of each book in the *titles* table in a slightly more user-friendly fashion—for example, *Modern Cooking* instead of *mod_cook*. We could use the following SELECT statement:

```
SELECT
title,
price,
'Type' =
    WHEN type = 'mod_cook' THEN 'Modern Cooking',
    WHEN type = 'trad_cook' THEN 'Traditional Cooking'
    WHEN type = 'psychology' THEN 'Psychology'
    WHEN type = 'business' THEN 'Business'
    WHEN type = 'popular_comp' THEN 'Popular Computing'
    ELSE 'Not yet decided'
    END
FROM titles
```

In this example, because every condition after WHEN is testing for equality with the value in the *type* column, we can use an even simpler form. You can think of this simplification as factoring out the *type =* from every WHEN clause, and place the *type* column at the top of the CASE expression:

```
SELECT
title,
price,
'Type' = type
    WHEN 'mod_cook' THEN 'Modern Cooking',
    WHEN 'trad_cook' THEN 'Traditional Cooking'
    WHEN 'psychology' THEN 'Psychology'
    WHEN 'business' THEN 'Business'
```

(continued)

453

```
        WHEN 'popular_comp' THEN 'Popular Computing''
        ELSE 'Not yet decided'
        END
FROM titles
```

You can use CASE in some unusual places; because it's an expression, you can use it anywhere an expression is legal. Using CASE in a view is a nice technique that can make your database more usable to others. For example, in Chapter 7, we saw CASE in a view using CUBE to shield users from the complexity of "grouping NULL" values. Using CASE in an UPDATE statement can make the update easier. More importantly, CASE can allow you to make changes in a single pass of the data that would otherwise require you to do multiple UPDATE statements, each of which would have to scan the data.

The Transact-SQL documentation for the previous version of SQL Server (6.5) had a nice conceptual example that we've reproduced here. Although it works fine and illustrates CASE, we've rewritten the UPDATE statement with an equivalent formulation that might be more intuitive.

```
-- In this example, reviews have been turned in and big salary
-- adjustments are due. A review rating of 4 will double the
-- worker's salary, 3 will increase it by 60 percent, 2 will
-- increase it by 20 percent, and a rating lower than 2 will
-- result in no raise. A raise will not be given if the employee
-- has been at the company for less than 18 months.
UPDATE employee_salaries
    SET salary=
        CASE
            WHEN (review=4 AND
                (DATEDIFF(month, hire_date, GETDATE()) >= 18))
                THEN salary * 2.0
            WHEN (review=3 AND
                (DATEDIFF(month, hire_date, GETDATE()) >= 18))
                THEN salary * 1.6
            WHEN (review=2 AND
                (DATEDIFF(month, hire_date, GETDATE()) >= 18))
                THEN salary * 1.2
            ELSE salary
        END

-- This second formulation produces identical results, but it's
- more intuitive and clearer
UPDATE employee_salaries
    SET salary=
        CASE review
```

```
         WHEN 4 THEN salary * 2.0
         WHEN 3 THEN salary * 1.6
         WHEN 2 THEN salary * 1.2
         ELSE salary
      END
   WHERE (DATEDIFF(month, hire_date, GETDATE()) > 18)
```

Cousins of CASE

SQL Server provides three nice shorthand derivatives of CASE: COALESCE, NULLIF, and ISNULL. COALESCE and NULLIF are both part of the ANSI SQL-92 specification; they were added to version 6.0 at the same time that CASE was added. ISNULL() is a longtime SQL Server function. Following is the syntax for these functions.

COALESCE　This function is equivalent to a CASE expression that returns the first NOT NULL expression in a list of expressions.

```
COALESCE(expression1, expression2, ... expressionN)
```

If no non-null values are found, COALESCE returns NULL (which is what *expressionN* was, given that there were no non-null values). Written as a CASE expression, COALESCE looks like this:

```
CASE
   WHEN expression1 IS NOT NULL THEN expression1
   WHEN expression2 IS NOT NULL THEN expression2
ELSE expressionN
END
```

NULLIF　This function is equivalent to a CASE expression in which NULL is returned if *expression1 = expression2*.

```
NULLIF(expression1, expression2)
```

If the expressions aren't equal, *expression1* is returned. In Chapter 7, you saw that NULLIF can be handy if you use dummy values instead of NULL, but you don't want those dummy values to skew the results produced by aggregate functions. Written using CASE, NULLIF looks like this:

```
CASE
   WHEN expression1=expression2 THEN NULL
   ELSE expression1
END
```

ISNULL   This function is almost the mirror of NULLIF.

```
ISNULL(expression1, expression2)
```

ISNULL allows you to easily substitute an alternative expression or value for an expression that's NULL. In Chapter 7, we saw the use of ISNULL to substitute the string *'ALL'* for a grouping NULL when using CUBE and to substitute a string of question marks, *'????'* for a NULL value. By doing this, the results were more clear and intuitive to users. Written instead using CASE, ISNULL looks like this:

```
CASE
    WHEN expression1 IS NULL THEN expression2
    ELSE expression1
END
```

The second argument to ISNULL (the value to be returned if the first argument is NULL) can be an expression or even a SELECT statement. Say, for example, that we want to query the *titles* table. If a title has NULL for *price,* we want to instead use the lowest price that exists for any book. Without CASE or ISNULL, this isn't an easily written query. With ISNULL, it is easy:

```
SELECT title, pub_id, ISNULL(price, (SELECT MIN(price)
    FROM titles)) FROM titles
```

For comparison, here's an equivalent SELECT statement written with the longhand CASE formulation:

```
SELECT title, pub_id,
    CASE WHEN price IS NULL THEN (SELECT MIN(price) FROM titles)
    ELSE price
    END
FROM titles
```

PRINT

Transact-SQL, like other programming languages, provides printing capability through the PRINT and RAISERROR statements. We'll discuss RAISERROR momentarily, but first we'll take a look at the PRINT statement.

PRINT is the most basic way to display any character string up to 8000 characters. You can display a literal character string or a variable of type *char, varchar, nchar, nvarchar, datetime, or smalldatetime.* You can concatenate strings and use functions that return string or date values. In addition, PRINT can print any expression or function that is implicitly convertible to a character datatype. (Refer to Table 9-10 on page 480 to determine which datatypes are implicitly convertible.)

It seems like every time you learn a new programming language, the first assignment is to write the "Hello World" program. Using TRANSACT-SQL, it couldn't be easier:

```
PRINT 'Hello World'
```

Even before we saw PRINT, you could've produced the same output in your Query Analyzer screen with the following:

```
SELECT 'Hello World'
```

So what's the difference between the two? The PRINT returns a message, nothing more. The SELECT statement returns output like this:

```
-----------
Hello World

(1 row(s) affected)
```

The SELECT statement returns the string as a result set. That's why we get the *(1 row(s) affected)* message. When using the Query Analyzer to submit your queries and view your results, you might not see much difference between the PRINT and the SELECT statements. But for other client tools (besides ISQL, OSQL, and Query Analyzer), there could be a big difference. PRINT returns a message of severity 0, and you need to check the documentation for the client API that you're using to determine how messages are handled. For example, if you're writing an ODBC program, the results of a PRINT statement get handled by *SQLError()*.

On the other hand, a SELECT statement returns a set of data, just like selecting prices from a table. Your client interface might expect you to bind data to local (client-side) variables before you can use them in your client programs. Again, you'll have to check your documentation to know for sure. The important distinction to remember here is that PRINT returns a message and SELECT returns data.

PRINT is extremely simple, both in its use and in its capabilities. It's not nearly as powerful as, say, *printf()* in C. You can't give positional parameters or control formatting. For example, you *can't* do this:

```
PRINT 'Today is %s', GETDATE()
```

Part of the problem here is that *%s* is meaningless. In addition, the built-in function GETDATE() returns a value of type *datetime*, which can't be concatenated to the string constant. So, we can do this instead:

```
PRINT 'Today is ' + convert(char(30), GETDATE())
```

457

RAISERROR

RAISERROR is similar to PRINT but can be much more powerful than it. RAISERROR also sends a message (not a result set) to the client; however, i t allows you to specify the specific error number and severity of the message. It also allows you to reference an error number, the text for which you can add to the *sysmessages* table. RAISERROR makes it easy for you to develop international versions of your software. Rather than have multiple versions of your SQL code when you want to change the language of the text, you need only one version. You can simply add the text of the message in multiple languages. The user will see the message in the language used by the particular connection.

Unlike PRINT, RAISERROR accepts *printf*-like parameter substitution as well as formatting control. RAISERROR also can allow messages to be logged to the Windows NT event service, making them visible to the Windows NT event viewer, and it allows SQL Server Agent alerts to be configured for these events. In many cases, RAISERROR is preferable to PRINT, and you might choose to use PRINT only for quick-and-dirty situations. For production-caliber code, RAISERROR is usually a better choice. Here's the syntax:

```
RAISERROR ({msg_id | msg_str}, severity, state[, argument1
[, argument2]])
[WITH LOG]
```

After calling RAISERROR, the system function @@ERROR will return the value passed as *msg_id*. If no ID is passed, the error is raised with error number 50000, and @@ERROR will be set to that number. You can also set the severity level; an informational message should be considered severity 0 (or severity 10; 0 and 10 are used interchangeably for a historical reason that's not important). Only someone with the system administrator (SA) role can raise an error with a severity of 19 or higher. Errors of severity 20 and higher are considered *fatal*, and the connection to the client will automatically be terminated.

You must use the WITH LOG option for all errors of severity 19 or higher. For errors of severity 20 or higher, the message text isn't returned to the client. Instead, it's sent to the SQL Server error log, and the error number, text, severity, and state are written to the Windows NT event log. The SA can use the WITH LOG option with any error number or any severity level.

Errors written to the Windows NT event log from RAISERROR go to the application event log, with *MSSQLServer* as the source and *Server* as the category. These errors have event ID 17060. (Errors that SQL Server raises can have different event IDs, depending on which component they come from.) The type of message in the Windows NT event log depends on the severity used in the RAISERROR statement. Messages with severity 14 and lower are recorded as *informational messages,* severity 15 messages are *warnings,* and severity 16 and higher messages are *errors.* Note that the severity that's recorded in the event log is the number that's passed to RAISERROR, regardless of the stated severity in *sysmessages.* So, although we don't recommend it, you can raise a serious message as informational or a noncritical message as an error. If you look at the data section of the Windows NT event log for a message raised from RAISERROR, or if you're reading from it in a program, you'll notice that the error number appears first, followed by the severity level.

You can use any number from 1 through 127 as the *state* parameter. You might pass a line number that tells where the error was raised. But *state* has no real relevance to SQL Server.

> **TIP** There's a little-known way to cause ISQL.EXE or OSQL.EXE (the command-line query tools) to terminate. Raising any error with *state* 127 causes ISQL or OSQL to immediately exit, with a return code equal to the error number. (You can determine the error number from a batch command file with ERRORLEVEL.) You could write your application so that it does something similar—it's a simple change to the error-handling logic. This trick can be a useful way to terminate a set of scripts that would be run through ISQL or OSQL. You could get a similar result by raising a high-severity error to terminate the connection. But using a *state* of 127 is actually simpler, and no scary message will be written to the error log or event log for what is a planned, routine action.

You can add your own messages and text for a message in multiple languages by using the *sp_addmessage* stored procedure. By default, SQL Server uses U.S. English, but you can add languages. (SQL Server distinguishes U.S. English from British English because of locale settings, such as currency. The text of messages is the same.) The script \MSSQL7\INSTALL\INSTLANG.SQL adds locale settings for nine more languages but not the actual translated messages. Error numbers lower than 50000 are reserved for SQL Server use, so choose a higher number for your own messages.

Suppose we want to rewrite "Hello World" to use RAISERROR, and we want the text of the message to be able to appear in both U.S. English and German (language ID of 1). Here's how:

```
EXEC sp_addmessage 50001, 10, 'Hello World', @replace='REPLACE'
-- New message 50001 for U.S. English
EXEC sp_addmessage 50001, 10, 'Hallo Welt' , @lang='Deutsch',
    @replace='REPLACE'
-- New message 50001 for German
```

When RAISERROR is executed, the text of the message becomes dependent on the SET LANGUAGE setting of the connection. If the connection does a *SET LANGUAGE Deutsch*, the text returned for *RAISERROR (50001, 10, 1)* will be *Hallo Welt*. If the text for a language doesn't exist, the U.S. English text (by default) will be returned. For this reason, the U.S. English message must be added before the text for another language is added. If no entry exists, even in U.S. English, error 2758 results:

```
Msg 2758, Level 16, State 1
RAISERROR could not locate entry for error n in Sysmessages.
```

We could easily enhance the message to say whom the "Hello" is from by providing a parameter marker and passing it when calling RAISERROR. (For illustration, we'll use some *printf*-style formatting, *#6x*, to display the process number in hexadecimal format.)

```
EXEC sp_addmessage 50001, 10,
    'Hello World, from: %s, process id: %#6x', @replace='REPLACE'
```

When user *kalend* executes

```
DECLARE @parm1 varchar(30), @parm2 int
SELECT @parm1=USER_NAME(), @parm2=@@spid
RAISERROR (50001, 15, -1, @parm1, @parm2)
```

this error is raised:

```
Msg 50001, Level 15, State 1
Hello, World, from: kalend, process id: 0xc
```

FORMATMESSAGE

If you have created your own error messages with parameter markers, you might need to inspect the entire message with the parameters replaced by actual values. RAISERROR makes the message string available to the client but not to your SQL Server application. To construct a full message string from a parameterized message in the *sysmessages* table, you can use the function FORMATMESSAGE().

If we consider the last example from the preceding RAISERROR section, we can use FORMATMESSAGE to build the entire message string and save it in a local variable for further processing. Here's an example of the use of FORMATMESSAGE:

```
DECLARE @parm1 varchar(30), @parm2 int, @message varchar(100)
SELECT @parm1=USER_NAME(), @parm2=@@spid
SELECT @message = FORMATMESSAGE(50001, @parm1, @parm2)
PRINT 'The message is: ' + @message
```

This will return the following:

```
The message is: Hello World, from: kalend, process id:    0xc
```

Note that no error number or state information is returned.

Operators

Transact-SQL provides a large collection of operators for doing arithmetic, comparing values, doing bit operations, and concatenating strings. These operators are similar to those you might be familiar with in other programming languages. You can use Transact-SQL operators in any expression, including in the select list of a query, in the WHERE or HAVING clauses of queries, in UPDATE and IF statements, and in CASE expressions.

Arithmetic Operators

We won't go into much detail here because arithmetic operators are pretty standard stuff. If you need more information, please refer to the online documentation. Table 9-2 shows the arithmetic operators.

Symbol	Operation	Used with These Datatypes
+	Addition	*int, smallint, tinyint, numeric, decimal, float, real, money,* and *smallmoney*
?	Subtraction	*int, smallint, tinyint, numeric, decimal, float, real, money,* and *smallmoney*
*	Multiplication	*int, smallint, tinyint, numeric, decimal, float, real, money,* and *smallmoney*
/	Division	*int, smallint, tinyint, numeric, decimal, float, real, money,* and *smallmoney*
%	Modulo	*int, smallint,* and *tinyint*

Table 9-2.
Arithmetic operators in Transact-SQL.

As with other programming languages, in Transact-SQL you need to consider the datatypes you're using when performing arithmetic operations, or you might not get the results you expect. For example, which of the following is correct?

$$1 \div 2 = 0$$

$$1 \div 2 = 0.5$$

If the underlying datatypes are both integers (including *tinyint* and *smallint*), the correct answer is 0. If one or both of the datatypes are *float* (including *real*) or *numeric/decimal* with a nonzero scale, the correct answer is 0.5 (or 0.50000, depending on the precision and scale of the datatype). When an operator combines two expressions of different datatypes, the datatype precedence rules specify which datatype is converted to the other. The datatype with the lower precedence is converted to the datatype with the higher precedence.

Here's the precedence order for SQL Server datatypes:

```
datetime (highest)
smalldatetime
float
real
decimal
money
smallmoney
int
smallint
tinyint
bit
ntext
text
image
timestamp
nvarchar
nchar
varchar
char
varbinary
binary
uniqueidentifier (lowest)
```

As you can see from the above precedence list, an *int* multiplied by a *float* produces a *float*. You can explicitly convert to a given datatype by using the CAST() function or its predecessor, CONVERT(). These conversion functions are discussed later in this chapter.

The addition (+) operator is also used to concatenate character strings. In this example, we want to concatenate last names, followed by a comma and a space, followed by first names from the *authors* table (in *pubs*), and then return the result as a single column:

```
SELECT 'author'=au_lname + ', ' + au_fname FROM authors
```

Here's the abbreviated result:

```
author
------
White, Johnson
Green, Marjorie
Carson, Cheryl
O'Leary, Michael
```

Bit Operators

Table 9-3 shows the SQL Server bit operators.

Symbol	Meaning
&	Bitwise AND (two operands)
|	Bitwise OR (two operands)
^	Bitwise exclusive OR (two operands)
~	Bitwise NOT (one operand)

Table 9-3.

SQL Server bit operators.

The operands for two-operand bitwise operators can be any of the datatypes of the integer or binary string datatype categories (except for the *image* datatype); however, neither operand can be any of the datatypes of the binary string datatype category. Table 9-4 shows the supported operand datatypes.

Left Operand	Right Operand
binary	*int, smallint,* or *tinyint*
bit	*int, smallint, tinyint,* or *bit*
int	*int, smallint, tinyint, binary,* or *varbinary*
smallint	*int, smallint, tinyint, binary,* or *varbinary*
tinyint	*int, smallint, tinyint, binary,* or *varbinary*
varbinary	*int, smallint,* or *tinyint*

Table 9-4.

Datatypes supported for two-operand bitwise operators.

The single operand for the bitwise NOT operator must be one of the integer datatypes.

Often, you must keep a lot of indicator-type values in a database, and bit operators make it easy to set up bit masks with a single column to do this. The SQL Server system tables use bit masks. For example, the *status* field in the *sysdatabases* table is a bit mask. If we wanted to see all databases marked as read-only, which is the tenth bit or decimal 1024 (2^{10}), we could use this query:

```
SELECT "read only databases"=name FROM master..sysdatabases
WHERE status & 1024 > 0
```

This example is for illustrative purposes only. In general, you shouldn't query the system catalogs directly. Sometimes the catalogs need to change between product releases, and if you query directly, your applications can break because of these required changes. Instead, you should use the provided system catalog stored procedures and object property functions, which return catalog information in a standard way. If the underlying catalogs change in subsequent releases, the property functions are also updated, insulating your application from unexpected changes.

So for this example, to see whether a particular database was marked read-only, we could use the DATABASEPROPERTY function:

```
SELECT DATABASEPROPERTY('mydb', 'IsReadOnly')
```

A value of 1 returned would mean that *mydb* was set to read-only status.

Note that keeping such indicators as *bit* datatype columns can be a better approach than using an *int* as a bit mask. This approach is more straightforward—you don't always need to look up your bit-mask values for each indicator. To write the query above, you'd need to check the documentation for the bit-mask value for "read only." And many developers, not to mention end users, aren't that comfortable using bit operators and are likely to use them incorrectly. From a storage perspective, *bit* columns don't require more space than creating equivalent bit-mask columns requires. (Eight *bit* fields can share the same byte of storage.)

True, *bit* columns have a couple of restrictions that you don't have if you create a bit mask as an integer and use bit operators: for example, you can't create an index on a *bit* column. But you wouldn't typically want to do that with a "yes/no" indicator field anyway. If you have a huge number of indicator fields, using bit-mask columns of integers instead of *bit* columns might be a better alternative than dealing with hundreds of individual *bit* columns. However, there's nothing to stop you from having hundreds of *bit* columns. You'd have to have an awful lot of *bit* fields to actually exceed the column limit, because a table in SQL Server can have up to 1024 columns. If you frequently add new indicators, using a bit mask on an integer might be better. To add a new indicator, you can make use of an unused bit of an integer status field rather than do an ALTER TABLE and add a new column (which you must do if you use a *bit* column). The case for using a *bit* column boils down to clarity.

Comparison Operators

Table 9-5 shows the SQL Server comparison operators.

Symbol	Meaning
=	Equal to
>	Greater than
<	Less than
>=	Greater than or equal to
<=	Less than or equal to
<>	Not equal to (ANSI standard)
!=	Not equal to (not ANSI standard)
!>	Not greater than (not ANSI standard)
!<	Not less than (not ANSI standard)

Table 9-5.
SQL Server comparison operators.

Comparison operators are straightforward. Only a couple of related issues might be confusing to a novice SQL Server developer:

- When dealing with NULL, remember the issues with three-value logic and the truth tables that were discussed in Chapter 7. Also understand that NULL is an unknown.

- Comparisons of *char* and *varchar* data (and their Unicode counterparts) depend on the sort order at the SQL Server installation. Whether comparisons evaluate to TRUE depends on the sort order installed. Review the discussion of sort orders in Chapter 4, "Planning for and Installing SQL Server."

Logical and Grouping Operators (Parentheses)

The three logical operators (AND, OR, and NOT) are vitally important in expressions, especially in the WHERE clause. You can use parentheses to group expressions and then apply logical operations to the group. In many cases, it's impossible to correctly formulate a query without using parentheses. In other cases, you might be able to avoid them, but it's not very intuitive and it could result in bugs. You could construct a convoluted expression using some combination of string concatenations or functions, bit operations, or arithmetic operations instead of using parentheses. But there's no good reason to do this.

Using parentheses can make your code clearer, less prone to bugs, and more easily maintained. Because there's no performance penalty beyond parsing, you should use parentheses liberally. Below is an example query that you couldn't readily write without using parentheses. This query is simple, and in English the request is well understood. But you're also likely to get this query wrong in Transact-SQL if you're not careful, and it clearly illustrates just how easy it is to make a mistake.

```
Find authors who do not live in either Salt Lake City, UT, or Oakland, CA.
```

Following are four examples that attempt to formulate this query. Three of them are wrong. Test yourself: which one is correctly stated? (As usual, multiple correct formulations are possible—not just the one presented here.)

EXAMPLE 1

```
SELECT au_lname, au_fname, city, state FROM authors
WHERE
city <> 'OAKLAND' AND state <> 'CA'
OR
city <> 'Salt Lake City' AND state <> 'UT'
```

EXAMPLE 2

```
SELECT au_lname, au_fname, city, state FROM authors
WHERE
(city <> 'OAKLAND' AND state <> 'CA')
OR
(city <> 'Salt Lake City' AND state <> 'UT')
```

EXAMPLE 3

```
SELECT au_lname, au_fname, city, state FROM authors
WHERE
(city <> 'OAKLAND' AND state <> 'CA')
AND
(city <> 'Salt Lake City' AND state <> 'UT')
```

EXAMPLE 4

```
SELECT au_lname, au_fname, city, state FROM authors
WHERE
NOT
(
(city='OAKLAND' AND state='CA')
OR
(city='Salt Lake City' AND state='UT')
)
```

Hopefully, you can see that only Example 4 operates as wanted. This query would be impossible to write without some combination of parentheses, NOT, OR (including IN, a shorthand for OR), and AND.

You can also use parentheses to change the order of precedence in mathematical and logical operations. These two statements return different results:

```
SELECT 1.0 + 3.0 / 4.0      -- Returns 1.75
SELECT (1.0 + 3.0) / 4.0    -- Returns 1.00
```

The order of precedence is similar to what you learned back in algebra class (except for the bit operators). Operators of the same level are evaluated left to right. You use parentheses to change precedence levels to suit your needs, when you're unsure, or when you simply want to make your code more readable. Groupings with parentheses are evaluated from the innermost grouping outward. Table 9-6 shows the order of precedence.

Operation	Operators
Bitwise NOT	~
Multiplication/division/modulo	* / %
Addition/subtraction	+ ?
Bitwise exclusive OR	^
Bitwise AND	&
Bitwise OR	|
Logical NOT	NOT
Logical AND	AND
Logical OR	OR

Table 9-6.
Order of precedence, from highest to lowest.

If you didn't pick the correct example, you should easily see the flaw in Examples 1, 2, and 3 by examining the output. Both Examples 1 and 2 return every row. *Every* row is either not in CA or not in UT, because a row can be in only one or the other. A row in CA isn't in UT, so the expression returns TRUE. Example 3 is too restrictive—for example, what about the rows in San Francisco, CA? The condition *(city <> 'OAKLAND' and state <> 'CA')* would evaluate as *(TRUE and FALSE)* for San Francisco, CA, which, of course, is FALSE, so the row would be rejected when it *should* be selected, according to the desired semantics.

Scalar Functions

In Chapter 7, we looked at aggregate functions, such as MAX(), SUM(), and COUNT(). These functions operate on a set of values to produce a single aggregated value. In addition to aggregate functions, SQL Server provides *scalar functions*, which operate on a single value. *Scalar* is just a fancy term for *single value*. You can also think of the value in a single column of a single row as *scalar*. Scalar functions are enormously useful—the Swiss army knife of SQL Server. (You've probably noticed that scalar functions have been used in several examples already—we'd all be lost without them.)

You can use scalar functions anywhere an expression is legal, such as:

- In the select list.

- In a WHERE clause, including one defining a view.

- Inside a CASE expression.

- In a CHECK constraint.

- In the VALUES clause of an INSERT statement.

- In an UPDATE statement to the right of the SET clause.

- With a variable assignment.

- As a parameter inside another scalar function.

SQL Server provides too many scalar functions to remember. The best you can do is to familiarize yourself with those that exist, and then, when you encounter a problem and a light bulb goes on in your head to remind you about a function that will help, you can look at the online documentation for details.

Even with so many functions available, you'll probably find yourself wanting some functions that still don't exist. (And you probably still wouldn't be completely satisfied even if another couple hundred functions were added!) You might have a specialized need that would benefit from a specific function, and it would be great if we could write and add our own libraries of scalar functions.

Stored procedures and extended stored procedures come somewhat close and are extraordinarily useful, but even they fall short of the capability provided by scalar functions. And unlike scalar functions, stored procedures or extended stored procedures can't be used in a select list, in a view, or in a WHERE clause. But take heart—the SQL Server developers do appreciate the need for user-defined functions, and no doubt user-defined functions will make their way into some future SQL Server release. Until then, familiarize yourself with the functions provided and remember that functions can be nested within other functions—sometimes providing what virtually amounts to a separate function.

The following sections provide a list of the scalar functions that currently exist, some comments on them, and some examples of how they're used. First we'll look at the CAST() function in a bit of detail because it's especially important.

Conversion Functions

SQL Server provides three functions for converting datatypes: the generalized CAST() function, the CONVERT() function—which is analogous to CAST(), but has a slightly different syntax—and the more specialized STR() function.

> **NOTE** SQL Server 7 introduced the CAST() function as a synonym for CONVERT(), to comply with ANSI-92 specifications. You'll see CONVERT() used in older documentation and older code. This book uses CAST() whenever possible.

CAST() is possibly the most useful function in all of SQL Server. It allows you to change the datatype when you select a field, which can be essential for concatenating strings, joining columns that weren't initially envisioned as related, performing mathematical operations on columns that were defined as character but which actually contain numbers, and other similar operations. Like C, SQL is a fairly strongly typed language.

Some languages, such as Microsoft Visual Basic or PL/1 (Programming Language 1), allow you to almost indiscriminately mix datatypes. If you mix datatypes in SQL, however, you'll often get an error. (Some conversions are implicit, so, for example, you can add or join a *smallint* and an *int* without any such error; trying to do the same between an *int* and a *char*, however, produces an error.) Without a way to convert datatypes in SQL, you would have to return the values back to the client application, convert them there, and then send them back to the server. You might need to create temporary tables just to hold the intermediate converted values. All of this would be cumbersome and inefficient.

Recognizing this inefficiency, the ANSI committee added the CAST operator to SQL-92. Few, if any, mainstream products today have implemented CAST, but it seems like the SQL-92 specification for CAST is just a subset of SQL Server's CAST() function. In other words, SQL Server's CAST()—and the older CONVERT()—provides a superset of ANSI CAST functionality. When a member of the ANSI SQL committee was asked which new features in SQL-92 are the most useful and powerful, his reply was "CASE and CAST," and he lamented that few products had implemented either. Fortunately, SQL Server has included CASE since version 6.0, and it has always had all the functionality of CAST via the CONVERT() function—and, in SQL Server 7, the CAST function(). The CAST() syntax is simple:

```
CAST (original_expression AS desired_datatype)
```

Suppose that we want to concatenate the *job_id* (*smallint*) column of the *employee* table with the *lname* (*varchar*) column. Without CAST(), this would be impossible (unless it was done in the application). With CAST(), it's trivial:

```
SELECT lname + '-' + CAST(job_id AS varchar(2)) FROM employee
```

Here's the abbreviated output:

```
Accorti-13
Afonso-14
Ashworth-6
Bennett-12
Brown-7
Chang-4
Cramer-2
Cruz-10
Devon-3
⋮
```

Specifying a length shorter than the column or expression is a useful way to truncate the column. (You could use the SUBSTRING() function for this equally well, but you might find it more intuitive to use CAST().) Specifying a length when converting to *char, varchar, decimal*, or *numeric* isn't required, but it is recommended. Specifying a length better shields you from possible behavioral changes in newer releases of the product.

> **NOTE** Although behavioral changes generally don't occur by design, it's difficult to ensure 100 percent consistency of subtle behavioral changes between releases. The development team strives for such consistency, but it's nearly impossible to ensure that no behavioral side effects result when new features and capabilities are added. There's little point in relying on the current default behavior when you can just as easily be explicit about what you expect.

You might want to avoid CAST() when converting *float* or *numeric/decimal* values to character strings if you expect to see a certain number of decimal places. CAST() doesn't currently provide formatting capabilities for numbers. The older CONVERT() function has some limited formatting capabilities, which we'll see shortly. Formatting floating-point numbers and such when converting to character strings is another area that's ripe for subtle behavior differences. So if you need to transform a floating-point number to a character string in which you expect a specific format, you can use the other conversion function, STR(). The STR() function is a specialized conversion function that always converts from a number (*float, numeric,* and so on) to a character datatype, but it allows you to explicitly specify the length and number of decimal places that should be formatted for the character string. Here's the syntax:

```
STR(float_expression, character_length, number_of_decimal_places)
```

Remember that *character_length* must include room for a decimal point and a negative sign if they might exist. Also be aware that STR() rounds the value to the number of decimal places requested, while CAST() simply truncates the value if the character length is smaller than the size required for full display. Here's an example of STR():

```
SELECT discounttype, "Discount"=STR(discount, 7, 3) FROM discounts
```

And here's the output:

```
discounttype       Discount
------------       --------
Initial Customer     10.500
Volume Discount       6.700
Customer Discount     5.000
```

You can think of the ASCII() and CHAR() functions as special type-conversion functions, but we'll discuss them later in this chapter along with string functions.

If all you're doing is converting an expression to a specific datatype, you can actually use either CAST() or the older CONVERT(). However, the syntax of CONVERT() is slightly different, and allows for a third, optional argument. Here's the syntax for CONVERT():

```
CONVERT (desired_datatype[(length)], original_expression
    [, style])
```

CONVERT() has an optional third parameter, *style*. This parameter is most commonly used when converting an expression of type *datetime* or *smalldatetime* to type *char* or *varchar*. It can also be used when converting *float*, *real*, *money*, or *smallmoney* to a character datatype.

When converting a *datetime* expression to character, if the *style* argument isn't specified, the conversion will format the date with the default SQL Server date format (for example, Oct 3 1999 2:25PM). By specifying a *style* type, you can format the output as you want. You can also specify a shorter length for the character buffer being converted to, in order to perhaps eliminate the time portion or for other reasons. Table 9-7 shows the various values you can use as the *style* argument.

NOTE Although style 0 is the default when converting a *datetime* value to a character string, Query Analyzer (and OSQL) will use style 121 when displaying a *datetime* value.

As we approach the new millennium, using two-character formats for the year could be a bug in your application just waiting to happen! Unless you have a compelling reason not to do so, you should always use the full year (*yyyy*) for both the input and output formatting of dates to prevent any ambiguity. SQL Server has no problem dealing with the year 2000—in fact, the change in century isn't even a boundary condition in SQL Server's internal representation of dates.

But if you represent a year by specifying only the last two digits, the inherent ambiguity might cause your application to make an incorrect assumption. On input of a date formatted that way, SQL Server's default behavior is to interpret a two-digit year as 19*yy* if the value is greater than or equal to 50, and as 20*yy* if the value is less than 50. That might be OK now, but by the year 2051 you won't want a two-digit year of 51 to be interpreted as 1951 instead of 2051. (If you assume that your application will have been long since retired, think again. A lot of COBOL programmers in the 1960s didn't worry about the year 2000.)

SQL Server 7 allows you to change the cutoff year that determines how a two-digit year is interpreted. A two-digit year that is less than or equal to the last two digits of the cutoff year is in the same century as the cutoff year. A two-digit year that is greater than the last two digits of the cutoff year is in the century that precedes the cutoff year. You can change the cutoff year by using the Properties dialog box for your SQL server in the SQL Server Enterprise Manager and selecting the Server Properties tab. Or you can use the *sp_configure* stored procedure:

```
exec sp_configure 'two digit year cutoff', '2000'
```

In this example, since the *two digit year cutoff* is 2000, all two-digit years other than 00 are interpreted as occurring in the 20th century. With the default *two digit year cutoff* value of 2049, the two-digit year 49 is interpreted as 2049 and the two-digit year 50 is interpreted as 1950. You should be aware that although SQL Server uses 2049 as the cutoff year for interpreting dates, OLE Automation objects use 2030. You can use the *two digit year cutoff* option to provide consistency in date values between SQL Server and client applications. However, to avoid ambiguity with dates, you should always use four-digit years in your data.

You don't need to worry about how changing the *two digit year cutoff* value will affect your existing data. If data is stored using the *dateline* or *smalldatetime* datatypes, the full four-digit year is part of the internal storage. The *two digit year cutoff* value only controls how SQL Server interprets date constants such as '10/12/99'.

Day First or Month First

The *two digit year cutoff* controls how SQL Server interprets the '99' in '10/12/99', but there is another ambiguity in this date constant. Are we talking about October 12 or December 10? The SET option DATEFORMAT determines whether SQL Server interprets a numeric three-part date as month first, followed by day; or day first, followed by month; or even year first, followed by month. The default value of DATEFORMAT is controlled by the language you are using but can be changed using the SET DATEFORMAT command. There are six possible values for DATEFORMAT, which should be self-explanatory: *mdy*, *dmy*, *ymd*, *ydm*, *dym*, and *myd*. Only the first three are commonly used. Here's an example of changing the DATEFORMAT value to U.S. standard format:

```
SET DATEFORMAT mdy
```

Style Number Without Century (yy)	Style Number with Century (yyyy)	Output Type	Style
–	0 or 100	Default	mon dd yyyy hh:miAM (or PM)
1	101	USA	mm/dd/yyyy
2	102	ANSI	yyyy.mm.dd
3	103	British/ French	dd/mm/yyyy
4	104	German	dd.mm.yyyy
5	105	Italian	dd-mm-yyyy
6	106	–	dd mon yyyy
7	107	–	mon dd, yyyy
–	8 or 108	–	hh:mm:ss
–	9 or 109	Default + milliseconds	mon dd yyyy hh:mi:ss:mmmAM (or PM)
10	110	USA	mm-dd-yy
11	111	JAPAN	yy/mm/dd
12	112	ISO	yymmdd
–	13 or 113	Europe default + milliseconds	dd mon yyyy hh:mi:ss:mmm (24h)
14	114	–	hh:mi:ss:mmm (24h)
	20 or 120	ODBC canonical	yyyy-mm-dd hh:mi:ss((24h)
	21 or 121	ODBC canonical + milliseconds	yyyy-mm-dd hh:mi:ss.mmm(24h)

Table 9-7.
Values for the style *argument of the CONVERT() function when converting a* datetime *expression to a character expression.*

CONVERT() can also be useful if you insert the current date using the GETDATE() function but don't consider meaningful the time elements of the *datetime* datatype. (Remember that SQL Server doesn't currently have separate date and time datatypes.) You can use CONVERT() to format and insert *datetime*

data with only a date element. Without the time specification in the GETDATE()
value, the time will consistently be stored as 12:00AM for any given date. That
eliminates problems that can occur when searching or joining between columns
of *datetime*: for example, if the date elements are equal between columns but the
time element is not, an equality search will fail.

You can eliminate this equality problem by making the time portion
consistent. (You might consider using style 102, ANSI, when inserting dates.
This style is always recognizable, no matter what the SQL Server default language
and no matter what the DATEFORMAT setting.) Consider this:

```
CREATE TABLE my_date (Coll datetime)
INSERT INTO my_date VALUES (CONVERT(char(10), GETDATE(), 102))
```

In this example, the CONVERT() function converts the current date and
time value to a character string that doesn't include the time. However, because
the table we're inserting into expects a *datetime* value, the new character string
will be converted back to a *datetime* datatype, using the default time of midnight.

The optional *style* argument can also be used when converting *float*, *real*,
money, or *smallmoney* to a character datatype. When converting from *float* or
real, the style allows you to force the output to appear in scientific notation, and
also allows you to specify either 8 or 16 digits. When converting from a money
type to a character type, the style allows you to specify whether you want a
comma to appear every 3 digits and whether you want two digits to the right
of the decimal point, or four.

In Table 9-8, the column on the left represents the *style* values for *float* or
real conversion to character data.

Style Value	Output
0 (the default)	Six digits maximum. In scientific notation, when appropriate.
1	Always eight digits. Always scientific notation.
2	Always sixteen digits. Always scientific notation.

Table 9-8.
Values for the style *argument of the CONVERT() function when converting
a floating-point expression to a character datatype.*

In Table 9-9 on the following page, the column on the left represents the
style value for *money* or *smallmoney* conversion to character data.

Style Value	Output
0 (the default)	No commas every three digits to the left of the decimal point. Two digits to the right of the decimal point. For example, 4235.98.
1	Commas every three digits to the left of the decimal point. Two digits to the right of the decimal point. For example, 3,510.92.
2	No commas every three digits to the left of the decimal point. Four digits to the right of the decimal point. For example, 4235.9819.

Table 9-9.
Values for the style *argument of the CONVERT() function when converting a money expression to a character datatype.*

Here's an example from the *pubs* database. The *advance* column in the *titles* table represents how much advance was paid by the publisher for each book, and most of the amounts are greater than $1000. In the *titles* table, the value is stored as a *money* datatype. The following query returns the value of advance as a *money* value, a *varchar* value with the default style, and as *varchar* with each of the two optional styles:

```
select "Money" = advance,
     "Varchar" = convert(varchar(10), advance),
     "Varchar-1" = convert(varchar(10), advance, 1),
     "Varchar-2" = convert(varchar(10), advance, 2)
from titles
```

Here is the abbreviated output:

```
Money                 Varchar     Varchar-1   Varchar-2
--------------------  ----------  ----------  ----------
5000.0000             5000.00     5,000.00    5000.0000
5000.0000             5000.00     5,000.00    5000.0000
10125.0000            10125.00    10,125.00   10125.0000
5000.0000             5000.00     5,000.00    5000.0000
.0000                 0.00        0.00        0.0000
15000.0000            15000.00    15,000.00   15000.0000
NULL                  NULL        NULL        NULL
7000.0000             7000.00     7,000.00    7000.0000
8000.0000             8000.00     8,000.00    8000.0000
```

Be aware that when you use CONVERT(), the conversion occurs on the server and the value is sent to the client application in the converted datatype. Of course, it's also common for applications to convert between datatypes, but conversion at the server is completely separate from conversion at the client. It's the client that determines how to display the value returned. In the above example, the results in the first column have no comma and four decimal digits. This is how the Query Analyzer tool displays values of type *money* that it receives from SQL Server. If we run this same query using the command line ISQL tool, the (abbreviated) results look like this:

```
Money                   Varchar    Varchar-1  Varchar-2
--------------------------  ----------  ----------  ----------
            5,000.00 5000.00     5,000.00   5000.0000
            5,000.00 5000.00     5,000.00   5000.0000
           10,125.00 10125.00    10,125.00  10125.0000
            5,000.00 5000.00     5,000.00   5000.0000
                0.00 0.00        0.00       0.0000
           15,000.00 15000.00    15,000.00  15000.0000
              (null) (null)      (null)     (null)
            7,000.00 7000.00     7,000.00   7000.0000
            8,000.00 8000.00     8,000.00   8000.0000
```

NOTE In addition to determining how to display a value of a particular datatype, the client program determines whether the output should be left-justified or right-justified and how NULLs are to be displayed. We're frequently asked how to change this default output to, for example, print *money* values with four decimal digits in Query Analyzer. Unfortunately, Query Analyzer has its own set of predefined formatting specifications, and, for the most part, you can't change them. Other client programs, like report writers, might give you a full range of capabilities for specifying the output format, but Query Analyzer isn't a report writer.

For another example of how the display can be affected by the client, if we use the GETDATE() function to select the current date, it is returned to the client application as a *datetime* datatype. The client application will likely convert that internal date representation to a string for display. On the other hand, if we use GETDATE() but also explicitly use CONVERT() to make the *datetime* character data, the column is sent to the calling application as a character string already.

So let's see what one particular client will do with that returned data. The command-line program ISQL is a DB-Library program and uses functions in DB-Library for binding columns to character strings. DB-Library allows such bindings to automatically pick up locale styles based on the settings of the workstation running the application. (The option Use International Settings in the Client Network Utility must be checked for this to occur by default.) So a column returned internally as a *datetime* datatype would be converted by ISQL.EXE into the same format as the locale setting of Windows. A column containing a date representation as a character string wouldn't, of course, be reformatted.

When we issue the following SELECT statement with SQL Server configured for U.S. English as the default language and with Windows NT on the client configured as English (United States), the date and string look alike:

```
SELECT
'returned as date'=GETDATE(),
'returned as string'=CONVERT(varchar(20), GETDATE())

returned as date        returned as string
------------------      -------------------
Dec 3 1996  3:10PM      Dec  3 1996  3:10PM
```

But if we change the locale in the Regional Settings application of the Windows NT Control Panel to French (Standard), the same SELECT statement returns the following:

```
returned as date        returned as string
-----------------       -------------------
3 déc. 1998 15:10       Dec  3 1998  3:10PM
```

You can see that the value returned to the client in internal date format was converted at the client workstation in the format chosen by the application. The conversion that uses CONVERT() was formatted at the server.

NOTE Although we have used dates in these examples, the discussion is also relevant to formatting numbers and currency with different regional settings.

We could *not* use the command-line OSQL program to illustrate the same behavior. OSQL, like the Query Analyzer, is an ODBC-based program, and *datetime* values are converted to ODBC Canonical format, which is independent of any regional settings. Using OSQL, the above query would return the code at the top of the next page.

```
returned as date            returned as string
--------------------------  --------------------
1998-12-15 09:26:24.793     Dec 15 1998  9:26AM
```

The rest of the book primarily uses CAST( ) instead of CONVERT( ) when converting between datatypes. CONVERT( ) is only used when the *style* argument is needed.

Some conversions are automatic and implicit, and using CAST( ) is unnecessary (although OK). For example, converting between numbers with types *int, smallint, tinyint, float, numeric,* and so on, happens automatically and implicitly as long as an overflow doesn't occur, in which case you'd get an error for arithmetic overflow. Converting numbers with decimal places to integer datatypes results in the truncation of the values to the right of the decimal point—without warning. (Converting between decimal or numeric datatypes requires that you explicitly use CAST( ) if a loss of precision is possible.)

Other conversions, such as between character and integer data, can be performed explicitly only by using CAST( ). Conversions between certain datatypes are nonsensical—for example, between a *float* and a *datetime*—and attempting such an operation results in error 529, which states that the conversion is impossible.

Table 9-10 on the following page, reprinted from the SQL Server documentation, is one that you'll want to refer to periodically for conversion issues.

Date and Time Functions

Operations on *datetime* values are common, such as "get current date and time," "do date arithmetic—50 days from today is what date," or "find out what day of the week falls on a specific date." Programming languages such as C or Visual Basic are loaded with functions for operations like these. Transact-SQL also provides a nice assortment to choose from (Table 9-11 on page 481).

The *datetime* parameter is any expression with a SQL Server *datetime* datatype or one that can be implicitly converted, such as an appropriately formatted character string like "1996.10.31". The *datepart* parameter uses the encodings shown in Table 9-12 on page 481. Either the full name or the abbreviation can be passed as an argument.

From: \ To:	binary	varbinary	char	varchar	nchar	nvarchar	datetime	smalldatetime	decimal	numeric	float	real	int(INT4)	smallint(INT2)	tinyint(INT1)	money	smallmoney	bit	timestamp	uniqueidentifier	image	ntext	text
binary		◉	◉	◉	◉	◉	◉	◉	◉	◉	○	○	◉	◉	◉	◉	◉	◉	◉	◉	◉	○	○
varbinary	◉		◉	◉	◉	◉	◉	◉	◉	◉	○	○	◉	◉	◉	◉	◉	◉	◉	◉	◉	○	○
char	●	●		◉	◉	◉	◉	◉	◉	◉	◉	◉	◉	◉	◉	●	●	◉	●	◉	◉	◉	◉
varchar	●	●	◉		◉	◉	◉	◉	◉	◉	◉	◉	◉	◉	◉	●	●	◉	●	◉	◉	◉	◉
nchar	●	●	◉	◉		◉	◉	◉	◉	◉	◉	◉	◉	◉	◉	●	●	◉	●	◉	○	◉	◉
nvarchar	●	●	◉	◉	◉		◉	◉	◉	◉	◉	◉	◉	◉	◉	●	●	◉	●	◉	○	◉	◉
datetime	●	●	◉	◉	◉	◉		◉	●	●	●	●	●	●	●	●	●	●	◉	○	○	○	○
smalldatetime	●	●	◉	◉	◉	◉	◉		●	●	●	●	●	●	●	●	●	●	◉	○	○	○	○
decimal	◉	◉	◉	◉	◉	◉	◉	◉		★	★	◉	◉	◉	◉	◉	◉	◉	◉	○	○	○	○
numeric	◉	◉	◉	◉	◉	◉	◉	◉	★	★		◉	◉	◉	◉	◉	◉	◉	◉	○	○	○	○
float	◉	◉	◉	◉	◉	◉	◉	◉	◉	◉		◉	◉	◉	◉	◉	◉	◉	◉	○	○	○	○
real	◉	◉	◉	◉	◉	◉	◉	◉	◉	◉	◉		◉	◉	◉	◉	◉	◉	◉	○	○	○	○
int(INT4)	◉	◉	◉	◉	◉	◉	◉	◉	◉	◉	◉	◉		◉	◉	◉	◉	◉	◉	○	○	○	○
smallint(INT2)	◉	◉	◉	◉	◉	◉	◉	◉	◉	◉	◉	◉	◉		◉	◉	◉	◉	◉	○	○	○	○
tinyint(INT1)	◉	◉	◉	◉	◉	◉	◉	◉	◉	◉	◉	◉	◉	◉		◉	◉	◉	◉	○	○	○	○
money	◉	◉	●	●	●	●	◉	◉	◉	◉	◉	◉	◉	◉	◉		◉	◉	◉	○	○	○	○
smallmoney	◉	◉	●	●	●	●	◉	◉	◉	◉	◉	◉	◉	◉	◉	◉		◉	◉	○	○	○	○
bit	◉	◉	◉	◉	◉	◉	◉	◉	◉	◉	◉	◉	◉	◉	◉	◉	◉		◉	○	○	○	○
timestamp	◉	◉	◉	◉	○	○	◉	◉	◉	◉	○	○	◉	◉	◉	◉	◉	◉		○	◉	○	○
uniqueidentifier	◉	◉	◉	◉	◉	◉	○	○	○	○	○	○	○	○	○	○	○	○	○		○	○	○
image	◉	◉	○	○	○	○	○	○	○	○	○	○	○	○	○	○	○	○	○	○		○	○
ntext	○	○	●	●	◉	◉	○	○	○	○	○	○	○	○	○	○	○	○	○	○	○		○
text	○	○	◉	◉	●	●	○	○	○	○	○	○	○	○	○	○	○	○	○	○	○	○	

● Explicit conversion
◉ Implicit conversion
○ Conversion not allowed
★ Requires CONVERT when loss of precision or scale will occur

Table 9-10.
Conversion table from the SQL Server documentation.

Date Function	Return Type	Description
DATEADD (*datepart, number, datetime*)	*Datetime*	Produces a date by adding an interval to a specified date.
DATEDIFF (*datepart, datetime1, datetime2*)	*Int*	Returns the number of *datepart* "boundaries" crossed between two specified dates.
DATENAME (*datepart, datetime*)	*Varchar*	Returns a character string representing the specified *datepart* of the specified date.
DATEPART (*datepart, datetime*)	*Int*	Returns an integer representing the specified *datepart* of the specified date.
GETDATE()	*Datetime*	Returns the current system date and time in the SQL Server standard internal format for *datetime* values.

Table 9-11.
Date and time functions in Transact-SQL.

datepart (Full Name)	Abbreviation	Values
year	Yy	1753–9999
quarter	Qq	1–4
month	Mm	1–12
dayofyear	Dy	1–366
day	Dd	1–31
week	Wk	1–53
weekday	Dw	1–7 (Sunday–Saturday)
hour	Hh	0–23
minute	Mi	0–59
second	Ss	0–59
millisecond	Ms	0–999

Table 9-12.
Values for the datepart *parameter.*

As do other functions, the date functions provide more than simple convenience. Suppose that we needed to find all records entered on the second Tuesday of every month and all records entered within 48 weeks of today. Without SQL Server date functions, the only way we could accomplish such a query would be to select all the rows and return them to the application and then filter them there. With a lot of data and a slow network, this can get ugly. With the date functions, the process is simple and efficient, and only the rows that meet this criteria are selected. For this example, assume that the table *records* includes these columns:

```
Record_number    int
Entered_on       datetime
```

This query will return the desired rows:

```
SELECT Record_number, Entered_on
FROM records
WHERE
DATEPART(WEEKDAY, Entered_on)=3
-- Tuesday is 3rd day of week (in USA)
AND
DATEPART(DAY, Entered_on) BETWEEN 8 AND 14
-- The 2nd week is from the 8th to 14th
AND
DATEDIFF(WEEK, Entered_on, GETDATE()) <= 48
-- Within 48 weeks of today
```

NOTE The day of the week considered "first" is locale-specific and depends on the DATEFIRST setting.

SQL Server 7 also allows you to add or subtract an integer to or from a *datetime* value. This is actually just a shortcut for the DATEADD function, with a *datepart* of Day. For example, the following two queries are equivalent. They'll each return the date 14 days from today:

```
select dateadd(day, 14, getdate() )
```

```
select getdate() + 14
```

The date functions don't do any rounding. The DATEDIFF() function just subtracts the components from each date that correspond to the *datepart* specified. For example, to find the number of years between New Year's Day and New Year's Eve of the same year, this query would return a value of 0. Because the *datepart* is specifying years, SQL Server will subtract the year part of the two dates, and because they're the same, the result of subtracting them is 0:

```
select datediff(yy, 'Jan 1, 1998', 'Dec 31, 1998')
```

However, if we wanted to find the difference in years between New Year's Eve of one year and New Year's Day (the next day), the following query would return a value of 1, because the difference in the year part is 1:

```
select datediff(yy, 'Dec 31, 1998', 'Jan 1, 1999')
```

There's no built-in mechanism for determining whether two date values are actually the same day, unless you've forced all *datetime* values to use the default time of midnight. (We saw a technique for doing so earlier in this section.) If you want to compare two *datetime* values (@date1 and @date2) to determine whether they're on the same day, regardless of the time, one technique would be to use a three-part condition like this:

```
if (datepart(mm, @date1) = datepart(mm, @date2) and
    (datepart(dd, @date1) = datepart(dd, @date2) and
    (datepart(yy, @date1) = datepart(yy, @date2)
print 'The dates are the same'
```

Alternatively, we could use a trick. If two dates are really the same, they both occurred the same number of days after any other specific date. Because the DATEDIFF() function ignores the time when we use a *datepart* of Day, we could merely check to see whether DATEDIFF() returns the same value for the two dates. Note that we could use any date constant in this query, as long as we use the same one in both function calls:

```
if datediff(day, '1/1/99', @date1) = datediff(day, '1/1/99', @date2)
    print 'The dates are the same'
```

Math Functions

Transact-SQL math functions are straightforward and typical. Many are specialized and of the type you learned about in trigonometry class. (If you don't have an engineering or mathematical application, you probably won't use those.) A handful of math functions are useful in general types of queries in applications that aren't mathematical in nature. ABS(), CEILING(), FLOOR(), and ROUND() are most useful functions for general queries to find values within a certain range.

The random number function, RAND(), is useful to generate test data or conditions. (We'll see examples of RAND() in Chapter 12.)

Table 9-13 shows the complete list of math functions and a few simple examples. (Some of the examples use other functions in addition to the math ones to illustrate how to use functions within functions.)

Function	Parameters	Result
ABS	(*numeric_expr*)	Absolute value of the numeric expression. Results returned are of the same type as *numeric_expr*.
ACOS	(*float_expr*)	Angle (in radians) whose cosine is the specified approximate numeric (*float*) expression.
ASIN	(*float_expr*)	Angle (in radians) whose sine is the specified approximate numeric (*float*) expression.
ATAN	(*float_expr*)	Angle (in radians) whose tangent is the specified approximate numeric (*float*) expression.
ATN2	(*float_expr1, float_expr2*)	Angle (in radians) whose tangent is (*float_expr1/float_expr2*) between two approximate numeric (*float*) expressions.
CEILING	(*numeric_expr*)	Smallest integer greater than or equal to the numeric expression. Result returned is the integer portion of the same type as *numeric_expr*.
COS	(*float_expr*)	Trigonometric cosine of the specified angle (in radians) in an approximate numeric (*float*) expression.
COT	(*float_expr*)	Trigonometric cotangent of the specified angle (in radians) in an approximate numeric (*float*) expression.
DEGREES	(*numeric_expr*)	Degrees converted from radians of the numeric expression. Results are of the same type as *numeric_expr*.
EXP	(*float_expr*)	Exponential value of the specified approximate numeric (*float*) expression.

Table 9-13.
Math functions in Transact-SQL.

Function	Parameters	Result
FLOOR	(*numeric_expr*)	Largest integer less than or equal to the specified numeric expression. Result is the integer portion of the same type as *numeric_expr*.
LOG	(*float_expr*)	Natural logarithm of the specified approximate numeric (*float*) expression.
LOG10	(*float_expr*)	Base-10 logarithm of the specified approximate numeric (*float*) expression.
PI	( )	Constant value of 3.141592653589793.
POWER	(*numeric_expr, y*)	Value of numeric expression to the power of *y*, where *y* is a numeric datatype (*decimal, float, int, money, numeric, real, smallint, smallmoney,* or *tinyint*). Result is of the same type as *numeric_expr*.
RADIANS	(*numeric_expr*)	Radians converted from degrees of the numeric expression. Result is of the same type as *numeric_expr*.
RAND	([*seed*])	Random approximate numeric (*float*) value between 0 and 1, optionally specifying an integer expression as the seed.
ROUND	(*numeric_expr, length*)	Numeric expression rounded off to the length (or precision) specified as an integer expression (*tinyint, smallint,* or *int*). Result is of the same type as *numeric_expr*. ROUND( ) always returns a value even if *length* is illegal. If the specified length is positive and longer than the digits after the decimal point, 0 is added after the fraction digits. If the length is negative and larger than or equal to the digits before the decimal point, ROUND( ) returns 0.00.
SIGN	(*numeric_expr*)	Returns the positive (+1), zero (0), or negative (−1) sign of the numeric expression. Result is of the same type as *numeric_expr*.
SIN	(*float_expr*)	Trigonometric sine of the specified angle (measured in radians) in an approximate numeric (*float*) expression.

(continued)

Table 9-13. *continued*

Function	Parameters	Result
SQRT	(*float_expr*)	Square root of the specified approximate numeric (*float*) expression.
SQUARE	(*float_expr*)	Square of the specified approximate numeric (*float*) expression.
TAN	(*float_expr*)	Trigonometric tangent of the specified angle (measured in radians) in an approximate numeric (*float*) expression.

The following examples show some of the math functions at work:

EXAMPLE 1

Produce a table with the cosine, sine, and tangent of all angles in multiples of 10 from 0 through 180. Format the return value as a string of six characters, with the value rounded to four decimal places.

```
DECLARE @degrees smallint
DECLARE @radians float
SELECT @degrees=0
SELECT @radians=0
WHILE (@degrees <= 180)
BEGIN
    SELECT
    DEGREES=@degrees,
    RADIANS=STR(@radians, 7, 5),
    SINE=STR(SIN(@radians), 7, 5),
    COSINE=STR(COS(@radians), 7, 5),
    TANGENT=STR(TAN(@radians), 7, 5)
    SELECT @degrees=@degrees + 10
    SELECT @radians=RADIANS(CONVERT(float, @degrees))
END
```

> **NOTE** This example actually produces 19 different result sets because the SELECT statement is issued once for each iteration of the loop. These separate result statements are concatenated and appear as one result set in this example. That works fine for illustrative purposes, but you should avoid doing an operation like this in the real world, especially on a slow network. Every one of the result sets carries with it metadata to describe itself to the client application. Chapter 12 shows a better technique.

And here are the results concatenated as a single table:

```
DEGREES RADIANS SINE    COSINE  TANGENT
------- ------- ------- ------- -------
      0  0.0000  0.0000  1.0000  0.0000
     10  0.1745  0.1736  0.9848  0.1763
     20  0.3491  0.3420  0.9397  0.3640
     30  0.5236  0.5000  0.8660  0.5774
     40  0.6981  0.6428  0.7660  0.8391
     50  0.8727  0.7660  0.6428  1.1918
     60  1.0472  0.8660  0.5000  1.7321
     70  1.2217  0.9397  0.3420  2.7475
     80  1.3963  0.9848  0.1736  5.6713
     90  1.5708  1.0000  0.0000 *******
    100  1.7453  0.9848 -0.1736 -5.6713
    110  1.9199  0.9397 -0.3420 -2.7475
    120  2.0944  0.8660 -0.5000 -1.7321
    130  2.2689  0.7660 -0.6428 -1.1918
    140  2.4435  0.6428 -0.7660 -0.8391
    150  2.6180  0.5000 -0.8660 -0.5774
    160  2.7925  0.3420 -0.9397 -0.3640
    170  2.9671  0.1736 -0.9848 -0.1763
    180  3.1416  0.0000 -1.0000 -0.0000
```

EXAMPLE 2

Express in whole-dollar terms the range of prices (non-null) of all books in the *titles* table. This example combines the scalar functions FLOOR() and CEILING() inside the aggregate functions MIN() and MAX():

```
SELECT 'Low End'=MIN(FLOOR(price)),
    'High End'=MAX(CEILING(price))
FROM titles
```

And the result:

```
Low End   High End
-------   --------
2.00      23.00
```

EXAMPLE 3

Use the same *records* table that was used earlier in the date functions example. Find all records within 150 days of September 30, 1997. Without the absolute value function ABS(), you would have to use BETWEEN or to provide two search conditions and OR them to account for both 150 days earlier and 150 days later than that date. ABS() lets you easily reduce that to a single search condition.

```
SELECT Record_number, Entered_on
FROM records
WHERE
ABS(DATEDIFF(DAY, Entered_on, '1997.09.30')) <= 150
-- Plus or minus 150 days
```

String Functions

String functions make it easier to work with character data. They let you slice and dice character data, search it, format it, and alter it. Like other scalar functions, string functions allow you to perform functions directly in your search conditions and SQL batches that would otherwise need to be returned to the calling application for further processing. (Also, remember the concatenation operator, +, for concatenating strings. You'll use this operator often in conjunction with the string functions.)

The string functions appear in Table 9-14. For more detailed information, consult the online documentation.

Function	Parameters	Returns
ASCII	(*char_expr*)	Indicates the numeric code value of the leftmost character of a character expression.
CHAR	(*integer_expr*)	Character represented by the ASCII code. The ASCII code should be a value from 0 through 255; otherwise, NULL is returned.
CHARINDEX	('*pattern*', *expression*)	Returns the starting position of the specified exact pattern. A *pattern* is a *char_expr*. The second parameter is an *expression*, usually a column name, in which SQL Server searches for *pattern*.

Table 9-14.
String functions in Transact-SQL.

Function	Parameters	Returns
DIFFERENCE	(*char_expr1*, *char_expr2*)	Shows the difference between the values of two character expressions as returned by the SOUNDEX function. DIFFERENCE compares two strings and evaluates the similarity between them, returning a value 0 through 4. The value 4 is the best match.
LEFT	(*char_expression*, *int_expression*)	Returns *int_expression* characters from the left of the *char_expression*.
LEN	(*char_expression*)	Returns the number of characters, rather than the number of bytes, of *char_expression*, excluding trailing blanks.
LOWER	(*char_expr*)	Converts uppercase character data to lowercase.
LTRIM	(*char_expr*)	Removes leading blanks.
NCHAR	(*int_expression*)	Returns the Unicode character with code *int_expression*, as defined by the Unicode standard.
PATINDEX	('%*pattern*%', *expression*)	Returns the starting position of the first occurrence of *pattern* in the specified expression, or 0 if the pattern isn't found.
QUOTENAME	QUOTENAME ('*char_string*'[, '*quote_character*'])	Returns a Unicode string with *quote_character* used as the delimiter to make the input string a valid SQL Server delimited identifier.
REPLACE	('*char_expression1*', '*char_expression2*', '*char_expression3*')	Replaces all occurrences of *char_expression2* in *char_expression1* with *char_expression3*.
REPLICATE	(*char_expr*, *integer_expr*)	Repeats a character expression a specified number of times. If *integer_expr* is negative, NULL is returned.
REVERSE	(*char_expr*)	Returns the *char_expr* backwards. This function takes a constant, variable, or column as its parameter.

(continued)

Table 9-14. *continued*

Function	Parameters	Returns
RIGHT	(*char_expr,* *integer_expr*)	Part of a character string starting *integer_expr* characters from the right. If *integer_expr* is negative, NULL is returned.
RTRIM	(*char_expr*)	Removes trailing blanks.
SOUNDEX	(*char_expr*)	Returns a four-character (SOUNDEX) of two strings. The SOUNDEX function converts an alpha string to a four-digit code used to find similar-sounding words or names.
SPACE	(*integer_expr*)	Returns a string of repeated spaces. The number of spaces is equal to *integer_expr*. If *integer_expr* is negative, NULL is returned.
STR	(*float_expr* [, *length* [, *decimal*]])	Returns character data converted from numeric data. The *length* is the total length, including decimal point, sign, digits, and spaces. The *decimal* value is the number of spaces to the right of the decimal point.
STUFF	(*char_expr1, start, length, char_expr2*)	Deletes *length* characters from *char_expr1* at *start* and then inserts *char_expr2* into *char_expr1* at *start*.
SUBSTRING	(*expression, start, length*)	Returns part of a character or binary string. The first parameter can be a character or binary string, a column name, or an expression that includes a column name. The second parameter specifies where the substring begins. The third parameter specifies the number of characters in the substring.
UNICODE	('*nchar_expression*')	Returns the integer value, as defined by the Unicode standard, for the first character of *nchar_expression*.
UPPER	(*char_expr*)	Converts lowercase character data to uppercase.

ASCII() and CHAR() functions   The function name ASCII() is really a bit of a misnomer. ASCII is only a 7-bit character set and hence can deal with only 128 characters. The character parameter to this function doesn't need to be an ASCII character. The ASCII function returns the code point for the character set installed with SQL Server, so the return value can be from 0 through 255. For example, if SQL Server is installed with the ISO 8859-1 (Latin-1) character set, the statement

```
SELECT ASCII('Ä')
```

returns 196. (The character *Ä* isn't an ASCII character.)

The CHAR() function is handy for generating test data, especially when combined with RAND() and REPLICATE(). (We'll see an example in Chapter 12.) CHAR() is also commonly used for inserting control characters such as tabs and carriage returns into your character string. Suppose, for example, that we want to return authors' last names and first names concatenated as a single field, but with a carriage return (0x0D, or decimal 13) separating them so that without further manipulation in our application, the names occupy two lines when displayed. The CHAR() function makes this simple:

```
SELECT 'NAME'=au_fname + CHAR(13) + au_lname
FROM authors
```

Here's the abbreviated result:

```
NAME
--------
Johnson
White
Marjorie
Green
Cheryl
Carson
Michael
O'Leary
Dean
Straight
Meander
Smith
Abraham
Bennet
Ann
Dull
```

UPPER() and LOWER() functions   The UPPER() and LOWER() functions are useful if you must perform case-insensitive searches on a server that is case-sensitive. On a case-sensitive server, for example, this query finds no rows even though author name Cheryl Carson is included in that table:

```
SELECT COUNT(*) FROM authors WHERE au_lname='CARSON'
```

If we change the query to the following, the row will be found:

```
SELECT COUNT(*) FROM authors WHERE UPPER(au_lname)='CARSON'
```

If the value to be searched might be of mixed case, you need to use the function on both sides of the equation. This query would find the row on the case-sensitive server:

```
DECLARE @name_param varchar(30)
SELECT @name_param='cArSoN'
SELECT COUNT(*) FROM authors WHERE UPPER(au_lname)=UPPER(@name_param)
```

In these examples, even though we might have an index on *au_lname*, it won't be useful because the index keys aren't uppercase. (However, it would be possible to use triggers to maintain an uppercase copy of the column, index it, and then use it for searching.)

You'll also often want to use UPPER() or LOWER() in stored procedures in which character parameters are used. For example, in a procedure that expects *Y* or *N* as a parameter, you'll likely want to use one of these functions in case *y* is entered instead of *Y*.

TRIM functions   The functions LTRIM() and RTRIM() are handy for dealing with leading or trailing blanks. Recall that by default (and if you don't enable the ANSI_PADDING setting), a *varchar* datatype is automatically right-trimmed of blanks, but a fixed-length *char* isn't. Suppose that we want to concatenate the *type* column and the *title_id* column from the *titles* table, with a colon separating them but with no blanks. The following query doesn't work because the trailing blanks are retained from the *type* column:

```
SELECT type + ':' + title_id FROM titles
```

This returns (in part):

```
--------------------
business    :BU1032
business    :BU1111
business    :BU2075
```

```
business    :BU7832
mod_cook    :MC2222
mod_cook    :MC3021
UNDECIDED   :MC3026
popular_comp:PC1035
popular_comp:PC8888
popular_comp:PC9999
```

But RTRIM() returns what we want:

```
SELECT RTRIM(type) + ':' + title_id FROM titles
```

And the result (in part):

```
------------------
business:BU1032
business:BU1111
business:BU2075
business:BU7832
mod_cook:MC2222
mod_cook:MC3021
UNDECIDED:MC3026
popular_comp:PC1035
popular_comp:PC8888
popular_comp:PC9999
```

String manipulation functions Functions are useful for searching and manipulating partial strings that include SUBSTRING(), CHARINDEX(), PATINDEX(), STUFF(), REPLACE(), REVERSE(), and REPLICATE(). CHARINDEX() and PATINDEX() are similar, but CHARINDEX() demands an exact match, and PATINDEX() works with a regular expression search.

> **NOTE** You could use one or both of these functions as a replacement for LIKE as well. For example, instead of saying *WHERE name LIKE '%SMITH%'*, you could say *WHERE CHARINDEX('Smith', name) > 0*. Before SQL Server version 6.0, the CHARINDEX() formulation above was much faster than LIKE for an exact pattern match query such as this. But this is no longer true—they're equal in performance.

Suppose we want to change occurrences of the word "computer" within the *notes* field of the *titles* table and replace it with "Hi-Tech-Computers." Assume that SQL Server is case-sensitive and, for simplicity, that we know that "computer" won't appear more than once per column. We want to be careful that the word "computers," which is already plural, isn't also changed. We can't just rely on searching on "computer" with a trailing blank, because the word might fall at the end of the sentence followed by a period or a comma. The regular expression *computer[^s]* always finds the word "computer" and ignores "computers," so it'll work perfectly with PATINDEX().

Here's the data before the change:

```
SELECT title_id, notes
FROM titles
WHERE notes LIKE '%[Cc]omputer%'
```

```
title_id    notes
--------    ----------------------------------------------------------
BU7832      Annotated analysis of what computers can do for you: a
            no-hype guide for the critical user.
PC8888      Muckraking reporting on the world's largest computer
            hardware and software manufacturers.
PC9999      A must-read for computer conferencing.
PS1372      A must for the specialist, this book examines the
            difference between those who hate and fear computers
            and those who don't.
PS7777      Protecting yourself and your loved ones from undue
            emotional stress in the modern world. Use of computer
            and nutritional aids emphasized.
```

You might consider using the REPLACE() function to make the substitution. However, REPLACE() requires that we search for a specific string that can't include wildcards like [^s]. Instead, we can use the older STUFF() function, which has a slightly more complex syntax. STUFF() requires that we specify the starting location within the string to make a substitution. We can use PATINDEX() to find the correct starting location, and PATINDEX() allows wildcards:

```
UPDATE titles
SET notes=STUFF(notes, PATINDEX('%computer[^s]%', notes),
    DATALENGTH('computer'), 'Hi-Tech-Computers')
WHERE  PATINDEX('%computer[^s]%', notes) > 0
```

Here's the data after the change:

```
SELECT title_id, notes
FROM titles
WHERE notes LIKE '%[Cc]omputer%'
```

494

```
title_id    notes
--------    ------------------------------------------------------
BU7832      Annotated analysis of what computers can do for you: a
            no-hype guide for the critical user.
PC8888      Muckraking reporting on the world's largest Hi-Tech-
            Computers hardware and software manufacturers.
PC9999      A must-read for Hi-Tech-Computers conferencing.
PS1372      A must for the specialist, this book examines the
            difference between those who hate and fear computers
            and those who don't.
PS7777      Protecting yourself and your loved ones from undue
            emotional stress in the modern world. Use of Hi-Tech-
            Computers and nutritional aids emphasized.
```

Of course, we could have simply provided 8 as the *length* parameter of the string "computer" to be replaced. But we used yet another function, DATALENGTH(), which would be more realistic if we were creating a general-purpose, search-and-replace procedure. Note that DATALENGTH() returns NULL if the expression is NULL, so in your applications, you might go one step further and use DATALENGTH() inside the ISNULL() function to return 0 in the case of NULL.

The REPLICATE() function is useful for adding filler characters—such as for test data. (In fact, generating test data seems to be about the only practical use for this function.) The SPACE() function is a special-purpose version of REPLICATE(): it's identical to using REPLICATE with the space character. REVERSE() reverses a character string (a standard programming puzzle, for sure, but not too common in production applications). REVERSE() can be used in a few cases to store and, more importantly, to index a character column backward to get more selectivity from the index. But in general, these three functions are rarely used.

SOUNDEX() and DIFFERENCE() Functions

If you've ever wondered how telephone operators are able to give you telephone numbers so quickly when you call directory assistance, chances are they're using a SOUNDEX algorithm. The SOUNDEX() and DIFFERENCE() functions let you search on character strings that sound similar when spoken. SOUNDEX() converts each string to a four-character code. DIFFERENCE() can then be used to evaluate the level of similarity between the SOUNDEX values for two strings as returned by SOUNDEX(). For example, you could use these functions if you wanted to look at all rows that sound like "Erickson," and they would find "Erickson," "Erikson," "Ericson," "Ericksen," "Ericsen," and so on.

SOUNDEX algorithms are commonplace in the database business, but the exact implementation can vary from vendor to vendor. For SQL Server's SOUNDEX() function, the first character of the four-character SOUNDEX code is the first letter of the word, and the remaining three characters are single digits that describe the phonetic value of the first three consonants of the word with the underlying assumption that there's one consonant per syllable. Identical consonants right next to each other are treated as a single consonant. Only nine phonetic values are possible in this scheme, because only nine possible digits exist. SOUNDEX() relies on phonetic similarities between sounds to group consonants together. In fact, SQL Server's SOUNDEX() algorithm uses only seven of the possible nine digits. No SOUNDEX() code uses the digits 8 or 9.

Vowels are ignored, as are the characters "h" and "y," so "Zastrak" would have the same code as "Zasituryk." If no second or subsequent consonant exists, the phonetic value for it is 0. In addition, SQL Server's SOUNDEX() algorithm stops evaluating the string as soon as the first nonalphabetic character is found. So if you have a hyphenated or two-word name (with a space in between), SOUNDEX() will ignore the second part of the name. More seriously, SOUNDEX() stops processing names as soon as it finds an apostrophe. So "O'Flaherty", "O'Leary", and "O'Hara" all have the same SOUNDEX() code, namely O000.

DIFFERENCE() internally compares two SOUNDEX values and returns a score from 0 through 4 to indicate how close the match is. A score of 4 is the best match, and 0 means no matches were found. Executing *DIFFERENCE(a1, a2)* first generates the four-character SOUNDEX values for a1 (call it *sx_a1*) and a2 (call it *sx_a2*). Then if all four values of the SOUNDEX value *sx_a2* match the values of *sx_a1*, the match is perfect, and the level is 4. Note that this compares the SOUNDEX values by character position, not by actual characters.

For example, the names "Smythe" and "Smith" both have a SOUNDEX() value of S530, so their difference level is 4, even though the spellings differ. If the first character (a letter, not a number) of the SOUNDEX value *sx_a1* is the same as the first character of *sx_a2*, the starting level is 1. If the first character is different, the starting level is 0. Then each character in *sx_a2* is successively compared to all characters in *sx_a1*. When a match is found, the level is incremented and the next scan on *sx_a1* starts from the location of the match. If no match is found, the next *sx_a2* character is compared to the entire four-character list of *sx_a1*.

The above description of the algorithms should make it clear that SOUNDEX() at best provides an approximation. Even so, sometimes it works extremely well. Suppose we want to query the *authors* table for names that sound similar to "Larsen." We'll define *similar* to mean "have a SOUNDEX() value of 3 or 4":

```
SELECT au_lname,
Soundex=SOUNDEX(au_lname),
Diff_Larsen=DIFFERENCE(au_lname, 'Larson')
FROM authors
WHERE
DIFFERENCE(au_lname, 'Larson') >= 3
```

Here's the result:

```
au_lname    Soundex    Diff_Larsen
--------    -------    -----------
Carson      C625       3
Karsen      K625       3
```

In this case, we found two names that rhyme with "Larsen" and didn't get any bad hits of names that don't seem close. Sometimes you'll get odd results, but if you follow the algorithms above, you'll understand how these oddities occur. For example, do you think "Bennet" and "Smith" sound similar? Well, SOUNDEX() does. When you investigate, you can see why the two names have a similar SOUNDEX() value. The SOUNDEX values have a different first letter, but the *m* and *n* sounds are converted to the same digit, and both names include a *t,* which is converted to a digit for the third position. "Bennet" has nothing to put in the fourth position, so it gets a 0. For Smith, the *h* becomes a 0. So, except for the initial letter, the rest of the SOUNDEX() strings are the same. Hence, the match.

This type of situation happens often with SOUNDEX()—you'll get hits on values that don't seem close, although usually you won't miss the ones that are similar. So if you query the *authors* table for similar values (with a DIFFERENCE() value of 3 or 4) as "Smythe," you get a perfect hit on "Smith" as you'd expect, but you also get a close match for "Bennet," which is far from obvious:

```
SELECT au_lname,
Soundex=SOUNDEX(au_lname),
Diff_Smythe=DIFFERENCE(au_lname, 'Smythe')
FROM authors
WHERE
DIFFERENCE(au_lname, 'Smythe') >= 3
```

(continued)

```
au_lname    Soundex    Diff_Smythe
--------    -------    -----------
Smith       S530       4
Bennet      B530       3
```

Sometimes SOUNDEX() misses close matches altogether. This happens when consonant blends are present. For example, you might expect to get a close match between "Knight" and "Nite." But you'll get a low value of 1 in the DIFFERENCE() between the two:

```
SELECT
"SX_KNIGHT"=SOUNDEX('Knight'),
"SX_NITE"=SOUNDEX('Nite'),
"DIFFERENCE"=DIFFERENCE('Nite', 'Knight')


SX_KNIGHT    SX_NITE    DIFFERENCE
---------    -------    ----------
K523         N300       1
```

System Functions

System functions are most useful for returning certain metadata or configuration settings. Table 9-15 lists of some of the more commonly used system functions, and it's followed by a brief discussion of the interesting features of a few of them. For complete details, see the SQL Server online documentation.

Function	Parameters	Returns
APP_NAME	NONE	Returns the program name for the current connection if one has been set by the program before logging on.
COALESCE	(*expression1, expression2, ... expressionN*)	A specialized form of the CASE statement. Returns the first non-null expression.
COL_LENGTH	(*'table_name', 'column_name'*)	The defined (maximum) storage length of a column.
COL_NAME	(*table_id, column_id*)	The name of the column.

Table 9-15.
Some commonly used system functions.

Function	Parameters	Returns
DATALENGTH	(*'expression'*)	The length of an expression of any datatype.
DB_ID	([*'database_name'*])	The database identification number.
DB_NAME	([*database_id*])	The database name.
GETANSINULL	([*'database_name'*])	The default nullability for the database. Returns 1 when the nullability is the ANSI NULL default.
HOST_ID	NONE	The workstation identification number.
HOST_NAME	NONE	The workstation name.
IDENT_INCR	(*'table_or_view'*)	The increment value specified during creation of an identity column of a table or view that includes an identity column.
IDENT_SEED	(*'table_or_view'*)	The seed value specified during creation of an identity column of a table or view that includes an identity column.
INDEX_COL	(*'table_name'*, *index_id*, *key_id*)	The indexed column name(s).
ISDATE	(*expression_of_possible_date*)	Checks whether an expression is a *datetime* datatype or a string in a recognizable *datetime* format. Returns 1 when the expression is compatible with the *datetime* type; otherwise, returns 0.
ISNUMERIC	(*expression_of_possible_ number*)	Checks whether an expression is a numeric datatype or a string in a recognizable number format. Returns 1 when the expression is compatible with arithmetic operations; otherwise, returns 0.
ISNULL	(*expression, value*)	Replaces NULL entries with the specified value.

(continued)

Table 9-15. *continued*

Function	Parameters	Returns
NULLIF	(*expression1, expression2*)	A specialized form of CASE. The resulting expression is NULL when *expression1* is equivalent to *expression2*.
OBJECT_ID	(*'object_name'*)	The database object identification number.
OBJECT_NAME	(*object_id*)	The database object name.
STATS_DATE	(*table_id, index_id*)	The date when the statistics for the specified index (*index_id*) were last updated.
SUSER_ID	([*'login_name'*])	The user's login ID number.
SUSER_NAME	([*server_user_id*])	The user's login name.
SUSER_SID	([*'login_name'*])	The security identification number (SID) for the user's login name.
SUSER_SNAME	([*server_user_sid*])	The login identification name from a user's security identification number (SID).
USER_ID	([*'user_name'*])	The user's database ID number.
USER_NAME	([*user_id*])	The user's database username.

The DATALENGTH() function is most often used with variable-length data, especially character strings, and it tells you the actual storage length of the expression (typically a column name). A fixed-length datatype always returns the storage size of its defined type (which is also its actual storage size), which makes it identical to COL_LENGTH() for such a column. The DATALENGTH() of any NULL expression returns NULL. The OBJECT_ID(), OBJECT_NAME(), SUSER_ID(), SUSER_NAME() SUSER_SAME(), SUSER_SID(), USER_ID(), USER_NAME(), COL_NAME(), DB_ID(), and DB_NAME() functions are commonly used to more easily eliminate the need for joins between system catalogs and to get run-time information dynamically.

For example, recognizing that an object name is unique within a database for a specific user, we can use the statement on the next page to determine whether an object by the name "foo" exists for our current user ID; if so, we can drop it (assuming that we know it's a table).

```
IF (SELECT id FROM sysobjects WHERE id=OBJECT_ID('foo')
    AND uid=USER_ID() AND type='U') > 0
    DROP TABLE foo
```

System functions can be handy with constraints and views. Recall that a view can benefit from the use of system functions. For example, if the *accounts* table includes a column that is the system login ID of the user to whom the account belongs, we can create a view of the table that allows the user to work only with his or her own accounts. We do this simply by making the WHERE clause of the view something like this:

```
WHERE system_login_id=SUSER_SID()
```

Or if we want to ensure that updates on a table occur only from an application named CS_UPDATE.EXE, we can use a CHECK constraint in the following way:

```
CONSTRAINT APP_CHECK (APP_NAME()='CS_UPDATE.EXE')
```

For this particular example, the check is by no means foolproof, as the application must set the *app_name* in its login record. A rogue application could simply lie. To prevent casual use by someone running an application like ISQL.EXE, the above formulation might be just fine for your needs. But if you're worried about hackers, this formulation isn't appropriate. Other functions, such as SUSER_SID(), have no analogous way to be explicitly set, so they're better for security operations like this.

The ISDATE() and ISNUMERIC() functions can be useful to determine whether data is appropriate for an operation. For example, suppose that your predecessor didn't know much about using a relational database and defined a column as type *char* and then stored values in it that were naturally of type *money*. Then your predecessor compounded the problem by sometimes encoding letter codes in the same field as notes. You're trying to work with the data as is (eventually you'll clean it up, but you have a deadline to meet), and you need to get a sum and average of all the values, whenever a value that makes sense to use is present. (If you think this example is contrived, talk to a programmer in an MIS shop of a Fortune 1000 company with legacy applications and ask whether this situation sounds uncommon.) Suppose that the table has a *varchar(20)* column named *acct_bal* with these values:

```
acct_bal
--------
205.45
```

(continued)

```
E
(NULL)
B
605.78
32.45
8
98.45
64.23
8456.3
```

If you try to simply use the aggregate functions directly, you'll get error 409:

```
SELECT SUM(acct_bal), AVG(acct_bal)
FROM bad_column_for_money

Msg 409, Level 16, State 2
The sum or average aggregate operation cannot take a varchar
data type as an argument.
```

If you try to use CONVERT(), the columns that contain alphabetic characters will cause the CONVERT() to fail:

```
SELECT
"SUM"=SUM(CONVERT(money, acct_bal)),
"AVG"=AVG(CONVERT(money, acct_bal))
FROM bad_column_for_money

Msg 235, Level 16, State 0
Cannot convert CHAR value to MONEY. The CHAR value has incorrect
syntax.
```

But if you use both CONVERT() in the select list and ISNUMERIC() in the WHERE clause to choose only those values for which a conversion would be possible, everything works great:

```
SELECT
"SUM"=SUM(CONVERT(money, acct_bal)),
"AVG"=AVG(CONVERT(money, acct_bal))
FROM bad_column_for_money
WHERE ISNUMERIC(acct_bal)=1

SUM       AVG
--------  --------
9,470.66  1,352.95
```

Property Functions

You can think of property functions as a type of system function because they allow you access to metadata. In earlier versions of SQL Server, the only way to determine which options or properties an object had was to actually query a system table, and possibly even decode a bitmap *status* column. SQL Server 7 provides a set of functions that return information about databases, files, filegroups, indexes, objects, and datatypes.

For example, to determine whether a database has the *select into/bulkcopy* property set, we can use the DATABASEPROPERTY() function:

```
IF DATABASEPROPERTY('pubs', 'IsBulkCopy') = 1
    /* call a procedure than runs the BULK INSERT command */
else
    /* call a procedure that does something else */
```

Many of the properties that we can check for correspond to database options that can be set with the *sp_dboption* stored procedure. One example is the *select into/bulkcopy* option, which determines the value of the IsBulkCopy property. Other properties, such as IsInLoad, are set internally by SQL Server. For a complete list of all the possible database properties and their possible values, please see the SQL Server documentation. Also in the documentation, you'll find the complete list of properties and possible values for use with the following functions:

- COLUMNPROPERTY()
- FILEGROUPPROPERTY()
- FILEPROPERTY()
- INDEXPROPERTY()
- OBJECTPROPERTY()
- TYPEPROPERTY()

Niladic Functions

ANSI SQL-92 has a handful of what it calls *niladic* functions—a fancy way to indicate that these functions don't accept any parameters. Niladic functions were implemented for version 6.0 and map directly to one of SQL Server's system functions. Frankly, they were added to SQL Server 6.0 because they were mandated for conformance to the ANSI SQL-92 standard—all of their functionality was already provided. Table 9-16 on the following page shows niladic functions and their equivalent SQL Server system functions.

Niladic Function	Equivalent SQL Server System Function
CURRENT_TIMESTAMP	GETDATE()
SYSTEM_USER	SUSER_NAME()
CURRENT_USER	USER_NAME()
SESSION_USER	USER_NAME()
USER	USER_NAME()

Table 9-16.
Niladic functions and equivalent SQL Server functions.

If you execute the following two SELECT statements, you'll see that they return identical results:

```
SELECT CURRENT_TIMESTAMP, USER, SYSTEM_USER, CURRENT_USER,
SESSION_USER

SELECT GETDATE(), USER_NAME(), SUSER_NAME(),
USER_NAME(), USER_NAME()
```

Other Parameterless Functions

As mentioned earlier in the chapter, the older SQL Server documentation refers to a set of parameterless system functions as *global variables*, because they're designated by @@, which is similar to the designation for local variables. However, these values aren't variables, because you can't declare them and you can't assign them values.

These functions are global only in the sense that any connection can access their values. However, in many cases the value returned by these functions is specific to the connection. For example, @@ERROR represents the last error number generated for a specific connection, not the last error number in the entire system. @@ROWCOUNT represents the number of rows selected or affected by the last statement for the current connection.

Many of these parameterless system functions keep track of performance-monitoring information for your SQL Server. These include @@CPU_BUSY, @@IO_BUSY, @@PACK_SENT, and @@PACK_RECEIVED.

Some of these functions are extremely static, and others are extremely volatile. For example, @@VERSION represents the build number and code freeze date of the SQL Server executable (sqlservr.exe) that you're running. It will change only when you upgrade or apply a service pack. Functions like @@ROWCOUNT are extremely volatile. Take a look at the code on the next page and its results.

```
select * from publishers
select @@ROWCOUNT
select @@ROWCOUNT
```

And the results:

```
pub_id pub_name                      city                   state country
------ ------------------------      --------------------   ----- ----------

0736   New Moon Books                Boston                 MA    USA
0877   Binnet & Hardley              Washington             DC    USA
1389   Algodata Infosystems          Berkeley               CA    USA
1622   Five Lakes Publishing         Chicago                IL    USA
1756   Ramona Publishers             Dallas                 TX    USA
9901   GGG&G                         München                NULL  Germany
9952   Scootney Books                New York               NY    USA
9999   Lucerne Publishing            Paris                  NULL  France

(8 row(s) affected)


-----------

8

(1 row(s) affected)


-----------

1

(1 row(s) affected)
```

Note that the first time @@ROWCOUNT was selected, it returned the number of rows in the *publishers* table (8). The second time @@ROWCOUNT was selected, it returned the number of rows returned by the previous select @@ROWCOUNT (1). Any query you execute that affects rows will change the value of @@ROWCOUNT.

SEE ALSO For the complete list of parameterless functions, refer to the SQL Server documentation. You can access the full set of documentation from the startup menu of the SQL Server evaluation CD (included with this book). You don't have to actually install SQL Server to read the documentation on the CD.

Summary

This chapter discussed the programming extensions beyond typical implementations of SQL that make Transact-SQL a specialized programming language. These extensions include control of flow, conditional branching, looping, variables, logical operations, bitwise operations, and a variety of scalar functions. The extensions let you write sophisticated routines directly in Transact-SQL and execute them directly in the SQL Server engine. Without them, much more logic would need to be written into client applications, which would reduce performance because more conversation would need to take place across the network.

Having now discussed in some depth the basics of the SQL language and the Transact-SQL extensions, let's move on to using these extensions in stored procedures and triggers: Chapter 10.

BATCHES, TRANSACTIONS, STORED PROCEDURES, AND TRIGGERS

In this chapter, we'll use Transact-SQL for more than interactive queries. When we send a query to the server, we're sending a command batch to SQL Server. But we can do even more! For example, we can wrap up commands in a module that can be stored and cached at the server for later reuse (stored procedures), and we can create modules that automatically execute when some event occurs (triggers). This chapter takes a closer look at transactions and transaction boundaries and shows how changes by multiple users affect them.

Batches

A batch is one or several SQL Server commands that are dispatched and executed together. Because every batch sent from the client to the server requires handshaking between the two, sending a batch instead of sending separate commands can prove to be more efficient. Even a batch that doesn't return a result set (for example, a single INSERT statement) requires at least an acknowledgment that the command was processed and offers a status code for its level of success. At the server, the batch must be received, queued for execution, and so on.

Although commands are grouped and dispatched together for execution, each command is distinct from the others. Let's look at an example. Suppose you need to execute 150 INSERT statements. Executing all 150 statements in one batch requires the processing overhead to be incurred once rather than 150 times. In one real-world situation, an application that took 5 to 6 seconds to complete 150 individual INSERT statements was changed so that all 150 statements were sent as one batch. The processing time decreased to well under 0.5 second, more than a tenfold improvement. And this was on a LAN, not on a slow network like a WAN or the Internet, where the improvement would have been even more pronounced. (Try running an application with 150 batches to insert 150 rows over the Internet, and you'll be really sorry!)

Using a batch is a huge win. By using the Transact-SQL constructs that were presented in Chapter 9, such as conditional logic and looping, you can often perform sophisticated operations within a single batch and eliminate the need to carry on an extensive conversation between the client and the server. Those operations can also be saved on the server as a stored procedure, which allows them to execute even more efficiently. Using batches and stored procedures to minimize client/server conversations is crucial for achieving high-performing applications. And now that more applications are being deployed on slower networks—such as WANs, the Internet, and dial-up systems—instead of on LANs only, using batches and stored procedures is crucial.

Every SELECT statement (except for those used for assigning a value to a variable) generates a result set. Even a SELECT statement that finds zero rows returns a result set that describes the columns selected. Every time the server sends a result set back to the client application, it must send *metadata* as well as the actual data. The metadata describes the result set to the client. You can think of metadata in this way: "Here's a result set with eight columns. The first column is named *last_name* and is of type *char(30)*. The second column is...."

Obviously, then, executing a single SELECT statement with a WHERE clause formulated to find (in one fell swoop) all 247 rows that meet your criteria is much more efficient than separately executing 247 SELECT statements that each return one row of data. In the former case, one result set is returned. In the latter case, 247 result sets are returned—the performance difference is striking.

Using batches might seem like an obvious necessity, yet many programmers still write applications that perform poorly because they don't use batches. The problem is especially common for developers who have worked on ISAM or similar sequential files doing row-at-a-time processing. Unlike ISAM, SQL Server works best with *sets* of data, not individual rows of data, so that you can minimize conversations between the server and the client application.

There's actually a middle ground between using one SELECT statement that returns all your rows and using an individual batch to return each row.

Batches can contain multiple statements, each one returning its own metadata, so the ideal solution is to minimize your total number of statements. Multiple SELECTs within a single batch are still better than having each statement in its own batch, because each batch has the overhead of handshaking between the client and server.

Following is a simple batch, issued from Query Analyzer. Even though three unrelated operations are being performed, we can package them in a single batch to conserve bandwidth:

```
INSERT authors VALUES (etc.)
SELECT * FROM authors
UPDATE publishers SET pub_id= (etc.)
GO
```

All the statements within a single batch are parsed as a unit. This means that if you have a syntax error in any of the statements, none of the statements will execute. For example, consider this batch of two statements, which we can try to execute from Query Analyzer:

```
SELECT * FROM sales
SELECT * FOM titleauthor
GO
```

When you execute this batch, you'll get the following error:

```
Server: Msg 170, Level 15, State 1
Line 2: Incorrect syntax near 'fom'.
```

Even though the first SELECT statement is perfectly legal, because of the error in the second statement, no data is returned. If we separated this into two different batches, the first one would return a result set and the second one would return an error.

Now suppose that instead of mistyping the keyword FROM as *FOM*, we had mistyped the name of the table:

```
SELECT * FROM sales
SELECT * FROM titleautor
GO
```

SQL Server 7 introduces delayed name resolution, in which object names aren't resolved until execution time. Earlier versions of SQL Server resolved names at compile time, so the above batch would return an "Invalid Object Name" error, and nothing would be executed. In this example, SQL Server 7 returns the data from the first SELECT, followed by the error message at the top of the next page.

```
Server: Msg 208, Level 16, State 1
Invalid object name 'titleautor'.
```

However, if we had mistyped the object name in the first statement, execution of the batch would stop when the error was encountered. No data would be returned by any subsequent valid queries.

Normally when using Query Analyzer, everything in the query window is considered a single batch and is sent to SQL Server for parsing, compiling, and execution when you click the green EXECUTE button. However, Query Analyzer provides two ways around this. First, it allows you to highlight just a section of code in the query window so that when you click the EXECUTE button, only the highlighted text is sent as a batch to SQL Server. Alternatively, you can include the keyword GO between your queries.

If you use either of the text-based query tools (*osql* or *isql*), there's no green EXECUTE button to click. When using those tools, you must type *GO* on a line by itself to indicate that everything you've typed up to that point is a batch. The tool (*osql* or *isql*) will then send that batch to SQL Server for processing.

GO isn't an SQL command. It's the end-of-batch signal understood only by certain client tools. It's interpreted by the client to mean that everything since the last GO should be sent to the server for execution. SQL Server never sees the GO command and has no idea what it means. With a custom application, a batch is executed with a single *SQLExecute* from ODBC (or *dbsqlexec* from DB-Library).

If you include the GO command in your query window in Query Analyzer, Query Analyzer will break up your statement into the indicated batches behind the scenes. Each batch (as marked by the GO command) will be sent individually to SQL Server.

A collection of batches that we frequently want to execute together is sometimes called a *script*. Most of the client tools allow us a mechanism for loading a script that we've saved to a text file and for executing it. In Query Analyzer, we can use the File/Open command to load a script. From the command-line *osql* or *isql* programs, we can specify the */i* flag followed by a filename to indicate that the SQL Server batches to execute should come from the specified file.

The fact that the client tool processes GO and not SQL Server can lead to some unexpected behavior. Suppose you have a script containing several batches. During your testing, you want to comment out a couple of the batches, to ignore them for the time being. Your commented script might then look something like this:

```
SELECT * FROM authors
/*
GO
SELECT * FROM sales
GO
SELECT * FROM publishers
GO
*/
SELECT * FROM titles
GO
```

The intention here was to comment out the SELECT from the *sales* and *publishers* tables and to run the SELECT from *authors* and *titles* as a single batch. However, if you run this script from Query Analyzer, you'll find that you get exactly the opposite behavior! That is, you'll see the data from the *sales* and *publishers* tables, but not from *authors* or *titles*. If you look at this script from the perspective of the client tool, the behavior makes sense. The tool doesn't try to interpret any of your SQL statements; it just breaks the statements into batches to be sent to SQL Server. A batch is marked by a GO command at the beginning of a line. So, the above script contains four batches.

The first batch (everything before the first GO) is:

```
SELECT * FROM authors
/*
```

SQL Server generates an error message because there's an open comment with no corresponding close comment.

The second and third batches are:

```
SELECT * FROM sales
```

and

```
SELECT * FROM publishers
```

Both of these batches are perfectly legal, and SQL Server can process them and return results.

The fourth batch is:

```
*/
SELECT * FROM titles
```

SQL Server also generates an error for this last one, because it has a close comment without an open comment marker, and no data will be returned.

If you want to comment out statements within a script that can contain the end-of-batch GO command, you should use the alternative comment marker—the double dash—in front of every GO. Your script would then look like this:

```
SELECT * FROM authors
/*
--GO
SELECT * FROM sales
--GO
SELECT * FROM publishers
--GO
*/
SELECT * FROM titles
GO
```

With this revised script, the client tool won't recognize the GO as the end-of-batch marker, because it's not the first thing on a line. The client will consider this script to be one single batch and send it to SQL Server as such. SQL Server will then ignore everything between the open comment (/*) and the close comment (*/) and execute only the SELECT statements from *authors* and *titles*.

Transactions

Like a batch, a user-declared transaction typically consists of several SQL commands that read and update the database. However, a batch is basically a client-side concept, which controls how many statements are sent to SQL Server for processing at once. A transaction, on the other hand, is a server-side concept that deals with how much work SQL Server will do before it considers the changes committed. A multistatement transaction doesn't make any permanent changes in a database until a COMMIT TRANSACTION statement is issued. In addition, a transaction can undo its changes when a ROLLBACK TRANSACTION statement is issued.

Both batches and transactions can contain multiple commands. In fact, transactions and batches can have a many-to-many relationship. A single transaction can span several batches (although that's bad from a performance perspective), and a batch can contain multiple transactions. The following examples illustrate these possibilities. Note that you can use TRAN as an abbreviation for TRANSACTION.

The first script is one transaction spread across four batches:

```
BEGIN TRAN
INSERT authors VALUES (etc.)
GO
SELECT * FROM authors
GO
UPDATE publishers SET pub_id= (etc.)
GO
COMMIT TRAN
GO
```

This second script is one batch that contains two transactions:

```
BEGIN TRAN
INSERT authors VALUES (etc.)
SELECT * FROM authors
COMMIT TRAN
BEGIN TRAN
UPDATE publishers SET pub_id= (etc.)
INSERT publishers VALUES (etc.)
COMMIT TRAN
GO
```

Now let's look at a simple transaction in a little more detail. The BEGIN TRAN and COMMIT TRAN statements cause the commands between them to be performed as a unit:

```
BEGIN TRAN
INSERT authors VALUES (etc.)
SELECT * FROM authors
UPDATE publishers SET pub_id= (etc.)
COMMIT TRAN
GO
```

Transaction processing in SQL Server assures that all commands within a transaction are performed as a unit of work—even in the presence of a hardware or general system failure. Such transactions are referred to as having the ACID properties (atomicity, consistency, isolation, and durability). (For more information about the ACID properties, refer to the section on transaction processing in Chapter 2.)

Explicit and Implicit Transactions

By default, SQL Server treats each statement—whether dispatched individually or as part of a batch—as independent and immediately commits it. Logically, the only kind of statement that can be committed is a statement that changes something in the database, so talking about committing a SELECT statement is really meaningless. When we look at transaction isolation levels later in this section, we'll see that it's important in some cases to include SELECTs inside larger transactions. However, for the most part when we talk about transactions, we're talking about data modification statements (INSERT, UPDATE, and DELETE). If you want multiple statements to be part of a transaction, you must wrap the group of statements within BEGIN TRANSACTION and COMMIT or ROLLBACK TRANSACTION statements.

You can also configure SQL Server to implicitly start a transaction by using SET IMPLICIT_TRANSACTIONS ON or by turning the option on globally using *sp_configure 'user options', 2*. More precisely, take the previous value for the *'user options'* setting and OR it with (decimal) 2, which is the mask for IMPLICIT_TRANSACTIONS.

For example, if the previous value were (decimal) 8, you'd set it to 10, because 8|2 is 10. (The symbol used here is the vertical bar, not a forward or backward slash.) If bit operations like 8|2 are somewhat foreign to you, let SQL Server do the work. You can issue a SELECT 8|2 in Query Analyzer, and the value returned will be 10. (But be careful not to assume that you just add 2 to whatever is already there—for example, 10|2 is 10, not 12.)

If implicit transactions are enabled, all statements are considered part of a transaction and no work is committed until and unless an explicit COMMIT TRAN (or synonymously, COMMIT WORK) is issued. This is true even if all the statements in the batch have executed: you must issue a COMMIT TRANSACTION in a subsequent batch before any changes are considered permanent. Throughout the examples in this book, we assume that you have not set IMPLICIT_TRANSACTIONS on and that any multistatement transaction must begin with BEGIN TRAN.

Error Checking in Transactions

One of the most common mistakes that developers make with SQL Server is to assume that *any* error within a transaction will cause the transaction to automatically roll back. If conditional action results from a possible error, your multistatement transactions should check for errors by selecting the value of @@ERROR after each statement. If a nonfatal error is encountered and you don't take action on it, processing moves on to the next statement. Only fatal errors cause the batch to be automatically aborted.

> **TIP** Neither a query that finds no rows meeting the criteria of the WHERE clause nor a searched UPDATE statement that affects no rows is an error, and @@ERROR returns a 0 (meaning no error) for either case. If you want to check for "no rows affected," use @@ROWCOUNT, not @@ERROR.

Syntax errors always cause the entire batch to be aborted before execution even begins, and references to objects that don't exist (for example, a SELECT from a table that doesn't exist) cause a batch to stop execution at that point. Typically, you'll work out syntax errors and correct references to objects before you put an application into production, so these won't be much of an issue.

However, a syntax error on a batch dynamically built and executed using EXECUTE(*'string'*) can't be caught until execution. You can think of this EXECUTE(*'string'*) construct as a way of nesting batches. If the *string* consists of multiple statements, a syntax or object reference error will abort the inner batch only. Processing proceeds to the next statement in the outer batch. For example, consider the following script:

```
DECLARE @tablename sysname
SET @tablename = 'authours'
EXECUTE ('USE pubs SELECT * FROM ' + @tablename + ' PRINT "Inner Batch Done")
PRINT "Outer Batch Done"
```

This batch won't have an error detected at parse time, so SQL Server will attempt to execute it. The DECLARE and the SET will be executed successfully, but the nested batch inside the EXECUTE will have a problem. There's an error in the SELECT, because the table name *authours* doesn't exist in the *pubs* database. The inner batch will generate an error during its parsing phase, so the third statement in the inner batch (PRINT) will *not* be executed. However, the outer batch will continue, and the message "Outer Batch Done" will be printed.

Errors that occur in a production environment are typically resource errors that you probably won't encounter much, especially if you've sufficiently tested to make sure that your configuration settings and environment are appropriate. Out-of-resource errors occur when the system runs out of locks, when there isn't enough memory to run a procedure, when a database runs out of room, and so on. For these types of fatal errors, conditional action based on @@ERROR is moot because the batch will automatically be aborted.

The following errors are among the most common ones that you need to be concerned about:

- Lack of permissions on an object.

- Constraint violations.

- Duplicates encountered while trying to update or insert a row.

- Deadlocks with another user.

■ NOT NULL violations.

■ Illegal values for the current datatype.

Following is a SQL Server Internet newsgroup posting from a user who encountered a nonfatal execution error and assumed that the entire transaction should have been automatically aborted. When that didn't happen, the user assumed that SQL Server must have a grievous bug. Here's the posting:

> Using SQL 6.5 in the example below, the empty tables *b* and *c* each get an insert within one tran. The insert into table *c* is fine, but the insert to *b* fails a DRI reference, but the table *c* still has a row in it. Isn't this a major bug?! Should the tran not have been rolled back implicitly!?
>
> *—Keith*

```
create table a (
a char(1) primary key)

create table b (
b char(1) references a)

create table c (
c char(1))
go

create proc test as
begin transaction
insert c values ( 'X' )
Insert b values ( 'X' )   --Fails reference
commit transaction
go

exec test
go

select *
from c  --Returns  'X'  !!
```

The statements, however, are performing as expected; the bug exists in the way the user wrote the transaction. The transaction hasn't checked for errors for each statement and *unconditionally* commits at the end. So even if one statement fails with a nonfatal execution error (in this case, a foreign key violation occurred), execution proceeds to the next statement. Ultimately, the COMMIT is executed, so all the statements without errors are committed. That's exactly what the procedure has been told to do. If you want to roll back a transaction if *any* error occurs, you must check @@ERROR or use SET XACT_ABORT.

Here's an example of the procedure rewritten to perform error checking, with a branch to perform a rollback if any error is encountered:

```
CREATE PROC test as
BEGIN TRANSACTION
INSERT c VALUES ('X')
    IF (@@ERROR <> 0) GOTO on_error
INSERT b VALUES ('X')  -- Fails reference
    IF (@@ERROR <> 0) GOTO on_error
COMMIT TRANSACTION
RETURN(0)


on_error:
ROLLBACK TRANSACTION
RETURN(1)
```

This simple procedure illustrates the power of Transact-SQL. The system function @@ERROR can return a value for the connection after each statement. A value of 0 for @@ERROR means no error occurred. Given the data the user provided, the INSERT statement on table *b* will fail with a foreign key violation. The error message for that type of failure is error 547, with text such as this:

```
INSERT statement conflicted with COLUMN FOREIGN KEY constraint
'FK__b__b__723BFC65'. The conflict occurred in database 'pubs',
table 'a', column 'a'
```

Consequently, @@ERROR would be set to 547 following that INSERT statement. Therefore, the statement *IF (@@ERROR <> 0)* evaluates as TRUE, and execution follows the *GOTO* to the *on_error:* label. Here, the transaction is rolled back. The procedure terminates with a return code of 1 because the RETURN(1) statement was used. Had the branch to *on_error:* not been followed (by virtue of @@ERROR not being 0), the procedure would have continued line-by-line execution. It would have reached COMMIT TRANS-ACTION, and then it would have returned value 0 and never made it all the way to the *on_error:* section.

As you do with most programming languages, make sure that a status is returned from a procedure to indicate success or failure (or other possible outcomes) and that those return status codes are checked from the calling routines. In Keith's original code, an "EXEC test" invoked the procedure. This approach is perfectly legal and could be done equally well with a procedure that returns 0 for SUCCESS and 1 for FAILURE. However, merely using "EXEC test" won't directly provide information about whether the procedure performed as expected. A better method is to use a local variable to examine the return code from that procedure:

```
DECLARE @retcode int
EXEC @retcode=test
```

Following execution of the test procedure, the local variable *@retcode* has the value 0 (if no errors occurred in the procedure) or 1 (if execution branched to the *on_error:* section).

The SET XACT_ABORT option was added to SQL Server in version 6.5 to help users like Keith. If you set this option, any error—not just a fatal error (equivalent to checking @@ERROR <> 0 after every statement)—will terminate the batch. Here's another way to ensure that *nothing* is committed if *any* error is encountered:

```
CREATE PROC test AS
SET XACT_ABORT ON
BEGIN TRANSACTION
INSERT c VALUES ('X')
INSERT b VALUES ('X')  -- Fails reference
COMMIT TRANSACTION
GO

EXEC test
GO

SELECT * FROM c
```

The output:

```
(0 rows affected)
```

Note that the name of the XACT_ABORT option is a bit of a misnomer because the current batch, not simply the transaction, will be immediately aborted if an error occurs, just as it is when a fatal resource error is encountered. This has consequences that might not be immediately apparent. For example, if you issued two transactions within one batch, the second transaction would never be executed because the batch would be aborted before the second transaction got a chance to execute. More subtly, suppose we want to use good programming practice and check the return status of the procedure above. (Note that even though it doesn't explicitly do a RETURN(), every procedure has a return status by default, with 0 indicating SUCCESS.)

We could write a batch like this:

```
DECLARE @retcode int
EXEC @retcode=test
SELECT @retcode
```

Yet there's a subtle but important problem here. If the procedure has an error, the SELECT @RETCODE statement will never be executed: the entire batch will be aborted by virtue of the SET XACT_ABORT statement. This is why we recommend checking @@ERROR instead of using SET XACT_ABORT. Checking @@ERROR after each statement is a bit more tedious, but it gives you finer control of execution in your procedures.

No doubt, error handling will be improved in future releases. Unfortunately, error handling in SQL Server 7 can be somewhat messy and inconsistent. For example, there's no way to install a routine that means "Do this on any error" (other than SET XACT_ABORT, which aborts but doesn't let you specify the actions to be performed). Instead, you must use something similar to the preceding examples that check @@ERROR and then do a GOTO.

In addition, there's currently no easy way to determine in advance which errors might be considered fatal so that the batch can be aborted vs. which errors are nonfatal so that the next statement can be executed. In most cases, an error with a severity level of 16 or higher is fatal and the batch will be aborted. Syntax that refers to nonexistent functions are level-15 errors, yet the batch is still aborted. Although you can use @@ERROR to return the specific error number, no function such as @@SEVERITY is available to indicate the error's severity level. Instead, you must subsequently select from the *sysmessages* table to see the severity level of the last error. To further complicate matters, some level-16 errors aren't fatal. Table 10-1 on the following page lists the most common nonfatal level-16 errors. Note the %.*s placeholders in the error messages: SQL Server will substitute the actual names being referenced when it issues the error message.

Admittedly, the rules are hardly consistent, and this area is ripe for some attention in future releases. As you write your procedures, keep in mind that they could be automatically aborted due to an unexpected fatal error, or you could cause them to abort with a nonfatal error.

Error	Error Message
515	Attempt to insert the value NULL into column '%.*s', table '%.*s'; column doesn't allow nulls. %s fails.
544	Attempt to insert explicit value for *identity* column in table '%.*s' when IDENTITY_INSERT is set to OFF.
547	Attempt to execute %s statement conflicted with %s %s constraint '%.*s'. The conflict occurred in database '%.*s', table '%.*s'%s%.*s%s.
550	Attempt to insert or update failed because the target view either specifies WITH CHECK OPTION or spans a view that specifies WITH CHECK OPTION, and one or more rows resulting from the operation didn't qualify under the CHECK OPTION constraint.

Table 10-1.
Common nonfatal level-16 errors.

Transaction Isolation Levels

The isolation level at which your transaction runs determines your application's sensitivity to changes made by others; consequently, it also determines how long your transaction needs to hold locks to potentially protect against changes made by others. SQL Server 7 offers four isolation-level behaviors:

- READ UNCOMMITTED (dirty read)
- READ COMMITTED (default—READ COMMITTED is equivalent to the term CURSOR STABILITY, which is used by several other products such as IBM DB/2)
- REPEATABLE READ
- SERIALIZABLE

Your transactions will behave differently depending on which isolation level is set. The saying "Not to decide *is* to decide" applies here, because every transaction has an isolation level whether you've specified it or not. You should understand the levels and choose the one that best fits your needs.

NOTE The syntactical options listed above correspond to the SQL standard isolation levels, which were discussed in detail in Chapter 3 in the section about the transaction manager. In this section, we'll only look at information that wasn't covered earlier. See Chapter 3 if you need a refresher.

When using the READ UNCOMMITTED option, keep in mind that you should deal with inconsistencies that might result from dirty reads. Because share locks aren't issued and exclusive locks of other connections aren't honored (that is, the data pages can be read, even though they're supposedly locked), it's possible to get some spurious errors during execution when using the READ UNCOMMITTED option. A moment later, reexecuting the same command is likely to work without error.

To shield your end users from such errors, your client applications using isolation level 0 (dirty read) should be prepared to retry due to spurious 605, 606, 624, or 625 errors. One of these errors might get raised to falsely indicate that the database is inconsistent. In such a case, what frequently happens is that an update or insert rolls back along with its page allocations, so you read data pages that no longer exist and logically never did. Ordinarily, locking will prevent such inconsistencies, but READ UNCOMMITTED takes some shortcuts and the errors can still occur. The retry logic you use should be identical to the logic that you would use to retry on a deadlock condition (error 1205).

> **NOTE** Of course, you don't *have* to add retry logic, but without it the command will be aborted and your end user might see a scary and confusing message. Adding a good error handler can make your client application behave much better by enabling an automatic retry, and the user will never know when such an error is raised.

Nothing illustrates the differences and effects of isolation levels like seeing them for yourself with some simple examples. To run the following examples, you'll need to establish two connections to SQL Server. Remember that each connection is *logically* a different user, even if both connections use the same login ID. (Locks made by one connection affect the other connection, even if both are logged in as the same user.) In case you can't run these examples, the SQL scripts and output are shown here.

EXAMPLE 1

This example shows a dirty read. A simple command file on the companion CD, RUN_ISOLATION1.CMD, spawns two simultaneous OSQL.EXE sessions, running the scripts ISOLATION_CNX1.SQL and ISOLATION_CNX2.SQL. The command file assumes that you're connecting to SQL Server on your local workstation. If not, you'll have to edit the RUN_ISOLATION1.CMD file as follows: change the argument after the /S flag from a single dot (meaning local server) to the name of the SQL Server machine.

Following are the scripts and the output (in bold) as will be contained in the output files ISOLATION_CNX1.OUT and ISOLATION_CNX2.OUT after the command file has been executed.

> **NOTE** The procedures *sem_set* and *sem_wait* provide a simple synchronization mechanism between the two connections. They do nothing more than set a value and then poll for a value—a handy technique. You can create these procedures by running the SEMAPHORE.SQL script, which is included on the companion CD.
>
> But this mechanism won't always do the job as it does in this case. For example, if you put *set_sem* within a transaction, it could be aborted or rolled back. Also, for illustrative purposes, simple delays are sometimes used here to coordinate the two scripts. Relying on timing like this creates the potential for a race condition, and it's not how you'd want to program a production application.

```
-- ISOLATION_CNX2.SQL
USE pubs
GO


EXEC sem_wait 1     -- Wait until other connection says can start
BEGIN TRAN
    UPDATE authors SET au_lname='Smith'
    -- Give other connection chance to read uncommitted data
    WAITFOR DELAY "000:00:20"
ROLLBACK TRAN

EXEC sem_set 0     -- Tell other connection done
```

(23 rows affected)

```
-- ISOLATION_CNX1.SQL
-- Illustrate Read Uncommitted (aka "Dirty Read")
--
USE pubs
GO
EXEC sem_set 0     -- Clear semaphore to start
GO

-- First verify there's only one author named 'Smith'
```

```
SELECT au_lname FROM authors WHERE au_lname='Smith'
GO

au_lname
--------------------------
Smith

(1 row affected)

SET TRANSACTION ISOLATION LEVEL READ UNCOMMITTED

-- Signal other connection that it's OK to update, and then wait
-- for it to proceed. (Obvious possible race condition here;
-- this is just for illustration.)

EXEC sem_set 1
-- Wait 10 secs for other connection to update
WAITFOR DELAY "000:00:10"
-- Check again for authors of name 'Smith'.  Now find 23 of them,
-- even though the other connection doesn't COMMIT the changes.
SELECT au_lname FROM authors WHERE au_lname='Smith'

au_lname
--------------------------
Smith
Smith
Smith
Smith
Smith
Smith
Smith
Smith
Smith
Smith
Smith
Smith
Smith
Smith
Smith
Smith
Smith
Smith
Smith
Smith
```

(continued)

```
Smith
Smith

(23 rows affected)

IF (@@ROWCOUNT > 0)
    PRINT 'Just read uncommitted data !!'

Just read uncommitted data !!

-- Now the other connection will roll back its changes:
EXEC sem_wait 0

-- Now check again for authors of name 'Smith'.
-- Find only one now, because other connection did a rollback.
SELECT au_lname FROM authors WHERE au_lname='Smith'

au_lname
-------------------------
Smith

(1 row affected)
```

The previous scripts, running simultaneously, illustrate that by setting the isolation level to READ UNCOMMITTED, you can read data that logically never existed (a dirty read). The update to *Smith* was never committed by the ISOLATION_CNX2.SQL script, yet the other connection read it. Not only did the connection read the update, but it did so immediately and didn't have to wait for the exclusive lock of the second connection updating the data to be released.

In this example, concurrency is high; however, consistency of the data isn't maintained. By changing the isolation level back to the default (READ COMMITTED), the same scripts would never see more than one row containing *Smith*. But with READ COMMITTED, the connection reading the data must wait until the updating transaction is done, and this is the trade-off: higher consistency is achieved (the uncommitted rows aren't seen by others), but concurrency is reduced.

EXAMPLE 2

This example illustrates the semantic differences between selecting data under the default isolation level of READ COMMITTED (cursor stability) and under the isolation level of REPEATABLE READ. Use the command file

RUN_ISOLATION3.CMD to run these two scripts simultaneously. (As before, you'll need to edit the file if you don't have SQL Server on your local machine.) Output will be written to ISOLATION3_CNX1.OUT and ISOLATION3_CNX2.OUT.

```
-- ISOLATION3_CNX2.SQL

USE pubs
GO

-- Wait until other connection says can start, then sleep 10 secs
EXEC sem_wait 1

WAITFOR DELAY "000:00:10"
GO
UPDATE authors SET au_lname='Smith'
GO
(23 rows affected)

EXEC sem_set 0     -- Tell other connection done with first part.
EXEC sem_wait 1    -- Wait until other connection says can start,
                   -- then sleep 10 secs.
GO

WAITFOR DELAY "000:00:10"
GO

UPDATE authors SET au_lname='Jones'
GO
(23 rows affected)

-- ISOLATION3_CNX1.SQL
-- Illustrate Read Repeatable/Serializable (aka level 2 & 3)
USE pubs
GO

UPDATE authors SET au_lname='Doe' -- Make sure no Smith or Jones
(23 rows affected)

EXEC sem_SET 0    -- Clear semaphore to start
GO

-- First verify there are no authors named 'Smith'
SELECT au_lname FROM authors WHERE au_lname='Smith'
GO
```

(continued)

```
au_lname
----------------------------------------

(0 rows affected)
SET TRANSACTION ISOLATION LEVEL READ COMMITTED
GO

-- Signal other connection it's OK to update, then wait for it to
-- proceed. (Obvious possible race condition here; this is just
-- for illustration.)
EXEC sem_SET 1
GO

BEGIN TRAN
SELECT au_lname FROM authors WHERE au_lname='Smith'
GO

au_lname
----------------------------------------

(0 rows affected)
WAITFOR DELAY "000:00:15"

SELECT au_lname FROM authors WHERE au_lname='Smith'

au_lname
----------------------------------------
 Smith
 Smith
 Smith
 Smith
 Smith
 Smith
 Smith
 Smith
 Smith
 Smith
 Smith
 Smith
 Smith
 Smith
 Smith
 Smith
 Smith
 Smith
 Smith
```

```
Smith
Smith
Smith
Smith

(23 rows affected)

COMMIT TRAN
GO

EXEC sem_wait 0
EXEC sem_SET 1
GO

-- Now do the same thing, but with SERIALIZABLE isolation

SET TRANSACTION ISOLATION LEVEL SERIALIZABLE
GO

BEGIN TRAN
SELECT au_lname FROM authors WHERE au_lname='Jones'
GO

au_lname
---------------------------------------

(0 rows affected)

-- Wait for other connection to have a chance to make and commit
-- its changes
WAITFOR DELAY "000:00:15"

SELECT au_lname FROM authors WHERE au_lname='Jones'

au_lname
---------------------------------------

(0 rows affected)

COMMIT TRAN
GO

-- Now notice that Jones updates have been done
SELECT au_lname FROM authors WHERE au_lname='Jones'
GO
```

(continued)

527

```
au_lname
----------------------------------------
Jones
Jones
Jones
Jones
Jones
Jones
Jones
Jones
Jones
Jones
Jones
Jones
Jones
Jones
Jones
Jones
Jones
Jones
Jones
Jones
Jones
Jones
Jones

(23 rows affected)

EXEC sem_SET 0     -- Tell other connection done
```

As you can see, when the isolation level was set to READ COMMITTED, selecting the same data twice within a transaction yielded totally different results: first no Smiths were found, and then 23 of them appeared. If this were a banking transaction, these results would be unacceptable. For applications that are less sensitive to minor changes, or when business functions guard against such inconsistencies in other ways, this behavior might be acceptable.

After changing the isolation level to REPEATABLE READ, we got the same result (no Joneses) with both SELECT statements. Immediately after the transaction was committed, the other connection updated all the names to *Jones*. So when we again selected for *Jones* (immediately after the transaction was committed), the update took place—but at some cost. In the first case, the other connection was able to do the update as soon as the first SELECT was processed. It didn't have to wait for the second query and subsequent transaction to complete. In the second case, that second connection had to wait until the first connection completed the transaction in its entirety. In this example, concurrency was significantly reduced but consistency was perfect.

EXAMPLE 3

This example illustrates the semantic differences between selecting data under the isolation level of REPEATABLE READ and under the isolation level of SERIALIZABLE. Use the command file RUN_ISOLATION4.CMD to run these two scripts simultaneously. (Like before, you'll need to edit the file if SQL Server isn't on your local machine.) Output will be written to ISOLATION4_CNX1.OUT and ISOLATION4_CNX2.OUT.

```
-- ISOLATION4_CNX2.SQL
USE pubs
SET QUOTED_IDENTIFIER OFF
SET ANSI_DEFAULTS OFF
go


-- Wait until other connection says can start, then sleep 10 secs
EXEC sem_wait 1

WAITFOR DELAY "000:00:10"

INSERT titles VALUES ('BU2000', 'Inside SQL Server', 'popular_comp',
      '0877', 49.95, 5000, 10, 0, null, '12/31/98')
GO

EXEC sem_set 0     -- Tell other connection done with first part.
EXEC sem_wait 1    -- Wait until other connection says can start,
                   -- then sleep 10 secs.
GO

WAITFOR DELAY "000:00:10"
GO
INSERT titles VALUES ('BU3000', 'Inside Visual InterDev', 'popular_comp',
      '0877', 39.95, 10000, 12, 15000, null, '2/14/98')

GO
-- ISOLATION4_CNX1.SQL
-- Illustrate Read Repeatable vs. Serializable (aka levels 2 & 3)
--
USE pubs
```

(continued)

```
SET QUOTED_IDENTIFIER OFF
SET ANSI_DEFAULTS OFF
go


EXEC sem_set 0     -- Clear semaphore to start
GO

SET TRANSACTION ISOLATION LEVEL REPEATABLE READ
GO

BEGIN TRAN
SELECT title FROM titles WHERE title_id LIKE 'BU%'
GO

title
------------------------------------------------------------
The Busy Executive's Database Guide
Cooking with Computers: Surreptitious Balance Sheets
You Can Combat Computer Stress!
Straight Talk About Computers

-- Wait for other connection to make and commit its changes
WAITFOR DELAY "000:00:15"
SELECT title FROM titles WHERE title_id LIKE 'BU%'

title
------------------------------------------------------------
Inside SQL Server
The Busy Executive's Database Guide
Cooking with Computers: Surreptitious Balance Sheets
You Can Combat Computer Stress!
Straight Talk About Computers

COMMIT TRAN
GO

EXEC sem_wait 0
EXEC sem_set 1
GO

-- Now do the same thing, but with SERIALIZABLE isolation

SET TRANSACTION ISOLATION LEVEL SERIALIZABLE
GO
```

```
BEGIN TRAN
SELECT title FROM titles WHERE title_id LIKE 'BU%'
GO
```

```
title
------------------------------------------------------------
Inside SQL Server
The Busy Executive's Database Guide
Cooking with Computers: Surreptitious Balance Sheets
You Can Combat Computer Stress!
Straight Talk About Computers
```

```
-- Wait for other connection to have a chance to make and commit
-- its changes
EXEC sem_set 1
GO
SELECT title FROM titles WHERE title_id LIKE 'BU%'
```

```
title
------------------------------------------------------------
Inside SQL Server
The Busy Executive's Database Guide
Cooking with Computers: Surreptitious Balance Sheets
You Can Combat Computer Stress!
Straight Talk About Computers
```

```
COMMIT TRAN
GO
```

```
-- Now notice that the second
-- new title has been inserted after the COMMIT TRAN
SELECT title FROM titles WHERE title_id LIKE 'BU%'
GO
```

```
title
------------------------------------------------------------
Inside SQL Server
Inside Visual InterDev
The Busy Executive's Database Guide
Cooking with Computers: Surreptitious Balance Sheets
You Can Combat Computer Stress!
Straight Talk About Computers
```

As you can see, when the isolation level was set to REPEATABLE READ, phantoms were possible. Another connection could add new data so that reissuing the same SELECT within a transaction would return more rows the second time. (In this case, *Inside SQL Server* just mysteriously appeared; it's the phantom row.)

After changing the isolation level to SERIALIZABLE, we got the same result (five titles) with both SELECT statements. Immediately after the transaction committed, the other connection inserted a new book with the title *Inside Visual InterDev*. So when we again selected all the titles (immediately after the transaction was committed), the INSERT had taken place—but again, at some cost. In the first case, the other connection was able to do the INSERT as soon as the first SELECT was processed. It didn't have to wait for the second SELECT and subsequent transaction to complete. In the second case, that second connection had to wait until the first connection completed the transaction in its entirety. Just like in Example 2, concurrency was significantly reduced but consistency was perfect.

Another way to look at the difference between these isolation levels is to see what modification operations are possible once you've selected data within a transaction. In ISOLATION LEVEL REPEATABLE READ, the actual rows read can't be modified or deleted. However, new rows can be added to the range of data specified in the WHERE clause of the SELECT statement. All data read is locked so that no modifications can occur. However, since INSERT is adding new data, the locks on the existing data do not interfere. In ISOLATION LEVEL SERIALIZABLE, once your transaction has selected data within a transaction, no modifications are possible to that data, or to the covered range of data, by any other connection. SERIALIZABLE locks ranges of data, including data that didn't actually exist, so that INSERTs are not allowed.

Additional Characteristics of Transactions

In addition to isolation levels, it's important to understand the following characteristics of transactions.

First, a single UPDATE, DELETE, or INSERT/SELECT statement that affects multiple rows is always an atomic operation and must complete without error, or it's automatically rolled back. For example, if you performed a single UPDATE statement that updated all rows, but one row failed a constraint, the operation would be terminated with no rows updated. Because there's no way to do error checking for each row within such a statement, any error rolls back the statement. However, the batch isn't aborted. Execution proceeds to the next available statement in the batch. This will occur even in INSERT operations that are based on a SELECT statement (INSERT/SELECT or SELECT INTO).

Alternatively, a single UPDATE statement that updates hundreds of rows could fail to complete because of a system failure, possibly unrelated to SQL

Server. (For example, the power might go out, and your UPS system might not arrive until next Tuesday.) Because SQL Server considers the single UPDATE to be an atomic unit of work, when SQL Server comes back up and runs recovery on the database, it will be as if the UPDATE had never happened. If SQL Server doesn't know for sure that a transaction committed, it will be rolled back. Even if 999,999 rows out of a million had been updated before the failure, because a transaction is an all-or-nothing operation, we're left with nothing.

Like the statements mentioned earlier, modifications made by a trigger are always atomic with the underlying data modification statement. For example, if an update trigger attempts to update data but fails, the underlying data modification operation is rolled back. Both operations must succeed, or neither does.

It might not be obvious, but Example 2 (the REPEATABLE READ example) shows that a transaction can affect pure SELECT operations in which no data is modified. The transaction boundaries define the statements between which a specified isolation level will be assured. Two identical SELECT statements might behave differently if they were executed while wrapped by BEGIN TRAN/COMMIT TRAN with an isolation level of REPEATABLE READ than they would behave if they were executed together in the same batch, but not within a transaction.

Stored Procedures

Now that you've learned about batches and transactions, it's time to examine another important capability of Transact-SQL. Stored procedures enable you to cache commands at the server for later use. To create a stored procedure, you take a batch and wrap it inside a CREATE PROCEDURE *proc_name* AS statement. After that, you use Transact-SQL with nothing special except for declaring which parameters will be passed to the procedure.

To demonstrate how easy it is to create a stored procedure, we've written a simple procedure called *get_author* that takes one parameter, the *author_id*, and returns the names of any authors that have IDs equal to whatever character string is passed to the procedure:

```
CREATE PROC get_author @au_id varchar(11)
AS
SELECT au_lname, au_fname
FROM authors
WHERE au_id=@au_id
```

This procedure can be subsequently executed with syntax like the following:

```
EXEC get_author '172-32-1176'
or

EXEC get_author @au_id='172-32-1176'
```

You can see that the parameters can be passed anonymously by including values in order, or the parameters can be explicitly named so that the order in which they're passed isn't important.

If executing the procedure is the first statement in the batch, using EXEC is optional. However, it's probably always best to use the keyword EXEC (or EXECUTE) so that you won't wind up wondering why your procedure wouldn't execute (only to realize later that it's no longer the first statement of the batch).

In practice, you'll probably want a procedure like the one above to be a bit more sophisticated. Perhaps you'd want to search for author names that begin with a partial ID that you pass. If you choose not to pass anything, the procedure should show all authors rather than give you an error message stating that the parameter is missing. And maybe you'd like to return some value as a variable (distinct from the result set returned and from the return code) that you would use to check for successful execution.

You can do this by passing an *output* parameter, which has a *pass-by reference* capability. Passing an output parameter to a stored procedure is similar to passing a pointer when calling a function in C. Rather than passing a value, you pass the address of a storage area in which the procedure will cache a value. That value is subsequently available to the SQL batch after the stored procedure has executed. For example, you might want an output parameter to tell you the number of rows returned by a SELECT statement. While the @@ROWCOUNT system function provides this information, it's available for only the last statement executed. If the stored procedure executed many statements, you'd need to put this value away for safekeeping. An output parameter provides an easy way to do this.

Here's a simple procedure that selects all the rows from the *authors* table and all the rows from the *titles* table. It also sets an output parameter for each table based on @@ROWCOUNT. This value is subsequently available to the calling batch by checking the variables passed as the output parameters.

```
CREATE PROC count_tables @authorcount int OUTPUT,
@titlecount int OUTPUT
AS
```

```
SELECT * FROM authors
SET @authorcount=@@ROWCOUNT
SELECT * FROM titles
SET @titlecount=@@ROWCOUNT
RETURN(0)
```

The procedure would then be executed like this:

```
DECLARE @a_count int, @t_count int
EXEC count_tables @a_count OUTPUT, @t_count OUTPUT
```

> **TIP** Variables declared in a stored procedure are always local, so we could have used the same names for both the variables in the procedure and those passed by the batch as output parameters. In fact, this is probably the most common way to invoke them. However, the point here is to make it clear that the variables don't need to have the same name. Even with the same name, they are in fact different variables because their scoping is different.

This procedure will return all the rows from both tables. In addition, the variables *@a_count* and *@t_count* will retain the row counts from the *authors* and *titles* tables, respectively.

```
SELECT authorcount=@a_count, titlecount=@t_count
```

Here's the output:

```
authorcount     titlecount
-----------     ----------
23              18
```

When creating a stored procedure, you can reference a table, a view, or another stored procedure that doesn't currently exist. (In the latter case, you'll get a warning message informing you that a referenced object doesn't exist. As long as the object exists at the time the procedure is executed, all will be fine.)

Nested Stored Procedures

Stored procedures can be nested and can call other procedures. A procedure invoked from another procedure can also invoke yet another procedure. In such a transaction, the top-level procedure has a nesting level of 1. The first subordinate procedure has a nesting level of 2. If that subordinate procedure subsequently invokes another stored procedure, the nesting level will be 3, and so on, to a limit of 32 nesting levels. If the 32-level limit is reached, a fatal error will result, the batch will be aborted, and any open transactions will be rolled back.

The nesting-level limit prevents stack overflows that can result from procedures recursively calling themselves infinitely. The limit allows a procedure to recursively call itself only 31 subsequent times (for a total of 32 procedure calls). To determine how deeply a procedure is nested at runtime, you can select the value of the system function @@NESTLEVEL.

Unlike it does with nesting levels, SQL Server has no practical limit on the number of stored procedures that can be invoked from a given stored procedure. For example, a main stored procedure could invoke hundreds of subordinate stored procedures. If the subordinate procedures don't invoke other subordinate procedures, the nesting level never reaches a depth greater than 2.

An error in a nested (subordinate) stored procedure isn't necessarily fatal to the calling stored procedure. When invoking a stored procedure from another stored procedure, it's smart to use a RETURN statement and check the return value in the calling procedure. In this way, you can work conditionally with error situations (as shown in the factorial example next).

Recursion in Stored Procedures

Stored procedures can perform nested calls to themselves, a technique known as *recursion*. Only powerful programming languages such as C and Transact-SQL support recursion. Recursion is a technique by which the solution to a problem can be expressed by applying the solution to subsets of the problem. Programming instructors usually demonstrate recursion by having students write a factorial program using recursion to display a table of factorial values for *0!* through *10!*. Recall that a factorial of a positive integer n, written as $n!$, is the multiplication of all integers from 1 through n. For example:

```
8!     = 8 x 7 x 6 x 5 x 4 x 3 x 2 x 1 = 40320
```

(Zero is a special case—*0!* is defined as equal to 1.)

We can write a stored procedure that computes factorials, and we can do the recursive programming assignment in Transact-SQL.

> **NOTE** Recursion isn't necessarily the best way to solve this problem. An iterative (looping) approach is probably better. This example is simply for illustrative purposes.

```
-- Use Transact-SQL to recursively calculate factorial
-- of numbers between 0 and 12.
-- Parameters greater than 12 are disallowed as result
-- overflows the bounds of an int.

CREATE PROC factorial @param1 int
AS
DECLARE @one_less int, @answer int
IF (@param1 < 0 OR @param1 > 12)
    BEGIN
        -- Illegal parameter value. Must be between 0 and 12.
        RETURN -1
    END

IF (@param1=0 or @param1=1)
    SELECT @answer=1
ELSE
    BEGIN
    SET @one_less=@param1 - 1
    EXEC @answer=factorial @one_less -- Recursively call itself
    IF (@answer= -1)
        BEGIN
            RETURN -1
        END

    SET @answer=@answer * @param1
        IF (@@ERROR <> 0)
            RETURN -1
    END

RETURN(@answer)
```

Note that when the procedure is initially created, a warning message like the one shown below will indicate that the procedure is referencing a procedure that doesn't currently exist (which is itself, in this case):

```
Cannot add rows to Sysdepends for the current stored procedure
because it depends on the missing object 'factorial'. The stored
procedure will still be created.
```

Once the procedure exists, we can use it to display the standard factorial table that students generate in C programming classes:

```
DECLARE @answer numeric, @param int
SET @param=0
WHILE (@param <= 12)
```

(continued)

```
BEGIN EXEC @answer=factorial @param
    IF (@answer= -1) BEGIN
        RAISERROR('Error executing factorial procedure.', 16, -1)
        RETURN
    END
PRINT CONVERT(varchar, @param) + '! = ' + CONVERT(varchar(50), @answer)
SET @param=@param + 1
END
```

Here's the return table:

```
0! = 1
1! = 1
2! = 2
3! = 6
4! = 24
5! = 120
6! = 720
7! = 5040
8! = 40320
9! = 362880
10! = 3628800
11! = 39916800
12! = 479001600
```

We stopped at *12!* in the *factorial* procedure because *13!* is 6,227,020,800, which exceeds the range of a 32-bit (4-byte) integer. Even if we changed the parameter *@answer* to be type *decimal*, we would still be limited to *12!* because the value included in a RETURN statement must be type *int*. Another version of the procedure is given here, which uses an output parameter for the answer and introduces a new variable to hold the returned status of the procedure. You can use a *decimal* datatype with a scale of 0 as an alternative to *int* for integer operations that require values larger than the 4-byte *int* can handle.

```
CREATE PROC factorial @param1 decimal(38,0), @answer decimal(38,0) output
AS
DECLARE @one_less decimal(38,0), @status int

IF (@param1 < 0 OR @param1 >

32)
    BEGIN
        -- Illegal parameter value. Must be between 0 and 12.
        RETURN -1
    END
```

```
IF (@param1=0 or @param1=1)
    SET @answer=1
ELSE
    BEGIN
    SET @one_less=@param1 - 1
    EXEC @status=factorial @one_less, @answer output
    -- Recursively call itself
    IF (@status= -1)
        BEGIN
            RETURN -1
        END

    SET @answer=@answer * @param1

        IF (@@ERROR <> 0)
            RETURN -1
    END

RETURN  0
```

Even though this procedure has removed the range limit on the result by using a *decimal* datatype to hold the answer, we can only go to *32!* because we'd reach the maximum nesting depth of 32, which includes recursive calls. Allowing an initial parameter > 32 would result in the procedure terminating with error 217:

```
Maximum stored procedure nesting level exceeded (limit 32)
```

In C, you need to be sure that you don't overflow your stack when you use recursion. Using Transact-SQL shields you from that concern, but it does so by steadfastly refusing to nest calls more than 32 levels deep. You can also watch @@NESTLEVEL and take appropriate action before reaching the hard limit. As is often the case with a recursion problem, an iterative solution could be performed without the restriction of nesting or worries about the stack.

Here's an iterative approach. To illustrate that there's no restriction of 32 levels because it's simple iteration, we'll go two steps further, to *34!*. So this version uses an output parameter declared as *numeric(38,0)* instead of *int*. (This example also illustrates that a numeric datatype with a scale of 0 can be used as an alternative to *int* for integer operations that require values larger than the 4-byte *int* can handle.) We stop at *34!* because *35!* would overflow the precision of a *numeric(38,0)* variable. (Note that SQL Server must be started with the *-p* flag to increase the maximum precision to 38 digits instead of the default of 28.) The iterative solution appears on the following page.

```
-- Alternative iterative solution does not have the restriction
-- of 32 nesting levels
CREATE PROC factorial2 @param1 int, @answer NUMERIC(38,0) OUTPUT
AS
DECLARE @counter int
IF (@param1 < 0 OR @param1 > 34)
    BEGIN
    RAISERROR ('Illegal Parameter Value. Must be between 0 and 34',
        16, -1)
    RETURN -1
    END

SET @counter=1 SET @answer=1

WHILE (@counter < @param1 AND @param1 <> 0 ) BEGIN
    SET @answer=@answer * (@counter + 1)
    SET @counter=@counter + 1
        END

RETURN
GO

DECLARE @answer numeric(38, 0), @param int
SET @param=0
WHILE (@param <= 34)
BEGIN
    EXEC factorial2 @param, @answer OUTPUT
    PRINT CONVERT(varchar(50), @param) + '! = '
        + CONVERT(varchar(50), @answer)
    SET @param=@param + 1
END
```

And here's the output table:

```
0! = 1
1! = 1
2! = 2
3! = 6
4! = 24
5! = 120
6! = 720
7! = 5040
8! = 40320
9! = 362880
10! = 3628800
11! = 39916800
12! = 479001600
```

```
13! = 6227020800
14! = 87178291200
15! = 1307674368000
16! = 20922789888000
17! = 355687428096000
18! = 6402373705728000
19! = 121645100408832000
20! = 2432902008176640000
21! = 51090942171709440000
22! = 1124000727777607680000
23! = 25852016738884976640000
24! = 620448401733239439360000
25! = 15511210043330985984000000
26! = 403291461126605635584000000
27! = 10888869450418352160768000000
28! = 304888344611713860501504000000
29! = 8841761993739701954543616000000
30! = 265252859812191058636308480000000
31! = 8222838654177922817725562880000000
32! = 263130836933693530167218012160000000
33! = 8683317618811886495518194401280000000
34! = 295232799039604140847618609643520000000
```

Nested Transaction Blocks

It's syntactically acceptable for blocks of BEGIN TRANSACTION followed by COMMIT or ROLLBACK to be nested within other such blocks. You can also do this kind of nesting with calls to nested stored procedures. However, the semantics of such a formulation might not be what you'd expect if you think that the transactions are truly nested: they aren't. But the behavior is reasonable and predictable. A ROLLBACK rolls back all levels of the transaction, not only its inner block. A COMMIT TRAN does nothing to commit the transaction if the statement isn't part of the outermost block. If the COMMIT TRAN is part of the outermost block, it commits all levels of the transaction.

So the behavior of a COMMIT or a ROLLBACK isn't too orthogonal when the transaction blocks are nested. Only the outermost COMMIT is able to commit the transaction, but any ROLLBACK will roll back the entire transaction at all levels. If this weren't true, a ROLLBACK in an outer transaction wouldn't be able to perform its job, because the data would have already been committed. This behavior allows stored procedures (and triggers) to be executed automatically and in a predictable way without your needing to check the transaction state. A nested stored procedure that does a ROLLBACK will roll back the entire transaction, including work done by the top-level procedure.

In addition, the blocks of BEGIN TRAN and COMMIT or ROLLBACK are determined only by what actually executes, not by what's present in the batch. If conditional branching occurs (via IF statements, for example) and one of the statements doesn't execute, the statement isn't part of a block.

A common misconception about ROLLBACK is that it changes the flow of control, causing, for example, an immediate return from a stored procedure or a batch. However, flow of control continues to the next statement, which, of course, could be an explicit RETURN. ROLLBACK affects only the actual data; it doesn't affect local variables or SET statements. If local variables are changed during a transaction, or if SET statements are issued, those variables and options *do not* revert to the values they had before the transaction started. Variables and SET options aren't part of transaction control.

The system function @@TRANCOUNT will return the depth of executed BEGIN TRAN blocks. You can think of the behavior of COMMIT and ROLLBACK in this way: ROLLBACK performs its job for all levels of transaction blocks whenever @@TRANCOUNT is 1 or greater. A COMMIT commits changes *only* when @@TRANCOUNT is 1.

NOTE Beginning on page 544, you'll see several examples of nesting transaction blocks. For illustration, the value of @@TRANCOUNT is shown in the comments. If this discussion isn't totally clear to you, you should work through these examples by hand to understand why the value of @@TRANCOUNT is what it is, why it changes, and why the behavior of COMMIT or ROLLBACK acts in a way that depends on the @@TRANCOUNT value.

Executing a BEGIN TRAN statement always increments the value of @@TRANCOUNT. If no transaction is active, @@TRANCOUNT is 0. Executing a COMMIT TRAN decrements the value of @@TRANCOUNT. Executing a ROLLBACK TRAN rolls back the entire transaction and sets @@TRANCOUNT to 0. Executing either a COMMIT or a ROLLBACK when there's no open transaction (@@TRANCOUNT is 0) results in error 3902 or 3903, which states that the COMMIT or ROLLBACK request has no corresponding BEGIN TRANSACTION. In this case, @@TRANCOUNT is not decremented, so it can never go below 0.

Other errors, not of your making, are fatal as well—for example, running out of memory, filling up the transaction log (if you don't have it set to auto-grow), or terminating because of a deadlock. Such errors cause an open transaction to automatically roll back. If that occurs, @@TRANCOUNT will return 0, signaling that no open transaction exists.

The following incidents cause fatal errors:

- The system runs out of resources.

- The log runs out of space.

- Deadlock conditions exist.

- Protection exceptions occur (that is, sufficient permissions are unavailable on an object).

- A stored procedure can't run (for example, it's not present or you don't have privileges).

- The maximum nesting level of stored procedure executions has been reached.

You can't plan precisely for all of these situations, and even if you could, a new release could likely add another one. In a production environment, fatal errors should be few and far between. But as is true in nearly all programming, it's up to you to decide whether you want to try to plan for every conceivable problem that could happen and then deal with each specifically, or whether you'll accept the system default behavior. In SQL Server, the default behavior would typically be to raise an error for the condition encountered and then, when the COMMIT or ROLLBACK is executed, raise another that says it has no corresponding transaction.

One possibility is to write some retry logic in your client application to deal with a possible deadlock condition. For the other error conditions, you might decide to go with the default error behavior. If your applications are deployed with proper system management, such errors should be nonexistent or rare. You could also check @@TRANCOUNT easily enough before executing a ROLL-BACK or COMMIT to ensure that a transaction to operate on is open.

The nesting of transaction blocks provides a good reason for you *not* to name the transaction in a ROLLBACK statement. If, in a rollback, any transaction other than the top-level transaction is named, error 6401 will result:

```
Cannot rollback XXX - no transaction or savepoint of that name found.
```

It's fine to name the transaction in the BEGIN TRAN block, however. A COMMIT can also be named, and it won't prompt an error if it's not paired in the top-level branch, because it's basically a NO-OP in that case anyway (except that it decrements the value returned by @@TRANCOUNT).

One reason for naming your BEGIN TRAN statements is to allow your COMMIT and ROLLBACK statements to be self-documenting. ROLLBACK TRAN doesn't require a transaction name, but you can include one as a way of emphasizing that you are rolling back the entire transaction. The following batch will result in an error. The statement ROLLBACK TRAN B will fail, with error 6401. The subsequent ROLLBACK TRAN A will succeed because it's the top-level transaction block. Remember, though, that we'd get the same behavior if we simply used ROLLBACK TRAN instead of ROLLBACK TRAN A.

```
-- To start with, verify @@TRANCOUNT is 0
SELECT @@TRANCOUNT
BEGIN TRAN A
    -- Verify @@TRANCOUNT is 1
    SELECT @@TRANCOUNT
    -- Assume some real work happens here
    BEGIN TRAN B
        -- Verify @@TRANCOUNT is 2
        SELECT @@TRANCOUNT
        -- Assume some real work happens here
    ROLLBACK TRAN B
-- @@TRANCOUNT is still 2 because the previous ROLLBACK
-- failed due to error 6401
SELECT @@TRANCOUNT -- Assume some real work happens here
ROLLBACK TRAN A
-- This ROLLBACK succeeds, so @@TRANCOUNT is back to 0
SELECT @@TRANCOUNT
```

The following example is arguably an improvement over the previous attempt. The first ROLLBACK will execute and the second ROLLBACK will fail, with error 3903:

```
Server: Msg 3903, Level 16, State 1
The ROLLBACK TRANSACTION request has no corresponding BEGIN TRANSACTION.
```

The first ROLLBACK did its job, and there is no open transaction:

```
-- To start with, verify @@TRANCOUNT is 0
SELECT @@TRANCOUNT
BEGIN TRAN A
    -- Verify @@TRANCOUNT is 1
    SELECT @@TRANCOUNT
    -- Assume some real work happens here
    BEGIN TRAN B
        -- Verify @@TRANCOUNT is 2
        SELECT @@TRANCOUNT
        -- Assume some real work happens here
    ROLLBACK TRAN -- Notice the tran is unnamed but works
    -- That ROLLBACK terminates transaction. @@TRANCOUNT is now 0.
    SELECT @@TRANCOUNT
-- The following ROLLBACK will fail because there is no open
-- transaction (that is, @@TRANCOUNT is 0)
ROLLBACK TRAN
-- @@TRANCOUNT does not go negative. It remains at 0.
SELECT @@TRANCOUNT
```

If you syntactically nest transactions, be careful not to nest multiple ROLL-BACK statements in a way that would allow more than one to execute. To illustrate that COMMIT behaves differently than ROLLBACK, note that the following example will run without error. However, the statement COMMIT TRAN B doesn't commit any changes. It does have the effect of decrementing @@TRANCOUNT, however.

```
-- To start with, verify @@TRANCOUNT is 0
SELECT @@TRANCOUNT
BEGIN TRAN A
    -- Verify @@TRANCOUNT is 1
    SELECT @@TRANCOUNT
    -- Assume some real work happens here
        BEGIN TRAN B
            -- Verify @@TRANCOUNT is 2
            SELECT @@TRANCOUNT
            -- Assume some real work happens here
        COMMIT TRAN B
-- The COMMIT didn't COMMIT anything, but does decrement
-- @@TRANCOUNT
    -- Verify @@TRANCOUNT is back down to 1
    SELECT @@TRANCOUNT
    -- Assume some real work happens here
COMMIT TRAN A
```

(continued)

```
-- The COMMIT on previous line does commit the changes and
-- closes the transaction.
-- Since there's no open transaction, @@TRANCOUNT is again 0.
SELECT @@TRANCOUNT
```

In summary, nesting transaction blocks is perfectly valid, but you must understand the semantics. If you understand when @@TRANCOUNT is incremented, decremented, and set to 0, and you know the simple rules for COMMIT and ROLLBACK, you can pretty easily produce the effect you want.

Savepoints

Often, users will nest transaction blocks, only to find that the behavior isn't what they want. What they *really* want is for a *savepoint* to occur in a transaction. A savepoint provides a point up to which a transaction can be undone—it might have been more accurately named a "rollback point." A savepoint doesn't commit any changes to the database—only a COMMIT statement can do that.

SQL Server allows you to use savepoints via the SAVE TRAN statement, which doesn't affect the @@TRANCOUNT value. A rollback to a savepoint (not a transaction) doesn't affect the value returned by @@TRANCOUNT, either. However, the rollback must explicitly name the savepoint: using ROLLBACK without a specific name will always roll back the entire transaction.

In the first nested transaction block example shown on the preceding pages, a rollback to a transaction name failed with error 6401 because the name wasn't the top-level transaction. Had the name been a savepoint instead of a transaction, no error would've resulted, as this example shows:

```
-- To start with, verify @@TRANCOUNT is 0
SELECT @@TRANCOUNT
BEGIN TRAN A
    -- Verify @@TRANCOUNT is 1
    SELECT @@trancount
    -- Assume some real work happens here
    SAVE TRAN B
-- Verify @@TRANCOUNT is still 1. A savepoint does not affect it.
        SELECT @@TRANCOUNT
        -- Assume some real work happens here
    ROLLBACK TRAN B
-- @@TRANCOUNT is still 1 because the previous ROLLBACK
-- affects just the savepoint, not the transaction
SELECT @@TRANCOUNT
-- Assume some real work happens here
```

```
ROLLBACK TRAN A
-- This ROLLBACK succeeds, so @@TRANCOUNT is back to 0
SELECT @@TRANCOUNT
```

Stored Procedure Parameters

Stored procedures take parameters, and you can give parameters default values. If you don't supply a default value when creating the procedure, an actual parameter will be required when executing the procedure. If you don't pass a required parameter, an error like this will result:

```
Msg 201, Level 16, State 2
Procedure sp_passit expects parameter @param1, which was not supplied.
```

You can pass values by explicitly naming the parameters or by furnishing all the parameter values anonymously but in correct positional order. You can also use the keyword DEFAULT as a placeholder in passing parameters. NULL can also be passed as a parameter (or defined to be the default). Here's a simple example with results in bold:

```
CREATE PROCEDURE pass_params
@param0 int=NULL,     -- Defaults to NULL
@param1 int=1,        -- Defaults to 1
@param2 int=2         -- Defaults to 2
AS
SELECT @param0, @param1, @param2
GO

EXEC pass_params              -- PASS NOTHING - ALL Defaults
(null)    1    2

EXEC pass_params 0, 10, 20    -- PASS ALL, IN ORDER
0    10    20

EXEC pass_params @param2=200, @param1=NULL
-- Explicitly identify last two params (out of order)
(null)    (null)    200

EXEC pass_params 0, DEFAULT, 20
-- Let param1 default. Others by place.
0    1    20
```

Executing Batches, or What's Stored About a Stored Procedure?

Typically, when a batch of Transact-SQL commands is received from a client connection, the following high-level actions are performed:

Step One: Parse Commands and Create the Sequence Tree

The command parser checks for proper syntax and translates the Transact-SQL commands into an internal format that can be operated on. The internal format is known as a *sequence tree* or *query tree*. The command parser handles these language events.

Step Two: Compile the Batch

An execution plan is generated from the sequence tree. The entire batch is compiled, queries are optimized, and security is checked. The execution plan contains the necessary steps to check any constraints that exist. If a trigger exists, the call to that procedure is appended to the execution plan. (Recall that a trigger is really a specialized type of stored procedure. Its plan is cached, and the trigger doesn't need to be recompiled every time data is modified.)

The execution plan includes the following:

- The complete set of necessary steps to carry out the commands in the batch or stored procedure.
- The steps needed to enforce constraints. (For example, for a foreign key, this would involve checking values in another table.)
- A branch to the stored procedure plan for a trigger, if one exists.

Step Three: Execute

During execution, each step of the execution plan is dispatched serially to a manager that's responsible for carrying out that type of command. For example, a data definition command (in DDL), such as CREATE TABLE, is dispatched to the DDL manager. DML statements, such as SELECT, UPDATE, INSERT, and DELETE, go to the DML manager. Miscellaneous commands, such as DBCC and WAITFOR, go to the utility manager. Calls to stored procedures (for example, EXEC *sp_who*) are dispatched to the stored procedure manager. A statement with an explicit BEGIN TRAN interacts directly with the transaction manager.

Contrary to what you might think, stored procedures don't permanently store the execution plan of the procedure. (This is a feature—the execution plan is relatively dynamic.) Think for a moment about why it's important for the execution plan to be dynamic. As new indexes are added, preexisting indexes are dropped, constraints are added or changed, and triggers are added or changed; or as the amount of data changes, the plan can easily become obsolete.

So, what's stored about a stored procedure?

The SQL statements that were used to create the procedure are stored in the system table *syscomments*. The first time a stored procedure is executed after SQL Server was last restarted, the SQL text is retrieved and an execution plan is compiled. The execution plan is then cached in SQL Server's memory, and it remains there for possible reuse until it's forced out in a least recently used (LRU) manner.

Hence, a subsequent execution of the stored procedure can skip not only Step 1, *parsing,* but also Step 2, *compiling,* and go directly to Step 3, *execution.* Steps 1 and 2 always add some overhead and can sometimes be as costly as actually executing the commands. Obviously, if you can eliminate the first two steps in a three-step process, you've done well. That's what stored procedures let you do.

When you execute a stored procedure, if a valid execution plan exists in the procedure cache; it will be used (eliminating the parsing and compiling steps). When the server is restarted, no execution plans will be in the cache; so the first time the server is restarted, a stored procedure will be compiled.

TIP You can preload your procedure cache with execution plans for stored procedures by defining a startup stored procedure that executes the procedures you want to have compiled and cached.

After a procedure executes, its plan remains in the cache and is reused the next time any connection executes the same procedure. In addition, because multiple connections might try to execute the same plan concurrently, a part of the plan (called the shareable portion) is reentrant. Each concurrent user of that plan also requires an execution context. If you think of this in traditional programming terms, this execution context is needed to contain the dirty data.

The execution context tends to be fairly small compared to the plans. The execution contexts are themselves serially reusable for certain plans that don't contain special operators. Figures 10-1 and 10-2 on the following page show execution with and without a stored procedure.

EXECUTE Stored Procedure

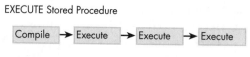

Figure 10-1.
Efficient execution with a stored procedure.

EXECUTE Batch (Without Stored Procedure)

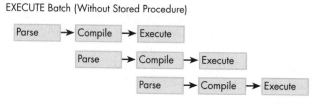

Figure 10-2.
Less efficient execution without a stored procedure.

Step Four: Recompile Execution Plans

By now it should be clear that the SQL code for stored procedures persists in the database, but execution plans don't. Execution plans are cached in memory. But sometimes they can be invalidated and a new plan generated.

So, when is a new execution plan compiled?

The short answer to this question is, whenever SQL Server needs to! This can include the following cases:

- When a copy of the execution plan isn't available in memory.

- When an index on a referenced table is dropped.

- When updated statistics are available for any table used by the procedure. (Chapter 14 covers statistics in detail.)

- When a table referenced in the procedure is altered using ALTER TABLE.

- When the table has been specifically identified, using *sp_recompile*, to force recompilation of any stored procedures referencing it. The system procedure *sp_recompile* increments the schema column of *sysobjects* for a given table. This invalidates any plans that reference the table, as described in the previous examples. You don't specify a procedure to be recompiled; instead, you simply supply the name of a table to *sp_recompile*, and all execution plans or procedures referencing the table will be invalidated.

■ When the stored procedure was created using the WITH RECOMPILE option. A stored procedure can be created using WITH RECOMPILE to ensure that its execution plan will be recompiled for every call and will never be reused. Using WITH RECOMPILE can be useful if procedures take parameters and the values of the parameters differ widely, resulting in a need for different execution plans to be formulated. For example, if a procedure is passed a value to be matched in the WHERE clause of a query, the best way to carry out that query can depend on the value passed. SQL Server maintains statistics for each index as a histogram to help it decide whether the index is selective enough to be useful.

For one given value, an index might be highly selective, and the distribution statistics might indicate that only 5 percent of the rows have that value. SQL Server might decide to use that index because it would exclude many pages of data from having to be visited. Using the index would be a good strategy, and the cached plan for the procedure might include the instructions to use the index. However, using another value, the index might not be so selective. Rather than use only the index to visit most of the data pages (ultimately doing more I/O because you're reading both the index and the data), you'd be better off simply scanning the data and not reading the index.

For example, suppose we have a nonclustered index on the *color* column of our *automobile* table. Forty percent of the cars are blue, 40 percent are red, and 5 percent each are yellow, orange, green, and purple. It's likely that a query based on color should scan the table if the color being searched on is blue or red; but it should use the index for the other colors. Without using the WITH RECOMPILE option, the execution plan created and saved would be based on the color value the first time the procedure was executed.

So if we passed *yellow* to the procedure the first time it executed, we'd get a plan that used an index. Subsequently, if we passed *blue*, we might be able to use the previous plan that was created for *yellow*. In this case, however, we'd be traversing a nonclustered index to access a large percentage of rows in the table. This could end up being far more expensive than simply scanning the entire table. In such a case, when there's a lot of variance in the distribution of data and execution plans are based on the parameters passed, it makes sense to use the WITH RECOMPILE option.

This example also shows that two execution plans for the same procedure can be different. Suppose we're not using WITH RECOMPILE, and we execute the procedure for both *blue* and *green* simultaneously from two different connections. Assume for a moment that no plan is cached. (Each will generate a new plan, but one plan will use the index and the other won't.) When a subsequent request for *red* arrives, the plan it would use is a matter of chance. And if two simultaneous calls come in for *red* and each plan is available, the two equivalent requests will execute differently because they'll use different plans. If, as you're processing queries, you see significant deviations in the execution times of apparently identical procedures, think back to this example.

■ When the stored procedure is executed using the WITH RECOMPILE option. This case is similar to the preceding one, except that here the procedure isn't created with the option, but rather the option is specified when the procedure is called. The WITH RECOMPILE option can always be added upon execution, forcing a new execution plan to be generated. The new plan is then available for subsequent executions (not using WITH RECOMPILE).

Storage of Stored Procedures

With each new stored procedure, a row is created in the *sysobjects* table, as occurs for all database objects. The text of a stored procedure (including comments) is stored in *syscomments*552 which is typically useful. This allows procedures like *sp_helptext* to display the source code of a stored procedure so that you can understand what's going on, and it allows stored procedure editors and debuggers to exist.

For most users and developers, the fact that the full text of a procedure is stored in clear text is definitely a feature of SQL Server. Prior to SQL Server 7, a real limit existed on the size of the text for a stored procedure because of the amount of text that *syscomments* could store for a given stored procedure.

In the *syscomments* table prior to SQL Server 7, the *text* column was defined as *varchar(255)*. Any given procedure could have many rows in *syscomments*, with comment chunks in lengths of up to 255 characters, and those chunks were sequenced by the *colid* field. But *colid* was rather shortsightedly defined as a *tinyint*, to ostensibly save a byte. Because the maximum value a *tinyint* could take is 255, up to 255 chunks of text could be included, each of which could be up to 255 bytes in size. Hence, the maximum size of the text used to create a stored procedure was 255 × 255, or 65,025 bytes (roughly 64 KB).

SQL Server 7 still has a limit, but it's not likely to be one you'll run up against soon. The *syscomments.text* field can now hold up to 8000 bytes, and *colid* is a *smallint*. Any one procedure should then be able hold 8000 × 32,768 bytes, or 250 MB. There's one more limiting factor, however, and that's the maximum size of a batch. To create the procedure, the client must send the complete definition to SQL Server in the CREATE PROCEDURE statement, and this must be sent as a single batch. SQL Server has a limit on batch size, which is 65,536 times the network packet size. Because the default value for network packet size is 4096, that gives us a batch size of 256 MB. So really, the limit of the size of your procedure text isn't worth worrying about right away.

Encrypting Stored Procedures

With the rollout of version 6.0, SQL Server developers learned somewhat painfully that some users didn't appreciate that the text of stored procedures was available in the *syscomments* system table. Several ISVs had already built integrated solutions or tools that created stored procedures to use with earlier versions of SQL Server. In most cases, these solutions were sophisticated applications, and the ISVs viewed the source code as their proprietary intellectual property. They had correctly noticed that the text of the procedure in *syscomments* didn't seem to do anything. If they set the text field to NULL, the procedure still ran fine—so that's what these ISVs did. This way, they wouldn't be publishing their procedure source code with their applications.

Unfortunately, when it came time to upgrade a database to version 6.0, this approach exposed a significant problem for their applications. The internal data structures for the sequence plans had changed between versions 4.2 and 6.0. ISVs had to re-create procedures, triggers, and views to generate the new structure. Although SQL Server's Setup program was designed to do this automatically, it accomplished the tasks by simply extracting the text of the procedure from *syscomments* and then dropping and re-creating the procedure using the extracted text. It's no surprise that this automatic approach failed for procedures in which the creator had deleted the text.

When the developers learned of this problem after the release of the beta version of SQL Server 6.0, they immediately understood why developers had felt compelled to delete the text. Nonetheless, they couldn't undo the work that had already been done. Developers with these ISVs had to dig out their original stored procedure creation scripts and manually drop and re-create all their procedures. While perhaps possible, it wasn't practical to create a converter program that would operate purely on the internal data structures used to represent procedures and views. Attempting this would have been like developing a utility to run against an executable program and have it backward-engineer the precise source code (more than a disassembly) that was used to create the binary. The SQL source code compilation process is designed to be a descriptive process that produces the executable, not an equation that can be solved for either side.

Following the version 6.0 beta release, but before the final release of version 6.0, the developers added the ability to *encrypt* the text stored in *syscomments* for stored procedures, triggers, and views. This allowed programmers to protect their source code without making it impossible for the upgrade process to re-create stored procedures, triggers, and views in the future. You can now protect your source code by simply adding the modifier WITH ENCRYPTION to CREATE PROCEDURE. No decrypt function is exposed (which would defeat the purpose of hiding the textlike source code). Internally, SQL Server can read this encrypted text and upgrade the sequence trees when necessary. Because the text isn't used at runtime, no performance penalty is associated with executing procedures created using WITH ENCRYPTION.

NOTE You give up some capabilities when you use WITH ENCRYPTION. For example, you can no longer use the *sp_helptext* stored procedure or object editors that display and edit the text of the stored procedure, and you can't use a source-level debugger for Transact-SQL, like the one available in the Enterprise edition of Microsoft Visual Basic or Microsoft Visual C++. Unless you are concerned about someone seeing your procedures, you shouldn't use the WITH ENCRYPTION option.

If you create a procedure, trigger, or view using WITH ENCRYPTION, the *texttype* column of *syscomments* will have its third bit set. (The *texttype* value will be OR'ed with decimal number 4.) For now, this simply means that the decimal value of *texttype* would be 6—the only other bit to be set would be the second one (decimal 2), indicating that the text in that procedure resulted from a CREATE statement and not a user-supplied comment. If you want to programmatically determine whether a procedure is encrypted, it's safer to check the value of the third bit by AND'ing it with 4 than it is to look for the value of 6. New bits could get added in the future, and the value of 6 might no longer be accurate.

To illustrate their effects on *syscomments*, we created two procedures—one encrypted and one not—in the following example:

```
CREATE PROCEDURE cleartext
AS
SELECT * FROM authors
GO

CREATE PROCEDURE hidetext WITH ENCRYPTION
AS
SELECT * FROM authors
GO

SELECT sysobjects.name, sysobjects.id,
        number, colid, texttype, language, text
FROM syscomments, sysobjects
WHERE sysobjects.id=syscomments.id AND
(
sysobjects.id=OBJECT_ID('hidetext') OR
sysobjects.id=OBJECT_ID('cleartext')
)
```

Here's the output:

```
name        id             number colid  texttype language text
----------  -------------  ------ ------  -------- -------- -----------------------
cleartext   110623437      1      1       2        0        CREATE PROCEDURE
cleartext
AS
SELECT * FROM authors
hidetext    126623494      1      1       6        0        ????????????????????????
????????????????????
????????????????????
?????????????????
```

To find created objects that have encrypted text, you can use a simple query:

```
-- Find the names and types of objects that have encrypted text
SELECT name, texttype FROM syscomments, sysobjects
WHERE sysobjects.id=syscomments.id
AND texttype & 4 > 0
```

Here's the output:

```
name      texttype
--------  --------
hidetext  6
```

If you try to run *sp_helptext* against an encrypted procedure, it will return a message stating that the text is encrypted and can't be displayed:

```
EXEC sp_helptext 'hidetext'
The object's comments have been encrypted.
```

Altering a Stored Procedure

SQL Server 7 allows you to alter the definition of a stored procedure. The syntax is almost identical to the syntax for creating the procedure initially, except that the keyword CREATE is replaced by the keyword ALTER.

The big difference is that the *procedure_name* used with ALTER PRO-CEDURE must already exist, and the definition specified replaces whatever definition the procedure had before. Just like when using the ALTER VIEW command, the benefit of ALTER PROCEDURE comes from the fact that the procedure's *object_id* won't change, so all the internal references to this procedure will stay intact. If other procedures reference this one, they'll be unaffected. If you've assigned permissions on this procedure to various users and roles, dropping the procedure removes all permission information. Altering the procedure keeps the permissions intact.

Temporary Stored Procedures

Temporary stored procedures allow an execution plan to be cached, but the object's existence and the text of the procedure are stored in the temporary database (*tempdb*) system tables—in *sysobjects* and *syscomments*. Recall that *tempdb* is re-created every time SQL Server is restarted, so these objects don't exist after SQL Server is shut down. During a given SQL Server session, you can reuse the procedure without permanently storing it. If you are familiar with the PREPARE/ EXECUTE model used by several other products, especially with the

Embedded SQL programming paradigm, you know that temporary procedures use a similar model.

Typically, you use a temporary stored procedure when you want to regularly execute the same task several times in a session, although you might use different parameter values, and you don't want to permanently store the task. You could conceivably use a permanent stored procedure and drop it when you're finished, but you'd inevitably run into cleanup issues if a stored procedure were still hanging around and the client application terminated without dropping the procedure. Because temporary stored procedures are deleted automatically when SQL Server is shut down (and *tempdb* is created anew at startup), cleanup isn't an issue.

Just as SQL Server has three types of temporary tables, it also has three types of temporary stored procedures: *private, global,* and those created from direct use of *tempdb.*

Private Temporary Stored Procedures

By adding a single pound sign (#) to the beginning of the stored procedure name (for example, *CREATE PROC #get_author AS...*), you can create the procedure from within any database as a private temporary stored procedure. Only the connection that created the procedure can execute it, and you can't grant privileges on it to another connection. The procedure exists for the life of the creating connection only; that connection can explicitly use DROP PROCEDURE on it to clean up sooner. Because the scoping of a private temporary table is specific only to the connection that created it, you won't encounter a name collision should you choose a procedure name that's used by another connection. As with temporary tables, you use your private version, and what occurs in other connections is irrelevant.

Global Temporary Stored Procedures

By prefixing two pound signs (##) to the stored procedure name (for example, *CREATE PROC ##get_author AS...*), you can create the procedure from within any database as a global temporary stored procedure. Any connection can subsequently execute that procedure without EXECUTE permission being specifically granted. Unlike private temporary stored procedures, only one copy of a global temporary stored procedure exists for all connections. If another connection created a procedure with the same name, the two names will collide and the CREATE PROCEDURE statement will fail. Permission to execute global temporary procedures defaults to public and can't be changed. You can issue a command to *deny* other users permission, but it will have no effect. Any user, on any connection, can execute a global temporary stored procedure.

A global temporary stored procedure exists until the creating connection terminates and all current execution of the procedure completes. Once the creating connection terminates, however, no further execution is allowed. Only those connections that have already started executing are allowed to finish.

Procedures Created from Direct Use of *tempdb*

Realizing that *tempdb* is re-created every time SQL Server is started, you can create a procedure in *tempdb* that fully qualifies objects in other databases. Procedures created in *tempdb* in this way can exist even after the creating connection is terminated, and the creator can specifically grant and deny execute permissions to specific users. To do this, the creator of the procedure must have CREATE PROCEDURE privileges in *tempdb*. Privileges in *tempdb* can be set up in one of two ways: you can set your privileges in *model* (the template database) so that they will be copied to *tempdb* when it is created at system restart, or you can set up an autostart procedure to set the *tempdb* privileges every time SQL Server is started. Here's an example of creating a procedure in *tempdb* and then executing it from the *pubs* database:

```
USE tempdb
GO

CREATE PROC testit AS
SELECT * FROM pubs.dbo.authors
GO

-- Executing the procedure created above from the pubs database
USE pubs
EXEC tempdb..testit
```

While we're on the subject of temporary objects, keep in mind that a private temporary table created within a stored procedure isn't visible to the connection after the creating procedure completes. It's possible, however, to create a local temporary table before executing a stored procedure and make the table visible to the stored procedure. The scoping of the temporary table extends to the current statement block and all subordinate levels.

NOTE You can use the @@NESTLEVEL system function to check for the visibility of temporary tables. A temporary table created at nest level 0 will be visible to all further levels on that connection. A table created within a procedure at nest level 1, for example, won't be visible when execution returns to the calling block at nest level 0. A global temporary table, or a table directly created in *tempdb* without using either # or ##, will be visible no matter what the nesting level.

System Stored Procedures and the Special *sp_* Prefix

SQL Server installs a large number of system stored procedures that are used mostly for administrative and informational purposes. In many cases, these are called behind the scenes by the SQL-DMO objects used by SQL Server Enterprise Manager and other applications. But the system stored procedures can also be called directly; only a few years ago, doing so was the primary mechanism by which SQL Server was administered. Old-time SQL Server users were indoctrinated into using system stored procedures.

With the great tools and interfaces that are a core part of SQL Server today, there's not much reason to work with these system stored procedures directly anymore. But it's good to be familiar with them—understanding them can help you understand the operations that occur on the system tables and can take much of the mystery out of what's going on behind the scenes with the graphical tools.

All the system stored procedure names begin with *sp_*, and most exist in the *master* database. This is more than just a convention. A procedure created in the *master* database that begins with *sp_* is uniquely able to be called from any other database without the necessity of fully referencing the procedure with the database name. This can be useful for procedures you create as well. The *sp_* magic works even for *extended stored procedures,* which are user-written calls to DLLs. By convention, extended stored procedure names begin with *xp_*, but the *sp_* prefix and its special property can be applied to them as well (but only when added to the *master* database). In fact, some extended procedures that are supplied as part of the product, such as those used to create Automation objects (for example, *sp_OACreate*), use the *sp_* prefix so that they can be called from anywhere, although they're actually functions in a DLL, not a Transact-SQL stored procedure.

The *sp_* prefix actually makes a procedure special in two ways. First, as already mentioned, a procedure whose name starts with *sp_* can be directly called from any database, without fully qualifying the name. Second, system tables referenced in your special procedures will always refer to the tables in the database from which the procedure was called. For example, the *sp_help* stored procedure lists all the objects from the *sysobjects* system table. But every database has its own sysobjects table, so which one is used? If you execute *sp_help* from the *pubs* database, you get a list of the objects in *pubs*; if you call *sp_help* from *msdb*, you get a list of objects in *msdb*, and so on.

Of course, if the *sp_* procedure references a table that exists only in the *master* database, such as *sysconfigures*, the table in *master* will be referenced no matter where you are when you call the procedure. This trick works only for system tables, however. If you create a user table called *MasterLookup* and reference it in an *sp_* stored procedure, SQL Server will look in only the *master* database to try to find the *MasterLookup* table. If it doesn't exist in *master*, you'll get an error message when executing your procedure.

> **WARNING** Microsoft strongly discourages any direct references to the system tables and suggests instead that you use only the pre-supplied stored procedures and the object property functions to get any system information you need. It's not guaranteed that the structures of the system tables will remain the same from one release to the next, or even between service packs. In fact, the Upgrade Wizard for converting SQL Server 6 to SQL Server 7 doesn't even attempt to upgrade any procedures that modify system tables.

If you look carefully through the SQL Server system tables, you'll find procedures beginning with *sp_* that are not among the documented system stored procedures. Typically, these procedures exist to be called by some other system stored procedure that is exposed; to support some SQL Server utility, such as SQL Server Enterprise Manager; or to provide statistics to the Microsoft Windows NT Performance Monitor. These procedures aren't documented for direct use because they exist only to support functionality exposed elsewhere—they don't provide that functionality independently.

There's nothing secret about these procedures, and their text is exposed clearly in *syscomments*. You're welcome to explore them to see what they do and use them if you want. But unlike the documented stored procedures, maintaining system stored procedures or striving to make them exhibit exactly consistent behavior isn't a commitment in future releases. Of course, if your applications were to become dependent on one of these procedures, you could certainly maintain your own version of it to perform exactly as you specify, or you could use one of them as a starting point and customize it to suit your needs (under a different name).

The SQL Server online documentation explains the specifics of each system stored procedure, so we don't need to cover that here. We'll just categorize and enumerate most of them to give you a general understanding of the types and number of procedures that exist. The name of the procedure usually reveals its purpose. But first, we'll look at how to autostart stored procedures.

Autostart Stored Procedures

Version 6 introduced the handy ability to mark a stored procedure as *autostart*. Autostart stored procedures are useful if you regularly want to perform housekeeping functions or if you have a background daemon procedure that's always expected to be running. Another handy use for an autostart procedure is to have it assign some privileges in *tempdb*. Or the procedure can create a global temporary table and then sleep indefinitely using WAITFOR. This will ensure that such a temporary table will always exist, because the calling process is the first thing executed, and it never terminates.

You can easily make a stored procedure start automatically—you use the system stored procedure *sp_procoption*. This procedure allows you to turn options for stored procedures on or off. In version 7 of SQL Server, the only available option is called *startup*. The syntax of the command to enable a procedure to automatically execute on SQL Server startup is as follows:

```
sp_procoption procedure_name, startup, true
```

You can remove the *startup* option by executing the same procedure and changing the value to FALSE. A procedure that's autostarted runs in the context of a system administrator account. (The procedure can use SETUSER to impersonate another account.) A procedure with the *startup* option set to TRUE must be in the *master* database and be owned by the database owner (dbo) in *master*. You can, of course, reference objects in other databases from within the startup procedure, or even call procedures that exist in other databases. A startup procedure is launched asynchronously, and it can execute in a loop for the entire duration of the SQL Server process. This allows several such procedures to be launched simultaneously at startup. When a startup procedure is running, it's seen as an active user connection.

A single startup procedure can nest calls to other stored procedures, consuming only a single user connection. Such execution of the nested procedures is synchronous, as would normally be the case. (That is, execution in the calling procedure doesn't continue until the procedure being called completes.) Typically, a stored procedure that's autostarted won't generate a lot of output. Errors, including those raised with RAISERROR, will be written to the SQL Server error log, and any result sets generated will seemingly vanish. If you need the stored procedure to return result sets, you should use a stored procedure that calls the main stored procedure with INSERT/EXEC to insert the results into a table.

If you want to prevent a procedure with the *startup* option from executing, you can start the server using trace flag 4022 or as a minimally configured server using the *-f* switch to SQLSERVR.EXE. (Add *-T4022* or *-f* as a parameter to SQL Server using the Services dialog box in the Windows NT Control Panel. You can also set the *-T4022* flag by using the SQL Server Properties dialog box in Enterprise Manager. You'll need to right-click the name of your server and choose Properties to get to this dialog box.) These safeguards allow you to recover from problems. (Consider the illustrative but perhaps absurd example of someone including a procedure that executes the SHUTDOWN command. If you had given such a procedure the *autostart* option, SQL Server would have immediately shut itself down before you could do anything about it!)

The following sections discuss the broad categories for grouping stored procedures: System, Catalog, SQL Server Agent, Replication, and Extended.

System Stored Procedures

System stored procedures aid in the administration of your system, and they sometimes modify the system tables. You shouldn't configure the system to allow direct modification of the system tables because a mistake can render your database useless. That's why direct modification of system tables is prohibited by default. If modification is necessary, a system stored procedure that is known to do the job correctly is provided.

Listed here are the SQL Server system stored procedures, which can be further divided into four categories: general, security, cursor, and distributed query procedures. Each procedure's name gives you a clue about its function. The general system procedures follow:

sp_addextendedproc	*sp_droptype*	*sp_helpserver*
sp_addmessage	*sp_executesql*	*sp_helpsort*
sp_addtype	*sp_fulltext_catalog*	*sp_helptext*
sp_addumpdevice	*sp_fulltext_column*	*sp_helptrigger*
sp_altermessage	*sp_fulltext_database*	*sp_indexoption*
sp_attach_db	*sp_fulltext_service*	*sp_lock*
sp_attach_single_file_db	*sp_fulltext_table*	*sp_monitor*
sp_autostats	*sp_getbindtoken*	*sp_processmail*

sp_bindefault
sp_bindrule
sp_bindsession
sp_certify_removable
sp_configure
sp_create_removable
sp_createstats
sp_datatype_info
sp_dbcmptlevel
sp_dboption
sp_depends
sp_detach_db
sp_dropdevice
sp_dropextendedproc
sp_dropmessage

sp_help
sp_helpconstraint
sp_helpdb
sp_helpdevice
sp_helpextendedproc
sp_helpfile
sp_helpfilegroup
sp_help_fulltext_catalogs
sp_help_fulltext_catalogs_cursor
sp_help_fulltext_columns
sp_help_fulltext_columns_cursor
sp_help_fulltext_tables
sp_help_fulltext_tables_cursor
sp_helpindex
sp_helplanguage

sp_procoption
sp_recompile
sp_refreshview
sp_rename
sp_renamedb
sp_serveroption
sp_setnetname
sp_spaceused
sp_tableoption
sp_unbindefault
sp_unbindrule
sp_updatestats
sp_validname
sp_who

And here are the security stored procedures:

sp_addalias
sp_addapprole
sp_addgroup
sp_addlinkedsrvlogin
sp_addlogin
sp_addremotelogin
sp_addrole
sp_addrolemember
sp_addserver
sp_addsrvrolemember
sp_adduser
sp_approlepassword
sp_change_users_login
sp_changedbowner
sp_changegroup
sp_changeobjectowner
sp_dbfixedrolepermission

sp_defaultdb
sp_defaultlanguage
sp_denylogin
sp_dropalias
sp_dropapprole
sp_dropgroup
sp_droplinkedsrvlogin
sp_droplogin
sp_dropremotelogin
sp_droprole
sp_droprolemember
sp_dropserver
sp_dropsrvrolemember
sp_dropuser
sp_grantdbaccess
sp_grantlogin
sp_helpdbfixedrole

sp_helpgroup
sp_helplogins
sp_helpntgroup
sp_helpremotelogin
sp_helprole
sp_helprolemember
sp_helpprotect
sp_helpsrvrole
sp_helpsrvrolemember
sp_helpuser
sp_password
sp_remoteoption
sp_revokedbaccess
sp_revokelogin
sp_setapprole
sp_srvrolepermission
sp_validatelogins

SQL Server 7 has a set of procedures available for finding information about existing cursors (called *cursor procedures*). Here's the list:

sp_cursor_list

sp_describe_cursor_columns

sp_describe_cursor_tables

SQL Server supports *distributed queries,* which access data from multiple heterogeneous data sources. You can store this data in either the same or different computers, and you can access it by using OLE DB. Here are the stored procedures available for managing distributed queries:

sp_addlinkedserver	*sp_columns_ex*	*sp_primarykeys*
sp_addlinkedsrvlogin	*sp_droplinkedsrvlogin*	*sp_serveroption*
sp_catalogs	*sp_indexes*	*sp_table_privileges_ex*
sp_column_privileges_ex	*sp_linkedservers*	*sp_tables_ex sp_foreignkeys*

Catalog Stored Procedures

Applications and development tools commonly need access to information about table names, column types, datatypes, constraints, privileges, and configuration options. All this information is stored in the system tables (system catalogs). But system tables might require changes between releases to support new features, so directly accessing the system tables could result in your application breaking from a new SQL Server release.

For this reason, SQL Server provides *catalog stored procedures,* a series of stored procedures that extract the information from the system tables, providing an abstraction layer that insulates your application. If the system tables are changed, the stored procedures that extract and provide the information will also be changed to ensure that they operate consistently (from an external perspective) from one release to another. Many of these procedures also map nearly identically to ODBC calls. The SQL Server ODBC driver calls these procedures in response to those function calls. While it's fine to directly query the system catalogs for ad hoc use, if you're deploying an application that needs to get information from the system tables, use these catalog stored procedures:

sp_column_privileges	*sp_pkeys*	*sp_statistics*
sp_columns	*sp_server_info*	*sp_stored_procedures*
sp_databases	*sp_special_columns*	*sp_table_privileges*
sp_fkeys	*sp_sproc_columns*	*sp_tables*

SQL Server Agent Stored Procedures

SQL Enterprise Manager uses SQL Server Agent stored procedures to set up alerts and schedule tasks for execution. If your application needs to carry out tasks like these, you can call the following procedures directly. They must be called from or qualified by the *msdb* database. SQL Server Agent stored procedures appear below:

sp_add_alert	*sp_help_jobhistory*
sp_add_category	*sp_help_jobschedule*
sp_add_job	*sp_help_jobserver*
sp_add_jobschedule	*sp_help_jobstep*
sp_add_jobserver	*sp_help_notification*
sp_add_jobstep	*sp_help_operator*
sp_add_notification	*sp_help_targetserver*
sp_add_operator	*sp_help_targetservergroup*
sp_add_targetservergroup	*sp_helptask*
sp_add_targetsvrgrp_member	*sp_manage_jobs_by_login*
sp_addtask	*sp_msx_defect*
sp_apply_job_to_targets	*sp_msx_enlist*
sp_delete_alert	*sp_post_msx_operation*
sp_delete_category	*sp_purge_jobhistory*
sp_delete_job	*sp_purgehistory*
sp_delete_jobschedule	*sp_reassigntask*
sp_delete_jobserver	*sp_remove_job_from_targets*
sp_delete_jobstep	*sp_resync_targetserver*
sp_delete_notification	*sp_start_job*
sp_delete_operator	*sp_stop_job*
sp_delete_targetserver	*sp_update_alert*
sp_delete_targetservergroup	*sp_update_category*
sp_delete_targetsvrgrp_member	*sp_update_job*
sp_droptask	*sp_update_jobschedule*
sp_help_alert	*sp_update_jobstep*
sp_help_category	*sp_update_notification*
sp_help_downloadlist	*sp_update_operator*
sp_helphistory	*sp_update_targetservergroup*
sp_help_job	*sp_updatetask*

Web Assistant Procedures

SQL Server provides a number of procedures for creating and managing Web pages. These procedures are typically called from within the Web Assistant Wizard, but they're documented and you can call them directly. You can consider them a subcategory of the SQL Server Agent procedures because SQL Server Agent handles much of the automatic updating of Web pages. Here is the list of the Web assistant procedures:

sp_dropwebtask

sp_enumcodepages

sp_makewebtask

sp_runwebtask

Replication Stored Procedures

You use replication stored procedures to set up and manage publication and subscription tasks. SQL Server Enterprise Manager typically provides a front end to these procedures, but you can also call them directly. SQL Server has many replication stored procedures; frankly, it's hard to manually use replication with these procedures. (You *can* do it, though, if you're determined.) Everything SQL Server Enterprise Manager does ultimately uses these system stored procedures. We urge you to use SQL Server Enterprise Manager or SQL-DMO if you need to customize replication administration into your application. The following list contains the replication stored procedures:

sp_add_agent_parameter	*sp_changemergearticle*
sp_add_agent_profile	*sp_changemergefilter*
sp_addarticle	*sp_changemergepublication*
sp_adddistpublisher	*sp_changemergepullsubscription*
sp_adddistributiondb	*sp_changemergesubscription*
sp_adddistributor	*sp_changepublication*
sp_addmergearticle	*sp_changesubscriber*
sp_addmergefilter	*sp_changesubscriber_schedule*
sp_addmergepublication	*sp_changesubstatus*
sp_addmergepullsubscription	*sp_change_subscription_properties*
sp_addmergepullsubscription_agent	*sp_deletemergeconflictrow*
sp_addmergesubscription	*sp_distcounters*

sp_addpublication

sp_addpublication_snapshot

sp_addpublisher70

sp_addpullsubscription

sp_addpullsubscription_agent

sp_addsubscriber

sp_addsubscriber_schedule

sp_addsubscription

sp_addsynctriggers

sp_article_validation

sp_articlecolumn

sp_articlefilter

sp_articlesynctranprocs

sp_articleview

sp_browsereplcmds

sp_changearticle

sp_changedistpublisher

sp_changedistributiondb

sp_changedistributor_password

sp_changedistributor_property

sp_generatefilters

sp_getmergedeletetype

sp_get_distributor

sp_grant_publication_access

sp_help_agent_default

sp_help_agent_parameter

sp_help_agent_profile

sp_help_publication_access

sp_helparticle

sp_helparticlecolumns

sp_helpdistpublisher

sp_helpdistributiondb

sp_helpdistributor

sp_helpmergearticle

sp_helpmergearticleconflicts

sp_drop_agent_parameter

sp_drop_agent_profile

sp_droparticle

sp_dropdistpublisher

sp_dropdistributiondb

sp_dropdistributor

sp_dropmergearticle

sp_dropmergefilter

sp_dropmergepublication

sp_dropmergepullsubscription

sp_dropmergesubscription

sp_droppublication

sp_droppullsubscription

sp_dropsubscriber

sp_dropsubscription

sp_dsninfo

sp_dumpparamcmd

sp_enumcustomresolvers

sp_enumdsn

sp_enumfullsubscribers

sp_helpsubscription

sp_helpsubscription_properties

sp_link_publication

sp_mergedummyupdate

sp_mergesubscription_cleanup

sp_publication_validation

sp_refreshsubscriptions

sp_reinitmergepullsubscription

sp_reinitmergesubscription

sp_reinitpullsubscription

sp_reinitsubscription

sp_removedbreplication

sp_replcmds

sp_replcounters

sp_repldone

(continued)

567

sp_helpmergeconflictrows   *sp_replflush*
sp_helpmergedeleteconflictrows   *sp_replicationdboption*
sp_helpmergefilter   *sp_replication_agent_checkup*
sp_helpmergepublication   *sp_replshowcmds*
sp_helpmergepullsubscription   *sp_repltrans*
sp_helpmergesubscription   *sp_revoke_publication_access*
sp_helppublication   *sp_script_synctran_commands*
sp_helppullsubscription   *sp_scriptdelproc*
sp_helpreplicationdb   *sp_scriptinsproc*
sp_helpreplicationdboption   *sp_scriptupdproc*
sp_helpsubscriber   *sp_subscription_cleanup*
sp_helpsubscriberinfo   *sp_table_validation*

Extended Stored Procedures

Extended stored procedures allow you to create your own external routines in a language such as C and have SQL Server automatically load and execute those routines just like a regular stored procedure. As with stored procedures, you can pass parameters to extended stored procedures, and they can return results, return status, or both. This allows you to extend SQL Server capabilities in powerful ways. Many SQL Server features introduced in the last few years have been implemented using extended stored procedures. These features include additions to SQL Server Enterprise Manager, login integration with Windows NT domain security, the ability to send or receive e-mail messages, and the ability to create a Web page based on a query.

Extended stored procedures are DLLs that SQL Server can dynamically load and execute. Extended stored procedures aren't separate processes spawned by SQL Server—they run directly in the address space of SQL Server. The DLLs are created using the Open Data Services (ODS) API, which SQL Server also uses.

Writing an extended stored procedure sounds harder than it really is, which is probably why these procedures are somewhat underused. But writing one can be as simple as writing a wrapper around a C function. For example, consider the formatting capabilities in SQL Server's PRINT statement, which are limited and don't allow parameter substitution. The C language provides the *sprintf* function, which is powerful for formatting a string buffer and includes parameter substitution. It's easy to wrap the C *sprintf* function and create an extended stored procedure that calls it, resulting in the procedure *xp_sprintf.* To show you how easy this is, below is the entire source code for the procedure *xp_sprintf*. Note that most of this code is setup code, and at the heart is the call to the C run-time function *sprintf()*:

```
// XP_SPRINTF
//
// Format and store a series of characters and values into an
// output string using sprintf
//
// Parameters:
//     srvproc - the handle to the client connection
//
// Returns:
//     XP_NOERROR or XP_ERROR
//
// Side Effects:
//
//
 SRVRETCODE xp_sprintf( SRV_PROC * srvproc )
{
    int numparams;
    int paramtype;
    int i;
    char string [MAXSTRLEN];
    char format[MAXSTRLEN];
    char values[MAXARGUMENTS][MAXSTRLEN];
    char szBuffer[MAXSTRLEN];

    // Get number of parameters
    //
    numparams=srv_rpcparams(srvproc);

    // Check number of parameters
    //
    if (numparams < 3)
    {
        // Send error message and return

        //
        LoadString(hModule, IDS_ERROR_PARAM, szBuffer,
            sizeof(szBuffer));
        goto ErrorExit;
    }
```

(continued)

```
paramtype=srv_paramtype(srvproc, 1);
if (paramtype != SRVVARCHAR)
{
    // Send error message and return
    //
    LoadString(hModule, IDS_ERROR_PARAM_TYPE, szBuffer,
        sizeof(szBuffer));
    goto ErrorExit;
}

if (!srv_paramstatus(srvproc, 1))
{
    // Send error message and return
    //
    LoadString(hModule, IDS_ERROR_PARAM_STATUS, szBuffer,
        sizeof(szBuffer));
    goto ErrorExit;
}

for (i = 2; i <= numparams; i++)
{
    paramtype=srv_paramtype(srvproc, i);

    if (paramtype != SRVVARCHAR)
    {
        // Send error message and return
        //
        LoadString(hModule, IDS_ERROR_PARAM_TYPE, szBuffer,
            sizeof(szBuffer));
        goto ErrorExit;
    }
}

for (i=0; i < MAXARGUMENTS; i++)
{
    memset(values[i], 0, MAXSTRLEN);

    srv_bmove(srv_paramdata(srvproc, i + 3),
            values[i],
            srv_paramlen(srvproc, i + 3));
}

memset(string, 0, MAXSTRLEN);
srv_bmove(srv_paramdata(srvproc, 2), format,
```

```
        srv_paramlen(srvproc, 2));
    format[srv_paramlen(srvproc, 2)]='\0';

    // This is the heart of the function -- it simply wraps sprintf
    // and passes back the string
    sprintf(string, format,
        values[0],  values[1],  values[2],  values[3],  values[4],
        values[5],  values[6],  values[7],  values[8],  values[9],
        values[10], values[11], values[12], values[13], values[14],
        values[15], values[16], values[17], values[18], values[19],
        values[20], values[21], values[22], values[23], values[24],
        values[25], values[26], values[27], values[28], values[29],
        values[30], values[31], values[32], values[33], values[34],
        values[35], values[36], values[37], values[38], values[39],
        values[40], values[41], values[42], values[43], values[44],
        values[45], values[46], values[47], values[48], values[49]);

    srv_paramset(srvproc, 1, string, strlen(string));

    return XP_NOERROR;

ErrorExit:
    srv_sendmsg(srvproc,
                SRV_MSG_ERROR,
                SPRINTF_ERROR,
                SRV_INFO,
                (DBTINYINT) 0,
                NULL,
                0,
                0,
                szBuffer,
                SRV_NULLTERM);

    return XP_ERROR;
}
```

Because extended stored procedures run in the same address space as SQL Server, they can be efficient; however, a badly behaved extended stored procedure could crash SQL Server, although this unlikely. A server crash would probably result from someone's maliciousness rather than carelessness. But this is a definite area for concern, and you should understand the issues that are covered in the rest of this section.

An extended stored procedure runs on the thread that called it. Each calling thread executes using the Windows NT structured exception handling constructs (most notably, *try-except*). When a thread is poorly written and performs a bad operation, such as trying to reference memory outside its address space, it is terminated. But only that single connection is terminated, and SQL Server remains unaffected. Any resources held by the thread, such as locks, are automatically released.

In actual use, extended stored procedures don't introduce significant stability issues into the environment. Nonetheless, it's certainly possible for an extended stored procedure to twiddle some data structure within SQL Server (to which it would have access because the procedure is part of SQL Server's address space) that could disrupt SQL Server's operation or conceivably even corrupt data. If you're unlucky, this could happen as the result of a bug in the extended stored procedure; however, it's more likely that the procedure would cause an access violation and have its thread terminated with no ill effects.

A procedure could conceivably cause data corruption, but such data structures aren't exposed publicly, so it would be hard to write a malicious procedure. It is possible, however, and given the propensity of some malicious people to create viruses, we can't rule this problem out (although no documented cases describe this happening). The ultimate responsibility for protecting your data has to rest with your system administrator, who has control over which, if any, extended stored procedures can be added to the system.

A Word of Warning

Although extended stored procedures can be terrific additions to your applications and in most cases do not negatively impact your system's behavior, exceptions do exist. You can save yourself hours of grief if you keep the following in mind:

- Be sure to include full error checking and exception handling. An unhandled exception will usually bring down SQL Server along with generating a Dr. Watson dump.

- Be sure to stress test your extended procedures thoroughly. Don't assume that, because they are not running on SQL Server itself, you don't have to be concerned about how SQL Server will behave with hundreds or thousands of users accessing it.

- Read and follow the guidelines in Microsoft Knowledge Base article Q190987, entitled "Extended Stored Procedures: What Everyone Should Know," which is included on the CD.

Only someone with the *sysadmin* role can register an extended stored procedure with the system (using *sp_addextendedproc*), and only a system administrator can grant others permission to execute the procedure. Extended stored procedures can be added only to the *master* database (eliminating their ability to be easily transferred to other systems via a dump and load of databases, for example). Administrators should allow use of only the procedures that have been thoroughly tested and proven to be safe and nondestructive.

Ideally, administrators could also have access to the source code and build environment of the extended stored procedure to verify that it bears no malicious intent. (Some people say they don't even want their SQL Server administrator to be able to do this—because that person might not be trustworthy. If that's the case, you have bigger problems. If you can't trust your system administrator, you'd better get a new one!)

Even without extended stored procedures, an administrator can disrupt a SQL Server environment in many ways. (Munging the system tables would be a good start.) Of course, you can decide that no one will ever add extended stored procedures to your system. That's certainly a safe approach, but you give up a powerful capability by taking this route. (It's kind of like deciding never to ride in a car to avoid having an accident.)

Even if you prohibit foreign extended stored procedures from your system, don't go overboard with a sweeping rule that would prevent use of even the procedures provided by Microsoft to implement new features. Could one of these procedures have a bug that could disrupt SQL Server? Sure, but a bug is no more likely to occur than if the code for these procedures had simply been statically linked into the SQLSERVR.EXE file rather than implemented as a DLL and loaded on demand. (Of course, Microsoft procedures are thoroughly tested before their release. The chance of a catastrophic bug occurring is pretty low.) The fact that these are *extended* stored procedures in no way increases the risk of bugs. It's an engineering decision—and a smart one—that allows Microsoft to add more features to the product in a way that doesn't require extra change to the core product or additional resource use by environments that don't call these features.

By convention, most of the extended stored procedures provided as part of the product begin with *xp_*. Unlike the *sp_* prefix, no special properties are associated with *xp_*. In fact, several extended stored procedures begin with *sp_* (for example, *sp_getbindtoken*), which allows them to be called from any database without being fully qualified (so we could just call it with *EXEC sp_getbindtoken* instead of *EXEC master.dbo.xp_getbindtoken*). To ascertain whether a procedure is a regular stored procedure or an extended stored procedure, you shouldn't rely on the prefix of the name. Use the function

OBJECTPROPERTY(). For example, the following should return 1, indicating that *sp_getbindtoken* is an extended procedure:

```
USE MASTER
SELECT OBJECTPROPERTY(object_id('sp_getbindtoken'), 'IsExtendedProc')
```

If you substitute a "real" stored procedure name for *sp_getbindtoken*, like *sp_help*, the function will return a 0.

As was the case with stored procedures, some extended stored procedures that are installed are not documented for direct use. These procedures exist to support functionality elsewhere—especially for SQL Server Enterprise Manager, SQL-DMO, and replication—rather than to provide features directly themselves.

Following are the extended stored procedures that are provided and documented for direct use. First, here are the general extended stored procedures:

xp_cmdshell

xp_sprintf

xp_sscanf

Here are the administration and monitoring extended stored procedures:

xp_logevent	*xp_msver*
xp_snmp_getstate	*xp_snmp_raisetrap*
xp_sqlinventory	*xp_sqlmaint*

These are the integrated security-related extended stored procedures:

xp_enumgroups	*xp_grantlogin*
xp_loginconfig	*xp_logininfo*
xp_revokelogin	

And finally, the SQL mail-related extended stored procedures:

xp_deletemail	*xp_findnextmsg*
xp_readmail	*xp_sendmail*
xp_startmail	*xp_stopmail*

SQL Server Profiler Extended Procedures

SQL Server Profiler provides a graphical user interface to a set of extended stored procedures for monitoring dozens of aspects of SQL Server's internal behavior. You can also use these extended stored procedures to create your own applications that monitor SQL Server. We'll be discussing SQL Server Profiler in Chapter 15, but to complete our list of extended procedures, here are the ones for working with SQL Server Profiler:

xp_sqltrace	*xp_trace_getuserfilter*	*xp_trace_addnewqueue*
xp_trace_getwritefilter	*xp_trace_deletequeuedefinition*	*xp_trace_loadqueuedefinition*
xp_trace_destroyqueue	*xp_trace_pausequeue*	*xp_trace_enumqueuedefname*
xp_trace_restartqueue	*xp_trace_enumqueuehandles*	*xp_trace_savequeuedefinition*
xp_trace_eventclassrequired	*xp_trace_setappfilter*	*xp_trace_flushqueryhistory*
xp_trace_setconnectionidfilter	*xp_trace_generate_event*	*xp_trace_setcpufilter*
xp_trace_getappfilter	*xp_trace_setdbidfilter*	*xp_trace_getconnectionidfilter*
xp_trace_setdurationfilter	*xp_trace_getcpufilter*	*xp_trace_seteventclassrequired*
xp_trace_getdbidfilter	*xp_trace_seteventfilter*	*xp_trace_getdurationfilter*
xp_trace_sethostfilter	*xp_trace_geteventfilter*	*xp_trace_sethpidfilter*
xp_trace_geteventnames	*xp_trace_setindidfilter*	*xp_trace_getevents*
xp_trace_setntdmfilter	*xp_trace_gethostfilter*	*xp_trace_setntnmfilter*
xp_trace_gethpidfilter	*xp_trace_setobjidfilter*	*xp_trace_getindidfilter*
xp_trace_setqueryhistory	*xp_trace_getntdmfilter*	*xp_trace_setqueueautostart*
xp_trace_getntnmfilter	*xp_trace_setqueuecreateinfo*	*xp_trace_getobjidfilter*
xp_trace_setqueuedestination	*xp_trace_getqueueautostart*	*xp_trace_setreadfilter*
xp_trace_getqueuedestination	*xp_trace_setserverfilter*	*xp_trace_getqueueproperties*
xp_trace_setseverityfilter	*xp_trace_getreadfilter*	*xp_trace_setspidfilter*
xp_trace_getserverfilter	*xp_trace_setsysobjectsfilter*	*xp_trace_getseverityfilter*
xp_trace_settextfilter	*xp_trace_getspidfilter*	*xp_trace_setuserfilter*
xp_trace_getsysobjectsfilter	*xp_trace_setwritefilter*	*xp_trace_gettextfilter*

Triggers

A trigger is a special type of stored procedure that is fired on an event-driven basis rather than by a direct call. Here are some common uses for triggers:

- To maintain data integrity rules that extend beyond simple referential integrity.

- To keep running totals updated.

- To keep a computed column updated.

- To implement a referential action, such as cascading deletes.

- To maintain an audit record of changes.

- To invoke an external action, such as beginning a reorder process if inventory falls below a certain level or sending e-mail or a pager notification to someone who needs to perform an action because of data changes.

A trigger can be set up to fire when data is changed in some way—that is, via an INSERT, an UPDATE, or a DELETE statement. Multiple triggers can be defined on a table for each event, and each trigger can invoke many stored procedures as well as carry out many different actions based on the values of a given column of data. However, there is no way to control the order of firing of triggers on the same table. For example, if you have three INSERT triggers on the *inventory* table, they will all be executed whenever rows are inserted into the table, but they could be executed in any order. If it is crucial that certain steps happen in a prescribed order, you should reconsider whether you really need to split the steps into multiple triggers.

A single trigger can be created to execute for any or all the INSERT, UPDATE, and DELETE actions, which modify data. Currently, SQL Server offers no trigger on a SELECT statement, since SELECT does not modify data. In addition, triggers can exist only on base tables, not on views. (Of course, data modified through a view does cause a trigger on the underlying base table to fire.)

A trigger is executed once for each UPDATE, INSERT, or DELETE statement, regardless of the number of rows it affects. Although it is sometimes thought that a trigger is executed once per row or once per transaction, neither of these assumptions is correct, strictly speaking. Let's see a simple example of this. The script below creates and populates a small table with three rows. It will then build a trigger on the table to be fired when a DELETE statement is executed for this table:

```
CREATE TABLE test_trigger
(col1 int,
 col2 char(6) )
GO
INSERT INTO test_trigger VALUES (1, 'First')
INSERT INTO test_trigger VALUES (2, 'Second')
INSERT INTO test_trigger VALUES (3, 'Third')
INSERT INTO test_trigger VALUES (4, 'Fourth')
INSERT INTO test_trigger VALUES (5, 'Fifth')
GO
CREATE TRIGGER delete_test
ON test_trigger FOR DELETE
AS
PRINT 'You just deleted a row!'
GO
```

Now let's put the trigger to the test. What do you think would happen when the following statement is executed?

```
DELETE test_trigger
WHERE col1 = 0
```

If you execute this statement, you'll see the following message:

```
You just deleted a row!
```

The message appears because the DELETE statement is a legal DELETE from the *test_trigger* table. The trigger is fired once no matter how many rows are affected, even if the number of rows is 0! To avoid executing code that is meaningless, it is not uncommon for the first statement in a trigger to check to see how many rows were affected. We have access to the @@ROWCOUNT function, and if the first thing the trigger does is check its value, it will reflect the number of rows affected by the data modification statement that caused the trigger to be fired. So we could change the trigger to something like this:

```
CREATE TRIGGER delete_test
ON test_trigger FOR DELETE
AS
IF @@rowcount = 0 RETURN
PRINT 'You just deleted a row!'
```

The trigger will still fire, but it will end almost as soon as it begins. You can also inspect our trigger's behavior if many rows are affected. What do you think would happen when the following statement is executed?

```
DELETE test_trigger
```

A DELETE without a WHERE clause means all the rows will be removed, and we get the following message:

```
You just deleted a row!

(5 row(s) affected)
```

Again, the trigger was only fired once, even though more than one row was affected.

If a statement affects only one row or is a transaction unto itself, the trigger will exhibit the *characteristics* of per-row or per-transaction execution. For example, if a WHILE loop were set up to perform an UPDATE statement repeatedly, an update trigger would execute each time the UPDATE statement was executed in the loop.

A trigger fires after the data modification statement has performed its work but before that work is committed to the database. Both the statement and any modifications made in the trigger are implicitly a transaction (whether or not an explicit BEGIN TRANSACTION was declared). Therefore, the trigger can roll back the data modifications that caused the trigger to fire. A trigger has access to the before image and after image of the data via the special pseudotables *inserted* and *deleted*. These two tables have the same set of columns as the underlying table being changed. You can check the before and after values of specific columns and take action depending on what you encounter. These tables are not physical structures—SQL Server constructs them from the transaction log. In fact, you can think of the *inserted* and *deleted* tables as views of the transaction log. This is why an unlogged operation such as a bulk copy or SELECT INTO does not cause triggers to fire. For regular logged operations, a trigger will always fire if it exists and has not been disabled. A trigger can be disabled by using the DISABLE TRIGGER clause of the ALTER TABLE statement.

The *inserted* and *deleted* pseudotables cannot be modified directly because they don't actually exist. As mentioned earlier, the data from these tables can be queried only. The data they appear to contain is based entirely on modifications made to data in an actual, underlying base table. The *inserted* and *deleted* pseudotables will contain as many rows as the INSERT, UPDATE, or DELETE statement affected. Sometimes it is necessary to work on a row-by-row basis within the pseudotables, although, as usual, a set-based operation is generally preferable to row-by-row operations. You can perform row-by-row operations by executing the underlying INSERT, UPDATE, or DELETE in a loop so that any single execution affects only one row, or you can perform the operations by opening a cursor on one of the *inserted* or *deleted* tables within the trigger.

Rolling Back a Trigger

Executing a ROLLBACK from within a trigger is different from executing a ROLLBACK from within a nested stored procedure. In a nested stored procedure, a ROLLBACK will cause the outermost transaction to abort, but the flow of control continues. However, if a trigger results in a ROLLBACK (because of a fatal error or an explicit ROLLBACK command), the entire batch is aborted.

Suppose that the following pseudocode batch is issued from the Query Analyzer:

```
begin tran
delete....
update....
insert.... -- This starts some chain of events that fires a trigger
           -- that rolls back the current transaction
update.... -- Execution never gets to here - entire batch is
           -- aborted because of the rollback in the trigger
if....commit  -- Neither this statement nor any of the following
              -- will be executed
else....rollback
```

```
begin tran....
insert....
if....commit
else....rollback

GO              -- isql batch terminator only

select ...      -- Next statement that will be executed is here
```

As you can see, once the trigger in the first INSERT statement aborts the batch, SQL Server not only rolls back the first transaction but skips the second transaction completely and continues execution following the GO.

Misconceptions about triggers include the belief that the trigger cannot do a SELECT statement that returns rows and that it cannot execute a PRINT statement. Although you can use SELECT and PRINT in a trigger, doing these operations is usually a dangerous practice unless you control all the applications that will work with the table that includes the trigger. Otherwise, applications not written to expect a result set or a print message following a change in data might fail because that unexpected behavior occurs anyway. For the most part, you should assume the trigger will execute invisibly, and that if all goes well, users and application programmers will never even know that a trigger was fired.

Be aware that if a trigger modifies data in the same table on which the trigger exists, using the same operation (INSERT, UPDATE or DELETE) won't, by default, fire that trigger again. That is, if you have an UPDATE trigger for the *inventory* table that updates the *inventory* table within the trigger, the trigger will not be fired a second time. You can change this behavior by allowing triggers to be recursive. This is controlled on a database-by-database basis by setting the option *recursive triggers* to TRUE. It's up to the developer to control the recursion and make sure it terminates appropriately. However, it will not cause an infinite loop if the recursion isn't terminated because, just like stored procedures, triggers can be nested only to a maximum level of 32. Even if recursive triggers have not been enabled, if separate triggers exist for INSERT, UPDATE, and DELETE statements, one trigger on a table could cause other triggers on the same table to fire (but only if *sp_configuration 'nested triggers'* is set to 1, as we'll see in a moment).

A trigger can also modify data on some other table. If that other table has a trigger, whether or not that trigger also fires depends on the current *sp_configuration* value for the *nested triggers* option. If that option is set to 1 (TRUE), which is the default setting, triggers will cascade to a maximum chain of 32. If an operation would cause more than 32 triggers to fire, the batch will be aborted and any transaction will be rolled back. This prevents an infinite cycle from being encountered. If your operation is hitting the limit of 32 firing triggers, you should probably look at your design—you've reached a point at which there are no longer any simple operations, so you're probably not going to be ecstatic with the performance of your system. If your operation truly is so complex that you need to perform further operations on 32 or more tables to modify any data, you could call stored procedures to perform the actions directly rather than enabling and using cascading triggers. Although valuable, overused cascading triggers can make your system a nightmare to maintain.

We'll see some actual examples of real triggers, including recursive triggers and the use of the IF UPDATE( ) conditional statement, in Chapter 12.

Debugging Stored Procedures and Triggers

By now, it should be obvious that stored procedures and triggers can represent a significant portion of your application's code. Even so, for a long time, no decent debugger support existed for stored procedures. (The typical debugging tool was the liberal use of PRINT statements.) Some ISVs jumped in and helped by adding some "pseudo-debugging" products—but these products didn't have access to the actual SQL Server execution environment. They typically added debugging support by doing tricks behind the scenes, such as adding additional PRINT statements or adding SELECT statements to get the current values of variables. Although some of these products were helpful, they had significant limitations: typically, they couldn't step into nested stored procedures or into triggers. A Transact-SQL debugger was always prominent on the wish list of SQL Server customers. Anybody who has done any serious coding in Transact-SQL will know firsthand how frustrating it is not to have a proper debugger and probably has spent many late nights putting PRINT statements into stored procedures.

Still, it didn't make sense for the SQL Server developers to write a new SQL Server–specific debugger because there were already too many debuggers on the market. If you're like most programmers, you want to do your work in one development environment. For example, if you are a C programmer, you probably want to use the same debugger on your SQL code that you use on your C code. Or if you program in Visual Basic, you probably will want to use the Visual Basic development environment for debugging. Fortunately, this environment-specific debugging capability now exists and its availability is rapidly expanding. If you are a developer in Microsoft Visual C++, Microsoft Visual J++, or Visual Basic, you can now debug Transact-SQL using the same debugger you use in those environments.

To accomplish this, the SQL Server developers defined a DLL and a set of callbacks that SQL Server would load and call at the beginning of each SQL statement. In essence, they defined a set of debug events that would allow them to control the execution on a statement-by-statement basis within SQL Server. This has come to be known as the SQL Server Debug Interface, or SDI. The interface that originally shipped with the version 6.5 release was a work in progress. SDI's first customer was Visual C++ version 4.2. SQL Server 6.5 shipped several months before Visual C++ 4.2, and, of course, the developers didn't get the interface quite right. Specs are never perfect, and they nearly always get tweaked— at a minimum—during implementation. This was certainly true for SDI, so to use it with Visual C++ version 4.2 or later you need SQL Server version 6.5 with Service Pack 1 or later. The developers debugged the debugging interface using the Visual C++ team as guinea pigs, and now other development tools are adding support for SDI. Today, SDI is available with Visual C++, Visual Basic, Visual J++, and other development tools from Microsoft. (The exact packaging is always subject to change, but in general, the debugger support for Transact-SQL is available only in each product's Enterprise edition.)

Although the interface is quite likely to change in future releases, it is also made available via a technical note to ISVs that want to add SQL Server debugger support. SDI is a specialized interface of interest only to those writing debuggers, so it is not considered a general feature of SQL Server.

With the existence of SDI, you now have a real debugging environment for Transact-SQL if you're using Microsoft Visual Studio. For example, as a C/C++ developer using Visual Studio, you can:

- Perform line-by-line debugging of all your Transact-SQL code.

- Step directly from your C code executing on your client machine into the Transact-SQL code executing remotely at the SQL Server machine.

- Remotely debug your procedures, with the actual execution of the procedures happening at the SQL Server machine and your debugging environment happening locally. (Or if you prefer, you can do it all from one machine.)

■ Set breakpoints anywhere in your SQL code.

■ Watch the contents of SQL Server local variables and certain system functions. You can even examine function values that are not used in your SQL code: for example, you can watch current status codes using @@ERROR or the number of rows selected using @@ROWCOUNT.

■ Modify the values of most variables in a watch window, testing conditional logic in your code more easily. (Note that variables with datatypes for which there is no direct mapping in C cannot be edited in a watch window.)

■ Examine the values of parameters passed to stored procedures.

■ Step into or over nested procedures. And if a statement causes a trigger to fire, you can even step into the trigger.

■ Use Visual Studio to edit your procedures and save them to the server. This makes it easy to fix bugs on the fly. SQL keywords and comments in your code are color coded, as they would be in C, to make them easier to spot.

■ Optionally send results of your SQL statements to the result window directly in Visual Studio.

The SDI is implemented via the pseudo–extended stored procedure *sp_sdidebug*. (The *sp_* convention was used so that the procedure could be called from any database without being fully qualified.) By "pseudo," we mean that, like a normal extended stored procedure, you will see an entry in the *sysobjects* table of type *X* for *sp_sdidebug*. But unlike a normal extended stored procedure, the code for *sp_sdidebug* is internal to SQL Server and does not reside in a separate DLL. This is true for a few other procedures as well, such as the remote cursor calls made by ODBC and DB-Library cursor functions. This was done so that new capabilities could be added to the server without having to change the tabular data stream (TDS) protocol that describes result sets back to the client application. It also eliminates the need for new keywords (potentially breaking a few applications) when the commands are of the sort that would not be executed directly by an application anyway.

You should never call *sp_sdidebug* directly. The procedure exists to load a DLL that the provider of the debugger would write and to toggle debugging on and off for the specific SQL Server connection being debugged. When debugging is enabled, the DLL is given access to internal state information for the SQL Server connection being debugged. All of the APIs defined in the interface are synchronous calls, and they are called in the context of the thread associated with the connection, which allows for callbacks to SQL Server to occur in the context of the client's thread. The internal Process Status Structure (PSS) in SQL Server holds status information for the connection being debugged, and the DLL is then able to read this structure to determine local variable, parameter, system function, and symbol information.

The debugging support of the Enterprise editions of the programming tools seems pretty normal if you are already familiar with the environment. Typically, the biggest problem people have with debugging Transact-SQL is getting it configured in the first place. Here are some tips that might help to you in debugging Transact-SQL from Visual Studio:

- You must use the Enterprise edition, not the Professional or Standard edition.

- Run SQL Server under a user account, not as Local System. You can change this in the Services applet of the Windows NT Control Panel. If SQL Server is running under the local account, break-points are ignored. While you're running the Services applet, also make sure that the RPC Service and the RPC Locator Service are running. You might consider setting them to start automatically. Make sure that the user account that is doing the debugging has access to the *sp_sdidebug* stored procedure. By default, only a system administrator has permission to run this procedure.

- SQL Server Debugging must be enabled in each of the Visual Studio components from which you want to allow debugging. Check the documentation for the particular programming environment for details. For example, in Visual Basic 6 (Enterprise edition) select Add Ins and then Add In Manager. Toward the bottom, there will be a selection for the VB tsql debugger; select it and then click the Loaded/Unloaded box. This will add the debugger to the Add In list. Do not debug on a production server. Due to the added overhead and break-in nature of the debugging product, you could adversely affect other users.

For simple debugging, you might find yourself still using the PRINT statement; for tougher problems, you might come to regard the new debugging capability as a lifesaver. Ron Soukup demonstrated this capability at the

SQL Server Professional Developer Conference in September 1996, and this five-minute sidebar of his two-hour presentation seemed to generate more interest than anything else he covered!

Execute("*any string*")

The ability to formulate and then execute a string dynamically in SQL Server is a subtle but powerful capability. Using this capability, you can avoid additional round-trips to the client application by formulating a new statement to be executed directly on the server. You can pass a string directly, or you can pass a local variable of type *char* or *varchar*. This capability is especially useful if you need to pass an object name to a procedure or if you want to build an SQL statement from the result of another SQL statement. For example, suppose that we had partitioned our database to have multiple tables similar to the *authors* table. We could write a procedure like the one shown below to pass the name of the table we want to insert into. The procedure would then formulate the INSERT statement by concatenating strings, and then it would execute the string it formulated:

```
CREATE PROC add_author
@au_id char(11),
@au_lname varchar(20),
@au_fname varchar(20),
@tabname varchar(30) AS

BEGIN
DECLARE @insert_stmt varchar(255)
SELECT @insert_stmt="INSERT " + @tabname + " (au_id,
    au_lname, au_fname, contract) VALUES ('" + @au_id +
    "','" + @au_lname + "','" + @au_fname + "', 1)"
EXECUTE (@insert_stmt)
END

EXEC add_author '999-99-1234', 'Pike', 'Neil', 'authors'
```

Working with Text and Image Data

SQL Server provides binary large object (BLOB) support via the *ntext*, *text*, and *image* datatypes. If you work with these datatypes, you might want to use the additional statements provided by SQL Server along with the standard SELECT, INSERT, UPDATE, and DELETE statements. Because a single text column can be as large as 2 GB, you frequently need to work with text data in chunks, and these additional statements (which we'll see in a moment) can help. (This topic could have been discussed earlier, when we discussed Transact-SQL programming. However, because you need some knowledge of isolation levels, transactions, and consistency issues to understand this topic, we waited until after we covered those issues.)

For simplicity's sake, most of the discussion will deal with the *text* datatype. But everything here is also relevant to the *image* and *ntext* datatypes. These three datatypes are essentially the same internally. Recall that *ntext*, *text*, and *image* datatypes are special because they are not stored on the same data page as the rest of the row. Instead, the data row holds only a 16-byte pointer to an *ntext*, *text*, or *image* structure.

Although the space required by *text* data is managed much more efficiently in SQL Server 7 than in earlier versions, functional drawbacks still exist. Although you can indeed use standard INSERT, UPDATE, DELETE, and SELECT statements with a *text* column, some significant restrictions apply. In a WHERE clause, you can search on the *text* column only with the LIKE operator or with the functions SUBSTRING() and PATINDEX(). Variables of type *text* cannot be manipulated. You can declare a parameter in a stored procedure to be of type *text* (or *ntext* or *image*), but you can't do much besides pass a value to the procedure initially. For example, you cannot subsequently assign different values to the parameter or return it as an OUTPUT parameter. Because of these limitations, you'll want to use these special datatypes only when another datatype isn't a reasonable option. If a *varchar(8000)* column can work for you, (or *varchar(4000)* for Unicode data) you can use it and avoid *text* or *ntext* altogether. But if you absolutely need a memo field, for example, and 8000 characters are not enough, you'll need to use *text* (or denormalize and use multiple *varchar* columns).

If a *text* column makes the most sense for you despite its drawbacks, you need to understand how to work effectively with text. When you can, it is easiest to work with *text* datatypes using standard SELECT, INSERT, UPDATE, and DELETE statements. But if your text data gets large, you're going to run into issues (such as how big a string your application can pass) that might make it necessary for you to deal with chunks of data at a time instead of the entire column.

The special statements for working with text data are WRITETEXT, READTEXT, and UPDATETEXT. Both READTEXT and UPDATETEXT let you work with chunks of a *text* column at a time. The WRITETEXT statement does not let you deal with chunks but rather with the entire column only.

WRITETEXT and UPDATETEXT will not log the text operations by default, although they can be instructed to log them. (The database must have the *select into/bulkcopy* option enabled for nonlogged operations.) An INSERT, UPDATE, or DELETE statement will always be logged, but these special text statements can be run without logging.

In general, nonlogged operations are not recommended for general use because they can compromise your database backup strategy. The situation is similar to nonlogged bulk copy. Nonlogged operations cannot be recovered at startup. A terminated nonlogged operation will leave the database in the state it was in before the operation began because logging (and hence rollback) of extent allocations still occurs. But the biggest downside is that in the face of a failure after a nonlogged operation, your database is only as good as your last full or differential backup and the transaction dumps up to the issuance of the nonlogged operation. You can't do further transaction dumps after a non-logged operation is performed. So think carefully about the appropriateness of nonlogged text and image operations. Also, if you use SQL Server replication to replicate *text* or *image* columns, the operations *must* be logged because the replication process looks for changes based on the transaction log.

The WRITETEXT, READTEXT, and UPDATETEXT statements all work with a *text pointer*. A text pointer is a unique *varbinary(16)* value for each *text* or *image* column of each row.

WRITETEXT

WRITETEXT completely overwrites an existing *text* or *image* column. You provide the column name (qualified by the table name), the text pointer for the specific column of a specific row, and the actual data to be written. The WITH LOG clause is optional, although it will always be used in the examples presented here. It might seem like a catch-22 when using WRITETEXT immediately, because you need to pass it a text pointer—but if the column is initially NULL, there *is* no text pointer. So how do you get one? You SELECT it with the TEXT-PTR() function. But if the *text* column has not been initialized, the TEXTPTR() function returns NULL. To initialize a text pointer for a column of a row with *text* or *image* data, you can perform some variation of the following:

- Explicitly insert a non-null value in the *text* column when you use an INSERT statement. Recognize that WRITETEXT will completely overwrite the column anyway, so the value can always be something like *A* or a blank space.

■ Define a default on the column with a non-null value like *A*. Then when you do the insert, you can specify DEFAULT or omit the column, which will result in the default value being inserted and the text pointer being initialized.

■ Update the row after inserting it, explicitly setting it to anything, even NULL.

You then select the text pointer into a variable declared as *varbinary(16)* and pass that to WRITETEXT. You can't use SELECT statements or expressions in the WRITETEXT statement. This means that the statement is limited to being executed one row at a time (although it can be done from within a cursor). The SELECT statement that gets the text pointer should be known to return only one row, preferably by using an exact match on the primary key value in the WHERE clause, because that will ensure that at most one row can meet the criteria. You can, of course, use @@ROWCOUNT to check this if you are not absolutely sure that the SELECT statement can return only one row. Before using the WRITETEXT statement, you should also ensure that you have a valid text pointer. If you find a row with the criteria you specified and the text pointer for that row was initialized, it will be valid. You can check it as a separate statement using the TEXTVALID() function. Or you can check that you do not have a NULL value in your variable that was assigned the text pointer, as we'll see in the following example. Make sure that you don't have an old text pointer value from a previous use, which would make the IS NOT NULL check be TRUE. In this example, we do one variable assignment and the variable starts out NULL, so we are sure that a non-null value means we have selected a valid text pointer:

```
-- WRITETEXT with an unprotected text pointer
DECLARE @mytextptr varbinary(16)
SELECT @mytextptr=TEXTPTR(pr_info)
    FROM pub_info WHERE pub_id='9999'
IF @mytextptr IS NOT NULL
    WRITETEXT pub_info.pr_info @mytextptr WITH LOG 'Hello Again'
```

In this example, the text pointer is not protected from changes made by others. Therefore, it is possible that the text pointer will no longer be valid by the time the WRITETEXT operation is performed. Suppose that you get a text pointer for the row with *pub_id='9999'*. But before you use it with WRITETEXT, another user deletes and reinserts the row for publisher 9999. In that case, the text pointer you are holding will no longer be valid. In the example above, the window for this occurrence is small, since we do the WRITETEXT immediately after getting the text pointer. *But there is still a window.* In your application, the window might be wider. If the text pointer is not valid when you do the WRITETEXT operation, you will get an error message like this:

```
Msg 7123, Level 16, State 1
Invalid text pointer value 000000000253f380.
```

You can easily see this for yourself if you add a delay (for example, *WAITFOR DELAY "00:00:15"*) after getting the text pointer and then delete the row from another connection. You'll get error 7123 when the WRITETEXT operation executes. If you think the chances of getting this error are slim, you can choose to simply deal with the error if it occurs. Frankly, because this seems to be what most applications that use text do, *text* columns are used in mostly low-concurrency environments. But even so, it's not good practice. (More likely, this is the general usage because the concurrency issue is not well understood.)

You should instead consider using transaction protection to ensure that the text pointer will not change from the time you read it until you use it, and to serialize access for updates so that you do not encounter frequent deadlocks. Many applications use TEXTVALID() to check right before operating—that's the right idea, but it's hardly foolproof. There is still a window between the TEXTVALID() operation and the use of the text pointer, during which the text pointer can be invalidated. The only way to close the window is to make both operations part of an atomic operation. This means using a transaction and having SQL Server protect the transaction with a lock. (For more about locking, see Chapter 13.)

By default, SQL Server will operate with Read Committed isolation and release a share (READ) lock after the page has been read. So simply putting the pointer in a transaction with the Read Committed isolation level, which is SQL Server's default, is not enough. You need to ensure that the lock is held until the text pointer is used. You could change the isolation level to Repeatable Read, which is not a bad solution, but this changes the isolation behavior for all operations on that connection, so it might have a more widespread effect than you intend. (Although you could, of course, then change it right back.) But even this is not ideal. This approach doesn't guarantee that you will subsequently be able to get the exclusive lock required to do the WRITETEXT operation; it ensures only that when you get to the WRITETEXT operation, the text pointer will still be valid. You won't be sure that you're not in the lock queue behind another connection waiting to update the same row and column. In that case, your transaction and the competing one would both hold a share lock on the same row and would both need to acquire an exclusive lock. Since both transactions are holding a share lock, neither can get the exclusive lock, and a *deadlock* results in one of the connections having its transaction automatically aborted. (In Chapter 13, you'll see that this is an example of a *conversion deadlock*.) If multiple processes are intending to modify the text and all transactions first request an update lock in a transaction when selecting the text pointer, conversion deadlocks will be avoided because only one process will get the update lock and the others will queue for it. But those users' transactions that need only to read the row will not be affected, since an update lock and a share lock are compatible.

Using the update lock on the text pointer is good for serializing access to the actual text data, even though the lock on the text data is distinct from the lock on the row with the text pointer. In this case, you essentially use the update lock on a text pointer as you'd use an intent lock for the text data. This is conceptually similar to the intent locks that SQL Server uses on a table when a page-locking or row-locking operation for that table will take place. That operation recognizes that rows, pages, and tables have an implicit hierarchy. You can think of text pointers and text data as having a similar hierarchy and use the update lock on the text pointer to protect access to the associated text data. Following is the improved version that protects the text pointer from getting invalidated and also reserves the transaction's spot in the queue so that it will get the exclusive lock that's necessary to change the column. This approach will avoid conversion deadlocks on the text pages:

```
-- WRITETEXT with a properly protected text pointer
BEGIN TRAN
DECLARE @mytextptr varbinary(16)
SELECT @mytextptr=TEXTPTR(pr_info)
    FROM pub_info (UPDLOCK) WHERE pub_id='9999'
IF @mytextptr IS NOT NULL
    WRITETEXT pub_info.pr_info @mytextptr WITH LOG 'Hello Again'
COMMIT TRAN
```

READTEXT

READTEXT is used in a similar way to WRITETEXT, except that READTEXT allows you to specify a starting position and the number of bytes to read. Its basic syntax appears on the next page.

```
READTEXT [[database.]owner.]table_name.column_name
    text_ptr offset size [HOLDLOCK]
```

Unlike with WRITETEXT, with READTEXT we do not need to work with the entire contents of the data. We can specify the starting position (*offset*) and the number of bytes to read (*size*). READTEXT is often used with the PATINDEX() function to find the offset at which some string or pattern exists, and it's also used with DATALENGTH() to determine the total size of the text column. But these functions cannot be used as the offset parameter directly. Instead, you must execute them beforehand and keep their values in a local variable, which you then pass. As mentioned in the discussion of WRITETEXT, you'll want to protect your text pointer from becoming invalidated. In the next example, you'll read text without updating it. So you can use the HOLDLOCK lock hint on the SELECT statement for the text pointer (or set the isolation level to Repeatable Read).

Sometimes people think that transactions are used only for data modifications, but notice that in this case you use a transaction to ensure read repeatability (of the text pointer) even though you are not updating anything. You can optionally add HOLDLOCK to the READTEXT statement to ensure that the text doesn't change until the transaction has completed. But in the example below, we'll read the entire contents with just one read and we will not be re-reading the contents, so there is no point in using HOLDLOCK here. This example finds the pattern *Washington* in the *pr_info* column for *pub_id* 0877 and returns the contents of that column from that point on:

```
-- READTEXT with a protected text pointer
BEGIN TRAN
DECLARE @mytextptr varbinary(16), @sizeneeded int, @pat_offset int
SELECT @mytextptr=TEXTPTR(pr_info),
    @pat_offset=PATINDEX('%Washington%',pr_info) - 1,
    @sizeneeded=DATALENGTH(pr_info) -
        PATINDEX('%Washington%',pr_info) - 1
    FROM pub_info (HOLDLOCK) WHERE pub_id='0877'

IF @mytextptr IS NOT NULL AND @pat_offset >= 0 AND
    @sizeneeded IS NOT NULL
    READTEXT  pub_info.pr_info @mytextptr @pat_offset @sizeneeded

COMMIT TRAN
```

NOTE If you run the preceding query using the Query Analyzer tool, you might not see the entire text result. The Query Analyzer has a default limit of 256 characters that can be returned for a text column. You can use the Query/Set Options command and go to the Format tab to change this limit.

The offset returned by PATINDEX() and the offset used by READTEXT unfortunately are not consistent. READINDEX treats the first character as offset 0. (This makes sense because you can think of an offset as how many characters you have to move to get to the desired position—to get to the first character, you don't need to move at all.) But PATINDEX() returns the value in terms of position, not really as an offset, and so the first character for it would be *1*. (You could actually call this a minor bug. But people have adapted to it, so changing it would cause more problems than it would solve at this point. You should assume that this acts as intended and adjust for it.) You need to fix this discrepancy by taking the result of PATINDEX() and subtracting 1 from it. PATINDEX() returns –1 if the pattern is not found. Since we subtract 1 from the value returned by PATINDEX(), if the pattern was not found, the variable *@pat_offset* would be –2. We simply check that *@pat_offset* is not negative.

You also need to specify how many bytes you want to read. If you want to read from that point to the end of the column, for example, you can take the total length as returned from DATALENGTH() and subtract the starting position, as shown in the preceding example. You cannot simply specify a buffer that you know is large enough to read the rest of the column into; that will result in error 7124:

```
The offset and length specified in the READTEXT command is greater
than the actual data length of %d.
```

If you could always perform a single READTEXT to handle your data, you'd probably not use it; instead, you could use SELECT. You need to use READTEXT when a *text* column is too long to reasonably bring back with just one statement. For example, the text size of the *pr_info* field for publisher 1622 is 18,518 bytes. We can't select this value in a program like the Query Analyzer because it's longer than the maximum expected row length for a result set, so it would be truncated. But we can set up a simple loop to show the text in pieces. To understand this process, you need to be aware of the system function @@TEXTSIZE, which returns the maximum amount of text or image data that you can retrieve in a single statement. (Of course, you need to make sure that the buffer in your application will also be large enough to accept the text.) You can read chunks smaller than the @@TEXTSIZE limit, but not larger.

NOTE The value for @@TEXTSIZE is unrelated to the setting in Query Analyzer for the maximum number of characters discussed in the previous note. @@TEXTSIZE is a server option, while the character limit controls the client tool's display.

You can change the value of @@TEXTSIZE for your connection by using SET TEXTSIZE *n*. The default value for @@TEXTSIZE is 64 KB. You should read chunks whose size is based on the amount of space available in your application buffer and based on the network packet size so that the text will fit in one packet, with an allowance for some additional space for metadata. For example, with the default network packet size of 4192 bytes (4 KB), a good read size would be about 4100 bytes, assuming that your application could deal with that size. You should also be sure that @@TEXTSIZE is at least equal to your read size. You can either check to determine its size or explicitly set it as we do in the example below. Also notice the handy use of the CASE statement for a variable assignment to initialize the *@readsize* variable to the smaller of the total length of the column and the value of @@TEXTSIZE. (In this example, we make the read size only 100 characters so that it displays easily in Query Analyzer or in a similar query window. But this is too small for most applications and is used here for illustration only.)

```
-- READTEXT in a loop to read chunks of text.
-- Instead of using HOLDLOCK, use SET TRANSACTION ISOLATION LEVEL
-- REPEATABLE READ (equivalent). Then set it back when done but
-- be sure to do so in a separate batch.
SET TRANSACTION ISOLATION LEVEL REPEATABLE READ
SET TEXTSIZE 100     --- Just for illustration; too small for
                     --- real world. 4000 would be a better value.
BEGIN TRAN

DECLARE @mytextptr varbinary(16), @totalsize int,
    @lastread int, @readsize int

SELECT
    @mytextptr=TEXTPTR(pr_info), @totalsize=DATALENGTH(pr_info),
    @lastread=0,
    -- Set the readsize to the smaller of the @@TEXTSIZE setting
    -- and the total length of the column
    @readsize=CASE WHEN (@@TEXTSIZE < DATALENGTH(pr_info)) THEN
        @@TEXTSIZE ELSE DATALENGTH(pr_info) END
```

```
            FROM pub_info WHERE pub_id='1622'

IF @mytextptr IS NOT NULL AND @readsize > 0
    WHILE (@lastread < @totalsize)
    BEGIN
        READTEXT pub_info.pr_info @mytextptr @lastread @readsize
        IF (@@error <> 0)
            BREAK     -- Break out of loop if an error on read
        -- Change offset to last char read
        SELECT @lastread=@lastread + @readsize
        -- If read size would go beyond end, adjust read size
        IF ((@readsize + @lastread) > @totalsize)
            SELECT @readsize=@totalsize - @lastread
    END

COMMIT TRAN
GO
--- Set it back, but in a separate batch
SET TRANSACTION ISOLATION LEVEL READ COMMITTED
```

Notice that in this example we need to ensure not only that the text pointer is still valid when we get to READTEXT but also that the column did not get changed *between* iterations of READTEXT. (If another connection simply updated the text in place, the text pointer would still be valid, although the read would be messed up since the contents and length were changed.) We could use HOLDLOCK both on the READTEXT statement as well as for protecting the text pointer. But for illustration, we instead changed the isolation level to REPEATABLE READ.

UPDATETEXT

UPDATETEXT is a big improvement to text processing. If you had only WRITETEXT, you would need to completely rewrite the entire column to make even a minor change. UPDATETEXT lets you work with text in pieces to insert, overwrite, or append data. Or you can copy data from another *text* column and append it or overwrite the column with it. Because of its additional capability and flexibility, the syntax for UPDATETEXT is a bit more complex:

```
UPDATETEXT table_name.dest_column_name dest_text_ptr
    offset delete_length [WITH LOG] [inserted_data |
    table_name.src_column_name src_text_ptr ]
```

The destination column name and text pointer parameters point to the column that you will be updating; these parameters are always used. Like you would with WRITETEXT, you should use the UPDLOCK hint to protect the text pointer from becoming invalid and to serialize access to the text pages to prevent a conversion deadlock. The source column name parameters are used only when you are copying data from another *text* column. Otherwise, you directly include in that spot the data you'll be adding or you omit the parameter if you are deleting data. The *offset* is the position at which you start your data modification. It should be NULL if you are appending to the current contents and 0 if you are starting from the beginning of the column. The *delete_length* parameter tells you how many bytes to delete (if any) starting from the offset parameter. Use NULL for this parameter if you will delete all contents from the offset up to the end of the column, and use 0 if you will delete no bytes. As with READTEXT, the first character of the column is considered to have a 0 offset.

UPDATETEXT can do everything, and it can do much more than WRITETEXT can do. So you might choose to use only READTEXT and UPDATETEXT and forget about WRITETEXT. (WRITETEXT existed in versions before UPDATETEXT appeared, so the former is maintained for backward compatibility, but there isn't much need for it now.)

Following are some examples that illustrate the use of UPDATETEXT better than further explanation.

EXAMPLE 1

Use UPDATETEXT to completely replace the contents of a column:

```
-- Use UPDATETEXT to completely overwrite a text column.
-- Alternative to WRITETEXT.
DECLARE @mytextptr varbinary(16)
BEGIN TRAN

SELECT @mytextptr=TEXTPTR(pr_info) FROM pub_info (UPDLOCK) WHERE
    pub_id='9999'
IF @mytextptr IS NOT NULL
    UPDATETEXT pub_info.pr_info @mytextptr 0 NULL WITH LOG
        "New text for 9999"

COMMIT TRAN
```

EXAMPLE 2

Use UPDATETEXT to delete characters off the end; first notice that publisher 0877, Binnet, has the following contents in the text column *pr_info*:

```
This is sample text data for Binnet & Hardley, publisher 0877 in
the pubs database. Binnet & Hardley is located in Washington,
D.C.
This is sample text data for Binnet & Hardley, publisher 0877 in
the pubs database. Binnet & Hardley is located in Washington,
D.C.
This is sample text data for Binnet & Hardley, publisher 0877 in
the pubs database. Binnet & Hardley is located in Washington,
D.C.
This is sample text data for Binnet & Hardley, publisher 0877 in
the pubs database. Binnet & Hardley is located in Washington,
D.C.
This is sample text data for Binnet & Hardley, publisher 0877 in
the pubs database. Binnet & Hardley is located in Washington,
D.C.
```

Because the text is repeated several times, we will delete all characters that follow the first occurrence of *D.C.* Here's how:

```
DECLARE @mytextptr varbinary(16), @pat_offset int
BEGIN TRAN
SELECT @mytextptr=TEXTPTR(pr_info),
    @pat_offset=PATINDEX('%D.C.%', pr_info)-1+4
    -- For offset, subtract 1 for offset adjust but add 4 for
    -- length of "D.C."
    FROM pub_info (UPDLOCK) WHERE pub_id='0877'

IF @mytextptr IS NOT NULL AND @pat_offset >= 0
    UPDATETEXT pub_info.pr_info @mytextptr @pat_offset NULL WITH LOG

COMMIT TRAN
```

The column now has these contents (only):

```
This is sample text data for Binnet & Hardley, publisher 0877 in
the pubs database. Binnet & Hardley is located in Washington,
D.C.
```

EXAMPLE 3

With the small amount of text here, it wouldn't be bad to simply rewrite the column with new text. But if this were a large *text* column (you could literally store the contents of *War and Peace* in a single *text* column), it would be extremely inefficient to rewrite the entire column just to make a minor change. In this example, we'll add the text "Kimberly Tripp is president of the company." to the current contents. We'll use UPDATETEXT to append text to the column:

```
DECLARE @mytextptr varbinary(16)
BEGIN TRAN
SELECT @mytextptr=TEXTPTR(pr_info) FROM pub_info (UPDLOCK)
    WHERE pub_id='0877'

IF @mytextptr IS NOT NULL
    UPDATETEXT pub_info.pr_info @mytextptr NULL NULL WITH LOG
        "Kimberly Tripp is president of the company."

COMMIT TRAN
```

And the result:

```
This is sample text data for Binnet & Hardley, publisher 0877 in
the pubs database. Binnet & Hardley is located in Washington,
D.C.Kimberly Tripp is president of the company.
```

That worked exactly as specified, but you might wish we had skipped a line and then included a tab before adding the new sentence. We can easily add both a vertical and a horizontal tab, as you can see in Example 4.

EXAMPLE 4

Use UPDATETEXT to insert some characters:

```
DECLARE @mytextptr varbinary(16), @pat_offset int,
    @mystring char(2)
BEGIN TRAN
SELECT
@mystring=char(13) + CHAR(9),    -- Vertical tab is code point 13.
                                 -- Tab is 9.
@pat_offset=PATINDEX('%Kim%', pr_info)-1,
@mytextptr=TEXTPTR(pr_info) FROM pub_info (UPDLOCK)
    WHERE pub_id='0877'

IF @mytextptr IS NOT NULL AND @pat_offset >= 0
    UPDATETEXT pub_info.pr_info @mytextptr @pat_offset 0 WITH LOG
        @mystring

COMMIT TRAN
```

And the result:

```
This is sample text data for Binnet & Hardley, publisher 0877 in
the pubs database. Binnet & Hardley is located in Washington,
D.C.
    Kimberly Tripp is president of the company.
```

Oops! We just learned that the president has gotten married and changed her last name from *Tripp* to *Tripp-Simonnet*. We need to fix that.

EXAMPLE 5

Use UPDATETEXT for search and replace:

```
-- UPDATETEXT for Search and Replace
DECLARE @mytextptr varbinary(16), @pat_offset int,
    @oldstring varchar(255), @newstring varchar(255),
    @sizeold int

BEGIN TRAN
SELECT @oldstring="Tripp", @newstring="Tripp-Simonnet"

SELECT @sizeold=DATALENGTH(@oldstring),
@pat_offset=PATINDEX('%' + @oldstring + '%', pr_info)-1,
@mytextptr=TEXTPTR(pr_info)
FROM pub_info (UPDLOCK) WHERE pub_id='0877'

IF @mytextptr IS NOT NULL AND @pat_offset >= 0
    UPDATETEXT pub_info.pr_info @mytextptr @pat_offset @sizeold
        WITH LOG @newstring

COMMIT TRAN
```

And the result:

```
This is sample text data for Binnet & Hardley, publisher 0877 in
the pubs database. Binnet & Hardley is located in Washington,
D.C.
    Kimberly Tripp-Simonnet is president of the company.
```

We used variables above and figured lengths and offsets using SQL Server's built-in functions. By doing this, we ensured that the procedure is pretty generic and that it can deal with changing the string to another string that is either longer or shorter than the original.

EXAMPLE 6

Suppose that we want to append the contents of the text for publisher Scootney (*pub_id* 9952) to the text for Binnet (*pub_id* 0877). If we did not have this option in UPDATETEXT, it would be necessary to bring all that text back to the client application, append it, and then send it back to the server. Over a slow network like the Internet, this would not be practical if the *text* columns were large. But with UPDATETEXT, the whole operation is done on the server. In this example, notice that we protect the text pointer for the target with UPDLOCK, since we'll be updating that row. We can use HOLDLOCK for the source row since we are reading it only and we want to ensure that it hasn't changed.

We'll use UPDATETEXT to copy and append one text column to another:

```
-- UPDATETEXT to copy and append another text column
DECLARE @target_textptr varbinary(16),
    @source_textptr varbinary(16)
BEGIN TRAN

SELECT @target_textptr=TEXTPTR(pr_info) FROM pub_info (UPDLOCK)
WHERE pub_id='0877'
SELECT @source_textptr=TEXTPTR(pr_info) FROM pub_info (HOLDLOCK)
WHERE pub_id='9952'

IF @target_textptr IS NOT NULL AND @source_textptr IS NOT NULL
    UPDATETEXT pub_info.pr_info @target_textptr NULL NULL
        WITH LOG pub_info.pr_info @source_textptr

COMMIT TRAN
```

Environmental Concerns

To finish this discussion of Transact-SQL programming, we'll briefly look at some of the environmental concerns that you need to be aware of in your programming—for example, we'll discuss case sensitivity, which can greatly affect your applications. We'll also look at nullability issues and ANSI compatibility.

Case Sensitivity

Various options and settings affect the semantics of your Transact-SQL statements. You must be sure that your Transact-SQL code can work regardless of the setting, or you must control the environment so that you know what the setting is.

Case sensitivity is by far the most common environmental problem, and it is simple to avoid. You should seriously consider doing most of your development in a case-sensitive environment, even if you will deploy your application mostly in a case-insensitive environment. The reason is simple: nearly all operations that work in a case-sensitive environment will also work in a case-insensitive environment, but the converse is not true. For example, if we write the statement *select * from authors* in the *pubs* database of a case-sensitive environment, it will work equally well in a case-insensitive environment. On the other hand, the statement *SELECT * FROM AUTHORS* will work fine in a case-insensitive environment but will fail in a case-sensitive environment. The table in *pubs* is actually named *authors*, which is lowercase. The only statement that would work in a case-sensitive environment but fail in a case-insensitive environment is the declaration of an object name, a column name, or a variable name. For example, with the statement *declare @myvar int*, another statement declaring *@MYVAR int* would work fine in a case-sensitive environment because the two names are distinct, but it would fail in a case-insensitive environment because the names would be considered duplicates.

The easiest way to determine whether your environment is case sensitive is to perform a SELECT statement with a WHERE clause that compares a lowercase letter with its uppercase counterpart—you wouldn't need to access a table to do this. The following simple SELECT statement returns 1 if the server is case sensitive and 0 if the server is case insensitive:

```
SELECT CASE
    WHEN ('A'='a') THEN 0
    ELSE 1
END
```

Case sensitivity is just one of the issues surrounding the character set used by SQL Server. The character set choice will affect both the rows selected and their ordering in the result set for a query such as this:

```
SELECT au_lname, au_fname FROM authors
    WHERE au_lname='José'
ORDER BY au_lname, au_fname
```

If you never use characters that are not in the standard ASCII character set, case sensitivity is really your primary issue. But if your data has special characters like the *é* in this example, be sure that you understand character-set issues. (For more information, see Chapter 4.)

Nullability and ANSI Compliance Settings

To pass the NIST test suite for ANSI SQL-92 compliance, various options had to be enabled in SQL Server because of subtle differences in semantics between the traditional SQL Server behavior and what is mandated by ANSI. We already covered the majority of these issues in earlier chapters. To preserve backward compatibility, the prior behavior couldn't simply be changed. So options were added (or in a few cases, previous options were toggled on) to change the semantics to comply with the ANSI SQL requirements. These options are summarized below, along with the statement used to change the behavior:

- Disable SQL Server's = NULL extension (*SET ANSI_NULLS ON*).

- Automatically display a warning if a truncation would occur because the target column is too small to accept a value. By default, SQL Server truncates without any warning (*SET ANSI_WARNINGS ON*).

- Always right-pad *char* columns, and don't trim trailing blanks that were entered in *varchar* columns, as SQL Server would do by default (*SET ANSI_PADDING ON*).

- Make statements implicitly part of a transaction, requiring a subsequent COMMIT or ROLLBACK (*SET IMPLICIT TRANSACTIONS ON*).

- Terminate a query if an overflow or divide-by-zero error occurs (*SET ARITHABORT ON*). By default, SQL Server returns NULL for these operators, issues a warning message, and proceeds.

- Close any open cursors upon COMMIT of a transaction. By default, SQL Server keeps the cursor open so that it can be reused without incurring the overhead of reopening it (*SET CURSOR_CLOSE_ON_COMMIT ON*).

- Allow identifier names to include SQL Server keywords if the identifier is included in double quotation marks, which by default is not allowed. This causes single and double quotation marks to be treated differently (*SET QUOTED_IDENTIFIER ON*).

- By default, create as NOT NULL a column in a CREATE TABLE statement that is not specified as NULL or NOT NULL. *SET ANSI_NULL_DFLT_ON ON* toggles this so that the column can be created with NULL. (We recommend that you always specify

NULL or NOT NULL so that this setting option is irrelevant.) The nullability of a column not explicitly declared is determined by the setting at the time the table was created, which could be different from the current setting.

All the previous options can be set individually, but you might want to avoid doing that because there are 256 (2^8) permutations to consider. You might want to set a few of the options individually, such as *SET ARITHABORT* or *SET ARITHIGNORE*. But by and large, you should either leave them all at their default settings or change them as a group to the ANSI SQL-92 behavior. These options can be enabled as a group by setting *SET ANSI_DEFAULTS ON*.

The ability to set these options on a per-connection basis makes life interesting for you as a SQL Server application programmer. Your challenge is to recognize and deal with the fact that these settings will change the behavior of your code. Basically, that means you need to adopt some form of the following four strategies:

- **The Optimistic Approach**   Hope that none of your users or the person doing database administration will change such a setting. Augment your optimism by educating users not to change these settings.

- **The Flexible Approach**   Try to write all your procedures to accommodate all permutations of the settings of all the various options (usually not practical).

- **The Hard-Line Approach**   Explicitly set your preferences at startup and periodically recheck them to determine that they have not been subsequently altered. Simply refuse to run if the settings are not exactly what you expect.

- **The Clean Room Approach**   Have a "sealed" system that prevents anyone from having direct access to change such a setting.

Whichever of these approaches you take is your choice, but recognize that if you don't think about the issue at all, you have basically settled for the Optimistic Approach. This approach is certainly adequate for many applications for which it's pretty clear that the user community would have neither the desire nor the ability to make environmental changes. But if you're deploying an application and the machine running SQL Server will be accessed by applications that you don't control, it is probably an overly simplistic approach. Philosophically, the Flexible Approach is nice, but it probably isn't realistic unless the application is quite simple.

You can change the SQL Server default values for the server as a whole by using *sp_configure 'user options'*. A specific user connection can then further refine the environment by issuing one of the specific SET statements we just discussed. The system function @@OPTIONS can then be examined by any connection to see the current settings for that connection. The @@OPTIONS function and the value to be set using *sp_configure 'user options'* are a bit mask with the values depicted in Table 10-2.

Decimal Value	Hexadecimal Value	Option and Description
2	0x0002	IMPLICIT_TRANSACTIONS. Controls whether a transaction is started implicitly when a statement is executed.
4	0x0004	CURSOR_CLOSE_ON_COMMIT. Controls behavior of cursors once a commit has been performed.
8	0x0008	ANSI_WARNINGS. Controls truncation and NULL in aggregate warnings.
16	0x0010	ANSI_PADDING. Controls padding of variables.
32	0x0020	ANSI_NULLS. Controls NULL handling by using equality operators.
64	0x0040	ARITHABORT. Terminates a query when an overflow or divide-by-zero error occurs during query execution.
128	0x0080	ARITHIGNORE. Returns NULL when an overflow or divide-by-zero error occurs during a query.
256	0x0100	QUOTED_IDENTIFIER. Differentiates between single and double quotation marks when evaluating an expression, allowing object names to include characters that would otherwise not conform to naming rules or would collide with a reserved word or a keyword.

Table 10-2.
Bit mask values for SQL Server options.

(continued)

Table 10-2. *continued*

Decimal Value	Hexadecimal Value	Option and Description
512	0x0200	NOCOUNT. Turns off the message returned at the end of each statement that states how many rows were affected by the statement.
1024	0x0400	ANSI_NULL_DFLT_ON. Alters the session's behavior to use ANSI compatibility for nullability. New columns defined without explicit nullability will be defined to allow NULLs.
2048	0x0800	ANSI_NULL_DFLT_OFF. Alters the session's behavior to not use ANSI compatibility for nullability. New columns defined without explicit nullability will be defined to prohibit NULLS.

By default, none of these options is enabled for SQL Server itself. So in a brand-new installation, the run value for *sp_configure 'user options'* will be 0. A system administrator can set this so that all connections have the same initial default settings. If you query the value of @@OPTIONS from an application that has not modified the environment, the value will also be 0. However, be aware that many applications, or even the SQL Server ODBC or OLE DB drivers that the application uses, might have changed the environment. Note that this includes the SQL Server Query Analyzer, which uses ODBC. To change the default behavior, simply set the corresponding bit by doing a bitwise OR with the previous value. For example, suppose that your run value is 512, which indicates that NOCOUNT is the only option turned on. You want to leave NOCOUNT enabled, but you also want to enable option value 32, which controls how NULLs are handled when using equality comparisons. You'd simply pass the decimal value 544 (or 0x220) to *sp_configure 'user options'*, which is the result of doing a bitwise OR between the two options (for example, SELECT 32|512).

You can examine current options that have been set using *DBCC USER OPTIONS.* The output is similar to the code on the following page.

```
Set Option      Value
----------      ----------
textsize        64512
language        us_english
dateformat      mdy
datefirst       7
arithabort      SET
nocount         SET
```

This DBCC command shows only options that have been set—it doesn't show all the current settings for *sp_configure 'user options'*. But you can also decode your current connection settings pretty easily from @@OPTIONS using something like this:

```
SELECT "IMPLICIT TRANSACTIONS", CASE WHEN
    (@@OPTIONS & 0x0002 > 0) THEN 'ON' ELSE 'OFF' END
UNION
SELECT "CURSOR_CLOSE_ON_COMMIT", CASE WHEN
    (@@OPTIONS & 0x0004 > 0) THEN 'ON' ELSE 'OFF' END
UNION
SELECT "ANSI_WARNINGS",CASE WHEN (@@OPTIONS & 0x0008 > 0) THEN
    'ON' ELSE 'OFF' END
UNION
SELECT "ANSI_PADDINGS", CASE WHEN (@@OPTIONS & 0x0010 > 0) THEN
    'ON' ELSE 'OFF' END
UNION
SELECT "ANSI_NULLS", CASE WHEN (@@OPTIONS & 0x0020 > 0) THEN 'ON'
    ELSE 'OFF' END
UNION
SELECT "ARITHABORT", CASE WHEN (@@OPTIONS & 0x0040 > 0) THEN 'ON'
    ELSE 'OFF' END
UNION
SELECT "ARITHIGNORE", CASE WHEN (@@OPTIONS & 0x0080 > 0)
    THEN 'ON' ELSE 'OFF' END
UNION
SELECT "QUOTED_IDENTIFIER", CASE WHEN (@@OPTIONS & 0x0100 > 0)
    THEN 'ON' ELSE 'OFF' END
UNION
SELECT "NOCOUNT", CASE WHEN (@@OPTIONS & 0x0200 > 0) THEN 'ON'
    ELSE 'OFF' END
UNION
SELECT "ANSI_NULL_DFLT_ON", CASE WHEN (@@OPTIONS & 0x0400 > 0)
    THEN 'ON' ELSE 'OFF' END
UNION
SELECT "ANSI_NULL_DFLT_OFF", CASE WHEN (@@OPTIONS & 0x0800 > 0)
    THEN 'ON' ELSE 'OFF' END
ORDER BY "OPTION"
```

Here's the result:

```
OPTION                        SETTING
----------------------        -------
ANSI_NULL_DFLT_OFF            OFF
ANSI_NULL_DFLT_ON             OFF
ANSI_NULLS                    OFF
ANSI_PADDINGS                 OFF
ANSI_WARNINGS                 OFF
ARITHABORT                    OFF
ARITHIGNORE                   OFF
CURSOR_CLOSE_ON_COMMIT        OFF
IMPLICIT TRANSACTIONS         OFF
NOCOUNT                       ON
QUOTED_IDENTIFIER             OFF
```

Unfortunately, running the previous SELECT statement will not give you a complete picture. As we saw in Chapter 5, many of the options, especially those involving NULL handling, can also be changed at the database level by using *sp_dboption*. To really get the full picture, you must examine @@OPTIONS for your current session in addition to *sp_dboption* for your current database.

Locale-Specific SET Options

Beware of the locale-specific SET options. SET DATEFORMAT and SET DATEFIRST change the recognized default date format. If DATEFORMAT is changed to *dmy* instead of the (U.S.) default *mdy*, a date such as *'12/10/98'* will be interpreted as October 12, 1998. A good strategy for dates is to always use the ISO format *yyyymmdd*, which is recognized no matter what the setting of DATEFORMAT is.

DATEFIRST affects what is considered the first day of the week. By default (in the United States), it has the value 7 (Sunday). Date functions that work with the day-of-week as a value between 1 and 7 will be affected by this setting. These day-of-week values can be confusing, since their numbering depends on the DATEFIRST value; but the values for DATEFIRST don't change. For example, as far as DATEFIRST is considered, Sunday's value is always 7. But having then designated Sunday (7) as DATEFIRST, if you executed the statement *SELECT DATEPART(dw,GETDATE())* and your date falls on a Sunday, the statement will return 1. You just defined Sunday to be the first day of the week, so 1 is correct.

Summary

Transact-SQL statements can be grouped together in batches, they can persist in the database, they can repeatedly execute as stored procedures, and they can be made to automatically fire as triggers. It is essential that you understand the differences between these functions and that you understand that their actions are not mutually exclusive.

Transact-SQL stored procedures can be quite complex, and they can become a significant portion of your application's source code. Fortunately, Visual Studio provides debugging support for SQL Server stored procedures.

Programming effectively with Transact-SQL also requires that you understand transactional topics, such as when transactions will be committed and when they can be rolled back. Since you'll likely be working in a multiuser environment, it is vital that you make the appropriate concurrency and consistency choices to suit the isolation level for your environment. Understanding isolation levels is also important for working with BLOBs in SQL Server using the special operators READTEXT, WRITETEXT, and UPDATETEXT. And no matter what task you are performing, it is important to realize that you must plan for various environmental options that will affect the behavior and semantics of your Transact-SQL code.

CURSORS

A relational database such as Microsoft SQL Server is naturally *set oriented*. This means that a given statement, such as SELECT, returns a set of results—often more than one row of data. On the other hand, most programming languages and many applications tend to be ultimately *record based*. For example, in an application that displays a list of customers, users scroll through the list and periodically drill down to get more detail about a customer and perhaps make some modifications. Then they might proceed to the next customer and do the operation again, and so on, one record at a time.

The incongruity between the set-oriented approach and the record-based approach is sometimes referred to as an *impedance mismatch*. To deal with this mismatch, SQL Server provides a significant bridge between the two models: cursors.

You can think of a cursor as a named result set in which a current position is always maintained as you move through the result set. For example, as you visually scan names in a printed phone book, you probably run your finger down the entries. Your finger acts like a cursor—it maintains a pointer to the current entry. You can think of the entries on the current page of the phone book as the result set from your query. The action of moving your finger through the listings on that page is similar to the action of a *scrollable cursor*—it moves forward and backward or up and down at different times, but it always maintains a current position on a particular row.

SQL Server has different types of cursors that you can choose based on your scrolling requirements and on how insulated you want the cursor to be from data changes made by others. Special cursor libraries in ODBC, OLE DB, and DB-Library have network optimizations that prevent each row fetched in a cursor from incurring the overhead of its own network conversation. Figure 11-1 on the following page shows how a cursor works.

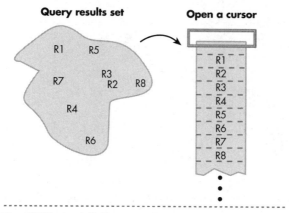

Use FETCH to scroll the cursor.

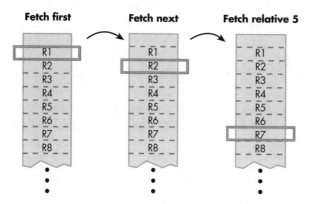

Figure 11-1.
SQL Server cursors bridge set-based and record-based models.

Cursor Basics

To work with a cursor, you take the following steps:

1. Declare the cursor using the DECLARE statement. You choose a cursor based on how sensitive you want it to be to the changes of others and on the level of scrolling you want. Then you specify the SELECT statement that will produce the cursor's result set. Often, the rows in the result set will be explicitly sorted using the ORDER

BY clause. Most database systems that provide cursors allow you to move only forward through the result set. SQL Server's scrollable cursors allow you to reposition the cursor to any row. They are also fully updatable.

2. Open the cursor. You can think of this step as executing the DE-CLARE statement from step 1.

3. Fetch rows in the cursor. The cursor position moves within the result set to get the next row or the previous row, to go back five rows, to get the last row, and so on. Typically, the FETCH statement is executed many times—at least once for every row in the result set. (The other cursor control statements tend to be executed only once per cursor.) In SQL Server, you typically check the system function @@FETCH_STATUS after each fetch. A 0 value indicates that the fetch was successful. A –1 value indicates that there are no more rows—that is, the fetch would move the cursor beyond the result set, either past the last row or before the first row. A value of –2 indicates that the row no longer exists in the cursor—it was deleted from the base table after the cursor was opened or it was updated in a way that no longer meets the criteria of the SELECT statement that generated the result set.

4. Update or delete the row of the table in which the cursor is positioned. This step is optional. Here's the syntax:

```
UPDATE table SET column = value WHERE CURRENT OF cursor_name
DELETE table WHERE CURRENT OF cursor_name
```

After the cursor is positioned at a specific row, that row is usually updated or deleted. Instead of supplying a WHERE clause that identifies a row in the table using values such as the primary key for the UPDATE or DELETE statement, you identify the row to be operated on by specifying CURRENT, which is the row the cursor points to. This type of operation is known as a *positioned update* (or a *positioned delete*).

5. Close the cursor. This ends the active cursor operation. The cursor is still declared, so you can reopen it without having to declare it again.

6. Deallocate the cursor to remove a cursor reference. When the last cursor reference is deallocated, SQL Server releases the data structures

comprising the cursor. (We'll see later in this chapter that you can have multiple references to the same cursor by using cursor variables.) Because internal data structures consume memory in the procedure cache, you should use the DEALLOCATE statement to clean up after you're done with the cursor. Think of DEALLOCATE as essentially "UNDECLARE"—the opposite of DECLARE, just as CLOSE is the opposite of OPEN. Below is an example of a simple cursor that fetches forward through the *authors* table and retrieves rows one by one. (For now, note that this is partly pseudocode—and highly inefficient—because we don't want to get immersed in the details quite yet.)

```
DECLARE au_cursor CURSOR FOR
SELECT * FROM authors ORDER by au_lname

OPEN au_cursor

WHILE (more rows)
FETCH NEXT FROM au_cursor      -- Do until end
CLOSE au_cursor
DEALLOCATE au_cursor
```

Of course, to get all the rows from the *authors* table, it would be a lot easier to issue the SELECT statement directly, which would return all the rows in one set. Using a cursor to return a simple result set is inappropriate, and this example served only to illustrate the basic flow of cursor operations. We'll talk about uses for cursors next.

Cursors and ISAMs

Before you proceed, you must understand something crucial about using cursors: You should never let cursors turn SQL Server into a network ISAM.

You might recall from Chapter 1 that the initial grand plan for SQL Server called for it to be a higher performance back end for Ashton-Tate's dBASE IV. dBASE was really a record-oriented, ISAM-like data management system (that is, it did sequential, row-by-row processing). It was not set based. At the time, SQL Server didn't use cursors, which made a difficult task even more difficult. The original plan to make the two record-oriented and set-based systems totally compatible and seamlessly interchangeable was doomed from the outset because of inherent differences in the models. If the original SQL Server had featured the rich cursor model it has now, cursors would have been heavily used to build the dBASE IV front end from the start. But it was probably better that the impedance mismatch became obvious. It forced the SQL Server development team to reexamine its basic goals and dramatically improve its plans. It also highlighted the importance of orienting oneself to work with sets of data, not individual records as one would do with an ISAM. Had cursors existed then, they probably would have been misused, with the result being a bad SQL Server front end.

Cursors can be an important tool when used prudently. However, because cursors are record oriented, developers who are familiar with ISAM systems (such as IMS, dBASE, VSAM, or the Microsoft Jet database engine used in Microsoft Access) are often tempted to use cursors to port an application from an ISAM system to SQL Server. Such a port can be done quickly, but this is also one of the fastest ways to produce a truly bad SQL Server application. In the basic cursor example shown previously, the operation to fetch each row of the *authors* table is much like an ISAM operation on the *authors* file. Using that cursor is an order of magnitude less efficient than simply using a single SELECT statement to get all authors. This type of cursor misuse is more common than you'd think. If you need to port an ISAM application to SQL Server, do a *deep port*—that is, go back and look at the basic design of the application and the data structures before you do the port. A *shallow port*—making SQL Server mimic an ISAM—is appropriate only if you're one of those programmers who believes that there's never time to do the port right but there's always time to do it over.

For example, even a modestly experienced SQL Server programmer who wants to show authors and their corresponding book titles would write a single SELECT statement similar to the one below that joins the appropriate tables. This SELECT statement is likely to yield subsecond response time even if all the tables are large, assuming that appropriate indexes exist on the tables.

```
SELECT A.au_id, au_lname, title
FROM authors A
JOIN titleauthor TA ON (A.au_id=TA.au_id)
JOIN titles T ON (T.title_id=TA.title_id)
ORDER BY A.au_id, title
```

> **NOTE** When we refer to response time, we mean the time it takes to begin sending results back to the client application—in other words, how long it takes until the first row is returned.

In the example above, all the join processing is done at the back end and a single result set is returned. Minimal conversation occurs between the client

application and the server—only the single request is received and all the qualifying rows are returned as one result set. SQL Server decides on the most efficient order in which to work with the tables and returns a single result set to
satisfy the request.

An ISAM programmer who doesn't know about an operation such as a join
would approach this problem by opening the *authors* "file" (as an ISAM
programmer would think of it) and then iterating for each author by scanning
the *titleauthor* "connecting file." This programmer would then traverse into the
titles file to retrieve the appropriate records. So rather than write the simple and
efficient SQL join described above, the programmer might see cursors as the
natural solution and write the code shown below. This solution works in a sense:
it produces the correct results. But it is truly horrific in terms of its relative complexity to write and its performance compared to the set-based join operation.
The join would be more than 100 times faster than this query.

```
DECLARE @au_id char(11), @au_lname varchar(40), @title_id char(6),
    @au_id2 char(11), @title_id2 char(6), @title varchar(80)

DECLARE au_cursor CURSOR FOR
    SELECT au_id, au_lname FROM authors ORDER BY au_id

DECLARE au_titles CURSOR FOR
    SELECT au_id, title_id FROM titleauthor ORDER BY au_id

DECLARE titles_cursor CURSOR FOR
    SELECT title_id, title FROM titles ORDER BY title

OPEN au_cursor
FETCH NEXT FROM au_cursor INTO @au_id, @au_lname

WHILE (@@FETCH_STATUS=0)
    BEGIN
    OPEN au_titles
    FETCH NEXT FROM au_titles INTO @au_id2, @title_id


    WHILE (@@FETCH_STATUS=0)
        BEGIN
        -- If this is for the current author, get
        -- titles too
        IF (@au_id=@au_id2)
            BEGIN
```

```
        OPEN titles_cursor
        FETCH NEXT FROM titles_cursor INTO
            @title_id2, @title

        WHILE (@@FETCH_STATUS=0)
            BEGIN
            -- If right title_id, display the values
            IF (@title_id=@title_id2)
                SELECT @au_id, @au_lname, @title

            FETCH NEXT FROM titles_cursor INTO
                @title_id2, @title
            END
            CLOSE titles_cursor
        END
        FETCH NEXT FROM au_titles INTO @au_id2, @title_id
        END

    CLOSE au_titles
    FETCH NEXT FROM au_cursor INTO @au_id,@au_lname
    END
CLOSE au_cursor

DEALLOCATE titles_cursor
DEALLOCATE au_titles
DEALLOCATE au_cursor
```

Although this cursor solution is technically correct and is similar to the way ISAM processing would be written, if your developers are writing SQL Server applications like this *stop them immediately* and educate them. It might be easy for a developer who is familiar with SQL to see that the join is much better, but a developer who is steeped in ISAM operations might see the cursor solution as more straightforward even though it is more verbose. This is much more than just a style issue. Even for this trivial example from *pubs* with only 25 rows of output, the join solution is orders of magnitude faster. SQL Server is designed for set operations, so whenever possible you should perform set operations instead of sequential row-by-row operations. In addition to the huge performance gain, join operations are simpler to write and are far less likely to introduce a bug.

Programmers familiar with the ISAM model do positioned updates. That is, they seek (or position) to a specific row, modify it, seek to another row, update it, and so forth. Cursors also offer positioned updates, but performance is far slower than what you can achieve using a single UPDATE statement that simultaneously affects multiple rows. Although the previous example showed a SELECT operation, you can also accomplish updates and deletes using subquery and join operations. (For details, see Chapter 8.)

Problems with ISAM-Style Applications

The main problems with the ISAM style of writing applications for SQL Server are as follows:

- The ISAM-style operation makes excessive requests to the SQL Server. When cursor operations are done in the client application, a huge increase in network traffic results. In the join solution example we just examined, one request was made to the server: the SQL query doing the join. But in ISAM-style code, if every OPEN and FETCH presents a command to the server, this simple example that produces fewer than 30 rows of output results in more than 1000 commands being sent to the SQL Server!

  For the sake of illustration, the procedure is written entirely with Transact-SQL cursors. But cursors are typically written from a client application, and every OPEN and every FETCH would indeed be a separate command and a separate network conversation. The number of commands grows large because of all the nested iteration that happens with the series of inner loops, as you'll see if you trace through the commands. Although this procedure is admittedly convoluted, it's not unlike ones that exist in real applications.

- It is almost always more expensive to use a cursor than it is to use set-oriented SQL to accomplish a given task. ISAM's only form of update is the positioned update, but this requires at least two round-trips to the server—one to position on the row and another to change it. In set-oriented SQL, the client application tells the server that it wants to update the set of records that meet specified criteria. Then the server figures out how to accomplish the update as a single unit of work. When you use a cursor, the client doesn't allow the server to manage retrieving and updating records.

  In addition, using a cursor implies that the server is maintaining client "state" information—such as the user's current result set at the server, usually in *tempdb*—as well as consumption of memory for the cursor itself. Maintaining this state unnecessarily for a large number of clients is a waste of server resources. A better strategy for using SQL Server (or any server resource in fact) is for the client application to get a request in and out as quickly as possible, minimizing the client state at the server between requests. Set-oriented SQL supports this strategy, which makes it ideal for the client/server model.

■ The ISAM-style application example uses a conversational style of communicating with the server, which often involves many network round-trips within the scope of a single transaction. The effect is that transactions take longer. Transactions handled in this way can require seconds or minutes between the BEGIN TRANSACTION and COMMIT TRANSACTION statements. These long-running transactions might work fine for a single user, but they scale much too poorly for multiple users if any update activity occurs.

To support transactional consistency, the database must hold locks on shared resources from the time the resources are first acquired within the transaction until the commit time. Other users must wait to access the same resources. If one user holds these locks longer, that user will affect other users more and increase the possibility of a deadlock. (For more on locking, see Chapter 13.)

SEE ALSO See Peter Hussey's whitepaper titled "Designing Efficient Applications for Microsoft SQL Server" to learn about programming interfaces that can be used for SQL Server development. It also covers such issues as appropriate uses for cursors. A copy of this document is included on the book's companion CD. You can also download it for free from http://www.microsoft.com/sql.

Cursor Models

The subject of cursors confuses many people, at least in part because several cursor models are available and those models have different options and capabilities. We can group these models into three categories: Transact-SQL cursors, API server cursors, and client cursors.

Transact-SQL Cursors

You use Transact-SQL cursors within SQL typically in a stored procedure or in a batch that needs to do row-by-row processing. Transact-SQL cursors use the familiar statements DECLARE CURSOR, OPEN *cursor*, and FETCH. At times, Transact-SQL cursors have been referred to as "ANSI cursors" because their syntax and capabilities fully implement—and go well beyond—the scrollable cursor functionality specified by ANSI SQL-92. The ANSI specification states that scrollable cursors are read-only. This isn't the way applications work, of course, so fortunately SQL Server allows scrollable cursors that can be updated. SQL Server provides backward scrolling, relative and absolute positioning within the result set, and many options regarding sensitivity to changes made by others, as well as positioned updates and deletes. Few other products implement even the ANSI specification for scrollable, read-only cursors, let alone a cursor model as rich as SQL Server's. The cursor functionality of SQL Server is without question the richest in the industry. The term "ANSI cursor" is rarely used anymore because it implies a feature that is commonplace in the industry; the extensive cursor functionality is unique to SQL Server and greatly exceeds that specified by ANSI.

API Server Cursors

The OLE DB provider for SQL Server, the ODBC driver for SQL Server, and the DB-Library programming libraries have special cursor functions that are optimized for cursor operations and better network use between a client application and a server application. For a high-performance application, it is important that there be no excessive conversation between the client and the server. The hallmark of high-quality client/server computing is to have the client issue a single, brief command and then have the server respond. If every row fetched in a cursor had to be individually requested over the network and had to provide all the metadata to describe the row fetched, performance would be abysmal.

The OLE DB provider and the ODBC driver that Microsoft provides for SQL Server fully implement these special cursor commands, as does the DB-Library programming interface. Higher level interfaces, such as RDO and ADO, also implement these functions. These capabilities have the cumbersome names "ODBC server cursors," "DB-Library server cursors," and "OLE DB server cursors," so they're all generally referred to in the documentation as "API server cursors."

API server cursors enable smarter communication between the calling client application and the SQL Server back end. Central to this is the interface's ability to specify a "fat" cursor. That is, instead of thinking of a cursor as pointing to a single row, imagine the cursor pointing to multiple rows. Take, for example, an application that displays a list box of 20 customers at a time. As the user scrolls through the list box, a FETCH requests the next 20 rows. Or perhaps it fetches the previous 20 rows, the last 20 rows, or the 20 rows thought to be about three-fourths of the way through the result set. The interface is provided by such function calls as SQLFetchScroll for ODBC and IRowset::GetNextRows for OLE DB. These functions make sense within those programming environments, and they are used instead of SQL statements such as DECLARE CURSOR and FETCH. These API functions allow options and capabilities, such as defining the "width" of the cursor (the number of rows), that cannot be expressed using Transact-SQL cursor syntax. Another important performance optimization of API server cursors is that metadata is sent only once for the cursor and not with every FETCH operation, as is the case with a Transact-SQL cursor statement.

Besides offering performance advantages (especially for operations across a network), API server cursors have other capabilities that Transact-SQL cursors do not have. API server cursors can be declared on a stored procedure if the procedure contains only one SELECT statement. You use API server cursors mostly in application code.

> **NOTE** Many APIs provide access to API server cursors, but in this chapter we'll look at them primarily in the context of Transact-SQL cursor syntax, which is the most widely readable syntax. But when a capability is available only via API server cursors, we'll point that out. The information on Transact-SQL cursors is also relevant to all forms of API server cursors. After reading the information here, you should consult the programming reference for the specific API you use to better understand the capabilities offered.

Client Cursors

If you consider that the job of a cursor is to set a position within a result set, it should be clear to you that this task can be performed (although possibly less efficiently) within the client application with no assistance from the server. SQL Server originally had no cursor support, and many application designers wrote their own client-side cursor libraries to do this type of operation. While SQL Server 4.2 did not have cursor support in the engine, it offered a rich set of cursor functions for DB-Library so that application programmers would not have to reinvent the wheel. These functions were implemented entirely on the client. No magic was performed, and these functions did nothing that other ISVs couldn't do. But the designers knew from the outset that they eventually wanted cursor support in the engine. They designed the API so that the bulk of the work could eventually be executed remotely at the server and that a new API or substantial changes to applications using the API would not be necessary.

Version 6.0 introduced scrollable cursor support directly in the engine. With this support, applications written using the DB-Library version 4.2 cursor library typically worked without any changes. In fact, they worked quite a bit better because of the server-side assistance that they got. Version 6.0 added an optimized ODBC driver that fully exploited SQL Server's support for scrollable cursors. With database management systems other than SQL Server (most of which do not have scrollable cursors), it's not unusual for an ODBC driver to take on these cursor functions, as DB-Library used to for SQL Server. But with the ODBC driver that ships with SQL Server, cursor operations use the back-end engine's capabilities.

With SQL Server, you tend to make use of cursors on the server. Because client cursors are more of a programming convenience, we won't cover them in much depth. Instead, we'll focus on the server. But be aware that you can still use the OLE DB or ODBC cursor library to do the cursor operations for you (using client cursors) instead of having them processed at the server.

Some people consider client cursors obsolete now that server cursors are available. But client cursors can make a lot of sense when properly used. For example, if you want your user interface to provide forward and backward scrolling but you want to use the more efficient default result set rather than a server cursor, you need a local buffering mechanism to cache the entire result set and provide the scrolling operations. You can write this mechanism yourself, but client cursors already provide it. Also, the Internet has brought new issues and challenges for "stateless" management of data. (That is, the connection to SQL Server is not persistent.) Client cursors can play a major part in these solutions. Although the introduction of server cursors in version 6.0 might have made client cursors obsolete, the Internet will probably drive future work into new and more sophisticated client-cursor solutions.

Default Result Sets

Do not fall into the habit of thinking that every result set is a cursor, at least of the type previously discussed, or you'll inch toward the dark side—always using cursors. Earlier we said that you can think of a cursor as a named result set. You can think of rows not returned in a cursor as the *default result set* or as just a result set. A default result set is really not a cursor. You can think of it as a fourth type of cursor if you remember that no cursor functionality at the server is involved.

A default result set is frequently referred to as a *firehose cursor* in discussions of the cursor capabilities of ODBC. Within the SQL Server ODBC driver, you use the same function call, SQLFetchScroll, to process rows from SQL Server whether they emanate from a cursor operation or simply from a default result set. With ODBC, if you request a cursor that is forward-only and read-only, with a row set size of 1, the driver doesn't ask for a cursor at all. Instead, it asks for a default result set, which is much more efficient than a cursor. The term "firehose" reflects the way that the server blasts rows to the client as long as the client keeps processing them so that there is room in the network buffer to send more results. In Chapter 3, we saw how results are sent from the server to the client, and this is exactly what happens with a firehose cursor. The fact that the same ODBC functions work for both cursor and noncursor results is a nice programming convenience, so we'll continue to use the term "firehose cursor." Just remember that from the SQL Server engine's perspective, it is not a cursor.

API Server Cursors vs. Transact-SQL Cursors

Although this book is not about OLE DB or ODBC programming, cursors are intrinsically related to those programming interfaces. This shouldn't be too surprising, since you know that a key motivation for including cursors in SQL Server was to bridge the impedance mismatch between the set operations of SQL Server and the ISAM operations of traditional programming languages. And traditional programming languages use ODBC or OLE DB (or higher level interfaces that build on them, such as RDO or ADO). For a complete description of API server cursors, see *Inside ODBC* (Microsoft Press, 1995) by Kyle Geiger. Kyle's discussion is obviously centered on ODBC, but he goes into significant depth to show the interaction between the ODBC calls and the server cursor functions. If you program with ODBC, Kyle's book is a must-read. But even if you use another interface that uses cursor functionality, there is plenty to be gained from Kyle's discussion.

SQL Server provides some specialized cursor functions that are called only internally by the OLE DB provider, the ODBC driver, or DB-Library. These functions look like stored procedures and have stubs in the *sysobjects* table, so you might see their names there (for example, *sp_cursor*). If you trace the functions going to SQL Server (using SQL Server Profiler, or perhaps a network sniffer), you will see these functions flowing from the client application. In fact, you can execute them directly from ad hoc tools such as the Query Analyzer, although you should not call them directly from your applications.

These functions are not really stored procedures; they are capabilities implemented directly in SQL Server. The code is compiled into SQLSERVR.EXE— it is not a stored procedure or an extended stored procedure. We'll refer to such functions as "pseudo–stored procedures." The stubs in *sysobjects* make cursor execution mimic the execution of a stored procedure so that there is no need for major changes to the tabular data stream (TDS) between client and server. Remember that when server cursor support was implemented in version 6.0, a major goal was to have SQL Server work seamlessly with applications that had been written to use the client cursor functions of DB-Library version 4.2, so implementing cursors without changing the TDS was a clever idea. These functions are not intended, or supported, for direct use by an application. They are invoked directly by the ODBC driver, the DB-Library programming libraries, and the native OLE DB provider for SQL Server.

The functions can also be used directly by an ISV that is trying to provide a gateway to another data source if that ISV wants the gateway to include support for scrollable cursors. The gateway can trap these calls and then mimic them in whatever way makes sense to the final destination. As far as we know, no such gateway yet achieves the level of transparency achieved with OLE DB, ODBC, and DB-Library. (Doing so would be far from trivial—writing a cursor library takes significant work. And such an effort would require technical assistance from Microsoft, since the interface hasn't been supported for third-party development. But since products such as gateways tend to be relatively expensive, high-level capabilities are expected, and such a capability would be highly valued.)

Transact-SQL cursors and API server cursors use the same code within SQL Server, although the Transact-SQL cursors do not directly call the pseudo–stored procedures. Because the procedures exist only for the sake of remoting the work from OLE DB, ODBC, and DB-Library, an SQL statement, which is already executing inside the engine, has no need to call the routines in that way. While Transact-SQL and API server cursors execute the same code and have many similarities, you should not think of them as alternative ways to do the same thing.

Appropriate Use of Cursors

When should you use cursors? A somewhat simplistic answer is, "Only when you have to." This is not a totally facetious answer, because if you can think of a set-based solution to a problem and avoid using a cursor, you should do that. Ordinarily, cursors should be near the bottom of your list of possible solutions. Remember that SQL Server is a relational database, so it is inherently set based. As we mentioned earlier, if you overuse cursors, you turn SQL Server into an ISAM-like product and severely cripple its power.

You should not interpret this warning as a blanket statement that you should never use cursors. Scrollable cursors were, in fact, near the top of the new features wish list of many members of the SQL Server development team. More important, cursors were near the top of the developer community's wish list. Cursors are extremely powerful and provide SQL Server capabilities that cannot be achieved with other products. So let's look at some situations in which cursors provide a great benefit.

Row-by-Row Operations

Transact-SQL cursors are great for row-by-row operations with a stored procedure or a single batch. For example, suppose we have some financial data that includes cash flows, and for each row of that data we want to return only rows having an internal rate of return (IRR) of more than 20 percent. IRR is a pretty involved financial function that requires iterating and converging to an answer, and we can't simply express it in the SELECT statement. But suppose we write an extended stored procedure for IRR so that we can pass it the cash flows and it will return the IRR. Then, for each row qualified by a query, we can calculate the IRR using columns in the row as input to the IRR extended procedure. Then we'll return only rows in which the IRR would be 20 percent or more. This is an appropriate use of Transact-SQL cursors. If we couldn't use a cursor, we'd have to return all the rows across the network to the client application so we could do the IRR operation there. (Or we'd have to consider other, more complex situations that could occur if cursors weren't available, such as problems arising from having another program running on the server.)

Because the cursor allows individual rows to be examined entirely at the server, we avoid sending multiple requests from the client. Because a SELECT statement does not work in this situation, the cursor allows the operation to return to the client only rows in which the IRR value is greater than 20 percent—

not all rows. If we had wanted to return all the rows, we could have simply returned the raw data to the client and computed the IRR with a client function. In the future, when SQL Server provides support for user-defined functions (UDFs), this problem can be solved without the cursor. This is one reason (of many) that UDFs are high on the list of desirable future enhancements.

With Transact-SQL cursors, FETCH is almost always done in a loop and the cursor is used to perform row-by-row processing on the entire result set. But you should not use Transact-SQL cursors across multiple batches. For example, don't issue singular FETCH commands as their own batches. If your application fetches rows, does some work, fetches more rows, and so on, you should use API server cursors, not Transact-SQL cursors.

Query Operations

Transact-SQL cursors are often used in conjunction with EXECUTE(*'string'*) to write and execute SQL statements based on the results of some query. For example, suppose we want to issue an UPDATE STATISTICS command for every table in a database that doesn't contain the string "lookup" in its name. Using Transact-SQL cursors, we can use the following generic batch to do the entire operation—without having to return the names of the tables to the calling client application, reformat them into the correct commands, and send them back to the server. Instead, the entire operation is done at the server; only the initial request is sent from the client application.

```
DECLARE tables_curs CURSOR FOR
    SELECT name FROM sysobjects
    WHERE type='U'
    AND name NOT LIKE '%lookup%'
OPEN tables_curs
DECLARE @tablename varchar(30), @output_msg varchar(80)
FETCH NEXT FROM tables_curs INTO @tablename
WHILE (@@FETCH_STATUS=0 )
    BEGIN
    EXEC ("UPDATE STATISTICS " + @tablename)
        IF (@@ERROR=0)
            SELECT @output_msg=
                'Statistics successfully updated on table '
                + @tablename
        ELSE
            SELECT @output_msg=
                'Failed to Update Statistics on table '
                + @tablename + ' @@ERROR=' +
                CONVERT(varchar, @@ERROR)
    PRINT @output_msg
    FETCH NEXT FROM tables_curs INTO @tablename
    END
```

```
CLOSE tables_curs
DEALLOCATE tables_curs
```

SQL Server 7 includes the system stored procedure *sp_updatestats* to update the statistics for *all* user-defined tables in a database. However, if you want to restrict the set of names for which you are updating statistics (as in our example where we didn't want to update statistics for lookup tables), the preceding cursor-based solution might be just what you need.

Scrolling Applications

The need for Transact-SQL cursors was not the biggest motivation for adding cursors to SQL Server. Rather, the crying need was for API server cursors to support "scrolling applications." Many of these applications originated from ISAM applications, or they started as single-user Microsoft FoxPro or dBASE applications (or they followed that paradigm—you know the type).

For example, think of an address book of the type used in your e-mail program. The user opens the address book and scrolls up or down to view the list of names. The user drags the scroll bar slider to the bottom and expects to be positioned at the last record. Dragging the slider to the beginning of the list, the user expects to be repositioned at the first record. Is this an appropriate use for a cursor? It depends on what you want to do with the information in the list. Here are some examples of how you might think about the problem.

EXAMPLE 1

A cursor is unnecessary if the address book includes only a few hundred entries, if it will be read-only, or if you're not concerned with sensitivity to changes in data (that is, you don't care whether the most up-to-date copy of the data is available). After the user's list box is initially populated, a few new names might be added or the information might change in some way. But for our purposes, it is unnecessary for the list box to exhibit dynamic behavior such as names appearing, disappearing, or changing as the user scrolls through the list. In this case and with these requirements, you can simply issue the query and get the results. You can easily buffer a few hundred rows of information on the client, so there is no need for cursors.

EXAMPLE 2

An API server cursor is appropriate if the address book has 100,000 entries. The user will probably look at only a few dozen entries and then quit. Should you select all 100,000 rows to populate the list box so that the user can see only a few dozen? In most cases, the answer is no. Using a cursor is reasonable in this situation; you can use an API server cursor.

Suppose the list box can display 20 names at a time. You can set the cursor width to 20 (a fat cursor) so that with any fetch forward or backward you get one list box worth of data. Or you can fetch 60 or 80 rows at a time so that the user can scroll by a few screenfuls within the application without having to ask the server for more rows. If the user moves the scroll bar slider to the bottom of the list, you fetch the bottom 20 rows by using LAST. If the user moves the slider to the top, you fetch the top 20 rows by using FIRST. And if the slider moves three-fourths of the way down the list, you can do some quick division and scroll to that point by using ABSOLUTE *n*. (For example, you can easily determine the total number of qualifying rows. If 100,000 rows are available and you want to scroll approximately three-fourths of the way down, you can do a FETCH ABSOLUTE 75000 statement.)

If you have to provide this type of application with a large amount of data, using a cursor makes sense. Of course, it might be better if the user is required to type in a few characters—that would allow the application to qualify the result set of the cursor. If you know that the user is interested only in names starting with *S*, for example, you can significantly reduce the size of the cursor by adding the appropriate criteria (for example, *name like ('S%')* in the cursor SELECT statement.

Choosing a Cursor

Although it might seem as if you have an overabundance of choices for your cursor model, the decision-making process is fairly straightforward. Follow these guidelines to choose the appropriate cursor for your situation:

- If you can do the operation with a good set-oriented solution, do so and avoid using a cursor. (In ODBC parlance, use a firehose cursor.)

- If you have decided that a cursor is appropriate and you will be doing multiple fetches over the network (such as to support a scrolling application), use an API server cursor. You'll use OLE DB, ODBC, RDO, DB-Library, ADO, or another API depending on your application needs.

- For the most part, avoid using client-side cursors and products or libraries that perform many cursor operations in the client application. Such applications tend to make excessive requests to the server and use the server inefficiently—the multitude of network round-trips makes for a slow, sluggish application.

Table 11-1 compares the ways cursors are declared and opened, and how operations are performed in Transact-SQL cursor statements; their rough equivalents among the pseudo–stored procedures used by the ODBC driver and DB-Library; and the ODBC and OLE DB cursor methods.

Transact-SQL Cursor Statement	Pseudo–Stored Procedure	ODBC Cursor Function	OLE DB Cursors
DECLARE/ OPEN	*sp_cursoropen*	SQLSetStmtAttr (SQL_ATTR_ CURSOR_TYPE) SQLSetStmtAttr (SQL_ATTR_ CONCURRENCY) SQLExecDirect or SQLExecute	Set row set properties such as DBPROP_ OTHERINSERT, DBPROP_OTHER UPDATEDELETE, DBPROP_OWN INSERT, or DBPROP_OWN UPDATEDELETE to control cursor behaviors
FETCH	*sp_cursorfetch*	SQLFetch or SQLExtendedFetch()	IRowset:: GetNextRows
UPDATE/ DELETE (positioned)	*sp_cursor*	SQLSetPos()	IRowsetChange:: SetData or IRowsetChange:: DeleteRows
CLOSE/ DEALLOC	*sp_cursorclose*	SQLCloseCursor	IRowset::Release

Table 11-1.
Equivalent Transact-SQL cursor statements, pseudo–stored procedures, ODBC cursor functions, and OLE DB cursor methods.

Cursor Membership, Scrolling, and Sensitivity to Change

In addition to understanding the cursor model (that is, Transact-SQL or API server cursors), you must understand some other key options that deal with the "membership" of the cursor and the behavior the cursor exhibits as you scroll through the result set. We can divide these options into the two categories listed at the top of the next page.

- **Cursor types** The API server cursors usually specify cursor behavior by dividing them into four different types: static, keyset, dynamic, and forward-only.

- **Cursor behaviors** The ANSI SQL-92 standard defines the keywords SCROLL and INSENSITIVE to specify the behavior of cursors. Some of the APIs also support defining a cursor's behavior using these terms. SQL Server 7 allows us to specify many more aspects of the cursor's behavior.

Transact-SQL cursors can use either the ANSI-specified syntax with INSENSITIVE and SCROLL options or the full range of cursor types, which we call Transact-SQL Extended Syntax. Prior to SQL Server version 7, only the ANSI syntax was available. However, since Transact-SQL Extended Syntax, which allows all the various options available through API cursors, provides much greater control and flexibility, we'll use that syntax in most of our examples. The ANSI specification does not define standards for several semantic issues related to sensitivity to changes made by others. (When the specification was written, it is likely that no one involved had implemented scrollable cursors. Even today, SQL Server is the only widely used product with scrollable cursors.) The issue of sensitivity to changes is further complicated in the client/server environment because using a FETCH statement means fetching across the network. When you use the ANSI specification to declare a cursor, the behavior characteristics are specified before the word *CURSOR*:

```
DECLARE cursor_name [INSENSITIVE] [SCROLL] CURSOR
FOR select_statement
[FOR {READ ONLY | UPDATE [OF column_list]}]
```

When implementing cursors, Microsoft engineers had to make a lot of decisions about subtle behavioral issues. They wanted efficient scrollable cursors that could be used for updating in a networked client/server environment. However, according to the ANSI specification, scrollable cursors are read-only! Fortunately, they were able to go way beyond the specification when they implemented scrollable, updatable cursors. In fact, Microsoft's original cursor specification went so far beyond the original ANSI specification that they started using the terminology of the four different cursor types (static, keyset, dynamic, and forward-only) even though the syntax allowed only the words INSENSITIVE and SCROLL. Since the new API-based syntax for declaring cursors actually uses these types in the declaration, that is the syntax we'll mainly use. Here's how to declare a cursor using Transact-SQL Extended Syntax:

```
DECLARE cursor_name CURSOR
[LOCAL | GLOBAL]
[FORWARD_ONLY | SCROLL]
[STATIC | KEYSET | DYNAMIC | FAST_FORWARD]
[READ_ONLY | SCROLL_LOCKS | OPTIMISTIC]
[TYPE_WARNING]
FOR select_statement
[FOR UPDATE [OF column_list]]
```

The keywords describe how membership in the cursor is maintained (that is, which rows qualify), the available scrolling capabilities, and the cursor's sensitivity to change. Notice that the keywords appear after the word *CURSOR* in the DECLARE statement. That is how the parser distinguishes the older ANSI cursor syntax from the new Transact-SQL Extended Syntax for cursors: in the former, the cursor qualifiers come before the word *CURSOR*; in the latter, the qualifiers come after.

Static Cursors

A static cursor is attached to a snapshot of the data that qualifies for the cursor. The snapshot is stored in *tempdb*. A static cursor is read-only, and the rows in the cursor and the data values of the rows never change when you fetch anywhere in the cursor because you operate on a private, temporary copy of the data. Membership in a static cursor is fixed—that is, as you fetch in any direction, new rows cannot qualify and old rows cannot change in such a way that they no longer qualify.

Before you use a static cursor, consider whether you need to use a cursor at all. If the data is static and read-only, it probably makes more sense to process it all in the client application as a default result set and not use a cursor. If the number of rows is too large to reasonably process on the client, creating this temporary table on the server can also prove to be an expensive undertaking.

If you use ANSI-style cursors and specify the modifier INSENSITIVE, the cursor will be static. Using Transact-SQL Extended Syntax, you can actually specify the keyword STATIC. A private temporary table is created for the SELECT statement you specify. Note that even the cursor cannot do positioned updates or deletes on this snapshot of data in the temporary table. For comparison, here are two cursor definitions for the same query, using the two syntax possibilities:

```
-- ANSI-style syntax for declaring static cursor
DECLARE my_cursor1 INSENSITIVE CURSOR
```

(continued)

```
FOR SELECT au_id, au_lname
FROM authors
where state != 'CA'

-- Transact-SQL Extended Syntax for declaring static cursor
DECLARE my_cursor1 CURSOR STATIC
FOR SELECT au_id, au_lname
FROM authors
where state != 'CA'
```

The result rows returned from the two cursors above are identical, with one minor behavioral difference. A static cursor defined using the ANSI syntax and the keyword INSENSITIVE is not scrollable—that is, you can fetch rows only in the forward direction. If you want the cursor to be scrollable, you must specify the SCROLL keyword. The Transact-SQL Extended Syntax creates static cursors that are scrollable by default.

You might want to use a static cursor for some "what if"–type operations on the data when you know that the changes will never be reflected in the base tables. If you want to carry out this type of operation, you can do a SELECT INTO in a temporary table and then declare a cursor on that table without specifying STATIC. If you specify a query that performs an aggregate function (such as SUM, MIN, MAX, GROUP BY, or UNION), the cursor might also have to be materialized in a temporary table and therefore will automatically be a static cursor.

Keyset Cursors

With a keyset cursor, a list of all the key values for the rows that meet the SELECT statement criteria is kept in *tempdb*. For example, if you declare a scrollable cursor on the *customer* table, the keyset is a list of those *cust_id* values that qualified for membership in the SELECT statement when the cursor was opened. Suppose that when the cursor was opened, the SELECT statement used to declare the cursor had a WHERE clause in this form:

```
WHERE cust_balance > 100000
```

Suppose also that customers 7, 12, 18, 24, and 56 (that is, rows with *cust_id* of those values) qualified. These keys are used whenever fetching is performed. Conceptually, further selection for the cursor takes this form

```
WHERE cust_id IN (7,12,18,24,56)
```

rather than this form:

```
WHERE cust_balance > 100000
```

(Internally, the SELECT statement is not issued again. This is for purposes of illustration only.) Membership in the keyset cursor is fixed. That is, these five identified rows are part of the cursor and no other rows are seen in subsequent fetching. Even if other rows that meet the SELECT statement criteria are subsequently inserted or updated, they are not seen by this cursor after it is opened.

In a keyset cursor as opposed to a static cursor, you can see changes to the data in the rows that meet the SELECT criteria when the cursor is opened. For example, if another user modifies the customer balance while you hold the cursor open and then fetch the row again, you see those changes (unless you hold locks to prevent such changes). In fact, even if the modification causes the row to no longer satisfy the criteria of *cust_balance > 100000*, you still see the row in a subsequent fetch. The row disappears only if it is actually deleted. The key value still exists because it was squirreled away in *tempdb,* but the row is gone. Default values, NULL values, blank spaces, or zeros (as appropriate) are supplied for the column values. But more important, the @@FETCH_STATUS system function returns a value of –2 in this case, indicating that the row no longer exists.

Because the keys are stored in *tempdb* when the cursor is open and membership is fixed, keyset cursors can fetch to an absolute position within the result set. For example, it is reasonable to fetch to row 104 of the cursor:

```
FETCH ABSOLUTE 104 FROM cursor
```

It shouldn't come as a surprise that a keyset cursor demands that a unique index exist on every table used in the SELECT statement for the cursor. The unique index is necessary to identify the keys. The index can be created directly (with CREATE INDEX), or it can exist as a result of a PRIMARY KEY or UNIQUE constraint.

> **N O T E** In SQL Server 7, every clustered index is treated as unique internally, even if you didn't specifically define the index to be unique. (We'll see more about internal index structures in Chapter 14.) For this reason, you can always define a keyset cursor on a table that has a clustered index.

If you declare a keyset cursor using Transact-SQL Extended Syntax on a table that doesn't have a unique index, you do not receive an error message or any warning unless the cursor was declared with the option TYPE_WARNING. Without that option specified, you just don't get a keyset cursor. Instead, the cursor is created as STATIC. Later in this chapter, we'll see the stored procedures that provide information about your currently available cursors.

Dynamic Cursors

You can think of a dynamic cursor as a cursor in which the SELECT statement is applied again in subsequent FETCH operations. That is, the cursor does not refetch specific rows, as in this statement:

```
WHERE cust_id IN (12,18,24,56,7)
```

Instead, conceptually, the WHERE clause is reapplied. For example:

```
WHERE cust_balance > 100000
```

This means that membership is *not* fixed—subsequent fetches might include newly qualifying rows, or previously qualifying rows might disappear. This can occur due to changes you have made within the cursor or due to changes made by others. If the cursor has not locked the rows of the result set (which is dependent on the concurrency options selected, as we'll see in a moment), the changes made by others are seen in your cursor when you do a subsequent fetch on the cursor. You see such changes only on a subsequent fetch. The image of data in the buffer from the last fetch is just that—a copy in memory of what the row or rows looked like when the last fetch was performed.

Since membership in a dynamic cursor is not fixed, there is no guarantee that subsequent fetches will always bring up the same information. For this reason, FETCH ABSOLUTE is not supported for cursors declared using the DYNAMIC keyword, even if you declare the cursor through the API. It doesn't make sense, for example, to simply fetch to row 104 if every subsequent fetch brings up a row 104 that contains different information. However, FETCH RELATIVE is supported with dynamic cursors, which sometimes surprises people. When used with a dynamic cursor, FETCH RELATIVE n starts fetching from the first row in the current cursor set and skips the first n rows from that point.

A cursor declared with an ORDER BY clause can be dynamic only if an index contains keys that match the ORDER BY clause. If no such index exists, the cursor automatically converts to either a keyset or a static cursor. As previously mentioned, you need a unique index on some column in the table to get a keyset cursor. So if you have a unique index that just doesn't happen to be on the columns in the ORDER BY, you get a keyset cursor. If there is no index that matches the ORDER BY and no unique index on any column, the cursor reverts to a static cursor.

Forward-Only Cursors

Forward-only cursors are dynamic cursors that allow only a FETCH type of NEXT. It's OK for you to think of SQL Server as having only three types of cursors (static, keyset, and dynamic). Forward-only is treated here as its own type because the Transact-SQL Extended Syntax, as well as API server cursors, specify forward-only at the same level as KEYSET and DYNAMIC.

Forward-only scrolling is consistent with the recommended use of Transact-SQL cursors to provide row-by-row processing within a stored procedure or batch. Such processing is usually from start to end—one way—so that rows are never refetched. If you use Transact-SQL cursors appropriately, you typically scroll forward-only to do a row-by-row operation and you do not revisit rows. Forward-only cursors are usually the fastest type of cursor, but a standard SELECT statement (not a cursor) is still significantly faster.

Fast Forward–Only Cursors

Transact-SQL Extended Syntax allows for a special type of forward-only cursor called a fast forward–only cursor. This type of cursor is always read-only, in addition to being forward-only. You can also specify fast forward–only cursors through the ODBC driver, and in fact this is the environment in which they provide the most benefit. Applications using the SQL Server ODBC driver can set the driver-specific statement attribute SQL_SOPT_SS_CURSOR_OPTIONS to SQL_CO_FFO or SQL_CO_FFO_AF. The SQL_CO_FFO_AF option specifies that an autofetch option also be enabled. Autofetch enables two optimizations that can significantly reduce network traffic:

- When the cursor is opened, the first row or batch of rows is automatically fetched from the cursor. This saves you from having to send a fetch request across the network.

- When a fetch hits the end of the cursor, the cursor is automatically closed. This saves you from having to send a separate close request across the network.

The most dramatic improvement comes when you process cursors with relatively small result sets that can be cached in the memory of an application. The fast forward–only cursor with autofetch enabled is the most efficient way to get a result set into an ODBC application.

The autofetch option is not available when you use Transact-SQL Extended Syntax. It is meant as an optimization when you declare and manage cursors through your client application.

Implicit conversion of fast forward–only cursors Fast forward–only cursors are implicitly converted to other cursor types in certain situations. If the SELECT statement joins one or more tables with triggers to tables without triggers, the cursor is converted to a static cursor. If a fast forward–only cursor is not read-only, it is converted to a dynamic cursor. If the SELECT statement is a distributed query that references one or more remote tables on linked servers, the cursor is converted to a keyset-driven cursor.

Other implicit conversions are also carried out when you work with Transact-SQL Extended Syntax cursors, depending on the structure of the underlying tables and the keywords used in the cursor's SELECT statement. We saw previously that a cursor declared as a keyset is implicitly converted to a static cursor if any of the underlying tables don't have a unique index. A cursor based on a SELECT statement that needs to build a *temp* table is implicitly converted to a static cursor. In you have any doubt whether SQL Server actually created the type of cursor you requested, you can use the cursor procedures described in the following sections to verify all of the cursor's properties.

Working with Transact-SQL Cursors

In the following sections, we'll discuss the cursor syntax for each of the cursor manipulation statements and then look at issues of locking and concurrency control. Throughout this discussion, we'll look at cursor functionality that is present in the server, which in some cases is available only through API server cursors.

DECLARE

Here again is the Transact-SQL Extended Syntax for declaring a cursor with a given name:

```
DECLARE cursor_name CURSOR
[LOCAL | GLOBAL]
[FORWARD_ONLY | SCROLL]
[STATIC | KEYSET | DYNAMIC | FAST_FORWARD]
[READ_ONLY | SCROLL_LOCKS | OPTIMISTIC]
[TYPE_WARNING]
FOR select_statement
[FOR UPDATE [OF column_list]]
```

A cursor is always limited in scope to the connection that declares it. Although the cursor is named, it is not visible to other connections and other connections can have cursors of the same name. This is true whether the cursor is declared as GLOBAL or LOCAL; it is always private to the connection.

Global and Local Cursors

By default, Transact-SQL cursors are global for the connection in which they are declared. This means that you can declare a cursor in one batch and use it in subsequent batches or fetch each row in its own batch. It also means that you can declare a cursor in a stored procedure and have access to the cursor outside of the stored procedure. This is not necessarily a good thing, because if the stored procedure is then called a second or subsequent time, it can get an error message when it tries to declare a cursor that already exists (from a previous execution using the same connection).

You can use the syntax for declaring a cursor to specify whether the cursor is global or local. As mentioned earlier, *global* means global to the connection for which the cursor was declared. A *local* cursor is local to the batch, stored procedure, or trigger in which it is declared, and no reference can be made to the cursor outside of that scope. If you need access to a cursor declared as local inside a stored procedure, you can pass the cursor as an output parameter to the batch that called the procedure. You'll see the details of this when we look at cursor variables and parameters.

Transact-SQL cursors are global by default in SQL Server. You can override this default at the database level by setting the database option *default to local cursor* to TRUE. Local cursors are implicitly deallocated when the batch, stored procedure, or trigger terminates unless it was passed back in an output parameter. If it is passed back in an output parameter, the cursor is deallocated when the last variable referencing it is deallocated or goes out of scope.

Specifying the Cursor's Result Set

A Transact-SQL cursor always has its result set generated from a SELECT statement. The SELECT statement can be ordered (ORDER BY), and it often is. An API server cursor can also be declared; the result set is the result of a stored procedure. This powerful capability, which is important for scrolling applications, is not available using the Transact-SQL syntax.

Specifying the Cursor's Behavior

In addition to specifying whether the cursor is local or global, the DECLARE statement also specifies what kind of directional movement is possible, using the keywords SCROLL and FORWARD_ONLY. When neither of these is specified,

FORWARD_ONLY is the default, unless a STATIC, KEYSET, or DYNAMIC keyword is specified. STATIC, KEYSET, and DYNAMIC cursors default to SCROLL.

The DECLARE statement also controls how much of the cursor's result set is stored in *tempdb* and how subject to change the cursor's result set is. These behaviors are specified using the STATIC, KEYSET, and DYNAMIC keywords, which we discussed earlier. The DECLARE statement uses the READ ONLY option to prevent updates from being made through this cursor by the connection that opened the cursor. A READ_ONLY cursor cannot be referenced in a WHERE CURRENT OF clause in an UPDATE or DELETE statement. This option overrides the cursor's default ability to be updated.

The READ ONLY option controls only whether the connection that opened the cursor can update the data through the cursor. It has no affect on what changes can be made to the cursor's data from other connections. Such changes are controlled by the STATIC, KEYSET, and DYNAMIC options. The READ ONLY option also controls the locks that are taken when rows are fetched through the cursor. The locking (or concurrency) options are discussed later.

It is worth pointing out that if the DECLARE statement includes a local variable, the variable's value is captured at declare time, not at open time. In the following example, the cursor uses a WHERE clause of *qty > 30*, not *qty > 5*:

```
DECLARE @t smallint
SELECT @t=30

DECLARE c1 CURSOR SCROLL FOR SELECT ord_num, qty FROM sales
    WHERE qty > @t

DECLARE @ordnum varchar(20), @qty smallint

SELECT @t=5
OPEN c1
```

OPEN

The OPEN statement opens the cursor, generating and populating temporary tables if needed:

```
OPEN cursor_name
```

If the cursor is keyset based, the keys are also retrieved when the cursor is opened. Subsequent update or fetch operations on a cursor are illegal unless the cursor opens successfully. You can call the system function @@CURSOR_ ROWS after the OPEN statement to retrieve the number of qualifying rows in the last opened cursor. Depending on the number of rows expected in the result set, SQL Server might populate the keyset cursor asynchronously on a separate thread. This allows fetches to proceed immediately, even if the keyset cursor is not fully populated. Table 11-2 shows the values returned by using @@CURSOR_ROWS and a description of each value.

Value	Description
-1	The cursor is dynamic. @@CURSOR_ROWS is not applicable.
$-m$	A keyset cursor is still in the process of being populated asynchronously. This value refers to the number of rows in the keyset so far. The negative value indicates that the keyset is still being retrieved. A negative value (asynchronous population) can be returned only with a keyset cursor.
n	This value refers to the number of rows in the cursor.
0	No cursors have been opened, or the last opened cursor has been closed.

Table 11-2.
Possible values returned by @@CURSOR_ROWS.

To set the threshold at which SQL Server generates keysets asynchronously (and potentially returns a negative value), you use the *cursor threshold* configuration option with *sp_configure*. Note that this is an "advanced option" and is not visible unless Show Advanced Options is also enabled with *sp_configure*. By default, the setting for this cursor threshold is –1, which means that the keyset is fully populated before the OPEN statement completes. (That is, the keyset generation is synchronous.) With asynchronous keyset generation, OPEN completes almost immediately and you can begin fetching rows while other keys are still being gathered. However, this can lead to some puzzling behaviors. For example, you can't really FETCH LAST until the keyset is fully populated. Unless you are generating large cursors, it's usually not necessary to set this option—synchronous keyset generation works fine and the behavior is more predictable. If you need to open a large cursor, however, this is an important capability for maintaining good response times.

FETCH

The FETCH statement fetches a row from the cursor in the specified direction:

```
FETCH [row_selector FROM] cursor_name [INTO @v1, @v2, ...]
```

A successful fetch results in the system function @@FETCH_STATUS returning the value 0. If the cursor is scrollable, *row_selector* can be NEXT, PRIOR, FIRST, LAST, ABSOLUTE *n*, or RELATIVE *n*. (We have seen one exception: a DYNAMIC cursor cannot FETCH ABSOLUTE.) If no *row_ selector* is specified, the default is NEXT. FETCH NEXT operations are by far the most common type of fetch for Transact-SQL cursors. This is consistent with their recommended use when row-by-row processing is needed with a stored procedure or batch. Such processing is nearly always from start to finish.

More exotic forms of fetch are also supported. ABSOLUTE *n* returns the *n*th row in the result set, with a negative value representing a row number counting backward from the end of the result set. RELATIVE *n* returns the *n*th row relative to the last row fetched, and a negative value indicates the row number is counted backward starting from the last row fetched. Fetches using NEXT, PRIOR, or RELATIVE operations are done with respect to the current cursor position.

RELATIVE 0 means "refetch the current row." This can be useful to "freshen" a "stale" row. The row number *n* specified in RELATIVE and ABSOLUTE fetch types can be a local variable or a parameter of type *integer, smallint,* or *tinyint.*

When a cursor is opened, the current row position in the cursor is logically before the first row. This causes the fetch options to have slightly different behaviors if they are the first fetch performed after the cursor is opened:

- FETCH NEXT is equivalent to FETCH FIRST.
- FETCH PRIOR does not return a row.
- FETCH RELATIVE is equivalent to FETCH ABSOLUTE if *n* is positive. If *n* is negative or 0, no row is returned.

The ANSI SQL-92 specification states that scrollable cursors must be read-only. There really isn't any rational reason for this, except that updatable scrollable cursors were considered too hard to implement to put into the standard. Fortunately, SQL Server scrollable cursors are indeed updatable—a quantum leap beyond what the standard specifies!

If the cursor is not scrollable, only NEXT (or no explicit parameter, which amounts to the same thing) is legal. When the cursor is opened and no fetch is done, the cursor is positioned before the first row—that is, FETCH NEXT returns the first row. When some rows are fetched successfully, the cursor is positioned on the last row fetched. When a FETCH request causes the cursor position to exceed the given result set, the cursor is positioned after the last row—that is, a FETCH PRIOR returns the last row. A fetch that causes the position to go outside the cursor range (before the first row or after the last row) causes the system function @@FETCH_STATUS to return the value −1.

> **TIP** Probably the most common and appropriate use of Transact-SQL cursors is to FETCH NEXT within a loop while @@FETCH_STATUS equals 0 (or <> −1). However, you must issue the first FETCH before checking the value of @@FETCH_STATUS and then reissue your FETCH within the loop. If your cursor is a keyset cursor, you must also check for a @@FETCH_STATUS of −2 after every row is read to verify that the row is still available. If a row is fetched but no longer exists with a keyset cursor, the row is considered "missing" and @@FETCH_STATUS returns −2. The row might have been deleted by some other user or by an operation within the cursor. A missing row has been deleted, not simply updated so that it no longer meets the criteria of the SELECT statement. (If that's the semantic you want, you should use a dynamic cursor.)

Missing rows apply to keyset cursors only. A static cursor, of course, never changes—it is merely a snapshot of the data stored in a temporary table and cannot be updated. A dynamic cursor does not have fixed membership. The row is not expected to be part of a dynamic cursor because rows come and go as the cursor is fetched, depending on what rows currently meet the query criteria. So there is no concept of a missing row for a dynamic cursor.

If an INTO clause is provided, the data from each column in the SELECT list is inserted into the specified local variable; otherwise, the data is sent to the client as a normal result set with full metadata using TDS. In other words, the result set of a Transact-SQL cursor is the same as any other result set. But doing 50 fetches back to the application in this way produces 50 result sets, which is inefficient. An error occurs from the fetch if the datatypes of the column being retrieved and the local variable being assigned are incompatible or if the length of the local variable is less than the maximum length of the column. Also, the number of variables and their order must exactly match those of the selected columns in the SELECT statement that defines the cursor.

UPDATE

The UPDATE statement updates the table row corresponding to the given row in the cursor:

```
UPDATE table_name SET assignment_list WHERE CURRENT OF cursor_name
```

This is referred to as a *positioned update*. Using Transact-SQL cursors, a positioned update (or a *positioned delete*) operates only on the last row fetched and can affect only one row. (API server cursors can update multiple rows in a single operation. You can think of this capability as an array of structures that can all be applied in one operation. This is a significant capability, but it makes sense to use it only from an application programming language.)

An update involving a column that is used as a key value is treated internally as a delete/insert—as though the row with the original key values was deleted and a new row with the modified key values was inserted into the table.

DELETE

The following is a positioned delete:

```
DELETE FROM table_name WHERE CURRENT OF cursor_name
```

This statement deletes from the given table the row corresponding to the current position of the cursor. This is similar to a positioned update. Using Transact-SQL cursors, however, you can't perform positioned inserts. Since a cursor can be thought of as a named result set, it should be clear that you do not insert into a cursor but into the table (or view) that the cursor is selecting from.

CLOSE

The CLOSE statement closes the cursor:

```
CLOSE cursor_name
```

After the cursor is closed, it can no longer be fetched from or updated/deleted. Closing the cursor deletes its keyset while leaving the definition of the cursor intact. (That is, a closed cursor can be reopened without being redeclared.) The keyset is regenerated during the next OPEN. Similarly, closing a static cursor deletes the temporary table of results, which can be regenerated when the cursor is reopened. Closing a dynamic cursor doesn't have much effect because neither the data nor the keys are materialized.

ANSI specifies that cursors are closed when a COMMIT statement is issued, but this is not SQL Server's default behavior. In the types of applications in which cursors are most appropriate (what you might call scrolling applications), it is common to make a change and want both to commit it and to keep working within the cursor. Having the cursor close whenever a COMMIT is issued seems inefficient and rather pointless. But if you want to be consistent with ANSI on this, you can use the following SET option, which provides this "feature" by closing all open cursors when a COMMIT or a ROLLBACK occurs.

```
SET CURSOR_CLOSE_ON_COMMIT ON
```

Note that when you use API server cursors with ODBC, the default is to close the cursor on COMMIT; ODBC followed the ANSI lead here. But the SQL Server ODBC driver and the SQL Server OLE DB provider both set the CURSOR_CLOSE_ON_COMMIT option to OFF. You can also control this behavior at the database level with the database option *close cursor on commit*.

> **NOTE** Unlike earlier versions of SQL Server, version 7 always closes cursors on a ROLLBACK, regardless of the value of the CURSOR_CLOSE_ON_COMMIT option. The only exception is cursors that are defined as STATIC (or INSENSITIVE, if you're using the older ANSI cursor syntax). Static cursors are not closed on ROLLBACK if the CURSOR_CLOSE_ON_COMMIT setting is OFF.

DEALLOCATE

DEALLOCATE, which is not part of the ANSI specification, is a cleanup command:

```
DEALLOCATE cursor_name
```

When the last cursor reference is deallocated, SQL Server releases the data structures comprising the cursor. As we'll see shortly, with cursor variables you can have additional references to a cursor besides the original cursor name specified in the DECLARE statement. You can deallocate one of the references, but if other references to the same cursor exist, you can still access the cursor's rows using those other references.

Once the last reference to a cursor is deallocated, the cursor cannot be opened until a new DECLARE statement is issued. Although it's considered standard practice to close a cursor, if you DEALLOCATE the last reference to an open cursor it is automatically closed. The existence of DEALLOCATE is basically a performance optimization. Without it, when would a cursor's resources be cleaned up? How would SQL Server know that you are really done using the cursor? Probably the only alternative would be to do the cleanup anytime a CLOSE is issued. But then all the overhead of a new DECLARE would be necessary before a cursor could be opened again. Although it is yet another command to issue, providing a separate DEALLOCATE command lets you close and reopen a cursor without redeclaring it.

Simplest Cursor Syntax

In its simplest form, with no other options declared, this example cursor is forward-only (a dynamic cursor subtype):

```
DECLARE my_curs CURSOR FOR SELECT au_id, au_lname FROM authors
```

If you try any fetch operation other than FETCH NEXT (or simply FETCH, since NEXT is the default if no modifier is specified), you get an error like this:

```
Msg 16911, Level 16, State 1
fetch: The fetch type FETCH_LAST cannot be used with forward-
only cursors
```

Transact-SQL cursors can scroll only to the NEXT row (forward-only) unless the SCROLL option is explicitly stated or the type of cursor is specified as STATIC, KEYSET, or DYNAMIC, in which case any fetch operation is legal.

Fully Scrollable Transact-SQL Cursors

Here is a an example of a fully scrollable Transact-SQL cursor:

```
DECLARE my_curs CURSOR SCROLL FOR SELECT au_id, au_lname
    FROM authors
OPEN my_curs
FETCH ABSOLUTE 6 FROM my_curs
```

Here's the output:

```
au_id         au_lname
-----------   --------------
427-17-2319   Dull
```

NOTE To keep our examples focused on the central point, they don't check @@FETCH_STATUS or @@ERROR. Real production-caliber code, of course, would check.

If the cursor is scrollable, but not every table listed in the SELECT statement has a unique index, the cursor is created as a static (read-only) cursor, although it is still scrollable. The results of the SELECT statement are copied into a temporary table when the cursor is opened. Unless the FOR UPDATE OF clause is used (or the cursor is declared with the option TYPE_WARNING), you receive no indication that this will occur. An error results after the DECLARE cursor statement is issued:

```
CREATE TABLE foo
(col1    int,
col2     int)
-- No indexes on this table
GO

DECLARE my_curs2 SCROLL CURSOR FOR SELECT col1, col2 FROM foo
FOR UPDATE OF col1
```

This returns:

```
Msg 16929, Level 16, State 1
Cursor is read only
```

WARNING The error above is a compile-time error, which means that the cursor is not created at all. The error message seems to indicate that the cursor was created as read-only instead of updatable as requested, but that is not what happens. A subsequent attempt to open this cursor yields an error message that the cursor does not exist.

Some options don't make sense when used together. For example, you can't declare a cursor using FOR UPDATE OF and combine that with either STATIC or READ_ONLY. This generates an error message when the cursor is declared. Remember that the STATIC option and READ_ONLY are not quite equivalent. When STATIC is specified, the results are copied into a temporary table when the cursor is opened. From then on, the results are returned from this temporary table in the server and the updates done by other users are not reflected in the cursor rows. A dynamic or keyset cursor can be READ_ONLY but not STATIC. As you scroll, you might see values that have been changed by other users since the cursor was opened. A cursor declared with these characteristics doesn't allow positioned updates or deletes via the cursor, but it doesn't prevent updates or deletes made by others from being visible.

Beware the Dynamic Cursor

Because a dynamic cursor has no guaranteed way of keeping track of which rows are part of the cursor's result set, you can end up with badly behaving dynamic cursors. For example, suppose you have a nonunique clustered index on a table for which you have declared a dynamic cursor. Internally, SQL Server makes the clustered index keys unique if necessary by adding a unique suffix to each duplicate value. If you use a positioned update to update the clustered keys to a value that already exists, SQL Server adds the next unique suffix in sequence. (That is, the second occurrence of any value gets a suffix of 1, the next occurrence gets a 2, and so on.) That means that the row has to move to a place in the table after the last row with that key in order to maintain the clustered ordering sequence. If you fetch through the cursor one row at a time and update the keys to values that already exist, you can end up revisiting the same row, or rows, over and over. In fact, you could end up in an infinite loop. This code does just that:

```
create table bad_cursor_table
(a char(3), b int identity)
go
create clustered index idx on bad_cursor_table(a)
go
insert into bad_cursor_table (a)  values ('1')
insert into bad_cursor_table (a)  values ('2')
insert into bad_cursor_table (a)  values ('3')
insert into bad_cursor_table (a)  values ('4')
go
declare bad_cursor cursor dynamic for select * from bad_cursor_table
open bad_cursor
fetch bad_cursor
while (@@fetch_status = 0) begin
    update bad_cursor_table
    set a = 'new'
    where current of bad_cursor
    fetch bad_cursor
end
```

If you execute this code, you'll see the value of column *b*, which you are not changing, cycle through the values 1 to 4 over and over as each update moves the updated row to the end of the table. The solution to this problem is to always create a clustered index on a truly unique column, or else to not create dynamic cursors on tables without a declared unique index.

Concurrency Control with Transact-SQL Cursors

If you use a cursor that's not in the scope of a transaction, locks are not held for long durations by default. A shared lock is briefly requested for the fetch operation and then immediately released. If you subsequently attempt to update through the cursor, optimistic concurrency control is used to ensure that the row being updated is still consistent with the row you fetched into the cursor.

```
DECLARE my_curs SCROLL CURSOR FOR SELECT au_id, au_lname
FROM authors
OPEN my_curs
FETCH ABSOLUTE 6 FROM my_curs
-- This would return: 427-17-2319 Dull
-- Assume some other user modifies this row between this and
-- the next statement:
UPDATE authors SET au_lname='Kronenthal' WHERE CURRENT OF my_curs
```

This returns:

```
Msg 16934, Level 16, State 1
Optimistic concurrency check failed, the row was modified outside
of this cursor
```

With optimistic concurrency control, locks are not held on the selected data, so concurrency increases. At the time of the update, the current row in the table is compared to the row that was fetched into the cursor. If nothing has changed, the update occurs. If a change is detected, the update does not occur and error message 16934 is returned. The term "optimistic" is meant to convey that the update is attempted with the *hope* that nothing has changed. A check is made at the time of the update to ensure that, in fact, nothing has changed. (It's not so optimistic that it forgoes the check.) In this case, although a change is detected and the update is refused, no locks are issued to prevent such a change. You could decide to go ahead and update the row, even though it failed the optimistic concurrency check. To do so, you would fully qualify the update with a normal WHERE clause specifying the unique key instead of issuing a positioned update (*WHERE CURRENT OF my_curs*). For example:

```
UPDATE authors
SET au_lname='Kronenthal'
WHERE au_id='427-17-2319'
```

Although here we are looking at this situation via the Transact-SQL syntax, in the real world you are much more likely to encounter this situation using API server cursors. In such a case, you might use optimistic concurrency control. If a conflict is encountered, you can display a message to your end user—something like "The row has subsequently changed. Here is the new value [which you could refetch to get]. Do you still want to go ahead with your update?"

There are actually two types of optimistic concurrency. With Transact-SQL cursors, if the table has a timestamp column defined, a cursor update uses it to determine whether the row has been changed since it was fetched. (Recall that a timestamp column is an automatic increasing value that is updated for any change to the row. It is unique within the database, but it bears no relationship to the system or calendar's date and time.) When the update is attempted, the current timestamp on the row is compared to the timestamp that was present when the row was fetched. The timestamp is automatically and invisibly fetched into the cursor even though it was not declared in the select list. Be aware that an update will fail the optimistic concurrency check even if a column not in the cursor has been updated since the row was fetched. The update to that column (not in the cursor) will increase the timestamp, making the comparison fail. But this happens only if a timestamp column exists on the table being updated.

If there is no timestamp column, optimistic concurrency control silently reverts to a "by-value" mode. Since no timestamp exists to indicate whether the row has been updated, the values for *all* columns in the row are compared to the current values in the row at the time of the update. If the values are identical, the update is allowed. Notice that an attempt to update a column in a row that is not part of the cursor causes optimistic concurrency control to fail, whether it is timestamp based or value based. You can also use traditional locking in conjunction with a cursor to prevent other users from changing the data that you fetch.

Although optimistic concurrency is the default for updatable cursors, you can designate this kind of locking explicitly by using the keyword OPTIMISTIC in your DECLARE statement.

Optimistic concurrency control works quite well in environments with relatively low update contention. With high update activity, optimistic concurrency control might not be appropriate; for example, you might not be able to get an update to succeed because the row is being modified by some other user. Whether optimistic or pessimistic (locking) concurrency control is more appropriate depends on the nature of your application. An address book application with few updates is probably well-suited to optimistic concurrency control. An application used to sell a product and keep track of inventory is probably not.

As another example, if you write an application to sell reserved tickets for a flight and sales are brisk, optimistic concurrency control is probably not appropriate. Here is what the telephone conversation between the ticket agent and customer might sound like if you use optimistic concurrency control:

Caller: "I'd like two tickets to Honolulu for January 15."

Ticket agent: "OK, I have two seats on flight number 1 leaving at 10 A.M."

Caller: "Great, I'll take them."

Ticket agent: "Oops. I just tried to reserve them, and they've been sold by another agent. Nothing else seems to be available on that date."

SEE ALSO Locking is discussed in detail in Chapters 13 and 14.

If you want to make sure that no other users have changed the data you have fetched, you can force SQL Server to hold update locks on data that is fetched while the cursor is open or until the next fetch. You can do this by specifying the SCROLL_LOCKS option in the cursor's DECLARE statement. These update locks prevent other users from updating the cursor's row or reading the row through another cursor using SCROLL_LOCKS, but they do not prevent other users from reading the data. Update locks are held until the next row is fetched or until the cursor is closed, whichever occurs first. If you need full pessimistic currency control, you should read the cursor row inside a transaction; these locks are held until the transaction is either committed or rolled back. Here is an example of a cursor that holds scroll locks while the cursor is open, ensuring that another user cannot update the fetched row:

```
DECLARE my_curs CURSOR SCROLL SCROLL_LOCKS FOR SELECT au_id, au_lname
    FROM authors
OPEN my_curs
FETCH ABSOLUTE 12 FROM my_curs
-- Pause to create window for other connection.
-- From other connection, try to update the row. E.g.,
-- UPDATE authors SET au_lname='Newest val' WHERE au_id='724-80-9391'.
-- The update will be blocked by a KEY UPDATE lock until this cursor is
-- closed. Refetch the row next and see that it has not changed.
-- The CLOSE cursor will release the SH_PAGE lock.
WAITFOR DELAY "00:00:20"
FETCH RELATIVE 0 FROM my_curs
-- RELATIVE 0 = "freshen" current row
CLOSE my_curs
DEALLOCATE my_curs
```

In this example, we are only reading data, not modifying it. When you do positioned updates or deletes, you might want to group all the cursor operations as a single transaction. To do that, you use an explicit BEGIN TRAN statement. The fetch requests a update (scroll) lock, and the lock is retained until the end of the transaction.

NOTE Don't get confused between update and scroll locks. Scroll locks for cursor processing are a special type of update lock. Both scroll and update locks prevent other processes from acquiring exclusive locks, update locks, or scroll locks, but they don't prevent simple share (read) locks. The real difference between update locks and scroll locks is the length of time the lock is held. If there is no surrounding transaction, scroll locks are released when a new row is fetched or the cursor is closed. If there is a surrounding transaction, the scroll lock is held until the end of the transaction. (This is a slight oversimplification. We'll discuss the difference between scroll and update locks in more detail in Chapter 13.)

The following example shows optimistic concurrency control within a transaction. This means we do not want to acquire scroll locks. A simple share lock on the row is acquired while the row is being read, but it is released as soon as the row is read. The script includes a couple of delays so that you can go to another connection and watch the locks. You'll see that the shared row locks are not held, although of course the exclusive locks, which are issued to carry out the actual update, are held until the transaction completes. This example also terminates the cursor and rolls back the transaction if either of the two update or fetch operations fail.

```
-- Be sure the default setting is in effect
SET TRANSACTION ISOLATION LEVEL READ COMMITTED
DECLARE my_curs CURSOR SCROLL FOR SELECT au_id, au_lname
    FROM authors
OPEN my_curs
BEGIN TRAN

FETCH FIRST FROM my_curs
IF (@@FETCH_STATUS <> 0) -- If not a valid fetch, get out
    GOTO OnError
-- Delay for 10 secs so can verify from another connection
-- and see no lock held using sp_lock
WAITFOR DELAY "00:00:10"
```

```
UPDATE authors SET au_lname='Row1 Name' WHERE CURRENT OF my_curs

IF (@@ERROR <> 0)
    GOTO OnError

FETCH LAST FROM my_curs

IF (@@FETCH_STATUS <> 0) -- If not a valid fetch, get out
    GOTO OnError

-- Delay for 10 secs so can verify from another connection
-- and see the exclusive KEY lock from previous update
WAITFOR DELAY "00:00:10"

UPDATE authors SET au_lname='LastRow Name' WHERE CURRENT OF my_curs
IF (@@ERROR <> 0)
    GOTO OnError
COMMIT TRAN
IF (@@ERROR=0)
PRINT 'Committed Transaction'
GOTO Done
OnError:
PRINT 'Rolling Back Transaction'
ROLLBACK TRAN
Done:
CLOSE my_curs
DEALLOCATE my_curs
```

The previous example uses a transaction, but it still uses optimistic concurrency control. If you want to be sure that a row doesn't change once you fetch it, you must hold the shared locks. You can do this using the HOLDLOCK hint in the SELECT statement or by setting the isolation level to Repeatable Read (or Serializable), as in this example:

```
SET TRANSACTION ISOLATION LEVEL REPEATABLE READ
DECLARE my_curs CURSOR SCROLL FOR SELECT au_id, au_lname
    FROM authors
OPEN my_curs
BEGIN TRAN

FETCH FIRST FROM my_curs
IF (@@FETCH_STATUS <> 0) -- If not a valid fetch, get out
    GOTO OnError
-- Delay for 10 secs so can verify from another connection
```

(continued)

```
-- and see shared KEY lock is held
WAITFOR DELAY "00:00:10"

UPDATE authors SET au_lname='Newer Row1 Name'
    WHERE CURRENT OF my_curs

IF (@@ERROR <> 0)
    GOTO OnError

FETCH LAST FROM my_curs

IF (@@FETCH_STATUS <> 0) -- If not a valid fetch, get out
    GOTO OnError

-- Delay for 10 secs so can verify from another connection
-- and see the exclusive KEY lock from previous update, and
-- shared KEY from most recent FETCH
WAITFOR DELAY "00:00:10"

UPDATE authors SET au_lname='Newer LastRow Name'
    WHERE CURRENT OF my_curs
IF (@@ERROR <> 0)
    GOTO OnError

COMMIT TRAN
IF (@@ERROR=0)
    PRINT 'Committed Transaction'
GOTO Done

OnError:
PRINT 'Rolling Back Transaction'
ROLLBACK TRAN

Done:
CLOSE my_curs
DEALLOCATE my_curs
```

This example holds onto shared locks on all the rows that have been fetched. You can be sure that once a row is fetched, another user cannot change it while the transaction is in process. However, you cannot be sure that you can update the row. If you take this example and run it simultaneously in two Query Analyzer windows, you almost certainly get the following error in one of the two windows:

```
Msg 1205, Level 13, State 1
Your server command (process id 14) was deadlocked with another
process and has been chosen as deadlock victim. Re-run your command
```

This is a classic *conversion deadlock,* which occurs when each process holds a shared lock on a row and each needs an exclusive lock on the same row. Neither can get the exclusive lock because of the other process's shared lock. No matter how long the two processes wait, no resolution occurs because neither can get the lock it needs. SQL Server terminates one of the processes so that the other can conclude. (Chapter 13 describes such deadlocks in more detail. It also differentiates between ROW and KEY locks, which we're treating as the same thing in this discussion.) To avoid conversion deadlocks, you should use scroll locks instead of shared locks for any data you are reading if you intend to update it later. A scroll lock or an update lock does not prevent another process from reading the data, but it ensures that the holder of the update lock is next in line for an exclusive lock for that resource and thus eliminates the conversion deadlock problem by serializing access for the update lock resource.

The following code is a modification of the previous example that uses the SCROLL_LOCKS keyword in the cursor declaration. This forces SQL Server to acquire an update lock on the row being fetched, which is held until the next row is fetched. No other process can acquire another update lock on this same row. Since we are updating the fetched row, the update lock is converted into an exclusive lock, which is held until the end of the transaction. If we run 2 (or even 200) instances of this simultaneously, we do not get a deadlock. The scroll (update) lock acquired the first time the row is fetched makes the multiple instances run serially, since they must queue and wait for the update lock to be released:

```
-- We will use SCROLL_LOCKS, which are held until the
-- next row is fetched or until they convert into EXCLUSIVE locks.
-- So we do not require REPEATABLE READ. We can use the default isolation
-- level of READ COMMITTED.
SET TRANSACTION ISOLATION LEVEL READ COMMITTED

DECLARE my_curs CURSOR SCROLL SCROLL_LOCKS FOR SELECT au_id, au_lname
    FROM authors
OPEN my_curs
BEGIN TRAN

FETCH FIRST FROM my_curs
IF (@@FETCH_STATUS <> 0) -- If not a valid fetch, get out
    GOTO OnError
```

(continued)

```
-- Delay for 10 secs to increase chances of deadlocks
WAITFOR DELAY "00:00:10"

UPDATE authors SET au_lname='Newer Row1 Name'
    WHERE CURRENT OF my_curs

IF (@@ERROR <> 0)
    GOTO OnError

FETCH LAST FROM my_curs

IF (@@FETCH_STATUS <> 0) -- If not a valid fetch, get out
    GOTO OnError

-- Delay for 10 secs to increase chances of deadlocks
WAITFOR DELAY "00:00:10"

UPDATE authors SET au_lname='Newer LastRow Name'
    WHERE CURRENT OF my_curs
IF (@@ERROR <> 0)
    GOTO OnError

COMMIT TRAN
IF (@@ERROR=0)
    PRINT 'Committed Transaction'
GOTO Done

OnError:
PRINT 'Rolling Back Transaction'
ROLLBACK TRAN

Done:
CLOSE my_curs
DEALLOCATE my_curs
```

> **NOTE** If we didn't do an explicit BEGIN TRAN in the example above, we would still get an UPDATE lock on the most recently fetched row. This lock would then move to subsequent rows and be released from the earlier ones as we continue to fetch.

Optimistic Concurrency Control vs. Locking

Whether you should use optimistic concurrency control, use scroll locks, or hold shared locks depends on the degree to which you experience update conflicts or deadlocks. If the system is lightly updated or the updates tend to be quite dispersed and few conflicts occur, optimistic concurrency control will offer the best concurrency since locks are not held. But some updates will be rejected, and you have to decide how to deal with that. If updates are frequently rejected, you should probably move to the more pessimistic and traditional mode of locking. Holding shared locks prevents rows from being changed by someone else, but it can lead to deadlocks. If you are getting frequent deadlocks, you should probably use scroll locks.

Note that the FOR UPDATE OF modifier of the DECLARE statement does not affect locking behavior, and it does not mean that scroll (update) locks are used. The modifier's only purpose is to allow you to ensure that the cursor is updatable and that the user has the necessary permissions to make updates. Normal optimistic concurrency is used if SCROLL_LOCKS is not specified, which means that a shared lock is acquired on the row being read and is released as soon as the read is completed. If a cursor cannot be updated, you get an error message when a cursor is declared with FOR UPDATE. It might be better that, if FOR UPDATE OF is specified, update locks rather than shared locks would be requested on the fetched data, although there is certainly a case to be made for not doing it this way. Although FOR UPDATE OF is specified, an update might never be made. If no update occurs, using shared locks is best because someone else can still declare the same cursor and there is no need to serialize the running of that batch. Concurrency therefore increases.

You should also realize that you do not have to issue the FOR UPDATE OF modifier to be able to do positioned updates via the cursor. You can update a cursor that does not have the FOR UPDATE OF modifier specified as long as the underlying declared cursor is updatable. A SELECT statement cannot be updated if it uses an aggregate function such as GROUP BY, HAVING, UNION, or CASE. But you do not get an error message stating that the SELECT statement cannot be updated until you actually try to do an update. By specifying FOR UPDATE OF in the DECLARE statement, you find out right away if the SELECT cannot be updated. You should consider always specifying FOR UPDATE OF for any cursor that you might later update.

If you will usually update fetched rows and there is contention for updates, you should use the SCROLL_LOCKS keyword. Yes, this serializes access to that resource, but the alternative is a high incidence of rejected updates with optimistic concurrency control or deadlocks with holding shared locks. Both of these require a lot of retries, which is wasteful. Using scroll locks in this type of scenario probably allows you to write the simplest application and gives you the best throughput for your system.

A final comment regarding concurrency options: if you use FOR UPDATE, you can update any column in the cursor. (You might be able to update any column if you don't specify the option, but you won't know that until you try the positioned update.) But if you use the FOR UPDATE OF *column_list* syntax and then try to update a column that is not in your specified list, you get error message 16932.

A lot of the discussion of cursor concurrency options ties in to modes and types of locking in SQL Server. You might consider rereading this section after you absorb all the details about locking in Chapter 13.

Cursor Variables

SQL Server 7 lets you declare variables with a type of cursor. Besides scalar (single-valued) variables, cursor variables are the only type of variable possible. To assign to a cursor variable, you use the SET statement. (Cursor variables cannot be assigned a value with an assignment SELECT, as scalar values can.) Cursor variables can be either the source or the target in SET assignment statements, and they can be used as the type for output parameters. They can be used in any of the cursor management statements: OPEN, FETCH, CLOSE, and DEALLOCATE. However, you cannot have a column in a table of type *cursor*, and input parameters to stored procedures cannot be cursors.

The following example declares a cursor and then sets a variable to reference the same result set:

```
DECLARE declared_cursor CURSOR FOR SELECT au_lname FROM authors
DECLARE @cursor_var cursor
SET @cursor_var = declared_cursor
```

The declared cursor and the cursor variable are almost synonymous. You can use either the declared name or the cursor variable name to open the cursor—they are two references to the same internal structure. You can open the cursor with this statement:

```
OPEN @cursor_var
```

Once you do this, the cursor is open. If you then try to open it with the declared name

```
OPEN declared_cursor
```

you get this error:

```
Msg 16905, Level 16, State 1
The cursor is already open.
```

If you issue one FETCH with the declared cursor, a subsequent FETCH from the cursor variable retrieves the next row. A CLOSE using either reference closes the cursor, and no more rows can be fetched. The only time the two references are treated differently is in the DEALLOCATE statement. Deallocating one of the references means only that you can no longer access the cursor using that reference. The internal data structures are not freed until the last reference is deallocated. If the cursor has not yet been closed, only the deallocation of the last reference closes it.

You can have more than one cursor variable referencing the same cursor, as the following example shows:

```
DECLARE declared_cursor CURSOR LOCAL
FOR SELECT title_id, price from titles
DECLARE @cursor_var_a CURSOR
DECLARE @cursor_var_b CURSOR
SET @cursor_var_a = declared_cursor
SET @cursor_var_b = @cursor_var_a
OPEN @cursor_var_a       -- opens declared cursor
FETCH @cursor_var_b      -- fetches row 1 from declared_cursor
FETCH declared_cursor    -- fetches row 2
DEALLOCATE declared_cursor
-- keeps cursor open since other references remain,
-- but can't use declared_cursor name to reference the cursor
```

One main use of cursor variables is for output parameters. There are four stored procedures for retrieving information about cursors, and each returns its information in a cursor. We'll look at these procedures in the next section.

Obtaining Cursor Information

Along with the wealth of cursor functionality in SQL Server 7, you have access to a function and several procedures that provide you with information about your cursors. However, these procedures are not always easy to use, so we have provided some additional procedures that go beyond what is offered with the installed SQL Server product.

CURSOR_STATUS

The CURSOR_STATUS() function determines the state of a particular cursor or cursor variable. Five possible values can be returned from this function, and the meaning of the values is slightly different depending on whether the argument is a cursor name or a cursor variable. The function takes two arguments; the first one indicates a global cursor, a local cursor, or a cursor variable (which is always local). The syntax appears at the top of the next page.

```
CURSOR_STATUS
(
{'local', 'cursor_name'}
| {'global', 'cursor_name'}
| {'variable', 'cursor_variable'}
)
```

Table 11-3 shows the five possible return values and their meanings.

Return Value	Cursor Name	Cursor Variable
1	The cursor is open, and for static and keyset cursors the result set has at least one row; for dynamic cursors, the result set can have zero, one, or more rows.	The cursor allocated to this variable is open, and for static and keyset cursors the result set has at least one row; for dynamic cursors, the result set can have zero, one, or more rows.
0	The result set of the cursor is empty. (Dynamic cursors never return this result.)	The cursor allocated to this variable is open, but the result set is empty. (Dynamic cursors never return this result.)
−1	The cursor is closed.	The cursor allocated to this variable is closed.
−2	Not applicable.	No cursor was assigned to this OUTPUT variable by the previously called procedure. *OR* A cursor was assigned by the previously called procedure, but it was in a closed state when the procedure completed. Therefore, the cursor is deallocated and not returned to the calling procedure. *OR* There is no cursor assigned to a declared cursor variable.
−3	A cursor with the specified name does not exist.	A cursor variable with the specified name does not exist. *OR* If one exists it has not yet had a cursor allocated to it.

Table 11-3.

Meanings of return values from the CURSOR_STATUS() function.

We'll use the CURSOR_STATUS( ) function below when we check the output parameter from the *sp_describe_cursor* stored procedure.

sp_describe_cursor

This procedure provides information on one cursor or cursor variable whose name must be passed to the procedure. Even though only one row of information is returned, you must supply the procedure with an output parameter of type *cursor*. After executing the procedure, you must use the cursor FETCH command to retrieve the information from the returned cursor. Here's the syntax for calling the stored procedure:

```
sp_describe_cursor [@cursor_return =] output_cursor_variable OUTPUT
{
[, [@cursor_source =] N'local', [@cursor_identity =] N'local_cursor_name'] |
[, [@cursor_source =] N'global',
[@cursor_identity =] N'global_cursor_name'] |
[, [@cursor_source =] N'variable', [@cursor_identity =]
N'input_cursor_variable']
}
```

Here's an example of using the procedure and then accessing the data returned in the cursor variable. *Authors_cursor* is the cursor for which we want information and *@Report* is a cursor variable to hold the results.

```
DECLARE authors_cursor CURSOR KEYSET FOR
SELECT au_lname
FROM authors
WHERE au_lname LIKE 'S%'

OPEN authors_cursor

-- Declare a cursor variable to hold the cursor output variable
-- from sp_describe_cursor
DECLARE @Report CURSOR

-- Execute sp_describe_cursor into the cursor variable
EXEC master.dbo.sp_describe_cursor
    @cursor_return = @Report OUTPUT,
    @cursor_source = 'global',
    @cursor_identity = 'authors_cursor'

-- Verify that the cursor variable contains information

IF cursor_status('variable', '@Report') != 1
    print 'No information available from the cursor'
```

(continued)

```
ELSE BEGIN

-- Fetch all the rows from the sp_describe_cursor output cursor
    WHILE (@@fetch_status = 0)
    BEGIN
        FETCH NEXT from @Report
    END
END

-- Close and deallocate the cursor from sp_describe_cursor
IF cursor_status('variable','@Report') >= -1
BEGIN
    CLOSE @Report
    DEALLOCATE @Report
END

GO

-- Close and deallocate the original cursor
CLOSE authors_cursor
DEALLOCATE authors_cursor
GO
```

Here's some of the information returned:

```
reference_name cursor_scope status model concurrency scrollable open_status
-------------- ------------- ------ ----- ----------- ---------- -----------
authors_cursor 2               0     2      3            1          1

cursor_rows fetch_status column_count row_count last_operation
----------- ------------ ------------ --------- --------------
0           0             1            0          1
```

Table 11-4 shows some of the return values.

Function	Return Values
CURSOR_SCOPE	1 = LOCAL 2 = GLOBAL
STATUS	The same values as reported by the CURSOR_STATUS() system function, described above.

Table 11-4.

Meaning of values returned by sp_describe_cursor.

(continued)

Table 11-4. *continued*

Function	Return Values
MODEL	1 = Static 2 = Keyset 3 = Dynamic 4 = Fast forward
CONCURRENCY	1 = Read-only 2 = Scroll locks 3 = Optimistic
SCROLLABLE	0 = Forward-only 1 = Scrollable
OPEN_STATUS	0 = Closed 1 = Open
CURSOR_ROWS	Number of qualifying rows in the result set.
FETCH_STATUS	The status of the last fetch on this cursor, as indicated by the @@FETCH_STATUS function. 0 = The fetch was successful. −1 = The fetch failed or is beyond the bounds of the cursor. −2 = The requested row is missing. −9 = There was no fetch on the cursor.
COLUMN_COUNT	The number of columns in the cursor result set.
ROW_COUNT	The number of rows affected by the last operation on the cursor, as indicated by the @@ROWCOUNT function.
LAST_OPERATION	The last operation performed on the cursor. 0 = No operations have been performed on the cursor. 1 = OPEN 2 = FETCH 3 = INSERT 4 = UPDATE 5 = DELETE 6 = CLOSE 7 = DEALLOCATE

sp_cursor_list

This procedure returns the same information as *sp_describe_cursor*, but it does so for all cursors. You can specify whether you want all global cursors, all local cursors, or both. Here's the syntax:

```
sp_cursor_list [@cursor_return =] cursor_variable_name OUTPUT,
[@cursor_scope =] cursor_scope
```

You can actually create your own stored procedure as a wrapper around *sp_cursor_list*. This allows you to avoid the declaration of the *@Report* cursor output parameter every time you want to look at cursor properties. You also do not have to code the repeated fetching of rows using this cursor variable. Here's an example of what such a procedure might look like. It uses a default of 3 for the value of *scope*, which means all cursors, but you can override that when you call this new *sp_cursor_info* procedure, and you can pass a 1 to indicate local cursors only or a 2 to indicate global cursors only:

```
use master
go
create proc sp_cursor_info
(@scope int = 3)
as
-- Declare a cursor variable to hold the cursor output variable
-- from sp_cursor_list.

DECLARE @Report CURSOR
-- Execute sp_cursor_list into the cursor variable.

EXEC master.dbo.sp_cursor_list @cursor_return = @Report OUTPUT,

@cursor_scope = @scope

-- Fetch all the rows from the sp_cursor_list output cursor.
WHILE (@@FETCH_STATUS = 0)
BEGIN
    FETCH NEXT from @Report
END

-- Close and deallocate the cursor from sp_cursor_list.
CLOSE @Report
DEALLOCATE @Report
GO
```

The procedure returns individual cursor rows, one for each cursor available in the session. You can expand this procedure even further to populate a temporary table with the values in the returned row. You can then use the CASE functionality to translate the integer code numbers returned into meaningful strings. The companion CD includes a script to build such a procedure, called *sp_cursor_details*, which calls *sp_cursor_list* and receives the results into a cursor variable. By creating the *sp_cursor_list* and *sp_cursor_details* procedures in your *master* database, you can execute *sp_cursor_details* just like any other system-supplied stored procedure. It will always return at least one row of information because internally it uses a cursor called @Report to process the results of *sp_describe_cursor*. If you haven't created any cursors of your own, *sp_cursor_details* will return output similar to the output below. (This output has been split into three sets of columns so it all fits on the page of the book, but the output in SQL Server Query Analyzer would be all on one line.

```
Cursor Reference   Declared Name                    Scope     Status
-----------------  -------------------------        --------  --------------
@Report             _MICROSOFT_SS_0301113436        local     closed

Model        LOCKING     Scrolling      Open Qualifying Rows Fetch Status
-----------  ----------  ------------   ---- ---------------- -------------
dynamic      read-only   scrollable     no    0                no fetch done

Columns Rows for last operation Last operation Handle
------- ----------------------- -------------- -----------
14       0                       OPEN           301113436
```

sp_describe_cursor_tables

This procedure reports on the tables accessed by a given cursor. It returns its output in a cursor variable, with one row for each table in the specified cursor. It returns such information as the name of the table and any optimizer hints specified for the table. See the SQL Server online documentation for more details.

sp_describe_cursor_columns

This procedure reports the attributes of the columns in the result set of a given cursor. It returns its output in a cursor variable, with one row for each column in the SELECT list of the specified cursor. The information it returns includes the name of the column, the datatype, the ordinal position of the column, and the name of the table from which the cursor is selected. See the SQL Server online documentation for more details.

Summary

This chapter described server cursors in detail. Cursors are important tools that help you bridge the impedance mismatch between the set-oriented world of SQL Server and traditional record-oriented programming languages. When used properly, cursors are invaluable. When overused or used inappropriately, they can cause you to have a bad experience with SQL Server. SQL Server provides fully scrollable, updatable cursors. Other mainstream products typically provide only forward-only cursors; if they do allow full scrolling, they do not allow updates. The cursor capabilities in SQL Server are currently far richer than those of any other RDBMS. SQL Server cursors implement and go well beyond the functionality in ANSI SQL-92.

SQL Server has four main cursor models: static, keyset, dynamic, and forward-only. Cursors can be accessed via syntax used directly in Transact-SQL or via function calls used in the programming interfaces to SQL Server (ODBC, OLE DB, and so on). These two types of cursors are called Transact-SQL cursors and API server cursors. Transact-SQL cursors are typically used if a batch or stored procedure must do some row-by-row processing. API server cursors are often appropriate for scrolling applications. Cursors allow positioned updates and deletes. They can use optimistic concurrency control or locking (also known as pessimistic concurrency control). This chapter focused on the Transact-SQL syntax, but the key points are relevant no matter what cursor interface you use with SQL Server.

TRANSACT-SQL EXAMPLES AND BRAINTEASERS

In this chapter, we'll look at some relatively common programming tasks that aren't as simple as you might think. If you find a solution here for something you need to do, that's great. But the real goal is to give you some insight into the power and flexibility of Transact-SQL. For some examples, we'll offer multiple solutions, often with different performance characteristics. Keep in mind that there are often many ways to solve a problem.

Using Triggers to Implement Referential Actions

As we discussed in Chapter 6, SQL Server implements FOREIGN KEY (or REFERENCES) constraints. If you attempt a data modification that would break a relationship—for example, if you attempt to delete the primary key row while foreign key references exist—the data modification is disallowed and the command is aborted. In other words, no action is taken—in fact, ANSI SQL-92 calls this the NO ACTION referential action. (Colloquially, NO ACTION is often referred to as RESTRICT, but technically this is incorrect. ANSI uses RESTRICT for security and permissions issues.)

> **NOTE** A FOREIGN KEY constraint can of course be directed toward a UNIQUE constraint, not just a PRIMARY KEY constraint. But there is no performance difference if the referenced table is declared using UNIQUE. In this section, we'll refer only to PRIMARY KEY in the referenced table for simplicity.

Keep in mind that a FOREIGN KEY constraint affects two tables, not just one. It affects the *referenced* table as well as the *referencing* table. While the constraint is declared on the referencing table, a modification that affects the primary key of the referenced table checks to see whether the constraint has been violated. A declared foreign key results in checks for the following actions whenever a data modification occurs in either the referencing or referenced table. (None of these actions is allowed by a FOREIGN KEY constraint.)

- Inserting a row in a referencing table so that the value of a foreign key does not match a primary key value in the referenced table.

- Updating a foreign key value in a row in a referencing table when no matching primary key value is in the referenced table.

- Updating a primary key value in a row in a referenced table so that a foreign key in a row in the referencing table no longer has a matching primary key value.

- Deleting a row in a referenced table so that a foreign key in a row in the referencing table no longer has a matching primary key value.

In addition to the NO ACTION referential action used in SQL Server 7, the SQL-92 standard specifies three additional referential actions for modifying the primary key side of a relationship: SET NULL, SET DEFAULT, and CASCADE. The four referential actions have the following characteristics:

- **NO ACTION** Disallows the action if the FOREIGN KEY constraint would be violated. This is the only referential action implemented by SQL Server 7 for a declared FOREIGN KEY constraint, and it's the only one that must be implemented for a product to claim to be "SQL-92 conformant."

- **SET NULL** Updates the referencing table so that the foreign key columns are set to NULL. Obviously, this requires that the columns be defined to allow NULL.

- **SET DEFAULT** Updates the referencing table so that the foreign key columns are set to their DEFAULT values. The columns must have DEFAULT values defined.

- **CASCADE** Updates the referencing table so that the foreign key columns are set to the same values that the primary key was changed to, or deletes the referencing rows entirely if the primary key row is deleted.

A declared FOREIGN KEY constraint, rather than a trigger, is generally the best choice for implementing NO ACTION. The constraint is easy to use and eliminates the possibility of a bug in a trigger that you write. You can use triggers to implement any of the other referential actions not currently available with declared FOREIGN KEY constraints.

You can also use a trigger to customize the referential actions in other ways. For example, you can customize error messages to make them more informative than the generic messages sent with a violation of a declared constraint.

Recall that constraint violations are tested before triggers fire. If a constraint violation is detected, the statement is aborted and execution never gets to the trigger (and the trigger never fires). Therefore, you cannot use a declared FOREIGN KEY constraint to ensure that a relationship is never violated by the update of a foreign key and then also use a trigger to perform a cascading action (or other such action) when the primary key side of the same relationship is changed. If you use triggers to implement CASCADE, SET NULL, or SET DEFAULT behavior for changes to the referenced table, you must also use triggers to restrict invalid inserts and updates to the referencing table. You can and should still declare PRIMARY KEY or UNIQUE constraints on the table to be referenced, however. It's relatively easy to write triggers to perform referential actions, as we'll see in the upcoming examples. For the sake of readability, you can still declare the FOREIGN KEY constraint in your CREATE TABLE scripts but then disable the constraint using ALTER TABLE NO CHECK so that it is not enforced. In this way, you ensure that the constraint still appears in the output of *sp_help <table>* and similar procedures.

> **NOTE** Although we're about to see triggers that perform referential actions, you might want to consider another option entirely. If you want to define constraints and still have update and delete capability beyond NO ACTION, a good alternative is using stored procedures that exclusively perform the update and delete operations. A stored procedure can easily perform the referential action (within the scope of a transaction) before the constraint would be violated. No violation occurs because the corresponding "fix-up" operation is already performed in the stored procedure. If an INSERT or UPDATE statement is issued directly (and you can prevent that in the first place by not granting such permissions), the FOREIGN KEY constraint still ensures that the relationship is not violated.

Here is an example of using triggers to implement a referential action. Rather than simply implementing NO ACTION, we want to implement ON DELETE CASCADE and ON UPDATE SET DEFAULT for the foreign key relationship between *titleauthor* and *titles*. We must create the following three triggers (or suitable alternatives):

```
-- 1. INSERT and UPDATE trigger on referencing table.
-- Disallow any insert or update if the foreign key title_id
-- here in the referencing table titleauthor does not match
-- the primary key title_id in the referenced table titles.
CREATE TRIGGER INS_UPD_titleauthor
    ON titleauthor
    FOR INSERT, UPDATE
AS
-- Do any rows exist in the inserted table that do not have
-- a matching ID in titles?
IF EXISTS
    (SELECT * FROM inserted WHERE inserted.title_id NOT IN
        (SELECT titles.title_id FROM titles) )
    BEGIN
    RAISERROR('No matching title found. Statement will be
aborted.', 16, 1)
    ROLLBACK TRAN
    END
GO


-- 2. If primary key in referenced table titles is changed,
-- update any rows in titleauthor to the DEFAULT value.
-- This implements ON UPDATE SET DEFAULT. Notice this trigger could
-- be easily changed to set the column to NULL instead of DEFAULT,
-- which would implement ON UPDATE SET NULL.
CREATE TRIGGER UPD_titles
    ON titles
    FOR UPDATE
AS
    DECLARE @counter int
    IF UPDATE(title_id)
        BEGIN
        UPDATE titleauthor
        SET titleauthor.title_id=DEFAULT
        FROM titleauthor, deleted
        WHERE titleauthor.title_id=deleted.title_id

        SET @COUNTER=@@ROWCOUNT
        -- If the trigger resulted in modifying rows of
```

```
        -- titleauthor, raise an informational message
        IF (@counter > 0)
            RAISERROR('%d rows of titleauthor were updated to
DEFAULT title_id as a result of an update to titles table',
10, 1, @counter)
        END
GO


-- 3. DELETE of referenced table titles will CASCADE to referencing
-- table titleauthor and delete any rows that referenced the row
-- deleted
CREATE TRIGGER DelCascadeTrig
    ON titles
    FOR DELETE
AS
    DECLARE @counter int
    DELETE titleauthor
    FROM titleauthor, deleted
    WHERE titleauthor.title_id=deleted.title_id
    SET @counter=@@ROWCOUNT

    IF (@counter > 0)
        RAISERROR('%d rows of titleauthor were deleted as a result
of a delete to the titles table', 10, 1, @counter)
GO
```

N O T E For these examples to run, you must drop or suspend the
existing FOREIGN KEY constraints on *titleauthor* that reference *titles*
as well as FOREIGN KEY constraints on two other tables (*sales* and
roysched) that reference *titles*. The code on the companion CD does this.

The following is a cascading update trigger on the *titles* (referenced) table
that updates all rows in the *titleauthor* table with matching foreign key values.
The cascading update is tricky. It requires that you associate both the before and
after values (from the *inserted* and *deleted* pseudotables) to the referencing table.
In a cascading update, you by definition change that primary key or unique value.
This means that typically the cascading update works only if one row of the
referenced table is updated. If you change the values of multiple primary keys
in the same update statement, you lose the ability to correctly associate the
referencing table. You can easily restrict an update of a primary key to not affect
more than one row by checking the value of the @@ROWCOUNT function,
as follows:

```
CREATE TRIGGER UpdCascadeTrig1
    ON titles
```

(continued)

665

```
        FOR UPDATE
AS
    DECLARE @num_affected int, @title_id varchar(11),
        @old_title_id varchar(11)
    SET @num_affected=@@ROWCOUNT
    IF (@num_affected=0)      -- No rows affected, so nothing to do
        RETURN

    IF UPDATE(title_id)
        BEGIN
        IF (@num_affected=1)
            BEGIN
            SELECT @title_id=title_id FROM inserted
            SELECT @old_title_id=title_id FROM deleted
            UPDATE titleauthor
            SET title_id=@title_id
            FROM titleauthor
            WHERE titleauthor.title_id=@old_title_id
            SELECT @num_affected=@@ROWCOUNT
            RAISERROR ('Cascaded update in titles of Primary Key
                from %s to %s to %d rows in titleauthor', 10, 1,
                @old_title_id, @title_id, @num_affected)
            END
        ELSE
            BEGIN
            RAISERROR ('Cannot update multiple Primary Key values
                in a single statement due to Cascading Update
                trigger in existence.', 16, 1)
            ROLLBACK TRANSACTION
            END
        END
```

The inability to update more than one primary key value at a time is not a limitation—if anything, it might save you from making a mistake. You typically won't want to make mass updates to a primary key. If you declare a PRIMARY KEY or UNIQUE constraint (as you should), mass updates usually won't work because of the constraint's need for uniqueness. Although such an update is rare, you might want to set the value to some expression, such as multiplying all Customer ID values by 1000 to renumber them. For such unusual cases, you can easily perform the UPDATE in a loop, one row at a time, and use a cascading trigger.

Another situation in which you might want to update multiple primary keys in the same statement is if you have a mail-order customer list that uses the customer phone number as the primary key. As phone companies add numbers to accommodate fax machines, e-mail, and cellular phones, some area codes run out of possible numbers, which leads to the creation of new area codes. If a mail-order company needs to keep up with such changes, it must update the primary key for all customers getting new area codes. If you assume that the phone number is stored as a character string of 10 digits, you must update the first three characters only. If the new area code is 425, for example, your update statement would look something like this:

```
UPDATE customer_list
    SET phone = '425' +  substring(phone, 4, 10)
    WHERE zip IN (list of affected zip codes)
```

This UPDATE would affect the primary key of multiple rows, and it would be difficult to write a trigger to implement a cascade operation (perhaps into an *orders* table).

You might think that you can write a trigger to handle multiple updates to the primary key by using two cursors to step through the *inserted* and *deleted* tables at the same time. However, this won't work. There's no guarantee that the first row in the *deleted* table corresponds to the first row in the *inserted* table, so you cannot determine which old foreign key values in the referencing tables should be updated to which new values.

Although it is logically the correct thing to do, you are not required to create a PRIMARY KEY or UNIQUE constraint on a referenced table. (Unless, of course, if you are going to actually declare a FOREIGN KEY constraint to reference a column in the referenced table.) And there is no hard-and-fast requirement that the constraint be unique. (However, not making it unique violates the logical relationship.) In fact, the "one row only" restriction in the previous cascading trigger is a tad more restrictive than necessary. If uniqueness were not required on *title_id*, the restriction could be eased a bit to allow the update to affect more than one row in the *titles* table as long as all affected rows were updated to the same value for *title_id*. When uniqueness on *titles.title_id* is required (as should usually be the case), the two restrictions are actually redundant. Since all affected rows are updated to the same value for *title_id*, you no longer have to worry about associating the new value in the referencing table, *titleauthor*. There is only one value. The trigger looks like this:

```
CREATE TRIGGER UpdCascadeTrig2
    ON titles
    FOR UPDATE
AS
    DECLARE @num_distinct int, @num_affected int,
        @title_id varchar(11)
    SET @num_affected=@@ROWCOUNT
```

(continued)

```
    IF (@num_affected=0)        -- No rows affected, so nothing to do
        RETURN

    IF UPDATE(title_id)
        BEGIN
        SELECT @num_distinct=COUNT(DISTINCT title_id) FROM inserted
        IF (@num_distinct=1)
            BEGIN
            -- Temporarily make it return just one row
             SET ROWCOUNT 1
            SELECT @title_id=title_id FROM inserted
            SET ROWCOUNT 0       -- Revert ROWCOUNT back
            UPDATE titleauthor
            SET titleauthor.title_id=@title_id
            FROM titleauthor, deleted
            WHERE titleauthor.title_id=deleted.title_id
            SELECT @num_affected=@@ROWCOUNT
            RAISERROR ('Cascaded update of Primary Key to value in
                titles to %d rows in titleauthor', 10, 1,
                @title_id, @num_affected)
            END
        ELSE
            BEGIN
            RAISERROR ('Cannot cascade a multirow update that
                changes title_id to multiple different values.', 16, 1)
            ROLLBACK TRANSACTION
            END
        END
```

Using *COUNT(DISTINCT title_id) FROM inserted* ensures that even if multiple rows are affected, they are all set to the same value. So *@title_id* can pick up the value of *title_id* for any row in the inserted table. You use the *SET ROWCOUNT 1* statement to limit the subsequent SELECT to only the first row. This is not required, but it's good practice and a small optimization. If you don't use *SET ROWCOUNT 1*, the assignment still works correctly but every inserted row is selected and you end up with the value of the last row (which, of course, is the same value as any other row). Note that you can't use the TOP clause in a SELECT statement that assigns to a variable. It's not good practice to do a SELECT or a variable assignment that assumes that just one row is returned unless you're sure that only one row *can* be returned. You can also ensure a single returned row by doing the assignment like this:

```
SELECT @title_id=title_id FROM titles GROUP BY title_id HAVING
    COUNT(DISTINCT title_id)=1
```

Because the previous IF allows only one distinct *title_id* value, you are assured that the preceding SELECT statement returns only one row.

In the previous two triggers, you first determine whether any rows were updated; if not, you do a RETURN. This illustrates something that might not be obvious: a trigger fires even if no rows were affected by the update. Recall that the plan for the trigger is appended to the rest of the statements' execution plan. You don't know the number of rows affected until execution. This is a feature, not a bug; it allows you to take action when you expect some rows to be affected but none are. Having no rows affected is not an error in this case. However, you can use a trigger to return an error when this occurs. The previous two triggers use RAISERROR to provide either a message that indicates the number of rows cascaded or an error message. If no rows are affected, we don't want any messages to be raised, so we return from the trigger immediately.

Recursive Triggers

SQL Server 7 allows triggers to recursively call themselves if the database option *recursive triggers* is set to TRUE. This means that if a trigger modifies the table on which the trigger is based, the trigger might fire a second time. But then, of course, the trigger modifies the table and fires the trigger again, which modifies the table and fires the trigger again...and so on. This process does not result in an infinite loop because SQL Server has a maximum nesting depth of 32 levels; after the 32nd call to the trigger, SQL Server generates the error shown next. The batch stops executing, and all data modifications since the original one that caused the trigger to be fired are rolled back.

```
Server: Msg 217, Level 16, State 1, Procedure up_rt1, Line 4
Maximum stored procedure nesting level exceeded (limit 32).
```

Writing recursive routines is not for the faint of heart. You must be able to determine what further actions to take based on what has already happened, and you must make sure that the recursion stops before the nesting reaches its limit. Let's look at a simple example. Suppose we have a table that keeps track of budgets for various departments. Departments are members (or children) of other departments, so the budget for a parent department includes the budgets for all its child departments. If a child department's budget increases or decreases, the change must be propagated to the parent department, the parent's parent, and so forth. The code at the top of the following page creates a small budget table and inserts three rows into it.

```
CREATE TABLE BUDGET
    (dept_name      varchar(30)    not null,
     parent_name    varchar(30)    null,
     budget_amt     money          not null)
GO
INSERT INTO budget values ('Internal Training', 'Training', $10)
INSERT INTO budget values ('Training', 'Services', $100)
INSERT INTO budget values ('Services', NULL, $500)
GO
```

The following trigger is fired if a single row in the budget table is updated. If the department is not the highest-level department, its parent name is not NULL, so you can adjust the budget for the parent department by the same amount that the current row was just updated. (The amount of the change is equal to the new amount in the inserted table minus the old amount in the deleted table.) That new update causes the trigger to fire again. If the next department has a non-null parent, the update is applied again. The recursion stops when you get to the highest level and the parent department is null. In that case, the trigger simply returns and all work is done.

```
CREATE TRIGGER update_budget
ON budget FOR update AS

IF (@@rowcount > 0 BEGIN
    PRINT 'Only one row can be updated at a time'
    ROLLBACK TRAN
    RETURN
END
IF (SELECT parent_name FROM inserted) IS NULL RETURN
UPDATE budget
    SET budget_amt = budget_amt + (SELECT budget_amt FROM inserted) -
                                  (SELECT budget_amt FROM deleted)
WHERE dept_name = (SELECT parent_name FROM inserted)
```

Brainteasers

Sometimes a reasonable and straightforward question posed in English can be difficult to write in SQL. In Chapter 7, we saw a great example of this—the query "Show me the stores that have sold every book title." Although the question is simple in English, it's tricky to get right in SQL. But enhancements to the SQL standard, many of which have not yet been implemented, as well as existing and future extensions unique to SQL Server will make many queries much easier to write. The addition of CASE, allowing the use of DISTINCT and UNION in views and subqueries, and full outer-join support in the two releases prior to SQL Server 7 have dramatically shortened the usual list of "tricky" queries. We'll now look at some examples based on real-world queries. When applicable, we'll look at a formulation that uses pure ANSI-standard SQL as well as one that uses a SQL Server extension.

Generating Test Data

Nothing tricky here, but because generating test data is a common need and some of the later solutions depend on test data, we'll look at a few simple techniques. (Of course, it's preferable to use an actual dataset of representative values for testing rather than generated test data before you deploy a production application. But sometimes it's more practical to generate test data when you need something "quick and dirty.")

If you need a bunch of rows and you don't care about the distribution of values, you can easily create a table using default values for every column and the Identity property on a column that will act as the primary key. You can then set a counter to loop as many times as necessary to achieve the number of rows you want and execute the special INSERT...DEFAULT VALUES statement. This example creates 1000 rows in table *xyz*:

```
-- Method 1.  Simple DEFAULT values on table.
CREATE TABLE xyz
(
col1    int         PRIMARY KEY IDENTITY(1, 1) NOT NULL,
col2    int         NOT NULL DEFAULT 999,
col3    char(10)    NOT NULL DEFAULT 'ABCEFGHIJK'
)
GO

DECLARE @counter int
SET @counter=1
WHILE (@counter <= 1000)
    BEGIN
    INSERT xyz DEFAULT VALUES
    SET @counter=@counter+1
    END


    SELECT * FROM xyz
```

(continued)

```
col1    col2    col3
----    ----    -----------
1       999     ABCEFGHIJK
2       999     ABCEFGHIJK
3       999     ABCEFGHIJK
4       999     ABCEFGHIJK
5       999     ABCEFGHIJK
⋮
999     999     ABCEFGHIJK
1000    999     ABCEFGHIJK
```

Usually, you want some distribution in the data values; the RAND( ) function, the modulo operator, and the functions CONVERT( ), CHAR( ), and REPLICATE( ) come in handy for this purpose. RAND( ) is a standard random number generator that's just like the function used in C, which RAND( ) calls. Because RAND( ) returns a *float* with a value between 0 and 1, you typically multiply it and convert the result to an integer so that you can use the modulo operator to indicate the range of values. For example, if you want a random integer from 0 through 9999, the following expression works nicely:

```
(CONVERT(int, RAND( ) * 100000) % 10000)
```

If you want to include negative numbers (for example, a range from –9999 through 9999), you can use RAND( ) to flip a coin and generate 0 or 1 (by doing modulo 2) and then use CASE to multiply half of the numbers by –1.

```
CASE
WHEN CONVERT(int, RAND( ) * 1000) % 2 = 1 THEN
    (CONVERT(int, RAND( ) * 100000) % 10000 * -1)
ELSE CONVERT(int, RAND( ) * 100000) % 10000
END
```

To use character data, you should generate a random number from 0 through 25 (since the English alphabet has 26 letters) and add that number to 64, which is the ASCII value for *A*. The result is the ASCII value for a character from *A* through *Z*. You can perform this operation a specified number of times or in a loop to generate as many characters as you want. Usually, after you indicate a few lead characters, you can use filler characters for the rest of a field. The REPLICATE( ) function is a nice tool to use for the filler. (If you want to be sure that different executions of the routine return different random numbers, you should seed the RAND( ) function by including an integer value between the parentheses. You can use *@@spid*, the *object_id* of the newly created table, or any other "almost random" integer value.)

The most common way to generate character data is to use local variables for the generated data inside a WHILE loop that does INSERT statements using the variables. Here's an example:

```
-- Method 2.    Generate random data in a loop.
IF (ISNULL(OBJECT_ID('random_data'), 0)) > 0
    DROP TABLE random_data
GO

CREATE TABLE random_data
(
col1        int PRIMARY KEY,
col2        int,
col3        char(15)
)
GO

DECLARE @counter int, @col2 int, @col3 char(15)
/* Insert 1000 rows of data  */
-- Seed random generator
SELECT @counter=0, @col2=RAND(@@spid + cpu + physical_io)
FROM master..sysprocesses where spid=@@spid

WHILE (@counter < 1000)
    BEGIN
    SELECT @counter=@counter + 10,    -- Sequence numbers by 10
    @col2=
        CASE        -- Random integer between -9999 and 9999
            WHEN CONVERT(int, RAND() * 1000) % 2 = 1
            THEN (CONVERT(int, RAND() * 100000) % 10000 * -1)
            ELSE CONVERT(int, RAND() * 100000) % 10000
        END,
    @col3=        -- Four random letters followed by random fill letter
        CHAR((CONVERT(int, RAND() * 1000) % 26 ) + 65) -- 65 is 'A'
            + CHAR((CONVERT(int, RAND() * 1000) % 26 ) + 65)
            + CHAR((CONVERT(int, RAND() * 1000) % 26 ) + 65)
            + CHAR((CONVERT(int, RAND() * 1000) % 26 ) + 65)
            + REPLICATE(CHAR((CONVERT(int, RAND() * 1000) % 26 )
            + 65), 11)

    INSERT random_data VALUES (@counter, @col2, @col3)
    END
GO
```

(continued)

```
-- Limit number of rows for illustration only
SELECT * FROM random_data WHERE COL1 < 200

col1    col2     col3
----    -----    ---------------
10      -5240    LXDSGGGGGGGGGGGG
20      9814     TTPD000000000000
30      3004     IEYXEEEEEEEEEEEE
40      -9377    MITDAAAAAAAAAAAA
50      -3823    ISGMUUUUUUUUUUUU
60      -4249    DHZQQQQQQQQQQQQQ
70      2335     XBJKEEEEEEEEEEEE
80      -4570    ILYWNNNNNNNNNNNN
90      4223     DHISDDDDDDDDDDDD
100     -3332    THXLWWWWWWWWWWWW
110     -9959    ALHFLLLLLLLLLLLL
120     4580     BCZNGGGGGGGGGGGG
130     6072     HRTJ000000000000
140     -8274    QPTKWWWWWWWWWWWW
150     8212     FBQABBBBBBBBBBBB
160     8223     YXAPLLLLLLLLLLLL
170     -9469    LIHCAAAAAAAAAAAA
180     -2959    GYKRZZZZZZZZZZZZ
190     7677     KWWBJJJJJJJJJJJJ
```

You can also set up the table with a DEFAULT that includes the random data expression and then use the DEFAULT VALUES statement. This method is a combination of the previous two methods. All the complexity of the random values is segregated to the CREATE TABLE command and the INSERT is again a simple loop that uses DEFAULT VALUES. In the example below, we use a CASE statement in a DEFAULT clause of a CREATE TABLE command:

```
-- Method 3.    Generate random values for DEFAULT.
CREATE TABLE random_data
(
col1    int      PRIMARY KEY IDENTITY(10,10) NOT NULL,
col2    int      NOT NULL DEFAULT CASE
                 -- Random integer between -9999 and 9999
                 WHEN CONVERT(int, RAND() * 1000) % 2 = 1
                 THEN (CONVERT(int, RAND() * 100000) % 10000 * -1 )
                 ELSE CONVERT(int, RAND() * 100000) % 10000
                 END,
col3    char(15) NOT NULL DEFAULT
```

```
                  CHAR((CONVERT(int, RAND() * 1000) % 26 ) + 65)
                  -- 65 is 'A'
                  + CHAR((CONVERT(int, RAND() * 1000) % 26 ) + 65)
                  + CHAR((CONVERT(int, RAND() * 1000) % 26 ) + 65)
                  + CHAR((CONVERT(int, RAND() * 1000) % 26 ) + 65)
                  + REPLICATE(CHAR((CONVERT(int, RAND() * 1000)
                       % 26) + 65), 11)
)
GO

DECLARE @counter int
SET @counter=1
WHILE (@counter <= 1000)
    BEGIN
    INSERT random_data DEFAULT VALUES
    SET @counter=@counter + 1
    END

-- Limit number of rows for illustration only
SELECT * FROM random_data WHERE col1 <= 200
```

col1	col2	col3
10	-6358	LCNLMMMMMMMMMMM
20	-2284	SSAITTTTTTTTTTT
30	-1498	NARJAAAAAAAAAAA
40	-1908	EINLZZZZZZZZZZZ
50	-716	KNIOFFFFFFFFFFF
60	-8331	WZPRYYYYYYYYYYY
70	-2571	TMUBEEEEEEEEEEE
80	-7965	LILNCCCCCCCCCCC
90	9728	IXLOBBBBBBBBBBB
100	878	IPMPPPPPPPPPPPP
110	-2649	QXPAPPPPPPPPPPP
120	-4443	EBVHKKKKKKKKKKK
130	6133	VRJWXXXXXXXXXXX
140	-5154	HMHXLLLLLLLLLLL
150	-480	RNLVQQQQQQQQQQQ
160	-2655	SEHXTTTTTTTTTTT
170	-8204	JVLHZZZZZZZZZZZ
180	-3201	PTWGBBBBBBBBBBB
190	-7529	TDCJXXXXXXXXXXX
200	2622	ANLDHHHHHHHHHHH

Getting Rankings

To get the five highest values or five lowest values in a dataset, you can use the TOP clause in a SQL Server 7 SELECT statement. (TOP was discussed in Chapter 7). The TOP clause also lets you specify WITH TIES. It's not always clear what that means, so an example might help. The following SELECT statement returns the rows with the five highest values for the *ytd_sales* column, including any ties:

```
SELECT TOP 5 WITH TIES title_id, ytd_sales, title
FROM titles
ORDER BY ytd_sales DESC
```

Here are the results:

```
title_id ytd_sales    title
-------- ---------    -----
MC3021   22246        The Gourmet Microwave
BU2075   18722        You Can Combat Computer Stress!
TC4203   15096        Fifty Years in Buckingham Palace Kitchens
PC1035   8780         But Is It User Friendly?
BU1032   4095         The Busy Executive's Database Guide
BU7832   4095         Straight Talk About Computers
PC8888   4095         Secrets of Silicon Valley
TC7777   4095         Sushi, Anyone?
(8 row(s) affected)
```

You end up with more than the five rows you requested. SQL Server returned the first five rows after sorting the data, and because additional rows had the same value as the fifth row returned (4095), it kept returning rows as long as there were equivalent *ytd_sales* values. The WITH TIES clause requires that the data be sorted using ORDER BY. A more "formal" definition of TOP *n* WITH TIES and ORDER BY *c* DESC is "return all rows that have a value of *c* for which there are at most *n*–1 greater values of *c*." So, in the dataset above, *n* is 5 and *c* is *ytd_sales*. The value 22246 has 0 rows with a greater value of *ytd_sales*, and 18722 has only one value greater. The last value returned, 4095, has only four values that are greater.

Another way to think of this concept of "the number of distinct values greater than a given value" is as the rank of the value. A value for which there are no greater values has a rank of 1, and a value for which there are two greater values has a rank of 3. The query above returns all the rows with a rank of 5 or less, using the TOP clause. However, it's not so simple to get a list of the rows with a rank of 5 or less along with an integer indicating the actual rank value. Let's look at several possible solutions to this problem.

Approach 1: The Standard SQL Approach Using a View

First let's look again at the *titles* table. Suppose you want to assign a rank value to all rows in the table based on their *ytd_sales* values (with the highest value getting the top rank). You can do this by performing a ranking of the values by nesting a SELECT inside the select list. For each row in the outer SELECT, the inner SELECT returns the number of rows in the table with values equal to or greater than the column being ranked. This "rows rank" value is then correlated back to the main query. The view can be queried to obtain any rank.

Performance suffers on large tables because a table must be scanned for every row. Ties are assigned equal rank; unique numbers are not guaranteed unless the columns are known to be unique. In the next example, the next nontie value's rank is one higher, not lower. Notice that we completely disregard rows with NULL values for *ytd_sales*.

```
CREATE VIEW ranked_sales (rank, title_id, ytd_sales, title)
AS
SELECT
(SELECT COUNT(DISTINCT T2.ytd_sales) FROM titles AS T2
    WHERE T2.ytd_sales >= T1.ytd_sales ) AS rank,
title_id,
ytd_sales,
title
FROM titles AS T1 WHERE ytd_sales IS NOT NULL
GO

SELECT * FROM ranked_sales WHERE rank <= 10 ORDER BY rank
GO

rank  title_id  ytd_sales  title
----  --------  ---------  ----------------------------------------
1     MC3021    22246      The Gourmet Microwave
2     BU2075    18722      You Can Combat Computer Stress!
3     TC4203    15096      Fifty Years in Buckingham Palace
                           Kitchens
4     PC1035    8780       But Is It User Friendly?
5     BU1032    4095       The Busy Executive's Database Guide
5     BU7832    4095       Straight Talk About Computers
5     PC8888    4095       Secrets of Silicon Valley
5     TC7777    4095       Sushi, Anyone?
6     PS3333    4072       Prolonged Data Deprivation: Four Case
                           Studies
7     BU1111    3876       Cooking with Computers: Surreptitious
                           Balance Sheets
```

(continued)

```
8       PS7777    3336      Emotional Security: A New Algorithm
9       PS2091    2045      Is Anger the Enemy?
10      MC2222    2032      Silicon Valley Gastronomic Treats
```

Approach 2: The Standard SQL Approach Without Using a View

This approach is basically the same as the first approach, but it saves you the step of creating the view, at the possible cost of being a bit harder to understand. Instead of using a view, you use a derived table (by adding a SELECT in the FROM clause). Performance is identical to that of the view approach, however. (That is, it's not too good.) The results are also identical, so we won't show them here.

```
SELECT rank, title_id, ytd_sales, title
FROM (SELECT
    T1.title_id,
    ytd_sales,
    T1.title,
        (SELECT COUNT(DISTINCT T2.ytd_sales) FROM titles AS T2
        WHERE T1.ytd_sales <= T2.ytd_sales) AS rank
        FROM titles AS T1) AS X
    WHERE ytd_sales IS NOT NULL
    ORDER BY rank
```

Approach 3: Using a Temporary Table with an *identity* Column and No Ties

If you want to assign a unique number even in the case of ties, or if you know that ties will not occur, you can create a temporary table with an *identity* column and then SELECT into the temporary table in an ordered fashion. This gives you a materialized table with rankings. This approach is conceptually easy to understand, and it's fast. Its only downside is that it does not recognize tied values. It's not ANSI-standard SQL, but the approach takes advantage of SQL Server–specific features. This approach can be useful with other sequential operations, as we'll see later.

```
CREATE TABLE #ranked_order
(
rank            int           IDENTITY NOT NULL PRIMARY KEY,
title_id        char(6)       NOT NULL,
ytd_sales       int           NOT NULL,
title           varchar(80)   NOT NULL
)
GO
```

```
INSERT #ranked_order
    SELECT title_id, ytd_sales, title FROM titles WHERE ytd_sales
    IS NOT NULL ORDER BY ytd_sales DESC

SELECT * FROM #ranked_order

DROP TABLE #ranked_order
```

rank	title_id	ytd_sales	title
1	MC3021	22246	The Gourmet Microwave
2	BU2075	18722	You Can Combat Computer Stress!
3	TC4203	15096	Fifty Years in Buckingham Palace Kitchens
4	PC1035	8780	But Is It User Friendly?
5	BU1032	4095	The Busy Executive's Database Guide
6	BU7832	4095	Straight Talk About Computers
7	PC8888	4095	Secrets of Silicon Valley
8	TC7777	4095	Sushi, Anyone?
9	PS3333	4072	Prolonged Data Deprivation: Four Case Studies
10	BU1111	3876	Cooking with Computers: Surreptitious Balance Sheets
11	PS7777	3336	Emotional Security: A New Algorithm
12	PS2091	2045	Is Anger the Enemy?
13	MC2222	2032	Silicon Valley Gastronomic Treats
14	PS1372	375	Computer Phobic AND Non-Phobic Individuals: Behavior Variations
15	TC3218	375	Onions, Leeks, and Garlic: Cooking Secrets of the Mediterranean
16	PS2106	111	Life Without Fear

Approach 4: Using a Temporary Table with an *identity* Column and Ties

With standard SQL solutions, if the query focuses on four rows with two rows tied for second rank, then one row has the rank of first, two rows are second, and one row is third. No row is ranked fourth. An alternative way to rank them is to make one row first, two rows second, no row third, and one row fourth. (This is how standings in a golf tournament are posted if two players tie for second place.) After populating the temporary table, you can query the table for the lowest rank for a given value and correlate that value back to the main query with a nested SELECT.

```
-- Approach 4A. Create a temp table with an identity, and then do
-- an ordered select to populate it.
-- Do a nested select correlated back to itself to find the lowest
-- rank for a given value.
CREATE TABLE #ranked_order
(
rank          int          IDENTITY NOT NULL,
title_id      char(6)      NOT NULL,
ytd_sales     int          NOT NULL,
title         varchar(80)  NOT NULL
)
GO

INSERT #ranked_order
    SELECT title_id, ytd_sales, title FROM titles WHERE ytd_sales
        IS NOT NULL ORDER BY ytd_sales DESC

SELECT B.rank, A.title_id, B.ytd_sales , A.title
FROM
(SELECT MIN(T2.rank) AS rank, T2.ytd_sales FROM #ranked_order AS T2
    GROUP BY T2.ytd_sales) AS B,
#ranked_order AS A
WHERE A.ytd_sales=B.ytd_sales
ORDER BY B.rank

DROP TABLE #ranked_order

rank  title_id  ytd_sales  title
----  --------  ---------  ----------------------------------------
1     MC3021    22246      The Gourmet Microwave
2     BU2075    18722      You Can Combat Computer Stress!
3     TC4203    15096      Fifty Years in Buckingham Palace Kitchens
4     PC1035    8780       But Is It User Friendly?
5     BU1032    4095       The Busy Executive's Database Guide
5     BU7832    4095       Straight Talk About Computers
5     PC8888    4095       Secrets of Silicon Valley
5     TC7777    4095       Sushi, Anyone?
9     PS3333    4072       Prolonged Data Deprivation: Four Case
                           Studies
10    BU1111    3876       Cooking with Computers: Surreptitious
                           Balance Sheets
11    PS7777    3336       Emotional Security: A New Algorithm
12    PS2091    2045       Is Anger the Enemy?
13    MC2222    2032       Silicon Valley Gastronomic Treats
```

14	PS1372	375	Computer Phobic AND Non-Phobic Individuals: Behavior Variations
14	TC3218	375	Onions, Leeks, and Garlic: Cooking Secrets of the Mediterranean
16	PS2106	111	Life Without Fear

You can slightly modify the SELECT on the temporary table and explicitly indicate where ties exist and how many values were tied. (The creation and population of the temporary table are identical, so we'll show just the SELECT statement.)

```
-- Approach 4B. Same as above, explicitly noting the ties.
SELECT B.rank,
CASE B.number_tied
    WHEN 1 THEN ' '
    ELSE '('+ CONVERT(varchar, number_tied) + ' Way Tie)'
    END AS tie,
A.title_id,
B.ytd_sales,
A.title
FROM
(SELECT MIN(T2.rank) AS rank, COUNT(*) AS number_tied, T2.ytd_sales
FROM #ranked_order AS T2 GROUP BY T2.ytd_sales) AS B,
#ranked_order AS A
WHERE A.ytd_sales=B.ytd_sales
ORDER BY B.rank
```

rank	tie	title_id	ytd_sales	title
1		MC3021	22246	The Gourmet Microwave
2		BU2075	18722	You Can Combat Computer Stress!
3		TC4203	15096	Fifty Years in Buckingham Palace Kitchens
4		PC1035	8780	But Is It User Friendly?
5	(4 Way Tie)	BU1032	4095	The Busy Executive's Database Guide
5	(4 Way Tie)	BU7832	4095	Straight Talk About Computers
5	(4 Way Tie)	PC8888	4095	Secrets of Silicon Valley
5	(4 Way Tie)	TC7777	4095	Sushi, Anyone?
9		PS3333	4072	Prolonged Data Deprivation: Four Case Studies
10		BU1111	3876	Cooking with Computers: Surreptitious Balance Sheets

(continued)

681

11		PS7777	3336	Emotional Security: A New Algorithm
12		PS2091	2045	Is Anger the Enemy?
13		MC2222	2032	Silicon Valley Gastronomic Treats
14	(2 Way Tie)	PS1372	375	Computer Phobic AND Non-Phobic Individuals: Behavior Variations
14	(2 Way Tie)	TC3218	375	Onions, Leeks, and Garlic: Cooking Secrets of the Mediterranean
16		PS2106	111	Life Without Fear

Approach 5: Using a Cursor

As a rule, you should try to perform a set operation (preferably using a single SELECT statement) wherever possible. A nonprocedural set operation is usually simpler to write (which means that there's less chance of introducing a bug), and it lets the SQL Server optimizer find an efficient way to carry out the request. In some cases, however, the problem is a naturally sequential operation. The SELECT statement (set operation) might require a correlated subquery or self-join to solve the problem, so that data is visited multiple times to provide the result. A cursor approach can work well in this case because it can solve the problem with one pass through the data. It can be more efficient than using the single SELECT statement for sequential operations such as a ranking operation. (However, it is not faster than the temporary table approaches.) It takes more work to correctly program this approach, but you gain considerable control and flexibility. You can also use any of the three rules for dealing with ties:

1. Give ties a duplicate rank value, and rank the next nonduplicate value one higher.

2. Always assign a unique rank value, even in the case of ties.

3. Assign a duplicate rank value but rank the next nonduplicate value according to its overall standing, not simply one higher.

Approach 5A: Using a cursor with rule 1 for ties

```
-- Approach 5A. Use cursors and deal with ties like the standard
-- SQL approaches did.
-- Assign a duplicate rank value, and simply increment the next
-- nonduplicate.
DECLARE @rank int, @title_id char(6), @ytd_sales int,
```

```
      @title varchar(80), @last_rank int, @last_ytd_sales money,
      @counter int
SELECT @rank=1, @last_rank=1, @last_ytd_sales=0, @counter=1
DECLARE rank_cursor CURSOR FOR SELECT title_id, ytd_sales,
      title FROM titles WHERE ytd_sales IS NOT NULL
      ORDER BY ytd_sales DESC
OPEN rank_cursor
FETCH NEXT FROM rank_cursor INTO @title_id, @ytd_sales, @title
WHILE (@@FETCH_STATUS <> -1)
BEGIN

      IF (@counter=1)       -- For first row, just display values
                            -- and set last values
          BEGIN
          SELECT rank=@rank, title_id=@title_id,
              ytd_sales=@ytd_sales, title=@title
          END
      ELSE
          BEGIN
          -- If current sales is same as last, assign the same rank
          IF (@ytd_sales=@last_ytd_sales)
              SELECT rank=@last_rank, title_id=@title_id,
                  ytd_sales=@ytd_sales, title=@title
          ELSE      -- Otherwise, increment the rank
              BEGIN
              SELECT rank=@last_rank+1, title_id=@title_id,
                  ytd_sales=@ytd_sales, title=@title
              SELECT @rank=@last_rank + 1
              END
          END
 -- Set values to current row
SELECT @counter=@counter + 1, @last_rank=@rank,
      @last_ytd_sales=@ytd_sales
FETCH NEXT FROM rank_cursor INTO @title_id, @ytd_sales, @title
END

CLOSE rank_cursor
DEALLOCATE rank_cursor
```

rank	title_id	ytd_sales	title
1	MC3021	22246	The Gourmet Microwave
2	BU2075	18722	You Can Combat Computer Stress!
3	TC4203	15096	Fifty Years in Buckingham Palace Kitchens

(continued)

683

4	PC1035	8780	But Is It User Friendly?
5	BU1032	4095	The Busy Executive's Database Guide
5	BU7832	4095	Straight Talk About Computers
5	PC8888	4095	Secrets of Silicon Valley
5	TC7777	4095	Sushi, Anyone?
6	PS3333	4072	Prolonged Data Deprivation: Four Case Studies
7	BU1111	3876	Cooking with Computers: Surreptitious Balance Sheets
8	PS7777	3336	Emotional Security: A New Algorithm
9	PS2091	2045	Is Anger the Enemy?
10	MC2222	2032	Silicon Valley Gastronomic Treats
11	PS1372	375	Computer Phobic AND Non-Phobic Individuals: Behavior Variations
11	TC3218	375	Onions, Leeks, and Garlic: Cooking Secrets of the Mediterranean
12	PS2106	111	Life Without Fear

Approach 5B: Using a cursor with rule 2 for ties

```
-- Approach 5B. Use cursors and always assign next row an
-- incremented rank value, even if it's a tie.
DECLARE @rank int, @title_id char(6), @ytd_sales int,
    @title varchar(80)
SELECT @rank=1
DECLARE rank_cursor CURSOR FOR SELECT title_id, ytd_sales, title
FROM titles WHERE ytd_sales IS NOT NULL ORDER BY ytd_sales DESC
OPEN rank_cursor
FETCH NEXT FROM rank_cursor INTO @title_id, @ytd_sales, @title
WHILE (@@FETCH_STATUS <> -1 )
    BEGIN
    SELECT rank=@rank, title_id=@title_id, ytd_sales=@ytd_sales,
        title=@title
    SELECT @rank=@rank + 1
FETCH NEXT FROM rank_cursor INTO @title_id, @ytd_sales, @title
END

CLOSE rank_cursor
DEALLOCATE rank_cursor
```

```
rank  title_id  ytd_sales  title
----  --------  ---------  ----------------------------------------
1     MC3021    22246      The Gourmet Microwave
2     BU2075    18722      You Can Combat Computer Stress!
3     TC4203    15096      Fifty Years in Buckingham Palace
                           Kitchens
```

4	PC1035	8780	But Is It User Friendly?
5	BU1032	4095	The Busy Executive's Database Guide
6	BU7832	4095	Straight Talk About Computers
7	PC8888	4095	Secrets of Silicon Valley
8	TC7777	4095	Sushi, Anyone?
9	PS3333	4072	Prolonged Data Deprivation: Four Case Studies
10	BU1111	3876	Cooking with Computers: Surreptitious Balance Sheets
11	PS7777	3336	Emotional Security: A New Algorithm
12	PS2091	2045	Is Anger the Enemy?
13	MC2222	2032	Silicon Valley Gastronomic Treats
14	PS1372	375	Computer Phobic AND Non-Phobic Individuals: Behavior Variations
15	TC3218	375	Onions, Leeks, and Garlic: Cooking Secrets of the Mediterranean
16	PS2106	111	Life Without Fear

Approach 5C: Using a cursor with rule 3 for ties

```
-- Approach 5C. Use cursors and deal with ties by assigning a
-- duplicate rank value, but then make the next nonduplicate
-- value its overall standing, not simply a rank of one higher.
-- For example, if 2 rows qualify for rank #1, then the 3rd row
-- will be #3 and no row will have rank #2.
DECLARE @rank int, @title_id char(6), @ytd_sales int,
    @title varchar(80), @last_rank int, @last_ytd_sales money,
    @counter int
SELECT @rank=1, @last_rank=1, @last_ytd_sales=0, @counter=1
DECLARE rank_cursor CURSOR FOR SELECT title_id, ytd_sales, title
FROM titles WHERE ytd_sales IS NOT NULL ORDER BY ytd_sales DESC
OPEN rank_cursor
FETCH NEXT FROM rank_cursor INTO @title_id, @ytd_sales, @title
WHILE (@@FETCH_STATUS <> -1)
    BEGIN

    IF (@counter=1)     -- For first row, just display values and
                        -- set last values
        BEGIN
        SELECT rank=@rank, title_id=@title_id,
            ytd_sales=@ytd_sales, title=@title
        END
    ELSE
        BEGIN
        -- If current sales are same as last, assign the same rank
```

(continued)

```
        IF (@ytd_sales=@last_ytd_sales)
            SELECT rank=@last_rank, title_id=@title_id,
                ytd_sales=@ytd_sales, title=@title
        ELSE    -- Otherwise, set the rank to the overall
                -- counter of how many rows have been visited
            BEGIN
            SELECT @rank=@counter
            SELECT rank=@rank, title_id=@title_id,
                ytd_sales=@ytd_sales, title=@title
            END
        END
    -- Set values to current row
    SELECT @counter=@counter+1, @last_rank=@rank,
        @last_ytd_sales=@ytd_sales
    FETCH NEXT FROM rank_cursor INTO @title_id, @ytd_sales, @title
    END

CLOSE rank_cursor
DEALLOCATE rank_cursor
GO
```

rank	title_id	ytd_sales	title
1	MC3021	22246	The Gourmet Microwave
2	BU2075	18722	You Can Combat Computer Stress!
3	TC4203	15096	Fifty Years in Buckingham Palace Kitchens
4	PC1035	8780	But Is It User Friendly?
5	BU1032	4095	The Busy Executive's Database Guide
5	BU7832	4095	Straight Talk About Computers
5	PC8888	4095	Secrets of Silicon Valley
5	TC7777	4095	Sushi, Anyone?
9	PS3333	4072	Prolonged Data Deprivation: Four Case Studies
10	BU1111	3876	Cooking with Computers: Surreptitious Balance Sheets
11	PS7777	3336	Emotional Security: A New Algorithm
12	PS2091	2045	Is Anger the Enemy?
13	MC2222	2032	Silicon Valley Gastronomic Treats
14	PS1372	375	Computer Phobic AND Non-Phobic Individuals: Behavior Variations
14	TC3218	375	Onions, Leeks, and Garlic: Cooking Secrets of the Mediterranean
16	PS2106	111	Life Without Fear

WARNING Unlike the other approaches, the cursor solution produces multiple result sets because of the multiple FETCH operations. Therefore, you get as many result sets as rows (16 in the example here). Every result set requires that metadata be passed between the server and client. With a slow network connection, this can be a huge drag on performance. The cursor solution might be a good choice on the machine running SQL Server or on a LAN, but it will perform poorly over dial-up lines if the result set contains many rows. Of the approaches we've presented, the temporary table approaches are best if they meet your needs for dealing with ties. They are intuitive and efficient, and they return a single result set.

Finding Differences Between Intervals

Suppose we have a table with two columns that records data for measured temperatures. The first column is the datetime at which the measurement was taken, and the second column is the temperature. We want to find the change in temperature between one interval and the next, and we want it expressed as the absolute value of the number of degrees that changed per minute. There is no preexisting primary key, such as *measurement_id*. It's unlikely that duplicate measurements exist for any single time (that is, the datetime field is probably unique), but we don't know this for sure. And the intervals between data measurements are not consistent. In fact, the data was not inserted in order (although a clustered index exists, so if data were selected without an ORDER BY, it would seem to be in order). Like the rankings problem presented earlier, this problem can be solved using standard (but tricky) SQL—you can use a temporary table or use cursors. In fact, you can think of this as another type of ranking problem—but here, you want to see the differences between adjacent ranks.

First we'll set up the table with some fairly random data. We really don't care whether the temperature values are realistic or how much they might fluctuate in even a few minutes. (So if you run this example and see temperatures of −100° F or a 40-degree change in temperature in five minutes, don't worry. These readings might not be from Earth!)

NOTE It's worthwhile to set up the routine to generate test data, even though in this case it would be quicker to manually insert 20 rows of data. Once the routine is working and you've checked your solution on the small table, you can easily change the constant in the WHILE loop to add much more data. This is important because many solutions perform well with small amounts of data but can degrade badly with large amounts of data. (This can be especially true if a solution uses correlated subqueries or self-joins, or if it does table scans.)

```
-- diff_intervals.sql
IF NULLIF(OBJECT_ID('measurements'), 0) > 0
    DROP TABLE measurements
GO

CREATE TABLE measurements
(
when_taken      datetime      NOT NULL,
temperature     numeric(4, 1)  -- (Fahrenheit)
)
CREATE CLUSTERED INDEX measurements_idx01
    ON measurements (when_taken)
GO

DECLARE @counter int, @whendate datetime, @val numeric(4, 1),
    @randdiff smallint, @randmins smallint
SELECT @counter=1, @whendate=GETDATE(), @val=50.0
/* Insert 20 rows of data.  Change constant if you want more.  */
WHILE (@counter <= 20)
    BEGIN
    INSERT measurements VALUES (@whendate, @val)
    -- Get a random number between -20 and 20 for change in
    -- temperature. This will be added to the previous value,
    -- plus RAND() again to give a fractional component.
      SELECT
      @randdiff=CASE
      WHEN CONVERT(int, RAND() * 100) % 2 = 1 THEN
          CONVERT(int, RAND() * 1000) % 21 * -1
      ELSE CONVERT(int, RAND() * 1000) % 21
      END,
    -- Get a random number between 0 and 10080 (the number of mins
    -- in a week). This will be added to the current GETDATE()
    -- value. Since GETDATE() returns a value to the millisecond,
    -- it's unlikely there will ever be a duplicate, though it
    -- is possible if the result of the addition and the current
    -- GETDATE() value happen to collide with the addition in
    -- another row. (That's intentional; we are not assuming
    -- that dups are automatically prevented.)
      @randmins=CONVERT(int, RAND() * 100000) % 10080
    SELECT @counter=@counter + 1,
    @whendate=DATEADD(mi, @randmins, GETDATE()),
```

```
        @val=@val + @randdiff + RAND()
        END

SELECT * FROM measurements

when_taken                      temperature
--------------------------      -----------
1999-02-17 12:31:41.203         50.0
1999-02-17 16:07:41.243         48.0
1999-02-17 23:56:41.233         55.7
1999-02-18 00:13:41.243         32.8
1999-02-18 13:40:41.273         -18.2
1999-02-18 20:35:41.283         27.2
1999-02-18 21:53:41.243         34.6
1999-02-19 01:21:41.283         -34.6
1999-02-19 22:52:41.253         16.8
1999-02-20 03:56:41.283         -27.8
1999-02-20 06:56:41.283         38.1
1999-02-21 08:28:41.243         67.6
1999-02-21 20:43:41.283         -7.0
1999-02-22 19:12:41.293         20.9
1999-02-23 05:59:41.273         .4
1999-02-23 07:33:41.243         58.1
1999-02-23 09:25:41.243         65.6
1999-02-23 16:04:41.283         7.0
1999-02-23 16:05:41.253         2.2
1999-02-23 20:59:41.253         30.9
```

Approach 1: Using Standard SQL

This approach is similar to the rankings solution. We assign a ranking to each row and then join the table back to itself on the ranking value less 1. If duplicate datetime values exist, this approach still computes the differential to the previous (nonduplicate) measurement, which might or might not be how you'd want to deal with it. As with the rankings solution, we can use this approach either as a view or as a derived table. Since a view is easier for most people to understand, we'll write it that way.

As in the top *n* and rankings problems, this approach is a good brainteaser, but it's not a good performer if the table is anything but very small. (This approach would also be problematic if duplicate datetime values could exist.)

```
CREATE VIEW rankdates (when_taken, temperature, daterank)
AS
SELECT when_taken, temperature,
```

(continued)

```
        (SELECT COUNT(DISTINCT when_taken) FROM measurements AS T1
        WHERE T1.when_taken <= T0.when_taken) AS rank
   FROM measurements AS T0
   GO


   SELECT * FROM rankdates ORDER BY daterank
   GO
```

when_taken	temperature	daterank
1999-02-17 12:31:41.203	50.0	1
1999-02-17 16:07:41.243	48.0	2
1999-02-17 23:56:41.233	55.7	3
1999-02-18 00:13:41.243	32.8	4
1999-02-18 13:40:41.273	-18.2	5
1999-02-18 20:35:41.283	27.2	6
1999-02-18 21:53:41.243	34.6	7
1999-02-19 01:21:41.283	-34.6	8
1999-02-19 22:52:41.253	16.8	9
1999-02-20 03:56:41.283	-27.8	10
1999-02-20 06:56:41.283	38.1	11
1999-02-21 08:28:41.243	67.6	12
1999-02-21 20:43:41.283	-7.0	13
1999-02-22 19:12:41.293	20.9	14
1999-02-23 05:59:41.273	.4	15
1999-02-23 07:33:41.243	58.1	16
1999-02-23 09:25:41.243	65.6	17
1999-02-23 16:04:41.283	7.0	18
1999-02-23 16:05:41.253	2.2	19
1999-02-23 20:59:41.253	30.9	20

```
-- Correlate each value with the one right before it
SELECT
P1_WHEN=V1.when_taken, P2_WHEN=V2.when_taken,
P1=V1.temperature, P2=V2.temperature,
DIFF=(V2.temperature - V1.temperature)
FROM rankdates AS V1 LEFT OUTER JOIN rankdates AS V2
ON (V2.daterank=V1.daterank + 1)
GO
```

P1_WHEN	P2_WHEN	P1	P2	DIFF
1999-02-17 12:31:41.203	1999-02-17 16:07:41.243	50.0	48.0	-2.0
1999-02-17 16:07:41.243	1999-02-17 23:56:41.233	48.0	55.7	7.7
1999-02-17 23:56:41.233	1999-02-18 00:13:41.243	55.7	32.8	-22.9

1999-02-18 00:13:41.243	1999-02-18 13:40:41.273	32.8	-18.2	-51.0
1999-02-18 13:40:41.273	1999-02-18 20:35:41.283	-18.2	27.2	45.4
1999-02-18 20:35:41.283	1999-02-18 21:53:41.243	27.2	34.6	7.4
1999-02-18 21:53:41.243	1999-02-19 01:21:41.283	34.6	-34.6	-69.2
1999-02-19 01:21:41.283	1999-02-19 22:52:41.253	-34.6	16.8	51.4
1999-02-19 22:52:41.253	1999-02-20 03:56:41.283	16.8	-27.8	-44.6
1999-02-20 03:56:41.283	1999-02-20 06:56:41.283	-27.8	38.1	65.9
1999-02-20 06:56:41.283	1999-02-21 08:28:41.243	38.1	67.6	29.5
1999-02-21 08:28:41.243	1999-02-21 20:43:41.283	67.6	-7.0	-74.6
1999-02-21 20:43:41.283	1999-02-22 19:12:41.293	-7.0	20.9	27.9
1999-02-22 19:12:41.293	1999-02-23 05:59:41.273	20.9	.4	-20.5
1999-02-23 05:59:41.273	1999-02-23 07:33:41.243	.4	58.1	57.7
1999-02-23 07:33:41.243	1999-02-23 09:25:41.243	58.1	65.6	7.5
1999-02-23 09:25:41.243	1999-02-23 16:04:41.283	65.6	7.0	-58.6
1999-02-23 16:04:41.283	1999-02-23 16:05:41.253	7.0	2.2	-4.8
1999-02-23 16:05:41.253	1999-02-23 20:59:41.253	2.2	30.9	28.7
1999-02-23 20:59:41.253	NULL	30.9	NULL	NULL

NOTE If you're interested in the derived table solution, go back to the rankings problem and note the difference between a view and a derived table; it should be easy to see how the derived table solution can be done here as well.

Approach 2: Materializing Rankings and Using a Self-Join

Conceptually, this solution is similar to the standard SQL approach. But rather than using a true view, we'll materialize the rankings as a temporary table, similar to the approach in one of the rankings solutions. Then we'll do the self-join with the temporary table. The advantage, of course, is that we create the rankings only once instead of many times. This is faster because the identity value simply assigns the rank in the order that the rows are presented.

In SQL Server 7, this solution performs about as quickly as the standard SQL solution. The results are the same, so we won't bother repeating the output. The standard SQL approach takes 84 logical reads with this dataset; the temporary table approach here takes 40 logical reads to create the *temp* table and 52 logical reads to access it. Because so little data is involved, no more than two physical reads occur in either of these solutions.

```
CREATE TABLE #rankdates (
when_taken datetime,
temperature numeric(4, 1),
daterank int IDENTITY PRIMARY KEY)
GO
```

(continued)

```
INSERT #rankdates (when_taken, temperature)
    SELECT when_taken, temperature
    FROM measurements
    ORDER BY when_taken ASC
GO


SELECT
P1_WHEN=V1.when_taken, P2_WHEN=V2.when_taken,
P1=V1.temperature, P2=V2.temperature,
DIFF=(V2.temperature - V1.temperature)
FROM #rankdates AS V1 LEFT OUTER JOIN #rankdates AS V2
ON (V2.daterank=V1.daterank + 1)
GO
```

Approach 3: Using a Cursor

This is a sequential operation, so a cursor works well:

```
DECLARE @lastval int, @currdate datetime, @currval numeric(4, 1),
    @counter int
SELECT @counter=1
DECLARE diffprev CURSOR
FOR SELECT when_taken, temperature FROM measurements
    ORDER BY when_taken ASC
OPEN diffprev
FETCH NEXT FROM diffprev INTO @currdate, @currval
WHILE (@@FETCH_STATUS <> -1)
BEGIN
    IF (@counter=1)      -- For first row, just get value and return
            SELECT WHEN_TAKEN=@currdate, "CURR_VALUE"=@currval,
                RANK=@counter, "PREV_VALUE"=NULL, "DIFF"=NULL
    ELSE
            SELECT WHEN_TAKEN=@currdate, "CURR_VALUE"=@currval,
                RANK=@counter, "PREV_VALUE"=@lastval,
                "DIFF"=@currval - @lastval
    SELECT @lastval=@currval, @counter=@counter + 1
    FETCH NEXT FROM diffprev INTO @currdate, @currval
END


CLOSE diffprev
DEALLOCATE diffprev
GO
```

From the perspective of logical I/Os, the cursor approach is nearly as efficient as Approach 2, which materializes the rankings using a temporary table and an identity value and then does a self-join. However, over a slow network, the performance of Approach 2 appears to be an order of magnitude faster than this cursor approach. In this solution, each FETCH is treated as a separate result set, so you get 20 result sets, each with one row, instead of just one result set with 20 rows, as in Approach 2. The cursor approach does, however, give you ultimate flexibility. For example, suppose that the time differential between two points is less than five seconds and you want to throw out that point and use the differential to the next point instead. This would be difficult to write in pure SQL, but it is easy with a cursor.

Keeping Running Totals

You can keep running totals by making some small changes to the techniques used for the time series problems—it's the same sort of problem. Consider the following table:

col1	value	running_tot
1	10	0
2	15	0
3	63	0
4	72	0
5	75	0
6	20	0
7	21	0
8	34	0
9	76	0
10	2	0

Suppose you want to store the running total of the *value* column in the *running_tot* column:

col1	value	running_tot
1	10	10
2	15	25
3	63	88
4	72	160
5	75	235
6	20	255
7	21	276
8	34	310
9	76	386
10	2	388

You can adapt any of the solutions for the time series problem to fit this situation. But you can also opt for another, highly efficient solution that uses an underutilized feature of the UPDATE statement. This solution uses only one logical read to compute all the values. (No solution can do less than one logical read.) It uses a variation of the SET clause, which sets a column to an expression, and then it sets a variable to the new value of the column. You can think of the processing as happening right to left: first you assign to the column, and then you assign to the variable.

```
-- running_tot.sql
DECLARE @run_total int
SELECT @run_total=0
UPDATE running_tot
    SET @run_total = running_tot = @run_total + value
FROM running_tot
```

Sampling Every *n* Rows

You can easily adapt the time series and differences between intervals solutions to check the value of every *n*th row. For example, suppose you want to find every fifth row. By using a solution that materializes the rankings in a temporary table, you can select from the temporary table with modulus 5. Or, using a cursor solution, you can use *FETCH RELATIVE 5*. Note that the idea of sampling is not too "relational," since there is no logically implied order of rows stored in the table (although physically this exists if a clustered index is present).

Finding Rows with Matching Columns

Suppose you want to look in a table for all rows that have duplicate values in multiple nonkey columns. For example, in the following table, *match_cols*, you want to find duplicate rows (except for *row_num*). It isn't enough to simply identify the *col2* and *col3* values that are duplicates (COUNT and GROUP BY would make that a piece of cake); you must identify the specific rows that contain the duplicates. This is a pretty common need in data-scrubbing–type situations.

In the example that follows, rows 3 and 10 are duplicates. (Note that *row_num* is a primary key, so the entire row is never a duplicate. You want to find duplicates across only the other columns.) With only 10 rows in the following example, you can easily spot the other duplicates (rows 4 and 6). But the example on the CD creates 5000 rows of data, again with letters *A* through *D* for *col2* and *col3*. (Since there are four letters and two columns, there are 4^2—or 16—possible combinations.) Depending on which solution you choose, this operation can prove expensive for even 5000 rows—not to mention real-world datasets of perhaps 5 million rows!

```
row_num    col2    col3
-------    ----    ----
1          A       A
2          C       C
3          B       D
4          D       B
5          D       C
6          D       B
7          A       C
8          A       D
9          B       A
10         B       D
```

Approach 1: Using a Self-Join

The self-join solution seems the most intuitive—much more so than using a subquery. But with larger amounts of data, it is not very efficient. It performs nested iteration, and the second virtual table must be scanned for each row in the first. With no useful index available for the duplicate columns, this is a full table scan and is unacceptable. Even with a useful index, such as the one for the example on the CD, the second virtual table must be scanned for each row in the first (and "scanned" here does not refer to a full table scan—the index is used). This is expensive. Response time isn't too bad with this number of rows—the results return within a few seconds. Approaches 2, 3, and 4 are more expensive in terms of logical reads, but not enough to definitely recommend one over another.

```
-- The self-join solution
SELECT DISTINCT A.row_num, A.col2, A.col3
FROM match_cols AS A, match_cols AS B
WHERE A.col2=B.col2 AND A.col3=B.col3 AND A.row_num <> B.row_num
ORDER BY A.col2, A.col3
```

Approach 2: Using a Correlated Subquery

We can use GROUP BY...COUNT as an inner query to identify known duplicate values. We can then correlate the query to an outer query of the same table to find the specific rows with those values known to have a count greater than 1 (and that are therefore duplicates). Because the inner query uses the EXISTS operator, the optimizer knows that as soon as one value is found, it can return TRUE.

```
-- The subquery solution
SELECT A.row_num, A.col2, A.col3 FROM match_cols AS A
WHERE EXISTS
(SELECT B.col2, B.col3 FROM match_cols AS B
    WHERE B.col2=A.col2
    AND   B.col3=A.col3
    GROUP BY B.col2, B.col3 HAVING COUNT(*) > 1)
ORDER BY A.col2, A.col3
```

Approach 3: Materializing the Nonunique Values and Joining to the Result

Intuitively, join solutions seem preferable to subquery solutions and correlated subquery solutions. For this problem, it would be nice to have a table with just the known nonunique columns and then do a simple equijoin to it. This approach is kind of a hybrid between the self-join and the correlated subquery solutions. We can easily do this using a temporary table. (This feels like cheating, so stay tuned for another approach.)

```
-- The temp table solution - materialize rows that are known to
-- have dups
SELECT col2, col3 INTO #mytemp
FROM match_cols
GROUP BY col2, col3 HAVING COUNT(*) > 1

-- Now simply do an equijoin to the temp table
SELECT #mytemp.col2, #mytemp.col3, match_cols.row_num
FROM #mytemp
JOIN match_cols
ON (#mytemp.col2=match_cols.col2 AND #mytemp.col3=match_cols.col3)
ORDER BY 1, 2, 3
```

This solution is fast. Since there are just 16 possible combinations and thus 16 ways to make duplicates, the temporary table contains only 16 rows. This becomes the outer table for the join. The main table, *match_cols*, is scanned (using an index) once for each of those 16 rows. So rather than the scan counts of 5000 we saw in the previous solutions, the scan count is only 16. This solution is by far the fastest yet, but it's a procedural solution. It would be much more satisfying to do this with a pure SQL query that is also efficient.

Approach 4: Using Derived Tables

This fast, pure SQL solution is conceptually like the solution that used a temporary table. But rather than explicitly creating and populating the temporary table, we use a derived table. The derived table performs the query for the duplicate values (again finding 16). Then *match_cols* is joined to the derived table. After the optimizer chooses the best join order, the table is processed internally, almost identically to the temporary table situation. Using derived tables is a great solution. If you thought of this solution yourself, you get a gold star.

```
-- The derived table solution
SELECT A.row_num, A.col2, A.col3 FROM match_cols AS A
-- Join the table to a virtual table that has one row for any row
-- combinations known not to be unique (count greater than 1)
JOIN
(SELECT col2, col3 FROM match_cols AS B
            GROUP BY col2, col3 HAVING COUNT(*) > 1) AS B
ON (A.col2=B.col2 AND A.col3=B.col3)
ORDER BY A.col2, A.col3, A.row_num
```

A Related Approach for Data Scrubbing

Often, a technique for finding rows with duplicate columns and deleting duplicates is used for data scrubbing—simply to eliminate duplicate rows. If you want to delete duplicate rows, you can create a new table that has a unique index, with the IGNORE_DUP_KEY option on the columns to be checked for duplicates. Then you use the INSERT...SELECT command to populate the new table and discard all the duplicate rows. This is a fast and easy solution. (It won't work if you want to identify the rows and not delete them, however. To identify and not delete, you can use the previous solutions and convert them to DELETE operations.) This solution gets rid of duplicates but doesn't identify them:

```
-- Data scrubbing
-- Use a unique index with IGNORE_DUP_KEY to throw out the duplicate
-- rows. This isn't quite a solution to the problem at hand, as it
-- doesn't identify the duplicate rows, but it does eliminate them.
CREATE TABLE #match_cols
(
row_num     int,
col2        char(1),
col3        char(1)
)
GO

CREATE UNIQUE INDEX #match_col2_idx ON #match_cols (col2, col3) WITH
IGNORE_DUP_KEY
GO

-- Note many dups in original table
```

(continued)

```
SELECT "COUNT(*)"=COUNT(*), col2, col3
FROM match_cols
GROUP BY col2, col3

COUNT(*)     col2     col3
--------     ----     ----
264          A        A
339          A        B
304          A        C
334          A        D
329          B        A
309          B        B
319          B        C
341          B        D
312          C        A
320          C        B
300          C        C
341          C        D
297          D        A
297          D        B
304          D        C
290          D        D

-- Supposedly selects ALL from the original table,
-- but duplicates will get silently thrown away
INSERT #match_cols
    SELECT * FROM match_cols

-- No dups in new table
SELECT "COUNT(*)"=COUNT(*), col2, col3
FROM #match_cols
GROUP BY col2, col3

COUNT(*)     col2     col3
--------     ----     ----
1            A        A
1            A        B
1            A        C
1            A        D
1            B        A
1            B        B
1            B        C
1            B        D
1            C        A
1            C        B
```

```
1          C        C
1          C        D
1          D        A
1          D        B
1          D        C
1          D        D
```

Putting Data on a Web Page

If you need a fast way to copy data to a simple but functional Web page, you can choose from several third-party tools. But you can do this easily (and for free) using the special stored procedure *sp_makewebtask* (which wraps the extended stored procedure *xp_makewebtask*). This procedure has a GUI front end—the Web Assistant Wizard—but you can also call it directly. We'll use this solution next to present a table of authors on a Web page. (You can get as fancy as you want—the online documentation discusses several optional parameters.) We'll specify the name of the HTML file to be created and write a query to get the data. You can also specify several formatting options, links to other URLs, and links to pages of related text or image data contained for each row. In this example, the entries in the *pr_info* and *logo* columns are hyperlinks to the actual text and image data:

```
sp_makewebtask @outputfile="c:\tmp\pub_info.htm",
@query="SELECT pub_id, pr_info, pub_id, logo, pub_id FROM pub_info",
@blobfmt="%2%FILE=c:\tmp\pubtxt_.html%4%FILE=c:\tmp\pubimg_.gif"
```

Figure 12-1 on the following page shows how the resulting Web page looks in Microsoft Internet Explorer.

Expanding a Hierarchy

Let's say you want to expand a hierarchy (such as an organization chart), prepare a bill of materials, or navigate a tree structure. This problem doesn't lend itself naturally to the use of standard SQL. Suppose we have a simple table of employees. It uses a self-reference in which each employee is associated with his or her manager's row in the same table.

```
CREATE TABLE emp_mgr
(
emp_no          int             NOT NULL PRIMARY KEY,
emp_name        varchar(25)     NOT NULL,
emp_title       varchar(25)     NOT NULL,
mgr_no          int             REFERENCES emp_mgr (emp_no)
)
```

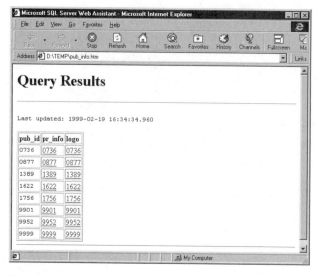

Figure 12-1.
Viewing a table of authors via Internet Explorer.

If we want to provide a list of employees, with each employee's manager name and title on the same line, it's easy. A self-join works like this:

```
SELECT
E.emp_no, E.emp_name AS Employee, E.emp_title,
M.mgr_no, M.emp_name AS Manager, M.emp_title AS Mgr_title
FROM
    emp_mgr AS E
JOIN
    emp_mgr AS M
ON (E.mgr_no=M.emp_no)
ORDER BY E.emp_no
```

```
emp_no Employee       emp_title        mgr_no Manager        Mgr_title
------ -----------    ---------------  ------ -------------- -------------
16     Dave Edgerton  VP-Operations    99     Mark Burke     President
73     Rick Eckhart   Albany Plant     16     Dave Edgerton  VP-Operations
                      Manager
99     Mark Burke     President        10050  John Smith     CEO
643    Greg Chapman   VP-Sales &       99     Mark Burke     President
                      Marketing
```

700

692	Ethel Knoll	Staff Accountant	7437	Rachel Hunt	Senior Cost Accountant	
865	Ron Simms	Terre Haute Plant Manager	16	Dave Edgerton	VP-Operations	
935	Deb Kerns	Mechanical Engineer	86145	Adam Smale	Chief Engineer	
1803	John Jacobs	Cash Flow Management	9543	Jill Hansen	Treasurer	
2037	Keith Teeter	Civil Engineer	28762	Jeff Cullerton	Electrical Engineer	
2345	Mike Jackson	Charlotte Plant Manager	16	Dave Edgerton	VP-Operations	
3260	Lee Chao	VP-R&D	99	Mark Burke	President	
4096	Hillary Loews	Staff Accountant	7437	Rachel Hunt	Senior Cost Accountant	
4318	Phyllis Brown	VP-Human Resources	99	Mark Burke	President	
4378	Kurt Phillips	Electrical Engineer	86145	Adam Smale	Chief Engineer	
4673	Kurt Johansen	Fremont Plant Manager	16	Dave Edgerton	VP-Operations	
6298	Wes Thomas	Mechanical Engineer	8548	Lee Roberts Johnson	Chief Engineer	
6578	Karl Johnson	Chief Engineer	4673	Kurt Johansen	Fremont Plant Manager	
7210	Ajay Kumar	Electrical Engineer	9763	Takeshi Sato	Chief Engineer	
7437	Rachel Hunt	Senior Cost Accountant	8576	Phil Kertzman	Corporate Controller	
8548	Lee Roberts Johnson	Chief Engineer	865	Ron Simms	Terre Haute Plant Manager	
8576	Phil Kertzman	Corporate Controller	20240	Sue Ferrel	VP-Finance	
9543	Jill Hansen	Treasurer	20240	Sue Ferrel	VP-Finance	
9763	Takeshi Sato	Chief Engineer	2345	Mike Jackson	Charlotte Plant Manager	
9871	Mike Baker	Staff Accountant	1803	John Jacobs	Cash Flow Management	
10050	John Smith	CEO	10050	John Smith	CEO	
11456	Paul Good	Civil Engineer	935	Deb Kerns	Mechanical Engineer	
20240	Sue Ferrel	VP-Finance	99	Mark Burke	President	

(continued)

23756	Pete Fuller	Civil Engineer	56432	Walt White	Mechanical Engineer
28762	Jeff Cullerton	Electrical Engineer	8548	Lee Roberts Johnson	Chief Engineer
56432	Walt White	Mechanical Engineer	6578	Karl Johnson	Chief Engineer
84521	Leland Teng	Civil Engineer	9763	Takeshi Sato	Chief Engineer
86145	Adam Smale	Chief Engineer	73	Rick Eckhart	Albany Plant Manager
92314	Billy Bob Jones	Mechanical Engineer	7210	Ajay Kumar	Electrical Engineer

If we want to show the hierarchy and the reporting relationships, it's not so easy. As we've seen, returning a bunch of result sets back to the client application is inefficient and should be avoided. In the old days, you couldn't really avoid doing it this way. Now, however, you can use a temporary table and sequence it with IDENTITY to hold the order of the reporting relationship. When we finish traversing the hierarchy, we need to join to that temporary table with a single, simple SELECT. (We use the SPACE( ) function and string concatenation to produce a simple report of the following form, showing each employee's reporting relationship. This is not central to the main solution, of course.)

A Borrowed Solution

This solution is credited to Rick Vicik. It uses a temporary table as a stack to keep track of all the items for which processing has begun but is not complete. When an item has been fully traversed, it is removed from the stack. This is a nice approach because it can work to an arbitrary and unknown number of levels. And by slightly modifying it (or making it a procedure and passing parameters), you can start at a given level and end at a given level.

Rick's original solution to this problem is in the SQL Server documentation under the topic "Expanding Hierarchies." The following approach is a slight refinement. Rick's solution dates from several years back, before the existence of IDENTITY. It relies on multiple PRINT statements to present the output.

```
Manager -> Employees
John Smith,   CEO
    Mark Burke,   President
        Dave Edgerton,   VP-Operations
            Rick Eckhart,   Albany Plant Manager
                Adam Smale,   Chief Engineer
                    Deb Kerns,   Mechanical Engineer
                        Paul Good,   Civil Engineer
                    Kurt Phillips,   Electrical Engineer
            Ron Simms,   Terre Haute Plant Manager
                Lee Roberts Johnson,   Chief Engineer
                    Wes Thomas,   Mechanical Engineer
                    Jeff Cullerton,   Electrical Engineer
                        Keith Teeter,   Civil Engineer
            Mike Jackson,   Charlotte Plant Manager
                Takeshi Sato,   Chief Engineer
                    Ajay Kumar,   Electrical Engineer
                        Billy Bob Jones,   Mechanical Engineer
                    Leland Teng,   Civil Engineer
            Kurt Johansen,   Fremont Plant Manager
                Karl Johnson,   Chief Engineer
                    Walt White,   Mechanical Engineer
                        Pete Fuller,   Civil Engineer
        Greg Chapman,   VP-Sales & Marketing
        Lee Chao,   VP-R&D
        Phyllis Brown,   VP-Human Resources
        Sue Ferrel,   VP-Finance
            Phil Kertzman,   Corporate Controller
                Rachel Hunt,   Senior Cost Accountant
                    Ethel Knoll,   Staff Accountant
                    Hillary Loews,   Staff Accountant
            Jill Hansen,   Treasurer
                John Jacobs,   Cash Flow Management
                Mike Baker,   Staff Accountant
```

Here is the batch, with comments, that produced this hierarchy:

```
-- Variables to keep track of reporting level and the current emp
DECLARE @level int, @current int

-- This table will act as a stack. We push employees onto the stack
-- until we process all their reports.
CREATE TABLE #stack
(depth_level int, emp_no int)
```

(continued)

```
-- This temp table will be used to hold the reporting chain.
-- The identity automatically sequences it and allows us to
-- ultimately return the hierarchy as just a single result set.
CREATE TABLE #orgchart
(seq_no          int     IDENTITY
org_level        int     NOT NULL
emp_id           int     NOT NULL
)

-- Assume we know with certainty that only one employee
-- (the CEO) can have himself as manager.
-- Can change this however makes sense, but need some way to
-- know where to start.
-- We'll set ROWCOUNT to 1 to be sure, but it is not necessary
-- since we know this.
-- In this batch, we'll assume we start with level 1 as the
-- depth_level.
SET ROWCOUNT 1
SELECT @level=1, @current=emp_no FROM emp_mgr WHERE emp_no=mgr_no
SET ROWCOUNT 0

INSERT INTO #stack (depth_level, emp_no) VALUES (@level, @current)

WHILE (@level > 0)     -- Do if any levels remain
    BEGIN

       -- See whether there are any rows for the level we're on
       IF EXISTS (SELECT * FROM #stack WHERE depth_level=@level)
          BEGIN

              -- Get FIRST emp_no at current level
              SET ROWCOUNT 1
              SELECT @current=emp_no FROM #stack
              WHERE depth_level=@level
              SET ROWCOUNT 0

              -- Put the employee in a temp table so
              -- we can later do a single select and join.
              -- We could SELECT here for every employee, but
              -- all those result sets are inefficient.
              -- The orgchart temp table is automatically sequenced
              -- via an identity. That's the key to the temp table
              -- providing a solution here.
              INSERT INTO #orgchart (ORG_LEVEL, EMP_ID)
                  SELECT @level, @current
```

704

```
      -- Delete row just processed from the stack
      DELETE FROM #stack
      WHERE depth_level=@level AND emp_no=@current

      -- Get new rows for stack by finding anyone reporting to
      -- current: except for the top employee who reports to self
      INSERT INTO #stack
          SELECT @level + 1, emp_no
          FROM emp_mgr
          WHERE mgr_no=@current
          AND mgr_no <> emp_no

      -- If any rows were found and inserted, there is a level
      -- below this employee, so increment level
      IF @@ROWCOUNT > 0
          SELECT @level=@level + 1

      END
  ELSE
      -- There are no levels below this employee, so pop up one
      SELECT @level=@level - 1
  END

-- Now just join to the #org_chart to get emp_names and titles.
-- Concatenate employees and managers into one string, indented by
-- level. Use SPACE()*level*5 to indent 5 spaces per level, except
-- for level 1.
SELECT "Manager -> Employees"=
SPACE((O.org_level - 1) * 5) + E.emp_name + ',      '+ E.emp_title
FROM #orgchart AS O
JOIN emp_mgr AS E ON (E.emp_no=O.emp_id)
ORDER BY O.SEQ_NO

DROP TABLE #stack, #orgchart
```

You can also solve this problem in a straightforward but tedious way using cursors. You simply FETCH through the chain for each employee to find all employees who report to him or her. This solution requires many fetches, which of course means many result sets.

SEE ALSO David Rozenshtein has written extensively on the topic of tree processing in SQL. (His book *Optimizing Transact-SQL,* coauthored by Anatoly Abramovich and Eugene Birger, is on the Suggested Reading list at the end of this book.) One of his solutions might be more efficient than this, but the solution above is plenty efficient.

Selecting Instead of Iterating

One common need is to perform some operation for every value, from 1 to *n*. In Chapter 9, we used the trigonometry functions to produce a listing of sine/cosine/tangent for every 10 degrees between 0 and 180. We took the obvious route and wrote a simple loop. However, that approach results in every row being its own result set. As we've discussed many times, sending many result sets when one will do is inefficient, and it is also more cumbersome to process in the client application. To refresh your memory, here's the solution from Chapter 9:

```
DECLARE @angle smallint
SELECT @angle=0
WHILE (@angle <= 180)
BEGIN
    SELECT
    ANGLE=@angle,
    SINE=STR(SIN(@angle), 7, 4),
    COSINE=STR(COS(@angle), 7, 4),
    TANGENT=STR(TAN(@angle), 7, 4)

    SELECT @angle=@angle + 10
END
```

Since it's common to iterate in this way, a simple table of ordered numbers can come in handy:

```
-- Create the seq_num table
CREATE TABLE seq_num
(seq_num INT PRIMARY KEY NOT NULL)

-- Populate the seq_num table with values from -500 through 500
DECLARE @counter int
SELECT @counter= -500
WHILE (@counter <= 500)
    BEGIN
    INSERT seq_num VALUES (@counter)
    SELECT @counter=@counter + 1
    END

-- If doing this for real, you might as well set FILLFACTOR to 100
```

We can select or join to this handy *seq_num* table rather than iterating. The following solution runs much faster than the solution from Chapter 9. It returns a single result set, and it's easier to write:

```
SELECT
    ANGLE=seq_num * 10,
    SINE=STR(SIN(seq_num * 10), 7, 4),
    COSINE=STR(COS(seq_num * 10), 7, 4),
    TANGENT=STR(TAN(seq_num * 10), 7, 4)
FROM seq_num
WHERE seq_num BETWEEN 0 AND 18
```

```
ANGLE    SINE       COSINE    TANGENT
-----    -------    -------   -------
0         0.0000     1.0000    0.0000
10       -0.5440    -0.8391    0.6484
20        0.9129     0.4081    2.2372
30       -0.9880     0.1543   -6.4053
40        0.7451    -0.6669   -1.1172
50       -0.2624     0.9650   -0.2719
60       -0.3048    -0.9524    0.3200
70        0.7739     0.6333    1.2220
80       -0.9939    -0.1104    9.0037
90        0.8940    -0.4481   -1.9952
100      -0.5064     0.8623   -0.5872
110      -0.0442    -0.9990    0.0443
120       0.5806     0.8142    0.7131
130      -0.9301    -0.3673    2.5323
140       0.9802    -0.1978   -4.9554
150      -0.7149     0.6993   -1.0223
160       0.2194    -0.9756   -0.2249
170       0.3466     0.9380    0.3696
180      -0.8012    -0.5985    1.3387
```

Getting a Row Count of a Table

Let's say you want to get the number of rows in a table, without qualification. Using the *seq_num* table of the last example, the obvious way to check the number of rows is to do this:

```
SELECT COUNT(*) FROM seq_num
```

While this is the most obvious solution, it's not the fastest one. The table still requires a scan (via some index or a full table scan). The number of rows in the table is maintained, and can be relied on to be accurate, in the *sysindexes* table. Recall that every table has at least one entry, and the entry has a value of 0 for *indid* if no clustered index is present. If a clustered index exists, the table has a value of 1 for *indid*. It does not have both values, although it of course includes other rows for all nonclustered indexes. You can put together a fast, simple query to find the number of rows by searching on the table and the *indid* of 0 or 1 (knowing that both cannot be present). This approach executes with only two or three logical reads—even for very large tables:

```
-- Faster way to get count of all rows in table
SELECT rows
FROM sysindexes
WHERE id=OBJECT_ID("seq_num")
AND indid < 2    -- If the table has no clustered index, the entry
                 -- will be 0 for the table. If the table has a
                 -- clustered index, the entry will instead be 1 for
                 -- the clustered index. So it will be either 0 or 1,
                 -- not both. Hence, specifying it as < 2 finds it
                 -- either way.
```

Of course, if you need to qualify the count (for example, if you need to get the count for all rows with positive values), you can do this only with COUNT(*). The *sysindexes.rows* trick works only to get a count of all rows in the table, without qualification.

Storing Computed Columns

If you need to select a column that is the result of a computation on data in other columns (for example, *SELECT QTY, PRICE, REV = QTY * PRICE*), you can do so easily with SQL Server 7: you define a column in a table to be a computed column. However, since the computed column is not physically stored, it cannot be indexed. If you find that you frequently search on a computed column, you might want to have an index on that computed value to speed retrieval. For example, you might want to maintain a customer's current balance in the specific customer row rather than recompute it each time you need it. Or you might need to maintain a SOUNDEX() value for each name in a table if your telephone operators use it for information retrieval. Here is a table definition that automatically generates the soundex value for each *cust_name* every time it is accessed:

```
CREATE TABLE customer_sx
(
cust_name        char(20),
soundex_value    as SOUNDEX(cust_name)
)
```

One problem with this approach is that the computed column (*soundex_value*) is not actually stored with the table; it is a virtual column that is computed only when it is accessed. For this reason, you cannot put an index on the column to aid telephone operators in their searches. Instead, you can use a trigger that maintains a SOUNDEX() value, as shown below. The table is clustered to enable names that sound similar to be stored together. Whenever the *cust_name* column is changed or a new customer is added, the SOUNDEX() value is updated.

```
-- soundex_trig.sql
CREATE TABLE customer_sx
(
cust_name        char(20),
soundex_value    char(4)    NULL
)
CREATE CLUSTERED INDEX sounds_like ON customer_sx (soundex_value)
GO

CREATE TRIGGER maintain_soundex ON customer_sx
FOR INSERT, UPDATE
AS
    UPDATE soundex_name SET soundex_value=SOUNDEX(inserted.cust_name)
        FROM customer_sx, inserted
        WHERE customer_sx.cust_name=inserted.cust_name
GO
```

Using Pivot Tables (Cross-Tabs)

Suppose you have a simple table called *cross_tab* with sales values for different years and quarters:

year	qtr	value		year	qtr	value
1990	1	15		1993	1	20
1990	2	26		1993	2	35
1990	3	37		1993	3	47
1990	4	48		1993	4	58
1991	1	19		1994	1	25
1991	2	25		1994	2	36
1991	3	37		1994	3	49
1991	4	48		1994	4	50
1992	1	15		1995	1	31
1992	2	29		1995	2	45
1992	3	32		1995	3	57
1992	4	44		1995	4	68

You need to provide summary data—one line for each year, values for all four quarters in the year, and the year's total. The query on the following page does the trick.

```
SELECT year,
q1=(SELECT value FROM cross_tab WHERE year=c.year AND qtr=1),
q2=(SELECT value FROM cross_tab WHERE year=c.year AND qtr=2),
q3=(SELECT value FROM cross_tab WHERE year=c.year AND qtr=3),
q4=(SELECT value FROM cross_tab WHERE year=c.year AND qtr=4),
total=(SELECT SUM(value) FROM cross_tab WHERE year=c.year)
FROM cross_tab c
GROUP BY year
```

year	q1	q2	q3	q4	total
1990	15	26	37	48	126
1991	19	25	37	48	129
1992	15	29	32	44	120
1993	20	35	47	58	160
1994	25	36	49	50	160
1995	31	45	57	68	201

If multiple data points exist for a given year and quarter (which in this case isn't possible since those two columns make up the primary key in the *cross_tab* table), you can modify the query slightly to use SUM for each quarter, not just for the total. Here is the modified query, which works when multiple entries can exist for any year/quarter combination. It works fine on the *cross_tab* table, too, but it contains extra SUMs.

```
SELECT year,
q1=(SELECT SUM(value) FROM cross_tab WHERE year=c.year AND qtr=1),
q2=(SELECT SUM(value) FROM cross_tab WHERE year=c.year AND qtr=2),
q3=(SELECT SUM(value) FROM cross_tab WHERE year=c.year AND qtr=3),
q4=(SELECT SUM(value) FROM cross_tab WHERE year=c.year AND qtr=4),
total=(SELECT SUM(value) FROM cross_tab WHERE year=c.year)
FROM cross_tab c
GROUP BY year
```

This is the type of solution that most people used prior to CASE being added to SQL Server 6. But all those SELECT statements do not make for a highly efficient solution. In fact, running this query with just the 24 data rows in this example requires more than 30 scans (not full table scans).

Using CASE, you make only a single pass through the *cross_tab* table. The scan count is 1, and the logical reads value is only 1! Obviously, this solution is much more efficient.

```
SELECT
year=c.year,
SUM(CASE qtr WHEN 1 THEN value ELSE 0 END) AS q1,
SUM(CASE qtr WHEN 2 THEN value ELSE 0 END) AS q2,
```

```
SUM(CASE qtr WHEN 3 THEN value ELSE 0 END) AS q3,
SUM(CASE qtr WHEN 4 THEN value ELSE 0 END) AS q4
FROM cross_tab c
GROUP BY year
```

Unfortunately, this solution doesn't quite meet the original specifications of the query: it doesn't calculate the total for the year. If you're going to throw the results in a spreadsheet, it's OK as it is—you can let the spreadsheet calculate that total value for the year based on the previous four columns.

It would be nice to do something like the following, but it's not supported— you can't treat a column heading as a column name as this example does:

```
SELECT
year=c.year,
SUM(CASE qtr WHEN 1 THEN value ELSE 0 END) AS q1,
SUM(CASE qtr WHEN 2 THEN value ELSE 0 END) AS q2,
SUM(CASE qtr WHEN 3 THEN value ELSE 0 END) AS q3,
SUM(CASE qtr WHEN 4 THEN value ELSE 0 END) AS q4
SUM (q1 + q2 + q3 + q4) AS total
FROM cross_tab c
GROUP BY year
```

We need to find a hybrid of the two methods. Here is the obvious solution: use the more efficient CASE solution, and for the *total* column that can't be solved with the single CASE pass, do a SELECT inside the SELECT:

```
SELECT
year=c.year,
SUM(CASE qtr WHEN 1 THEN value ELSE 0 END) AS q1,
SUM(CASE qtr WHEN 2 THEN value ELSE 0 END) AS q2,
SUM(CASE qtr WHEN 3 THEN value ELSE 0 END) AS q3,
SUM(CASE qtr WHEN 4 THEN value ELSE 0 END) AS q4,
(SELECT SUM(value) FROM cross_tab WHERE year=c.year) AS total
FROM cross_tab c
GROUP BY year
```

This adds 6 to the scan count and another 6 logical reads. But it's more efficient than the first solution, and it meets the query specification.

Still, we know that there's an easy way to compute the total for one year. It's a simple query to write:

```
SELECT year, SUM(value)
FROM cross_tab
GROUP BY year
```

It would be nice to use the result of this query and join it to the fast query. Then we'd have the best of both worlds. Below we do just that—we make the query for the year totals a derived table and then join to it:

```
SELECT
c.year AS year,
SUM(CASE qtr WHEN 1 THEN value ELSE 0 END) AS q1,
SUM(CASE qtr WHEN 2 THEN value ELSE 0 END) AS q2,
SUM(CASE qtr WHEN 3 THEN value ELSE 0 END) AS q3,
SUM(CASE qtr WHEN 4 THEN value ELSE 0 END) AS q4,
MIN(y.VAL) AS total
FROM cross_tab AS c
JOIN
    (SELECT year, SUM(value) AS VAL
    FROM cross_tab c
    GROUP BY year) AS y
    ON (y.year=c.year)

GROUP BY c.year
```

This is the most efficient solution we could devise. (You might be more clever and find a better one.) Note one tricky thing here: we used *MIN(y.VAL)* instead of *SUM(y.VAL)*. If we used SUM, we'd get four times the value for each year, because the row from the derived table would be projected to every row for each year—and there are four quarters in each year. We don't want the sum of all yearly totals; we want just one total for the entire year. But we can't mix nonaggregates in the SELECT list because we need to use GROUP BY. So the solution is to use one value for each year, which we do by using MIN. MAX would work just as well. The MIN, MAX, and AVG for each year's total would of course be the same, since only one total can exist for the year.

Here is one more solution to the problem. The idea comes from an article by Steve Roti that appeared several years ago in *DBMS* magazine. He constructed a "unit matrix" table that looks like this:

```
Qtr    Q1    Q2    Q3    Q4
---    --    --    --    --
1      1     0     0     0
2      0     1     0     0
3      0     0     1     0
4      0     0     0     1
```

After constructing and carefully populating the table (named *pivot* in the example that follows), you can use it to join to the *cross_tab* table via the *Qtr* column. The value for each column can be multiplied by its respective quarter.

For example, since only one quarter in any given row has a value of 1 and each of the others has a value of 0, multiplying yields the desired result. The column retains the value (by multiplying it by 1) for the respective quarter but sets it to 0 for a different quarter (by multiplying by 0). This is a clever and efficient solution, but not as efficient as the CASE and derived table solution. And it does require that you fabricate the unit matrix table, although this is not difficult to do. Without CASE, this would be the best solution:

```
SELECT year,
q1=SUM(value * Q1),
q2=SUM(value * Q2),
q3=SUM(value * Q3),
q4=SUM(value * Q4),
total=SUM(value)
FROM cross_tab JOIN pivot
ON (cross_tab.qtr=pivot.Qtr)
GROUP BY year
```

Integrating SQL Server with E-Mail

SQL Server has the unique ability to directly send and receive e-mail. At first blush, many people don't grasp the significance of this. But this feature can perform such functions as alerting you about an important data value or automatically sending a new order to your supplier when inventory reaches a certain level. SQL Server can also receive mail—you can e-mail a query to SQL Server and it will return the results to you, or you can have the body of the e-mail message stored in a database for later use.

Automatically Sending Mail Based on an Event

The following is a trigger for the bug database at Microsoft called RAID that the SQL Server development team uses. If a serious, "severity 1" bug is entered or when an existing bug is elevated to "sev 1," the database sends e-mail to the development team's e-mail alias:

```
-- raidtrigger.sql
CREATE trigger OnCheckBugs ON Bugs
 FOR INSERT, UPDATE, DELETE
 AS
  DECLARE @test int
  DECLARE @recipients varchar(255), @message varchar(255),
     @subject varchar(50)
  -- Send mail for any newly activated sev 1 bugs on a version
```

(continued)

```
-- that has been released
IF EXISTS (SELECT * FROM inserted WHERE
   inserted.Severity='1' AND inserted.Status='ACTIVE')

   BEGIN
   -- If row was already sev 1 and ACTIVE (and is just being
   -- edited), don't resend mail
   IF EXISTS (SELECT * FROM deleted WHERE
       deleted.Severity='1' AND deleted.Status='ACTIVE')
       RETURN

   -- UPDATE NEXT LINE FOR ALL WHO SHOULD GET THE MAIL
   -- Separate with semicolons
   SELECT @recipients='SQLDevTeam;johnsmith;janedoe'

   -- Make subject line of mail the severity, bug number,
   -- & bug database
   SELECT @subject='Sev' + inserted.Severity + '  Bug ' +
       CONVERT(varchar(6), inserted.BugID)
       + ' activated in ' + DB_NAME() FROM inserted

   -- Make message the component area, who opened bug, & its title
   SELECT @message='Component: ' + RTRIM(Component) +
       ' Opened By: ' + RTRIM(inserted.OpenedBy) +
       'Version: ' + OpenedRev + char(13) +
       'Title: ' + RTRIM(inserted.Title) FROM inserted

   EXECUTE master..xp_sendmail    @recipients= @recipients,
                                  @message=    @message,
                                  @subject=    @subject,
                                  @no_output=  TRUE
   END

RETURN
```

Processing Incoming Mail

In the SQL Server group, each developer sends a brief weekly e-mail message to the group reporting on his or her work. Suppose developers want to keep this e-mail train but don't want it cluttering up their e-mail Inbox folders. Suppose they also want to be able to query on it in a structured way by putting the mail automatically into a SQL Server database. They could create a form that populates a database, but the e-mail tradition is well established, informal, and well liked (as much as any demand for status reports is ever well liked).

The following procedure uses the *xp_readmail* capabilities of SQL Server 6.5. It processes mail and reads only mail with the string *stat* (written as uppercase, lowercase, or mixed case) in the subject line. It then inserts attributes such as the sender, datetime sent, and exact subject line into a table. The body of the message is inserted into a text column.

```
USE pubs   -- For example case, make table in pubs database
GO
CREATE TABLE mailstore
(
Msg_ID    varchar(64)  NOT NULL PRIMARY KEY,
Sent_By   varchar(20)  NOT NULL,  -- REFERENCES employees(emp_email)
Subject   varchar(40)  NOT NULL DEFAULT 'No Subject',
Recvd     datetime     NOT NULL DEFAULT GETDATE(),
Msg_Text  text         NULL
)
GO


USE MASTER
GO


DROP PROCEDURE sp_status_mail
GO


CREATE PROCEDURE sp_status_mail
    -- Process only unread mail
    @unread_msgs_only varchar(5)='false',
    -- Delete processed mail
    @delete_after_reading varchar(5)='false',
    -- Do not change mail read status
    @do_not_change_read_status varchar(5)='true',
    -- Process only "Stat" mail
    @only_read_stat_mail varchar(5)='true'

AS
DECLARE @status int,                -- MAPI Status
        @msg_id varchar(64),        -- MSG ID for each mail
        @originator varchar(255),   -- MAIL FROM
        @msgsubject varchar(255),   -- MAIL SUBJECT
        @msgtext varchar(255),      -- BUFFER FOR MAIL TEXT
        @messages int,              -- Counter for messages processed
        @mapifailure int,           -- Indicator if MAPI error
        @maildate varchar(255),     -- MAIL SENT Date
        @skip_bytes int,            -- Pointer for where to read next
```

(continued)

```
                                          -- text chunk
             @msg_length int,             -- Total size of message text
             @textptr varbinary(16)       -- TextPointer

SELECT @messages=0
SELECT @mapifailure=0


WHILE (1=1)
    BEGIN  -- BEGIN NEXT MSG LOOP
        EXEC @status=master.dbo.xp_findnextmsg
            @msg_id=@msg_id OUTPUT,
            @unread_only=@unread_msgs_only

        IF @status <> 0
        BEGIN
            SELECT @mapifailure=1
            BREAK    -- If any MAPI error, bail out
        END

        IF (@msg_id IS NULL)  -- If msg_id is NULL, it's not a
                              -- valid received message so continue
                              -- with the next message
        BREAK

        SELECT @skip_bytes=0, @msg_length=0

        EXEC @status=master.dbo.xp_readmail
            @msg_id=@msg_id,
            @originator=@originator OUTPUT,
            @subject=@msgsubject OUTPUT,
            @date_received=@maildate OUTPUT,
            @message=@msgtext OUTPUT,
            @skip_bytes=@skip_bytes OUTPUT,
            @msg_length=@msg_length OUTPUT,
            @peek=@do_not_change_read_status

        IF @status <> 0
            BEGIN
                SELECT @mapifailure=1
                BREAK     -- If any MAPI error, bail out
            END

  -- If flag is set, care only about mail that has "stat" in the
  -- subject line. So forget rest and continue.
  -- Do not count an "uninteresting" message as one processed.
```

```
IF (LOWER(@only_read_stat_mail)='true' AND
    LOWER(@msgsubject) NOT LIKE '%stat%')
    CONTINUE

-- Count how many messages processed
SELECT @messages=@messages + 1

-- The sender field might be an address or a name.
-- If it's a name, get the address. Must turn off expand
-- to friendly names. Then, if there is a < in originator,
-- parse for the address using only charindex.

SELECT @originator=CASE
    WHEN (@originator NOT LIKE '%<%' OR @originator
        NOT LIKE '% %')
        THEN @originator
    ELSE SUBSTRING(@originator,
        (charindex('<', @originator) + 1),
        (charindex('@', @originator) -
        (charindex('<', @originator) + 1)))
    END

-- Insert message into a table

INSERT pubs.dbo.mailstore
    (Sent_By, Msg_ID, Subject, Recvd, Msg_Text)
VALUES (@originator, @msg_id, @msgsubject, @maildate,
    @msgtext)

-- If MSG_ID already there, continue and try the next
-- message: error 2627 is a violation of a unique or PK
-- constraint due to duplicates, and error 2601 is same but
-- just due to a unique index

IF (@@ERROR IN (2627, 2601))
    BEGIN
        RAISERROR ('MSG ID: %s already exists. Skipping to
            next message.', 16, 1, @msg_id)
        CONTINUE
    END

-- Get the textptr from last row inserted
SELECT @textptr=TEXTPTR(Msg_Text)
FROM pubs.dbo.mailstore WHERE Msg_ID=@msg_id
```

(continued)

717

```
-- If non-null textptr and skip_bytes show there is more
-- to read, keep reading message text until done, and
-- append with UPDATETEXT

WHILE ((@textptr IS NOT NULL) AND
    (@skip_bytes < @msg_length))
    BEGIN    -- BEGIN READ-ALL-TEXT-LOOP
        EXEC @status=master.dbo.xp_readmail
            @msg_id=@msg_id,
            @message=@msgtext OUTPUT,
            @skip_bytes=@skip_bytes OUTPUT,
            @msg_length=@msg_length OUTPUT

        IF @status <> 0
            BEGIN
                SELECT @mapifailure=1
                BREAK    -- If any MAPI error, bail out
            END

        UPDATETEXT pubs.dbo.mailstore.Msg_Text
            @textptr  NULL  0  WITH LOG  @msgtext
    END    -- END READ-ALL-TEXT-LOOP

-- If broke out of text loop because of MAPI failure,
-- break out of next message processing too

IF @mapifailure=1
    BREAK

-- If delete flag is ON, delete this message

IF (LOWER(@delete_after_reading)='true')
    BEGIN
        EXEC @status=master.dbo.xp_deletemail @msg_id
        IF @status <> 0
            BEGIN
                SELECT @mapifailure=1
                BREAK    -- If any MAPI error, bail out
            END
    END

END -- END NEXT MSG LOOP

/* Finished examining the contents of Inbox */
```

```
IF @mapifailure=0      -- No MAPI errors. Success!
    BEGIN
        RAISERROR(15079, -1, -1, @messages)
        RETURN(0)
    END
ELSE                   -- MAPI errors. Bailed out.
    BEGIN
        RAISERROR ('MAPI Error. Terminated Procedure', 16, 1)
        RETURN(-100)
    END
```

Copying Text to Sequenced *varchar* Columns

The text datatype is sometimes awkward to work with. Many functions don't operate on text, stored procedures are limited in what they can do with text, and some tools don't deal with it well. Instead of having a single, huge text column, sometimes it's easier to work with a sequenced set of rows with a *varchar* column. In SQL Server 7, *varchar* columns can be up to 8000 bytes. Although the code that follows can produce columns of that size, that might still be too big to work with effectively. Although all SQL Server's string functions will work on these columns, if you want to print out each column, you might want to find something smaller that fits your needs better. The code produces columns of length 200. You can take this code and substitute *varchar(8000)* or any other length up to 8000 for the *varchar(200)* used.

So how can you copy a text column, which can hold up to $2^{31}-1$ characters, to multiple *varchar(200)* columns and make sure they are sequenced correctly within a single SQL batch? You can, of course, read the data out to a program and then reinsert it. But then you would need to do a lot of copying of large amounts of data between processes. This is far from ideal.

The following procedure operates on the *pub_info* table from the *pubs* database. For a given *pub_id*, the procedure takes the text column of the row and does successive READTEXT operations in chunks of 200 until the entire text column has been read. After creating the procedure, we use a cursor to iterate for each row of *pub_info* and copy the text column into multiple rows of a temporary table. When we're done for a given *pub_id*, we take the temporary table's contents and add it to the permanent table. We truncate the temporary table and move on to the next *pub_id* value.

```
-- copy_text_to_varchar.sql
-- Be sure the pub_info table has the text columns added.
-- If necessary, run \MSSQL\INSTALL\PUBTEXT.BAT to add the text
```

(continued)

```
-- columns. (Run from that directory.)
--
-- Proc get_text does READTEXT in a loop to read chunks of text
-- no larger than 200, or the column size or @@TEXTSIZE, and
-- produces as many rows as necessary to store the text column
-- as a series of sequenced varchar(200) rows
CREATE PROC get_text @pub_id char(4)
AS

DECLARE @mytextptr varbinary(16), @totalsize int, @lastread int,
    @readsize int
-- Use a TRAN and HOLDLOCK to ensure that textptr and text are
-- constant during the iterative reads
BEGIN TRAN
SELECT @mytextptr=TEXTPTR(pr_info), @totalsize=DATALENGTH(pr_info),
    @lastread=0,
    -- Set the readsize to the smaller of the @@TEXTSIZE settings,
    -- 200, and the total length of the column
    @readsize=CASE WHEN (200 < DATALENGTH(pr_info)) THEN 200
    ELSE DATALENGTH(pr_info) END
    FROM pub_info (HOLDLOCK) WHERE pub_id=@pub_id

-- If debugging, uncomment this to check values
-- SELECT @mytextptr, @totalsize, @lastread, @readsize

-- Do READTEXT in a loop to get next 200 characters until done
IF @mytextptr IS NOT NULL AND @readsize > 0
    WHILE (@lastread < @totalsize)
    BEGIN
        -- If readsize would go beyond end, adjust readsize
        IF ((@readsize + @lastread) > @totalsize)
            SELECT @readsize = @totalsize - @lastread

        -- If debugging, uncomment this to check values
        -- SELECT 'valid ptr?'=textvalid('pub_info.pr_info',
        --     @mytextptr), 'totalsize'=@totalsize,
        --     'lastread'=@lastread, 'readsize'=@readsize

        READTEXT pub_info.pr_info @mytextptr @lastread @readsize
        IF (@@ERROR <> 0)
            BREAK    -- Break out of loop if an error on read
        -- Change offset to last char read
        SELECT @lastread=@lastread + @readsize

    END
```

```
COMMIT TRAN
GO

IF EXISTS (SELECT * FROM tempdb.dbo.sysobjects
    WHERE name='##mytmptext' AND type='U')
    DROP TABLE ##mytmptext
GO

-- Intermediate temp table that READTEXT will use.
-- This table is truncated after each pub_id value, so the Identity
-- property sequences the rows for each publisher separately.
CREATE TABLE ##mytmptext
(
seq_no          int       IDENTITY,
text_chunk      text
)
GO

IF EXISTS (SELECT * FROM sysobjects
    WHERE name='newprinfo' AND type='U')
    DROP TABLE newprinfo
GO

-- This is the new table that pub_info is copied to.
-- It keeps chunks of text and is sequenced for each pub_id.
CREATE TABLE newprinfo
(
pub_id          char(4)     NOT NULL,
seq_no          int         NOT NULL,
text_chunk      varchar(200),
CONSTRAINT PK PRIMARY KEY (pub_id, seq_no)
)
GO

-- Having created the procedure get_text, iterate for each pub_id
-- value, temporarily sequencing them in the temp table. Once done
-- for a given pub_id, copy them to the new permanent table. Then
-- truncate the temp table for use with reseeded Identity for next
-- pub_id row.
DECLARE @pub_id char(4)
DECLARE iterate_prinfo CURSOR FOR
    SELECT pub_id FROM pub_info ORDER BY pub_id

OPEN iterate_prinfo
    FETCH NEXT FROM iterate_prinfo INTO @pub_id
```

(continued)

```
WHILE (@@FETCH_STATUS <> -1)
    BEGIN
    TRUNCATE TABLE ##mytmptext

    INSERT ##mytmptext
        EXEC get_text @pub_id

    INSERT newprinfo (pub_id, seq_no, text_chunk)
        SELECT @pub_id, SEQ_NO,
        CONVERT(varchar(200), TEXT_CHUNK)
        FROM ##mytmptext ORDER BY SEQ_NO

    FETCH NEXT FROM iterate_prinfo INTO @pub_id
    END

CLOSE iterate_prinfo
DEALLOCATE iterate_prinfo
GO

-- Simply verify contents of the new table
SELECT * FROM newprinfo ORDER BY pub_id,seq_no
GO
```

A subset of the output looks like the following:

```
pub_id   seq_no   text_chunk
------   ------   ------------------------------------------------
0736     1        This is sample text data for New Moon Books,
                  publisher 0736 in the pubs database. New Moon
                  Books is located in Boston, Massachusetts.
                  This is sample text data for New Moon Books,
                  publisher 0736 in
0736     2        the pubs database. New Moon Books is located in
                  Boston, Massachusetts.
                  This is sample text data for New Moon Books,
                  publisher 0736 in the pubs database. New Moon
                  Books is located in Boston, Massach
0736     3        usetts.
                  This is sample text data for New Moon Books,
                  publisher 0736 in the pubs database. New Moon
                  Books is located in Boston, Massachusetts.
                  This is sample text data for New Moon Books,
                  publish
```

Instantiating and Executing an Automation Object

SQL Server doesn't (yet) support user-defined functions (UDFs). It does let you write call-outs to extended procedures, which are your own DLLs written using the ODS API. Writing extended procedures isn't too difficult, but it's still too daunting a task for many programmers.

Many development tools, such as Microsoft Visual Basic 6 and Microsoft Visual C++ 6, make it easy to create Automation objects. Using Visual Basic, it can be as easy as calling one of the built-in functions and saving it as an Automation procedure. If you can do that, you can run that Automation procedure from SQL Server.

At the SQL Server Professional Developer Conference in September 1996, Ron Soukup demonstrated how to use Visual Basic to create an internal rate of return (IRR) function. For you non-MBAs, IRR is a financial term for the percentage return, based on a set of cash flows, that would be required for the cash flows to have a net present value (NPV) of 0. In other words, the IRR is the interest rate implicitly earned on an investment consisting of payments (negative values) and income (positive values) that occur at regular periods, such that total income equals total payments. Calculating IRR is not easy, and it requires an iterative solution—you start with a guess and move toward the solution. Visual Basic provides many nice financial functions; SQL Server does not. So it is natural to want to use one of these Visual Basic functions, and this is what the following example does. This solution assumes that you have previously used Visual Basic to create the object GET_IIR used here (which takes about three mouse clicks to do—you simply load the IRR function provided by the software).

```
-- VB_IRR.SQL
-- Use an OLE object named GET_IIR previously created from VB
-- as an internal rate of return (IRR) function
DECLARE
@pObj int,       -- Will be used as an OUTPUT parameter to hold
                 -- the object token when the object is created
@hr int          -- Return code

DECLARE @source varchar(30)      -- Output variable for source of an
                                 -- error
DECLARE @desc varchar(200)       -- Output variable for error string
DECLARE @IRR float               -- Output variable for IRR value
                                 -- (VB doesn't have a decimal)
```

(continued)

```
-- Instantiate the object
EXEC @hr=sp_OACreate "GetIRR.CGetIRR", @pObj OUT
    IF @hr <> 0 GOTO Err

-- Call the IRR method
-- Takes variable number of parameters as cash flows
EXEC @hr=sp_OAMethod @pObj, "GetIRR", @IRR OUT,
            -900, 100, 300, 300, 200, 200
    IF @hr <> 0 GOTO Err

-- Convert the float column to a decimal
SELECT "IRR"=CONVERT(DECIMAL(5, 3), @IRR)
GOTO Done

Err:
    RAISERROR ('Error in calculating Net Present Value. ', 16, 1)
    -- Get error info from OLE object
    EXEC sp_OAGetErrorInfo NULL, @source OUT, @desc OUT
    SELECT hr=CONVERT(BINARY(4), @hr), source=@source,
        description=@desc

Done:
    -- Destroy the object instance
    EXEC sp_OADestroy @pObj
```

Because most of the preceding code is template code, you can cut and paste it for use with another object (except for the call to *sp_OAMethod*, of course). Using Automation gives you a lot of flexibility. However, these procedures are not particularly fast when they are run from within the SQL Server context. Because of reentrance issues within SQL Server's threaded environment, they must be protected with mutexes, so only one such procedure runs at a given time and other executions of that same object are serialized. For many uses, though, this will suffice, and it fills a nice niche until true UDFs are available.

Here's another example using *sp_OAcreate* that doesn't require you to create any functions of your own. It uses a function that is already available in Microsoft Excel applications to check the spelling of individual words. A stored procedure is created to do spell checking within your SQL Server application, which uses the CheckSpelling method with *sp_OAMethod*.

```
USE master
GO
CREATE PROCEDURE SP_OA_SPELLER @TEST_VALUE VARCHAR(255) = "default"
AS

DECLARE @object int              -- Object variable
DECLARE @hr int                  -- Error variable
```

```
DECLARE @property varchar(255)        -- Error property variable
DECLARE @return int                   -- Return error value
DECLARE @output varchar(255)          -- Error output variable
DECLARE @source varchar(255)          -- Error source variable
DECLARE @description varchar(255)     -- Error description variable

SET nocount on                        -- Turn row counting off
-- Create an object
EXEC @hr = sp_OACreate 'Excel.Application', @object OUT
IF @hr <> 0
BEGIN
    PRINT 'OLE Automation Error Information'
    EXEC @hr = sp_OAGetErrorInfo @object, @source OUT, @description OUT
    IF @hr = 0
    BEGIN
        SELECT @output = '  Source: ' + @source
        PRINT @output
        SELECT @output = '  Description: ' + @description
        PRINT @output
    END
    ELSE BEGIN
        PRINT '  sp_OAGetErrorInfo failed.'
        RETURN
    END
END
-- Get a property by calling the spelling method
EXEC @hr = sp_OAMethod @object, 'CheckSpelling', @return OUTPUT, @TEST_VALUE
IF @hr <> 0
BEGIN
    PRINT 'OLE Automation Error Information'
    EXEC @hr = sp_OAGetErrorInfo @object, @source OUT, @description OUT
    IF @hr = 0
    BEGIN
        SELECT @output = '  Source: ' + @source
        PRINT @output
        SELECT @output = '  Description: ' + @description
        PRINT @output
    END
    ELSE BEGIN
        PRINT '  sp_OAGetErrorInfo failed.'
        RETURN
    END
END
ELSE BEGIN
    IF @return <> 0
```

```
                SELECT 'The word >>> ' + @TEST_VALUE + ' <<< was spelled correctly'
        ELSE
                SELECT 'The word >>> ' + @TEST_VALUE + ' <<< was misspelled'
END
-- Destroy the object
EXEC @hr = sp_OADestroy @object
IF @hr <> 0
BEGIN
    PRINT 'OLE Automation Error Information'
    EXEC @hr = sp_OAGetErrorInfo @object, @source OUT, @description OUT
    IF @hr = 0
    BEGIN
        SELECT @output = '  Source: ' + @source
        PRINT @output
        SELECT @output = '  Description: ' + @description
        PRINT @output
    END
    ELSE BEGIN
        PRINT '  sp_OAGetErrorInfo failed.'
        RETURN
    END
END
```

Note that most of this stored procedure code is error checking. The real work happens in just one place—the call to *sp_OAMethod*. The SQL stored procedure can be called by simply passing it a string to be spell checked.

```
EXEC sp_oa_speller 'mispell'

OUTPUT:
The word >>> mispell <<< was misspelled
```

Summary

This chapter covered how to implement referential actions via triggers, generate test data, and solve various types of statistical or time series problems. It showed standard SQL solutions as well as the use of SQL Server extensions. It also presented solutions to problems that are difficult to solve in SQL, such as expanding a hierarchy or pivoting a table. The chapter presented real-world solutions for use of the *xp_mail* functionality, as well as examples of running Automation objects from SQL Server. It also showed a solution for cracking a text column into multiple sequenced rows of *varchar* datatypes.

LOCKING

Locking is a crucial function of any multiple-user database system, including Microsoft SQL Server. As you know, SQL Server manages multiple users simultaneously and ensures that all transactions observe the properties of the specified isolation level. At the highest isolation level, Serializable, SQL Server must make the multiple-user system yield results that are indistinguishable from those of a single-user system. It does this by automatically locking data to prevent changes made by one user from unexpectedly affecting work being done by another user on the same database at the same time.

The Lock Manager

SQL Server can lock data using several different modes. For example, read operations acquire shared locks and write operations acquire exclusive locks. Update locks are acquired during the initial portion of an update operation when the data is read. The SQL Server lock manager acquires and releases these locks. It also manages compatibility between lock modes, resolves deadlocks, and escalates locks if necessary. It controls locks on tables, on the pages of a table, on index keys, and on individual rows of data. Locks can also be held on system data—data that's private to the database system, such as page headers and indexes.

The lock manager provides two separate locking systems. The first system affects all fully shared data and provides row locks, page locks, and table locks for tables, data pages, text pages, and leaf-level index pages. The second system is used internally for index concurrency control, controlling access to internal data structures, and retrieving individual rows of data pages. It uses latches, which are less resource intensive than locks and provide performance optimization. You could use full-blown locks for all locking, but because of their complexity, they would slow down the system if they were used for all internal needs. If you examine locks using the *sp_lock* system stored procedure or a similar mechanism that gets information from the *syslockinfo* table, you cannot see latches—you see only information about locks for fully shared data.

Another way to look at the difference between locks and latches is that locks ensure the *logical* consistency of the data and latches ensure the *physical* consistency. Latching happens when you place a row physically on a page or move data in other ways, such as compressing the space on a page. SQL Server must guarantee that this data movement can happen without interference.

The Lock Manager and Isolation Levels

SQL Server supports all four transaction isolation levels specified by ANSI and ISO: Serializable, Repeatable Read, Read Committed, and Read Uncommitted. (See Chapter 3 and Chapter 10 for details.) To achieve the Serializable isolation level, phantoms must be prevented because the transaction's behavior must be identical to what would have occurred had the transaction run on a single-user system. SQL Server provides serializability, which you can set using SET TRANSACTION ISOLATION LEVEL SERIALIZABLE. To support serializability, SQL Server locks index ranges using a special type of lock called a *key-range lock*. Such locks are held until the end of the transaction to prevent phantoms. If no index exists, the lock manager uses a table lock to guarantee serializability.

The lock manager provides fairly standard two-phase locking services. Although the names are similar, two-phase locking (2PL) and the two-phase commit (2PC) protocol are not directly related, other than by the obvious fact that 2PC must use 2PL services. In two-phase locking, a transaction has a "growing" phase, during which it acquires locks, and a "shrinking" phase, during which it releases locks. To achieve serializability, all acquired locks are held until the end of the transaction and then are dropped all at once.

For a lower isolation level, such as Committed Read, locks can be released sooner—when the use of the object is completed. For example, if a range of data is being queried in the table, there will probably be shared locks outstanding. With Committed Read isolation, a shared lock is released as soon as the scan moves off one piece of data and onto the next. Exclusive locks, on the other hand, are always held until the end of the transaction so that the transaction can be rolled back if necessary.

With Serializable or Repeatable Read isolation, shared locks must be held until the end of the transaction to guarantee that the data that was read will not change or that new rows meeting the criteria of the query cannot be added while the transaction is in progress. Like shared locks, latches are not tied to the boundaries of a transaction because they are used to provide mutual exclusion (mutex) functionality rather than to directly lock data. For example, during a row insert in a table with a clustered index, the nearby index page is latched to prevent other inserts from colliding. The latches are needed to provide mutual exclusion only during long periods of time (that is, periods with more than a few instruction cycles).

Spinlocks

For shorter-term needs, SQL Server achieves mutual exclusion using a latch, implemented with a spinlock. Spinlocks are used purely for mutual exclusion and never to lock user data. They are even more lightweight than latches, which are lighter than the full locks used for data and index leaf pages. The spinlock is the only place in SQL Server in which processor-specific assembly language is used. A spinlock is implemented in a few lines of assembly language specific to each processor type (such as *x86*/Pentium or Alpha). The requester of a spinlock repeats its request if the lock is not immediately available. (That is, the requestor "spins" on the lock until it is free.)

Spinlocks are often used as mutexes within SQL Server when a resource is usually not busy. If a resource is busy, the duration of a spinlock is short enough that retrying is better than waiting and then being rescheduled by Microsoft Windows NT, which results in context switching between threads. The savings in context switches more than offsets the cost of spinning, as long as you don't have to spin too long. Spinlocks are used for situations in which the wait for a resource is expected to be brief (or if no wait is expected).

Deadlocks

A deadlock occurs when two processes are waiting for a resource and neither process can advance because the other process prevents it from getting the resource. A true deadlock is a catch-22 in which, without intervention, neither process can ever progress. When a deadlock occurs, SQL Server intervenes automatically.

> **NOTE** A simple wait for a lock is not a deadlock. When the process that's holding the lock completes, the waiting process gets the lock. Lock waits are normal, expected, and necessary in multiple-user systems.

In SQL Server, two main types of deadlocks can occur: a cycle deadlock and a conversion deadlock. Figure 13-1 on page 731 shows an example of a cycle deadlock. Process A starts a transaction, acquires an exclusive table lock on the *authors* table, and requests an exclusive table lock on the *publishers* table. Simultaneously, process B starts a transaction, acquires an exclusive lock on the *publishers* table, and requests an exclusive lock on the *authors* table. The two processes become deadlocked—caught in a "deadly embrace." Each process holds a resource needed by the other process. Neither can progress, and, without intervention, both would be stuck in deadlock forever. You can actually generate the deadlock using the SQL Server Query Analyzer, as follows:

1. Open a query window, and change your database context to the *pubs* database. Execute the following batch for process A:

```
BEGIN TRAN
UPDATE authors SET contract = 0
GO
```

2. Open a second window, and execute this batch for process B:

```
BEGIN TRAN
UPDATE publishers SET city = 'Redmond', state = 'WA'
GO
```

3. Go back to the first window, and execute this update statement:

```
UPDATE publishers SET city = 'New Orleans', state = 'LA'
GO
```

At this point, the query should block. It is not deadlocked yet, however. It is waiting for a lock on the *publishers* table, and there is no reason to suspect that it won't eventually get that lock.

4. Go back to the second window, and execute this update statement:

```
BEGIN TRAN
UPDATE authors SET contract = 1
GO
```

At this point, a deadlock occurs. The first connection will never get its requested lock on the *publishers* table because the second connection will not give it up until it gets a lock on the *authors* table. Since the first connection already has the lock on the *authors* table, we have a deadlock. One of the processes received this error message (of course, the actual process ID reported will probably be different):

```
Server: Msg 1205, Level 13, State 1, Line 1
Your transaction (process ID #12) was deadlocked with another
process and has been chosen as the deadlock victim. Rerun your
transaction.
```

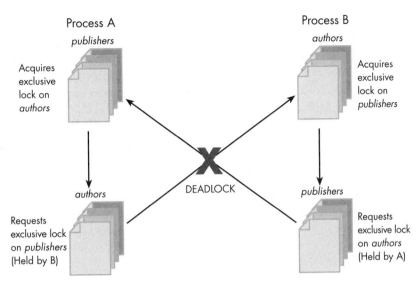

Figure 13-1.
A cycle deadlock resulting from each of two processes holding a resource needed by the other.

Figure 13-2 on the following page shows an example of a conversion deadlock. Process A and process B each hold a shared lock on the same page within a transaction. Each process wants to promote its shared lock to an exclusive lock but cannot do so because of the other process's lock. Again, intervention is required.

SQL Server automatically detects deadlocks and intervenes through the lock manager, which provides deadlock detection for regular locks. Latches are not involved in deadlock detection because SQL Server uses deadlock-proof algorithms when it acquires latches. When SQL Server detects a deadlock, it terminates one process's batch, rolling back the transaction and releasing all that process's locks to resolve the deadlock.

In SQL Server 7, a separate thread called LOCK_MONITOR checks the system for deadlocks every 5 seconds. The lock monitor also uses an internal counter called a *deadlock detection counter* to determine whether to check the system for deadlocks more often. The deadlock detection counter starts at a value of 3 and is reset to 3 if a deadlock occurs. If the LOCK_MONITOR thread finds no deadlocks when it checks at the end of its 5-second cycle, it decrements the deadlock detection counter. If the counter has a value greater than 0, the lock manager requests that the lock monitor also check all the locks for a deadlock cycle if a process requests a lock resource and is blocked. Thus, after 20 seconds of not finding any deadlocks, the deadlock detection counter is 0 and the lock manager stops requesting deadlock detection every time a process blocks on a lock. The deadlock detection counter stays at 0 most of the time and the checking for deadlocks happens only at the 5-second intervals of the lock monitor.

This LOCK_MONITOR thread checks for deadlocks by inspecting the list of waiting locks for any cycles, which indicate a circular relationship between processes holding locks and processes waiting for locks. Typically, the process chosen as the *victim* is the process that has just requested a lock and initiated the check for deadlocks. If a deadlock is encountered during the normal execution of the lock monitor, the first process whose termination will break the deadlock cycle is typically chosen as the victim. However, certain operations are marked as *golden,* or unkillable. For example, a process involved in rolling back a transaction cannot be chosen as a deadlock victim because the changes being rolled back could be left in an indeterminate state, causing data corruption.

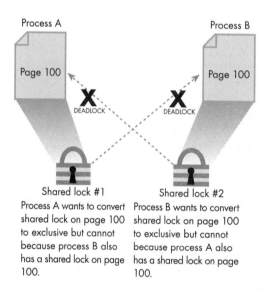

Figure 13-2.

A conversion deadlock resulting from two processes wanting to promote their locks on the same resource within a transaction.

In SQL Server 6.5, the lock manager checked for deadlocks every time a process began waiting for a lock resource. This provided rapid deadlock detection, but it wasted a lot of resources looking for deadlocks even in systems or situations in which they were rare. In earlier SQL Server releases, other algorithms were used to choose the deadlock victim (such as choosing the process that had consumed fewer CPU cycles). Those algorithms made a noble attempt at fairness, but they often resulted in another deadlock because yet another process might have been queued up for the resource that was part of the deadlock circular chain of lock requests. The result would be a chain reaction.

Using the SET DEADLOCK_PRIORITY LOW | NORMAL statement, you can make a process sacrifice itself as the victim if a deadlock is detected. If a process has a deadlock priority of LOW, it terminates when a deadlock is detected even if it is not the process that closed the loop. However, there is no counterpart SET option to set a deadlock priority to HIGH. As much as you might want your own processes to always come out the winner in a deadlock situation, this feature has not yet been implemented in SQL Server.

> **NOTE** The lightweight latches and spinlocks used internally do not have deadlock detection services. Instead, deadlocks on latches and spinlocks are avoided rather than resolved. Avoidance is achieved via strict programming guidelines used by the SQL Server development team. These lightweight locks must be acquired in a hierarchy, and a process must not have to wait for a regular lock while holding a latch or spinlock. For example, one coding rule is that a process holding a spinlock must never directly wait for a lock or call another service that might have to wait for a lock, and a request can never be made for a spinlock that is higher in the acquisition hierarchy. By establishing similar guidelines for your development team for the order in which SQL Server objects are accessed, you can go a long way toward avoiding deadlocks in the first place.

In the example in Figure 13-1, the cycle deadlock could have been avoided if the processes had decided on a protocol beforehand—for example, if they had decided to always access the *customer* table first and the *parts* table second. Then one of the processes would get the initial exclusive lock on the table being accessed first, and the other process would wait for the lock to be released. One process waiting for a lock is normal and natural. (Remember, waiting is not a deadlock.)

You should always try to have a standard protocol for the order in which processes access tables. If you know that the processes might need to update the row after reading it, they should initially request an update lock, not a shared lock. If both processes request an update lock rather than a shared lock, the process that is granted an update lock is assured that the lock can later be promoted to an exclusive lock. The other process requesting an update lock has to wait. The use of an update lock serializes the requests for an exclusive lock. Other processes needing only to read the data can still get their shared locks and read. Since the holder of the update lock is guaranteed an exclusive lock, the deadlock is avoided. We'll look in more detail at the compatibility of locks later in this chapter; additional information on deadlocks is presented in Chapter 14.

By the way, the time that your process holds locks should be minimal so other processes don't wait too long for locks to be released. Although you don't usually invoke locking directly, you can influence locking by keeping transactions as short as possible. For example, don't ask for user input in the middle of a transaction. Instead, get the input first and then quickly perform the transaction.

Locks and Memory

Locks are not on-disk structures—you won't find a lock field directly on a data page or a table header—because it would be too slow to do disk I/O for locking operations. Locks are internal memory structures—they consume part of the memory used for SQL Server. Each locked data resource (a row, index key, page, or table) requires 32 bytes of memory to keep track of the database, the type of lock, and the information describing the locked resource. Each process holding a lock also must have a lock owner block of 32 bytes. Sometimes a single transaction can have multiple lock owner blocks; a scrollable cursor sometimes uses several. Also, one lock can have many lock owner blocks, as in the case of a shared lock. Finally, each process waiting for a lock has a lock waiter block of another 32 bytes.

> **NOTE** In this context, we use the term "process" to refer to a SQL Server subtask. Every user connection is referred to as a process, as are the checkpoint manager, the lazywriter, the log writer, and the lock monitor. But these are only subtasks within SQL Server, not processes from the perspective of Windows NT, which considers the entire SQL Server engine to be a single process with multiple threads.

Lock Types for User Data

Now we'll examine four aspects of locking user data. First, we'll look at the mode of locking (the type of lock). We already mentioned shared, exclusive, and update locks, and we'll go into more detail about these modes as well as others. Next, we'll look at the granularity of the lock, which specifies how much data is covered by a single lock. This can be a row, a page, an index key, a range of index keys, an extent, or an entire table. The third aspect of locking is the duration of the lock. As mentioned earlier, some locks are released as soon as the data has been accessed and some locks are held until the transaction commits or rolls back. For example, cursor scroll locks are held until a new FETCH operation is executed. The fourth aspect of locking concerns the ownership of the lock (the scope of the lock). Locks can be owned by a session, a transaction, or a cursor.

Lock Modes

SQL Server uses several locking modes, including shared locks, exclusive locks, update locks, and intent locks.

Shared Locks

Shared locks are acquired automatically by SQL Server when data is read. Shared locks can be held on a table, a page, an index key, or an individual row. Many processes can hold shared locks on the same data, but no process can acquire an exclusive lock on data that has a shared lock on it (unless the process requesting the exclusive lock is the same process as the one holding the shared lock). Normally, shared locks are released as soon as the data has been read, but you can change this by using query hints or a different transaction isolation level.

Exclusive Locks

SQL Server automatically acquires exclusive locks on data when it is modified by an insert, update, or delete operation. Only one process at a time can hold an exclusive lock on a particular data resource; in fact, as we'll see when we discuss lock compatibility, no locks of any kind can be acquired by a process if another process has the requested data resource exclusively locked. Exclusive locks are held until the end of the transaction. This means that the changed data is normally not available to any other process until the current transaction commits or rolls back. Other processes can decide to read exclusively locked data by using query hints.

Update Locks

Update locks are really not a separate kind of lock; they are a hybrid between shared and exclusive locks. They are acquired when SQL Server executes a data modification operation but first needs to search the table to find the resource that will be modified. Using query hints, a process can specifically request update locks, and in that case they prevent the conversion deadlock situation presented in Figure 13-2.

Update locks provide compatibility with other current readers of data, allowing the process to later modify data with the assurance that the data hasn't been changed since it was last read. An update lock is not sufficient to allow you to change the data—all modifications require that the data resource being modified has an exclusive lock. An update lock acts as a serialization gate to queue future requests for the exclusive lock. (Many processes can hold shared locks for a resource, but only one process can hold an update lock.) As long as a process holds an update lock on a resource, no other process can acquire an update lock or an exclusive lock for that resource; instead, another process requesting an update or exclusive lock for the same resource must wait. The process holding the update lock can acquire an exclusive lock on that resource because the update lock prevents lock incompatibility with any other processes. You can think of update locks as "intent-to-update" locks, which is essentially the role they perform. Used alone, update locks are insufficient for updating data—an exclusive lock is still required for actual data modification. Serializing access for the exclusive lock lets you avoid conversion deadlocks.

Don't let the name fool you: update locks are not just for update operations. SQL Server uses update locks for any data modification operation that requires a search for the data prior to the actual modification. Such operations include qualified updates and deletes, as well as inserts into a table with a clustered index. In the latter case, SQL Server must first search the data (using the clustered index) to find the correct position at which to insert the new row. While SQL Server is only searching, it uses update locks to protect the data; only after it has found the correct location and begins inserting does it escalate the update lock to an exclusive lock.

Intent Locks

Intent locks are not really a separate mode of locking; they are a qualifier to the modes previously discussed. In other words, you can have *intent shared locks, intent exclusive locks,* and even *intent update locks.* Because SQL Server can acquire locks at different levels of granularity, a mechanism is needed to indicate that a component of a resource is already locked. For example, if one process tries to lock a table, SQL Server needs a way to determine whether a row (or a page) of that table is already locked. Intent locks serve this purpose. We'll discuss them in more detail when we look at lock granularity.

Special Lock Modes

SQL Server offers three additional lock modes: *schema stability locks, schema modification locks,* and *bulk update locks.* When queries are compiled, schema stability locks prevent other processes from acquiring schema modification locks, which are taken when a table's structure is being modified. A bulk update lock is acquired when the BULK INSERT command is executed or when the *bcp* utility is run to load data into a table. In addition, the copy operation must request this special lock by using the TABLOCK hint. Alternatively, the table can set the table option called *table lock on bulk load* to true, and then any bulk copy IN or BULK INSERT operation automatically requests a bulk update lock.

Another lock mode that you might notice is the SIX lock. This mode is never requested directly by the lock manager but is the result of a conversion. If a transaction is holding a shared (S) lock on a resource and later an IX lock is needed, the lock mode will be indicated as SIX. For example, suppose you are operating at the Repeatable Read transaction isolation level and you issue the following batch:

```
BEGIN TRAN
SELECT * FROM bigtable
UPDATE bigtable
    SET col = 0
    WHERE keycolumn = 100
```

Assuming the table is large, the SELECT statement will acquire a shared table lock. (If there are only a few rows in *bigtable*, SQL Server will acquire individual row or key locks.) The UPDATE statement will then acquire a single exclusive key lock to do the update of a single row, and the X lock at the key level will mean an IX lock at the page and table level. The table will then show SIX when viewed through *sp_lock*.

Table 13-1 shows most of the lock modes, as well as the abbreviations used in the output of *sp_lock*.

Abbreviation	Lock Mode	Description
S	Shared	Allows other processes to read but not change the locked resource.
X	Exclusive	Prevents another process from modifying or reading data in the locked resource (unless the process is set to the Read Uncommitted isolation level).
IS	Intent shared	Indicates that a component of this resource is locked with a shared lock. This lock can be acquired only at the table or page level.
IX	Intent exclusive	Indicates that a component of this resource is locked with an exclusive lock. This lock can be acquired only at the table or page level.
SIX	Shared with intent exclusive	Indicates that a resource holding a shared lock also has a component (a page or row) locked with an exclusive lock.
Sch-S	Schema stability	Indicates that a query using this table is being compiled.
Sch-M	Schema modification	Indicates that the structure of the table is being changed.
BU	Bulk update	Used when a bulk copy operation is copying data into a table and the TABLOCK hint is being applied (either manually or automatically).

Table 13-1.
SQL Server lock modes.

Lock Granularity

SQL Server can lock user data resources (not system resources, which are protected with latches) at the table, page, or row level. SQL Server also locks index keys and ranges of index keys. Figure 13-3 shows the possible lock levels in a table. Note that if the table has a clustered index, the data rows are at the leaf level of the clustered index, and they are locked with key locks instead of row locks.

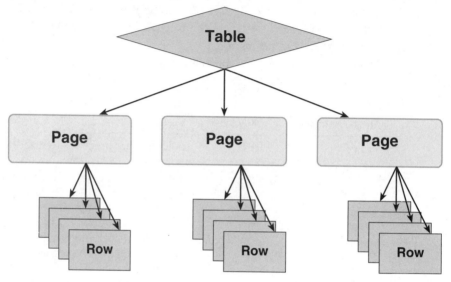

Figure 13-3.
Levels of granularity for SQL Server locks.

The *syslockinfo* table keeps track of each lock by storing the type of resource locked (such as a row, key, or page), the mode of the lock, and an identifier for the specific resource. When a process requests a lock, SQL Server compares the lock requested to the resources already listed in the *syslockinfo* table and looks for an exact match on the resource type and identifier. (The lock modes don't have to be the same to yield an exact match.) However, if one process has a row exclusively locked in the *authors* table, another process might try to get a lock on the entire *authors* table. Since these are two different resources, SQL Server does not find an exact match unless additional information is already stored in *syslockinfo*. This is what intent locks are for. The process that has the exclusive lock on a row of the *authors* table also has an intent exclusive lock on the page containing the row and another intent exclusive lock on the table containing the row. When the second process attempts to acquire the exclusive lock on the table, it finds a conflicting row already in the *syslockinfo* table on the same lock resource (the *authors* table).

Key Locks

SQL Server 7 supports two kinds of key locks, whose use depends on the isolation level of the current transaction. If the isolation level is Read Committed or Repeatable Read, SQL Server tries to lock the actual index keys accessed while processing the query. With a table that has a clustered index, the data rows are the leaf level of the index, and you will see key locks acquired. If the table is a heap, you might see key locks for the nonclustered indexes and row locks for the actual data.

If the isolation level is Serializable, the situation is special. We want to prevent phantoms, which means that if we have scanned a range of data within a transaction, we need to lock enough of the table to make sure that no one can insert a value into the range that was scanned. For example, we can issue the following query within an explicit transaction:

```
SELECT * FROM employees
WHERE salary BETWEEN 30000 AND 50000
```

Locks must be acquired to make sure that no new rows with salary values between 30000 and 50000 are inserted before the end of the transaction. Earlier versions of SQL Server guaranteed this by locking whole pages or even the entire table. In many cases, however, this was too restrictive—more data was locked than the actual WHERE clause indicated, resulting in unnecessary contention. SQL Server 7 uses key range locks, which are associated with a particular key value in an index and indicate that all values between that key and the previous one in the index are locked.

Suppose we have an index on the *lastname* field in the *employee* table. We are in TRANSACTION ISOLATION LEVEL SERIALIZABLE and we issue this SELECT statement:

```
SELECT *
FROM members
WHERE last_name BETWEEN 'Delaney' AND 'DuLaney'
```

If *Dallas*, *Donovan*, and *Duluth* are sequential leaf-level index keys in the table, the second two of these (*Donovan* and *Duluth*) acquire key range locks (although only one row, for *Donovan*, is returned in the result set). The key range locks prevent any inserts into the ranges ending with the two key range locks. No values greater than *Dallas* and less than or equal to *Donovan* can be inserted, and no values greater than *Donovan* and less than or equal to *Duluth* can be inserted. Note that the key range locks imply an open interval starting at the previous sequential key and a closed interval ending at the key on which the lock is placed. These two key range locks prevent anyone from inserting either *Delany* or *Delanie*, which are in the range specified in the WHERE clause. However, the key range locks would also prevent anyone from inserting *DeLancey* (which is greater than *Dallas* and less than *Donovan*) even though *DeLancey* is not in the query's specified range. Key range locks are not perfect, but they do give much greater concurrency than locking whole pages or tables, which was the only possibility in previous SQL Server versions.

Additional Lock Resources

Locking is also done on *extents*—units of disk space that are 64 KB in size (eight pages of 8 KB each). This kind of locking occurs automatically when a table or an index needs to grow and a new extent must be allocated. You can think of an extent lock as another type of special purpose latch, but it does show up in the output of the *sp_lock* procedure. Extents can have both shared extent and exclusive extent locks.

When you examine the output of *sp_lock*, notice that each process holds a lock on at least one database. These are always shared locks and are used by SQL Server for determining when a database is in use. Generally, you don't need to be concerned with extent or database locks, but you might see them if you are running *sp_lock* or perusing *syslockinfo*.

Identifying Lock Resources

When the lock manager tries to determine whether a requested lock can be granted, it checks the *syslockinfo* table to determine whether a matching lock with a conflicting lock mode already exists. It compares locks by looking at the database id (dbid), the object id (objid), the type of resource locked, and the description of the specific resource referenced by the lock. The lock manager knows nothing about the meaning of the resource description. It simply compares the strings identifying the lock resources to look for a match. If it finds a match, it knows that resource is already locked; it then uses the lock compatibility matrix to determine whether the current lock is compatible with the one being requested. Table 13-2 shows all the lock resources, the abbreviations used in the output of *sp_lock*, and the information used to define the actual resource locked.

Resource	Abbreviation	Resource Description	Example
Database	DB	None; the database is always indicated in the *dbid* column for every locked resource.	
Table	TAB	The table ID.	261575970 (Note that *sp_lock* shows the table ID in its own column rather than in the resource description column.)
Extent	EXT	File number:page number of the first page of the extent.	1:96
Page	PAG	File number:page number of the actual table or index page.	1:104
Index Key	KEY	A hashed value derived from all the key components and the locator. For a non-clustered index on a heap, where columns *c1* and *c2* are indexed, the hash would contain contributions from *c1*, *c2*, and the RID.	ac0001a10a00
Index Key Range	KEY	Same as Index Key.	ac0001a10a00
Row	RID	File number:page number: slot number of the actual row.	1:161:3

Table 13-2.
Lockable resources in SQL Server.

Note that key locks and key range locks have identical resource descriptions. When we look at some examples of output from the *sp_lock* procedure, you'll see that you can distinguish between these types of locks by the value in the lock mode column.

Lock Duration

The length of time that a lock is held depends primarily on the mode of the lock and the transaction isolation level in effect. The default isolation level for SQL Server is Read Committed. At this level, shared locks are released as soon as SQL Server has read and processed the locked data. An exclusive lock is held until the end of the transaction, whether it is committed or rolled back. An update lock is held until the end of the transaction unless it has been promoted to an exclusive lock, in which case the exclusive lock remains for the duration of the transaction. If your transaction isolation level is Repeatable Read or Serializable, shared locks have the same duration as exclusive locks. That is, they are not released until the transaction is over.

In addition to changing your transaction isolation level, you can control the lock duration by using query hints. We'll discuss query hints for locking and for other purposes in Chapter 14.

Lock Ownership

Lock duration can also be affected by the lock ownership. There are three types of lock owners: transactions, cursors, and sessions. These are available through the *req_ownertype* column in the *syslockinfo* table. (This information is not visible through the *sp_lock* stored procedure.) A *req_ownertype* value of 1 indicates that the lock is owned by transaction, and its duration is as discussed above. Most of our locking discussion, in fact, deals with locks owned by a transaction. A cursor lock has a *req_ownertype* value of 2. If a cursor is opened using a locking mode of SCROLL_LOCKS, a cursor lock is held on every row fetched until the next row is fetched or the cursor is closed. Even if the transaction commits before the next fetch, the cursor lock is not released. Locks owned by a session have a *req_ownertype* value of 3. A session lock is one taken on behalf of a process that is outside the scope of a transaction. The most common example is a database lock, as discussed earlier. A process acquires a session lock on the database when it issues the USE database command, and that lock isn't released until another USE command is issued or until the process is disconnected.

Viewing Locks

To see the locks currently outstanding in the system as well as those that are being waited for, examine the *syslockinfo* system table or execute the system stored procedure *sp_lock*. (The *syslockinfo* table is not really a system table. It is not maintained on disk because locks are not maintained on disk. Rather, it is materialized in table format based on the lock manager's current accounting of locks each time *syslockinfo* is queried.) Another way to watch locking activity is with the excellent graphical representation of locking status provided by SQL Server Enterprise Manager. (Even those of you who think GUIs are for wimps can appreciate SQL Server Enterprise Manager's view of locking.)

The following examples show what each of the lock types and modes discussed earlier look like when reported by the *sp_lock* procedure. Note that the call to the *sp_lock* procedure is preceded by the keyword EXECUTE, which is required when the call to a stored procedure is not the first thing in a batch. Note also that the *sp_lock* procedure is given an argument of @@spid, which refers to the process ID of the current process (the server process ID). We don't want to see all the locks in the system, only those held by our process.

Example 1: SELECT with Default Isolation Level

SQL BATCH

```
USE PUBS
SET TRANSACTION ISOLATION LEVEL READ COMMITTED
BEGIN TRAN
SELECT * FROM authors
WHERE au_lname = 'Ringer'
EXEC sp_lock @@spid
COMMIT TRAN
```

OUTPUT OF *sp_lock*

spid	dbid	ObjId	IndId	Type	Resource	Mode	Status
11	1	0	0	DB		S	GRANT
11	2	0	0	DB		S	GRANT
11	5	0	0	DB		S	GRANT
11	1	117575457	0	TAB		IS	GRANT

Every time we run the *sp_lock* procedure, we acquire locks in the master database to generate the output to be displayed. If you look at the *dbid* column in the output, you'll see locks in database 1 (*master*) and database 2 (*tempdb*). We won't show those locks in the output for the rest of the examples. If we ignore the locks in *master* and *tempdb*, we'll see that the only lock in the *pubs* database is the session-level database lock. No locks on the *authors* table are held at this point because the batch was doing only select operations that acquired shared locks. By default, the shared locks are released as soon as the data has been read, so by the time *sp_lock* is executed, the locks are no longer held.

Example 2: SELECT with Repeatable Read Isolation Level

SQL BATCH

```
USE PUBS
SET TRANSACTION ISOLATION LEVEL REPEATABLE READ
BEGIN TRAN
SELECT * FROM authors
WHERE au_lname = 'Ringer'
EXEC sp_lock @@spid
COMMIT TRAN
```

OUTPUT OF *sp_lock*

spid	dbid	ObjId	IndId	Type	Resource	Mode	Status
11	5	117575457	2	PAG	1:123	IS	GRANT
11	5	117575457	1	PAG	1:96	IS	GRANT
11	5	0	0	DB		S	GRANT
11	5	117575457	2	KEY	(d5f329a7dcdc)	S	GRANT
11	5	117575457	2	KEY	(4c62318cf11f)	S	GRANT
11	5	117575457	1	KEY	(3dc1b1ecb5be)	S	GRANT
11	5	117575457	1	KEY	(37fdb5efbcbe)	S	GRANT
11	5	117575457	0	TAB		IS	GRANT

Because the *authors* table has a clustered index, the rows of data are all index rows in the leaf level. The locks on the individual rows are marked as key locks instead of row locks. There are also key locks at the leaf level of the nonclustered index on the table. You can tell the two indexes apart by the value in the *IndId* field: the data rows have an *IndId* value of 1, and the nonclustered index rows have an *IndId* value of 2. Because the transaction isolation level is Repeatable Read, the shared locks are held until the transaction is finished. Note that the two rows and two index rows have shared (S) locks, and the data and index pages, as well as the table itself, have intent shared (IS) locks.

Example 3: SELECT with Serializable Isolation Level

SQL BATCH

```
USE PUBS
SET TRANSACTION ISOLATION LEVEL SERIALIZABLE
BEGIN TRAN
SELECT * FROM authors
WHERE au_lname = 'Ringer'
```

```
EXEC sp_lock @@spid
COMMIT TRAN
```

OUTPUT OF *sp_lock*

spid	dbid	ObjId	IndId	Type	Resource	Mode	Status
11	5	117575457	2	PAG	1:123	IS	GRANT
11	5	117575457	1	PAG	1:96	IS	GRANT
11	5	0	0	DB		S	GRANT
11	5	117575457	2	KEY	(d5f329a7dcdc)	IS-S	GRANT
11	5	117575457	2	KEY	(4c62318cf11f)	IS-S	GRANT
11	5	117575457	1	KEY	(3dc1b1ecb5be)	IS-S	GRANT
11	5	117575457	1	KEY	(37fdb5efbcbe)	IS-S	GRANT
11	5	117575457	2	KEY	(d5968ed3b619)	IS-S	GRANT
11	5	117575457	0	TAB		IS	GRANT

The locks held with the Serializable isolation level are almost identical to those held with the Repeatable Read isolation level. The main difference is in the mode of the lock. The two-part mode IS-S indicates a key range lock in addition to the lock on the key itself. The first part (IS) is the lock on the range of keys between (and including) the key holding the lock and the previous key in the index. The key range locks prevent other transactions from inserting new rows into the table that meet the condition of this query; that is, no new rows with a last name of *Ringer* can be inserted. There are three key locks in the nonclustered index on *au_lname* (*IndId* = 2) because three different ranges need to be locked. SQL Server must lock the range from the key preceding the first *Ringer* in the table up to the first *Ringer*, it must lock the range between the two instances of *Ringer*, and it must lock the range from the second *Ringer* to the next key in the index. (So actually nothing between *Ringer* and the previous key, *Panteley*, and nothing between *Ringer* and the next key, *Smith*, could be inserted into the table. For example, we could not insert an author with the last name *Pattin* or *Singh*.)

Example 4: Update Operations

SQL BATCH

```
USE PUBS
SET TRANSACTION ISOLATION LEVEL READ COMMITTED
BEGIN TRAN
UPDATE authors
SET contract = 0
WHERE au_lname = 'Ringer'
EXEC sp_lock @@spid
COMMIT TRAN
```

OUTPUT OF *sp_lock*

spid	dbid	ObjId	IndId	Type	Resource	Mode	Status
11	5	117575457	1	PAG	1:96	IX	GRANT
11	5	0	0	DB		S	GRANT
11	5	117575457	1	KEY	(3dc1b1ecb5be)	X	GRANT
11	5	117575457	1	KEY	(37fdb5efbcbe)	X	GRANT
11	5	117575457	0	TAB		IX	GRANT

The two rows in the leaf level of the clustered index are locked with X locks. The page and the table are then locked with IX locks. We discussed earlier that SQL Server actually acquires update locks while it looks for the rows to update. However, these are escalated to X locks when the actual update is done, and by the time the *sp_lock* procedure is run, the update locks are gone. Unless you actually force update locks with a query hint, you might never see them in the output of *sp_lock*.

Example 5: Creating a Table

SQL BATCH

```
USE PUBS
SET TRANSACTION ISOLATION LEVEL READ COMMITTED
BEGIN TRAN
SELECT *
INTO newTitles
FROM titles
WHERE price < 5
EXEC sp_lock @@spid
COMMIT TRAN
```

OUTPUT OF *sp_lock*

spid	dbid	ObjId	IndId	Type	Resource	Mode	Status
7	5	0	0	DB	[BULK-OP-LOG]	S	GRANT
7	5	0	0	DB		S	GRANT
7	5	0	0	DB	[BULK-OP-DB]	S	GRANT
7	5	1	0	TAB		IX	GRANT
7	5	3	0	TAB		IX	GRANT
7	5	2	0	TAB		IX	GRANT
7	5	0	0	PAG	1:199	X	GRANT

7	5	0	0	PAG	1:198	X	GRANT
7	5	0	0	PAG	1:197	X	GRANT
7	5	0	0	PAG	1:196	X	GRANT
7	5	0	0	PAG	1:195	X	GRANT
7	5	0	0	PAG	1:194	X	GRANT
7	5	0	0	PAG	1:193	X	GRANT
7	5	0	0	EXT	1:192	X	GRANT
7	5	0	0	PAG	1:166	X	GRANT
7	5	0	0	PAG	1:165	X	GRANT
7	5	3	2	KEY	(0693cc100b75)	X	GRANT
7	5	3	2	KEY	(3790f0cf7f55)	X	GRANT
7	5	2	1	KEY	(0257f4438466)	X	GRANT
7	5	3	2	KEY	(242ad7320fa2)	X	GRANT
7	5	3	2	KEY	(e794778e397a)	X	GRANT
7	5	1061578820	0	TAB		Sch-M	GRANT
7	5	1	2	KEY	(269dc7159f33)	X	GRANT
7	5	3	1	KEY	(024e7788d08c)	X	GRANT
7	5	3	1	KEY	(02567f88d08c)	X	GRANT

(etc.)

Very few of these locks are actually acquired on elements of the new table. In the *ObjId* column, notice that most of the objects have an ID of less than 100, which means that they are system tables. As the new *newTitles* table is built, SQL Server acquires locks on *sysobjects* and *syscolumns* to record information about this new table. Also notice the schema modification (Sch-M) lock on the new table as well as extent (EXT) locks. While the table is built, the extents are not marked as belonging to the table; you can see that the *ObjId* is 0. In the output above, the extent ID is shown as 1:192. This means that page 192 in file 1 is the first page of the extent. You can also see that the subsequent seven pages (193–199) in this extent are all exclusively locked while the table is being created.

Example 6: Row Locks

SQL BATCH

```
USE PUBS
SET TRANSACTION ISOLATION LEVEL READ COMMITTED
BEGIN TRAN
UPDATE newTitles
SET price = 3.99
WHERE type = 'business'
EXEC sp_lock @@spid
ROLLBACK TRAN
```

OUTPUT OF *sp_lock*

spid	dbid	ObjId	IndId	Type	Resource	Mode	Status
13	1	0	0	DB		S	GRANT
13	2	0	0	DB		S	GRANT
13	5	0	0	DB		S	GRANT
13	5	1077578877	0	RID	1:184:0	X	GRANT
13	5	1077578877	0	PAG	1:184	IX	GRANT
13	5	1077578877	0	TAB		IX	GRANT
13	1	117575457	0	TAB		IS	GRANT

There are no indexes on the *newTitles* table, so the lock on the actual row meeting our criterion is an exclusive (X) lock on the row (RID). As expected, IX locks are taken on the page and the table.

Lock Compatibility

Two locks are compatible if one lock can be granted while another lock on the same object by a different process is outstanding. On the other hand, if a lock requested for an object is not compatible with a lock currently being held, the requesting connection must wait for the lock. For example, if a shared page lock exists on a page, another process requesting a shared page lock for the same page is granted the lock because the two lock types are compatible. But a process that requests an exclusive lock for the same page is not granted the lock because an exclusive lock is not compatible with the shared lock already held. Table 13-3 summarizes the compatibility of locks in SQL Server.

Lock compatibility comes into play between locks on different resources, such as table locks and page locks. A table and a page obviously represent an implicit hierarchy since a table is made up of multiple pages. If an exclusive page lock is held on one page of a table, another process cannot get even a shared table lock for that table. This hierarchy is protected using intent locks. A process acquiring an exclusive page lock, update page lock, or intent exclusive page lock first acquires an intent exclusive lock on the table. This intent exclusive table lock prevents another process from acquiring the shared table lock on that table. (Remember that intent exclusive and shared locks are not compatible.)

Requested Mode	Existing Granted Mode								
	IS	S	U	IX	SIX	X	Sch-S	Sch-M	BU
IS	Yes	Yes	Yes	Yes	Yes	No	Yes	No	No
S	Yes	Yes	Yes	No	No	No	Yes	No	No
U	Yes	Yes	No	No	No	No	Yes	No	No
IX	Yes	No	No	Yes	No	No	Yes	No	No
SIX	Yes	No	No	No	No	No	Yes	No	No
X	No	No	No	No	No	No	Yes	No	No
Sch-S	Yes	Yes	Yes	Yes	Yes	Yes	Yes	No	Yes
Sch-M	No	No	No	No	No	No	No	No	No
BU	No	No	No	No	No	No	Yes	No	Yes

Table 13-3.
Yes *indicates that the lock held is compatible with the lock requested;* No *means that they're not compatible.*

Similarly, a process acquiring a shared row lock must first acquire an intent shared lock for the table, which prevents another process from acquiring an exclusive table lock. Or if the exclusive table lock already exists, the intent shared lock is not granted and the shared page lock has to wait until the exclusive table lock is released. Without intent locks, process A can lock a page in a table with an exclusive page lock and process B can place an exclusive table lock on the same table and hence think that it has a right to modify the entire table, including the page that process A has exclusively locked.

NOTE At the risk of stating the obvious, lock compatibility is an issue only when the locks affect the same object. For example, two or more processes can each hold exclusive page locks simultaneously as long as the locks are on different pages or different tables.

Even if two locks are compatible, the requester of the second lock might still have to wait if an incompatible lock is waiting. For example, suppose that process A holds a shared page lock. Process B requests an exclusive page lock and must wait because the shared page lock and the exclusive page lock are not compatible. Process C requests a shared page lock that is compatible with the shared page already outstanding to process A. However, the shared page lock cannot be immediately granted. Process C must wait for its shared page lock because process B is ahead of it in the lock queue with a request (exclusive page) that is not compatible.

By examining the compatibility of locks not only to those processes granted but also to those processes waiting, SQL Server prevents *lock starvation,* which occurs when requests for shared locks keep overlapping so that the request for the exclusive lock can never be granted.

Bound Connections

Remember that the issue of lock contention applies only between different processes (also called *connections*). A process holding locks on a resource does not lock itself from the resource—only other processes are prevented access. But any other process (or connection to SQL Server) can actually execute as the same application and user. It is common for applications to have more than one connection to SQL Server. Every such connection is treated as an entirely different SQL Server process, and by default no sharing of the "lock space" occurs between connections, even if they belong to the same user and the same application. (Again, in this context, "process" means a SQL Server subtask, not a Windows NT process.)

However, two different connections can share a lock space and hence not lock each other out. This capability is known as a *bound connection.* With a bound connection, the first connection asks SQL Server to give out its bind token. The bind token is passed by the application (using a client-side global variable, a shared memory, or another method) for use in subsequent connections. The bind token acts as a "magic cookie" so that those other connections can share the lock space of the original connection. Locks held by bound connections do not lock each other. (The *sp_getbindtoken* and *sp_bindsession* system stored procedures get and use the bind token.)

Bound connections are especially useful if you are writing an extended stored procedure, which is a function written in your own DLL, and that extended stored procedure needs to call back into the database to do some work.

Without a bound connection, the extended stored procedure collides with its own calling process's locks. When multiple processes share a lock space and a transaction space by using bound connections, a COMMIT or ROLLBACK affects all the participating connections.

Here's an example of using bound connections between two different windows in SQL Server's Query Analyzer. Since we don't have a controlling application to declare and store the bind token in a client-side variable, we have to actually copy it from the first session and paste it into the second. So, in your first query window, you execute this batch:

```
DECLARE @token varchar(30)
EXEC sp_getbindtoken @token
SELECT @token
GO
```

This should return something like the following:

```
----------------------------------------
dPe---5---.?j0U<_WP?1HMK-3/D8;@1
```

Normally, you wouldn't have to look at this messy string; your application would just store it and pass it on without your ever having to see it. But for a quick example using the Query Analyzer, it's necessary to actually see the value. You use your keyboard or mouse to select the token string that you received and use it in the following batch in a second Query Analyzer window:

```
EXEC sp_bindsession 'dPe---5---.?j0U<_WP?1HMK-3/D8;@1'
GO
```

Now go back to the first query window and begin a transaction that locks some data. You can use something like this:

```
USE pubs
BEGIN TRAN
UPDATE titles
SET price = $100
GO
```

This should exclusively lock every row in the *titles* table. Now go to the second query window and select from the locked table:

```
SELECT title_id, price FROM titles
GO
```

You should be able to see all the $100 prices in the *titles* table, just as if you were part of the same connection as the first query. Besides sharing lock space, the bound connection also shares transaction space. You can execute a ROLLBACK TRAN in the second window even though the first one began the transaction. If the first connection tries to then issue a ROLLBACK TRAN, it gets this message:

```
Server: Msg 3903, Level 16, State 1, Line 1
The ROLLBACK TRANSACTION request has no corresponding BEGIN
TRANSACTION.
```

Row-Level vs. Page-Level Locking

The debate over whether row-level locking is better than page-level locking or vice versa has been one of those near-religious wars and warrants a few comments here. Although some people would have you believe that one is always better, it's not really that simple.

Prior to SQL Server version 7, the smallest unit of data that SQL Server could lock was a page. Even though many people argued that this was unacceptable and it was impossible to maintain good concurrency while locking entire pages, many large and powerful applications were written and deployed using only page-level locking. If they were well designed and tuned, concurrency was not an issue, and some of these applications supported hundreds of active user connections with acceptable response times and throughput. However, with the change in page size from 2 KB to 8 KB for SQL Server 7, the issue has become more critical. Locking an entire page means locking four times as much data as in previous versions. SQL Server 7 implements full row-level locking, so any potential problems due to lower concurrency with the larger page size should not be an issue. However, locking isn't free. Considerable resources are required to manage locks. Recall that a lock is an in-memory structure of about 32 bytes, with another 32 bytes for each process holding the lock and each process waiting for the lock. If you need a lock for every row and you scan a million rows, you need more than 30 MB of RAM just to hold locks for that one process.

Beyond the memory consumption issues, locking is a fairly processing-intensive operation. Managing locks requires substantial bookkeeping. (Recall that, internally, SQL Server uses a lightweight mutex called a spinlock to guard resources, and it uses latches—also lighter than full-blown locks—to protect non-leaf-level index pages. These performance optimizations avoid the overhead of full locking.) If a page of data contains 50 rows of data, all of which will be used, it is obviously more efficient to issue and manage one lock on the page than to manage 50. That's the obvious benefit of page locking—a reduction in the number of lock structures that must exist and be managed.

If two different processes each need to update a few separate rows of data and some of the rows needed by each process happen to exist on the same page, one process must wait until the page locks of the other process are released. If, in this case, you use row-level locking instead of page-level locking, the other process does not have to wait. The finer granularity of the locks means that no conflict occurs in the first place because each process is concerned with different rows. That's the obvious benefit of row-level locking. Which of these obvious benefits wins? Well, the decision isn't clear cut, and it depends on the application and the data. Each type of locking can be shown to be superior for different types of applications and usage.

The stored procedure *sp_indexoption* lets you manually control the unit of locking within an index. It also lets you disallow page locks or row locks within an index. Since these options are available only for indexes, there is no way to control the locking within the data pages of a heap. (But remember that if a table has a clustered index, the data pages are part of the index and are affected by the *sp_indexoption* setting.) The index options are set for each table or index individually. Two options, AllowRowLocks and AllowPageLocks, are both set to TRUE initially for every table and index. If both of these options are set to FALSE for a table, only full table locks are allowed.

Lock Escalation

SQL Server automatically escalates row, key, or page locks to coarser table locks as appropriate. This escalation protects system resources—it prevents the system from using too much memory for keeping track of locks—and increases efficiency. For example, after a query acquires many row locks, the lock level can be escalated to a table lock. If every row in a table must be visited, it probably makes more sense to acquire and hold a single table lock than to hold many row locks. A single table lock is acquired and the many row locks are released. This escalation to a table lock reduces locking overhead and keeps the system from running out of locks. Recall that a lock is a memory structure. Because there is a finite amount of memory, there must be a finite number of locks. You can configure SQL Server for the maximum number of locks your system is expected to need, but the default is for the *locks* configuration parameter to be tuned automatically by SQL Server.

As mentioned earlier, SQL Server determines at runtime whether to lock rows, pages, or the entire table. The locking of rows (or keys) is heavily favored if at all possible. The type of locking chosen is based on the number of rows and pages to be scanned, the number of rows on a page, the isolation level in effect, the update activity going on, the number of users on the system needing memory for their own purposes, and so on. Perhaps the best of both worlds would be to "deescalate" locks—that is, to start at a coarser level of locking and change to more granular locks if and only if there is a conflict for the coarse lock.

For example, suppose you have two processes that each update a few rows. Process A might start with page locking. If no other process requests a lock of the same page, no contention occurs, so the additional overhead of doing locking for every row does not happen. But if process B asks for a lock on one of the pages locked by process A, those held locks can be deescalated to row locks for only the rows that are actually needed. After failing to obtain the page-level lock, process B might then try to get a lock on only the specific rows it needs rather than on the entire page. If the rows needed are not the same between the processes, there is no contention and each gets its own row locks. But if there is no contention for rows, the reduced overhead of locking only at the page level can be realized. You can begin the locking at an even coarser level, such as at the table level, and deescalate as needed to a page, and then further to a row, and conceptually even further to perhaps a column level, although this might be stretching the model.

A deescalation locking strategy is being considered for future releases. As of version 7, SQL Server uses predominantly row-level locking. As mentioned, sometimes page locks or a table lock are chosen initially, or if too many individual row locks are acquired, SQL Server dynamically escalates those to a table lock. In version 7, lock escalation converts many individual row or page locks to a table lock; escalation never converts row locks to page locks. Lock deescalation is not implemented.

Locking Hints and Trace Flags

Just as you can specify hints on queries to direct the optimizer to choose a certain index or strategy in its query plan, you can specify hints for locking. For example, if you know that your query will scan so many rows that its page locks will escalate to table locks, you can direct the query to use table locks in the first place, which is more efficient. We'll look at locking hints and locking contention issues in detail in Chapter 14.

For now, armed with the knowledge of locking you've gained here, you can observe the locking activity of your system to understand how and when locks occur. Trace flag 1204 provides detailed information about deadlocks, and this information can help you understand why locks are occurring and how to change the order of access to objects to reduce them. Trace flag 1200 provides detailed locking information as every request for a lock is made. (But its output is voluminous.) You'll see details about these trace flags in Chapter 14.

Summary

SQL Server lets you manage multiple users simultaneously and ensure that transactions observe the properties of the chosen isolation level. Locking guards data and the internal resources that make it possible for a multiple-user system to operate like a single-user system. In this chapter, we looked at the locking mechanisms in SQL Server, including full locking for data and leaf-level index pages and lightweight locking mechanisms for internally used resources.

We also looked at the types and modes of locks as well as lock compatibility and lock escalation. It is important to understand the issues of lock compatibility if you want to design and implement high-concurrency applications. We also looked at deadlocks and discussed ways to avoid them.

PERFORMANCE AND TUNING

4141 417b000c 015858

585858 5858585

585858585858585

4304030603030

0xc2b000

xc2b000   pg=0 nextobjid=

revpg=0 objid=4

d=0 freeoff=30

0410x17b000c 015858

OPTIMIZING QUERY PERFORMANCE

If you want to end up with a poorly performing application or a complete project failure, you should wait until the end of the project to deal with performance concerns. If, however, you want your application to be the best it can be, you must consider performance throughout the development cycle. In fact, you must consider performance before you even write your first line of code.

Every chapter of this book has included some information on performance. If you've turned directly to this chapter in hopes of finding the secret to improving your lackluster application, you'll be disappointed. We can offer only guidelines for you to keep in mind, along with some pointers that refer back to earlier information or to other helpful materials.

Microsoft SQL Server systems can be brilliantly fast with well-designed, well-implemented applications. It can support workloads of the type and size that no one dreamed possible back in 1988 when SQL Server first became available. But with a poorly planned or poorly implemented system, SQL Server can perform horribly. Statements like "SQL Server is slow" are not uncommon. (Nor are such statements about other database products.) Anytime you hear this from someone who has deployed a production application, your first thought should be that the person has dropped the ball somewhere along the line—or that SQL Server is unsuitable for the task at hand. (SQL Server can handle most systems, but some are still beyond its reach.)

If this is the first chapter you've turned to, please stop and go back at least to Chapter 3. All of the chapters from Chapter 3 to this one are relevant to performance issues. You might also revisit Chapter 11, which is about cursors, and Chapter 13, on locking. A thorough understanding of cursors and locking is a prerequisite for understanding the material in this chapter.

The Development Team

A software project's success depends on the experience and skill of the staff developing it. Your second SQL Server development project will be better than your first, no matter how smart you are, so don't make your first project one that will have thousands of concurrent users, manage tens of gigabytes of data, and replicate data to 10 other servers. If you tackle such an extensive project your first time out, you'll probably fail (or at least finish late and over budget). And although it's useful to have experience working with other systems and environments, you can't expect successful SQL Server development on the first try.

The smartest companies start with a small, less-than-mission-critical system before moving many applications over to SQL Server. If management will not allow you the luxury of working on a "practice" system, you should at least try to augment your team with an experienced consultant or two. Look for someone who, at a minimum, is a Microsoft Certified Systems Engineer (MCSE) who has taken both SQL Server exams for electives. In 1999, Microsoft is introducing a Microsoft Certified DBA (MCDBA) certification, which would indicate a similar level of qualification. This book, while it provides much useful information, can't replace other training. And skills such as database design, which transcend SQL Server specifically, are essential for a project's success.

> **SEE ALSO** The Microsoft course called "Performance Tuning and Optimization of Microsoft SQL Server" is worthwhile. Microsoft develops this course with input from the SQL Server development group. The course is available at Microsoft Certified Technical Education Centers (CTECs). For more information, go to http://www.microsoft.com/ctec.

Application and Database Design

The biggest performance gains come from changes to the application and database design. You might change your configuration settings and add heftier hardware and be thrilled when performance doubles, but changes to the application can often result in even larger performance increases. There are as many approaches to software development as there are pages in this book. No single approach is the right approach—yours must be tailored to the size of the project, your team, and the skill level of the team members.

Take a look at the list of suggestions on the facing page for planning and implementing good performance in your system. We'll explain these items in detail in this chapter and in Chapter 15.

- Develop expertise on your development team.
- Understand that there is no substitute for solid application and database design.
- State performance requirements for peak, not average, use.
- Consider perceived response time for interactive systems.
- Prototype, benchmark, and test throughout the development cycle.
- Create useful indexes.
- Choose appropriate hardware.
- Use cursors judiciously.
- Use stored procedures almost always.
- Minimize network round-trips.
- Understand concurrency and consistency tradeoffs.
- Analyze and resolve locking (blocking) problems.
- Analyze and resolve deadlock problems.
- Monitor and tune queries using SQL Server Profiler.
- Monitor system using Performance Monitor.
- Review and adjust Windows NT settings.
- Review and adjust SQL Server configuration settings.
- Make only one change at a time, and measure its effect.
- Do periodic database maintenance.

Normalize Your Database

We'll assume that if you're reading this book, you understand the concept of normalization and terms such as *third normal form*. (If you don't, see Candace Fleming and Barbara Vonhalle's *Handbook of Relational Database Design* and Michael Hernandez's *Database Design for Mere Mortals*. A plethora of other books about database design and normalization are also available.)

A normalized database eliminates functional dependencies in the data so that updating the database is easy and efficient. But querying from that database might require a lot of joins between tables, so common sense comes into play. If the most important and time-critical function your system must perform is fast querying, it often makes sense to back off from a normalized design in favor of one that has some functional dependencies. (That is, the design is not in third normal form or higher.) Think of normalization as typically being good for updating but potentially bad for querying. Start with a normalized design and then look at all the demands that will be placed on the system.

> **NOTE** There really isn't a binary concept of being "normalized" or "not normalized." There are only degrees of normalization. It is common to refer to a database that is at least in third normal form as "normalized" and to refer to a database at a lower level of normalization as "unnormalized" or "denormalized." To keep the discussion simple, we'll use the terms in that way, as imprecise as that might be. (The terms "unnormalized" and "denormalized" have slightly different meanings. An *unnormalized* database is one that has never been normalized. A *denormalized* database is one that was normalized at some point, but for specific performance-related reasons the design was backed down from the normalized version. Our apologies to those who make a living doing entity-relationship diagrams and are horrified by the loose use of these terms.)

If you understand the data elements you need to record and you understand data modeling, producing a normalized design is not difficult. But it might take some time to learn about the way a business operates. If you already understand the underlying processes to be modeled and know how to do data modeling, the mechanics of producing a normalized database design are quite straightforward.

Once you produce a normalized design, which you can also think of as the *logical design,* you must decide if you can implement the design nearly "as is" or if you need to modify it to fit your performance characteristics. A lot of people have trouble with this. Rather than try to articulate specific performance characteristics, they generalize and strive for "as fast as possible" or "as many users as we can handle." Although goals can be difficult to articulate precisely, you should at least set relative goals. You should understand the tradeoffs between update and query performance, for example. If a salesperson must call up all of a customer's records while the customer is waiting on the phone, that action should be completed within a few seconds. Or if you want to run a bunch of batch processes and reports for your manufacturing operation each night and you have a window of four hours in which to do it, you have a pretty clear objective that must be met.

Evaluate Your Critical Transactions

One thing that you should do immediately is look at your critical transactions—that is, transactions whose performance will make or break the system. (In this context, we use the term "transaction" loosely; it means any operation on the database.) Which tables and joins will be required for your critical transactions? Will data access be straightforward or complicated?

For example, if it is imperative that a given query have less than a 2-second response time but your normalized design would require a seven-way join, you should look at what denormalizing would cost. If tables are properly indexed, the query is well qualified, the search parameters are quite selective, and not a lot of data needs to be returned, the quick response might be possible. But you should note any seven-way joins and consider other alternatives. (You should probably look for alternatives any time you get beyond a four-way join.)

In our example, you might decide to carry a little redundant information in a couple of tables to make it just a three-way join. You'll incur some extra overhead to correctly update the redundant data in multiple places, but if update activity is infrequent or less important and the query performance is essential, altering your design is probably worth the cost. Or you might decide that rather than compute a customer's balance by retrieving a large amount of data, you can simply maintain summary values. You can use triggers to update the values incrementally when a customer's records change. (For example, you can take the old value and add to or average it but not compute the whole thing from scratch each time.) When you need the customer balance, it is available, already computed. You incur extra update overhead for the trigger to keep the value up-to-date, and you need a small amount of additional storage.

Proper indexes are extremely important for getting the query performance you need. But you must face query-vs.-update tradeoffs similar to those described earlier because indexes speed up retrieval but slow down updating. Chapter 8 explains the extra work required when your updates require index maintenance. (Because of the way that nonclustered indexes are stored and updated, the overhead of index maintenance is not nearly as severe in SQL Server 7 as in previous versions of the product.) You might want to lay out your critical transactions and look for the likely problems early on. If you can keep joins on critical transactions to four tables or less and make them simple equijoins on indexed columns, you'll be in good shape.

None of these considerations are new, nor are they specific to SQL Server. Back in the mainframe days, there was a technique known as "completing a CRUD chart." CRUD stands for Create-Retrieve-Update-Delete. In SQL, this would translate as ISUD—Insert-Select-Update-Delete. Conceptually, CRUD is pretty simple. You draw a matrix with critical transactions on the vertical axis and tables with their fields on the horizontal axis. The matrix gets very big very quickly, so creating it in Microsoft Excel or in your favorite spreadsheet program can be helpful. For each transaction, you note which fields must be accessed and how they will be accessed, and you note the access as any combination of I, S, U, or D, as appropriate. You make the granularity at the field level so you can gain insight into what information you want in each table. This is the information you need if you decide to carry some fields redundantly in other tables to reduce the number of joins required. Of course, some transactions require many tables to be accessed, so be sure to note whether the tables are accessed sequentially or via a join. You should also indicate the frequency and time of day that a transaction runs, its expected performance, and how critical it is that the transaction meet the performance metric.

How far you carry this exercise is up to you. You should at least go far enough to see where the potential hot spots are for your critical transactions. Some people try to think of every transaction in the system, but that's nearly impossible. And what's more, it doesn't matter: only a few critical transactions need special care so they don't lead to problems. (You shouldn't worry much about such things as noncritical reports that run only during off-hours.) For example, if you have to do frequent select operations simultaneously on the tables that are being updated the most, you might be concerned about locking conflicts. You need to consider what transaction isolation level to use and whether your query can live with Read Uncommitted and not conflict with the update activity.

If you are doing complex joins or expensive aggregate functions—SUM(), AVG(), and so on—for common or critical queries, you should explore techniques such as the following and you should understand the tradeoffs between query performance improvement and the cost to your update processes:

- Add logically redundant columns to reduce the number of tables to be joined.

- Use triggers to maintain aggregate summary data, such as customer balances, the highest value, and so forth. Such aggregates can usually be incrementally computed quickly. The update performance impact can be slight, but the query performance improvement can be dramatic.

Keep Table Row Lengths and Keys Compact

When you create tables, you must understand the tradeoffs of using variable-length columns. (See Chapter 6.) As a general rule, data with substantial variance in the actual storage length is appropriate for variable-length columns. Also remember that the more compact the row length, the more rows will fit on a given page. Hence, a single I/O operation with compact rows is more efficient than an I/O operation with longer row lengths—it returns more rows and the data cache allows more rows to fit into a given amount of memory.

As with tables, when you create keys you should try to make the primary key field compact because it frequently occurs as a foreign key in other tables. If no naturally compact primary key exists, you might consider using an *identity* or *uniqueidentifier* column as a surrogate. And recall that if the primary key is a composite of multiple columns, the columns are indexed in the order that they are declared to the key. The order of the columns in the key can greatly affect how selective, and hence how useful, the index is.

Your clustered key should also be as compact as possible. If your clustered key is also your primary key (which is the default when you declare a PRIMARY KEY constraint), you might already have made it compact for the reason mentioned above. There are additional considerations for your clustered key because SQL Server automatically keeps the clustered key in all nonclustered indexes, along with the corresponding nonclustered key. For example, if your clustered index is on *zipcode* and you have a nonclustered index on *employee_id*, every row in the nonclustered index stores the corresponding *zipcode* value along with the *employee_id* value. We discussed the structure of indexes in Chapters 3 and 6, and we'll look at it again later in this chapter when we look at how to choose the best indexes.

Occasionally, a table will have some columns that are infrequently used or modified and some that are very hot. In such cases, it can make sense to break the single table into two tables; you can join them back together later. This is kind of the reverse of denormalization as you commonly think of it. In this case, you do not carry redundant information to reduce the number of tables; instead, you increase the number of tables to more than are logically called for to put the hot columns into a separate, narrower table. With the more compact row length, you get more rows per page and potentially a higher cache-hit ratio. As with any deviation from the normalized model, however, you should do this only if you have good reason. After you complete a CRUD chart analysis, you might see that while your customer table is frequently accessed, 99 percent of the time this access occurs just to find out a customer's credit balance. You might decide to maintain this balance via a trigger rather than by recomputing it each time the query occurs. Information such as customer addresses, phone numbers, e-mail addresses, and so on are large fields that make the table have a wide row length. But not all that information is needed for critical transactions—only the customer balance is needed. In this case, splitting the table into two might result in the difference between fitting, say, 150 rows on a page instead of only 2 or 3 rows. A more narrow table means a greater likelihood that the customer balance can be read from cache rather than by requiring physical I/O.

Planning for Peak Usage

People often ask questions like, "Can SQL Server handle our system? We do a million transactions a day." To answer this question, you have to know exactly what transactions they have in mind. You also need to know the system's peak usage. If a million transactions a day are nicely spread out over 24 hours, that's less than 12 transactions per second. In general, a 12-TPS (transactions-per-second) system would be adequate. But if 90 percent of the million transactions come between 2 P.M. and 3 P.M., it's a very different situation. You'll have rates of about 275 TPS during that hour and probably peaks of more than 350 TPS. You can use benchmarks, such as Debit-Credit, in which SQL Server performs over 1500 TPS, but all transactions are different. It is meaningless to refer to transactions per second in SQL Server or any other system without also talking about the types of transactions. This is precisely the reason that standardized tests are available from the Transaction Processing Council for comparing database performance.

Regardless of the specific transactions, though, you must design and build your system to handle peak usage. In the case above, the important consideration is peak usage, which determines whether you should target your system to a volume of 350 TPS for unevenly distributed usage or to only 12 TPS with usage spread out evenly. (Most systems experience peaks, and daily usage is not so nicely spread out.)

Perceived Response Time for Interactive Systems

Systems are often built and measured without the appropriate performance goals in mind. When measuring query performance, for example, most designers tend to measure the time that it takes for the query to complete. By default, this is how SQL Server decides to cost query performance. But this might not be the way your users perceive system performance. To users, performance is often measured by the amount of time that passes between pressing the Enter key and getting some data. As a program designer, you can use this to your advantage. For example, you can make your application begin displaying results as soon as the first few rows are returned; if many rows will appear in the result set, you don't have to wait until they are all processed. You can use such approaches to dramatically improve the user's perception of the system's responsiveness. Even though the time required to get the last row might be about the same with both approaches, the time it takes to get the first row can be different—and the *perceived* difference can translate into the success or failure of the project.

By default, SQL Server optimizes a query based on the total estimated cost to process the query to completion. Recall from Chapter 3 that if a significant percentage of the rows in a table must be retrieved, it is better to scan the entire table than to use a nonclustered index to drive the retrieval. (A clustered index, of course, would be ideal because the data would be physically ordered already. The discussion here pertains only to the performance tradeoff of scan-and-sort vs. using a nonclustered index.)

Retrieving a page using the nonclustered index requires traversing the B-tree to get the address of a data page or the clustering key and then retrieving that page (by using the RID to directly access it or traversing the clustered index to find the data page) and then traversing the nonclustered B-tree again to get the location information for the next data page and retrieving it...and so on. Many data pages are read many times each, so the total number of page accesses can be more than the total number of pages in the table. If your data and the corresponding nonclustered index are not highly selective, SQL Server usually decides not to use that nonclustered index. That is, if the index is not expected to eliminate more than about 90 percent of the pages from consideration, it is typically more efficient to simply scan the table than to do all the extra I/O of reading B-trees for both the nonclustered and clustered indexes as well as the data pages. And by following the index, each data page must frequently be accessed multiple times (once for every row pointed to by the index). Subsequent reads are likely to be from cache, not from physical I/O, but this is still much more costly than simply reading the page once for all the rows it contains (as happens in a scan).

Scanning the table is the strategy SQL Server chooses in many cases, even if a nonclustered index is available that could be used to drive the query, and even if it would eliminate a sort to return the rows based on an ORDER BY clause. A scan strategy can be much less costly in terms of total I/O and time. However, the choice of a full scan is based on SQL Server's estimate of how long it would take the query to complete in its entirety, not how long it would take for the first row to be returned. If an index exists with a key that matches the ORDER BY clause of the query and the index is used to drive the query execution, there is no need to sort the data to match the ORDER BY clause (because it's already ordered that way). The first row is returned faster by SQL Server chasing the index even though the last row returned might take much longer than if the table were simply scanned and the chosen rows sorted.

In more concrete terms, let's say that a query that returns many rows takes 1 minute to complete using the scan-and-sort strategy and 2 minutes using a nonclustered index. With the scan-and-sort strategy, the user doesn't see the first row until all the processing is almost done—for this example, about 1 minute. But with the index strategy, the user sees the first row within a subsecond—the time it takes to do, say, five I/O operations (read two levels of the nonclustered index, two levels of the clustered index, and then the data page). Scan-and-sort is faster in total time, but the nonclustered index is faster in returning the first row.

SQL Server provides a query hint called FAST that lets SQL Server know that having the first *n* rows returned quickly is more important than the total time, which would be the normal way query plans get costed. Later in this chapter, we'll look at some techniques for speeding up slow queries and discuss when it is appropriate to use the query hint. For now, you should understand the issues of *response time* (the time needed to get the first row) vs. *throughput* (the time needed to get all rows) when you think about your performance goals. Typically, highly interactive systems should be designed for best response time, and batch-oriented systems should be designed for best throughput.

Prototyping, Benchmarking, and Testing

As you make changes to your application design or hardware configuration, you should measure the effects of these changes. A simple benchmark test to measure differences is a tremendous asset. The benchmark system should correlate well with the expected performance of the real system, but it should be relatively easy to run. If you have a development "acceptance test suite" that you run before checking in any significant changes, you should add the benchmark to that test suite.

> **TIP** You should measure performance with at least a proxy test; otherwise, you're setting yourself up for failure. Optimism without data to back it up is usually misguided.

Your benchmark doesn't have to be sophisticated initially. You can first create your database and populate it with a nontrivial amount of data—thousands of rows at a minimum. The data can be randomly generated, although the more representative you can make the data the better. Ideally, you should use data from the existing system, if there is one. For example, if a particular part represents 80 percent of your orders, you shouldn't make all your test data randomly dispersed. Any differences in the selectivity of indexes between your real data and the test data will probably cause significant differences in the execution plans you choose. You should also be sure that you have data in related tables if you use FOREIGN KEY constraints. As we explained earlier in this book, the enforcement of FOREIGN KEY constraints requires that those related tables (either referenced or referencing) be accessed if you are modifying data in a column that is participating in the constraint. So the execution plan is sometimes considerably more complicated due to the constraints than might be apparent, and a plethora of constraints can result in a system that has no simple operations.

As a rule of thumb, you should start with at least enough data so the difference between selecting a single row based on its primary key by using an index is dramatically faster than selecting such a row using a table scan. (This assumes that the table in production will be large enough to reflect that difference.) Remember that the system will perform much differently depending on whether I/O operations are physical or from the cache. So don't base your conclusions on a system that is getting high cache-hit ratios unless you have enough data to be confident that this behavior also will be true for your production system. In addition, keep in mind that running the same test multiple times might yield increasingly short response times. If you are testing on a dedicated machine, no other processes will be using SQL Server's memory, and the data you read in from the disk the first time will already be in cache for subsequent tests.

TIP If you want to run your tests repeatedly under the same conditions, use the command DBCC DROPCLEANBUFFERS after each test run to remove all data from memory.

Early in the development process, you should identify areas of lock contention between transactions and any specific queries or transactions that take a long time to run. The SQL Server Profiler, discussed in Chapter 15, can be a wonderful tool for tracking down your long-running queries. And if table scans will be a drain on the production system, you should have enough data early on so that the drain is apparent when you scan. If you can run with several thousand rows of data without lock contention problems and with good response time on queries, you're in a good position to proceed with a successful development cycle. Of course, you must continue to monitor and make adjustments as you ramp up to the actual system and add more realistic amounts of data and simultaneous users. And, of course, your system test should take place on an ongoing basis before you deploy your application. It's not a one-time thing that you do the night before you go live with a new system.

> **TIP** Before you roll out your production system, you should be able to conduct system tests with the same volumes of data and usage that the real system will have when it goes live. Crossing your fingers and hoping is not good enough. Two tools in the Microsoft BackOffice Resource Kit might prove useful for this purpose. The *filltabl* utility populates a specified table with any number of rows of random data. A load simulator (*sqlls*) lets you run one or more SQL scripts with up to 64 operating system threads executing each script. These and other tools from the BackOffice Resource Kit are written for the previous version of SQL Server, but they will work with SQL Server 7.

Obviously, if your smallish prototype is exhibiting lock contention problems or the queries do not perform well within your desired goals, it's unlikely that your real system will perform as desired. Run the stored procedures that constitute your critical transactions. You can use a simple tool like OSQL.EXE to dispatch them. First run each query or transaction alone—time it in isolation and check the execution plans (*SET SHOWPLAN_TEXT ON*). Then run multiple sessions to simulate multiple users, either by manually firing off multiple OSQL commands or by using the SQL Load Simulator mentioned above. (A bit later, we'll look at how to analyze and improve a slow-running query.)

Also, based on your CRUD chart analysis (or on any other analysis of critical transactions), you should identify tasks that will run at the same time as your critical transactions. Add these tasks to your testing routine to determine whether they will lead to contention when they run simultaneously with your critical transactions. For example, suppose *proc_take_orders* is your critical transaction. When it runs, some reports and customer status inquiries will also run. You should run some mixture of these types of processes when you analyze *proc_take_orders*. This will help you identify potential lock contention issues or other resource issues, such as high CPU usage or low cache.

You might also want to use the SQL Server benchmark kit, which is available on the companion CD as well as at the Microsoft Web site (http://www.microsoft.com/sql). Although the transaction in the kit will probably not be directly applicable to your situation, the benchmark framework provides the infrastructure you need to launch and coordinate multiple client tasks simultaneously to time their work for throughput and response time. The kit also provides some sample code for populating the test database. Other custom benchmarking tools are available from other companies (such as Dynameasure from Bluecurve, Inc. at http://www.bluecurve.com.)

A Rant on Development Methodologies

How much you spec, how you spec, when you start coding, and the role of prototyping are all matters on which there is no consensus; there is no one right answer. What's right for one team or project might be wrong for another. You must remember that the point of development is to ship products or deploy applications. Your ultimate purpose is not to produce specs and design documents.

The spec exists to clearly articulate and document how a module or system should work. It ensures that the developer thinks through the approach before writing code. It is also vitally important to others who come in later and are new to the system. While writing the design document, the developer might have to write some quick prototype code to help think through an issue. Or the developer should at least write some pseudocode and include it as part of the document.

Any development task that will take more than a couple of days to implement deserves a simple design document. Ideally, such a document should be at most 15 pages, and often about 3 succinct pages are ideal for even a complex component. The best design documents can be read in one sitting, and the reader should come away understanding clearly how the system will be built. The document should be reviewed by other developers before coding begins. This is best done in a positive, informal atmosphere in which others can contribute ideas. And, of course, in a healthy environment, developers are continually bouncing ideas off their peers.

The document should assume that the reader already knows *why* a module or component is needed. The document provides the *how*. Too many specs have 40 pages describing the market need for something or why a potential product would be really cool, and then they have 1 page that says, in essence, "We'll figure it out when we code it up."

No one can write a perfect spec up front. Prototyping the spec in an iterative fashion works far better. Areas that are clear don't need a prototype; use prototypes for areas fraught with risk, for your critical transactions, and for critical areas of the system in which multiple approaches are possible or reasonable. For the tricky stuff that you can't describe or predict a best performance, prototypes provide enormous benefits.

A useful prototype can be "quick and dirty." If you don't worry about all the failure cases and every conceivable state in which something can exist, useful prototype code can often be produced in 5 percent of the time it takes to create production-caliber code (in which you must worry about those things). However, the production code might be 10 times better because you have recognized and corrected deficiencies early on. You'll either junk the prototype code or use it for the skeleton of the real system. Prototyping lets you learn and prove or disprove ideas, and then you can update the spec based on what you learn. And if you're selling your ideas to management or customers, your prototype can be useful to demonstrate proof of your concept.

As we mentioned before, every nontrivial development task deserves a brief design document. You need enough documentation to lay out the framework and system architecture and to detail how pieces fit together. But at the detailed levels, it's better to simply comment the source code liberally while you write and modify it. External design documentation rarely gets updated in a timely manner, so it quickly becomes useless. No one has much use for worthless comments (like adding *incrementing i* before the statement *i++* in C). Rather, comments should describe the approach and intent of each routine, the expected inputs and outputs, and any side effects that might occur by changing the code. Explain operations when their purpose is not obvious. Don't assume that your readers will immediately grasp all the subtleties. And when you change something after the fact, add a comment about what you changed, when you changed it, and why. A module should be commented well enough so that testers or technical writers can gain a good understanding of what is going on just from reading the comments, even if they are not skilled programmers.

Creating Useful Indexes

Creating useful indexes is one of the most important tasks you can do to achieve good performance. Indexes can dramatically speed up data retrieval and selection, but they are a drag on data modification because along with changes to the data, the index entries must also be maintained and those changes must be logged. The key to creating useful indexes is understanding the uses of the data, the types and frequencies of queries performed, and how queries can use indexes to help SQL Server find your data quickly. A CRUD chart or similar analysis technique can be invaluable in this effort. You might want to quickly review the difference between clustered and nonclustered indexes because the difference is crucial in deciding what kind of index to create.

Clustered and nonclustered indexes are similar at the upper (node) levels—both are organized as B-trees. Index rows above the leaf level contain index key values and pointers to pages the next level down. Each row keeps track of the first key value on the page it points to. Figure 14-1 shows an abstract view of an index node for an index on a customer's last name. The entry *Johnson* indicates page 1:200 (file 1, page 200), which is at the next level of the index. Since *Johnson* and *Jones* are consecutive entries, all the entries on page 1:200 have values between *Johnson* (inclusive) and *Jones* (exclusive).

Key	Page Number
Jackson	1:147
Jensen	1:210
Johnson	1:200
Jones	1:186
Juniper	1:202

Figure 14-1.
An index node page.

The leaf, or bottom, level of the index is where clustered and nonclustered indexes differ. For both kinds of indexes, the leaf level contains every key value in the table on which the index is built, and those keys are in sorted order. In a clustered index, the leaf level is the data level, so of course every key value is present. This means that the data in a table is sorted in order of the clustered index. In a nonclustered index, the leaf level is separate from the data. In addition to the key values, the index rows contain a bookmark indicating where to find the actual data. If the table has a clustered index, the bookmark is the clustered index key that corresponds to the nonclustered key in the row. (If the clustered key is composite, all parts of the key are included.)

Remember that clustered indexes are guaranteed to be unique in SQL Server 7; if you don't declare them as unique, SQL Server adds a uniqueifier to every duplicate key to turn the index into a unique composite index. If our index on last name is a nonclustered index and the clustered index on the table is the zip code, a leaf-level index page might look something like Figure 14-2 on the following page. The number in parentheses after the zip code is the uniqueifier and appears only when there are duplicate zip codes.

Key	Locator
Johnson	98004(1)
Johnson	06801(3)
Johnston	70118
Johnstone	33801(2)
Johnstone	95014(2)
Johnstone	60013
Jonas	80863(2)
Jonas	37027
Jonasson	22033(4)

Figure 14-2.

A leaf-level index page.

Choose the Clustered Index Carefully

Clustered indexes are extremely useful for range queries (for example, *WHERE sales_quantity BETWEEN 500 and 1000*) and for queries in which the data must be ordered to match the clustering key. Only one clustered index can exist per table, since it defines the physical ordering of the data for that table. Since you can have only one clustered index per table, you should choose it carefully based on the most critical retrieval operations. Because of the clustered index's role in managing space within the table, nearly every table should have one. And if a table has only one index, it should probably be clustered.

If a table is declared with a primary key (which is advisable), by default the primary key columns form the clustered index. Again, this is because almost every table should have a clustered index, and if the table has only one index, it should probably be clustered. But if your table has several indexes, some other index might better serve as the clustered index. This is often true when you do single-row retrieval by primary key. A nonclustered, unique index works nearly as well in this case and still enforces the primary key's uniqueness. So save your clustered index for something that will benefit more from it by adding the keyword NONCLUSTERED when you declare the PRIMARY KEY constraint.

Make Nonclustered Indexes Highly Selective

A query using an index on a large table is often dramatically faster than a query doing a table scan. But this is not always true, and table scans are not all inherently evil. Nonclustered index retrieval means reading B-tree entries to determine the data page that is pointed to and then retrieving the page, going back to the B-tree, retrieving another data page, and so on until many data pages are read over and over. (Subsequent retrievals can be from cache.) With a table scan, the pages are read only once. If the index does not disqualify a large percentage of the rows, it is cheaper to simply scan the data pages, reading every page exactly once.

The query optimizer greatly favors clustered indexes over nonclustered indexes, because in scanning a clustered index the system is already scanning the data pages. Once it is at the leaf of the index, the system has gotten the data as well. So there is no need to read the B-tree, read the data page, and so on. This is why nonclustered indexes must be able to eliminate a large percentage of rows to be useful (that is, they must be highly selective), whereas clustered indexes are useful even with less selectivity.

Indexing on columns used in the WHERE clause of frequent or critical queries is often a big win, but this usually depends on how selective the index is likely to be. For example, if a query has the clause *WHERE last_name = 'Stankowski'*, an index on *last_name* is likely to be very useful; it can probably eliminate 99.9 percent of the rows from consideration. On the other hand, a nonclustered index will probably not be useful on a clause of *WHERE sex = 'M'* because it eliminates only about half of the rows from consideration; the repeated steps needed to read the B-tree entries just to read the data require far more I/O operations than simply making one single scan through all the data. So nonclustered indexes are typically not useful on columns that do not have a wide dispersion of values.

Think of selectivity as the percentage of qualifying rows in the table (qualifying rows/total rows). If the ratio of qualifying rows to total rows is low, the index is highly selective and is most useful. If the index is used, it can eliminate most of the rows in the table from consideration and greatly reduce the work that must be performed. If the ratio of qualifying rows to total rows is high, the index has poor selectivity and will not be useful. A nonclustered index is most useful when the ratio is around 5 percent or less—that is, if the index can eliminate

95 percent of the rows from consideration. If the index has less than 5 percent selectivity, it probably will not be used; either a different index will be chosen or the table will be scanned. Recall that each index has a histogram of sampled data values for the index key, which the optimizer uses to estimate whether the index is selective enough to be useful to the query.

Tailor Indexes to Critical Transactions

Indexes speed data retrieval at the cost of additional work for data modification. To determine a reasonable number of indexes, you must consider the frequency of updates vs. retrievals and the relative importance of the competing types of work. If your system is almost purely a decision-support system (DSS) with little update activity, it makes sense to have as many indexes as will be useful to the queries being issued. A DSS might reasonably have a dozen or more indexes on a single table. If you have a predominantly online transaction processing (OLTP) application, you need relatively few indexes on a table—probably just a couple carefully chosen ones.

Look for opportunities to achieve index coverage in queries, but don't get carried away. An index "covers" the query if it has all the data values needed as part of the index key. For example, if you have a query such as *SELECT emp_name, emp_sex FROM employee WHERE emp_name LIKE 'Sm%'* and you have a nonclustered index on *emp_name*, it might make sense to append the *emp_sex* column to the index key as well. Then the index will still be useful for the selection, but it will already have the value for *emp_sex*. The optimizer won't need to read the data page for the row to get the *emp_sex* value; the optimizer is smart enough to simply get the value from the B-tree key. The *emp_sex* column is probably a *char(1)*, so the column doesn't add greatly to the key length, and this is good.

Every nonclustered index is a covering index if all you are interested in is the key column of the index. For example, if you have a nonclustered index on first name, it covers all these queries:

- Select all the first names that begin with *K*.

- Find the first name that occurs most often.

- Determine whether the table contains the name *Melissa*.

In addition, if the table also has a clustered index, every nonclustered index includes the clustering key. So it can also cover any queries that need the clustered key value in addition to the nonclustered key. For example, if our nonclustered index is on the first name and the table has a clustered index on the last name, the following queries can all be satisfied by accessing only leaf pages of the B-tree:

- Select Tibor's last name.

- Determine whether any duplicate first and last name combinations exist.

- Find the most common first name for people with the last name *Wong*.

You can go too far and add all types of fields to the index. The net effect is that the index becomes a virtual copy of the table, just organized differently. Far fewer index entries fit on a page, I/O increases, cache efficiency is reduced, and much more disk space is required. The covered queries technique can improve performance in some cases, but you should use it with discretion.

A unique index (whether nonclustered or clustered) offers the greatest selectivity (that is, only one row can match), so it is most useful for queries that are intended to return exactly one row. Nonclustered indexes are great for single-row accesses via the PRIMARY KEY or UNIQUE constraint values in the WHERE clause.

Indexes are also important for data modifications, not just for queries. They can speed data retrieval for selecting rows, and they can speed data retrieval needed to find the rows that must be modified. In fact, if no useful index for such operations exists, the only alternative is for SQL Server to scan the table to look for qualifying rows. Update or delete operations on only one row are common; you should do these operations using the primary key (or other UNIQUE constraint index) values to be assured that there is a useful index to that row and no others.

A need to update indexed columns can affect the update strategy chosen. For example, to update a column that is part of the key of the clustered index on a table, you must process the update as a delete followed by an insert rather than as an update-in-place. When you decide which columns to index, especially which columns to make part of the clustered index, consider the effects the index will have on the update method used. (Review the discussion of updates in Chapter 8.)

Pay Attention to Column Order

At the risk of stating the obvious, an index can be useful to a query only if the criteria of the query match the columns that are leftmost in the index key. For example, if an index has a composite key of *last_name,first_name*, that index is useful for a query such as *WHERE last_name = 'Smith'* or *WHERE last_name = 'Smith' AND first_name = 'John'*. But it is not useful for a query such as *WHERE first_name = 'John'*. Think of using the index like a phone book. You use a phone book as an index on last name to find the corresponding phone number. But the standard phone book is useless if you know only a person's first name because the first name might be located on any page.

Put the most selective columns leftmost in the key of nonclustered indexes. For example, an index on *emp_name,emp_sex* is useful for a clause such as *WHERE emp_name = 'Smith' AND emp_sex = 'M'*. But if the index is defined as *emp_sex,emp_name*, it isn't useful for most retrievals. The leftmost key, *emp_sex*, cannot rule out enough rows to make the index useful. Be especially aware of this when it comes to indexes that are built to enforce a PRIMARY KEY or UNIQUE constraint defined on multiple columns. The index is built in the order that the columns are defined for the constraint. So you should adjust the order of the columns in the constraint to make the index most useful to queries; doing so will not affect its role in enforcing uniqueness.

Index Columns Used in Joins

Index columns are frequently used to join tables. When you create a PRIMARY KEY or UNIQUE constraint, an index is automatically created for you. But no index is automatically created for the referencing columns in a FOREIGN KEY constraint. Such columns are frequently used to join tables, so they are almost always among the most likely ones on which to create an index. If your primary key and foreign key columns are not naturally compact, consider creating a surrogate key using an identity column (or a similar technique). As with row length for tables, if you can keep your index keys compact, you can fit many more keys on a given page, which results in less physical I/O and better cache efficiency. And if you can join tables based on integer values such as an identity, you avoid having to do relatively expensive character-by-character comparisons. Ideally, columns used to join tables are integer columns—fast and compact.

Join density is the average number of rows in one table that match a row in the table it is being joined to. You can also think of density as the average number of duplicates for an index key. A column with a unique index has the lowest possible density (there can be no duplicates) and is therefore extremely selective for the join. If a column being joined has a large number of duplicates, it has a high density and is not very selective for joins.

Joins are frequently processed as nested loops. For example, if while joining the *orders* table with *order_items* the system starts with the *orders* table (the outer table) and then for each qualifying order row, the inner table is searched for corresponding rows. Think of the join being processed as, "Given a specific row in the outer table, go find all corresponding rows in the inner table." If you think of joins in this way, you'll realize that it is important to have a useful index on the inner table, which is the one being searched for a specific value. For the most common type of join, an equijoin that looks for equal values in columns of two tables, the optimizer automatically decides which is the inner table and which is the outer table of a join. The table order that you specify for the join doesn't matter in the equijoin case. However, the order for outer joins must match the semantics of the query, so the resulting order is dependent on the order specified. We'll talk about join strategies later in this chapter.

Create or Drop Indexes as Needed

If you create indexes but find that they aren't used, you should drop them. Unused indexes slow data modification without helping retrieval. You can determine whether indexes are used by watching the plans produced via the SHOWPLAN options; this is easy if you are analyzing a large system with many tables and indexes. There might be thousands of queries that can be run and no way to run and analyze the SHOWPLAN output for all of them. An alternative is to use the Index Tuning Wizard to generate a report of current usage patterns. The wizard is designed to determine which new indexes to build, but you can use it simply as a reporting tool to find out what is happening in your current system. We'll look at the wizard later in this chapter.

Some batch-oriented processes that are query intensive can benefit from certain indexes. Such processes as complex reports or end-of-quarter financial closings often run infrequently. If this is the case, remember that creating and dropping indexes is simple. Consider a strategy of creating certain indexes in advance of your batch processes and then dropping them when those batch processes are done. In this way, the batch processes benefit from the indexes but do not add overhead to your OLTP usage.

Using Stored Procedures and Caching Mechanisms

You should try using stored procedures whenever possible, rather than passing ad hoc SQL statements from your applications. Chapters 3 and 10 discussed the efficiencies that stored procedures bring in terms of not requiring compilation of an execution plan for each execution. Plans can be reused and stay cached and available for subsequent use. Saving recompile time was something to consider with previous versions of SQL Server, although it was not the most important reason to use stored procedures. In many queries, especially complex joins on large tables, the time spent on compilation was frequently insignificant compared to the time needed for execution. So it was much more crucial that the best plan be chosen, even if that meant a recompilation. The picture has changed somewhat in SQL Server 7. The query optimizer now has many more processing options, and compilation and optimization time can end up being a more significant percentage of total execution time. It is even more crucial now that you know when recompilation will take place and try to avoid it, if at all possible.

Choosing Appropriate Hardware

We don't advise trying to solve performance problems simply by "killing them with hardware." A powerful system cannot compensate for basic inefficiencies in the application or database design. Nevertheless, appropriate hardware is extremely important. (We discussed some hardware issues in Chapter 4.) Remember that SQL Server performance, from the hardware perspective, is a function of the integer processing (CPU) power, the amount of memory in the system, and the I/O capacity of the system. A system must be well matched. Even a system with tremendous CPU capacity might run SQL Server slower than a system with less CPU power if the first system has too little memory or I/O capacity. And when you put together your system, you should think carefully about not just the I/O capacity but also the fault tolerance capabilities. RAID solutions provide varying capabilities of increased I/O performance and fault tolerance. You should decide up front on the appropriate level of RAID for your system. (Chapter 4 also discusses RAID levels.)

SQL Server 7 can save on recompilation using four new mechanisms to make plan caching accessible in a wider set of scenarios:

- Ad hoc caching

- Autoparameterization

- The *sp_executesql* procedure

- The prepare and execute method

NOTE The information on caching query plans was adapted from a preliminary copy of a whitepaper by Peter Carlin. We are indebted to him for his assistance.

Ad Hoc Caching

SQL Server caches the plans from ad hoc queries, and if a subsequent batch matches exactly, the cached plan is used. This feature requires no extra work to use, but it is limited to exact textual matches. For example, if the three queries shown on the following page are submitted, the first and third queries will use the same plan but the second one will need to generate a new plan.

Using Cursors Judiciously

If you intend to use cursors heavily in your application, make sure you've closely read Chapter 11. Used properly, cursors provide valuable features not found in any other mainstream database product. But, as discussed in Chapter 11, cursors are misused in many systems, turning SQL Server into a network ISAM instead of a relational database. This problem is common if a system is being ported from a mainframe using VSAM (or a similar method) or upsized from a data store such as Btrieve or Microsoft FoxPro. In such cases, the cursor model of one-row-at-a-time processing seems familiar to developers with an ISAM background. Converting the ISAM calls to cursor calls looks easy, and it is. But you can easily create a bad application. You should approach your application in terms of set operations and nonprocedural code, and you should avoid the temptation of simply doing a quick port from an ISAM and using cursors extensively.

```
INSERT mytable VALUES (1.0)
INSERT mytable VALUES (2.0)
INSERT mytable VALUES (1.0)
```

Autoparameterization

For simple queries, SQL Server guesses which constants might really be parameters and attempts to treat them as parameters. If this is successful, subsequent queries that follow the same basic template can use the same plan. Four templates can be used for autoparameterization. (Note that *key-expression* is an expression involving only column names, constants, AND operators, and comparison operators (<, >, =, <=, >=, and <>).)

```
INSERT table VALUES ({constant | NULL | DEFAULT}, ...)
DELETE table WHERE key-expression
UPDATE table SET colname = constant WHERE key-expression
SELECT {* | column-list} FROM table WHERE key-expression ORDER BY column-list
```

For example, these two queries will use the same plan:

```
SELECT firstname, lastname, salary FROM employees WHERE employee_id = 1000
SELECT firstname, lastname, salary FROM employees WHERE employee_id = 5
```

Internally, SQL Server parameterizes these queries as

```
SELECT firstname, lastname, salary FROM employees WHERE employee_id = @p
```

SQL Server can allow other queries of the same template to use the same plan only if the template is *safe*. A template is safe if the plan selected will not change even if the actual parameters change. This ensures that autoparameterization won't degrade a query's performance.

The SQL Server query processor is much more conservative about deciding whether a template is safe than an application can be. SQL Server guesses which values are really parameters, whereas your application should actually know. Rather than rely on autoparameterization, you should use one of the following two mechanisms to mark parameters when they are known.

The *sp_executesql* Procedure

The stored procedure *sp_executesql* is halfway between ad hoc caching and stored procedures. Using *sp_executesql* requires that you identify the parameters but doesn't require all the persistent object management needed for stored procedures.

Here's the general syntax for the procedure:

```
sp_executesql @batch_text,@batch_parameter_definitions,
    param1,...paramN
```

Repeated calls with the same *batch_text* use the cached plan, with the new parameter values specified. The same cached plan is used in all the following cases:

```
sp_executesql 'insert mytable values(@p)','@p float',1.0
sp_executesql 'insert mytable values(@p)','@p float',2.0
sp_executesql 'insert mytable values(@p)','@p float',1.0
```

ODBC and OLE DB expose this functionality via *SQLExecDirect* and *ICommandWithParameters*. (The ODBC and OLE DB documentation provide more details.)

The Prepare and Execute Method

This last mechanism is like *sp_executesql* in that parameters to the batch are identified by the application, but there are some key differences. The prepare and execute method does not require the full text of the batch to be sent at each execution. Rather, the full text is sent once at prepare time; a handle that can be used to invoke the batch at execute time is returned. ODBC and OLE DB expose this functionality via *SQLPrepare/SQLExecute* and *ICommandPrepare*. You can also use this mechanism via ODBC and OLE DB when cursors are involved. When you use these functions, SQL Server is informed that this batch is meant to be used repeatedly.

Sharing Cached Plans

To allow users to share plans and thus maximize the effectiveness of the caching mechanisms, all users should execute in the same environment. Don't change SET options or database settings in the middle of an application or connection.

For all of the caching mechanisms, reusing a cached plan avoids recompilation and optimization. This saves compilation time, but it means that the same plan is used regardless of the particular parameter values passed in. If the optimal plan for a given parameter value is not the same as the cached plan, the optimal execution time will not be achieved. For this reason, SQL Server is very conservative about autoparameterization. When an application uses *sp_executesql*, prepare and execute, or stored procedures, the application developer is responsible for determining what should be parameterized. You should parameterize only constants whose range of values does not drastically affect the optimization choices.

The SQL Server Performance Monitor includes a counter called SQL Server: SQL Statistics that has several counters dealing with autoparameterization. You can monitor these counters to determine whether there are many unsafe or failed autoparameterization attempts. If these numbers are high, you can inspect your applications for situations in which the application can take responsibility for explicitly marking the parameters.

When to Use Stored Procedures and Other Caching Mechanisms

Keep the following in mind when you are deciding whether to use stored procedures or one of the other mechanisms:

- **Stored procedures**   Use when multiple applications are executing batches in which the parameters are known.

- **Ad hoc caching**   Useful in limited scenarios. Don't design an application to use this.

- **Autoparameterization**   Use for applications that cannot be easily modified. Don't design an application to use this.

- **The *sp_executesql* procedure**   Use when a single user *might* use the same batch multiple times and when the parameters are known.

- **The prepare and execute method**   Use when multiple users are executing batches in which the parameters are known, or when a single user will definitely use the same batch multiple times.

Recompiling Stored Procedures

In spite of the benefits of the mechanisms just discussed, you should still use stored procedures whenever possible. Besides giving you the benefits of precompilation, they minimize network traffic by reducing the text that needs to be sent from your application to SQL Server, and they provide a security mechanism to control who can access data and under what conditions. Stored procedures can be recompiled automatically or manually under various circumstances. (Chapter 10 discussed some of these issues.)

You can actually watch automatic recompilation occurring by using SQL Server Profiler: Choose to trace the event in the Stored Procedures category called SP:Recompile. If you also trace the event called SP:StmtStarting, you can see at what point in the procedure it is being recompiled. In particular, you might notice that stored procedures can be recompiled multiple times during their execution. For example, if you build a temporary table and later create an index on that table, and then add data to the table, your stored procedure will be recompiled numerous times. One way to avoid this is to include all data definition statements dealing with your temporary tables, as well as the insertion of rows into the temporary tables, right at the beginning of the procedure. So if the procedure must be recompiled, it won't happen more than once. Another way to prevent recompilations is to include the query hint KEEPPLAN in your statements that access the temporary tables. We'll discuss query hints in detail later in this chapter.

Although we've been assuming that recompilation is something you will usually want to avoid, this is not always the case. If you know that updated statistics can improve the query plan, or if you know that you have wildly different possible parameter values, recompilation can be a good thing.

> **TIP** If you want to run your tests repeatedly under the same conditions so that you can measure performance when you start with no cached plans, you can use the command DBCC FREEPROCCACHE after each test run to remove all cached plans from memory.

Limiting the Number of Plans in Cache

SQL Server will try to limit the number of plans for any particular stored procedure. Since plans are reentrant, this is much easier to do in SQL Server 7 than in previous versions. Although the online documentation states that there can be at most two compiled plans for any procedure (at most one for parallel plans—that is, those that will be executed on multiple processors—and one for nonparallel plans), this is not completely true. Other situations will cause multiple plans for the same procedure to be stored. The most likely situation is a difference in certain SET options, database options, or configuration options. For example, a stored procedure that concatenates strings might compile the concatenation differently depending on whether the option CONCAT_NULL_YIELDS_NULL is on or off, or whether the corresponding database option is true or false. If a user executes the procedure with the option on, that person will use a different plan than if the option is off.

The system table *syscacheobjects* keeps track of the compiled objects in cache at any time. This table is accessible only by system administrators, but you can write your own stored procedures to provide information for your own tuning and testing purposes. You can use a procedure called *sp_procs_in_cache* (which is on this book's companion CD) to return a list of all procedure plans in cache and the number of times each plan occurs. The list is organized by database. If you execute the procedure without passing a parameter, you see procedures in your current database only. Alternatively, you can provide a specific database name or use the parameter *all* to indicate that you want to see procedure plans in cache from all databases. If you want to pull different information out of *syscacheobjects*, you can customize the procedure in any way you like. Remember to create the procedure in the master database so that it can be called from anywhere. Also remember to grant appropriate permissions if anyone other than a system administrator will be running it.

Running the *sp_procs_in_cache* procedure shows the two different types of stored procedure plans: *compiled plans* and *executable plans*. A compiled plan is the part of a plan that is reentrant and can be shared by multiple users. You can think of an executable plan as an instance of the compiled plan that contains information describing a particular process that is executing the procedure. In most cases, both compiled and executable plans remain in the memory cache, subject of course to memory pressure from other processes or applications. In other cases, such as when a compiled plan contains a sort operation, execution plans do not remain in cache at all after execution.

Other Benefits of Stored Procedures

Beyond the significant performance and security advantages, stored procedures can provide a valuable level of indirection between your applications and the database design. Suppose your application calls a procedure such as *get_customer_balance* and expects a result set to be returned. If the underlying database is then changed, the application can be totally unaffected and unaware of the change as long as the procedure also changes to return the result set as expected. For example, if you decide to denormalize your database design to provide faster query performance, you can change the stored procedure to respecify the query. If many applications call the procedure, you can simply change the stored procedure once and never touch the application. In fact, a running application doesn't even need to be restarted—it executes the new version of the stored procedure the next time it is called.

Another good reason to use stored procedures is to minimize round-trips on the network (that is, the conversational TDS traffic between the client application and SQL Server for every batch and result set). If you will take different actions based on data values, try to make those decisions directly in the procedure. (Strictly speaking, you don't need to use a stored procedure to do this—a batch also provides this benefit.) Issue as many commands as possible in a batch. You can try a simple test by inserting 100 rows first as a single batch and then as every insert in its own batch (that is, 100 batches). You'll see a performance improvement of an order of magnitude even on a LAN, and on a slow network the improvement will be stunning. While LAN speeds of 10 megabits per second (Mbps) are fast enough that the network is generally not a significant bottleneck, speeds can be tremendously different on a slow network. A modem operating at 28.8 kilobits per second (Kbps) is roughly 300 times slower than a LAN. Although WAN speeds vary greatly, they typically can be 100 to 200 times slower than a LAN. The fast LAN performance might hide inefficient network use. You can often see a prime example of this phenomenon when you use cursors. Fetching each row individually might be tolerable on a LAN, but it is intolerable when you use dial-up lines.

If a stored procedure has multiple statements, by default SQL Server sends a message to the client application at the completion of each statement to indicate the number of rows affected for each statement. This is known as a DONE_IN_PROC message in TDS-speak. However, most applications do not need DONE_IN_PROC messages. So if you are confident that your applications do not need these messages, you can disable them, which can greatly improve performance on a slow network when there is otherwise little network traffic. (One particular application deployed on a WAN had an order-of-magnitude performance improvement after suppressing the DONE_IN_PROC messages. This made the difference between a successful deployment and a fiasco.)

You can use the connection-specific option *SET NOCOUNT ON* to disable these messages for the application. While they are disabled, you cannot use the ODBC SQLRowCount() function or its OLE DB equivalent. However, you can toggle NOCOUNT on and off as needed, and you can use *SELECT @@ROWCOUNT* even when NOCOUNT is on. You can also suppress the sending of DONE_IN_PROC messages by starting the server with trace flag 3640, which lets you suppress what might be needless overhead without touching your application. However, some ODBC applications depend on the DONE_IN_PROC message, so you should test your application before using trace flag 3640 in production—it can break applications that are written implicitly to expect that token.

You should keep an eye on the traffic between your client applications and the server. An application designed and tuned for slow networks works great on a fast network, but the reverse is not true. If you use a higher-level development tool that generates the SQL statements and issues commands on your behalf, it is especially important to keep an eye on what's moving across the network. You can use the SQL Server Profiler to watch all traffic into the server. If you want to watch both commands in and responses sent, you can start the server from the command line with trace flags 4032 and 4031, which respectively display the server's receive and send buffers (for example, *sqlservr –c –T4031 –T4032*). Enabling these two flags dumps all conversation to and from the server to standard output for the *sqlservr* process, which is the monitor if you start it from a console window. (Note that the output can get huge.) Whether you use SQL Server Profiler or these trace flags, you can get all the exact commands and data being sent. Just to monitor network traffic, though, this might be over-kill; a network sniffer such as Network Monitor (available with Microsoft Windows NT Server and Microsoft Systems Management Server) can work better if you want only to monitor network traffic. Network Monitor is easy to use, and even a networking neophyte can set it up quickly and with a few mouse clicks watch the traffic between machine pairs.

Concurrency and Consistency Tradeoffs

If you are designing a multiple-user application that will both query and modify the same data, you need a good understanding of concurrency and consistency. Concurrency is the ability to have many simultaneous users operating at once. The more users who can work well simultaneously, the higher your concurrency. Consistency is the level at which the data in multiple-user scenarios exhibits the same behavior that it would if only one user were operating at a time. Consistency is expressed in terms of isolation levels. At the highest isolation level, Serializable, the multiple-user system behaves identically to what would exist if users submitted their requests serially—that is, as if the system made every user queue up and run operations one at a time (serially). At the Serializable level you have a greater need to protect resources, which you do by locking and which reduces concurrency. (Locking is discussed in Chapter 13. You should also understand transactional concepts, which are presented in Chapter 10.)

In many typical environments, an ongoing struggle occurs between the OLTP demands on the database and the DSS demands. OLTP is characterized by relatively high volumes of transactions that modify data. The transactions tend to be relatively short and usually don't query large amounts of data. DSS is read-intensive, often with complex queries that can take a long time to complete and thus hold locks for a long time. The exclusive locks needed for data modification with OLTP applications block the shared locks used for DSS. And DSS tends to use many shared locks and often holds them for long periods, stalling the OLTP applications, which then must wait to acquire the exclusive locks required for updating. DSS also tends to benefit from many indexes and often from a denormalized database design that reduces the number of tables to be joined.

Large numbers of indexes are a drag on OLTP because of the additional work to keep them updated. And denormalization means redundancy—a tax on the update procedures.

You need to understand the isolation level required by your application. Certainly, you do not want to request Serializable (or, equivalently, use the HOLDLOCK or SERIALIZABLE hint) if you need only Read Committed. And it might become clear that some queries in your application require only Read Uncommitted (dirty read), since they look for trends and don't need guaranteed precision. If that's the case, you potentially have some flexibility in terms of queries not requiring shared locks, which keeps them both from being blocked by processes modifying the database and from blocking those modifying processes. But even if you can live with a dirty-read level, you should use it only if necessary. This isolation level means that you might read data that logically never existed; this can create some weird conditions in the application. (For example, a row that's just been read will seem to vanish because it gets rolled back.) If your application can live with a dirty-read isolation level, it might be comforting to have that as a fallback. However, you should probably first try to make your application work with the standard isolation level of Read Committed and fall back to dirty read only if necessary.

Resolving Blocking Problems

Many applications suffer poor performance because processes are backed up waiting to acquire locks or because of deadlocks. A smooth, fast application should minimize the time spent waiting for locks, and it should avoid deadlocks. The most important step you can take is to first understand how locking works.

A process *blocks* when it stalls while waiting to acquire a lock that is incompatible with a lock held by some other process. This condition is often, but erroneously, referred to as a "deadlock." As long as the process being stalled is not, in turn, stalling the offending process—which results in a circular chain that will never work itself out without intervention—you have a blocking problem, not a deadlock. If the blocking process is simply holding on to locks or is itself blocked by some other process, this is not a deadlock either. The process requesting the lock must wait for the other process to release the incompatible lock; when it does, all will be fine. Of course, if the process holds that lock excessively, performance still grinds to a halt and you must deal with the blocking problem. Your process will suffer from bad performance and might also hold locks that stall other processes; every system on the network will appear to hang.

The following guidelines will help you avoid or resolve blocking problems:

■ Keep transactions as short as possible. Ideally, a BEGIN TRAN... COMMIT TRAN block will include only the actual DML statements that must be executed. To the extent possible, do conditional logic, variable assignment, and other "setup" work before the BEGIN TRAN. The shorter the transaction lasts, the shorter the time that locks will be held. Keep the entire transaction within one batch if possible.

■ Never add a pause within a transaction for user input. This rule is basically a part of the previous one, but it is especially important. Humans are slow and unreliable compared to computers. Do not add a pause in the middle of the transaction to ask a user for input or to confirm some action. The person might decide to get up to take a coffee break, stalling the transaction and making it hold locks that cause blocking problems for other processes. If some locks must be held until the user provides more information, you should set timers in your application so that even if the user decides to go to lunch, the transaction will be aborted and the locks will be released. Similarly, give your applications a way to cancel out of a query if such an action is necessary. Alternatively, you can use the LOCK_TIMEOUT session option to control when SQL Server automatically cancels out of a locking situation. We'll look at this option later in this chapter.

■ When you process a result set, process all rows as quickly as possible. Recall from Chapter 3 that an application that stops processing results can prevent the server from sending more results and stall the scanning process, which requires locks to be held much longer.

■ For browsing applications, consider using cursors with optimistic concurrency control. An address book application is a good example of a browsing application: users scroll around to look at data and occasionally update it. But the update activity is relatively infrequent compared to the time spent perusing the data. Using scrollable cursors with the OPTIMISTIC locking mode is a good solution for such applications. Instead of locking, the cursor's optimistic concurrency logic determines whether the row has changed from the copy that your cursor read. If the row has not changed, the update is made without holding locks during the lengthy period in which the user is perusing the data. If the row has changed, the UPDATE statement produces an error and the application can decide how to respond. Although you were strenuously cautioned in Chapter 11 about the misuse of cursors, they are ideally suited to browsing applications.

You can also easily implement your own optimistic locking mechanism without using cursors. Save the values of the data you selected and add a WHERE clause to your update that checks whether the values in the current data are the same as those you retrieved. Or, rather than use the values of the data, use a SQL Server *timestamp* column—an ever-increasing number that's updated whenever the row is touched, unrelated to the system time. If the values or timestamp are not identical, your update will not find any qualifying row and will not affect anything. You can also detect changes with @@ROW-COUNT and decide to simply abort, or more typically, you can indicate to the user that the values have changed and then ask whether the update should still be performed. But between the time the data was initially retrieved and the time the update request was issued, shared locks are not held, so the likelihood of blocking and deadlocks is significantly reduced.

Indexes and Blocking

We've already recommended that you choose your indexes wisely, strictly for performance reasons. However, concurrency concerns are also a reason to make sure you have good indexes on your tables. (Of course, better concurrency can also lead to better performance.) We saw in Chapter 13 that SQL Server acquires row (or key) locks whenever possible. However, this does not always mean that no other rows are affected if you are updating only one row in a table. Remember that to find the row to update, SQL Server must first do a search and acquire UPDATE locks on the resources it inspects. If SQL Server does not have a useful index to help find the desired row, it uses a table scan. This means every row in the table acquires an update lock, and the row actually being updated acquires an exclusive lock, which is not released until the end of the transaction. The following page shows a small example that nevertheless illustrates the crucial relationship between indexes and concurrency.

```
USE pubs
go
DROP TABLE t1
go
/* First create and populate a small table. */
CREATE TABLE t1 (a int)
go
INSERT INTO t1 VALUES (1)
INSERT INTO t1 VALUES (3)
INSERT INTO t1 VALUES (5)
go

BEGIN tran
UPDATE t1
SET a = 7 WHERE a = 1

EXEC sp_lock @@spid
/* The output here should show you one X lock, on a RID; that is the
   row that has been updated. */
/* In another query window, run this batch before rollback is
   issued: */

USE pubs
UPDATE t1
SET a = 10
WHERE a = 3

/* Execute the rollback in the first window. */
ROLLBACK TRAN
```

You should have noticed that the second connection was unable to proceed. To find the row where a = 3, it tries to scan the table, first acquiring update locks. However, it cannot obtain an update lock on the first row, which now has a value of 7 for *a*, because that row is exclusively locked. Since SQL Server has no way to know whether that is a row it is looking for without being able to even look at it, this second connection blocks. When the rollback occurs in the first connection, the locks are released and the second connection can finish.

Let's see what happens if we put an index on the table. We'll run the same script again, except we'll build a nonclustered index on column *a*.

```
USE pubs
go
DROP TABLE t1
go
```

```
/* First create and populate a small table. */
CREATE TABLE t1 ( a int)
Go
CREATE INDEX idx1 ON t1(a)
go
INSERT INTO t1 VALUES (1)
INSERT INTO t1 VALUES (3)
INSERT INTO t1 VALUES (5)
go

BEGIN tran
UPDATE t1
SET a = 7 WHERE a = 1

EXEC sp_lock @@spid

/* In this case, the output should show you three X locks (one again on
a RID) and two KEY locks. When the key column a is changed, the leaf
level of the nonclustered index is adjusted. Since the leaf level of
the index keeps all the keys in sorted order, the old key with the
value 1 is moved from the beginning of the leaf level to the end,
because now its value is 7. However, until the transaction is over, a
ghost entry is left in the original position and the key lock is
maintained. So there are two key locks: one for the old value and one
for the new. */
/* In another query window, run this batch before rollback is issued: */

USE pubs
UPDATE t1
SET a = 10
WHERE a = 3

/* Execute the rollback in the first window. */
ROLLBACK TRAN
```

This time the second query succeeded, even though the first query held
X locks on the keys in the leaf level of the index. The second connection was
able to generate the lock resource string for the keys it needed to lock, and then
only request locks on those particular keys. Since the keys the second connection requested were not the same as the keys that the first connection locked,
there was no conflict over locking resources and the second connection could
proceed.

Resolving Deadlock Problems

Deadlocks befuddle many programmers and are the bane of many applications. A deadlock occurs when, without some intervening action, processes cannot get the locks they need no matter how long they wait. Simply waiting for locks is *not* a deadlock condition. SQL Server automatically detects the deadlock condition and terminates one of the processes to resolve the situation. The process gets the infamous error message 1205 indicating that it was selected as the "victim" and that its batch and the current transaction have been canceled. The other process can then get the locks it needs and proceed. The two general forms of deadlocks are *cycle deadlocks* and *conversion deadlocks*. (See Chapter 13 for more information about these two kinds of deadlocks.)

Cycle Deadlock Example

If you repeatedly run the following two transactions simultaneously from different OSQL.EXE sessions, you are nearly assured of encountering a "deadly embrace" (cycle deadlock) almost immediately from one of the two processes. It should be clear why: one of the processes gets an exclusive lock on a row in the *authors* table and needs an exclusive lock on a row in the *employee* table. The other process gets an exclusive lock on the row in *employee*, but it needs an exclusive lock for the same row in *authors* that the first process has locked.

```
-- Connection 1
USE pubs
WHILE (1=1)
BEGIN
    BEGIN TRAN
    UPDATE employee SET lname='Smith' WHERE emp_id='PMA42628M'
    UPDATE authors SET au_lname='Jones' WHERE au_id='172-32-1176'
    COMMIT TRAN
END

-- Connection 2
USE pubs
WHILE (1=1)
BEGIN
    BEGIN TRAN
    UPDATE authors SET au_lname='Jones' WHERE au_id='172-32-1176'
    UPDATE employee SET lname='Smith' WHERE emp_id='PMA42628M'
    COMMIT TRAN
END
```

The result is the dreaded error 1205 (shown below) from one of the connections. The other connection continues along as if no problem occurred.

```
Msg 1205, Level 13, State 2
Your server command (process id 12) was deadlocked with another
process and has been chosen as deadlock victim. Re-run your command
```

If you simply rewrite one of the batches so that both batches first update *authors* and then update *employee*, the two connections will run forever without falling into a cycle deadlock. Or you can first update *employee* and then update *authors* from both connections. Which table you update first doesn't matter, but the updates must be consistent and you must follow a known protocol. If your application design specifies a standard protocol for accessing the tables consistently, one of the connections gets the exclusive page lock on the first table and the other process must wait for the lock to be released. Simply waiting momentarily for a lock is normal and usually fast, and it happens frequently without your realizing it. It is *not* a deadlock.

Conversion Deadlock Example

Now run the following transaction simultaneously from two different OSQL.EXE sessions. You're running the same script, so it's obvious that the two processes follow a consistent order for accessing tables. But this example quickly produces a deadlock. A delay has been added so that you encounter the race condition more quickly, but the condition is lurking there even without the WAITFOR DELAY—the delay just widens the window.

```
USE pubs
SET TRANSACTION ISOLATION LEVEL REPEATABLE READ
BEGIN TRAN
SELECT * FROM authors WHERE au_id='172-32-1176'
-- Add 5 sec sleep to widen the window for the deadlock
WAITFOR DELAY "00:00:05"
UPDATE authors SET au_lname='Updated by '
    + CONVERT(varchar, @@spid) WHERE au_id='172-32-1176'
COMMIT TRAN
```

You can correct this example in a couple of ways. Does the isolation level need to be Repeatable Read? If Read Committed is sufficient, simply change the isolation level to get rid of the deadlock and to provide better concurrency. If you use Read Committed isolation, the shared locks can be released after the SELECT, and then one of the two processes can acquire the exclusive lock it needs. The other process waits for the exclusive lock and acquires it as soon as the first process finishes its update. All operations progress smoothly, and the queuing and waiting happen invisibly and so quickly that it is not noticeable to the processes.

But suppose that you need Repeatable Read (or Serializable) isolation. In this case, you should serialize access by using an update lock, which you request using the UPDLOCK hint. Recall from Chapter 13 that an update lock is compatible with a shared lock for the same resource. But two update locks for the same resource are not compatible, and update and exclusive locks are also not compatible. Acquiring an update lock does not prevent others from reading the same data, but it does ensure that you are first in line to upgrade your lock to an exclusive lock if you subsequently decide to modify the locked data. (The important issue here is that the exclusive lock can be acquired, so this technique works equally well even if that second statement is a DELETE and not an UPDATE, as in this example.)

By serializing access to the exclusive lock, you prevent the deadlock situation. The serialization also reduces concurrency, but that's the price you must pay to achieve the high level of transaction isolation. A modified example follows; multiple simultaneous instances of this example will not deadlock. Try running about 20 simultaneous instances and see for yourself. None of the instances deadlock and all complete, but they run serially. With the built-in 5-second sleep, it takes about 100 seconds for all 20 connections to complete because one connection completes about every 5 seconds. This illustrates the lower concurrency that results from the need for higher levels of consistency (in this case, Repeatable Read).

```
USE pubs
SET TRANSACTION ISOLATION LEVEL REPEATABLE READ
BEGIN TRAN
SELECT * FROM authors (UPDLOCK) WHERE au_id='172-32-1176'
-- Add 5 sec sleep to widen the window for the deadlock
WAITFOR DELAY "00:00:05"
UPDATE authors SET au_lname='Updated by '
    + CONVERT(varchar, @@spid) WHERE au_id='172-32-1176'
COMMIT TRAN
```

As a general strategy, add the UPDLOCK hint (or some other serialization) if you discover during testing that conversion deadlocks are occurring. Or add UPDLOCK from the outset because you detect from your CRUD analysis that deadlocks are likely, and then try backing it off during multiple-user testing to see if it is absolutely necessary. Either approach is viable. If you know that in most cases the read-for-update (discussed later) will follow with an actual update, you might opt for the UPDLOCK hint from the outset and see if you can back it off later. But if the transaction is short and you will later update the data in most cases, there isn't much point in backing off the update lock. The shared lock will need to upgrade to an exclusive lock, so getting the update lock in the first place makes good sense.

Preventing Deadlocks

Deadlocks can usually be avoided, although you might have to do some detailed analysis to solve the problems that cause them. Sometimes the cure is worse than the ailment, and you're better off handling deadlocks rather than totally preventing them, as we'll discuss in the next section. Preventing deadlocks (especially conversion deadlocks) requires a thorough understanding of lock compatibility. These are the main techniques you can use to prevent deadlocks:

- To prevent cycle deadlocks, make all processes access resources in a consistent order.
- Reduce the transaction isolation level if it's suitable for the application.
- To prevent conversion deadlocks, explicitly serialize access to a resource.

Deadlock prevention is a good reason to use stored procedures. By encapsulating the data access logic in stored procedures, it's easier to impose consistent protocols for the order in which resources (for example, tables) are accessed, which can help you avoid cycle deadlocks. But in so doing, you do not reduce the likelihood of conversion deadlocks. As noted above, conversion deadlocks are best dealt with by serializing access to a resource or by lowering the transaction isolation level if appropriate. The most common scenario for conversion deadlocks is the read-for-update situation. If a resource will be read within a transaction requiring Repeatable Read or Serializable isolation and will be updated later, you should request an update lock on the read using the UPDLOCK hint. The update lock will let other users read the data but will prevent them from updating the data or doing a read-for-update. The net effect is that once the update lock is acquired, the process will be next in line for the exclusive lock needed to actually modify it.

Handling Deadlocks

The cost of serializing access is that other users wanting to read-for-update (or actually update or delete) must wait. If you are not experiencing deadlocks, serializing access might needlessly reduce concurrency. You might have a case in which a transaction often does a read-for-update but only infrequently does the update. In this case, deadlocks might be infrequent. The best course of action might be to *not* prevent deadlocks and simply deal with them when they occur.

Preventing deadlocks can significantly reduce concurrency because the read-for-update would be blocked. Instead, you can simply write your applications to handle deadlocking. Check for deadlock message 1205, and retry the transaction. With retry logic, you can live with moderate deadlock activity without adding a lot of serialization to the application. It's still a good idea to keep count of how often you experience deadlocks; if the incidence is high, the wasted effort and constant retrying are likely to be worse than the cost of preventing the deadlock in the first place. How you write the deadlock handler will depend on the language or tool you use to build your application. But an application that is prone to deadlocks should have a deadlock handler that retries. Such a handler must be written in the host language. There is no way to do a retry directly within a stored procedure or a batch, since deadlock error 1205 terminates the batch.

Volunteering to Be the Deadlock Victim

Recall from Chapter 13 that the LOCK_MONITOR process in SQL Server typically chooses as the deadlock victim the process that made the final lock request that closed the loop and created a circular chain. But a process can also offer to "sacrifice itself" as the victim for deadlock resolution. You can make this happen by using the *SET DEADLOCK_PRIORITY LOW | NORMAL* statement. If a process has a deadlock priority of LOW and the other participating process is NORMAL (the default), the LOW process is chosen as the victim even if it was not the process that closed the loop.

In the deadlock examples shown earlier, you saw that the default victim is the process that you started second, since it closes the loop. However, adding *SET DEADLOCK_PRIORITY LOW* to one of the connections (and not the other) indicates that it will be selected as the victim, even if it was started first. You might find this useful if, for example, you are doing reporting and OLTP on the same database and you occasionally have deadlocks, and you know that one process is more important than the other. You set the less important process to LOW. It might also be useful if one application was written with a good deadlock handler and the other was not. Until the application without the handler can be fixed, the "good" application can make the simple change of volunteering itself and then handle a deadlock with retry logic when the deadlock occurs later.

Watching Locking Activity

Locking problems often result from locks that you don't even realize are being taken. You might be updating only table A, but blocking issues arise on table B because of relationships that you don't realize exist. If, for example, a foreign key relationship exists between table A and table B and the update on A is causing some query activity to B, some shared locks must exist. Or a trigger or a nested call to another procedure might cause some locking that isn't obvious to you.

In cases like these, you must be able to watch locks to look for locking operations that you weren't aware of. The graphical lock display of SQL Server Enterprise Manager is the most convenient way to watch locking in many cases. However, SQL Server Enterprise Manager provides only a snapshot of the *current* state of locking; you can miss a lot of locking activity that occurs in the time it takes you to refresh the display.

Identifying the Culprit

As with most debugging situations, the hardest part of solving a problem with locking is understanding the problem. If you get complaints that "the system is hung," it's a good bet that you have a blocking problem. Most blocking problems happen because a single process holds locks for an extended period of time. A classic case (as we discussed earlier) is an interactive application that holds locks until the user at the other end takes an action, such as clicking a button to commit the transaction or scrolling to the end of the output, which causes all the results to be processed. If the user goes to lunch and doesn't take that action, everyone else might as well grab lunch too, because they're not going to get much work done. Locks pile up, and the system seems to hang. The locks in the system are reported in the pseudo–system table, *syslockinfo* in the *master* database. (We'll discuss a related pseudo–system table, *sysprocesses*, later in the chapter.)

> **NOTE** The pseudo–system tables are not maintained as on-disk structures. Locking and process data are by definition relevant only at runtime. So *syslockinfo* and *sysprocesses* are presented as system tables, and although they can be queried just like other system tables, they do not have on-disk storage as normal tables do.

A big challenge in trying to identify the cause of blocking is that when you experience such problems, you probably have hundreds or thousands of locks piled up. At these times, it's hard to see the trees through the forest. Usually, you just want to see which process is holding up everyone else. Once you identify it, of course, you need to immediately get it out of the way, either by forcing it to complete or, if necessary, by issuing the KILL command on the connection. The longer-term solution is to rework the application so that it will not hold locks indefinitely.

SQL Server Enterprise Manager, shown in Figure 14-3, provides a graphical way to watch locking activity; this is the best method most of the time. From the Management folder, choose Current Activity. You can look at locks either by process or by object. If you select the Locks / Process ID option, the graphic shows which processes are blocked and which processes are blocking. When you double-click on the process in the right pane, you see the last command the process issued. This is what Figure 14-3 shows. You can then send a message to the offending user to complete the transaction (although this is a short-term solution at best). Or you can kill the process from SQL Server Enterprise Manager—which isn't ideal, but sometimes it's the best short-term course of action. You can select a particular process from the left pane, under the Locks / Process ID option, and the right pane will show all the locks held by that process.

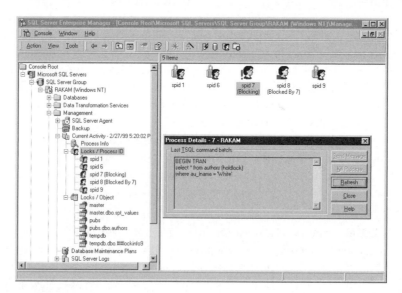

Figure 14-3.
Viewing the last batch issued by a blocking process in SQL Server Enterprise Manager.

Alternatively, you can select the Locks/Objects option under Current Activity. The left pane displays a graphic of each locked object. If you then select one of these objects, the right pane shows which processes have that object locked. Again, when you double-click on the process in the right pane, you see the last command the process issued.

But sometimes even SQL Server Enterprise Manager can get blocked by locking activity in *tempdb*, so it's useful to know how to monitor-lock the old-fashioned way, by using system stored procedures or querying directly from the *syslockinfo* table. You start by running *sp_who2* and *sp_lock*. Most people are familiar with *sp_who* but not *sp_who2*, which works in almost the same way but formats the output in a more readable way and contains more of the columns from the *sysprocesses* table. However, *sysprocesses* contains additional information that neither *sp_who* nor *sp_who2* reports, so you might even want to write your own *sp_who3*! We'll look at the *sysprocesses* table in more detail later in this chapter.

The *BlkBy* column of the *sp_who2* output shows the ID (*spid*) of a blocking process. The procedure *sp_lock* provides a formatted and sorted listing of *syslockinfo* that decodes the lock types into mnemonic forms (such as *update_page* instead of *type 7*). In Chapter 13, we looked at output from *sp_lock* to watch the various types and modes of locking. If your users say that the system is hung, try to log on and execute *sp_who2* and *sp_lock*. If you can log on and execute these procedures, you immediately know that the system is not hung. If you see a nonzero *spid* in the *BlkBy* column of the *sp_who2* output or if the Status value is WAIT in the *sp_lock* output, blocking is occurring. It's normal for some blocking to occur—it simply indicates that one process is waiting for a resource held by another. If such contention didn't exist, you wouldn't even need to lock. But if you reissue the query for lock activity a moment later, you expect to find that same blockage cleared up. In a smoothly running system, the duration that locks are held is short, so long pileups of locks don't occur.

When a major lock pileup occurs, you can get a lengthy chain of processes blocking other processes. It can get pretty cumbersome to try to track this manually. You can create a procedure like the following to look for the process at the head of a blocking chain:

```
CREATE PROCEDURE sp_leadblocker
AS
IF EXISTS
    (SELECT * FROM master.dbo.sysprocesses
    WHERE spid IN (SELECT blocked FROM master.dbo.sysprocesses))
    SELECT
```

(continued)

```
        spid, status, loginame=SUBSTRING(SUSER_NAME(suid), 1, 12),
        hostname=substring(hostname, 1, 12),
            blk=CONVERT(char(3), blocked),
        dbname=SUBSTRING(DB_NAME(dbid), 1, 10), cmd, waittype
        FROM master.dbo.sysprocesses
        WHERE spid IN (SELECT blocked FROM master.dbo.sysprocesses)
            AND blocked=0
ELSE
SELECT "No blocking processes found!"
```

Once you identify the connection (*spid*) causing the problem, check to see the specific locks that it is holding. You can query from *syslockinfo* for this, but simply running *sp_lock spid* will probably give you exactly what you need. There might be multiple separate lock chains, in which case the batch will return more than one *spid*. You can follow the same procedure for each one.

The *syslockinfo* Table

If a lot of blocking is going on, you might want to take a look at all locks held that are blocking other users. You can use the procedure *sp_blockinglocks* (which is not a part of the installed SQL Server product but is included on the companion CD) to print out a list of all locks held that are blocking other processes. The procedure examines the *syslockinfo* table for resources that have more than one lock listed and are held by different processes with different status values. For example, if process 12 has an X lock on the *sales* table with a status of GRANT and process 13 is trying to read from that table, the output of *sp_blockinglocks* looks like this:

spid	dbid	ObjId	IndId	Type	Resource	Mode	Status
12	5	437576597	0	TAB		X	GRANT
13	5	437576597	0	TAB		IS	WAIT

It can also be useful to see the last command issued by a blocking process; you can do this by double-clicking on a process ID in the Current Activity panes of SQL Server Enterprise Manager. Use *DBCC INPUTBUFFER (spid)* for this—which is the same thing SQL Server Enterprise Manager does when you double-click on a process. DBCC INPUTBUFFER reads the memory from within the server that was used for the last command. So DBCC INPUTBUFFER can access whatever command is still in the buffer for a given connection, even if it has already been executed.

Usually, by this point you have enough of a handle on the problem to turn your attention to the application, which is where the resolution will ultimately lie. But if you need or want to go a bit further, you can find out the depth at which the connection is nested within a transaction. Blocking problems often happen because the connection doesn't realize the nested depth and hasn't applied the correct pairing of COMMIT commands. (Chapter 10 discusses the scoping and nesting levels of transactions.) A connection can determine its own nesting depth by querying @@TRANCOUNT. Starting with SQL Server 7, you can also determine the nesting level of any current connection, not just your own. This involves inspecting the *sysprocesses* table directly because the information is not included in either *sp_who* or *sp_who2*.

The *sysprocesses* Table

As we mentioned, some columns in the *sysprocesses* table don't show up in the output of either *sp_who* or *sp_who2*. Table 14-1 depicts these columns.

Column Name	Data Type	Description
waittype	*binary(2)*	The *waittypes* of 1 through 15 correspond to the mode of lock being waited on. (See list on the following page.) Hex values 0x40 through 0x4f correspond to miscellaneous waits. 0x81 is a wait to write to the log. 0x400 through 0x40f are latch waits. 0x800 is a wait on a network write.
waittime	*int*	Indicates current wait time in milliseconds. Value is 0 when the process is not waiting.
lastwaittype	*nchar(32)*	A string indicating the name of the last or current wait type.
waitresource	*nchar(32)*	A textual representation of a lock resource.
memusage	*int*	Indicates number of pages in the memory cache that are currently allocated to this process. A negative number means that the process is freeing memory allocated by another process.
login_time	*datetime*	Indicates time when a client process logged on to the server. For system processes, indicates time when SQL Server startup occurred.

Table 14-1. *(continued)*

Columns in the sysprocesses *table that aren't available via* sp_who *or* sp_who2.

Table 14-1. *continued*

Column Name	Data Type	Description
ecid	*smallint*	An execution context ID that uniquely identifies the subthreads operating on behalf of a single process.
open_tran	*smallint*	Indicates current transaction nesting depth for the process.
sid	*binary(85)*	A globally unique identifier (GUID) for the user.
hostprocess	*nchar(8)*	The workstation process ID number.
nt_domain	*nchar(128)*	The Windows NT domain for the client.
nt_username	*nchar(128)*	The Windows NT username for the process.
net_address	*nchar(12)*	An assigned unique identifier for the network interface card on each user's workstation.
net_library	*nchar(12)*	The name of the client's network library DLL.

The procedure *sp_who2* translates the *dbid* into a database name and translates the numeric value for its status into a string. The most common status values you'll see are BACKGROUND, ROLLBACK, DORMANT (used when a connection is being retained while waiting for Remote Procedure Call [RPC] processing), SLEEPING, and RUNNABLE.

The values that the *sysprocesses* table holds in the *waittype* column are the same ones you'll see in the *req_mode* column of *syslockinfo*. They can be translated as follows:

```
Lock Mode  value
---------  -----------
Sch-S      1
Sch-M      2
IS         3
SIU        4
IS-S       5
IX         6
SIX        7
S          8
U          9
```

```
IIn-Nul    10
IS-X       11
IU         12
IS-U       13
X          14
BU         15
```

The Trace Flag for Analyzing Deadlock Activity

Trace flags are useful for analyzing deadlock situations. When a process is part of a deadlock, the victim process realizes that the deadlock occurred when it gets error message 1205. Any other process participating in the deadlock is unaware of the situation. To resolve the deadlock, you probably want to see *both* processes; trace flag 1204 provides this information.

The following is a fragment of the output from SQLSERVR.EXE, which was started from the command line using –T1204. This example uses the conversion deadlock script that we used previously—issuing the same batch from two connections—to illustrate the output of trace flag 1204. To capture deadlock information, SQL Server must be started from a command prompt. You can specify a special location for the error log, which will contain all the same information that is displayed on the command screen while SQL Server is running.

```
sqlservr -c -T1204 -eDEADLOCKTRACE.out
```

```
1999-01-19 15:20:11.70 spid2    *** Deadlock Detected ***
1999-01-19 15:20:11.70 spid2    ==> Process 8 chosen as deadlock victim
1999-01-19 15:20:11.70 spid2    == Deadlock Detected at: 1999-01-19 15:20:11.70
1999-01-19 15:20:11.70 spid2    == Session participant information:
1999-01-19 15:20:11.70 spid2    SPID: 7 ECID: 0 Statement Type: UPDATE Line #: 7
1999-01-19 15:20:11.70 spid2    Input Buf:  S E T   T R A N S A C T I O N   I
                                S O L A T I O N   L E V E L   R E P E A T A B L
                                E   R E A D   B E G I N   T R A N   S E L E C
                                T   *   F R O M   a u t h o r s   W H E R E   a
                                u _ i d = ' 1 7 2 - 3 2 - 1 1 7 6 '    - - A d
                                d   s l e e p   t o   w i d e n   t h e   w i n
                                d o w   f o r   t h e   d e a d l o c k   W A I
                                T F O R   D E L A Y   " 0 0 : 0 0 : 0 5 "   U P
                                D A T E
1999 01-19 15:20:11.70 spid2    SPID: 8 ECID: 0 Statement Type: UPDATE Line #: 7
```
(continued)

```
1999-01-19 15:20:11.70 spid2     Input Buf:  S E T  T R A N S A C T I O N  I
                                 S O L A T I O N  L E V E L  R E P E A T A B L
                                 E  R E A D  B E G I N  T R A N  S E L E C
                                 T  *  F R O M  a u t h o r s  W H E R E  a
                                 u _ i d = ' 1 7 2 - 3 2 - 1 1 7 6 '   - - A d
                                 d  s l e e p  t o  w i d e n  t h e  w i n
                                 d o w  f o r  t h e  d e a d l o c k  W A I
                                 T F O R  D E L A Y  " 0 0 : 0 0 : 0 5 "  U P
                                 D A T E
1999-01-19 15:20:11.71 spid2
1999-01-19 15:20:11.71 spid2     == Deadlock Lock participant information:
1999-01-19 15:20:11.71 spid2     == Lock: KEY: 5:117575457:1 (0afe9ce59186)
1999-01-19 15:20:11.71 spid2     Database: pubs
1999-01-19 15:20:11.71 spid2     Table: authors
1999-01-19 15:20:11.71 spid2     Index: UPKCL_auidind
1999-01-19 15:20:11.71 spid2      - Held by: SPID 7 ECID 0 Mode "U"
1999-01-19 15:20:11.71 spid2      - Requested by: SPID 8 ECID 0 Mode "U"
1999-01-19 15:20:11.71 spid2     == Lock: KEY: 5:117575457:1 (0afe9ce59186)
1999-01-19 15:20:11.71 spid2     Database: pubs
1999-01-19 15:20:11.71 spid2     Table: authors
1999-01-19 15:20:11.71 spid2     Index: UPKCL_auidind
1999-01-19 15:20:11.71 spid2      - Held by: SPID 8 ECID 0 Mode "S"
1999-01-19 15:20:11.71 spid2      - Requested by: SPID 7 ECID 0 Mode "X"
```

This output shows the *spid* for both processes affected, shows a fragment of their input buffer (but not the entire command), and notes that neither process can upgrade its locks because of the circular relationship. Process 8 requests an update lock on a key that process 7 already has an update lock on. At the same time, process 7 requests an exclusive lock on a key that process 8 already has a shared lock on. Thus the two processes are in a circular relationship. The output can help you solve the problem—you know the processes involved and the locks that could not be acquired, and you have an idea of the commands being executed.

You might also notice, if you scrutinize the trace flag output in the error log carefully, that trace flag 1206 is turned on. Used in conjunction with trace flag 1204, this flag produces some of the actual object name information that you see in the output above. SQL Server automatically enables this flag when 1204 is turned on.

NOTE The number assigned to trace flag 1204 is intended to be easy to remember. Recall that error 1205 is the well-known error message an application receives when it is chosen as the deadlock victim.

Segregating OLTP and DSS Applications

Sometimes it makes sense to split up your OLTP and DSS applications. This can be an excellent strategy if your DSS applications don't need immediate access to information. This is a reason for the recent popularity of data warehousing, data marts, and other data management systems (although these concepts have been around for years).

You can use a separate database (on the same server or on different servers) for DSS and OLTP, and the DSS database can be much more heavily indexed than the OLTP database. The DSS database will not have exclusive locks holding up queries, and the OLTP database's transactions will not get held up by the shared locks of the DSS. SQL Server's built-in replication capabilities make it relatively easy to publish data from the OLTP server and subscribe to it from your reporting server. SQL Server's replication capabilities can propagate data in near real time, with latency between the servers of just a few seconds. However, for maintaining a DSS server, it is best to propagate the changes during off-peak hours. Otherwise, the locks acquired during propagation at the subscribing site will affect the DSS users, just as any other update activity would. In addition, if for most of the day the DSS server is only executing SELECT queries, you can enable the database option *read only*. This means that SQL Server will not acquire or check locks for any queries because they will all be shared and therefore compatible. Completely bypassing lock maintenance can lead to noticeable performance improvements for the SELECT queries.

Optimizing Queries

Monitoring and tuning of queries are essential to optimizing performance. Knowing how the query optimizer works can be helpful as you think about how to write a good query or what indexes to define. However, you should guard against outsmarting yourself and trying to predict what the optimizer will do. You might miss some good options this way. Try to write your queries in the most intuitive way you can and then try to tune them only if their performance doesn't seem good enough.

The big gains in query performance usually do not come from syntactic changes in the query but rather from a change in the database design or in indexing—or from taking a completely different approach to the query. For example, you might have to choose among the following approaches: writing a pretty complex query using a self-join or multilevel correlated subquery, using a cursor, or creating a solution that involves temporary tables. (We saw some of these techniques in Chapter 12.) Invariably, the only way you can determine which solution is best is to try all the queries. You might be surprised by the results.

Rather than trying to learn a bunch of tricks to do up front, you should be much more interested in doing the basics right. That is, you need to be sure that you've set up a good database structure—including perhaps some denormalization based on your CRUD analysis—and that you've created in advance what appear to be useful indexes. From there, you can test your queries and study the query plans generated for any queries that seem problematic. (This is why we've looked at general database design strategies and indexing before discussing how the query optimizer works.)

Nevertheless, insight into how the optimizer works is certainly useful. It can help you understand the guidelines on which indexes to create, as well as the query plans you will examine in the SQL Server Query Analyzer. For each table involved in the query, the query optimizer evaluates the search arguments and considers which indexes are available to narrow the scan of a table. That is, the optimizer evaluates to what extent the index can exclude rows from consideration. The more rows that can be excluded, the better, since that leaves fewer rows to process.

Joins can be processed using one of three methods: nested iteration, hashing, or merging. For any of these methods, the optimizer decides on the order in which the tables should be accessed. Because a nested iteration is a loop, order is important. The fewer the iterations through the loops, the less processing will be required. So it is useful to start with the table (or tables) that can exclude the most rows as the outer loops. The general strategy is to make the outer table limit the search the most, which results in the fewest total iterations (scans). With hash or merge joins, SQL Server builds an in-memory structure from one of the tables. To conserve memory resources, it tries to determine which is the smaller table or which will have the smallest number of qualifying rows after the WHERE conditions are applied. This table is typically chosen as the first table to be processed. (We'll see more on each of these join strategies later in the chapter.)

For each combination of join strategy, join order, and indexes, the query optimizer estimates a cost, taking into account the number of logical reads and the memory resources that are required and available. Then the optimizer compares the cost of each plan and chooses the plan with the lowest estimate. You can think of query optimization as happening in three main phases: query analysis, index selection, and join selection (although there is a lot of overlap between the index selection and join selection phases). The following sections discuss each phase.

Query Analysis

During the first phase of query optimization, query analysis, the query optimizer looks at each clause of the query and determines whether it can be useful in limiting how much data must be scanned—that is, whether the clause is useful as a search argument (SARG) or as part of the join criteria. A clause that can be used as a search argument is referred to as *sargable,* or *optimizable,* and can make use of an index for faster retrieval.

A SARG limits a search because it specifies an exact match, a range of values, or a conjunction of two or more items joined by AND. A SARG contains a constant expression (or a variable that is resolved to a constant) that acts on a column by using an operator. It has the form

```
column inclusive_operator <constant or variable>
```

or

```
<constant or variable> inclusive_operator column
```

The column name can appear on one side of the operator, and the constant or variable can appear on the other side. If a column appears on both sides of the operator, the clause is not sargable. Sargable operators include =, >, <, =>, <=, BETWEEN, and sometimes LIKE. LIKE is sargable depending on the type of wildcards (regular expression) used. For example, *LIKE 'Jon%'* is sargable but *LIKE 'Jon%'* is not because the wildcard (%) at the beginning prevents the use of an index. Here are some SARG examples:

```
name = 'jones'

salary > 40000

60000 < salary

department = 'sales'

name = 'jones' AND salary > 100000

name LIKE 'dail%'
```

A single SARG can include many conditions if they are AND'ed together. That is, one index might be able to operate on all the conditions that are AND'ed together. In the example above, there might be an index on (*name,salary*), so the entire clause *name = 'jones' AND salary > 100000* can be considered one SARG and can be evaluated for qualifying rows using one index. If OR is used instead of AND in this example, a single index scan cannot be used to qualify both terms. The reason should be clear—if the lead field in the index key is *name*, the index is useful for finding just the *'jones'* entries. If the criteria is AND *salary*, the second field of the index also qualifies those rows. But if the criteria is OR *salary*, the index is not useful because all the rows would need to be examined, not just the *'jones'* entries.

The phone book analogy also applies. If you want to find *people with the name "jones" AND that live on 5th Avenue*, using the phone book can help greatly reduce the size of your search. But if you want to find *people with the name "Jones" OR that live on 5th Avenue,* you have to scan every entry in the book. (This assumes that you have only one phone book that is sorted alphabetically by name. If you have two phone books, and one is sorted by name and one is sorted by street, that's another story, which we'll discuss a bit later.)

An expression that is not sargable cannot limit the search. (That is, every row must be evaluated.) So an index is not useful to nonsargable expressions. Typical nonsargable expressions include negation operators such as NOT, !=, <>, !>, !<, NOT EXISTS, NOT IN, and NOT LIKE. Don't extrapolate too far and think that this means using a nonsargable clause always results in a table scan. An index is not useful to the nonsargable clause, but there might be indexes useful to other SARGs in the query. Queries often have multiple clauses, so a great index for one or more of the other clauses might be available. Here are some examples of nonsargable clauses:

```
name <> 'jones'

salary !> 40000

NOT(60000 < salary)

name LIKE '%jon%'

name = 'jones' OR salary > 100000
```

> **NOTE** The last example above is not a single search argument, but each expression on either side of the OR is individually sargable. So a single index won't be used to evaluate both expressions, as it might if the operator is AND. A separate index can still be useful to each expression.

Unlike previous versions of SQL Server, expressions involving computations are not always nonsargable. SQL Server 7 can do scalar simplification in some cases. The following table shows examples of expressions that the SQL

Server optimizer will simplify, along with the resultant simplified expression that is used to determine the usefulness of an index:

Original Expression	Simplified Expression
WHERE price * 12 = sales/costs	WHERE price = sales/costs/12
WHERE salary * 1 > 40000	WHERE salary > 40000

The simplified expression is not guaranteed to be exactly equivalent to the original, particularly if you have a mixture of datatypes and implicit conversions are occurring. However, the simplified expression is used only during optimization, to detect and measure the usefulness of a particular index. When determining whether a particular row actually qualifies for the result set, SQL Server always uses the original expression.

Expressions that apply a function to a column are not sargable, and in SQL Server 7, the optimizer does not attempt to internally convert them to something that is sargable. In some cases, however, you might be able to write an equivalent expression. For example, suppose you have an index on the *lname* column of the *newemployee* table. The following two queries return the same results, but the first one does not use an index and the second one does:

```
SELECT * FROM newemployee WHERE substring(lname,1,1) = 'K'

SELECT * FROM newemployee WHERE lname LIKE 'K%'
```

Future versions of SQL Server will address more issues of nonsargable clauses.

Index Selection

During the second phase of query optimization, index selection, the query optimizer determines whether an index exists for a sargable clause, assesses the index's usefulness by determining the selectivity of the clause (that is, how many rows will be returned), and estimates the cost to find the qualifying rows. An index is potentially useful if its first column is used in the search argument and the search argument establishes a lower bound, upper bound, or both to limit the search. In addition, if an index contains every column referenced in a query, even if none of those columns is the first column of the index, the index is considered useful.

An index that contains all the referenced columns is called a *covering index* and is one of the fastest ways to access data. The data pages do not have to be accessed at all, which can mean a substantial savings in physical I/O. For example, suppose we have an index on last name, first name, and date of hire. The query at the top of the following page is covered by this index.

```
SELECT lname, hire_date
FROM employee
WHERE fname = 'Sven'
```

You might have more covering indexes than you are aware of. In SQL Server 7, a nonclustered index contains the clustered index key as part of the row locator. So if the *employee* table has a clustered index on the employee ID (*emp_id*) column, the nonclustered index on *lname* contains both the last name and the ID for every data row, stored in the leaf level of the index. Thus, the following is also a covered query:

```
SELECT emp_id, fname, lname
FROM employee
WHERE lname LIKE 'B%'
```

Index Statistics

After the query optimizer finds a potentially useful index that matches the clause, it evaluates the index based on the selectivity of the clause. The optimizer checks the index's statistics—the histogram of values accessible through the index's row in the *sysindexes* table. The histogram is created when the index is created on existing data, and the values are refreshed each time UPDATE STATISTICS runs. If the index is created before data exists in the table, no statistics appear. The statistics will be misleading if they were generated when the dispersion of data values was significantly different from what appears in the current data in the table. However, SQL Server detects if statistics are not up-to-date, and by default it automatically updates them during query optimization.

Statistics are a histogram consisting of an even sampling of values for the index key (or the first column of the key for a composite index) based on the current data. The histogram is stored in the *statblob* field of the *sysindexes* table, which is of type *image*. (As you know, *image* data is actually stored in structures separate from the data row itself. The data row merely contains a pointer to the *image* data. For simplicity's sake, we'll talk about the index statistics as being stored in the *image* field called *statblob*.) To fully estimate the usefulness of an index, the optimizer also needs to know the number of pages in the table or index; this information is stored in the *dpages* column of *sysindexes*.

The statistics information also includes details about the uniqueness of the data values encountered, referred to as the *density*, which provides a measure of how selective the index is. Recall that the more selective an index is, the more useful it is, because higher selectivity means that more rows can be eliminated from consideration. A unique index, of course, is the most selective—by definition, each index entry can point to only one row. A unique index has a density value of $1/\textit{number of rows in the table}$.

Density values range from 0 through 1. Highly selective indexes have density values of 0.10 or lower. For example, a unique index on a table with 8345 rows has a density of 0.00012 (1/8345). If there is a nonunique nonclustered index with a density of 0.2165 on the same table, each index key can be expected to point to about 1807 rows (0.2165 × 8345). This is probably not selective enough to be more efficient than just scanning the table, so this index is probably not useful. Because driving the query from a nonclustered index means that the pages must be retrieved in index order, an estimated 1807 data page accesses (or logical reads) are needed if there is no clustered index on the table and the leaf level of the index contains the actual RID of the desired data row. The only time a data page doesn't need to be reaccessed is for the occasional coincidence that can occur when two adjacent index entries happen to point to the same data page.

Assume in this example that about 40 rows fit on a page, so there are about 209 total pages. The chance of two adjacent index entries pointing to the same page is only about 0.5 percent (1/209). The number of logical reads for just the data pages, not even counting the index I/O, is likely to be close to 1807. If there is also a clustered index on the table, a couple of additional page accesses will be needed for each nonclustered key accessed. In contrast, the entire table can be scanned with just 209 logical reads—the number of pages in the table. In this case, the optimizer looks for better indexes or decides that a table scan is the best it can do.

The statistics histogram records steps (samples) for only the lead column of the index. This optimization takes into account the fact that an index is useful only if its lead column is specified in a WHERE clause. The density information stored in the *statblob* field consists of two types of information, called *density* values and *all_density* values. The values are computed based on the number of rows in the table, the cardinality of the indexed columns (the number of distinct values), the number of nonfrequent (NF) values (values that appear no more than once in the histogram step boundaries), and the cardinality of NF values. This will become clearer when we see some actual statistics information.

SQL Server defines *density* and *all_density* as follows:

- *density* = (*NF count/distinct NF count*)/(*number of rows*)

- *all_density* = 1/*cardinality of index keys*

Statistics for a single column consist of one histogram, one *all_density* value, and one *density* value. The multicolumn statistics for one set of columns in a composite index consist of one histogram for the first column in the index, one *density* value for the first column, and *all_density* values for each prefix combination of columns (including the first column alone). The fact that density information is kept for all columns helps you decide how useful the index is for joins.

Suppose, for example, that an index is composed of three key fields. The density on the first column might be 0.50, which is not too useful. But as you look at more columns in the key, the number of rows pointed to is fewer (or in the worst case, the same) as the first column, so the density value goes down. If you're looking at both the first and second columns, the density might be 0.25, which is somewhat better. And if you examine three columns, the density might be 0.03, which is highly selective. (It doesn't make sense to refer to the density of only the second column. The lead column density is always needed.)

The histogram contains up to 300 values of a given key column. In addition to the histogram, the *statblob* field contains the following information:

- The time of the last statistics collection
- The number of rows used to produce the histogram and density information
- The average row length
- Densities for other combinations of columns

The following example uses the *authors* table in the *pubs* database. Assume that we have built a nonclustered composite index (*idx3*) on *state* and *au_lname* in addition to an existing clustered index on *au_id*. We can use DBCC SHOW_STATISTICS to display the statistics information for this index:

```
DBCC SHOW_STATISTICS(authors, idx3)
```

We see the following results:

Updated	Rows	Rows Sampled	Steps	Density	Average key length
Jan 20 1999	23	23	23	4.3478262E-2	9.6956511

All density	Columns
0.125	state
4.5454547E-2	state, au_lname
4.3478262E-2	state, au_lname, au_id

```
(3 row(s) affected)
```

```
Steps
-----
CA
CA
CA
CA
CA
CA
CA
CA
CA
CA
CA
CA
CA
CA
IN
KS
MD
MI
OR
TN
UT
UT
```

(23 row(s) affected)

This output indicates that the statistics for this index were last updated on January 20, 1999. It also indicates that the table currently has 23 rows. There are eight distinct values for state, but two of them occur in multiple steps, so only six of them are nonfrequent. In this data set, all the NF key values actually occur only once in the data, so the NF count is the same as the unique NF count, and density is computed as 6/6/23, or 4.3478262E-2. The *all_density* value for the *state* column is 1/8, or 0.125. For the combination of *state* and *au_lname*, there is only one duplicate, so there are 22 unique values, and 1/22 is 4.5454547E–2. Notice that there is also an *all_density* value for the combination of *state*, *au_lname*, and *au_id*. Since this table has a clustered index on *au_id*, that key appears along with every nonclustered index key and can be used in determining density information. Since the addition of *au_id* makes the three-valued key unique, *all_density* is 1/23, or 4.3478262E–2. (In this case, this is the same as the density for first column, but this won't always be true.)

In addition to statistics on indexes, SQL Server 7 can also keep track of statistics on columns with no indexes. Knowing the density, or the likelihood of a particular value occurring, can help the optimizer determine an optimum processing strategy, even if SQL Server can't use an index to actually locate the values. We'll discuss column statistics in more detail when we look at statistics management later in this section.

Query optimization is probability-based, which means that its conclusions can be wrong. It can sometimes make decisions that are not optimal, even if those decisions make sense from a probability standpoint. (As an analogy, you can think of national election polls, which show how accurate relatively small samples can be for predicting broader results. But the famous headline "Dewey Defeats Truman!" proves that predictions based on sample populations can also be wrong.)

NOTE The information about the meaning of the SHOW_ STATISTICS values, as well as information about statistics on columns, was adapted from a preliminary copy of a whitepaper by Lubor Kollar. We are indebted to him for his assistance.

Index Cost

The second part of determining the selectivity of a clause is calculating the estimated cost of the access methods that can be used. Even if a useful index is present, it might not be used if the optimizer determines that it is not the cheapest access method. One of the main components of the cost calculation, especially for queries involving only a single table, is the amount of logical I/O, which refers to the number of page accesses that are needed. Logical I/O is counted whether the pages are already in the memory cache or must be read from disk and brought into the cache. The term is sometimes used to refer to I/O from cache, as if a read were either logical or physical, but this is a misnomer. As discussed in Chapter 3, pages are always retrieved from the cache via a request to the Buffer Manager, so all reads are logical. If the pages are not already in the cache, they must be brought in first by the Buffer Manager. In those cases, the read is also physical. Only the Buffer Manager, which serves up the pages, knows whether a page is already in cache or must be accessed from disk and brought into cache. The ratio of how much I/O is already in the cache and does not require a physical read is referred to as the *cache-hit ratio*, an important metric to watch.

The optimizer evaluates indexes to estimate the number of likely "hits" based on the density and step values in the statistics. Based on these values, the optimizer estimates how many rows qualify for the given SARG and how many logical reads would retrieve those qualifying rows. It might find multiple indexes that can find qualifying rows, or it might determine that just scanning the table and checking all the rows is best. It chooses the access method that it predicts will require the fewest logical reads.

Whether the access method uses a clustered index, one or more nonclustered indexes, a table scan, or another option determines the estimated number of logical reads. This number can be very different for each method. Using an index to find qualifying rows is frequently referred to as *an index driving the scan*. When a nonclustered index drives the scan, the query optimizer assumes that the page containing each identified qualifying row is probably not the same page accessed the last time. Because the pages must be retrieved according to the order of the index entries, retrieving the next row with a query driven by a nonclustered index will likely require that a different page than the one that contained the previous row be fetched because the two rows probably don't reside on the same page. They might reside on the same page by coincidence, but the optimizer correctly assumes that typically this will not be the case. (With 5000 pages, the chance of this occurring is 1/5000.) If the index is not clustered, data order is random with respect to the index key.

If the scan is driven from a clustered index, the next row is probably located on the same page as the previous row, since the index leaf is, in fact, the data. The only time this is not the case when you use a clustered index is when the last row on a page has been retrieved; the next page must be accessed, and it will contain the next bunch of rows. But moving back and forth between the index and the data pages is not required.

There is, of course, a chance that a specific page might already be in cache when you use a nonclustered index. But a logical read will still occur, even if the scan does not require physical I/O (a read from disk). Physical I/O is an order of magnitude more costly than I/O from cache. But don't assume that only the cost of physical I/O matters—reads from the cache are still far from free. In some of the advanced examples in Chapter 12, different solutions for the small *pubs* database each use about the same number of physical reads because the tables are small enough to all be cached. But the solutions have widely different needs for logical I/O, and the performance differences are quite dramatic.

To minimize logical I/O, the query optimizer tries to produce a plan that will result in the fewest number of page operations. In doing so, the optimizer will probably minimize physical I/O as well. For example, suppose we need to resolve a query with the following SARG:

```
WHERE Emp_Name BETWEEN 'Smith' AND 'Snow'
```

The relevant index entries for a nonclustered index on *Emp_Name* appear at the top of the following page.

```
Index_Key (Emp_Name)      Found on Page(s)
--------------------      --------------------
Smith                     1:267, 1:384, 1:512
Smyth                     1:267
Snow                      1:384, 1:512
```

If this table is a heap, when we use this nonclustered index, six logical reads are required to retrieve the data pages in addition to the I/O necessary to read the index. If none of the pages is already cached, the data access results in three physical I/O reads, assuming that the pages remain in the cache long enough to be reused for the subsequent rows (which is a good bet).

Suppose that all the index entries are on one leaf page and the index has one intermediate level. In this case, three I/O reads (logical and probably physical) are necessary to read the index (one root level, one intermediate level, and one leaf level). So chances are that driving this query via the nonclustered index requires about nine logical I/O reads, six of which are probably physical if the cache started out empty. The data pages are retrieved in the following order:

Page 1:267 to get row with Smith
Page 1:384 for Smith
Page 1:512 for Smith
Page 1:267 (again) for Smyth
Page 1:384 (again) for Snow
Page 1:512 (again) for Snow

The number of logical reads is more if the table has a clustered index (for example, on the zip code field). Our leaf-level index entries might look like this:

```
Index_Key (Emp_Name)      Clustered Key(s)
--------------------      --------------------
Smith                     06403, 20191, 98370
Smyth                     37027
Snow                      22241, 80863
```

For each of the six nonclustered keys, we have to traverse the clustered index. You typically see about three to four times as many logical reads for traversing a nonclustered index for a table that also has a clustered index. However, if the indexes for this table are re-created so that a clustered index existed on the *Emp_Name* column, all six of the qualifying rows are probably located on the same page. The number of logical reads is probably only three (the index root, the intermediate index page, and the leaf index page, which is the data page), plus the final read that will retrieve all the qualifying rows. This scenario should make it clear to you why a clustered index can be so important to a range query.

With no clustered index, you have a choice between doing a table scan and using one or more nonclustered indexes. The number of logical I/O operations required for a scan of the table is equal to the number of pages in the table. A table scan starts at the first page and uses the Index Allocation Map (IAM) to access all the pages in the table. As the pages are read, the rows are evaluated to see whether they qualify based on the search criteria. Clearly, if the table from the previous example had fewer than nine total data pages, fewer logical reads would be necessary to scan the whole thing than to drive the scan off the nonclustered index (which was estimated to take nine logical reads).

The estimated logical reads for scanning qualifying rows is summarized in Table 14-2. The access method with the least estimated cost is chosen based on this information.

Access Method	Estimated Cost (in Logical Reads)
Table scan	The total number of data pages in the table.
Clustered index	The number of levels in the index plus the number of data pages to scan. (Data pages to be scanned = number of qualifying rows / rows per data page.)
Nonclustered index on a heap	The number of levels in the index plus the number of leaf pages plus the number of qualifying rows (a logical read for the data page of each qualifying row). The same data pages are often retrieved (from cache) many times, so the number of logical reads can be much higher than the number of pages in the table.
Nonclustered index on a table with a clustered index	The number of levels in the index plus the number of leaf pages plus the number of qualifying rows times the cost of searching for a clustered index key.
Covering nonclustered index	The number of levels in the index plus the number of leaf index pages (qualifying rows / rows per leaf page). The data page need not be accessed because all necessary information is in the index key.

Table 14-2.
The cost of data access for tables with different index structures.

Using Multiple Indexes

In SQL Server 7, the optimizer can decide to use two or more nonclustered indexes to satisfy a single query. When more than one index is considered useful because of two or more SARGs, the cost estimate changes a bit from the formulas given in Table 14-1. In addition to the I/O cost of finding the qualifying rows in each index, there is an additional cost of finding the intersection of the indexes so that SQL Server can determine which data rows satisfy all search conditions. Since each nonclustered index key contains a locator for the actual data, the results of the two index searches can be treated as worktables and joined together on the locator information.

Suppose we have the following query and we have indexes on both the *lastname* and *firstname* columns. In this case, we have a clustered index on ID number, which is a unique value.

```
SELECT firstname, lastname, ID_num FROM employees
WHERE lastname BETWEEN 'Smith' AND 'Snow'
AND firstname BETWEEN 'Daniel' and 'David'
```

If the query optimizer decides to use both indexes, it builds two worktables with the results of each index search:

```
Index_Key (lastname)    Locator(Clustered Key)
--------------------    ----------------------
Smith                   66-712403
Smith                   87-120191
Smith                   76-137027
Smyth                   11-983770
Snow                    43-220191
Snow                    21-780863


Index_Key (firstname)   Locator(Clustered Key)
--------------------    ----------------------
Daniel                  11-983770
Daniel                  77-321456
Danielle                66-712403
David                   29-331218
```

These worktables are joined on the row locator information, which is unique for each row. (Even if you don't declare a clustered index as unique, SQL Server adds a special uniqueifier where needed so there is always a unique row locator in every nonclustered index.) From the information above, we can see that only two rows have both their first name and last name values in the requested range. The result set is:

```
firstname    lastname           ID_num
----------   ----------------   ---------
Daniel       Smythe             11-983770
Danielle     Smith              66-712403
```

In this example, the data in the two indexes is enough to satisfy the query. If we also want to see information such as address and phone number, the query optimizer uses the locator to find the actual data row by traversing the clustered index. It can also use multiple indexes if a single table has multiple SARGs that are OR'ed together. In this case, SQL Server finds the UNION of the rows returned by each index to determine all the qualifying rows. If we take the same query and data and write an OR query instead of an AND, we can demonstrate the main differences:

```
SELECT firstname, lastname, ID_num FROM employees
WHERE lastname BETWEEN 'Smith' AND 'Snow'
OR firstname BETWEEN 'Daniel' and 'David'
```

SQL Server can use the two indexes in the same way and build the same two worktables. However, it must UNION the two worktables together and remove duplicates. Once it removes the duplicates, it uses the locators to find the rows in the table. All the result rows will have either a first name or a last name in the requested range, but not necessarily both. For example, we can return a row for Daniel Delaney or Bridgette Smith. If we don't remove duplicates, we end up with Daniel Smythe and Danielle Smith showing up twice because they meet both conditions of the SARGs.

Unusable Statistics

In two cases, the query optimizer can't use the statistics to estimate how many rows will satisfy a given SARG. First, if there are no statistics available, SQL Server obviously can't come up with any cost estimate. However, this situation is rare in SQL Server 7 because by default every database has the two options *auto create statistics* and *auto update statistics* set to TRUE. As we'll see later, you can turn this behavior off at the table level or the database level, but it is usually not recommended. The second situation in which there are no usable statistics is if the values in a SARG are variables. Consider this example:

```
DECLARE @name varchar(30)
SET @name = 'Zelda'
SELECT firstname, lastname, ID_num FROM employees
WHERE lastname > @name
```

When the preceding query is optimized, the SET statement has not been executed and the value of *@name* is unknown. No specific value can be used to compare the steps in the index's statistics information, so the query optimizer must guess.

NOTE Don't confuse variables with parameters, even though their syntax is nearly identical. A variable's value is never known until the statement is actually executed; it is never known at compile time. Stored procedure parameters are known when the procedure is compiled because compilation and optimization don't even take place until the procedure is actually called with specific values for the parameters.

If the query optimizer can't use the statistics for either of the reasons mentioned, the server uses fixed percentages, shown below, depending on the operator. These fixed percentages can be grossly inaccurate for your specific data, however, so make sure that your statistics are up-to-date.

Operator	Percentage of Rows
=	10
>	30
<	30
BETWEEN	10

When the SARG involves an equality, the situation is usually handled in a special way. The 10 percent estimate shown above is actually used only in the unusual case in which there are no statistics at all. If there are statistics, they can be used. Even if we don't have a particular value to compare against the steps in the statistics histogram, the density information can be used. That information basically tells the query optimizer the expected number of duplicates, so when the SARG involves looking for one specific value, it assumes that the value occurs the average number of times. An even more special case occurs when the query optimizer recognizes an equality in the WHERE clause and the index is unique. Because this combination yields an exact match and always returns at most one row, the query optimizer doesn't have to use statistics. For queries of one row that use an exact match such as a lookup by primary key, a unique nonclustered index is highly efficient. In fact, many environments probably shouldn't "waste" their clustered index on the primary key. If access via the complete primary key is common, it might be beneficial to specify NONCLUSTERED when you declare the primary key and save the clustered index for another type of access (such as a range query) that can benefit more from the clustered index.

Join Selection

Join selection is the third major step in query optimization. If the query is a multiple-table query or a self-join, the query optimizer evaluates join selection and selects the join strategy with the lowest cost. It determines the cost using a number of factors, including the expected number of reads and the amount of memory required. It can use three basic strategies for processing joins: nested loop joins, merge joins, and hash joins. In each method, the tables to be joined (or subsets of tables that have already been restricted by applying SARGs) are called the join inputs.

Nested Loop Joins

Joins are usually processed as nested iterations—a set of loops that take a row from the first table and use that row to scan the inner table, and so on, until the result that matches is used to scan the last table. The number of iterations through any of the loops equals the number of scans that must be done. (This is not a table scan, since it is usually done using an index. In fact, if no useful index is available to be used for an inner table, nested iteration probably isn't used and a hash join strategy is used instead.) The result set is narrowed down as it progresses from table to table within each iteration in the loop. If you've done programming with an ISAM-type product, this should look familiar in terms of opening one "file" and then seeking into another in a loop. To process this join

```
WHERE dept.deptno=empl.deptno
```

you use pseudocode that looks something like this:

```
    DO (until no more dept rows);
        GET NEXT dept row;
            {
            begin
 // Scan empl, hopefully using an index on empl.deptno
                GET NEXT empl row for given dept
            end
    }
```

Merge Joins

Merge joins were introduced in SQL Server 7. You can use a merge join when the two join inputs are both sorted on the join column. Consider the query we looked at in the previous section:

```
WHERE dept.deptno=empl.deptno
```

If both the *department* table and the *employee* table have clustered indexes on the *deptno* column, the query is a prime candidate for a merge join. You can think of merge joins as taking two sorted lists of values and merging them. Suppose you have two piles of contractor information. One pile contains the master contract that each contractor has signed, and the second contains descriptions of each project that the contractor has worked on. Both piles are sorted by contractor name. You need to merge the two piles of paperwork so each contractor's master contract is placed with all the project descriptions for that contractor. You basically need to make just one pass through each stack.

Going back to the *employee* and *department* query, our pseudocode would look something like this:

```
GET one dept row and one empl row
DO (until one input is empty);
    IF dept_no values are equal
        Return values from both rows
    ELSE IF empl.dept_no < dept.dept_no
        GET new employee row
    ELSE GET new department row
    GET NEXT dept row;
```

The query optimizer usually chooses the merge join strategy when both inputs are already sorted on the join column. In some cases, even if a sort must be done on one of the inputs, the query optimizer might decide that it is faster to sort one input and then do a merge join than to use any of the other available strategies. If the inputs are both already sorted, little I/O is required to process a merge join if the join is one to many. A many-to-many merge join uses a temporary table to store rows instead of discarding them. If there are duplicate values from each input, one of the inputs must rewind to the start of the duplicates as each duplicate from the other input is processed.

Hash Joins

Hash joins, also introduced in SQL Server 7, can be used when no useful index exists on the join column in either input. Hashing is commonly used in searching algorithms (as discussed in detail in Donald Knuth's classic *The Art of Computer Programming: Sorting and Searching*). We'll look at a simplified definition here. Hashing lets you determine whether a particular data item matches an already existing value by dividing the existing data into groups based on some property. You put all the data with the same value in what we can call a *hash bucket*. Then, to see if a new value has a match in existing data, you simply look in the bucket for the right value.

For example, suppose you need to keep all your wrenches organized in your workshop so that you can find the right size and type when you need it. You can organize them by size property and put all half-inch wrenches (of any type) together, all 10-mm wrenches together, and so on. When you need to find a 15-mm box wrench, you simply go to the 15-mm drawer to find one (or see whether the last person who borrowed it has returned it). You don't have to look through all the wrenches, only the 15-mm ones, which greatly reduces your searching time. Alternatively, you can organize your wrenches by type and have all the box wrenches in one drawer, all the socket wrenches in another drawer, and so on.

Hashing data in a table is not quite so straightforward. You need a property by which to divide the data into sets of manageable size with a relatively equal membership. For integers, the hashing property might be something as simple as applying the modulo function to each existing value. If you decide to hash on the operation modulo 13, every value is put in a hash bucket based on its remainder after dividing by 13. This means you need 13 buckets because the possible remainders are the integers 0 through 12. (In real systems, the actual hash functions are substantially more complex; coming up with a good hash function is an art as well as a science.)

When you use hashing to join two inputs, SQL Server uses one input, called the *build input*, to actually build the hash buckets. Then, one row at a time, it inspects the other input and tries to find a match in the existing buckets. The second input is called the *probe input*. Suppose we use modulo 3 as the hash function and join the two inputs shown in Figure 14-4 on the following page. (The rows not matching the SARGs are not shown, so the two inputs are reduced in size quite a bit.) Here is the query:

```
SELECT Name, Manager
FROM employee.dept_no empl JOIN department.dept_no dept
ON dept.deptno=empl.deptno
WHERE <SARGs>
```

Department	
dept_no	Manager
2	Laszlo
5	Wehland
6	Graeffe
8	Waymire
10	Aebi
13	Soukup
15	Berenson

Employee		
ID	Name	dept_no
1	Pike	2
2	Delaney	6
3	Harvey	7
4	Moran	10
5	Rogerson	14
6	Karaszi	13
7	Fields	11
8	Robertson	4
9	Pfeiff	1
10	Hotz	7
11	Dwyer	2
12	Talmadge	12

Figure 14-4.

Two inputs to a hash join operation.

When processing hash joins, SQL Server tries to use the smaller input as the build input, so in this case we'll assume that the hash buckets have been built based on the *department* table values. The buckets are actually stored as linked lists, in which each entry contains only the columns from the build input that are needed. In this case, all we have to keep track of is the department number and manager name. The collection of these linked lists is called the *hash table*. Our hash table is shown in Figure 14-5. Our pseudocode looks something like this:

```
Allocate an Empty Hash Table
For Each Row in the Build Input
    Determine the hash bucket by applying the hash function
    Insert the relevant fields of the record into the bucket
For Each Record in the Probe Input
    Determine the hash bucket
    Scan the hash bucket for matches
    Output matches
Deallocate the Hash Table
```

Applying this algorithm to our two inputs, we get these results:

```
Name        Manager
--------    -------
Pike        Laszlo
Delaney     Graeffe
Moran       Aebi
Dwyer       Laszlo
```

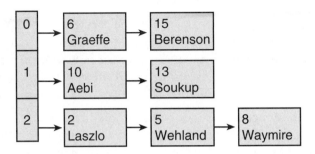

Figure 14-5.
A hash table built from the smaller (build) input.

Hashing Variations

Although you can use hashing effectively when there are no useful indexes on your tables, the query optimizer might not always choose it as the join strategy because of its high cost in terms of memory required. Ideally, the entire hash table should fit into memory; if it doesn't, SQL Server must split both inputs into partitions, each containing a set of buckets, and write those partitions out to disk. As each partition (with a particular set of hash buckets) is needed, it is brought into memory. This increases the amount of work required in terms of I/O and general processing time. In the academic literature, you might see this type of hashing operation referred to as a *Grace hash*; the name comes from the project for which this technique was developed. SQL Server has another alternative, somewhere in between keeping everything in memory and writing everything out to disk. Partitions are only written out as needed, so you might have some partitions in memory and some out on disk.

To effectively use hashing, SQL Server must be able to make a good estimate of the size of the two inputs and choose the smaller one as the build input. Sometimes, during execution SQL Server will discover that the build input is actually the larger of the two. At that point, it can actually switch the roles of the build and probe input midstream, in a process called *role reversal*. Determining which input is smaller isn't too hard if there are no restrictive SARGs, as in this query:

```
SELECT Name, Manager
FROM employee.dept_no empl JOIN department.dept_no dept
ON dept.deptno=empl.deptno
```

SQL Server knows the sizes of the inputs because *sysindexes* keeps track of the size of each table. However, consider the case in which additional conditions are added to the query, as in this example:

```
WHERE empl.phone like '425%'
```

It would help the query optimizer to know what percentage of the employees have phone numbers starting with 425. This is a case in which column statistics can be helpful. Statistics can tell the query optimizer the estimated number of rows that will meet a given condition, even if there is no actual index structure to be used.

> **NOTE** Hash and merge join can be used only if the join is an equijoin—that is, if the join predicate compares columns from the two inputs for an equality match. If the join is not based on an equality, as in the example below, a nested loops join is the only possible strategy:
>
> ```
> WHERE table1.col1 BETWEEN table2.col2 AND table2.col3,
> ```

The hashing and merging strategies can be much more memory intensive than the nested loops strategy, and since the query optimizer takes into account all available resources, you might notice that a system with little available memory might not use the hash and merge joins as often as systems with plenty of memory. Desktop installations are particularly vulnerable to memory pressure because you are more likely to have many competing applications running simultaneously. Although the online documentation states that the desktop edition of SQL Server does not support hash and merge joins at any time, this is not true. Because in most situations there is limited memory for a desktop installation, the query optimizer is much more pessimistic when it decides to use one of these two strategies.

Multiple-Table Joins

According to some folklore, SQL Server "does not optimize" joins of more than four tables. There was some truth to this in earlier versions of SQL Server, but in SQL Server 7 optimization doesn't happen in the same way at all. There are so many different possible permutations of join strategies and index usage that the query optimizer goes through multiple optimization passes, each considering a larger set of the possible plans. On each pass, it keeps track of the best plan so far and uses a cost estimate to reduce the search in succeeding passes. If your query contains many tables, the query optimizer is likely to interrupt the last pass before completion because the last pass is quite exhaustive. The cheapest plan found will then be used.

Other Processing Strategies

Although our discussion of the query optimizer has dealt mainly with the choice of indexes and join strategies, it makes other decisions as well. It must decide how to process queries with GROUP BY, DISTINCT, and UNION, and it must decide how updates should be handled—either row at a time or table at a time. We discussed update strategies in Chapter 8. Here we'll briefly discuss GROUP BY, DISTINCT, and UNION.

GROUP BY Operations

In prior versions of SQL Server, a GROUP BY operation was processed in only one way. SQL Server sorted the data (after applying any SARGs) and then formed the groups from the sorted data. SQL programmers noticed that queries involving grouping returned results in sorted order, although this was merely a byproduct of the internal grouping mechanism. In SQL Server 7, you can use hashing to organize your data into groups and compute aggregates. The pseudocode looks like this:

```
For Each Record in the Input
    Determine the hash bucket
    Scan the hash bucket for matches
    If a match exists
        Aggregate the new record into the old
        Drop the new record
    Otherwise
        Insert the record into the bucket
Scan and Output the Hash Table
```

If the query optimizer chooses to use hashing to process the GROUP BY, the data does not come back in any predictable order. (The order actually depends on the order in which records appear in the hash table, but without knowing the specific hash function, you can't predict this order.) If you use a lot of GROUP BY queries, you might be surprised that sometimes the results come back sorted and sometimes they don't. If you absolutely need your data in a particular order, you should use ORDER BY in your query.

> **NOTE** If a database has its compatibility level flag set to 60 or 65, the query processor automatically includes an ORDER BY in the query. This allows you to mimic the behavior of older SQL Server versions.

DISTINCT Operations

As with GROUP BY queries, the only technique for removing duplicates in previous versions of SQL Server was to first sort the data. In SQL Server 7, you can use hashing to return only the distinct result rows. The algorithm is much like the algorithm for hashing with GROUP BY, except that an aggregate does not need to be maintained.

```
For Each Record in the Input
    Determine the hash bucket
    Scan the hash bucket for matches
    If a match exists
        Drop the new record
    Otherwise
        Insert the record into the bucket
            and return the record as output
```

UNION Operations

The UNION operator in SQL Server has two variations for combining the result sets of two separate queries into a single result set. If you specify UNION ALL, SQL Server returns all rows from both as the final result. If you don't specify ALL, SQL Server removes any duplicates before returning the results. For performance reasons, you should carefully evaluate your data, and if you know that the inputs are not overlapping, with no chance of duplicates, you should specify the ALL keyword to eliminate the overhead of removing duplicates. If SQL Server has to find the unique rows, it can do so in three ways: It can use hashing to remove the duplicates in a UNION, just the way it does for DISTINCT; it can sort the inputs and then merge them; or it can concatenate the inputs and then sort them to remove the duplicates.

For GROUP BY, DISTINCT, and UNION operations, your best bet is to let the query optimizer decide whether to use hashing or sorting and merging. If you suspect that the query optimizer might not have made the best choice, you can use query hints to force SQL Server to use a particular processing strategy and compare the performance with and without the hints. In most cases, the query optimizer will have made the best choice after all.

Maintaining Statistics

As we've seen, the query optimizer uses statistics on both indexed and nonindexed columns to determine the most appropriate processing strategy for any particular query. Whenever an index is created on a table containing data (as opposed to an empty table), the query optimizer collects statistics and stores them for that index in *sysindexes.statblob*. By default, the statistics are automatically updated whenever the query optimizer determines that they are out-of-date. In addition, the query optimizer generates statistics on columns used in SARGs when it needs them, and it updates them when needed.

The histogram for statistics on an index key or statistics on a nonindexed column is a set of up to 300 values for that column. SQL Server composes this set of values by taking either all occurring values or a sampling of the occurring values and then sorting that list of values and dividing it into as many as 299 approximately equal intervals. The endpoints of the intervals become the 300 histogram steps, and the query optimizer's computations assume that the actual data has an equal number of values between any two adjacent steps. These step values are stored in the *statblob* column of *sysindexes*. Even if the table or sample has more than 300 rows, the histogram might have fewer than 300 steps to achieve uniformity of step size.

You can specify the sampling interval when the indexes or statistics are initially created or at a later time using the statistics management tools. You can specify the FULLSCAN option, which means that all existing column values are sorted, or you can specify a percentage of the existing data values. By default, SQL Server uses a computed percentage that is a logarithmic function of the size of the table. If a table is less than 8 MB in size, a FULLSCAN is always done. When sampling, SQL Server randomly selects pages from the table by following the IAM chain. Once a particular page has been selected, all values from that page are used in the sample. Since disk I/O is the main cost of maintaining statistics, using all values from every page read minimizes that cost.

Statistics on nonindexed columns are built in exactly the same way as statistics on indexes. The system procedure *sp_helpindex* shows column statistics as well as indexes on a table. If the statistics are created automatically, their names are very distinctive, as shown in this example:

```
index_name                 index_description                       index_keys
------------------------    ------------------------------------    --------------

UPKCL_auidind              clustered, unique, primary key          au_id
                           located on PRIMARY
aunmind                    nonclustered located on PRIMARY         au_lname,
                                                                   au_fname
s1                         nonclustered, statistics                state
                           located on PRIMARY
_WA_Sys_au_fname_07020F21  nonclustered, statistics,               au_fname
                           auto create located on PRIMARY
```

Here we have two indexes and two sets of statistics. The name of the explicitly generated statistics is *s1*. The name of the system-generated statistics is *_WA_Sys_au_fname_07020F21*. To avoid long-term maintenance of unused statistics, SQL Server ages out the statistics that are automatically created on nonindexed columns. After it updates the column statistics more than a certain number of times, the statistics are dropped rather than updated again. The *StatVersion* column of the *sysindexes* table shows how many times the statistics have been updated. Once *StatVersion* exceeds an internally generated threshold, the statistics are dropped. If they are needed in the future, they can be created again. There is no substantial cost difference between creating statistics and updating them. Statistics that are explicitly created (such as *s1* in the preceding example) are not automatically dropped.

Statistics are automatically updated when the query optimizer determines they are out-of-date. This basically means that sufficient data modification operations have occurred since the last time they were updated to minimize their usefulness. The number of operations is tied to the size of the table and is usually something like 500 + 0.2 * (number of rows in the table). This means that the table must have at least 500 modification operations before statistics are updated during query optimization; for large tables, this threshold can be much larger.

You can also manually force statistics to be updated in one of two ways. You can run the UPDATE STATISTICS command on a table or on one specific index or column statistics. Or you can also execute the procedure *sp_updatestats*, which runs UPDATE STATISTICS against all user-defined tables in the current database.

You can create statistics on nonindexed columns using the CREATE STATISTICS command or by executing *sp_createstats*, which creates single-column statistics for all eligible columns for all user tables in the current database. This includes all columns except computed columns and columns of the *ntext*, *text*, or *image* datatypes, and columns that already have statistics or are the first column of an index.

Every database is created with the database options *auto create statistics* and *auto update statistics* set to true, but either one can be turned off. You can also turn off automatic updating of statistics for a specific table in one of two ways:

- **sp_autostats**   This procedure sets or unsets a flag for a table to indicate that statistics should or should not be updated automatically. You can also use this procedure with only the table name to find out whether the table is set to automatically have its index statistics updated.

- **UPDATE STATISTICS**   In addition to updating the statistics, the option WITH NORECOMPUTE indicates that the statistics should not be automatically recomputed in the future. Running UPDATE STATISTICS again without the WITH NORECOMPUTE option enables automatic updates.

However, setting the database option *auto update statistics* to FALSE overrides any individual table settings. In other words, no automatic updating of statistics takes place. This is not a recommended practice unless thorough testing has shown you that you don't need the automatic updates or that the performance overhead is more than you can afford.

The Index Tuning Wizard

We've seen that the query optimizer can come up with a reasonably effective query plan even in the absence of well-planned indexes on your tables. However, this does not mean that a well-tuned database doesn't need good indexes. The query plans that don't rely on indexes frequently consume additional system memory, and other applications might suffer. In addition, having appropriate indexes in place can help solve many blocking problems.

Designing the best possible indexes for the tables in your database is a complex task; it not only requires a thorough knowledge of how SQL Server uses indexes and how the query optimizer makes its decisions, but it requires that you be intimately familiar with how your data will actually be used. SQL Server 7 provides two tools to help you design the best possible indexes.

The Query Analyzer includes a tool called Index Analyzer, which you can access by choosing Perform Index Analysis from the Query menu. The index analyzer recommends indexes for the queries that you've included in the current workspace. It assumes that all your existing indexes will stay in place, so it might end up not recommending any new ones. It never recommends a clustered index because the optimum choice for a clustered index must take more than a single query into account. The index analyzer displays a dialog box with its recommendations and lets you choose whether to implement the recommendations. You cannot postpone the creation of the indexes or save a script of the CREATE INDEX statements to be used. If you need to do either of these, you can use the Index Tuning Wizard.

You can access the Index Tuning Wizard from the Wizards list in the Enterprise Manager or from SQL Server Profiler under the Tools menu. The wizard tunes a single database at a time, and it bases its recommendations on a workload file that you provide. The workload file can be a file of captured trace events that contains at least the RPC and SQL Batch starting or completed events, as well as the text of the RPCs and batches. It can also be a file of SQL statements. If you use the SQL Server Profiler to create the workload file, you can capture all SQL statement submitted by all users over a period of time. The wizard can then look at the data access patterns for all users, for all tables, and make recommendations with everyone in mind.

The book's companion CD includes a whitepaper with more details about this wizard. The CD also includes a sample database called *orders*, which is in two files: *orders_data.mdf* and *orders_log.ldf*. You can use the procedure *sp_attachdb* to add the *orders* database to your system. Finally, the CD includes a sample workload file (*Orders_Workload.sql*) composed of SQL statements that access the *orders* database.

When the wizard gets a workload file, it tunes the first 32 KB of parsable queries and produces five reports. You can make the analysis more exhaustive or less. You can choose to have the wizard keep all existing indexes, or you can have it come up with a totally new set of index recommendations, which might mean dropping some or all of your existing indexes.

After the wizard generates its reports, which you can save to disk, you can implement the suggestions immediately, schedule the implementation for a later time, or save the script files for the creation (and optional dropping) of indexes. Once the scripts are saved, you can run them later or just inspect them to get ideas of possible indexes to create.

You can also use the wizard purely for analyzing your existing design. One of the reports, Index Usage Report (Current Configuration), shows what percentage of the queries in the submitted workload make use of each of your existing indexes. You can use this information to determine whether an index is being used at all and get rid of any unused indexes along with their space and maintenance overhead.

The current version of the wizard cannot completely tune cross-database queries. It inspects the local tables involved in the queries for index recommendations, but it ignores the tables in other databases. Also, if you are using Unicode data, the wizard does not recognize Unicode constants (such as *N'mystring'*) in your queries and cannot optimize for them. Future versions of the wizard will address these issues and probably add new features as well.

NOTE If you're going to use SQL Server Profiler to capture a workload file, you should consider tracing events at several periods throughout the day. This can give you a more balanced picture of the kinds of queries that are actually being executed in your database. If you define your trace using the SQL Server Profiler extended procedures, you can set up a SQL Server Agent job to start and stop the trace at predefined times, appending to the same workload file each time.

Monitoring Query Performance

Before you think about taking some action to make a query faster, such as adding an index or denormalizing, you should understand how a query is processed. You should also get some baseline performance measurements so you can compare behavior both before and after making your changes. SQL Server provides these tools (SET options) for monitoring queries:

- STATISTICS IO
- STATISTICS TIME
- Showplan

You enable any of these SET options before you run a query, and they will produce additional output. Typically, you run your query with these options set in a tool such as the Query Analyzer. When you are satisfied with your query, you can cut and paste the query into your application or into the script file that creates your stored procedures. If you use the SET commands to turn these options on, they apply only to the current connection. The Query Analyzer provides check boxes you can use to turn any or all of these options on and off for all connections.

STATISTICS IO

Don't let the term *statistics* fool you. STATISTICS IO doesn't have anything to do with the statistics used for storing histograms and density information in *sysindexes*. This option provides statistics on how much work SQL Server did to process your query. When this option is set to ON, you get a separate line of output for each query in a batch that accesses any data objects. (You don't get any output for statements that don't access data, such as PRINT, SELECT the value of a variable, or call a system function.) The output from SET STATISTICS IO ON includes the values Logical Reads, Physical Reads, Read Ahead Reads, and Scan Count.

Logical Reads
This value indicates the total number of page accesses needed to process the query. Every page is read from the data cache, whether or not it was necessary to bring that page from disk into the cache for any given read. This value is always at least as large and usually larger than the value for Physical Reads. The same

page can be read many times (such as when a query is driven from an index), so the count of Logical Reads for a table can be greater than the number of pages in a table.

Physical Reads

This value indicates the number of pages that were read from disk; it is always less than or equal to the value of Logical Reads. The value of the Buffer Cache Hit Ratio, as displayed by Performance Monitor, is computed from the Logical Reads and Physical Reads values as follows:

Cache-Hit Ratio = (Logical Reads − Physical Reads) / Logical Reads

Remember that the value for Physical Reads can vary greatly and decreases substantially with the second and subsequent execution because the cache is loaded by the first execution. The value is also affected by other SQL Server activity and can appear low if the page was preloaded by read ahead activity. For this reason, you probably won't find it useful to do a lot of analysis of physical I/O on a per-query basis. When looking at individual queries, the Logical Reads value is usually more interesting because the information is consistent. Physical I/O and achieving a good cache-hit ratio is crucial, but they are more interesting at the all-server level. Pay close attention to Logical Reads for each important query, and pay close attention to physical I/O and the cache-hit ratio for the server as a whole.

STATISTICS IO acts on a per-table, per-query basis. You might want to see the *physical_io* column in *sysprocesses* corresponding to the specific connection. This column shows the cumulative count of synchronous I/O that has occurred during the *spid*'s existence, regardless of the table. It even includes any Read Ahead Reads that were made by that connection.

Read Ahead Reads

The Read Ahead Reads value indicates the number of pages that were read into cache using the read ahead mechanism while the query was processed. These pages are not necessarily used by the query. If a page is ultimately needed, a logical read is counted but a physical read is not. A high value means that the value for Physical Reads is probably lower and the cache-hit ratio is probably higher than if a read ahead was not done. In a situation like this, you shouldn't infer from a high cache-hit ratio that your system can't benefit from additional memory. The high ratio might come from the read ahead mechanism bringing much of the needed data into cache. That's a good thing, but it could be better if the data simply remains in cache from previous use. You might achieve the same or a higher cache-hit ratio without requiring the Read Ahead Reads.

You can think of read ahead as simply an optimistic form of physical I/O. In full or partial table scans, the table's IAMs are consulted to determine which extents belong to the object. The extents are read with a single 64-KB scatter read, and because of the way that the IAMs are organized, they are read in disk order. If the table is spread across multiple files in a file group, the read ahead attempts to keep at least eight of the files busy instead of sequentially processing the files. Read ahead reads are asynchronously requested by the thread that is running the query; because they are asynchronous, the scan doesn't block while waiting for them to complete. It blocks only when it actually tries to scan a page that it thinks has been brought into cache and the read hasn't finished yet. In this way, the read ahead neither gets too ambitious (reading too far ahead of the scan) nor too far behind.

Scan Count

The Scan Count value indicates the number of times that the corresponding table was accessed. Outer tables of a nested loop join have a Scan Count of 1. For inner tables, the Scan Count might be the number of times "through the loop" that the table was accessed. The number of Logical Reads is determined by the sum of the Scan Count times the number of pages accessed on each scan. However, even for nested loop joins, the Scan Count for the inner table might show up as 1. SQL Server might copy the needed rows from the inner table into a worktable in cache and use this worktable to access the actual data rows. When this step is used in the plan, there is often no indication of it in the STATISTICS IO output. You must use the output from STATISTIC TIME, as well as information about the actual processing plan used, to determine the actual work involved in executing a query. Hash joins and merge joins usually show the Scan Count as 1 for both tables involved in the join, but these types of joins can involve substantially more memory. You can inspect the *memusage* value in sysprocesses while the query is being executed, but unlike the *physical_io* value, this is not a cumulative counter and is valid only for the currently running query. Once a query finishes, there is no way to see how much memory it used.

STATISTICS TIME

The output of SET STATISTICS TIME ON is pretty self-explanatory. It shows the elapsed and CPU time required to process the query. (In this context, it means the time not spent waiting for resources such as locks or reads to complete.) The times are separated into two components: the time required to parse and compile the query, and the time required to execute the query. For some of your testing, you might find it just as useful to look at the system time with *getdate()* before and after a query if all you need to measure is elapsed time. However, if you want to compare elapsed vs. actual CPU time or if you are interested in how long compilation and optimization took, you must use STATISTICS TIME.

Showplan

In SQL Server 7, there is not just a single option for examining the execution plan for a query. You can choose to see the plan in a text format, with or without additional performance estimates, or you can see a graphical representation of the processing plan.

SHOWPLAN_TEXT and SHOWPLAN_ALL

The two SET options SHOWPLAN_TEXT and SHOWPLAN_ALL let you see the estimated query plan without actually executing the query. Both options also enable the SET NOEXEC option, so you don't see any results from your query—you see only the way that SQL Server has determined is the best method for processing the query. SHOWPLAN_TEXT shows you all the steps involved in processing the query, including the type of join used, the order of table accesses, and which index or indexes are used for each table. Any internal sorts are also shown. SHOWPLAN_ALL provides this information plus estimates of the number of rows that are expected to meet the queries' search criteria, the estimated size of the result rows, the estimated CPU time, and the total cost estimate that was used to compare this plan to other possible plans.

> **WARNING** Since turning on SHOWPLAN TEXT or SHOW-PLAN ALL implies that NOEXEC is also on, you must set the SHOWPLAN option to OFF before you do anything else. For example, you must set SHOWPLAN_TEXT to OFF before setting SHOWPLAN_ALL to ON. You must also set these options to OFF before using the graphical Showplan, discussed on the next page.

The output from these options shows the order in which tables are accessed and how they are joined, which indexes are used, which tables are scanned, and what worktables are created. Showplan is your primary tool for determining which indexes are useful.

Typically, you add one or more indexes that you think might help speed up a query and then you use one of these Showplan options to see whether any of them were actually used. If an index is not going to be used (and you're not adding it to maintain a PRIMARY KEY or UNIQUE constraint), you might as well not add it. If an index is not useful for queries, the index is just overhead in terms of space and maintenance time. After you add indexes, be sure to monitor their effect on your updates, since indexes can add overhead to data modification (inserts, deletes, and updates).

If the index *is* useful, also consider whether it is worthwhile in terms of the effect on your data modification operations. If a change to indexing alone is not the answer, you should look at other possible solutions, such as using an index hint or changing the general approach to the query. (In Chapter 12, you saw that several different approaches can be useful to some queries—ranging from the use of somewhat tricky SQL to the use of temporary tables and cursors. If these approaches also fail, you should consider changes to the database design using the denormalization techniques discussed earlier.)

Graphical Showplan

SQL Server 7 provides a graphical representation of a query's estimated execution plan. Like the SET options for Showplan, by default your query is not executed when you choose to display the graphical Showplan output. You can choose to display this graphical information by choosing Display Estimated Execution Plan from the Query menu in the Query Analyzer or by clicking the corresponding toolbar button in the Query Analyzer. The graphical representation contains all the information available through SHOWPLAN_ALL, but not all of it is visible at once. You can, however, move your cursor over any of the icons in the graphical plan to see the additional performance estimates, as shown in Figure 14-6 on the following page.

Displaying the Actual Plan

All of the Showplan options discussed so far show the estimated query plan. As long as the query is not actually being executed, you can only see an estimate. Conditions such as memory resources might change before you actually run the query, so the estimated plan might not be the actual plan. If you need to see the actual plan at the time the query is executed, you have three options:

- Choose Show Execution Plan from the Query menu in the Query Analyzer. You'll see two tabs of results for every query you run until you deselect Show Execution Plan. The first tab shows the actual query output, and the second shows the graphical Showplan.

- Set STATISTICS PROFILE to ON. This option gives you the query results followed by the STATISTICS_ALL output in the same results pane.

- Set up a trace in the SQL Server Profiler to capture the Execution Plan events. This displays all the information from SHOWPLAN_ALL in the trace output for every query that is executed.

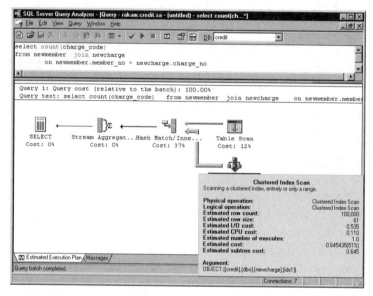

Figure 14-6.
Graphical Showplan and context-sensitive performance estimates.

Using Query Hints

As you know, locking and query optimization are done automatically by SQL Server. But because the query optimizer is probability-based, it sometimes makes wrong predictions. For example, to eliminate a deadlock, you might want to force an update lock. Or you might want to tell the query optimizer that you value the speed of returning the first row more highly than total throughput. You can specify these and other behaviors by using query hints. The word "hint" is a bit of a misnomer in this context, because the hint is handled as a directive rather than as a suggestion. SQL Server provides four general types of hints:

- **Join hints**   Specify the join technique that will be used.

- **Index hints**   Specify one or more specific indexes that should be used to drive a search or a sort.

- **Lock hints**   Specify a particular locking mode that should be used.

- **Processing hints**   Specify that a particular processing strategy should be used.

If you've made it this far in this book, you probably understand the various issues related to hints—locking, how indexes are selected, overall throughput vs. the first row returned, and how join order is determined. Understanding these issues is the key to effectively using hints and intelligently instructing SQL Server to deviate from "normal" behavior when necessary. Hints are simply syntactic hooks that override default behavior; you should now have insight into those behaviors so you can make good decisions about when such overrides are warranted.

Query hints should be used for special cases—not as standard operating procedure. When you specify a hint, you constrain SQL Server. For example, if you indicate in a hint that a specific index should be used, and later you add another index that would be even more useful, the hint prevents the query optimizer from considering the new index. In future versions of SQL Server, you can expect new query optimization strategies, more access methods, and new locking behaviors. If you bind your queries to one specific behavior, you forgo your chances of benefiting from such improvements. SQL Server offers the nonprocedural development approach—that is, you don't have to tell SQL Server *how* to do something. Rather, you tell it *what* to do. Hints run contrary to this approach. Nonetheless, the query optimizer isn't perfect and never can be. In some cases, hints can make the difference between a project's success and failure, if they are used judiciously.

When you use a hint, you must have a clear vision of how it might help. It's a good idea to add a comment to the query to justify the hint. Then test your hypothesis by watching the output of STATISTICS IO, STATISTICS TIME, and one of the Showplan options both with and without your hint.

> **TIP**   Since your data is constantly changing, a hint that worked well today might not indicate the appropriate processing strategy next week. In addition, SQL Server's optimizer is constantly evolving, and the next upgrade or service pack you apply might invalidate the need for that hint. You should periodically retest all queries that rely on hinting, to verify that the hint is still useful.

Join Hints

You can use join hints only when you use the ANSI-style syntax for joins—that is, when you actually use the word JOIN in the query. In addition, the hint comes between the type of join and the word JOIN, so you can't leave off the word INNER for an inner join. Here's an example of forcing SQL Server to use a HASH JOIN:

```
SELECT title_id, pub_name, title
FROM titles INNER HASH JOIN publishers
    ON titles.pub_id = publishers.pub_id
```

Alternatively, you can specify a LOOP JOIN or a MERGE JOIN. You can use another join hint, REMOTE, when you have defined a linked server and are doing a cross-server join. REMOTE specifies that the join operation is performed on the site of the right table (that is, the table after the word JOIN). This is useful when the left table is a local table and the right table is a remote table. You should use REMOTE only when the left table has fewer rows than the right table.

Index Hints

You can specify that one or more specific indexes be used by naming them directly in the FROM clause. You can also specify the indexes by their *indid* value, but this makes sense only when you specify *not* to use an index or to use the clustered index, whatever it is. Otherwise, the *indid* value is prone to change as indexes are dropped and re-created. You can use the value 0 to specify that no index should be used—that is, to force a table scan. And you can use the value 1 to specify that the clustered index should be used regardless of the columns on which it exists. The index hint syntax looks like this:

```
SELECT select_list
FROM table [(INDEX ({index_name | index_id}[, index_name | index_id ...]))]
```

This example forces the query to do a table scan:

```
SELECT au_lname, au_fname
FROM authors (INDEX(0))
WHERE au_lname LIKE 'C%'
```

This example forces the query to use the index named *aunmind*:

```
SELECT au_lname, au_fname
FROM authors (INDEX(aunmind))
WHERE au_lname LIKE 'C%'
```

The following example forces the query to use both indexes 2 and 3. Note, however, that identifying an index by *indid* is dangerous. If an index is dropped and re-created in a different place, it might take on a different *indid*. If you don't have an index with a specified ID, you get an error message. Also, you cannot specify index 0 (no index) along with any other indexes.

```
SELECT au_lname, au_fname
FROM authors (INDEX (2,3))
WHERE au_lname LIKE 'C%'
```

A second kind of index hint is FASTFIRSTROW, which tells SQL Server to use a nonclustered index leaf level to avoid sorting the data. This hint has been preserved only for backward compatibility; it has been superseded by the processing hint FAST *n*, which we'll discuss later.

Lock Hints

You can specify a lock type or duration with syntax similar to that for specifying index hints. Chapter 13 explains lock compatibility and other issues that are essential to using lock hints properly. Lock hints work only in the context of a transaction, so if you use these hints, you must use BEGIN TRAN/END TRAN blocks (or you must run with implicit transactions set to ON). The lock hint syntax is as follows:

```
SELECT select_list
FROM table_name [(lock_type)]
```

> **TIP** Remember to put the lock hint in parentheses; if you don't, it will be treated as an alias name for the table instead of as a lock hint.

You can specify one of the following keywords for *lock_type*:

HOLDLOCK Equivalent to the SERIALIZABLE hint described on the following page. This option is similar to specifying SET TRANSACTION ISOLATION LEVEL SERIALIZABLE , except the SET option affects all tables, not only the one specified in this hint.

UPDLOCK Takes update page locks instead of shared page locks while reading the table and holds them until the end of the transaction. Taking update locks can be an important technique for eliminating conversion deadlocks.

TABLOCK Takes a shared lock on the table even if page locks would be taken otherwise. This option is useful when you know you'll escalate to a table lock or if you need to get a complete snapshot of a table. You can use this option with HOLDLOCK if you want the table lock held until the end of the transaction block (REPEATABLE READ).

PAGLOCK Takes shared page locks when a single shared table lock might otherwise be taken. (There is no hint for taking an exclusive page lock. Instead, you hint to take an update page lock using UPDLOCK. Once the lock is acquired, you know that UPDLOCK can be automatically upgraded to an exclusive lock if required.)

TABLOCKX   Takes an exclusive lock on the table that is held until the end of the transaction block. (All exclusive locks are held until the end of a transaction, regardless of the isolation level in effect.)

ROWLOCK   Specifies that a shared row lock be taken when a single shared page or table lock is normally taken.

READUNCOMMITTED | READCOMMITTED | REPEATABLEREAD | SERIALIZABLE   These hints specify that SQL Server should use the same locking mechanisms as when the transaction isolation level is set to the level of the same name. However, the hint controls locking for a single table in a single statement, as opposed to locking of all tables in all statements in a transaction.

NOLOCK   Allows uncommitted, or dirty, reads. Shared locks are not issued by the scan, and the exclusive locks of others are not honored. This hint is equivalent to READUNCOMMITTED.

READPAST   Specifies that locked rows are skipped (read past). READPAST applies only to transactions operating at READ COMMITTED isolation and reads past row-level locks only.

Setting a Lock Timeout

Although it is not specifically a query hint, SET LOCK_TIMEOUT also lets you control SQL Server locking behavior. By default, SQL Server does not time out when waiting for a lock; it assumes optimistically that the lock will be released eventually. Most client programming interfaces allow you to set a general timeout limit for the connection so that a query is automatically canceled by the client if no response comes back after a specified amount of time. However, the message that comes back when the time period is exceeded does not indicate the cause of the cancellation; it could be because of a lock not being released, it could be because of a slow network, or it could just be a long running query.

Like other SET options, SET LOCK_TIMEOUT is valid only for your current connection. Its value is expressed in milliseconds and can be accessed by using the system function @@LOCK_TIMEOUT. This example sets the LOCK_TIMEOUT value to 5 seconds and then retrieves that value for display:

```
SET LOCK_TIMEOUT 5000
SELECT @@LOCK_TIMEOUT
```

If your connection exceeds the lock timeout value, you receive the following error message:

```
Server: Msg 1222, Level 16, State 50, Line 0
Lock request time out period exceeded.
```

Setting the LOCK_TIMEOUT value to 0 means that SQL Server does not wait at all for locks. It basically cancels the entire statement and goes on to the next one in the batch. This is not the same as the READPAST hint, which skips individual rows.

WARNING Exceeding the LOCK_TIMEOUT value does not automatically roll back a transaction, although it cancels the current statement. If you have a user-defined transaction containing multiple UPDATE statements, the first one might be canceled due to a lock timeout and the second one might succeed and commit. If this is unacceptable to your applications, you should program a check for error 1222 and then explicitly roll back the transaction. If you do not change the LOCK_TIMEOUT value, you don't have to worry about this behavior because locks will never time out.

The following example illustrates the difference between READPAST, READUNCOMMITTED, and setting LOCK_TIMEOUT to 0. All of these techniques let you "get around" locking problems, but the behavior is slightly different in each case.

1. In a new query window, execute the following batch to lock one row in the titles table:

```
USE pubs
BEGIN TRANSACTION
UPDATE titles
SET price = price * 0.1
WHERE title_id = 'BU1032'
```

2. Open a second connection, and execute the following statements:

```
USE pubs
SET LOCK_TIMEOUT 0
SELECT * FROM titles
SELECT * FROM authors
```

Notice that after error 1222 is received, the second select statement is executed, returning all the rows from the *authors* table.

3. Open a third connection, and execute the following statements:

```
USE pubs
SELECT * FROM titles (READPAST)
SELECT * FROM authors
```

SQL Server skips (reads past) only one row, and the remaining 17 rows of *titles* are returned, followed by all the *authors* rows.

4. Open a fourth connection, and execute the following statements:

```
USE pubs
SELECT * FROM titles (READUNCOMMITTED)
SELECT * FROM authors
```

In this case, SQL Server does not skip anything. It reads all 18 rows from *titles*, but the row for title BU1032 shows the dirty data that you changed in step 1. This data has not yet been committed and is subject to being rolled back.

NOTE The NOLOCK, READUNCOMMITTED, and READ-PAST table hints are not allowed for tables that are targets of delete, insert, or update operations.

Combining Hints

You can combine index and lock hints and use different hints for different tables, and you can combine HOLDLOCK with the level of shared locks. Here's an example:

```
BEGIN TRAN
SELECT title, au_lname
FROM titles (TABLOCK), titleauthor, authors (PAGLOCK, HOLDLOCK,
    INDEX(1))
WHERE titles.title_id=titleauthor.title_id
AND authors.au_id=titleauthor.au_id
```

Query Processing Hints

Query processing hints follow the word OPTION at the very end of your SQL statement and apply to the entire query. If your query involves a UNION, only the last SELECT in the UNION can include the OPTION clause. You can include more than one OPTION clause, but you can specify only one hint of each type. For example, you can have one GROUP hint and also use the RO-BUST PLAN hint. Here's an example of forcing SQL Server to process a GROUP BY using hashing:

```
SELECT type, count(*)
FROM titles
```

```
GROUP BY type
OPTION (HASH GROUP)
```

This example uses multiple query processing hints:

```
SELECT pub_name, count(*)
FROM titles JOIN publishers
    ON titles.pub_id = publishers.pub_id
GROUP BY pub_name
OPTION (ORDER GROUP, ROBUST PLAN, MERGE JOIN)
```

There are eight different types of processing hints, most of which are fully documented in SQL Server Books Online. The key aspects of these hints appear in the following list:

Grouping hints You can specify that SQL Server use a HASH GROUP or an ORDER GROUP to process GROUP BY operations.

Union hints You can specify that SQL Server form the UNION of multiple result sets by using HASH UNION, MERGE UNION, or CONCAT UNION. HASH UNION and MERGE UNION are ignored if the query specifies UNION ALL because UNION ALL does not need to remove duplicates. UNION ALL is always carried out by simple concatenation.

Join hints You can specify join hints in the OPTION clause as well as in the JOIN clause, and any join hint in the OPTION clause applies to all the joins in the query. OPTION join hints override those in the JOIN clause. You can specify LOOP JOIN, HASH JOIN, or MERGE JOIN.

FAST number_rows This hint tells SQL Server to optimize so that the first rows come back as quickly as possible, possibly reducing overall throughput. You can use this option to influence the query optimizer to drive a scan using a nonclustered index that matches the ORDER BY clause of a query rather than using a different access method and then doing a sort to match the ORDER BY clause. After the first *number_rows* are returned, the query continues execution and produces its full result set.

FORCE ORDER This hint tells SQL Server to process the tables in exactly the order listed in your FROM clause. However, if any of your joins is an OUTER JOIN, this hint might be ignored.

MAXDOP number Overrides the *max degree of parallelism* configuration option for only the query specifying this option. We'll discuss parallelism when we look at server configuration in Chapter 15.

ROBUST PLAN   Forces the query optimizer to attempt a plan that works for the maximum potential row size, even if it means degrading performance. This is particularly applicable if you have wide *varchar* columns. When the query is processed, some types of plans might create intermediate tables. Operators might need to store and process rows that are wider than any of the input rows, which might exceed SQL Server's internal row size limit. If this happens, SQL Server produces an error during query execution. If you use ROBUST PLAN, the query optimizer will not consider any plans that might encounter this problem.

KEEP PLAN   This option ensures that a query is not recompiled as frequently when there are multiple updates to a table. This can be particularly useful when a stored procedure does a lot of work with temporary tables, which might cause frequent recompilations.

Summary

This chapter walked you through performance-related topics that you should consider while designing and implementing a high-performance application. As a starting point, skilled team members are vital. More than anything else, a skilled and experienced staff is the best predictor and indicator of a project's potential success. You must establish performance criteria and prototype, test, and monitor performance throughout development.

We also reviewed techniques that you can use in database design and in making indexing decisions. We saw how to deal with lock contention issues and how to resolve deadlocks. We also discussed how the query optimizer chooses a plan and what you can do to ensure that it performs as well as possible.

As you make and monitor changes, remember to change just one variable at a time. When you change multiple variables at the same time, it becomes impossible to evaluate the effectiveness of any one of them. This goes for all changes, whether they are related to design, indexing, the use of an optimizer hint, or a configuration setting. This is a fundamental aspect of all performance optimization. In the next chapter, we'll look at configuration and performance monitoring.

CONFIGURATION AND PERFORMANCE MONITORING

In the previous chapter, we looked at the most important aspects of performance—those affected by design, prototyping, indexing, and query writing. You can also improve system performance by tuning your system configuration, but this is unlikely to yield as much gain as a design change. It's even more critical that your system not be misconfigured. You might see only a 5 percent improvement in performance by moving from a reasonable configuration to an ideal configuration, but a badly misconfigured system can kill your application's performance.

This chapter discusses configuration options for Microsoft Windows NT and Microsoft SQL Server. It includes guidelines for setting important values and suggests improvements (which are sometimes likely to be minor at best). You'll also learn how to use the two most essential monitoring tools: SQL Server Profiler and Performance Monitor.

Windows NT Configuration Settings

As mentioned above, a badly configured system can destroy performance. For example, a system with an incorrectly configured memory setting can break an application. SQL Server dynamically adjusts the most important configuration options for you; you should accept these defaults unless you have a good reason to change them. In certain cases, tweaking the settings rather than letting SQL Server dynamically adjust them might lead to a tiny performance improvement, but your time is probably better spent on application and database design, indexing, tuning queries, and other such activities.

Task Management

As we saw in Chapter 3, Windows NT schedules all threads in the system for execution. Each thread of every process has a priority, and Windows NT executes the next ready thread with the highest priority. By default, it gives active applications a higher priority. But this priority setting is not appropriate for a server application that's running in the background, such as SQL Server. To remedy this situation, SQL Server's installation program eliminates Windows NT's favoring of foreground applications by modifying the priority setting. (It's not a bad idea to periodically double-check this setting in case someone sets it back. From the Windows NT Control Panel, double-click on the System icon to open the System Properties dialog box. On the Performance tab, in the Application Performance section, slide the Select The Performance Boost For The Foreground Application control to the None setting.)

Resource Allocation

A computer running Windows NT Server for file and print services will want to use the most memory for file caching. But if it is also running SQL Server, it makes sense for more memory to be available for SQL Server's use. You can configure the server's resource allocation (and associated nonpaged memory pool usage) in the Server dialog box of the Network applet. Double-click on the Network icon on the Control Panel and click on the Services tab. The Server dialog box appears, as shown in Figure 15-1.

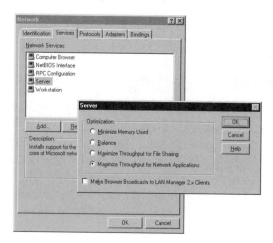

Figure 15-1.
Configuring the Server service settings.

The Maximize Throughput For Network Applications setting is best for running SQL Server. You need high network throughput with minimal memory devoted to file caching so more memory is available to SQL Server. When this option is set, network applications such as SQL Server have priority over the file cache for access to memory. Although you might expect that the Minimize Memory Used option would help, it minimizes the memory available for some internal network settings that are needed to support a lot of SQL Server users.

PAGEFILE.SYS Location

If possible, you should place the Windows NT page file on a different drive than the files used by SQL Server. This is vital if your system will be paging. However, an even better approach is to add memory or change the SQL Server memory configuration to effectively eliminate paging. So little page file activity will occur that the file's location will be irrelevant.

File System Selection

As we discussed in Chapter 4, whether you use the FAT or the NTFS file system doesn't have much effect on system performance. You should use NTFS for most cases for reasons of security and robustness, not performance.

Nonessential Services

You should disable any services you don't need, using the Services icon on the Control Panel. These unnecessary services add overhead to the system and use resources that could otherwise go to SQL Server. If possible, don't use the Windows NT server that's running SQL Server as the primary domain controller or backup domain controller (PDC or BDC), the group's file or print server, the Web server, the DHCP server, and so on. You should also consider disabling the Alerter, ClipBook Server, Computer Browser, Messenger, Network DDE, and Schedule services that are enabled by default but not needed by SQL Server.

Network Protocols

You should run only the network protocols you actually need for connectivity. Installing multiple network protocols (TCP/IP, NWLink, NetBEUI, DLC, and Appletalk) on your system is so easy that some systems run protocols that aren't even used. But this adds overhead. If you legitimately need to use multiple protocols, you should make sure that the highest binding is set for the most often used protocol. You set protocols and bind order via the Control Panel's Network icon.

SQL Server Configuration Settings

Configuration changes can degrade system performance just as easily as they can improve it. This is particularly true in version 7 of SQL Server, for which most performance-oriented configuration settings are fully automatic. SQL Server 7 has only 11 configuration options that are not considered "advanced," and none of these directly affects performance. To see all the configuration options, you must change the value of the Show Advanced Options setting:

```
EXEC sp_configure 'show advanced options', 1
GO
RECONFIGURE
GO
```

You should change configuration options only when you have a clear reason for doing so, and you should closely monitor the effects of each change to determine whether the change improved or degraded performance. Always make and monitor changes one at a time.

Serverwide Options

The serverwide options discussed here are set via the *sp_configure* system stored procedure. Many of them can also be set from SQL Server Enterprise Manager, but there is no single dialog box from which all configuration settings can be seen or changed. Most of the options that can be changed from the SQL Server Enterprise Manager user interface are controlled from one of the Properties tabs that you reach by right-clicking on your server. If you use the *sp_configure* stored procedure, no changes take effect until the RECONFIGURE command (or RECONFIGURE WITH OVERRIDE, in some cases) is issued. Some changes (dynamic changes) take effect immediately upon reconfiguration, but others do not take effect until the server is restarted. If an option's *run_value* and *config__value* as displayed by *sp_configure* are different, the server must be restarted for the *config_value* to take effect.

We won't look at every configuration option here—only those that relate directly to performance. In most cases, we'll discuss options that you should *not* change. Some of these are resource settings that relate to performance only in that they consume memory (for example, *open objects*). But if they are configured too high, they can rob a system of memory and degrade performance. We'll group the *sp_configure* settings by functionality. Keep in mind that SQL Server sets almost all of these options automatically, and your applications will work well without you ever looking at these options.

Memory Options

In previous versions of SQL Server, you had to manually configure memory options; this is not the case in SQL Server 7. In Chapter 3, we saw how SQL Server uses memory, including how memory is allocated for different uses within SQL Server and when data is read from or written to disk. But we did not discuss how much memory SQL Server actually uses for these various purposes or how to monitor the amount of the system's memory resources used by SQL Server.

min server memory **and** *max server memory*   By default, SQL Server automatically adjusts the total amount of the memory resources it will use. However, you can use the *min server memory* and *max server memory* configuration options to take manual control. The default setting for *min server memory* is 0 (MB), and the default setting for *max server memory* is 2147483647. If you use the *sp_configure* stored procedure to change both of these options to the same value, you basically take full control and tell SQL Server to use a fixed memory size. This mimics the memory configuration behavior in earlier versions of SQL Server. You can also use SQL Server Enterprise Manager to set a minimum and maximum value for memory, using the Memory tab of the SQL Server Properties dialog box (shown in Figure 15-2). Right-click on the name of your server, and choose Properties to bring up the dialog box.

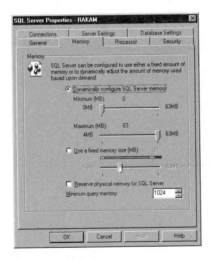

Figure 15-2.
The Memory tab of the SQL Server Properties dialog box.

You can set the minimum and maximum memory using slider bars. Note that the maximum allowed is slightly less than the amount of physical memory in the machine. The absolute maximum of 2147483647 MB previously mentioned is actually the largest value that can be stored in the integer field of the *sysconfigures* table. It is not related to the actual resources of your system. You can select a separate option button to indicate that you want to use a fixed size. Setting the minimum and maximum sliders to the same value has the same effect.

set working set size   The dialog box also includes a check box labeled Reserve Physical Memory For SQL Server. Selecting this is equivalent to setting the configuration option *set working set size* to 1, which reserves physical memory space for SQL Server that is equal to the server memory setting. Do this only if you don't want SQL Server to dynamically adjust its memory usage. Setting *set working set size* means that the operating system does not swap out SQL Server pages even if they can be used more readily by another process when SQL Server is idle. If the Windows NT virtual memory manager must page, it must do so from other processes. This setting defaults to 0, which allows the Windows NT virtual memory manager to determine the working set size of SQL Server.

As we've mentioned, you should generally let SQL Server take full control over the memory values, but if your server might be inactive for long periods, you can manually set *min server memory* so that when someone finally submits a query, memory will be available and the query can be processed quickly. If you have other critical applications on your server that might have inactive periods, you can manually set *max server memory* so that SQL Server will not use too much system memory and so that when the other application becomes active again, memory will be available for it to use.

When SQL Server uses memory dynamically, the lazywriter queries the system periodically to determine the amount of free physical memory available. The lazywriter expands or shrinks the buffer cache to keep the operating system's free physical memory at 5 MB plus or minus 200 KB to prevent paging. If less than 5 MB is free, the lazywriter releases memory to the operating system that usually goes on the free list. If more than 5 MB of physical memory is free, the lazywriter recommits memory to the buffer cache. The lazywriter recommits memory to the buffer cache only when it repopulates the free list; a server at rest does not grow its buffer cache.

SQL Server also releases memory to the operating system if it detects that too much paging is taking place. You can tell when SQL Server increases or decreases its total memory use by using SQL Server Profiler to monitor the Server Memory Change event (in the Misc. category). An event is generated whenever SQL Server's memory increases or decreases by 1 MB or 5 percent of the maximum server memory, whichever is greater. You can look at the value of the data element called Event Sub Class to see whether the change was an increase or a decrease. An Event Sub Class value of 1 means a memory increase; a value of 2 means a memory decrease. We'll discuss SQL Server Profiler in more detail later in this chapter.

extended memory size   A third memory option, called *extended memory size*, is intended for SQL Server Enterprise edition running under future versions of Windows NT, which will support a full 64-bit address space. The extended memory size option refers to Enterprise Memory Architecture (EMA), which allows memory beyond the 3-GB range (or 2-GB range on Alpha processors) to be treated as a second-level cache. However, with certain hardware, you can use this feature with Windows NT 4. Pentium II Xeon chips ship with a special driver called PSE-36 (which was codeveloped by Microsoft and Intel) that allows up to 64 GB of memory to be used. Of course, you must have a machine that can support that much memory, but this feature will let you take advantage of memory well beyond the current limits. Although the *extended memory size* option is visible in all editions of SQL Server 7, its setting is ignored unless you are running the Enterprise edition.

user connections   SQL Server 7 dynamically adjusts the number of simultaneous connections to the server if the *user connections* configuration setting is left at its default of 0. Even if you set this value to a different number, SQL Server does not actually allocate the full amount of memory needed for each user connection until a user actually connects. When SQL Server starts up, it allocates an array of pointers with as many entries as the configured value for user connections. Each entry uses less than 1000 bytes of memory. When a user connects to SQL Server, it is allocated 24 KB for three memory objects of one page (8 KB) each. These memory objects keep track of things such as the Process Status Structure (PSS) for each connection and the context area needed by the User Mode Scheduler (UMS) to keep track of the user's context as it moves the wait queue to a CPU and back again.

You should always let SQL Server dynamically adjust the value of the *user connections* option. If you configure the value too low, future connections will be denied access to SQL Server. Even if you are trying to limit actual simultaneous users, this can backfire because connections are not the same as users. One user can open multiple connections through the same application. If you're using a query tool such as the SQL Server Query Analyzer, each time you click the New Query button you start a new connection to the server that counts against the total.

locks   The *locks* configuration option sets the number of available locks (of all types). The default is 0, which means that SQL Server adjusts this value dynamically. It starts by allocating 2 percent of the memory allotted SQL Server to an initial pool of lock structures. When the pool of locks is exhausted, it allocates additional locks. The dynamic lock pool does not allocate more than 40 percent of the memory allocated to SQL Server. If too much memory is being used for locks, SQL Server escalates row locks into table locks wherever possible. You should leave this value at its default. If you manually supply a value for the maximum number of locks, once that number of locks is reached, any query that requests additional lock resources will receive an error message and the batch will terminate.

Scheduling Options

SQL Server 7 has a completely new algorithm for scheduling user processes, which uses special UMS threads (as described in Chapter 3). There is one UMS thread per processor, and the UMS makes sure that only one process can run on a scheduler at any given time. The UMS manages assignment of user connections to UMS threads to keep the number of users per CPU as balanced as possible. Four configuration options affect the behavior of the scheduler: *lightweight pooling*, *affinity mask*, *priority boost*, and *max worker threads*.

lightweight pooling   By default, SQL Server operates in thread mode, which means that the UMS schedules Windows NT threads. However, SQL Server also lets user connections run in fiber mode; fibers are less expensive to manage than threads. The *lightweight pooling* option has a value of 0 or 1; 1 means that SQL Server should run in fiber mode. Using fibers can yield a minor performance advantage, perhaps as much as a 5 percent increase in throughput when all of the available CPUs are operating at 100 percent. However, the tradeoff is that certain operations, such as running queries on linked servers or executing extended stored procedures, must run in thread mode. The cost of switching from fiber to thread mode for those connections can be noticeable, and in some cases can offset any benefit of operating in fiber mode.

  If you are running in an environment with multiple CPUs, all of which are operating at 100 percent capacity, and if Performance Monitor shows a lot of context switching, setting *lightweight pooling* to 1 might have some performance benefit. With a system using more than four processors, the performance improvements should be even greater.

affinity mask   You can use the *affinity mask* setting to bind all the threads (or fibers) handled by one UMS thread to a certain processor. You should avoid doing this because this setting prevents Windows NT from using whatever processor is currently most available; each UMS must then schedule its threads on the same processor.

You can also use this setting to limit the number of processors that SQL Server can use. Previous versions of SQL Server had a configuration option called *SMP concurrency* that specified a maximum number of processors that SQL Server would use. That option is no longer available, but if you want to test the benefit of limiting the number of processors SQL Server uses, you can use *affinity mask* to disable the use of some of the processors. For example, on an eight-processor system, setting *affinity mask* to 63 decimal or 00111111 binary means that SQL Server can use only processors 0 through 5. Two processors are reserved for other, non–SQL Server activity.

The *affinity mask* option was added in version 6.5 at the request of some major customers who ran SMP hardware with more than four processors. These sites were accustomed to similar options on UNIX or mainframe systems. Most sites do not need this option. To learn more about this setting, see the SQL Server documentation on the companion CD.

priority boost If the *priority boost* setting is enabled, SQL Server runs at a higher Windows NT scheduling priority. The default is 0, which means that SQL Server runs at normal priority whether you are running it on a single-processor machine or on an SMP machine. Enabling the *priority boost* option will allow the SQL Server process to run at high priority. There are probably few sites or applications for which setting this option will make much difference, so we recommend leaving it alone. But if your machine is totally dedicated to running SQL Server, you might want to enable this option (set it to 1) to see for yourself. It can potentially offer a performance advantage on a heavily loaded, dedicated system. Contrary to some folklore, this setting does not make SQL Server run at the highest Windows NT priority.

max worker threads SQL Server uses the Windows NT thread services by keeping a pool of worker threads (or fibers) that take requests off the queue. It attempts to evenly divide the worker threads among the UMS schedulers so the number of threads available to each UMS is the setting of *max worker threads* divided by the number of CPUs. With 100 or fewer users, there are usually as many worker threads as active users (not just connected users who are idle). With more users, it often makes sense to have fewer worker threads than active users. Although some user requests have to wait for a worker thread to become available, total throughput increases because less context switching occurs.

The *max worker threads* setting is somewhat autoconfigured. The default is 255, which does not mean that 255 worker threads are in the pool. It means that if a connection is waiting to be serviced and no thread is available, a new thread is created if the thread total is currently below 255. If this setting is configured to 255 but the highest number of simultaneously executing commands is, say, 125, the actual number of worker threads will not exceed 125. It might be less than that because SQL Server destroys and trims away worker threads that are no longer being used. You should probably leave this setting alone if your system is handling 100 or fewer simultaneous connections. In that case, the worker thread pool will not be greater than 100.

Even systems that handle 4000 or more connected users run fine with the default setting of 255. When thousands of users are simultaneously connected, the actual worker thread pool is usually well below 255 since from the back-end database perspective most connections are idle, even though the user might be doing plenty of work on the front end.

Disk I/O Options

No options are available for controlling SQL Server's disk read behavior. All the tuning options to control read-ahead in previous versions of SQL Server are now handled completely internally. Two options are available to control disk write behavior. One controls the number of simultaneous write requests that can be issued, and the other controls the frequency with which the checkpoint process writes to disk.

max async IO The *max async IO* option controls how many outstanding I/O operations SQL Server can have at a time. This number is specific to the speed of the I/O system of the hardware. The default setting of 32 is reasonable for most systems, but it is too low for systems with good I/O subsystems and high OLTP transaction rates. As usual, you shouldn't change the default capriciously, but this setting probably warrants changing for such systems.

This setting governs the checkpoint, lazywriter, and recovery processes, since only during these operations do multiple outstanding I/O operations come into play. During the checkpoint process, large numbers of pages might need to be flushed. Recall that asynchronous I/O is never used for writing to the log because write-ahead logging demands synchronous I/O to ensure recoverability. If you have a fast RAID system and your checkpoint process flushes many pages (that is, if you have a high OLTP-type application), you can change this value and then measure the difference by monitoring the throughput of your application or benchmark test. (The SQL Server Benchmark Kit on the companion CD is a good proxy test for this setting, since this setting is more a function of what your hardware can handle rather than specific to your application.) You can gauge your system's effectiveness with asynchronous I/O during the checkpoint process by watching the Checkpoint Writes/sec counter of the SQLServer: Buffer Manager object.

On systems with a fast I/O subsystem—multiple disks in a fast RAID environment—a setting of 32 might be too low to fully drive the hardware's capability, but you should change the setting only if you will empirically measure the result. If you set it too high, you might flood the system and hurt throughput. The large numbers of outstanding write operations issued by a checkpoint might result in other read activity being starved. Correctly setting this value results in throttling the checkpoint process, so you should see a less than 10 percent reduction in throughput even on a heavily loaded OLTP system while the checkpoint process is active. The whitepaper on the companion CD titled "Microsoft SQL Server 7.0 Performance Tuning Guide" includes the following advice:

> A rule of thumb for setting *max async I/O* for SQL Servers running on larger disk subsystems is to multiply the number of physical drives available to do simultaneous I/O by 2 or 3. Then watch Performance Monitor for signs of disk activity or queuing issues. The negative impact of setting this configuration option too high is that it may cause Checkpoint to monopolize disk subsystem bandwidth that is required by other SQL Server I/O operations, such as reads.

recovery interval   The *recovery interval* option can be automatically configured. SQL Server setup sets it to 0, which means autoconfiguration. In the current version, this means a recovery time of less than one minute, but that might change in later releases or service packs. This option lets the DBA control the checkpoint frequency by specifying the maximum number of minutes that recovery should take.

In earlier versions of SQL Server, the recovery interval was set in terms of minutes; the default was 5. In practice, this meant a checkpoint every 30,000 log records, which was almost always much less than every 5 minutes because the implementation was not scaled for today's faster systems. In SQL Server 7, recovery is more likely to match the recovery interval option, assuming that the system was busy before it came down. For databases with more than 20 MB of log records, the recovery interval directly corresponds to the checkpoint frequency. Thus, a recovery interval of 5 means that checkpoints occur only every 5 minutes and all dirty pages are written to disk.

Query Processing Options
SQL Server 7 introduces several options for controlling the resources available for processing queries. As with all the other tuning options, your best bet is to leave these options at their default values unless thorough testing indicates that a change might help.

min memory per query When a query requires additional memory resources, the number of pages it gets is determined partly by the *min memory per query* option. This minimum memory value for the sort is specified in kilobytes. Most people think this option is relevant only for sort operations that specifically request using an ORDER BY clause, but it also applies to internal memory needed by merge join operations and by hash merge and hash grouping operations. In SQL Server 7, sort and hash operations receive memory in a much more dynamic fashion than in previous versions, so you rarely need to adjust this value. In fact, on larger machines, your sort and hash queries typically get much more than the *min memory per query* setting, so you don't restrict yourself unnecessarily. If you need to do a lot of hashing or sorting, however, and you have few users or a lot of available memory, you might improve performance by adjusting this value. On smaller machines, setting this value too high can cause virtual memory to page, which hurts server performance.

query wait The *query wait* option controls how long a query that needs additional memory waits, if that memory is not available. A setting of –1 means that the query waits 25 times the estimated execution time of the query. A value of 0 or more specifies the number of seconds that a query waits. If the wait time is exceeded, SQL Server generates error 8645:

```
Server: Msg 8645, Level 17, State 1, Line 1
A time out occurred while waiting for memory resources to execute the
query. Re-run the query.
```

Even though memory is allocated dynamically, SQL Server can still run out if the memory resources on the machine are exhausted. If your queries time out with error 8645, you can try increasing the paging file size or even add more physical memory. You can also try tuning the query by creating more useful indexes so that hash or merge operations aren't needed.

index create memory The *min memory per query* option applies only to sorting and hashing used during query execution; it does not apply to the sorting that takes place during index creation. Another option, *index create memory*, lets you allocate a specific amount of memory for index creation. Its value is also specified in kilobytes.

query governor cost limit You can use the *query governor cost limit* option to set a maximum length of time that a query will run. SQL Server will not execute queries that the optimizer estimates will take longer than this. The option is specified in seconds, but it might not map exactly to seconds on your machine. You should think of the value as an abstract cost of the query rather than an actual number of seconds. The cost figure was correlated to seconds on one test machine in the SQL Server development group, and no information is available on the exact specs of that machine.

You can come up with your own correlation using SQL Server Profiler. If you capture the *Misc: Execution Plan* events, the data element called Binary Data reflects the optimizer's estimated cost for each SQL statement. This value is compared to the *query governor cost limit* value. If you then also capture the Duration data for each SQL statement, you can compare the estimated cost with the actual duration. For example, if on the average, queries that show a cost (in the SQL Server Profiler trace) of 8 seconds take 10 seconds to run, you should specify a *query governor cost limit* of about 80 percent of what you'll really allow. If you want to block all queries that are estimated to take longer than 1 minute to run, you should set the option to 48 (80 percent of 60 seconds). We'll look at SQL Server Profiler in more detail later in this chapter.

max degree of parallelism and cost threshold for parallelism   Version 7 of SQL Server lets you run certain kinds of complex queries simultaneously on two or more processors. The queries must lend themselves to being executed in sections. Here's an example:

```
SELECT avg(charge_amt), category
FROM charge
GROUP BY category
```

If the *charge* table has 100,000 rows and there are 10 different values for *category*, SQL Server can split the rows into groups and have only a subset of the groups processed on each processor. For example, with a 4-CPU machine, categories 1 through 3 can be averaged on the first processor, categories 4 through 6 on the second processor, categories 7 and 8 on the third, and categories 9 and 10 on the fourth. Each processor can come up with averages for only its groups, and the separate averages are brought together for the final result.

During query optimization, SQL Server looks for queries that might benefit from parallel execution. It inserts exchange operators into the query execution plan to prepare the query for parallel execution. An exchange operator is an operator in a query execution plan that provides process management, data redistribution, and flow control. The two main types of exchange operators that you'll observe if parallel plans are generated are the *distribute* operator, which separates the processing into multiple streams, and the *gather* operator, which retrieves the separate results and combines them into a single result. Occasionally, you will also see a *redistribute* operator if the original streams need to be moved onto different processors at some point during the processing. Once exchange operators are inserted, the result is a parallel query execution plan. A portion of a parallel execution plan is shown in Figure 15-3 on the next page.

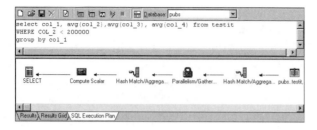

Figure 15-3.
A portion of a parallel query plan showing the gather *operator.*

A parallel query execution plan can use more than one thread; a serial execution plan, which is used by a nonparallel query, uses only a single thread. The actual number of threads used by a parallel query is determined at query plan execution initialization and is called the *degree of parallelism*. Even though a parallel plan might be developed, at execution time SQL Server might decide not to use it.

Data modification statements are always carried out on a single processor, but the search portion of the update, delete, and insert statements (in which SQL Server determines which rows to modify) might be still performed in parallel. In addition, even if the query is a SELECT query, parts of it might run single threaded within a parallel plan.

SQL Server automatically determines the best degree of parallelism for each instance of a parallel query execution by considering the following:

- Is SQL Server running on a computer with more than one processor? (Only computers with more than one processor can take advantage of parallel queries.)

- How many concurrent users are active on the server? SQL Server monitors its CPU use and adjusts the degree of parallelism at query startup time. It chooses lower degrees of parallelism if the CPUs are already busy. Parallel queries are valuable only if few users are on the system. Once a parallel query starts running, it consumes most of the CPU resources until it has completed.

- Is sufficient memory available for parallel query execution? Each query requires a certain amount of memory to execute. Executing a parallel query requires more memory than a nonparallel query. The amount of memory required for executing a parallel query is equivalent to the amount of memory required for serial query execution multiplied by the degree of parallelism. If the memory requirement of the parallel plan cannot be satisfied, SQL Server automatically executes the serial plan for the corresponding query.

■ What type of query is being executed? Queries that consume a lot of CPU cycles are the best candidates for a parallel query (for example, joins of large tables, substantial aggregations, and sorting of large result sets). With simple queries, which are often found in transaction processing applications, the additional coordination required to execute a query in parallel outweighs the potential performance boost.

■ Are a sufficient number of rows processed in the given stream? If the query optimizer determines that the number of rows in a stream is too low, it does not introduce exchange operators to distribute the stream.

Once a query starts executing on multiple threads for parallel execution, the query uses the same number of threads until completion. SQL Server reexamines the optimal number of thread decisions each time a parallel query execution plan is retrieved from the cache. One execution of a query can result in the use of a single thread, and another execution of the same query (at a different time) can result in using two or more threads.

Two configuration options are available for controlling parallel queries. The *max degree of parallelism* option indicates the maximum number of processors that are used to run queries in parallel. The default value of 0 means that SQL Server should use the number of available CPUs. A value of 1 means that SQL Server should suppress parallelism completely. Any other value restricts the degree of parallelism below the number of CPUs. If your computer has only one processor, the *max degree of parallelism* value is ignored.

The second configuration option for controlling parallelism is *cost threshold for parallelism.* You can specify that SQL Server should not even consider a parallel plan for a query with an estimated cost lower than this threshold. The unit of costing is the same one used by the *query governor cost limit* option. The default of 5 seconds is fine for most systems.

Be careful when you use either of these configuration options—they have serverwide impact. You can also use trace flag 8687 to turn off parallelism for individual connections

SQL Server Profiler lets you trace the degree of parallelism for each query captured. If you choose to monitor events in the SQL Operators category (Delete, Insert, Select, or Update), the Event Sub Class data is a number indicating the degree of parallelism for that query. The values at the top of the following page are possible for the Event Sub Class value for the SQL Operators events.

Value	Meaning
0	No parallelism was considered. For example, the computer executing the query contains only one processor or the estimated cost of the query execution is lower than the *cost threshold for parallelism* value.
1	Parallel execution was considered, but the query was executed using a serial plan because a parallel execution plan would have required an unavailable amount of resources.
>1	A portion of the query has been executed using a parallel execution plan with the degree of parallelism indicated.

Database Options

Several database options can affect performance. The *read only* and *single user* options affect performance because they eliminate locking in some cases. If your database is used only for decision support (for example, a data mart), it might make sense to set your database to *read only*, as follows:

```
EXEC sp_dboption 'dbname', 'read only', TRUE
```

In this way, no locking is performed in the database; this greatly reduces overhead. This option prevents changes from being made to the database. You can easily toggle it off to perform tasks such as bulk loading of data. For an operation in which the data is changed via large batch jobs that can run during off-hours and the normal workload is query only, *read only* is a good choice.

Even if your database is not read only, you might want to perform off-hour maintenance tasks and bulk loading operations with the *single user* option enabled, as shown here:

```
EXEC sp_dboption 'dbname', 'single user', TRUE
```

This option also eliminates the need for locking, since only one connection can use the database at a time. Of course, you need locking to make a multiple-user system behave like a single-user system. But in this case, it *is* a single-user system, so locking is not required. If you need to do a big bulk load and index creation at night while no one else is using the system, you can eliminate the need to take locks during the bulk load.

Two other options are particularly useful if you are running the SQL Server Desktop edition on a small machine and your resources are extremely limited: *autoclose* and *autoshrink*. The *autoclose* option causes the database to shut down cleanly and free resources after the last user exits. By default, it is set to TRUE for all databases when SQL Server runs on Windows 95 or Windows 98. The database reopens automatically when a user tries to use the database. The *autoshrink* option (discussed in Chapter 5) can be useful if your disk space resources are extremely limited, but there is a performance tradeoff. Shrinking a database is a CPU-intensive operation and takes a long time. All indexes on heaps affected by the shrink must be adjusted because the row locators change.

Finally, two database options control the automatic gathering of statistics: *auto create statistics* and *auto update statistics*. These were both discussed in Chapter 14.

Buffer Manager Options

In Chapter 3, we saw how the Buffer Manager (also known as the Cache Manager) uses a queue of "favored pages," which you can think of as a least-recently-used (LRU) algorithm, but no queue list of buffers is maintained in the order of most recent access. You can use the *pintable* option to directly influence the favoring behavior.

Pinning a Table in the Cache

You can permanently remove a table from the queue of pages examined by the lazywriter so that once they are read into the data cache, they are never forced from cache. (This favors them permanently, although it is really more than that: they are entirely exempted.) You can enable this option using the *sp_tableoption* stored procedure with the *pintable* option.

This option is not appropriate for most sites. But if you get very random cache hits and you have some relatively small tables that are hot compared to other larger tables, this option might be beneficial. If those small, hot tables keep getting forced out by the random access to larger tables and you have plenty of memory, you can pin those small tables. By pinning, you override the Buffer Manager. But you take away the pages in cache used for that table, so you give the Buffer Manager less memory to work with. Pinning the table does not initially read it in; pinning just makes the table "sticky" so that once a page of the table is in the cache, it doesn't get forced out. If you want the table preloaded and sticky, you can enable the option and then do *SELECT * FROM table* to read all the pages into cache. (The table shouldn't be so big that you eat up more memory than your system can afford to use.)

Monitoring Buffer Manager Performance

Two DBCC commands exist to monitor the performance of the Buffer Manager; they are known as SQLPERF(WAITSTATS) and SQLPERF(LRUSTATS). DBCC SQLPERF(WAITSTATS) not only provides an overview of the Buffer Manager, it helps identify where a transaction is delayed. It shows the total milliseconds of wait time and how much of the time is due to waiting for reads, waiting for different types of locks, waiting to add a log record to the log buffer, and waiting for log buffers to be physically written. The command DBCC SQLPERF(LRUSTATS) gives details on the lazywriter and the state of the cache, such as the cache-hit ratio, the size of the cache, the average number of pages scanned to find an available buffer, and the number of free pages. Although this information is available through the Performance Monitor, the DBCC SQLPERF command lets you capture the output to a table and save the data for analysis.

For example, to capture the DBCC SQLPERF(WAITSTATS) output, you can create a table with four columns and use the dynamic EXECUTE command to populate the table. The following script shows one way to define and populate such a table. It actually adds a fifth column to the table, which indicates the current date and time that the rows were inserted into the table.

```
CREATE TABLE waitstats
(wait_type      varchar (20),
requests        numeric(10,0),
wait_time       numeric(12,2),
signal_wait     numeric(12,0),
recorded_time   datetime DEFAULT getdate() )
GO
INSERT INTO waitstats (wait_type, requests, wait_time, signal_wait)
    EXEC ('DBCC SQLPERF(WAITSTATS)')
```

Startup Parameters on SQLSERVR.EXE

You can alter startup parameters used by the SQL Server process to tune performance by disabling the performance statistics collection or specifying trace flags.

Disabling the Performance Collection

Normally, SQL Server keeps performance statistics such as CPU usage and amount of I/O on a per-user basis. The values are materialized in the *sysprocesses* table (really just memory) when queried. If you never query or monitor these values, the work to keep track of them is unnecessary. You can eliminate the calls that produce these performance statistics by passing the *-x* startup flag to SQLSERVR.EXE. Or you can add *-x* as an additional parameter from the Setup program via the Set Server Options dialog box.

Specifying Trace Flags

We've discussed the use of trace flags several times, and we've seen how to enable them using DBCC TRACEON. You can also specify a trace flag at server startup; some trace flags make the most sense if they are specified serverwide rather than on a per-user basis. For example, trace flag 1204, which records information to the error log when a deadlock occurs, doesn't make sense for a specific connection because you probably have no idea ahead of time which connections will encounter deadlocks. To enable a trace flag serverwide, you add the flag as a parameter when you start SQL Server from the command line (for example, *sqlservr.exe -c -t1204*).

To support tracing on a per-user basis, a flag in the PSS must also be set to enable any of the trace flags that are tested with the original (non–user-specific) *TRACE* macro. Each place in the code that tests for these trace flags first determines whether the PSS flag is set before testing the trace-flag array. Many trace flags (such as 1081) don't make sense on a per-user basis. If you specify a lowercase *t*, SQL Server skips the per-user test to determine whether the trace flag is enabled. Using an uppercase *T* sets the PSS flag and requires per-user checking. A lowercase *t* flag is not enabled unless at least one uppercase *T* is also set or until some connection executes a DBCC TRACEON with –1 (which means that it is set for all connections).

System Maintenance

SQL Server requires much less regular system maintenance than most comparable products. (For example, because pages are automatically split, it maintains data clustering characteristics; most products that support data clustering make you do data reorganization to keep the data clustered.) However, you should perform a couple of regular maintenance tasks for performance reasons. You can easily schedule these tasks (such as updating statistics and rebuilding your clustered index) using SQL Executive or the Database Maintenance Plan Wizard.

In the earlier discussion of tuning queries, we explained the importance of index distribution statistics. If you have not enabled automatic updating of statistics, you should update statistics frequently so that any significant changes in the volumes or distribution of data are reflected. Although it is not essential to dump and reload tables to keep clustering properties intact, it can be useful to rebuild tables to reestablish fill factors and avoid page splits. The simple way that you can do this is by rebuilding the clustered index on the table using the DROP_EXISTING option that we discussed in Chapter 6. Using this option, the existing nonclustered indexes will not have to be re-created, since the clustering key will stay the same. You can also use the DBCC DBREINDEX command to rebuild all the indexes on a table. Rebuilding the clustered index helps keep a table from becoming fragmented and makes read ahead more effective. You can use DBCC SHOWCONTIG to determine how contiguous a table is.

Of course, you should also regularly do other tasks, such as performing backups and periodically checking the structural integrity of the database (for example, by using DBCC CHECKDB), but these are not performance-related tasks.

Monitoring System Behavior

Throughout this book, we've looked at statements that are useful for monitoring some aspect of SQL Server's performance. These include procedures such as *sp_who2*, *sp_lock*, *SET SHOWPLAN_TEXT ON*, DBCC SQLPERF, and various trace flags for analyzing deadlock issues. SQL Server Enterprise Manager provides a graphical display that is a combination of *sp_who2* and *sp_lock*, and you should make use of it. In addition, two other tools let you monitor the behavior of your SQL Server system: SQL Server Profiler and Performance Monitor.

SQL Server Profiler

SQL Server Profiler is new with SQL Server 7. It looks similar to the SQL Trace tool in version 6.5, but it has far greater capabilities. SQL Trace was basically an "ODS Sniffer," which itself was based on an earlier freeware product called SQLEye. SQLEye was essentially a filter that listened on the network using the ODS API for all the batches that were sent to a specified SQL Server. When SQLEye received an incoming batch, it could apply one of several filters to it and record in a file all batches that satisfied the filters' conditions. In version 6.5, the same developer who wrote SQLEye put a GUI wrapper around its configuration and specification commands and created the SQL Trace tool.

Because SQL Trace worked only at the ODS layer, it could capture only the commands that were actually being sent to SQL Server. Once SQL Server received the command, SQL Trace had no further knowledge of what SQL Server did with it. For example, if a client connection sent a batch to SQL Server that consisted of only a stored procedure call, that is all SQL Trace could capture and record. It could not record all the statements that were executed within the stored procedure, and it had no knowledge of other procedures that were called by the original stored procedure.

SQL Server Profiler belongs to a new generation of profiling tools. Not only can it keep track of every statement executed and every statement within every stored procedure, it can keep track of every time a table is accessed, every time a lock is acquired, and every time an error occurs. In fact, it can capture 68 predefined events, and you can configure 5 additional events of your own.

SQL Server Profiler relies on the concept of events. Event producers write to queues maintained by SQL Server. Event consumers read events off of the queues. Figure 15-4 shows the general relationship between producers and consumers. (Event *producers* are server components such as the lock manager, Buffer Manager, and ODS, which generate the events recorded in the queue.)

SQL Server Profiler is more than just the user interface that is available through the SQL Server Profiler icon. You use the interface for defining traces from a client machine, watching the events recorded by those client side traces, and replaying traces. SQL Server Profiler can also define server-side traces that run invisibly, using extended stored procedures. One of the advantages of server-side traces is that they can be configured to start automatically. We'll see more on server-side traces later.

Defining a Trace

We'll look at how to define a trace by using the SQL Server Profiler interface, but the details regarding the types of events, data elements available, and filters are equally applicable to server-side traces defined using the extended stored procedures. To start a new trace, choose New from the SQL Server Profiler File menu. You'll see a dialog box like the one shown in Figure 15-5 on the following page, with four tabs for defining the trace properties.

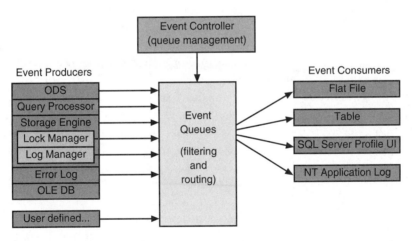

Figure 15-4.
The SQL Server Profiler architecture.

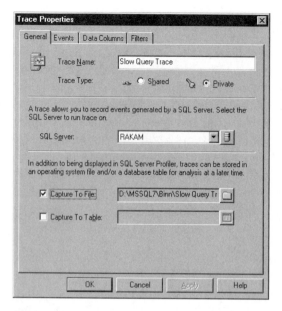

Figure 15-5.
The General tab of the Trace Properties dialog box.

You can define a trace as either shared or private. A private trace is available only to the operating system user (as opposed to the SQL Server user) who created it. Private and shared traces defined in the SQL Server Profiler interface are available only on the client machine on which they were defined, but you can export the definition to another client machine. Import and export options are available from the File menu. You can specify where you want the captured information to be saved. The captured events are always displayed in the SQL Server Profiler user interface, and when you define client-side traces, you cannot turn this off. In addition, you can save the events to either a file or a table within SQL Server. If you save to a table, the table is created automatically, with the appropriate columns defined to hold the data values that are being collected.

On the Events tab of the Trace Properties dialog box, you can select from the 68 available events, which are grouped into 12 categories. You can select an entire category or select events from within a category. The online documentation gives a complete description of each event.

On the Data Columns tab, you can specify which data items you want to record for each event. For example, you might want to keep track of only the SQL Server user, the application being used, and the text of the SQL statement being executed. Or you might want to record performance information such as the duration of the event, the table or index accessed, the severity of an error, and the start and end time of the event. Three data elements—Binary Data, Integer Data, and Event Sub Class—have different meanings depending on what event is being captured. For example, if you are capturing the Execution Plan event, Binary Data reflects the estimated cost of the query and Integer Data reflects the estimate of the number of rows to be returned. If you're capturing the Server Memory event, Event Sub Class data can be 1, which means that the server memory was increased, or it can be 2, which means it was decreased. The Integer Data column reflects the new memory size. Not all events have meaningful values for every possible data element. Again, full details are available in the online documentation.

> **NOTE** By default, you do not see all 68 events and 13 data elements listed in the Trace Properties dialog box. You see only a subset of the events and data elements. To see the complete list, you must close the dialog box and choose Options from the Tools menu. Select the All Event Classes and All Data Columns option buttons.

On the Filters tab of the Trace Properties dialog box, you can filter out events that aren't of interest. Three types of filters are available—name filters, range filters, and ID filters. Each possible data element can be filtered in only one of the three ways.

You use a name filter to include or exclude specific values. Typically, values entered in the Include box override values entered in the Exclude box. For example, if you enter *MS SQL Query Analyzer* in the Include box, you capture only events that originate through the Query Analyzer. All other events are ignored, regardless of what you entered in the Exclude box. The exception is when you use wildcards. You can enter *%SQL Server%* in the Include box to include all applications whose name includes that string, and then you can exclude specific applications that include that string, such as SQL Server Profiler. This is shown in Figure 15-6 on the following page. By default, all traces exclude events originating from SQL Server Profiler, because typically you don't want to trace the events that are involved in the actual tracing.

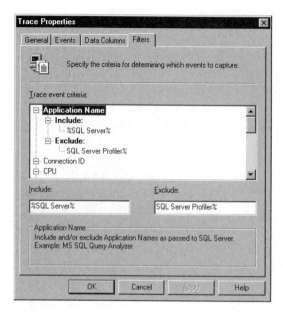

Figure 15-6.
The Filters tab of the Trace Properties dialog box.

A range filter takes a low value and a high value. Only events for which the filtered data element falls within the specified range are recorded. Probably the most common filter is for duration. If you are tracing your long-running queries, you are probably not interested in any queries that take less than a second to execute. You can enter 1000 (milliseconds) as the minimum duration and leave the maximum unspecified.

An ID filter lets you indicate specific values that you are interested in. For example, if you want to record only events that occur in a particular database, you can select one specific value for the Database ID filter. In the first release of SQL Server 7, you can choose only one specific value. If you want to trace two different databases, you must set up two separate traces. One of the data elements that allows an ID filter is the Object ID that an event is affecting (that is, the table being updated). If you want to record Object ID information but are not interested in when system tables are accessed, you can select a special check box for that purpose. As Figure 15-7 shows, you can either record events dealing with one specific Object ID or you can select the check box to indicate that you want all objects except the system tables.

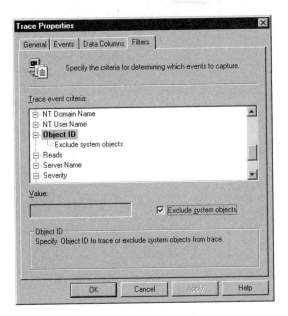

Figure 15-7.
Creating an Object ID filter.

The SQL Server online documentation provides full details of all the filters and which data elements allow which of the three types of filters.

Information gathered by SQL Server Profiler can be extremely useful for tracking all kinds of performance problems. By saving the captured events to a table, you can analyze usage patterns and query behavior using Transact-SQL stored procedures. By saving your captured events to a file, you can copy that file to another machine or e-mail it to a central location (or even to your support provider).

Gathering Diagnostic Information

A lot of the information that SQL Server Profiler gathers can help your support provider troubleshoot system problems. However, this information is usually not enough by itself. Support providers ask a standard set of questions when you call. A special utility in SQL Server 7 helps you gather this information with a single command: *sqldiag*. It can work with SQL Server Profiler if you have enabled automatic query recording, as shown here:

```
EXEC xp_trace_setqueryhistory 1
```

This procedure tells SQL Server to automatically keep track of the most recent 100 queries in an internal ring buffer. When the 101st query is recorded, it overwrites the first, so there are never more than 100 queries in the buffer. Once enabled, it autostarts every time SQL Server starts. The only way to stop the automatic recording of queries to the ring buffer is by running the *xp_trace_setqueryhistory* procedure with an argument of 0.

When you execute *sqldiag* from a command prompt while SQL Server is running, it gathers the following information:

- Text of all error logs

- Registry information

- DLL version information

- The contents of *master.dbo.sysprocesses*

- Output from the following SQL Server stored procedures:
  - ❏ *sp_configure*
  - ❏ *sp_who*
  - ❏ *sp_lock*
  - ❏ *sp_helpdb*
  - ❏ *xp_msver*
  - ❏ *sp_helpextendedproc*

- Input buffer from all active processes

- Any available deadlock information

- Microsoft Diagnostics Report for the server

The information is stored in a file called sqldiag.txt; you can specify a different filename in the command line for *sqldiag*. Executing *sqldiag* also places the contents of the internal ring buffer containing the most recent 100 queries in the file called sqldiag.trc. This is a normal SQL Server Profiler trace file, which you open and examine using SQL Server Profiler.

Obviously, if SQL Server is not running, some of the information in the above list won't be available. If SQL Server is down because of a severe system error, knowing the nature of the most recent queries could be of tremendous value. If you have enabled the ring buffer by using *xp_trace_setqueryhistory*, that information is available. Every time SQL Server encounters a system-generated error with a severity level greater than 17, it automatically dumps the contents of the ring buffer to a trace file called blackbox.trc. If the server has crashed with a severe error, you have a record of the final moments of activity.

Note that blackbox.trc is created only if the error is system generated. Also note that SQL Server always appends to the blackbox.trc file. If you encounter a situation in which frequent failures occur, this file will continue to grow. You must periodically delete this file or remove all its contents (perhaps after copying its contents to another location) to keep it from growing indefinitely.

If you use RAISERROR to generate an error of your own, even if you request a severity level greater than 17, blackbox.trc will not be created. However, you can use the command *xp_trace_flushqueryhistory* at any time to dump the ring buffer to a file of your choice. A complete description of this command is in the online documentation.

You can save and restart traces that you define using SQL Server Profiler. You can also copy the definition to another machine and start it from the SQL Server Profiler user interface there. If you want to start a particular trace programmatically (or automatically) or save the captured events someplace other than a SQL Server table or trace file, you must define a server-side trace using the *xp_trace_** extended stored procedures. You can include the calls to these procedures in any SQL Server stored procedure or batch.

To define a server-side trace, client programs can use the SQL Server Profiler extended stored procedure *xp_trace_addnewqueue*. They can use *xp_trace_setqueuedestination* to direct the output of the trace to one of four destinations: a file, the Windows NT application log, a table, or a forwarded server. The procedure *xp_sqltrace* is still available for backward compatibility, but the options for configuring traces using this procedure are much more limited, so you should use *xp_trace_addnewqueue* to define a trace.

Here are the steps for defining a trace from a client application:

1. Execute *xp_trace_addnewqueue* with the required parameters to create a trace queue and determine the columns to record. This is run once for each trace. An integer bit mask is used to specify all the data columns to be captured.

2. Execute *xp_trace_seteventclassrequired* with the required parameters to select the events to trace. This is run once for each event class for each trace. All events in the specified event class will be captured.

3. You can optionally execute the applicable *xp_trace_set** extended stored procedures to set any, none, or a combination of filters.

4. Execute *sp_setqueuedestination* with the required parameters to select a consumer for the trace data. This is run once for each destination for each trace.

5. Optionally, you can execute *xp_trace_savequeuedefinition* to save the trace queue definition.

6. Execute *xp_trace_startconsumer* with the required parameters to start the consumer, which sends the trace queue information to its destination.

Here's an example that creates a queue that writes events to a file and optionally saves the trace and marks it for autostart whenever SQL Server is restarted. (For full details on the arguments of all the extended procedure calls, see the online documentation.)

```
-- Declare variables.
declare @queue_handle int  -- queue handle to refer to this trace by
declare @column_value int  -- data column bit mask

-- Set the column mask for the data columns to capture.
SET @column_value = 1|16|32|128|512|4096|8192
-- 1 = Text
-- 16 = Connection ID
-- 32 = Windows NT username
-- 128 = Host
-- 512 = Application name
-- 4096 = Duration
-- 8192 = Start time


-- Create a queue.
exec xp_trace_addnewqueue 1000, 5, 95, 90, @column_value,
    @queue_handle output

-- Specify the event classes to trace.
exec xp_trace_seteventclassrequired @queue_handle,
    10 ,1 -- RPC:Completed
exec xp_trace_seteventclassrequired @queue_handle,
    12 ,1 -- SQL:BatchCompleted
exec xp_trace_seteventclassrequired @queue_handle,
    14 ,1 -- Connect
exec xp_trace_seteventclassrequired @queue_handle,
    16 ,1 -- Disconnect
exec xp_trace_seteventclassrequired @queue_handle,
    17 ,1 -- ExistingConnection

-- Create a filter that omits events created by
-- SQL Server Profiler and this script from the trace.
EXEC xp_trace_setappfilter @queue_handle, NULL,
    'SQL Server Profiler%'
EXEC xp_trace_settextfilter @queue_handle, NULL,
    'EXEC xp_trace%;SET ANSI%'
```

```
-- Configure the queue to write to a file.
exec xp_trace_setqueuedestination @queue_handle, 2, 1, NULL,
    'c:\temp\test_trace1.trc'

-- Start the consumer that actually writes to the file.
exec xp_trace_startconsumer @queue_handle

-- Display the queue handle; will need it later to stop the queue.
select @queue_handle

-- Save the definition as TestTrace1.
-- exec xp_trace_savequeuedefinition @queue_handle, "TestTrace1" ,1

-- Mark it for autostart.
-- exec xp_trace_setqueueautostart "TestTrace1" ,1
```

You might find it useful to have certain traces running constantly, but be careful about the amount of information you capture. Trace files can grow quite large if they are left running the entire time SQL Server is running. The companion CD contains an example of a SQL batch that stops a trace if it is running and restarts it with a new filename. You can use SQL Server Agent to run the batch periodically—for example, every four hours—so that each file contains only four hours' worth of trace information.

Tuning SQL Server Profiler

SQL Server Profiler uses a "pay as you go" model. There is no overhead for events that are not captured. Most events need very few resources. SQL Server Profiler becomes expensive only if you trace all 68 event classes and capture all data from those events. Early testing shows an absolute maximum of 5 to 10 percent overhead if you capture everything. In addition, most of the performance hit is due to a longer code path; the actual resources needed to capture the event data are not particularly CPU intensive.

You can tune the behavior and the resources required by SQL Server Profiler on the General tab of the Trace Properties dialog box. To the right of the server name is an icon of a server; if you click on that icon, you see the dialog box shown in Figure 15-8 on the following page, which shows four options. If you're defining a server-side trace using the extended procedure, these options are specified as parameters to the *xp_trace_addnewqueue* procedure.

The Number Of Rows To Buffer setting indicates the maximum number of events that can be buffered on the server queue to which the producers are writing. One consumer thread on the server consumes events to send back to whatever clients are collecting the events.

The Server Timeout setting indicates when to autopause after a producer has been backed up.

877

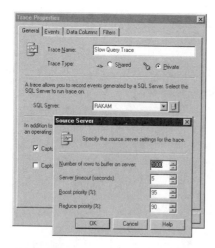

Figure 15-8.
Using the Source Server dialog box to set trace tuning options.

The Boost Priority setting indicates how full (by percentage) the queue can be before a boost in priority takes place. If the queue exceeds the setting, the consumer thread priority is boosted to consume events faster. Because the consumer thread can read events faster after the priority is boosted, either the number of events in the queue decreases or the queue fills more slowly.

The Reduce Priority setting is also expressed as a percentage. If the number of events drops below this level, the priority of the consuming thread will be reduced.

If the queue fills up, events back up on a producer-by-producer basis. When a producer is backed up for longer than the timeout setting, it is autopaused and an event is written to the trace so that you know that the trace was autopaused. Backed-up events and any events that occurred during the autopause are lost. When the queue opens up, producers begin producing events again. If the queue opens up before the timeout, backed-up events are written to the queue and no events are lost.

NOTE This discussion is just the tip of the iceberg as far as SQL Server Profiler is concerned. The online documentation offers much more information, but the best way to understand SQL Server Profiler's event tracing capabilities is to start using the tool. The SQL Server Profiler user interface comes with six predefined traces, so you can run one of them while you work through examples in this book. Save the traces to files, and then reopen the files to see what kinds of replaying are possible and how you can reorganize the events to get different perspectives on your server's behavior.

Performance Monitor

You can use SQL Server Profiler to monitor the behavior of your server on a query-by-query or event-by-event basis. But if you want to monitor your server's performance as an entire system, the best tool is Performance Monitor. This tool is extensible, which allows SQL Server to export its performance statistics so that you can monitor your entire system. That's crucial because such important statistics as CPU use must be monitored for the entire system, not just for SQL Server. In fact, many of the most important counters to watch while performance tuning SQL Server don't even belong to any of the SQL Server objects.

Performance Monitor comes with Windows NT. Traditionally, in mainframe and minicomputer systems, you had to buy a separate system monitor—at considerable expense—or use a hodgepodge of utilities, some to monitor the operating system and others to monitor the database. Then, if you worked on some other system, it didn't have the same set of tools you were accustomed to using.

In the SQL Server folder, click on the Performance Monitor icon to start Performance Monitor with a saved PMC file that allows certain counters to be preloaded. There is no separate Performance Monitor for use with SQL Server; the icon in the SQL Server folder calls the Windows NT Performance Monitor with a specific set of counters. You can also manually save your own settings in a PMC file and set up a shortcut in the same way.

Performance Monitor provides a huge set of counters. Probably no one understands all of them, so don't be intimidated. Peruse all the objects and counters and note which ones have separate instances. Use the Explain button for helpful information, or see the SQL Server and Windows NT documentation.

> **SEE ALSO** The whitepaper "Microsoft SQL Server 7.0 Performance Tuning Guide" on the companion CD discusses many of the Performance Monitor counters and explains how to determine the ideal value for your SQL Server. Also helpful is the Windows NT Workstation Resource Kit Version 4.0 (Chapters 9 through 16). Prior to Windows NT 4, the Performance Monitoring section of the resource kit was contained in a separate volume called *Optimizing Windows NT* by Russ Blake.

Performance Monitor Counters

In this section, we'll look at several important counters. We'll provide a brief explanation of how they can be useful and what actions you should consider based on the information they provide. Often, of course, the appropriate action is generic: for example, if CPU usage is high, you should try to reduce it.

The methods you can use to make such adjustments are varied and vast—from redesigning your application to reworking some queries, adding indexes, or getting faster or additional processors.

Object: Processor
Counter: % Processor Time

This counter monitors systemwide CPU usage. If you use multiple processors, you can set up an instance for each processor. Each processor's CPU usage count should be similar. If not, you should examine other processes on the system that have only one thread and are executing on a given CPU. Ideally, your system shouldn't consistently run with CPU usage of 80 percent or more, although short spikes of up to 100 percent are normal, even for systems with plenty of spare CPU capacity. If your system runs consistently above 80 percent or will grow to that level soon, or if it frequently spikes above 90 percent and stays there for 10 seconds or longer, you should try to reduce CPU usage.

First, consider making your application more efficient. High CPU usage counts can result from just one or two problematic queries. The queries might get high cache-hit ratios but still require a large amount of logical I/O. Try to rework those queries or add indexes. If the CPU usage count continues to be high, you might consider getting a faster processor or adding processors to your system. If your system is running consistently with 100 percent CPU usage, look at specific processes to see which are consuming the CPUs. It's likely that the offending process is doing some polling or is stuck in a tight loop; if so, the application needs some work, such as adding a sleep.

You should also watch for excessively low CPU usage, which indicates that your system is stalled somewhere. If locking contention is occurring, your system might be running at close to 0 percent CPU usage when no productive work is happening! Very low CPU usage can be a bigger problem than very high CPU usage. If you have poor overall throughput and low CPU usage, your application has a bottleneck somewhere and you must find and clear it.

Note that the Task Manager (Ctrl-Alt-Delete) in Windows NT 4 also provides a way to monitor CPU usage. The Task Manager is even easier to use than Performance Monitor.

Object: PhysicalDisk
Counter: Disk Transfers/sec

This counter shows physical I/O rates for all activity on the machine. You can set up an instance for each physical disk in the system or watch it for the total of all disks. SQL Server does most I/O in 8-KB chunks, although read-ahead I/O is essentially done with an I/O size of 64 KB. Watch this counter to be sure that you are not maxing out the I/O capacity of your system or of a particular disk. The I/O capacity of disk drives and controllers varies considerably depending on the hardware. But today's typical SCSI hard drive can do 80 to 90 random 8-KB reads per second, assuming that the controller can drive it that hard. If you see I/O rates approaching these rates *per drive,* you should verify that your specific hardware can sustain more. If not, add more disks and controllers, add memory, or rework the database to try to get a higher cache-hit ratio and require less physical I/O (via better design, better indexes, possible denormalization, and so on).

To see any of the counters from the PhysicalDisk object, you must reboot your computer with the Diskperf service started. You do this from the Devices applet in the Control Panel. Find Diskperf and change its startup option to Boot; then reboot the machine. After you're done monitoring, disable Diskperf.

Object: PhysicalDisk
Counter: Current Disk Queue Length

This counter indicates the number of reads that are currently outstanding for a disk. Occasional spikes are OK, especially when asynchronous I/O such as checkpoint kick in. But for the most part, the disks should not have a lot of queued I/O. Those operations, of course, must ultimately complete, so if more than one operation is queued consistently, the disk is probably overworked. You should either decrease physical I/O or add more I/O capacity.

Object: Memory
Counter: Pages/sec and Page Faults/sec

This counter watches the amount of paging on the system. As the system settles into a steady state, you want these values to be 0—that is, no paging going on in the system. In fact, if you allow SQL Server to automatically adjust its memory usage, it will reduce its memory resources when paging occurs. You should find that any paging that does occur is not due to SQL Server. If your system does experience regular paging, perhaps due to other applications running on the machine, you should consider adding more physical memory.

Object: Process
Counter: % Processor Time

Typically, you run this counter for the SQLServer process instance, but you might want to run it for other processes. It confirms that SQL Server (or some other process) is using a reasonable amount of CPU time. (It doesn't make much sense to spend a lot of time reducing SQL Server's CPU usage if some other process on the machine is using the larger percentage of the CPU to drive the total CPU usage near capacity.)

Object: Process
Counter: Virtual Bytes

Use this counter to see the total virtual memory being used by SQL Server, especially when a large number of threads and memory are being consumed. If this number gets too high, you might see Out Of Virtual Memory errors.

Object: Process
Counter: Private Bytes

This counter shows the current number of bytes allocated to a process that cannot be shared with other processes. It is probably the best Performance Monitor counter for viewing the approximate amount of memory committed by any threads within the *sqlservr.exe* process space.

Object: Process
Counter: Working Set

This counter shows the amount of memory recently used by a process. For the SQL Server process instance, this counter can actually be a valuable indicator of how much memory has been allocated within the SQL Server process space, especially for a dedicated server (because working-set trimming will likely not happen much). The value recorded by the working set should be very close to the value reported in the Task Manager, on the Processes tab, as the Mem Usage value for *sqlservr.exe*. Working Set is the current memory that SQL Server (and any components loaded in it) is currently accessing. It might not reflect the total amount of memory that SQL Server (and any component loaded in its process space) has allocated. Here, we use the term "allocated" to mean memory that has been committed to SQL Server. As long as no trimming has occurred, Working Set is the best counter for seeing how much memory has been allocated within the SQL Server process space.

Process: Private Bytes (described above) does not show all the memory committed, but the value can be more stable than Working Set if trimming occurs. You should consider monitoring both Private Bytes and Working Set. If you see Working Set dip below Private Bytes, you should look at Private Bytes. If Working Set dips below Private Bytes, the operating system must be trimming SQL Server's Working Set. This means other processes are competing for memory that SQL Server might need to get back, and you should evaluate what other processes are competing with SQL Server for memory resources.

Object: SQLServer: Buffer Manager
Counter: Buffer Cache Hit Ratio

There is no right value for the buffer cache-hit ratio since it is application-specific. If your system has settled into a steady state, ideally you want to achieve rates of 90 percent or higher, but this is not always possible if the I/O is random. Keep adding more physical memory as long as this value continues to rise or until you run out of money.

Object: SQLServer: Memory Manager
Counter: Total Server Memory

This counter can be useful, but it does not reflect all memory allocated within the SQL Server process space. It only reflects memory allocated in the SQL Server buffer pool. Note that the buffer pool is used much more extensively in version 7 than in previous versions (as discussed in Chapter 3). It is not just for data pages; it is also for other memory allocations within the server, including plans for stored procedures and for ad hoc queries. Certain components can get loaded into the SQL Server process space and allocate memory that is not under SQL Server's direct control. Examples of these are extended stored procedures, OLE Automation objects, and OLE DB provider DLLs. The memory space needed for these types of objects is included in SQL Server's Working Set, but not in the Total Server Memory counter.

Object: SQLServer: Cache Manager

This object contains counters for monitoring how the cache is being used for various types of objects, including ad hoc query plans, procedure plans, trigger plans, and prepared SQL plans. A separate Cache Hit Ratio counter is available for each type of plan, as is a counter showing the number of such objects and the number of pages used by the objects.

Object: SQLServer Buffer Manager
Counter: Page Reads/sec

Watch this counter in combination with the counters from the PhysicalDisk object. If you see rates approaching the capacity of your hardware's I/O rates (use 80 to 90 I/Os per disk per second as a guide), you should reduce I/O rates by making your application more efficient (via better design, better indexes, denormalization, and so on). Or you can increase the hardware's I/O capacity. This statistic measures only read operations, not writes, and it does so only for SQL Server, so you don't see the whole picture.

Object: SQLServer Buffer Manager
Counter: Checkpoint Writes/sec

Since the checkpoint process happens only at periodic intervals, you'll see a 0 value for this counter much of the time. During the checkpoint process, you should sustain as high an I/O rate as possible (perhaps hundreds per second) to get the checkpoint to complete as quickly as possible. If you have multiple disks and a fast controller, consider changing the *max async IO* option using *sp_configure* to try to sustain higher rates and shorter durations for the checkpoint. You can also use the *recovery interval* configuration option to affect the frequency of checkpointing.

Object: SQLServer: Buffer Manager
Counter: Page Writes/sec

This value keeps track of all physical writes done by SQL Server, for any reason. It includes checkpoint writes, lazywriter writes, and large block writes done during index creation or bulk copy operations. Separate counters are available for checkpoint writes and lazy writes; you're probably better off using these more specific counters.

Object: SQLServer: Databases
Counter: Log Flushes/sec

This value should be well below the capacity of the disk on which the transaction log resides. It is best to place the transaction log on a separate physical disk drive (or on a mirrored drive) so that the disk drive is always in place for the next write, since transaction log writes are sequential. There is a separate counter for each database, so make sure you are monitoring the right database instance.

Object: SQLServer: Databases
Counter: Transactions/sec

This counter measures actual transactions—either user-defined transactions surrounded by BEGIN TRAN and COMMIT TRAN or individual data modification statements if no BEGIN TRAN has been issued. For example, if you have a batch that contains two individual INSERT statements, this counter records two transactions. The counter has a separate instance for each database and there is no way to keep track of total transactions for all of SQL Server. Use it only as a general indication of your system's throughput. There is obviously no "correct" value—just the higher the better.

User-Defined Counters

SQL Server 7 offers 10 performance monitor counters for keeping track of any data or information that is useful to you. These counters are under the User Settable object. The only counter is called Query, and there are 10 instances to choose from. Ten stored procedures are available for specifying a value that Performance Monitor will chart for a particular instance. For example, if you want to use User Counter 1 to keep track of how many rows are in the *invoices* table, you can create triggers on the *invoices* table so that every time a row is inserted or deleted, the stored procedure *sp_user_counter1* is executed. You can include the following code in the triggers:

```
DECLARE @numrows int
SELECT @numrows = count(*) FROM invoices
EXEC sp_user_counter1 @numrows
```

Once it is assigned a value, the user counter maintains that value until a new value is assigned. User counters are much more passive in SQL Server 7 than in earlier versions. In version 6.5, the stored procedures for defining user counters contained whatever calculations were needed to generate the counter's value, and Performance Monitor continually polled the server to determine the value for the counter. Polling meant actually executing the stored procedure for the counter. It took place at whatever polling interval Performance Monitor was configured to use. If your stored procedure was complex, it could take longer than the polling interval to generate the new value, and the cost of generating the values could be quite expensive. In SQL Server 7, the stored procedure must be called explicitly to set a counter value.

Note that the value passed to the stored procedure must be a constant, a variable, or a parameterless system function starting with @@, and its datatype must be Integer.

Other Performance Monitor Counters

The counters mentioned in this chapter are just the tip of the iceberg. SQL Server has dozens of others, for monitoring almost every aspect of SQL Server behavior discussed in this book. The best way to learn about them is to experiment with Performance Monitor. Look through the list of available objects and counters, select a few for viewing, and see what results you get. You'll probably find a few that you'll want to monitor all the time, and others that you'll be interested in only occasionally. But do revisit the list of all available counters, because there are too many to remember. A month from now, you'll rediscover a counter that you completely overlooked the first time. You should also revisit the available objects and counters after every service pack upgrade, because new ones might be added as the SQL Server development team gets feedback.

Tables 15-1 through 15-5 on the following pages show some of the counters you might want to experiment with; the descriptions are adapted from the online documentation.

Counter	Description
Extents Allocated/sec	Number of extents allocated per second to database objects used for storing index or data records.
Forwarded Records/sec	Number of records per second fetched through forwarded record pointers.
Full Scans/sec	Number of unrestricted full scans per second. These can be either base-table or full-index scans.
Index Searches/sec	Number of index searches per second. These are used to start range scans and single index record fetches and to reposition an index.
Page Splits/sec	Number of page splits per second that occur as the result of overflowing index pages.
Pages Allocated/sec	Number of pages allocated per second to database objects used for storing index or data records.
Probe Scans/sec	Number of probe scans per second. These are used to find rows in an index or base table directly.
Range Scans/sec	Number of qualified range scans through indexes per second.
Skipped Ghosted Records/sec	Number of ghosted records per second skipped during scans.
Table Lock Escalations/sec	Number of times locks on a table were escalated.
Worktables Created/sec	Number of worktables created per second.

Table 15-1.
Counters for the Access Methods object.

Counter *	Description
Active Transactions	Number of active transactions for the database.
Bulk Copy Rows/sec	Number of rows bulk copied per second.
Bulk Copy Throughput/sec	Amount (in kilobytes) of data bulk copied per second.
Data File(s) Size (KB)	Cumulative size (in kilobytes) of all the data files in the database, including any automatic growth. This counter is useful for determining the correct size of *tempdb*, for example.
Log Cache Hit Ratio	Percentage of log cache reads satisfied from the log cache.
Log File(s) Size (KB)	Cumulative size (in kilobytes) of all the transaction log files in the database.
Log Growths	Total number of times the transaction log for the database has been expanded.
Log Shrinks	Total number of times the transaction log for the database has been shrunk.
Log Truncations	Total number of times the transaction log for the database has been truncated.
Percent Log Used	Percentage of space in the log that is in use.
Shrink Data Movement Bytes/sec	Amount of data being moved per second by autoshrink operations or by DBCC SHRINKDATABASE or DBCC SHRINKFILE statements.
Transactions/sec	Number of transactions started for the database per second.

*Separate instances of these counters exist for each database.

Table 15-2.
Counters for the Databases object.

Counter	Description
Average Wait Time (ms)	Average amount of wait time (in milliseconds) for each lock request that resulted in a wait.
Lock Requests/sec	Number of new locks and lock conversions per second requested from the lock manager.
Lock Timeouts/sec	Number of lock requests per second that timed out, including internal requests for NOWAIT locks.
Lock Wait Time (ms)	Total wait time (in milliseconds) for locks in the last second.
Lock Waits/sec	Number of lock requests per second that could not be satisfied immediately and required the caller to wait.
Number of Deadlocks/sec	Number of lock requests per second that resulted in a deadlock.

Table 15-3.
Counters for the Locks object.

Counter	Description
Connection Memory (KB)	Total amount of dynamic memory the server is using for maintaining connections.
Lock Memory (KB)	Total amount of dynamic memory the server is using for locks.
Maximum Workspace Memory (KB)	Maximum amount of memory available for executing processes such as hash, sort, bulk copy, and index creation operations.
Memory Grants Outstanding	Total number of processes per second that have successfully acquired a workspace memory grant.
Memory Grants Pending	Total number of processes per second waiting for a workspace memory grant.

Table 15-4.
Counters for the Memory Manager object.

(continued)

Table 15-4. *continued*

Counter	Description
Optimizer Memory (KB)	Total amount of dynamic memory the server is using for query optimization.
SQL Cache Memory (KB)	Total amount of dynamic memory the server is using for the dynamic SQL cache.
Target Server Memory (KB)	Total amount of dynamic memory the server is willing to consume.
Total Server Memory (KB)	Total amount (in kilobytes) of dynamic memory that the server is currently using.

Counter	Description
Auto-Param Attempts/sec	Number of autoparameterization attempts per second. Total should be the sum of the failed, safe, and unsafe autoparameterizations. Autoparameterization occurs when SQL Server attempts to reuse a cached plan for a previously executed query that is similar, but not exactly the same, as the current query.
Batch Requests/sec	Number of Transact-SQL command batches received per second.
Failed Auto-Params/sec	Number of failed autoparameterization attempts per second. This should be small.
Safe Auto-Params/sec	Number of safe autoparameterization attempts per second.
SQL Compilations/sec	Number of SQL compilations per second. Indicates the number of times the compile code path is entered. Includes compiles due to recompiles. Once SQL Server user activity is stable, this value should reach a steady state.
Unsafe Auto-Params/sec	Number of unsafe autoparameterization attempts per second. The table has characteristics that prevent the cached plan from being shared. These are designated as *unsafe*. The fewer of these that occur the better.

Table 15-5.
Counters for the SQL Statistics object.

Other Performance Monitoring Considerations

Any time you monitor performance, you also slightly alter performance simply because of the overhead cost of monitoring. It can be helpful to run Performance Monitor on a separate machine from SQL Server to reduce that overhead. The SQL Server–specific counters are obtained by querying SQL Server, so they use connections to SQL Server. (Performance Monitor always uses Windows NT Authentication to connect to the SQL Server.) It is best to monitor only the counters you are interested in.

Summary

Configuration alone can rarely turn your slow, plodding application into a screamer. In fact, you're more likely to misconfigure your system by taking manual control of the options that SQL Server sets automatically. Knowing what each configuration option does can keep you from misconfiguring your system.

In this chapter, we looked at the configuration options and discussed some guidelines for their use. We also discussed how to monitor the effects on your system's performance using SQL Server Profiler and Performance Monitor. SQL Server Profiler lets you determine which queries, procedures, or users have the biggest performance impact. Performance Monitor gives you a scientific method of holding constant all but one variable within the system as a whole so that you can measure the effect as you vary it.

SUGGESTED READING

Despite this book's considerable length, it doesn't touch on all important areas, and it assumes that readers have some knowledge of relational database management systems (RDBMS). This section includes other recommended resources for learning about the SQL language, the fundamentals of using Microsoft SQL Server, and related technologies. However, the most important resource that we can recommend is to read, cover to cover, the SQL Server documentation.

One of the CDs included with this book contains an evaluation copy of the complete SQL Server 7 product. You can read the online documentation right from the CD. The other CD contains some valuable whitepapers. Start there. This second CD also contains some tools for use with SQL Server as well as an online Transact-SQL language reference, compiled by a member of the SQL Server development team at Microsoft. Although the reference is a Microsoft Word file, it contains many cross-linked references and is intended for online use.

You can augment your reading with the following books and selections. We've listed them in order from introductory materials to the more detailed or specialized materials.

SQL (Osborne's Complete Reference Series) by James R. Groff and Paul N. Weinberg (Osborne McGraw-Hill, 1999). This book is an excellent primer for those users new to SQL.

An Introduction to Database Systems by C. J. Date (Addison-Wesley, 1994). A classic book, written by a giant in the field, covering general relational database concepts. A must for anyone in the database industry.

Microsoft SQL Server Training (Microsoft Press, 1996). Nice, self-paced training, with plenty of information about administration and security. Fairly introductory and suitable for those newer to SQL Server. The 1996 edition is based on SQL Server 6.5. The SQL Server 7 version is not available as of this writing but should be available soon. Check the Microsoft Press Web site (http://mspress.microsoft.com) periodically for details.

Database Design for Mere Mortals by Michael J. Hernandez (Addison-Wesley, 1997). A very readable approach to the daunting task of designing a relational database to solve real-world problems. The book is written in a database-independent format, so the details can be applied to SQL Server, as well as to other relational database management systems you might use.

Handbook of Relational Database Design by Candace C. Fleming and Barbara Vonhalle (Addison-Wesley, 1988). A fine book discussing general logical database design and data modeling approaches and techniques.

SAMS Teach Yourself Microsoft SQL Server 7.0 in 21 Days by Richard Waymire and Rick Sawtell (SAMS Publishing, 1999). A good first book on SQL Server 7 that gets readers up to speed quickly. Co-written in tutorial format by a program manager on the SQL Server development team at Microsoft, this title includes self-test questions for each of the 21 "days."

Database: Principles, Programming, Performance by Patrick O'Neil (Morgan Kaufmann Publishers, 1994). This thorough textbook provides excellent introductory materials, so we've placed it high on our list. It also covers a broad spectrum of information and carefully details many database topics, including buffer management and transaction semantics.

Understanding the New SQL: A Complete Guide by Jim Melton and Alan R. Simon (Morgan Kaufmann Publishers, 1993). An excellent reference, and one that we consult frequently for issues regarding ANSI SQL-92 semantics and conformance. (Jim Melton is an active participant in the SQL standards work and was the editor of the ANSI SQL-92 standard.) Although you can get the ANSI SQL-92 specification directly from ANSI, this book translates the standard into English.

A Guide to the SQL Standard by C. J. Date with Hugh Darwen (Addison-Wesley, 1993). Similar in purpose and focus to the Melton and Simon book, this book's coverage is more compact, provides additional insight into why something is the way it is, and provides more discussion of semantics. It is an especially good reference for issues about the use of NULL. We use this book hand in hand with the Melton and Simon book and find that the books' subtle differences in emphasis complement each other well.

Optimizing Transact-SQL: Advanced Programming Techniques by David Rozenshtein, Anatoly Abramovich, and Eugene Birger (Coriolis Group, 1996). Lots of clever queries and solutions written with Transact-SQL. (Note, however, that the solutions here were authored before SQL Server had the CASE statement, and CASE sometimes might provide easier, more straightforward solutions.)

Joe Celko's SQL for Smarties: Advanced SQL Programming by Joe Celko (Morgan Kaufmann Publishers, 1995). This is an excellent book to consult for insight into subtle but powerful ways to write nonintuitive queries. In places, this one is truly the SQL book for the Mensa crowd— it's loaded with mind-bending puzzles about how to write an SQL query to perform some nonobvious task. It contains many examples—probably more than any other book on this list—and you're likely to find solutions to problems similar in scope to ones you might face.

Hitchhiker's Guide to Visual Basic and SQL Server by William Vaughn (Microsoft Press, 1998). A good book discussing the various programming interfaces available through Microsoft Visual Basic, especially when accessing SQL Server.

Inside Microsoft Visual InterDev by Nicholas Evans, Ken Miller, and Ken Spencer (Microsoft Press, 1999). A complete guide to developing Web-based applications, with examples using SQL Server.

Inside ODBC by Kyle Geiger (Microsoft Press, 1995). The finest book available on ODBC, period. Written by the "Father of ODBC." A must for C programmers working with ODBC and SQL Server. It includes a fine discussion of cursors as well. Although this book is out of print, you might be able to find someone who has a copy on their bookshelf, or you can check at used bookstores.

Microsoft KnowledgeBase Various articles, containing helpful information, tips, and answers to common questions, are available from http://www.microsoft.com. The site is frequently updated and of high quality. A must for any serious developer using any Microsoft development product, not just SQL Server.

Microsoft Developer Network (MSDN) Library Various articles and resources are available from Microsoft. Like the Microsoft KnowledgeBase, MSDN contains information about all the Microsoft development products. A must for serious developers.

Microsoft Windows NT Workstation 4.0 Resource Kit (Microsoft Press, 1996). Especially useful are Chapters 9 through 16, which were written by Russ Blake and formerly available as a separate bound volume (in the version 3.5 Resource Kit). A great source of information for effectively using Performance Monitor. Also contains a thorough discussion of general performance issues (not specific to SQL Server).

Performance Tuning and Optimization of Microsoft SQL Server 6.5 Microsoft Authorized Training Course #665. We'd recommend this fine course to people interested in becoming the SQL Server performance experts of their teams. Available from authorized training centers. The SQL Server 7 version of the course is not available as of this writing. Check the Microsoft training and certification Web site (found at http://www.microsoft.com/train_cert) periodically for details.

Microsoft SQL Server 7 Unleashed by David Solomon, et al. (MacMillan Publishing, 1999). The *Unleashed* series is usually authored by a team of exceptional writers with years of experience in the subject matter. The breadth of information covered in this book is extensive, including chapters on security, clustering, backup and recovery, replication, Data Transformation Services, data warehousing, and programming interfaces.

Transaction Processing: Concepts and Techniques by Jim Gray and Andreas Reuter (Morgan Kaufmann Publishers, 1992). Without a doubt, the best book ever written for in-depth explanations of such issues as locking, logging and recovery, and transactional semantics. Unusual (and terrific!) in that it is packed with detailed information, yet still readable and understandable. Unlike many of the overly academic papers that seem more suitable for graduate school classes than for people trying to build actual solutions.

In Search of Clusters: The Ongoing Battle in Lowly Parallel Computing by Gregory F. Pfister (Prentice Hall, 1998). A good source of information regarding scalability limits of SMP systems, such as Amdahl's law, the Von Neumann bottleneck, and other considerations for SMP systems.

Transaction Processing Council (TPC) Web site and full disclosure reports Invaluable resources available at http://www.tpc.org. This is a good Web site to consult to stay abreast of current performance levels of competing hardware and software solutions. It also has plenty of information regarding the benchmarks. You also might want to order one of the full disclosure reports (FDRs) for a benchmark that uses SQL Server to determine the exact hardware and software configuration used. If you will plan to run a very large system, such an FDR can be a good template to use.

INDEX

Page numbers in italics refer to figures, tables, or code listings.

Ron Soukup

Ron Soukup is one of the original members of the SQL Server team at Microsoft. He joined Microsoft in 1989. Ron was general manager of the SQL Server group through the end of 1995, and he led the development and shipment versions 1.1, 1.11, 4.2 (OS/2), 4.21 (Windows NT), 6.0, and 6.5 beta. After delivering version 6.5 to beta test, Ron stepped down from his duties as general manager and the years of "ship crunch" for a while to spend more time with his wife, Kay, and their daughters, Kelly and Jamie. After a year away, Ron recently rejoined the SQL Server group, and currently manages the SQL Server Replication development team.

Ron has worked more than 18 years in computer and database systems, and he has experience with DB/2 (MVS), SQL/DS (VM), Oracle, Informix, Sybase, and Ingres systems. Prior to working at Microsoft, Ron held technical positions at United Airlines and AT&T. A longtime Chicagoan, Ron earned his B.S. and M.B.A. degrees from Northwestern University in Evanston, Illinois.

Kalen Delaney

Kalen Delaney has worked with SQL Server extensively since joining the technical support group at Sybase in 1987, shortly after the company's first public product release. Kalen soon began teaching Sybase's Performance and Tuning course, receiving the company's Instructor of the Year Award in 1990. Kalen left Sybase in 1992 to become an independent Microsoft SQL Server trainer and consultant; she quickly became the primary Subject Matter Expert (SME) for two Microsoft SQL Server 6.5 courses. Recently Kalen helped Microsoft develop training materials for bringing their product support specialists up to speed on the new capabilities and internal behavior of SQL Server 7.0 and began teaching that course to support engineers throughout the United States.

Kalen has worked more than 20 years in computer and database systems since earning her M.S. degree in computer science at the University of California, Berkeley. She has published numerous articles in *SQL Server Professional* and *NT Magazine* and currently writes a column for *SQL Server Magazine*. She lives with her husband and four children in the Pacific Northwest, a ferryboat ride from Microsoft's Redmond campus.

The manuscript for this book was prepared and submitted to Microsoft Press in electronic form. Text files were prepared using Microsoft Word 97. Pages were composed by Microsoft Press using Adobe PageMaker 6.52 for Windows, with text in Galliard and display type in Helvetica bold. Composed pages were delivered to the printer as electronic prepress files.

Cover Graphic Designer
Tim Girvin Design, Inc.

Cover Illustrator
Glenn Mitsui

Interior Graphic Artist
Alton Lawson

Manuscript Editors
Chrisa Hotchkiss, Ina Chang

Principal Compositors
Dan Latimer, Peggy Herman

Principal Proofreader/Copy Editor
Roger LeBlanc

Indexer
Richard Shrout

Editorial Assistant
Denise Bankaitis

The *bible* for Visual Basic data access.

U.S.A. **$49.99**
U.K. £46.99 [V.A.T. included]
Canada $71.99
ISBN 1-57231-848-1

The HITCHHIKER'S GUIDE TO VISUAL BASIC® AND SQL SERVER,™ Sixth Edition, is the definitive guide for developers who want to use Visual Basic to access SQL Server. Whether you're using earlier versions or the new Visual Basic 6.0 and the completely reengineered SQL Server 7.0 (which now runs on Windows® 95 and Windows 98), this book will help you decide which of the constantly evolving data access options is best for your situation. Author William Vaughn provides the same depth and breadth of coverage that have made earlier editions of this book indispensable. Plus, he introduces innovations that may well change the way you think about data access!

Microsoft®

mspress.microsoft.com

Unlock the power of
Microsoft Visual Studio

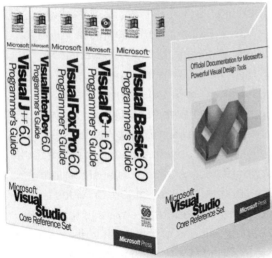

U.S.A. **$129.99**
U.K. £121.99 [V.A.T. included]
Canada $188.99
ISBN 1-57231-884-8

The MICROSOFT® VISUAL STUDIO® CORE REFERENCE SET contains the programmer's guide for each product in Microsoft Visual Studio 6.0:

- Microsoft Visual Basic® 6.0 Programmer's Guide

- Microsoft Visual C++® 6.0 Programmer's Guide

- Microsoft Visual FoxPro® 6.0 Programmer's Guide

- Microsoft Visual InterDev™ 6.0 Programmer's Guide

- Microsoft Visual J++® 6.0 Programmer's Guide

The answers that professionals need are close at hand in easy-to-use book form. And because they're from Microsoft's own Developer User Education groups, these volumes provide authoritative and complete information straight from the source. As a bonus, the *Microsoft Visual C++ 6.0 Programmer's Guide* contains a CD-ROM with helpful tools and samples for Visual C++ 6.0 programmers. Get this valuable set working for you today.

Microsoft Press® products are available worldwide wherever quality computer books are sold. For more information, contact your book or computer retailer, software reseller, or local Microsoft Sales Office, or visit our Web site at mspress.microsoft.com. To locate your nearest source for Microsoft Press products, or to order directly, call 1-800-MSPRESS in the U.S. (in Canada, call 1-800-268-2222).

Prices and availability dates are subject to change.

Microsoft®

mspress.microsoft.com

Build
collaborative
solutions
that **bridge**—and **extend**—
enterprise
resources.

Microsoft Press

Programming
Microsoft
Outlook
Microsoft **and**
Exchange

Build collaborative
business solutions
with Microsoft
Outlook 98/2000
and Microsoft
Exchange Server 5.5

Thomas Rizzo

Build and run core business services
across the enterprise using Microsoft's
powerful messaging and collaboration tools—
Outlook® 98, Outlook 2000, and Exchange
Server 5.5. This book offers detailed guid-
ance—plus a full cache of code and other
resources on CD—to help you build open,
extensible solutions for tracking, messaging,
workflow, knowledge management, and real-
time collaboration.

U.S.A.	**$49.99**
U.K.	£46.99 [V.A.T. included]
Canada	$74.99
ISBN 0-7356-0509-2	

Microsoft®

mspress.microsoft.com

MICROSOFT LICENSE AGREEMENT
Book Companion CD

IMPORTANT—READ CAREFULLY: This Microsoft End-User License Agreement ("EULA") is a legal agreement between you (either an individual or an entity) and Microsoft Corporation for the Microsoft product identified above, which includes computer software and may include associated media, printed materials, and "online" or electronic documentation ("SOFTWARE PRODUCT"). Any component included within the SOFTWARE PRODUCT that is accompanied by a separate End-User License Agreement shall be governed by such agreement and not the terms set forth below. By installing, copying, or otherwise using the SOFTWARE PRODUCT, you agree to be bound by the terms of this EULA. If you do not agree to the terms of this EULA, you are not authorized to install, copy, or otherwise use the SOFTWARE PRODUCT; you may, however, return the SOFTWARE PRODUCT, along with all printed materials and other items that form a part of the Microsoft product that includes the SOFT-WARE PRODUCT, to the place you obtained them for a full refund.

SOFTWARE PRODUCT LICENSE

The SOFTWARE PRODUCT is protected by United States copyright laws and international copyright treaties, as well as other intellectual property laws and treaties. The SOFTWARE PRODUCT is licensed, not sold.

1. **GRANT OF LICENSE.** This EULA grants you the following rights:

   a. **Software Product.** You may install and use one copy of the SOFTWARE PRODUCT on a single computer. The primary user of the computer on which the SOFTWARE PRODUCT is installed may make a second copy for his or her exclusive use on a portable computer.

   b. **Storage/Network Use.** You may also store or install a copy of the SOFTWARE PRODUCT on a storage device, such as a network server, used only to install or run the SOFTWARE PRODUCT on your other computers over an internal network; however, you must acquire and dedicate a license for each separate computer on which the SOFTWARE PRODUCT is installed or run from the storage device. A license for the SOFTWARE PRODUCT may not be shared or used concurrently on different computers.

   c. **License Pak.** If you have acquired this EULA in a Microsoft License Pak, you may make the number of additional copies of the computer software portion of the SOFTWARE PRODUCT authorized on the printed copy of this EULA, and you may use each copy in the manner specified above. You are also entitled to make a corresponding number of secondary copies for portable computer use as specified above.

   d. **Sample Code.** Solely with respect to portions, if any, of the SOFTWARE PRODUCT that are identified within the SOFT-WARE PRODUCT as sample code (the "SAMPLE CODE"):

      i. **Use and Modification.** Microsoft grants you the right to use and modify the source code version of the SAMPLE CODE, *provided* you comply with subsection (d)(iii) below. You may not distribute the SAMPLE CODE, or any modified version of the SAMPLE CODE, in source code form.

      ii. **Redistributable Files.** Provided you comply with subsection (d)(iii) below, Microsoft grants you a nonexclusive, royalty-free right to reproduce and distribute the object code version of the SAMPLE CODE and of any modified SAMPLE CODE, other than SAMPLE CODE, or any modified version thereof, designated as not redistributable in the Readme file that forms a part of the SOFTWARE PRODUCT (the "Non-Redistributable Sample Code"). All SAMPLE CODE other than the Non-Redistributable Sample Code is collectively referred to as the "REDISTRIBUTABLES."

      iii. **Redistribution Requirements.** If you redistribute the REDISTRIBUTABLES, you agree to: (i) distribute the REDISTRIBUTABLES in object code form only in conjunction with and as a part of your software application product; (ii) not use Microsoft's name, logo, or trademarks to market your software application product; (iii) include a valid copyright notice on your software application product; (iv) indemnify, hold harmless, and defend Microsoft from and against any claims or lawsuits, including attorney's fees, that arise or result from the use or distribution of your software application product; and (v) not permit further distribution of the REDISTRIBUTABLES by your end user. Contact Microsoft for the applicable royalties due and other licensing terms for all other uses and/or distribution of the REDISTRIBUTABLES.

2. **DESCRIPTION OF OTHER RIGHTS AND LIMITATIONS.**

   - **Limitations on Reverse Engineering, Decompilation, and Disassembly.** You may not reverse engineer, decompile, or disassemble the SOFTWARE PRODUCT, except and only to the extent that such activity is expressly permitted by applicable law notwithstanding this limitation.

   - **Separation of Components.** The SOFTWARE PRODUCT is licensed as a single product. Its component parts may not be separated for use on more than one computer.

   - **Rental.** You may not rent, lease, or lend the SOFTWARE PRODUCT.

   - **Support Services.** Microsoft may, but is not obligated to, provide you with support services related to the SOFTWARE PRODUCT ("Support Services"). Use of Support Services is governed by the Microsoft policies and programs described in the user manual, in "online" documentation, and/or other Microsoft-provided materials. Any supplemental software code provided to you as part of the Support Services shall be considered part of the SOFTWARE PRODUCT and subject to the terms and conditions of this EULA. With respect to technical information you provide to Microsoft as part of the Support Services, Microsoft may use such information for its business purposes, including for product support and development. Microsoft will not utilize such technical information in a form that personally identifies you.

- **Software Transfer.** You may permanently transfer all of your rights under this EULA, provided you retain no copies, you transfer all of the SOFTWARE PRODUCT (including all component parts, the media and printed materials, any upgrades, this EULA, and, if applicable, the Certificate of Authenticity), **and** the recipient agrees to the terms of this EULA.

- **Termination.** Without prejudice to any other rights, Microsoft may terminate this EULA if you fail to comply with the terms and conditions of this EULA. In such event, you must destroy all copies of the SOFTWARE PRODUCT and all of its component parts.

3. **COPYRIGHT.** All title and copyrights in and to the SOFTWARE PRODUCT (including but not limited to any images, photographs, animations, video, audio, music, text, SAMPLE CODE, REDISTRIBUTABLES, and "applets" incorporated into the SOFTWARE PRODUCT) and any copies of the SOFTWARE PRODUCT are owned by Microsoft or its suppliers. The SOFTWARE PRODUCT is protected by copyright laws and international treaty provisions. Therefore, you must treat the SOFTWARE PRODUCT like any other copyrighted material **except** that you may install the SOFTWARE PRODUCT on a single computer provided you keep the original solely for backup or archival purposes. You may not copy the printed materials accompanying the SOFTWARE PRODUCT.

4. **U.S. GOVERNMENT RESTRICTED RIGHTS.** The SOFTWARE PRODUCT and documentation are provided with RESTRICTED RIGHTS. Use, duplication, or disclosure by the Government is subject to restrictions as set forth in subparagraph (c)(1)(ii) of the Rights in Technical Data and Computer Software clause at DFARS 252.227-7013 or subparagraphs (c)(1) and (2) of the Commercial Computer Software—Restricted Rights at 48 CFR 52.227-19, as applicable. Manufacturer is Microsoft Corporation/One Microsoft Way/Redmond, WA 98052-6399.

5. **EXPORT RESTRICTIONS.** You agree that you will not export or re-export the SOFTWARE PRODUCT, any part thereof, or any process or service that is the direct product of the SOFTWARE PRODUCT (the foregoing collectively referred to as the "Restricted Components"), to any country, person, entity, or end user subject to U.S. export restrictions. You specifically agree not to export or re-export any of the Restricted Components (i) to any country to which the U.S. has embargoed or restricted the export of goods or services, which currently include, but are not necessarily limited to Cuba, Iran, Iraq, Libya, North Korea, Sudan, and Syria, or to any national of any such country, wherever located, who intends to transmit or transport the Restricted Components back to such country; (ii) to any end user who you know or have reason to know will utilize the Restricted Components in the design, development, or production of nuclear, chemical, or biological weapons; or (iii) to any end user who has been prohibited from participating in U.S. export transactions by any federal agency of the U.S. government. You warrant and represent that neither the BXA nor any other U.S. federal agency has suspended, revoked, or denied your export privileges.

DISCLAIMER OF WARRANTY

NO WARRANTIES OR CONDITIONS. MICROSOFT EXPRESSLY DISCLAIMS ANY WARRANTY OR CONDITION FOR THE SOFTWARE PRODUCT. THE SOFTWARE PRODUCT AND ANY RELATED DOCUMENTATION IS PROVIDED "AS IS" WITHOUT WARRANTY OR CONDITION OF ANY KIND, EITHER EXPRESS OR IMPLIED, INCLUDING, WITHOUT LIMITATION, THE IMPLIED WARRANTIES OF MERCHANTABILITY, FITNESS FOR A PARTICULAR PURPOSE, OR NONINFRINGEMENT. THE ENTIRE RISK ARISING OUT OF USE OR PERFORMANCE OF THE SOFTWARE PRODUCT REMAINS WITH YOU.

LIMITATION OF LIABILITY. TO THE MAXIMUM EXTENT PERMITTED BY APPLICABLE LAW, IN NO EVENT SHALL MICROSOFT OR ITS SUPPLIERS BE LIABLE FOR ANY SPECIAL, INCIDENTAL, INDIRECT, OR CONSEQUENTIAL DAMAGES WHATSOEVER (INCLUDING, WITHOUT LIMITATION, DAMAGES FOR LOSS OF BUSINESS PROFITS, BUSINESS INTERRUPTION, LOSS OF BUSINESS INFORMATION, OR ANY OTHER PECUNIARY LOSS) ARISING OUT OF THE USE OF OR INABILITY TO USE THE SOFTWARE PRODUCT OR THE PROVISION OF OR FAILURE TO PROVIDE SUPPORT SERVICES, EVEN IF MICROSOFT HAS BEEN ADVISED OF THE POSSIBILITY OF SUCH DAMAGES. IN ANY CASE, MICROSOFT'S ENTIRE LIABILITY UNDER ANY PROVISION OF THIS EULA SHALL BE LIMITED TO THE GREATER OF THE AMOUNT ACTUALLY PAID BY YOU FOR THE SOFTWARE PRODUCT OR US$5.00; PROVIDED HOWEVER, IF YOU HAVE ENTERED INTO A MICROSOFT SUPPORT SERVICES AGREEMENT, MICROSOFT'S ENTIRE LIABILITY REGARDING SUPPORT SERVICES SHALL BE GOVERNED BY THE TERMS OF THAT AGREEMENT. BECAUSE SOME STATES AND JURISDICTIONS DO NOT ALLOW THE EXCLUSION OR LIMITATION OF LIABILITY, THE ABOVE LIMITATION MAY NOT APPLY TO YOU.

MISCELLANEOUS

This EULA is governed by the laws of the State of Washington USA, except and only to the extent that applicable law mandates governing law of a different jurisdiction.

Should you have any questions concerning this EULA, or if you desire to contact Microsoft for any reason, please contact the Microsoft subsidiary serving your country, or write: Microsoft Sales Information Center/One Microsoft Way/Redmond, WA 98052-6399.